THE MOST
TRUSTED NAME
IN TRAVEL

ISRAEL

8th Edition

By Elianna Bar-El,
Shira Rubin & Karen Chernick

FrommerMedia LLC

Frommer's Israel, 8th Edition

Published by:
Frommer Media LLC

ISBN 978-1-62887-531-7 (paper), 978-1-62887-532-4 (e-book)

Editorial Director: Pauline Frommer
Editor: Pauline Frommer
Production Editor: Erin Geile
Cartographer: Roberta Stockwell and Liz Puhl
Photo Editor: Meghan Lamb
Indexer: Cheryl Lenser
Cover Design: Dave Riedy

Front cover: Dome of the Rock, the Russian church of Mary Magdalene, church steeples of the Old City, fortified wall of the Tower of David, and high-rise hotel of West Jerusalem. John Theodor / Shutterstock
Title page: Makhtesh Ramon Crater in Mitzpe Ramon. Mazur Travel / Shutterstock

For information on our other products or services, see www.frommers.com.

Frommer Media LLC also publishes its books in a variety of electronic formats. Some content that appears in print may not be available in electronic formats.

Manufactured in Malaysia

5 4 3 2 1

HOW TO CONTACT US

In researching this book, we discovered many wonderful places—hotels, restaurants, shops, and more. We're sure you'll find others. Please tell us about them, so we can share the information with your fellow travelers in upcoming editions. If you were disappointed with a recommendation, we'd love to know that, too. Please write to: Support@FrommerMedia.com

FROMMER'S STAR RATINGS SYSTEM

Every hotel, restaurant and attraction listed in this guide has been ranked for quality and value. Here's what the stars mean:

★ Recommended
★★ Highly Recommended
★★★ A must! Don't miss!

AN IMPORTANT NOTE

The world is a dynamic place. Hotels change ownership, restaurants hike their prices, museums alter their opening hours, and buses and trains change their routings. And all of this can occur in the several months after our authors have visited, inspected, and written about these hotels, restaurants, museums, and transportation services. Though we have made valiant efforts to keep all our information fresh and up-to-date, some few changes can inevitably occur in the periods before a revised edition of this guidebook is published. So please bear with us if a tiny number of the details in this book have changed. Please also note that we have no responsibility or liability for any inaccuracy or errors or omissions, or for inconvenience, loss, damage, or expenses suffered by anyone as a result of assertions in this guide.

CONTENTS

LIST OF MAPS v

ABOUT THE AUTHORS vi

1 THE BEST OF ISRAEL 1

Israel's Iconic Experiences 2

The Most Evocative Ancient Sites & Cities 5

The Best Ways to Experience Israel Like a Local 7

Israel's Best Restaurants 8

Israel's Best Hotels 10

2 SUGGESTED ITINERARIES 13

Israel in 2 Weeks 13

Israel in 1 Week 19

A Week in Israel with Young Kids 22

More Kid-Friendly Picks in Israel 25

The Regions in Brief 25

3 ISRAEL IN CONTEXT 28

Israel Today 28

Looking Back: Israel's History 29

Dateline 32

Eating & Drinking 36

Israeli Street Food Tips 37

Dining Bargains 39

When to Go 39

Israel Calendar of Holidays & Events 41

4 SETTLING INTO JERUSALEM 46

Orientation 46

Getting Connected in Jerusalem 50

The Neighborhoods in Brief 50

Getting Around 51

Fast Facts: Jerusalem 54

Where to Stay 55

Alternative Accommodations 55

Family-Friendly Hotels 65

Where to Eat 74

Jerusalem's Top Eateries 78

Sabbath Dining 83

Coffee & People-Watching 85

Street Meals 86

Jerusalem Nightlife 95

Best in Booze: A Distillery Tour 98

5 EXPLORING JERUSALEM 101

The Old City 104

The Hidden Wall 121

An Easy Walking Tour of the Old City 129

West Jerusalem Attractions 142

Other West Jerusalem Neighborhoods Worth a Visit 153

East Jerusalem Attractions 155

The People's Princess 160

Especially for Kids 163

Organized Tours 164

Outdoor Pursuits & Sports 165

The Shopping Scene 165

The Art of Bargaining 170

Wineries in the Hill Country 173

Side Trips Outside Jerusalem 174

Excursions to Bethlehem 175

6 THE DEAD SEA & MASADA 178
The Dead Sea 178
Dead Sea Safety 179
Masada 185
Into the Negev 188

7 THE GALILEE 192
Nazareth 193
Sweet Treats 202
Tiberias 205
Around the Sea of Galilee 221
Bed & Breakfasts in the Galilee 227
River Jordan Baptisms 229
Safed (Zefat) 230
Rosh Pina 241

8 TEL AVIV 246
Best Tel Aviv Experiences 249
Essentials 250
Fast Facts: Tel Aviv 257
Exploring Tel Aviv 257
Design Museum & Children's Museum in Holon 263
Organized Tours & Special Events 267
Outdoor Pursuits & Sports 268
Where to Stay 270
Private Rooms & Apartments 271
Where to Eat 288
Vegan Restaurants 290
Kid-Friendly Restaurants 294
Tel Aviv's Ice Cream Scene 303
Shopping 303
Tel Aviv & Jaffa After Dark 310
Day Trips from Tel Aviv 313

9 THE NORTHERN COASTAL PLAIN 316
Caesarea 316
Apollonia: A Secret Site 321
A Side Trip to Zichron Ya'acov 322
Haifa 323
Akko (Acre) 338

10 EILAT & PETRA 351
Eilat 351
Petra 362
Fast Facts: Petra 366
Walking Tour: Petra 368

11 PLANNING YOUR TRIP TO ISRAEL 379
Getting There 379
Getting Around 380
Tips on Accommodations 384
Tours & Escorted Trips 386
Fast Facts: Israel 392

INDEX 399

LIST OF MAPS

Israel in 2 Weeks 14
Israel in 1 Week 21
A Week in Israel with Young Kids 23
History of Israel 30
Old City Accommodations, Dining & Attractions 56
West Jerusalem Accommodations & Dining 63
Citywide Jerusalem Accommodations & Dining 76
Historic Jerusalem 103
Church of the Holy Sepulchre 124
Old City Walking Tour & Sites 130
Citywide Jerusalem Attractions 156
Masada 186
Galilee 194
Tel Aviv Accommodations, Dining & Attractions 272
The Northern Coast 317
Haifa 324
Akko (Acre)/Old Akko 339
Petra Walking Tour 370

ABOUT THE AUTHORS

Elianna Bar-El is a Southern California native calling Tel Aviv home for the past 13 years. She served as the editor for *Time Out Israel* for over a decade and has written for *Vogue, Architectural Digest, As Promised*, and more. You'll find her traveling, reading, eating, and vintage shopping (often all at once).

Shira Rubin is a foreign correspondent for the *Washington Post* based in Tel Aviv. She speaks English, Hebrew, Arabic, French, and Spanish.

Karen Chernick is a Tel Aviv -based writer who prides herself on knowing obscure historical facts about the cityscape, plus the best place to get lunch. She can often be found at recently opened art exhibitions, the market, or walking along the Mediterranean (a view that never gets old). Her stories about hidden gems and worth-splurging eats have been featured in *The Times* (UK), *Elle Decor, Smithsonian, Atlas Obscura, Haaretz*, and *The Times of Israel*, among other publications.

ABOUT THE FROMMER TRAVEL GUIDES

For most of the past 50 years, Frommer's has been the leading series of travel guides in North America, accounting for as many as 24% of all guidebooks sold. I think I know why.

Though we hope our books are entertaining, we nevertheless deal with travel in a serious fashion. Our guidebooks have never looked on such journeys as a mere recreation, but as a far more important human function, a time of learning and introspection, an essential part of a civilized life. We stress the culture, lifestyle, history, and beliefs of the destinations we cover, and urge our readers to seek out people and new ideas as the chief rewards of travel.

We have never shied from controversy. We have, from the beginning, encouraged our authors to be intensely judgmental, critical—both pro and con—in their comments, and wholly independent. Our only clients are our readers, and we have triggered the ire of countless prominent sorts, from a tourist newspaper we called "practically worthless" (it unsuccessfully sued us) to the many rip-offs we've condemned.

And because we believe that travel should be available to everyone regardless of their incomes, we have always been cost-conscious at every level of expenditure. Though we have broadened our recommendations beyond the budget category, we insist that every lodging we include be sensibly priced. We use every form of media to assist our readers, and are particularly proud of our feisty daily website, the award-winning Frommers.com.

I have high hopes for the future of Frommer's. May these guidebooks, in all the years ahead, continue to reflect the joy of travel and the freedom that travel represents. May they always pursue a cost-conscious path, so that people of all incomes can enjoy the rewards of travel. And may they create, for both the traveler and the persons among whom we travel, a community of friends, where all human beings live in harmony and peace.

Arthur Frommer

THE BEST OF ISRAEL

1

By Karen Chernick

For a country the size of New Jersey, Israel is startlingly diverse. When you find yourself in the silent, haunting desertscape near the Dead Sea, spotting ibexes on cliffs that are dotted with inaccessible caves—like those in which the Dead Sea Scrolls lay hidden for more than 18 centuries—it can be hard to believe that less than 60 minutes away is the 19th-century Eastern European time-warp world of Jerusalem's orthodox Mea Shearim quarter. And a few blocks from Mea Shearim, you'll find the labyrinthine medieval Arab bazaars of the Old City, with calls to prayer from the city's minarets punctuating your wanderings. Hop into a sherut (shared taxi) to Tel Aviv, and in an hour you're in a world of glass skyscrapers, surfboards, and bikinis on the beach. Travel 2½ hours to the north, and you can explore ruined Crusader castles in the green forests of the Galilee Mountains.

The Holy Land surprises visitors in other ways as well. Fifty years ago, the country was an austere, no-frills society—Israelis lived with few luxuries, and this spartan life was part of the national ideology. Today, Israeli society is frenetically inventive, the country's economy is booming, the standard of living has skyrocketed, and many surveys rank Israel's per-capita income among the top 20 in the world. Israel is becoming a nation with a lively sense of style and a taste for the good life. Deluxe accommodations have popped up all over the country, and visitors find an interesting array of restaurants, shopping opportunities, wineries, and microbreweries.

With the Israeli-Jordanian peace treaty, a journey to Israel can also easily include an excursion to the fabulous ancient Nabatean city of Petra in Jordan, camping with Bedouin in Jordan's wild Wadi Rum, or a stay at one of the excellent luxury spas on the Jordanian side of the Dead Sea. Relations with other neighbors in the region, with the notable exception of Egypt, still tend to be more fraught, so as with any destination in the Middle East you'll want to stay informed both before and during your trip.

Amid Israel's busy swirl of exoticism, ancient sites, markets, and crowded highways, you can still find young, idealistic kibbutzim and communities in the Negev, where new immigrants and old-timers are reclaiming the land from the desert as they learn how to live on it, appreciate its wonders, and make it truly their own.

Many travelers are attracted to Israel for reasons of faith, or to reconnect with their Jewish roots in the ancestral homeland of the Jewish people. Others are drawn by the history, pure and simple (although the history here is often anything but simple), and others find their bliss under the Mediterranean sun. Beneath it all is the feisty spirit of the Israelis themselves, who through a formidable work ethic and sometimes startling creativity make this little place a fascinating one with which to get acquainted. Roman ruins, biblical sites, beaches, and delicious food are all enticements, too. So it's no exaggeration at all to say that unlike most destinations for its size, Israel will amaze you.

ISRAEL'S iconic EXPERIENCES

- **Twilight from a Rooftop in Jerusalem's Old City:** Find a high vantage point where you can watch over the Old City and listen to the echoes of synagogue prayers, mosque chants and the Islamic call to temple, and church bells that usher in Jerusalem's aura of evening sanctity.
- **Visiting the Dome of the Rock and the Temple Mount (Haram Es Sharif):** Built by the early Islamic rulers of Jerusalem in A.D. 691 on the site of the Temple of Solomon, this shrine is one of the world's most beautiful structures and the centerpiece of this awesome, sacred compound. Take the time to experience the power of this extraordinary place on your own. Note that access to the Temple Mount is always subject to changing political conditions. See p. 114.
- **The Western Wall on the Eve of Sabbath:** Enter Jerusalem's Jaffa Gate before Shabbat and join the flow of worshippers making their way downhill through the bazaars and alleys of the Old City as they move toward the Western Wall. At the Wall, you'll feel the magnetism and charisma that this remnant of the ancient Temple possesses for millions in the Jewish world. See p. 105.
- **A Walking Tour of Tel Aviv's Bauhaus District:** Tel Aviv is Israel's bustling seaside metropolis, and while its long beach promenade is something to behold, so is its wealth of white Bauhaus architecture that has earned the city a UNESCO World Heritage designation. In fact, Tel Aviv boasts more original Bauhaus buildings, mostly from the 1930s and 1940s, than any other city in the world. Liebling Haus and the Bauhaus Center offer great walking tours all year long. See p. 267.
- **Getting Into the Dead Sea:** Float up top at the lowest place on earth, the Dead Sea. The water's high salinity makes it impossible to do anything but bob at the surface, and the feeling of weightlessness is uncanny. Visit one of the Dead Sea's public beaches, or find a spot where you can cover

The Dome of the Rock was built in the 7th century. It is the oldest still-standing Islamic monument on the planet.

The Dead Sea has that name because it was assumed that its high level of salinity would kill any creature that attempted to live in it. Scientists now know that some bacteria and fungi do survive in these waters.

yourself from head to toe in Dead Sea mud (coveted for its cosmetic properties). See p. 178.

- **An Evening Stroll Through Old Jaffa:** The beautifully preserved labyrinth of small streets in Old Jaffa is filled with galleries, shops, cafes, great restaurants, and vistas of minarets and Crusader ruins set against the sunset and the sea. It's a special Israeli mix of the ancient and the cutting edge. See p. 264.
- **Holy Week in Jerusalem:** Starting with the Palm Sunday procession into the Old City and continuing with the Stations of the Cross on Good Friday and the Easter Sunday rites of the Latin, Orthodox, Coptic, Ethiopian, and Armenian churches at the Holy Sepulchre Church, this is a time of passion and meaning for thousands of pilgrims.
- **Yad Vashem Memorial & Holocaust Museum:** A visit to this complex of memorials and museums in Jerusalem that commemorates the six million Jews who fell victim to the Nazis is an act of contemplation about the dangers of hatred and indifference to suffering. No visitor can leave unaffected. See p. 145.
- **Circling the Sea of Galilee:** This gemlike, turquoise lake set amid the mountains of Galilee is Israel's greatest natural treasure and was the landscape of Jesus's ministry. The eastern and northern shores are less developed and better reveal the lake's poetry. Explore biblical sites and watch twilight fall over this magical body of water from a eucalyptus-shaded beach. Kibbutz Ein Gev is perfect for overnighting and idyllic swimming. Rent a car for a few days and freewheel through the Galilee's olive groves, wineries, ruined Roman-era synagogues, Crusader castles, ancient churches, and the walled Casbah of Akko beside the Mediterranean. See chapter 7.

THE most evocative ANCIENT SITES & CITIES

Israel and neighboring Jordan are filled with ancient sites and cities from every part of their long histories. Some sites are famous places of pilgrimage; others were lost and forgotten until modern times. Now, dazzling physical monuments to the past are being recovered at a rapid pace.

- **City of David:** Just outside the present walls of Jerusalem, this is where most of Jerusalem was located from prehistoric to Old Testament times. Presently undergoing intensive, sometimes controversial, archaeological excavation, this area is now in the densely populated Arab neighborhood of Silwan. It is best visited on an organized tour or with a guide. See p. 118.
- **Capernaum, Tabgha & the Mount of Beatitudes:** This lyrically lovely corner of the Sea of Galilee was the center of Jesus's early ministry. It contains the sites of St. Peter's house, the Miracle of the Loaves and the Fishes, and the Sermon on the Mount. See chapter 7.
- **Akko:** This ancient city just north of Haifa (and easily accessible by train) isn't as well known among today's foreign tourists, but in the past it hosted the ancient Romans, Marco Polo, the Crusaders, and many other shapers of history. It is one of the oldest ports in the world. Worth a day trip for its historic ruins, fresh fish, and distinctive architecture. Don't miss the Subterranean Crusader City. See p. 338.

The City of David is still an active archaeological site, and new items found there are reshaping historians' understandings of what daily life was like in Jerusalem's biblical era, and before.

Gaze into the faces of the A.D. 6th century in Zippori, where archaeologists have unearthed a treasure trove of mosaics.

- **Basilica of the Nativity** (Bethlehem, West Bank): The site of Jesus's birth, this is the oldest surviving church in the Holy Land; the Persians spared it during their invasion in A.D. 614 because, according to legend, they were impressed by a representation of the Magi (fellow Persians) that decorated the building. See p. 175.
- **Caesarea** (on the coast between Tel Aviv and Haifa): Built by Herod as the great harbor and seaport of his kingdom, this was the splendid capital of Roman Judea and Byzantine-era Palestine. The vast Roman and Crusader ruins include amphitheaters, a hippodrome, and Crusader forts that are all the more romantic with Mediterranean waves lapping at the ancient stones. See p. 316.
- **Zippori** (Sepphoris, near Nazareth): This cosmopolitan Jewish-Hellenistic city, close to Nazareth, was the capital of the Galilee in Roman times. Especially interesting because the area was probably familiar to Jesus, Zippori's highlights include a colonnaded street, a mosaic synagogue floor, and a masterpiece mosaic portrait of a Roman-era woman dubbed "the *Mona Lisa* of the Galilee." See p. 199.
- **Korazim:** Once hidden by mountains of thistles, this Roman-Byzantine-era Jewish town in the hills just northeast of the Sea of Galilee is a beautiful place with sweeping views of the lake. Houses and an ancient synagogue adorned with beautifully carved black basalt detailing still stand. See p. 225.
- **Petra:** One of the great wonders of the world, yet forgotten for a thousand years, this legendary 2,000-year-old Nabatean city carved from the walls of a hidden desert canyon is the highlight of excursion tours into Jordan. The entire Petra experience, including the trek into the canyon, has an air of adventure and mystery. Stays of 1 or 2 nights are recommended. See chapter 10.

THE best WAYS TO EXPERIENCE ISRAEL LIKE A LOCAL

- **Sampling Food in an Open-Air Shuk, such as Tel Aviv's Carmel Market or Jerusalem's Machane Yehuda:** For some of the best eats that Israel has to offer, go straight to the source: one of the open air markets where seasonality is king (look for fresh green chickpeas in spring and figs in summer). Friday mornings will be the busiest as shoppers prepare for the Sabbath, so plan accordingly. Look on market side streets for cafes and lunch spots—a crowd is the best indication of whether a place is good. See chapters 8 and 5.
- **Watching the Sun Set over the Mediterranean:** Israel's entire coastline of white-sand beaches, cliffs, and bluffs faces directly west into the sunset. The Jewish day traditionally begins with the marking of sunset. Take a half-hour and find a spot to watch the sun sink into the sea—it's a memorable way to unwind and reflect.
- **Going with the Flow on the Sabbath:** The idea that every living thing must be allowed to rest for one-seventh of its existence is one of Judaism's ancient precepts. In modern Israel, most businesses and public transportation cease on Shabbat and *everyone* relaxes, if not rests. Join the national aura of Sabbath calm: Keep your Sabbath itinerary slow and restful. In Jerusalem, expect a city-wide shut down; in Tel Aviv, you'll find restaurants, art galleries, and movie theaters operating (under the philosophy that leisure is rest!).

Small mountains of spice are a feature at many Israeli markets. Pictured here is the Carmel market in Jerusalem.

Despite its small size, Israel is home to some 2,500 species of wildflowers. That's 1,000 more than the larger British Isles! Here, a field of red anemones bursts into bloom in front of the Mount of Beatitudes.

- **Wildflower-Watching in Late Winter:** After the winter rains, thousands of Israelis and travelers pour into the Galilee to enjoy the oceans of wildflowers, including the famous wild irises near Netanya and the Gilboa hills, that cover the normally parched landscape. In the Negev, people flock to see the bright red blossoming of anemones during a festival called *Darom Adom* (Red South). They're traditions akin to cherry-blossom viewing in Japan.
- **Sampling the Music Scene:** Israel possesses an oversupply of magnificent musicians; even smaller cities, such as Beersheba, are home to orchestras that would be the envy of world capitals. Check local tourist offices for information about concerts and festivals ranging from classical to jazz to traditional local music.
- **Ask Questions Everywhere:** Israelis and Palestinians live with passion. They have lots to say, and most speak at least some English. Ask polite questions. Don't impose your own views—just listen to the answers you get. You'll hear a mosaic of feelings that reflect Israel's ancient traditions and modern complexities.

ISRAEL'S best RESTAURANTS

- **Jerusalem's Machane Yehuda Market:** This enormous market for produce, spices, and exotic ingredients is dotted with tiny no-name, genuine eateries and a sprinkling of new boutique food shops and gourmet restaurants. Sip

Who says vegetarian food can't be varied? At Tzemah, each meal is a kaleidoscopic feast of different flavors, textures, spice levels, and colors.

fresh almond milk, munch sweet grapes or a bag of fresh-from-the-oven *ruggele* pastry, and let the aromas, sights, and mountains of foods overwhelm you. See p. 168.

- **Tzemah** (Jerusalem): The latest eatery opened by Jerusalemite celebrity chef Assaf Granit (known for restaurants such as Machneyuda, also a top choice), Tzemah is all about giving local produce the all-star treatment. Favorites on the menu include eggplant brulée with caramelized sugar on top, or the lychee ceviche. See p. 91.
- **Hummus Abu Hassan** (Jaffa): This humble hummus joint, one of the oldest in Israel and known nationwide, may not look like much from the outside—but appearances are deceptive. In fact, foodies have been known to make hummus pilgrimages just to dine at these crowded communal tables. There's no menu, but only a handful of hummus options, so see our suggestions before you sit down. A delicious and authentic experience. See p. 302.
- **Luna Bistro** (Nazareth): Ask most local Nazarenes to recommend the best place to eat and they'll point you towards Luna Bistro, a modern restaurant serving superb versions of traditional Galilean food. This woman-owned restaurant has something for every palate, from toddlers to vegans. See p. 201.
- **Hotel Montefiore Restaurant** (Tel Aviv): While the Hotel Montefiore is indeed a hotel (albeit a boutique one with just 12 rooms), Tel Avivians know the place better for its elegant gourmet restaurant. Whether you come for lunch, dinner, or a drink at the chic bar, you will have an unforgettably

flavorful experience. Reservations strongly recommended. See p. 293.

- **Decks** (Tiberias): With a setting that floats on the surface of the Sea of Galilee like a dream, Decks offers luxurious meats and fish expertly grilled over olive- and citrus-wood fires. As an extra, go on a complimentary post-dinner disco cruise. Decks is kosher and a great choice for a memorable evening at moderate-to-expensive prices. See p. 217.
- **Hellena** (Caesarea): With vistas of the sea, waves lapping at its terrace, and a great young chef designing its menu, this restaurant, set amid the ruins of Caesarea, may be the most romantic spot in Israel for a gourmet meal, especially when the sun sets over the Mediterranean. See p. 322.

A group of Israeli and Venetian artisans and designers worked together to transform two Ottoman-era manors into the exquisite Efendi Hotel.

ISRAEL'S best HOTELS

- **American Colony Hotel** (Jerusalem): This atmospheric, gardened enclave was once a 19th-century pasha's villa. As an international meeting place between East and West Jerusalem, it attracts journalists, writers, and archaeologists and may be the most romantic spot in the Middle East (outside Rick's Café in the film *Casablanca*). The hotel's Saturday afternoon lunch buffet is famous. See p. 72.
- **Abraham Hostel** (Jerusalem): A great new concept in hostels, the Abraham offers guests a lively spirit of camaraderie and lots of tours, ideas, and advice on how to really experience Jerusalem and Israel. Look for their equally stellar outposts in Tel Aviv, Nazareth, and Eilat. See p. 62.
- **Bat Shlomo Farmhouse & Winery** (Zichron Ya'acov): Tucked away in the northern hills of Zichron Ya'acov, this newly restored vineyard houses a small three-room villa with boutique-level attention to detail. Stays here include farm-to-table meals with a private chef, yoga classes, cooking workshops, and wine tastings. See box p. 322.
- **Carlton Hotel** (Tel Aviv): This beachfront hotel doesn't look like much from the outside, but it's packed with fine features like a rooftop pool, the Blue Sky by Meir Adoni restaurant, and a fantastic breakfast buffet at Carlton on the Beach. Guest rooms are recently renovated and most feature sea views. See p. 271.

The gardens are as potent a lure as the guest rooms at the Scots Hotel in Tiberias.

- **Efendi** (Akko): A romantic combination of luxury and authenticity, this beautifully restored villa/boutique hotel has helped turn historic but under-visited Akko into an overnight destination. See p. 348.
- **Fauzi Azar** (Nazareth): From its narrow entryway in Nazareth's old city, Fauzi Azar looks like a simple backpackers' hostel. But the open-air courtyard and the impressive Ottoman-era architecture of this former villa illustrate that this is no ordinary budget spot. Be sure to go to the upper-level living room where the frescoed ceiling and marble inlay floors are still intact. See p. 198.
- **Scots Hotel** (Tiberias): For many Israelis there is only place to stay in Tiberias, and that's this categorically beautiful hotel on the edge of the Sea of Galilee. Non-kosher, Scots is run by the Church of Scotland and combines restored stone 19th-century buildings with more modern structures and features a fabulous restaurant and world-class spa. Lush gardens invite lingering, as does the swimming pool with its Galilee sea views. See p. 213.
- **Shalom & Relax Hotel** (Tel Aviv): This modest hotel near—but not on—the seafront boardwalk makes up for its lack of Mediterranean views with, yes, relaxing amenities. Head to the hammock-packed roof deck for plush seating and free massages from the on-duty masseuse. See p. 276.
- **Setai Sea of Galilee** (Galilee): This resort, set right on the waters of the Sea of Galilee, offers private villas and a relaxing atmosphere that sets it apart from other accommodations along the lakefront. See p. 214.

The roof garden of the Waldorf Astoria follows the curvy contours of this landmarked building.

- **The Vera** (Tel Aviv): This five-story hotel on Tel Aviv's lively Lilienblum Street (conveniently parallel to plush Rothschild Boulevard) is all about the details: an open bar in the lobby with boutique Israeli wines, a verdant rooftop with daily yoga classes, and indulgent bath products. Great location and service. See p. 283.
- **Waldorf Astoria** (Jerusalem): Built as the Palace Hotel in 1928–29, this iconic Jerusalem structure is now a modern bastion of luxury with Ottoman-inspired interiors and a stellar level of service. See p. 67.

SUGGESTED ITINERARIES

2

By Elianna Bar-El

By and large, distances are not great in Israel; as a reference, the country's size is comparable to that of the state of New Jersey. Its small area makes it possible to get a quick taste of the desert, the Mediterranean coast, and even the Sea of Galilee on organized day trips from Jerusalem. To help you make the most of your time, this chapter offers three itineraries. The first is geared for those with 2 weeks or so to tour and explore Israel in considerable depth, covering all the major highlights. The second narrows the focus to just 1 week's worth of adventures. The third itinerary is specifically designed for families. The chapter also includes a summary of each region in the country for those who prefer to plan their own itineraries.

ISRAEL IN 2 WEEKS

This itinerary allows time to enjoy the beauty and variety of Israel's landscapes, and see its iconic sights. You'll have a solid block of time in which to explore Jerusalem, the jewel in the crown. When you're not in Tel Aviv and Jerusalem, it will be most convenient to get around in a rental car, though you could do the following itinerary using just public transportation.

Day 1: Tel Aviv & Jaffa

Head from Ben-Gurion Airport to your hotel, but try to get outside again as quickly as you can. Lots of sunlight will help get you into the rhythm of Israeli time. If you arrive in the early afternoon, head first to the **Jaffa Flea Market,** where vendors hawk everything from hand-made Kilim rugs to Judaica. In the cool of the evening, explore the **Old City of Jaffa** with its cobblestoned medieval streets, galleries, and eateries overlooking the sea.

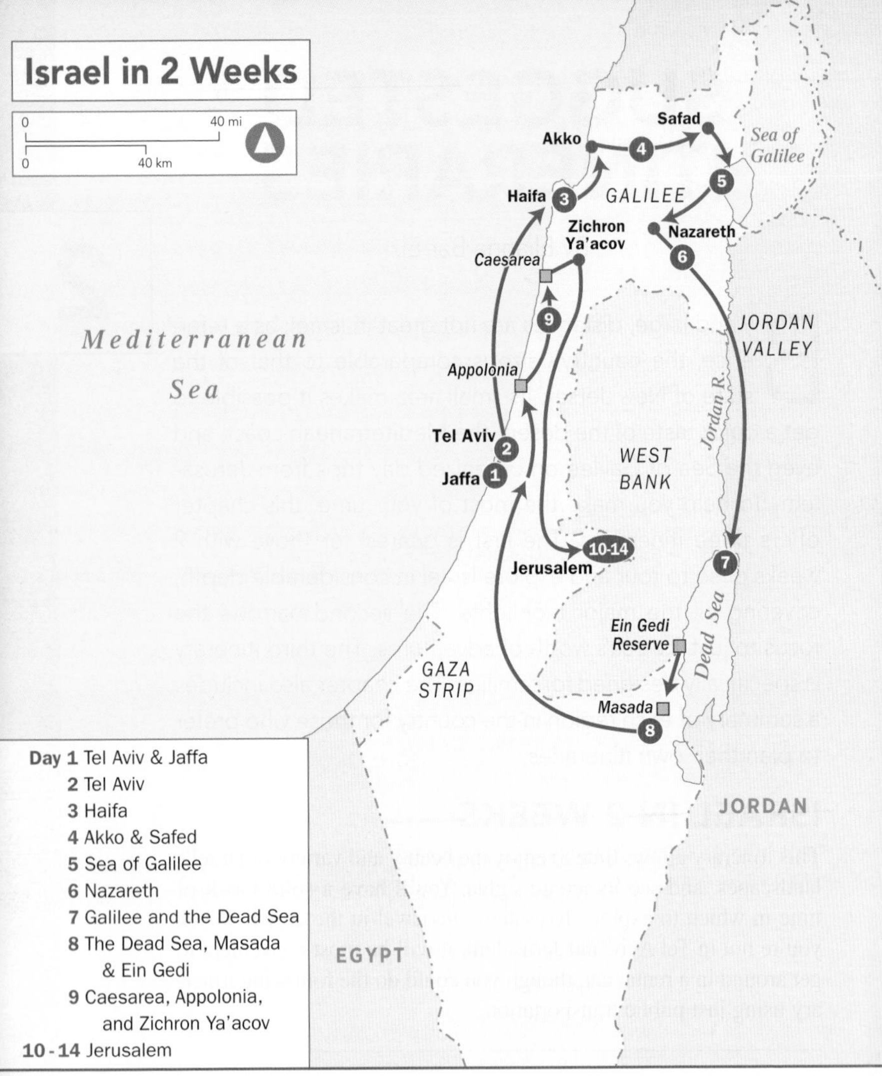

Day 2: Tel Aviv

Before you see Jerusalem, Masada, or the country's other iconic sites, it's important to get an understanding of who the Jewish people are, so you'll be better able to appreciate the dominant culture of Israel. And there's no better place for that than the biggest Jewish culture museum on the planet, **ANU: Museum of the Jewish People** (see p. 257). It's not in a central location, unfortunately, so you'll need to head out early to ensure you can dedicate at least 2 hours to this absorbing institution. Eat a big breakfast, too, as you'll be lunching late, after you travel back to the center of the city to the foodie mecca that is the **Carmel Market** (p. 307). Wandering there, and through the nearby bohemian **Neve**

Circles, repeating eight-pointed stars, and geometrical patterns with asymmetrical elements all have been woven into the landscape architecture of the Bahá'i Gardens in Haifa in an attempt to make these nature areas as conducive to spiritual practice as the temple they surround.

Tzedek neighborhood (p. 250), with its charming boutiques and galleries, will fill the afternoon. Finish the day with fresh seafood and a sunset at the beachfront **Manta Ray** restaurant (p. 301). If you have energy left, take a stroll on the adjacent boardwalk for major people-watching.

Day 3: Haifa

It should take about an hour and a half to drive from Tel Aviv to **Haifa** (p. 323) giving you a generous amount of time to explore this hilly port city, the third largest in Israel. Get your bearings by heading uphill first, to the resplendent **Bahá'i Gardens and Shrine** (p. 330), which are set on 19 terraces flowing down Mount Carmel. After lunch, head to the **Clandestine Immigration and Naval Museum** (p. 331), which tells the gripping story of how Jewish European refugees were infiltrated into British-blockaded Palestine between 1934 to 1948. Finish the day with dinner at the vibrant contemporary Arabic restaurant **Fattoush** (p. 337).

Day 4: Akko & Safed

Half an hour from Haifa is the walled Arabic port city of **Akko** (p. 338), famed for its ancient bazaars and mosques. Tour the town, and lunch there before moving on to the mystic, mountaintop city of **Safed** (p. 230). On the way, visit the ruined ancient synagogue at **Bar'am** (an evocative sight, p. 240) and if you have time, consider popping by one of the region's wineries, like **Abouhav** (www.abouhav-winery.com/t-en) with its 600-year-old cellar. Dine at **Bat Ya'ar Ranch Steak House** (p. 238), which has options for vegetarians, despite the name. It's not a typical Israeli restaurant but it's the best meal to be had in these parts.Spend the night in Safed or at a nearby kibbutz.

Day 5: The Sea of Galilee

It's possible to see several New Testament sites in the course of a morning, starting with the view-rich **Mount of the Beatitudes** (p. 224), where Jesus gave his Sermon on the Mount. Next would be **Capernaum** (p. 224), traditionally believed to be the home of the apostle Peter, and **Tabgha** (p. 222), which has a Benedictine monastery and the Church of the Multiplication of the Loaves and Fishes (marking where that biblical event is thought to have happened). Archeologists uncovered some of the most eye-popping ancient mosaics in Israel at Tabgha. Make your way to **Tiberias** (p. 205) for lunch and a cruise on the mysterious and lovely Lake Kinneret. In the evening, treat yourself to a meal at celeb-chef Assaf Granit–helmed restaurant **Lotte** (p. 212). Spend the night in or near Tiberias.

Day 6: Nazareth

Famous for the **Church of the Annunciation** and **Nazareth Biblical Village,** with its replicas of buildings from the time of Jesus, two-thirds of the day should be spent exploring Nazareth (it's a 30-min. drive from Tiberias). Then, pop in the car for a visit to **Zippori National Park**

(p. 204), which contains the ruins of an impressive Hellenistic-era metropolis. **Luna Bistro** (see p. 201), back in Nazareth, is where you want to have supper before bedding down for the night.

Day 7: Galilee to the Dead Sea

Travel south through the Jordan Valley to visit the vast archaeological park of Roman-era **Bet She'an.** Then make a stop at the famous zodiac mosaic floor of the 5th-century **Bet Alpha Synagogue** at **Kibbutz Heftziba** (p. 210) before making your way to a hotel near **Masada** (p. 185). You want to be in the vicinity of that famous Herodian fortress overnight, so you can start the trek to the top before the sun has risen. Doing so allows you to catch a spectacular sunrise and avoid the site's often blistering midday temperatures.

Day 8: The Dead Sea, Masada & Ein Gedi

After a very early tour of **Masada,** where the last Jewish resisters against Rome chose suicide over surrender, take a float in the otherworldly **Dead Sea** (p. 178). You may also have time for a waterfall-filled hike in the **Ein Gedi Reserve** (see p. 183), a canyon oasis where David hid from King Saul in ancient times, which now attracts nature lovers from all over the world. Return to the hotel you stayed in last night.

Day 9: Caesarea, Apollonia & Zichron Ya'acov

On your way to Jerusalem, visit the ancient Roman ruins of seaside **Caesarea** (p. 316)—and do so underwater if you have a scuba diving

Visitors take in the view from the summit of Masada.

Jerusalem Sightseeing

Tailor the Jerusalem suggestions in this tour to the days when sites are open. The Temple Mount is closed to visitors Friday and Saturday; much of West Jerusalem shuts for Shabbat. There are wonderful concerts, performances, and lectures (many in English); check the Friday editions of *The Jerusalem Post* or *Haaretz* for listings. Other online resources include www.itraveljerusalem.com, www.jerusalem.muni.il, and www.gojerusalem.com.

certificate. If not, the on-land archeological site is spectacular, as are the nearby remains of a 13th-century Crusader castle known as Apollonia. For the evening, backtrack a tad for dinner and a stay in the ever-charming and history-rich town of **Zichron Ya'acov** (p. 322).

Day 10: Jerusalem

After your 1½-hour drive to Jerusalem, drop your bags at your hotel, return the rental car, and grab some lunch. Since you need a full day to really experience the Old City (that will be tomorrow), your afternoon activity will be a visit to the **Israel Museum** (p. 142) to see the Dead Sea Scrolls and the other treasures it holds. Celebrate the end of your first day in Jerusalem with dinner at **Chakra** (p. 89), one of the city's most festive, and tasty, restaurants.

Day 11: The Old City

Get up early and go into the **Old City** to see the **Temple Mount** and the **Western Wall.** The magnificent **Dome of the Rock** and **Al Aqsa Mosque** are not open to non-Muslims but they are a sight to behold, both from afar and close up. Exit the Old City via the Damascus Gate and take a round-trip taxi to the **Mount of Olives,** which is best visited in the morning, when the sun will be behind you as you look (and photograph) west to the panorama of the Old and New cities. Afterward, explore the Old City bazaars; the **Crusader Church of St. Anne,** with its exquisite acoustics; and the **Church of the Holy Sepulchre.** See "The Old City" in chapter 5.

A worshipper lights a candle at the Church of the Holy Sepulchre.

Day 12: The New City

Go on **Egged Bus no. 99**'s Jerusalem Highlights tour, which takes you all over the city. Spend a somber afternoon at **Yad Vashem Holocaust Memorial & Museum** (p. 145). Consider a meal at the **Rooftop of the Mamilla Hotel** (p. 82), where the view and dishes are equally exquisite.

Day 13: More of New Jerusalem

Choose from the **Knesset** (p. 151), with its Chagall panels, or **Hadassah Hospital Ein Kerem** (p. 149), with its world-famous Chagall stained-glass windows. The latter will take you to **Ein Kerem** (p. 155), once the village of John the Baptist. Make a late afternoon visit to West Jerusalem's **Machane Yehuda** produce market, which is colorful and filled with great places to eat and stock up on signature treats to bring back home. Drop in to **Tzemah** (p. 91) or **Machneyuda Restaurant** (p. 89) for a bite of chef Assaf Granit's famous dishes and then walk over to **Thinkers Distillery** (p. 98) for some locally crafted bourbon, gin, or whiskey (also authentic souvenirs to bring back home!).

Day 14: A Last Look at Jerusalem

If you don't have to rush to the airport, either spend more time in the Old City, visit spots you may have missed elsewhere in the city, or head to **Huzot HaYotzer,** an artists' colony at the foot of the Old City Walls, where stunning, handmade works by Israeli artists can be found. For an extra special farewell meal, stop into **Eucalyptus** (p. 80) and relish the local ingredients and artistry of chef Moshe Basson.

ISRAEL IN 1 WEEK

This fast-paced itinerary covers all the heavy-hitters in Israel, though it only allows you to scratch the surface of these diverse, fascinating sights. You shouldn't need to rent a car to accomplish the following itinerary.

Day 1: Tel Aviv

Head from Ben-Gurion Airport to your hotel. Walk along the Tayelet seaside promenade and if it's warm enough (basically any time between March and late October), go for a swim. If you're there earlier in the day and have the energy, drop into the spellbinding **ANU Museum of the Jewish People** (p. 257). In the evening, take in the lively street scenes along **Dizengoff Street** or on and around **Rothschild Boulevard.** For the perfect first night dinner, score a reservation at contemporary Israeli restaurant **North Abraxas** (p. 295).

Day 2: Jaffa

Use your second morning in Tel Aviv to explore the city's ancient side in **Jaffa.** The Old City of Jaffa with its medieval streets, galleries, and

One of the many stalls at Jaffa's mesmerizing flea market.

eateries overlooking the sea is a must, but so is the flea market area behind the iconic **Clock Tower.** Tucked among the souvenir stalls and purveyors of furniture, rugs, and vintage maps are contemporary restaurants and shops featuring the wares of Israeli designers. Pop into **the Old Jaffa Visitor's Center** (p. 266) for its informative exhibits. In the afternoon, soak up Tel Aviv's phenomenal and extensive Bauhaus architecture, either on your own or by taking a guided, in-depth walking tour with the experts of the **Bauhaus Center** (p. 259).

Day 3: Jerusalem

Leave Tel Aviv very early so that you can follow the Old City itinerary suggested for day 11 of our 2-week tour (see p. 18).

Day 4: Jerusalem

Use your fourth day to continue your exploration of Jerusalem. In the morning, visit **Yad Vashem,** Israel's exhaustive, emotional national Holocaust memorial. Then journey back in time at the fantastic **Israel Museum,** home of the Dead Sea Scrolls and an array of impressive archaeological finds. By this point in your journey, you'll begin to see how truly varied Israel is. Consider staying overnight near Masada, so you can get an early start on day 5 and avoid the midday heat at the summit.

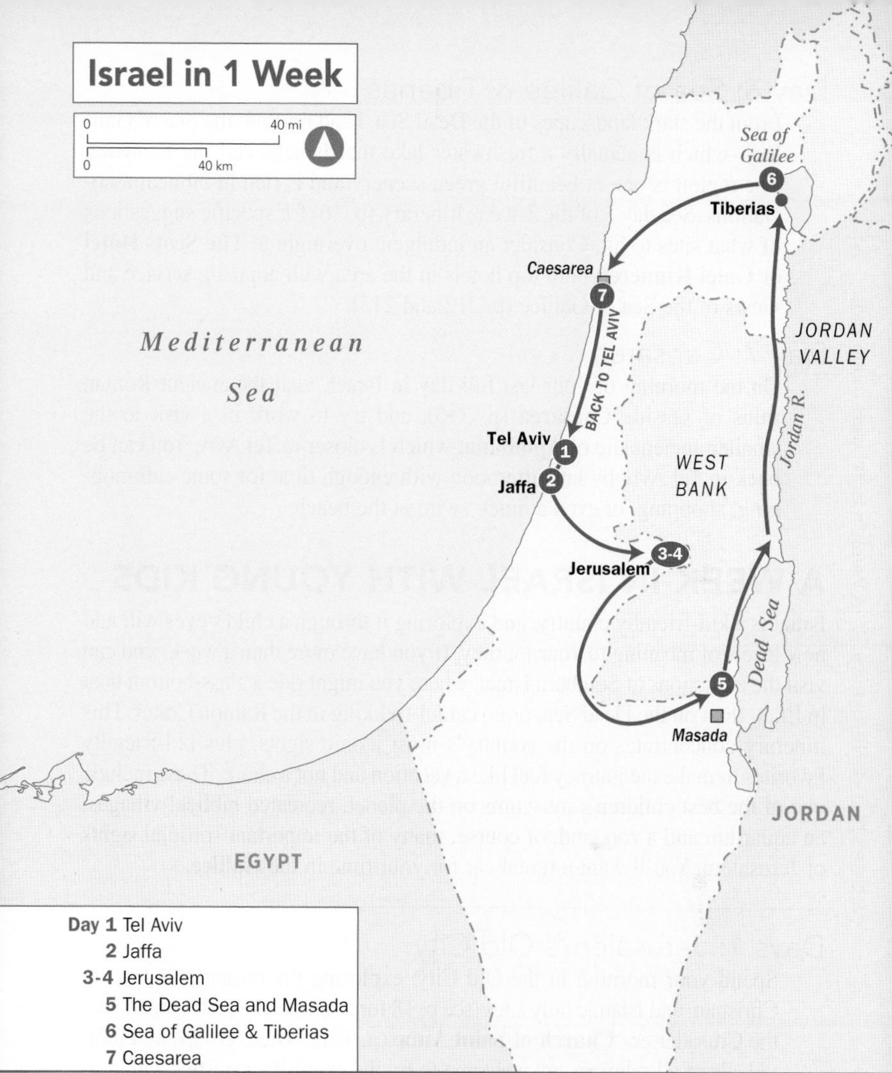

Day 5: The Dead Sea & Masada

You will get a sense of how human and natural history intertwine by visiting the ancient Jewish fortress of **Masada.** Take the cable car up for spectacular views of the desert and Dead Sea, and leave ample time to investigate the well-marked ruins on the summit. For your next stop, you'll float away, literally, in the **Dead Sea.** This geological wonder is close to Jerusalem but, figuratively, it's a million miles away. The lowest point on earth never fails to amaze. See chapter 6.

Day 6: Sea of Galilee & Tiberias

From the stark landscapes of the Dead Sea, head north to the Sea of Galilee—which is actually a freshwater lake that Israelis call the Kinneret. The region is one of beautiful green scenery and is rich in biblical associations. See day 5 of the 2-week itinerary (p. 16) for specific suggestions of what sites to hit. Consider an indulgent overnight at **The Scots Hotel** or **Galei Kinneret,** both top hotels in the area with amazing service and views of the Sea of Galilee (p. 212 and 213).

Day 7: Caesarea

On the morning of your last full day in Israel, visit the ancient Roman ruins of seaside **Caesarea** (p. 316), and try to work in a visit to the smaller ancient site of **Apollonia,** which is closer to Tel Aviv. You can be back in Tel Aviv by late afternoon with enough time for some cafe-hopping, shopping, or even a quick swim at the beach.

A WEEK IN ISRAEL WITH YOUNG KIDS

Israel is a kid-friendly country, and exploring it through a child's eyes will add new levels of meaning to your journey. If you have more than a week, you can visit the attractions of Southern Israel, where you might ride a glass-bottom boat in Eilat, float on the Dead Sea, or go camel-trekking in the Ramon Crater. This itinerary concentrates on the country's most iconic sights, plus kid-friendly favorites to make the journey feel like a vacation and not a chore. These include one of the best children's museums on the planet, recreated biblical villages, an aquarium and a zoo, and, of course, many of the important spiritual sights of Jerusalem. You'll want a rental car for your time in the **Galilee.**

Days 1: Jerusalem's Old City

Spend your morning in the Old City, exploring the bazaar and Jewish, Christian, and Islamic holy sites (see p. 18 for a sample day). Be sure to visit the Crusader-era **Church of Saint Anne** (p. 121), where groups and individuals of all religions are welcome to try the exquisite acoustics with religious songs of any tradition. If your curious child is a foodie-in-the-making,

Kids' Activities

No matter where you travel with your kids, always read the Friday *Haaretz/Herald Tribune* and *The Jerusalem Post* and check in with tourist information offices. Other online resources are www.itraveljerusalem.com, www.jerusalem.muni.il, www.gojerusalem.com, and www.tel-aviv.gov.il/en.

Especially during the summer and holidays, there are usually an array of street performers at night in Jerusalem's outdoor Mamilla Mall or Ben-Yehuda Street and on Tel Aviv's beach promenade, plus a smattering of puppet shows, performances, special museum exhibits and activities aimed at kids.

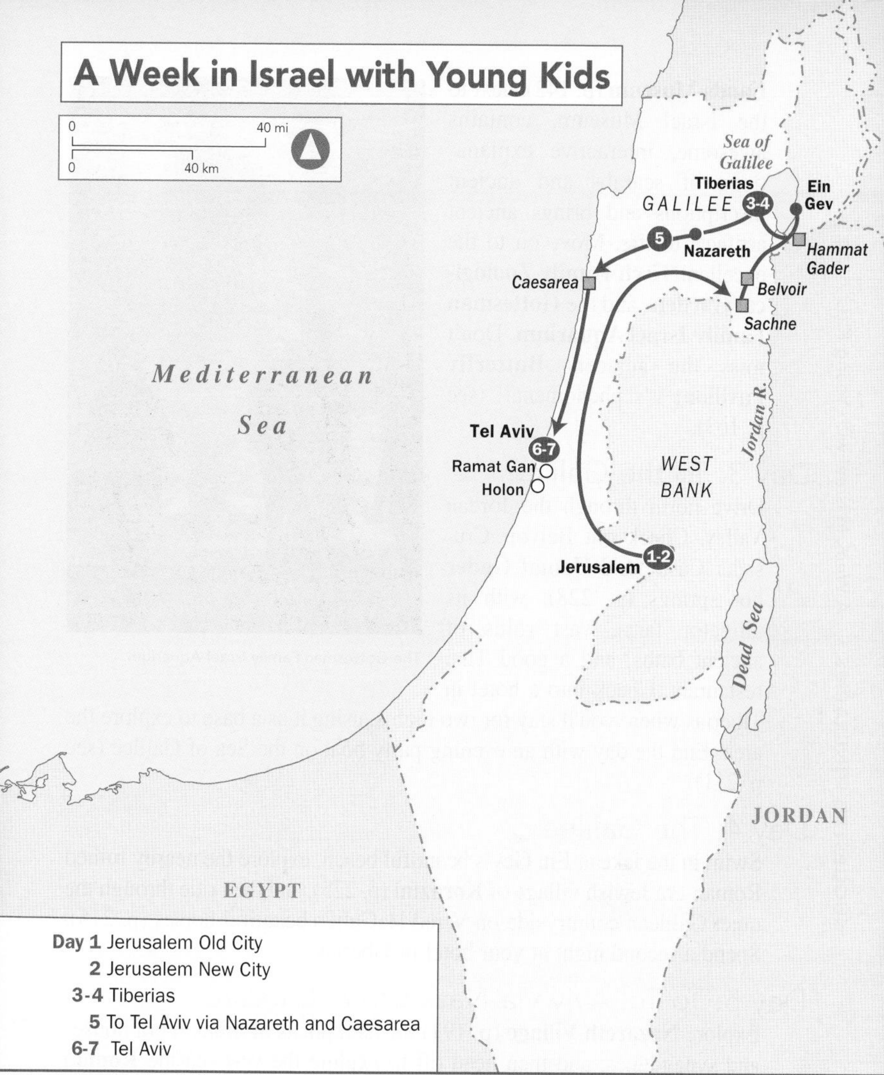

check out the Via Dolorosa between the fourth and fifth Stations of the Cross for shops selling simple kanafeh (an Arabic honey-infused cheese treat that will satisfy any sweet tooth). **Jaffar and Sweets** (p. 80) on the Suq Khan es-Zeit Bazaar is always a big hit. Head to Machne Yehuda Market for stalls upon stalls of interesting eats for an early dinner.

Day 2: Jerusalem's New City

Visit the **Israel Museum** (p. 142). Children will especially enjoy the Children's Museum; the wall of Chanukah menorahs from all over the world in the Judaica Wing; and the Billy Rose Sculpture Garden filled with works by Picasso, Rodin, and others. For older kids, the **Bible**

Lands Museum (p. 142), next to the Israel Museum, contains awesome, interactive explanations of scarabs and ancient inscriptions and brings ancient artifacts to life. Move on to the excellent **Tisch Family Zoological Gardens** and the **Gottesman Family Israel Aquarium.** Don't miss the adjacent **Butterfly Pavilion;** it's phenomenal! (see p. 163).

The Gottesman Family Israel Aquarium.

Day 3: To the Galilee

Drive north through the Jordan Valley. Check out Belvoir Crusader Castle and **Hamat Gader** hot springs (p. 228), with its alligator farm, vast ruins of ancient baths, and a good Thai restaurant. Check into a hotel in Tiberias where you'll stay for two nights, using it as a base to explore the area. End the day with an evening party boat on the Sea of Galilee (see p. 211).

Day 4: The Galilee

Swim in the lake at Ein Gev's beautiful beach, explore the nearby ruined Roman-era Jewish village of **Korazim** (p. 225), and then ride through the quiet Galilean countryside on Vered HaGalil's beautiful horses (p. 215). Spend a second night at your hotel in Tiberias.

Day 5: To Tel Aviv via Nazareth & Caesarea

Explore **Nazareth Village** (p. 197) for its replicas of biblical-era houses and synagogues, and then head off to explore the vast seaside **Roman and Crusader ruins at Caesarea** (p. 318), which includes a great multimedia presentation. Check into a beachfront hotel in **Tel Aviv**'s vibrant port area known as the **Namal.** The family-friendly stretch of north Tel Aviv is filled with outdoor jungle gyms, an indoor trampoline park called Sky Jump, splash pads in the summer, various activities, and restaurants with outdoor seating overlooking the Mediterranean. It's a win-win for parents and kids.

Day 6: Tel Aviv

There are so many kid-friendly museums in the area, it is truly a challenge to choose. From the **Children's Museum** of Holon's fascinating "Dialogue in the Dark" exhibit on blindness (p. 263) to the **Eretz Israel**

MORE kid-friendly picks IN ISRAEL

Dan Caesarea ★★ (Caesarea; p. 321) Set amid vast, lush gardens, with an enormous pool and a kid-size basketball court, this is a fun place to relax for a day or so while taking in the region. The nearby ancient ruins of Caesarea (p. 318) come alive with a modern, multimedia presentation.

Dan Carmel Haifa Hotel ★★ (Haifa; p. 335) The energetic children's summer staff and evening entertainment captivate kids, and the swimming pool is deliciously warm by August. The Dan Hotels' children's clubs are excellent throughout the country.

Nachsholim ★★★ (near Zichron Ya'acov; www.nahsholim.co.il/en) This kibbutz hotel is a winner for both kids and parents. The beach is rugged and wild with tide pools and the hotel is accommodating and convenient. There is the option for rooms in the kibbutz, or in the more recently built area that houses deluxe family units featuring private pools overlooking the sea.

Elma Arts Complex ★★★ (Zichron Ya'acov; p. 323) A sprawling architectural marvel with a host of family suites, the Elma is a great place for everyone to unwind in its vast expanse of grassy landscapes or poolside—all with glorious views. The on-site restaurant has its own menu of kid favorites, and the lobby and common areas are filled with Israeli art to ponder and ignite the imagination.

Museum's planetarium (p. 259) and more, there is plenty of ground to cover.

Day 7: Tel Aviv & Surroundings

In the nearby city of Holon, the **Israel Children's Museum** (p. 263) boasts world-class exhibits that initiate a dialogue and simulation with children to help them understand the daily lives of those who are blind, deaf, elderly, and have special needs. Each adult guide speaks from their own experiences and the result is truly thought-provoking for both adults and adolescents. Be sure to book in advance. There is also the wonderful drive-through **Safari Park** in nearby Ramat Gan (p. 261), where children find the thriving giraffe herd and colony of upside down bats endlessly fascinating. Take a late-afternoon Mediterranean swim. Head off to Ben-Gurion Airport for a late-night flight home or spend one last night in Tel Aviv.

The Regions in Brief

It doesn't take much time to get from one region of Israel to another (at some points, it's only 16km/10 miles wide), but you'll find the country is enormously varied. A quick review of the landscape will help you to decide where to spend your time.

JERUSALEM

The jewel in the crown. The city is many worlds: modern and timeless; Jewish and Arab; religious and secular. The walled, labyrinthine Old City has been named a World Heritage Site; in addition to being a perfectly preserved town with more than 4,000 years of history, it contains the great holy places of Judaism, Christianity, and Islam—the Temple Mount with the Dome of the Rock and the Al Aqsa Mosque, the Western Wall, and the Church of the Holy Sepulchre. Highlights of the New City include the remarkable Israel Museum, which houses the Dead Sea Scrolls, and Yad Vashem, the haunting Holocaust Memorial and Museum.

THE DEAD SEA

Easy to visit for a day by using Jerusalem as your base, the Dead Sea, the lowest point on the earth, is also a good place to visit for a few days as part of a jaunt into the Negev Desert. The almost impregnable Herodian Fortress of **Masada,** the most dramatic ancient site in the country, is perched on a plateau above the Dead Sea. It was here that the last Jewish resisters against Rome committed suicide rather than surrender. The beautiful canyon oasis of **Ein Gedi** is another attraction, as is the unique experience of floating in the mineral-heavy Dead Sea waters. The southern Israeli shore of the sea is lined with world-famous spas and hotels offering an array of therapeutic and beauty-treatment packages.

THE NEGEV

The southern part of Israel (nearly two-thirds of the country) is desert and semi-desert; it contains beautiful **nature reserves** and is great for hiking and nature tours. This part of the country, least visited by tourists, is perhaps the most mysterious. Long famous for its coral reef and laid-back snorkeling and diving opportunities, **Eilat,** at the southern tip of the Negev, is a world unto itself—a mirage rising out of the sand, with dozens of new high-rise mega hotels and restaurants grouped on the city's few miles of Red Sea shoreline. The **Sinai Coast of Egypt,** a bit farther south and easily accessible from Eilat, offers reefs that are even more spectacular, a landscape that is more dramatic and less developed, and hotels that are considerably less expensive.

TEL AVIV

Full of energy and a decidedly hedonistic vibe (many wonder how it can be in the same country as Jerusalem), Tel Aviv has top-of-the line restaurants; beautiful, if not packed, beaches; and a slew of visit-worthy cultural institutions including the Eretz Israel Museum, Tel Aviv Museum of Art, Liebling House, ANU Museum of the Jewish People, Habima Theatre, the Steinhardt Museum of Natural History, and more. Tel Aviv is a good first stop in Israel—you can spend a day at the beach to recover from jet lag before plunging into the rest of the country.

THE MEDITERRANEAN COAST

The ruined Roman- and Crusader-era city of **Caesarea** is the most dramatic archaeological site along the coast; farther north, the Old City of **Akko,** with its bazaars, cafes, and minarets beside the Mediterranean, is the most exotic site. **Kibbutzim** and moshav holiday villages, from Nachsholim, south of Haifa, right up to the northernmost coast, are good spots for a pleasant beach break from touring. A side day trip to **Zichron Ya'acov** and its charming wineries is a must-stop on the way up north.

HAIFA

Israel's third major city offers a spirit and face quite different from Jerusalem or Tel Aviv. It is an unassuming business and industrial city, but it's also beautifully laid out on the slopes of Mount Carmel, which overlooks a bustling harbor. The magnificent Bahá'i Gardens and fun tech and science museums for kids make Haifa a smart base for exploring the northwestern part of the country.

THE GALILEE

Israel's northern region is filled with a lovely countryside of forested mountains and olive groves dotted with Israeli-Arab cities and towns, kibbutzim, and the remains of ancient ruined cities, synagogues, and churches. At the heart of the region is the freshwater **Sea of Galilee,** a lyrically beautiful body of water made all the more special by its association with both New and Old Testament sites. The Galilee offers great hiking and nature trails, but it's also a good place to rent a car for a few days and freewheel.

THE WEST BANK/PALESTINIAN AUTHORITY AREAS

This was a countryside of classic biblical landscapes and ancient sites, but 20-plus years of political turmoil and war have made the West Bank difficult to visit at the best of times and outright dangerous at the worst of times. As of press time, the governments of most Western countries advise against visiting this

Visitors wander around the ancient city of Petra in Jordan.

area until the political situation improves, so it's best to consider this area off limits when planning your itinerary, although visits with organized Christian tour groups to Bethlehem are popular when the political situation allows.

PETRA, JORDAN

Israel's neighbor offers dramatic, totally unspoiled landscapes and magnificent sites from ancient times, such as the legendary rock-hewn city of **Petra** in the southern part of the country. Luxury and moderate hotels here are a bargain compared to those in Israel. The less-developed Jordanian side of the Dead Sea is dotted with hot springs and is home to a number of relaxing spas and hotels that offer a variety of unique therapeutic and beauty treatments. **Wadi Rum,** south of Petra, offers opportunities for camping and hiking with Bedouin guides in one of the most dramatic desertscapes in the world.

ISRAEL IN CONTEXT

By Karen Chernick

3

Israel lies on the tectonic plates where the continents of Africa and Asia, the East and the West, and the Heavenly and the Earthly all collide. No other place is quite like it.

Not only is Israel the birthplace of religions and ideas that lie at the heart of Western Civilization, but this tiny land encompasses incredible diversity on every level—deserts and forested mountains, awesome holy sites and hedonistic beaches, ancient walled cities and coral reefs in crystal-clear waters, medieval bazaars and sleek high-tech society. To millions of Jews, Christians, Muslims, and Bahá'ís, Israel is the Holy Land where Solomon reigned in all his glory, Jesus taught and performed miracles, Muhammad visited during a miraculous night journey from Mecca, and Bahá'u'lláh was exiled. Yet amid this swirl of charisma, history, legends, and spiritual pull, Israel is also a modern, lively, innovative country that's fun and fascinating for visitors.

ISRAEL TODAY

Israel has celebrated over 70 years of independence, but its identity is still being shaped. The country today has fulfilled its mission of becoming a haven where Jews from all over the world can live free from persecution. With its energetic spirit, high-tech and cultural achievements, innovative style, and endless absorption of new immigrants, Israel is clearly thriving. But Israel's security remains at risk, and with constant waves of immigration, the long-term identity of Israel is still a work in progress.

The population of Israel now stands at about 9,500,000: Approximately 7,000,000 Israeli citizens are Jewish; 1,995,000 are Arab Christians, Muslims, and Druze; and at least 472,000 are of other backgrounds or are international.

Israel's Jewish population comes from all over the world. **Israel's Arab citizens** form about 21% of the county's population and are the descendants of Palestinian Muslims and Christians who remained in the newly formed State of Israel after the 1948 partition of British Mandate Palestine and Israel's War of Independence.

These groups automatically became citizens of Israel when the state was created and now number close to 2 million. Israel's Arab population is centered in the Galilee, in predominantly Arab cities such as Nazareth, and in mixed Jewish/Arab cities such as Haifa, Akko, and Jaffa. The **Druze** people and the once-nomadic **Bedouin** peoples of the Negev and the Galilee are also part of the Israeli-Arab tapestry. Israel's Arab citizens are not required to complete military service; however, most Israeli Bedouins and Druze serve voluntarily, and a large number have received citations for valor.

Additionally, in East Jerusalem, which Israel captured and annexed in 1967 following the Six-Day War, live approximately 300,000 **East Jerusalem Palestinians** who hold permanent Israeli/Jerusalem resident IDs and reside in the homes and neighborhoods where they lived before 1967. Most East Jerusalem Palestinians are not Israeli citizens, both by their own choice and that of the Israeli government. East Jerusalem Palestinians, unlike the Palestinians of the West Bank and Gaza, have complete freedom to travel, work, and study inside Israel. Also, along with thousands of foreign workers from Asia, large numbers of asylum seekers from Sudan, Somalia, Eritrea, and elsewhere in Africa have come to Israel, adding to the mix of peoples, foods, and cultures you'll encounter as you travel through the country.

LOOKING BACK: ISRAEL'S HISTORY

Recorded Jewish history dates from the time of Abraham, between 2000 and 1800 B.C. Many elements of the patriarchal chronicles have been confirmed as accurate by recent archaeological discoveries, but other elements of this enormously distant past may never be historically documented. Modern scientific methods reveal that human beings have lived in the Holy Land since the Old Stone Age, some 100,000 years ago. But a history so deep and full of universal significance is almost impossible to grasp in its entirety. Here is an outline of the major periods and events up to the present.

A BRIEF LOOK AT THE PAST In Israel's museums and at Israel's archaeological sites, you will encounter the following terms used to define the many time periods in Israel's long history.

THE BRITISH MANDATE The Balfour Declaration in 1917 announced British support for the creation of a "national home" for the Jewish people in Palestine. In 1920, after Great Britain had captured the region of Palestine from the Ottoman Empire at the end of World War I, the League of Nations granted the British a "mandate" to govern Palestine. In 1922, Great Britain separated Trans-Jordan (present-day Jordan) from British Mandate Palestine and established a separate Arab country.

Within Palestine, huge progress was made during the first 20 years of British administration. Hospitals and schools were established in both Jewish and Arab areas, and in Jewish areas, dazzlingly modern planned communities,

History of Israel

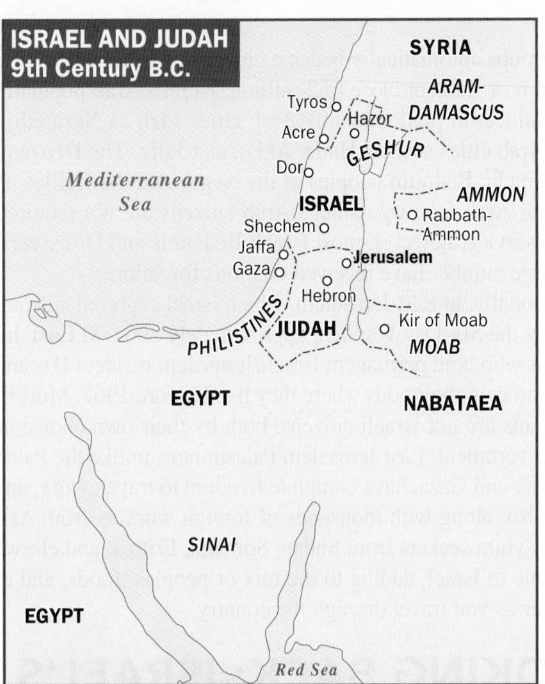

ISRAEL AND JUDAH
9th Century B.C.
SYRIA
ARAM-
DAMASCUS
Tyros
Hazor
Acre
GESHUR
Dor
Mediterranean
Sea
AMMON
ISRAEL
Rabbath-
Ammon
Shechem
Jaffa
Jerusalem
Gaza
Hebron
PHILISTINES
JUDAH
Kir of Moab
MOAB
EGYPT
NABATAEA
SINAI
EGYPT
Red Sea

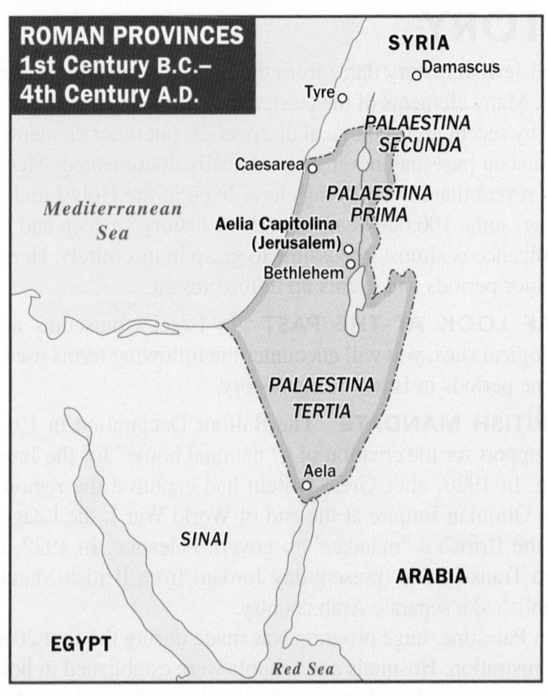

ROMAN PROVINCES
1st Century B.C.–
4th Century A.D.
SYRIA
Damascus
Tyre
PALAESTINA
SECUNDA
Caesarea
PALAESTINA
PRIMA
Mediterranean
Sea
Aelia Capitolina
(Jerusalem)
Bethlehem
PALAESTINA
TERTIA
Aela
SINAI
ARABIA
EGYPT
Red Sea

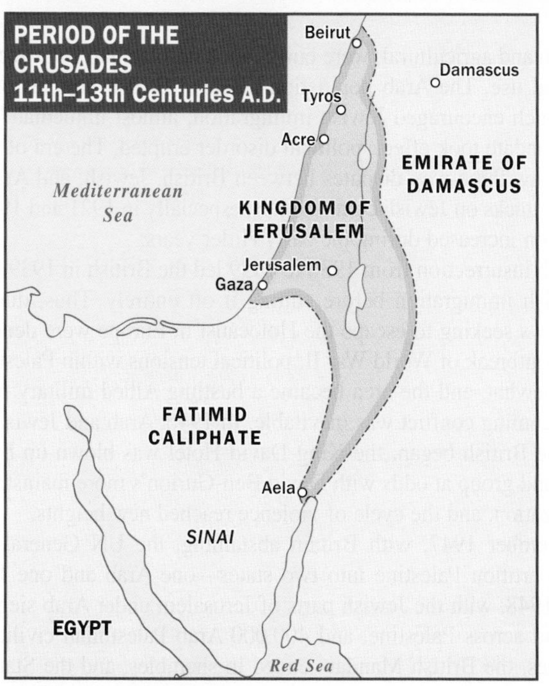
PERIOD OF THE CRUSADES 11th–13th Centuries A.D.
Beirut
Damascus
Tyros
Acre
EMIRATE OF DAMASCUS
Mediterranean Sea
KINGDOM OF JERUSALEM
Jerusalem
Gaza
FATIMID CALIPHATE
Aela
SINAI
EGYPT
Red Sea

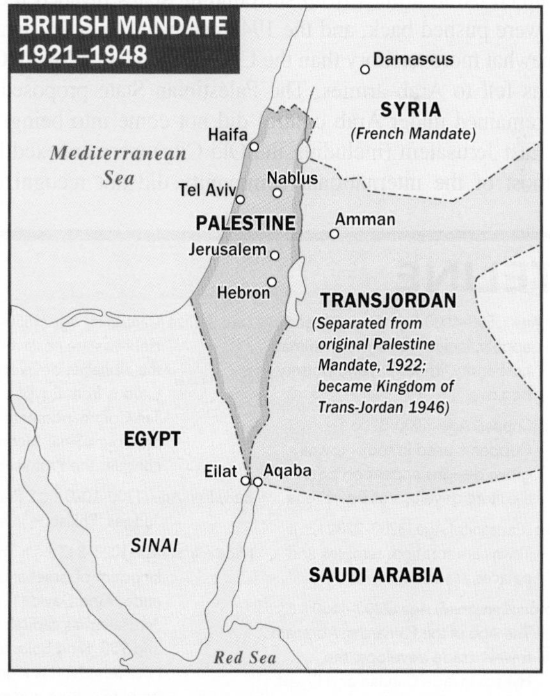
BRITISH MANDATE 1921–1948
Damascus
SYRIA
(French Mandate)
Haifa
Mediterranean Sea
Nablus
Tel Aviv
PALESTINE
Amman
Jerusalem
Hebron
TRANSJORDAN
(Separated from original Palestine Mandate, 1922; became Kingdom of Trans-Jordan 1946)
EGYPT
Eilat
Aqaba
SINAI
SAUDI ARABIA
Red Sea

both urban and agricultural, were built; much desolate land was reclaimed for agricultural use. The Arab population resented British policies of the early 1920s, which encouraged Jewish immigration; almost immediately after the British Mandate took effect, political disorder erupted. The era of the British Mandate saw three-way disputes between British, Jewish, and Arab factions and Arab attacks on Jewish communities, especially in 1921 and 1929. Jewish immigration increased during the early Hitler years.

An Arab insurrection from 1936 to 1939 led the British in 1939 to severely limit Jewish immigration before cutting it off entirely. Thus, during World War II, Jews seeking to escape the Holocaust in Europe were denied refuge. After the outbreak of World War II, political tensions within Palestine diminished somewhat, and the area became a bustling Allied military base. However, the coming conflict was inevitable. In 1946, Arab and Jewish terrorism against the British began, the King David Hotel was blown up by a Jewish underground group at odds with David Ben-Gurion's more mainstream Zionist organization, and the cycle of violence reached new heights.

In November 1947, with Britain abstaining, the UN General Assembly voted to partition Palestine into two states—one Arab and one Jewish. On May 14, 1948, with the Jewish parts of Jerusalem under Arab siege, fighting widespread across Palestine, and 400,000 Arab Palestinian civilians fleeing their homes, the British Mandate ended in shambles, and the State of Israel was proclaimed. Arab armies from surrounding states invaded the fledgling nation but were pushed back, and the 1949 cease-fire lines left Israel in control of somewhat more territory than the UN partition had allotted. Only a few Jewish areas fell to Arab armies. The Palestinian State proposed for those areas that remained under Arab control did not come into being. The West Bank and East Jerusalem (including the Old City) were annexed by Jordan, although most of the international community did not recognize this act.

DATELINE

Late Stone Age (7500–4000 B.C.): First villages appear, including Jericho. Animal husbandry, irrigation, and pottery begin.

Chalcolithic (Copper) Age (4000–3200 B.C.): Copper is used in tools; towns grow; designs appear on pottery; a culture develops at Beersheba.

Early Bronze (Canaanite) Age (3200–2200 B.C.): Towns are fortified; temples and palaces are built.

Middle Bronze (Canaanite) Age (2200–1550 B.C.): The Age of the Patriarchs; Abraham travels; trade develops; the Hyksos invade Canaan and Egypt.

Late Bronze (Canaanite) Age (1550–1200 B.C.): Hebrews are enslaved in Egypt; the alphabet develops; the Exodus from Egypt occurs; the Ten Commandments are delivered on Mount Sinai; Hebrew tribes conquer the Promised Land.

Early Iron Age (1200–1020 B.C.): Period of the Judges; Philistine invasion.

Middle Iron Age (1020–842 B.C.): The united kingdom of Israel and Judah under King David (1000 B.C.) with Jerusalem as capital; between 960 and 950, King Solomon builds the First Temple; it is a golden age of Israelite culture and power.

A portrait of David Ben-Gurion.

Jordan granted citizenship to all Palestinians under its control, the only Arab nation to do so. Egypt occupied but did not annex the Gaza Strip. Its inhabitants were declared stateless.

THE MAKING OF AN INDEPENDENT STATE In the beginning of the State of Israel's history, there was enormous exhilaration but also a grim determination. The double weight of the horrors of the Holocaust and the enormous casualties suffered in the War of Independence from 1948 to 1949 drove the country to protect every sand dune, to force life out of the desert, and to create a haven for any Jews who might again find themselves in danger. Life was austere. For years, food, clothing, razor blades, and paint were severely rationed, as the country struggled to survive as well as to feed and shelter the thousands of new immigrants who arrived each month. In less than a decade, the nation's population quadrupled as hundreds of thousands of Holocaust survivors and Jewish refugees from the Middle East arrived. Hundreds of thousands more were added in the 1960s as Jews fled North Africa.

Slowly, with enormous effort, conditions grew more stable. Basic housing was built, uprooted people began to develop new identities, and although life was still spartan (the founding fathers refused to allow television stations to

Late Iron Age (842–587 B.C.): Period of the later kings and prophets; the Kingdom of Israel is destroyed in 701 B.C. The Kingdom of Judah is destroyed in 587 B.C. by Babylonians; the First Temple in Jerusalem is destroyed.

Babylonian & Persian Periods (587–332 B.C.): Jewish captivity in Babylon, followed by Persian permission to return to Jerusalem; the Second Temple is built in 515 B.C.; times of Ezra and Nehemiah; public reading of the Torah begins.

Hellenistic & Maccabean Periods (332–37 B.C.): Conquest by Alexander the Great, followed by Hellenistic dynasties; the Maccabean revolt and liberation of Judea.

Roman Period (37 B.C.–A.D. 324): Herodian dynasty; birth of Jesus, his ministry, and crucifixion; Jewish revolt against Rome; the Second Temple and Jerusalem are destroyed (A.D. 70); fall of Masada (A.D. 73); Bar Kochba revolt against Rome (A.D. 132–35).

Byzantine Period (A.D. 324–640): Galilee Jews revolt against Byzantine domination; Jerusalem Talmud is completed; Persian invasion and sack of Jerusalem (A.D. 614); birth and rise of Islam in the Middle East.

continues

be established, claiming that the nation had more important things to attend to), the country began to flourish. Modern farming and irrigation, along with dedication, made the desert bloom, but even more important were Israel's developing industries (today, huge areas of hard-won agricultural land are being plowed for new cities and industrial zones).

WARS & THE SEARCH FOR PEACE During the Suez War of November 1956, Great Britain and France invaded Egypt to secure the Suez Canal, which Egypt had nationalized, and Israel (in coordination with the British and French recapture of Suez) conquered Egypt's Sinai Peninsula and the Gaza Strip, hoping to put an end to 9 years of Egyptian attacks on southern Israel. In exchange for the stationing of a UN peacekeeping force on the Egyptian side of the Israeli-Sinai border, and with promises of freedom to send its shipping through the Red Sea to Eilat, Israel withdrew entirely from the Sinai Peninsula and Gaza in early 1957. Ten years of relative peace followed, punctuated by periodic sniper attacks on the Galilee from Syrian batteries on the Golan Heights and Israeli retaliations.

In May 1967, the UN peacekeeping force that had maintained security on the Israeli-Egyptian border for 10 years was unilaterally ordered out by Egypt's president, Gamal Abdel Nasser, in violation of international guarantees. At the same time, Nasser blockaded the port of Eilat on the Red Sea, economically strangling Israel, while Syria stood ready to attack the Galilee from the Golan Heights. For Israelis, only too aware that the nation was less than 16km (10 miles) wide and that the Jordanian army in East Jerusalem was aimed point-blank at Jewish West Jerusalem, the agony of these weeks, while the Israeli government tried to rally international support, was unbearable. The pace of propaganda against Israel throughout the Arabic world reached new pitches of frenzy, and Arab armies in Egypt and Syria mobilized to deliver what was claimed would be a crushing blow. The Israelis dug mass

Arab Period (A.D. 640–1096): Jerusalem is conquered by Islamic armies (A.D. 638); Arab Empire capital is first at Damascus, later Baghdad; joint Christian-Muslim protectorate of holy places; Christian pilgrimage rights are curtailed.

The Crusades (1096–1291): First Crusade (1096–99); Crusader conquest of Jerusalem (1099); Crusader Kingdom established under Godfrey of Bouillon; Saladin recaptures Jerusalem for Islam (1187); the end of the Fourth Crusade (1202–04) sees the destruction of the Crusader Kingdom.

Mamluk & Ottoman Turkish Period (1291–1917): Mongols and Seljuks replace Arabs and Byzantines as rulers of the Holy Land; Ottomans conquer Palestine in 1517; Suleiman the Magnificent rebuilds Jerusalem's walls; thousands of Jews, expelled from Spain and Italy, find refuge in the Ottoman Empire; Safed, in the Galilee, becomes a center for Jewish scholarship; Napoleon's campaign in Egypt and Palestine (1799); movement to re-create a Jewish homeland is led by Theodor Herzl (1860–1904), who publishes "The Jewish State"; first Zionist Congress is held in Basel (1897).

graves in the parks of Tel Aviv in preparation for the civilian casualties of an Arab invasion.

In the early morning of June 5, 1967, Israel made a preemptive strike against the air forces of Egypt and Syria. At noon, Jordan, despite diplomatic pleas that it stay out of the conflict, began to shell West Jerusalem. In the **Six-Day War** that followed, Israel swept to an unimaginable victory, conquering the Sinai Peninsula, the Gaza Strip, the Golan Heights, East Jerusalem, and the entire West Bank. The Arab world was left in a state of shock. Suddenly Israel was no longer a struggling state hanging on tenaciously to its hard-won independence. Land areas under its control more than tripled. Israel's patriarch, David Ben-Gurion, by then in retirement, warned that all the conquered areas must be relinquished immediately, but in the euphoria of the day, his words made little sense to most Israelis. Many believed that peace would finally develop.

As the years passed, however, the Arab world continued to refuse to recognize Israel diplomatically, and the plight of the Palestinian refugees scattered throughout the Middle East continued to be ignored by the world at large. In the absence of a peace agreement that would trade most land captured in 1967 for peace, the occupation of the West Bank and the Gaza Strip began to seem less temporary. The small political movement for Jewish settlement of the Occupied Territories began to grow, although at first the Israeli government officially opposed it. Resentment grew among the Palestinians under occupation.

The country experienced a sharp change in fortune in October 1973. The **Yom Kippur War,** an unexpected simultaneous attack against Israel launched by Egypt and Syria, had a sobering effect on the entire nation. In the first days of the attack, the Golan Heights were almost retaken by Syria, and Egyptian forces, crossing the Suez Canal, overwhelmed Israeli troops in Sinai. More than 2,500 young Israelis were killed in 1 month, losses proportionately higher than the casualties the United States sustained during the entire Vietnam War. Egyptian and Syrian casualties were enormous. Although the war ended with Israeli forces closer than ever before to Cairo and Damascus, the high cost in lives shook the nation's confidence and tarnished the images of its leaders. In a backlash, voters turned against the Labor Party, which had led the state since its founding, and elected a government dominated by the right-of-center Likud led by Menachem Begin.

In 1977, Prime Minister Begin quietly set in motion a series of events that resulted in Egypt's President Anwar Sadat making a dramatic visit to Jerusalem. This led to a peace treaty with Egypt in March 1979, ending 30 years of war between the two countries. Accordingly, Israel returned the Sinai to Egypt. With peace established, it remains open to tourists from Israel, although the current turmoil in Egypt makes travel to Sinai uncertain.

The hopes for a regional peace agreement that the Egyptian-Israeli settlement raised were not quickly realized. No additional Arab countries came forward to negotiate. The 1982 invasion of southern Lebanon put further strains on Israel's relations with its neighbors. Deteriorating relations with

Palestinians in the West Bank and Gaza marked the 1980s, as more land was appropriated for Jewish settlements. In 1987, the Palestinian population of the West Bank and Gaza began daily commercial strikes and demonstrations. This uprising, the Intifada, continued through the early 1990s.

The 1990s brought a wave of almost a million immigrants from Ethiopia and the dissolving Soviet system and, in the summer of 1990, the Kuwait crisis. Israel was not a participant in the Allied coalition against Iraq in the Gulf War that followed, but Saddam Hussein declared that he would "incinerate half of Israel" with missile-borne chemical and bacteriological attacks if the Allied coalition moved against him. The United States asked Israel to refrain from retaliating if it came under attack and pledged that any Iraqi missile threat to Israel would be destroyed by American bombing within the first hours of war. Nevertheless, Israelis found themselves dashing for gas masks and sitting in makeshift sealed rooms, experiencing nightly Scud missile attacks for the entire 6 weeks of the Gulf War. Iraq's missiles turned out to be armed only with explosives instead of the chemical weapons Hussein had threatened, but the ordeal left its mark on Israeli society. Many Israelis came to believe it was worth taking risks to try to achieve peace. Others were more determined than ever to avoid any further concessions. The Oslo peace process began in 1991 and continued after President Bill Clinton arranged a White House peace process ceremony between newly elected Prime Minister Yitzhak Rabin and Palestinian leader Yasser Arafat in 1993.

THE PEACE PROCESS STALLS Negotiating directly with Palestinians and moderate Arab governments, Israel began a planned withdrawal from parts of the West Bank and Gaza in 1994. In the same year, **a peace treaty was signed with the Kingdom of Jordan.** The assassination of Prime Minister Rabin by a Jewish opponent of the peace process in 1995 was a blow for those who hoped for lasting peace.

After the assassination of Prime Minister Rabin, a Palestinian Intifada erupted from 2000 to 2005. In 2005, Prime Minister Ariel Sharon evacuated all Israeli settlements in Gaza but suffered a massive stroke before he could outline further plans. Since then, the conflict has continued on a course of uncertainty, punctuated by rocket attacks on southern Israeli towns from Gaza and by Israeli retaliation.

Tensions periodically erupt between Israel and the Hamas-controlled Gaza Strip. Rocket attacks by Hamas in July 2014 led Israel to launch a military operation dubbed Protective Edge; a cease-fire and fragile calm came only after 7 weeks of hostilities and losses on both sides. A similar scenario played out in May 2021. As is true elsewhere in the Middle East, politics can be volatile, and at press time the peace process seemed as stuck as ever.

EATING & DRINKING

In its earliest decades, Israeli food was by necessity a barebones affair. It was based on readily available produce and simple ingredients.

Today, Israelis are gourmands with an appreciation for good food and fine wine. The country is awash with young, imaginative Israeli chefs who are creating inventive haute cuisine menus rooted in ancient local food traditions and a mélange of Jewish Diaspora dishes including Yemenite, Mediterranean, and North African ingredients and traditions, often all blended. Tel Aviv is the foodie center, but food quality tends to be high nationwide.

Those expecting to find a Middle Eastern version of a Jewish delicatessen are likely to be disappointed, though. Very few restaurants serve the traditional Eastern European dishes that many think of when imagining Jewish food. Instead, typical Israeli cuisine draws on local traditions such as the *mezze,* a vast array of spiced salads and spreads that opens a lavish Middle Eastern–style feast. It includes the Arabic falafel and moves on to scrumptious *shawarma* (seasoned meat cooked on a spit) and kabobs, served with salads and sauces, all tucked into a pita sandwich. Palestinian *zaatar* (a traditional mix of local spices that includes dried hyssop and salt) flavors food throughout the country. Big, often very shareable fresh salads are available in cafes everywhere. For kosher travelers, Israel offers a rare chance to sample excellent kosher Indian food as well as an array of kosher Italian, French, Chinese, and sushi dishes. Vegan and vegetarian foods are also easy to find, increasingly so in the last decade.

But a big chunk of the Israeli cuisine experience is just being there. A great lamb chop, a plate of ordinary pasta, a grilled kabob, or even a falafel sandwich becomes a memorable meal if it's served on a starlit dock stretching into the Sea of Galilee or on a rooftop terrace in the heart of Jerusalem's Old City.

ISRAELI street food TIPS

Falafel, shawarma, or sabich (see below) tucked into a pita with chopped salad and pickles are the nation's most beloved fast foods. To make sure you sample the best the country has to offer, here are a few tips:

- A quality *falafel* (spiced chickpea fritter) sandwich should contain at least four falafels and your choice of a number of fresh salads and condiment sauces.
- Opt for places with long lines and falafels fried to order. You should be able to see falafels being fried, otherwise move on.
- A sandwich made with giant napkin-size Iraqi pita bread costs just a little bit extra and fills you up for most of the day.
- *Sabich*, a pita sandwich made with fried eggplant and hardboiled eggs, is a beloved Israeli street sandwich barely known outside the country's borders. Don't skip it.
- *Shawarma* (spiced turkey or lamb on a spit) should be freshly sliced from the spit. If the proprietor must turn on the flame to heat the spit, move on.
- Many stands offer hummus either as a separate sandwich choice or with falafel. Avoid it after noon on a hot summer day because it's unpasteurized.
- Falafel sandwiches, especially with lots of essential *techina* sauce, tend to be messy. Grab tons of napkins—*techina* stains are forever.

A collection of Israeli specialties, including shakshuka (top left), falafel (middle), and hummus (bottom right).

Dining Customs

THE SABBATH (SHABBAT) On Friday afternoons and afternoons before holidays, kosher restaurants close around 2pm in preparation for Shabbat (the Jewish Sabbath), which begins at sunset. Kosher restaurants won't reopen until Saturday evening after dark, or Sunday morning. Most non-kosher restaurants in cities and resort areas remain open on Shabbat.

If staying in a religiously observant area, like Jerusalem, check what meals your hotel provides between Friday dinner and Saturday breakfast. Most larger hotels serve kosher Friday-night meals and Saturday lunches prepared before the Sabbath (reserved in advance), but these can be expensive and bland. By Saturday evening after the sun sets and Shabbat is over, restaurants will be open again, but in summer, the end of Shabbat comes quite late. If you're kosher and don't want to go to the expense of reserving Shabbat hotel meals, eat a hearty lunch on Friday and buy food for the weekend in advance.

KOSHER FOOD According to the rigorous regulations of kashrut, only peaceful, non-predatory animals that chew their cud and have cleft hooves and birds that do not eat carrion may be used for food—and then, only if they have been killed instantly and humanely according to methods supervised by religious authorities. Only fish with fins and scales can be eaten, which means no shellfish. Pork, too, is forbidden. Kosher restaurants that serve milk will not

dining BARGAINS

- Look for weekday business lunch specials. In some restaurants, they go until 3 or 4pm. Remember—after the witching hour, when lunch turns to dinner, the price for the same dishes can double.
- In bigger cities such as Jerusalem, Tel Aviv, and Eilat, you'll find free tourist maps and brochures loaded with coupons offering discounts on many restaurants. Take into account, though, that the restaurants offering tourist coupons aren't necessarily the ones where locals find their best meals.
- Amazingly, kosher restaurants are not easy to find in all parts of Israel. Check out websites like **www.yeahthatskosher.com** or **www.eluna.com**, which review and list kosher options around the country.
- Fill up at hearty breakfast, and you might not even need lunch! Israeli hotels tend to put out vast morning spreads with fresh salads, eggs, cheeses, seasonal fruit, and baked goods.

serve any food containing meat or poultry, although they are permitted to serve fish. This means that cheese lasagna must be meatless. In restaurants serving meat, your coffee will be served with milk substitute and desserts won't contain milk products.

A restaurant may maintain a kosher menu, but if it prepares and cooks food or does business on Shabbat, it will generally not be able to receive a kashrut certificate.

Note: Never bring your own food (such as a cookie or a piece of baklava) to a meal at a kosher restaurant, as this may contaminate the kashrut status of the establishment.

Most kosher restaurants are more expensive than their non-kosher counterparts. If kashrut is not a concern, you can save a bit by seeking out non-kosher places. Glatt kosher and mehadrin (especially stringent supervision of kashrut) often mean an even higher price.

WHEN TO GO

Climate

Israel has two seasons: winter (late Oct to mid-Mar), which is cool to cold and when the rains occur, and summer (Apr–Oct), which is warm to hot and virtually rain-free. Winter in Israel starts with showers in October and advances to periodic heavy rainfall from November to March. Swimming is out in the Mediterranean during this time, except during occasional heat waves, although at times you can swim in Eilat and the Dead Sea in the winter. The Israeli winter doesn't normally involve snow, except on Mount Hermon on the Golan Heights.

During February and the beginning of March, the entire country turns green from the winter rains, and wildflower displays in the Galilee and Golan regions are truly spectacular. By late March, the flowers and the green fade. In the months that follow, the heat—and by the coast, humidity—gathers intensity, reaching its peak in July and August. By late September temperatures dip a bit, but summer-style heat can easily persist all month long.

Israel also experiences hot, dry desert winds at the beginning and end of the summer, although a *hamsin* can occur anytime from March to November. A *hamsin* (or *sharav*) heat wave means you must cut back on rushing around: Plan to be in air-conditioned museums, in the shadowy depths of a bazaar, or in the water during midday, and make sure you increase your water intake.

In winter, cold rain systems move in from the north. Because they are prevented from continuing south by the constant tropical highs over Africa, these storms can stall over Israel for days until they rain themselves out. Lots of warm socks, layered clothes (including a fleece liner), and a good raincoat and portable umbrella are necessary.

Israel's Average Temperatures

		JAN	FEB	MAR	APR	MAY	JUNE	JULY	AUG	SEPT	OCT	NOV	DEC
JERUSALEM	°F	43–53	44–57	47–61	53–69	60–77	63–81	66–84	66–86	65–82	60–78	54–67	47–56
	°C	6–12	7–14	8–16	12–21	16–25	17–27	19–29	19–30	18–28	16–26	12–19	8–13
TEL AVIV	°F	49–65	48–66	51–69	54–72	63–77	67–83	70–86	69–89	59–83	54–76	54–77	49–66
	°C	9–18	9–19	11–21	12–22	17–25	19–28	21–30	21–32	15–28	12–24	12–25	9–19
HAIFA	°F	49–63	47–64	47–70	55–78	58–76	64–82	68–86	70–86	68–85	60–80	56–74	48–65
	°C	9–17	8–18	8–21	13–26	14–24	18–28	20–30	21–30	20–29	16–27	13–23	9–18
TIBERIAS	°F	48–65	49–67	51–72	56–80	62–89	68–95	73–98	75–99	71–95	65–89	59–78	53–68
	°C	9–18	9–19	11–22	13–27	17–32	20–35	23–37	24–37	22–35	18–32	15–26	12–20
EILAT	°F	49–70	51–73	56–79	63–87	69–95	75–99	77–103	79–104	75–98	69–92	61–83	51–74
	°C	9–21	11–23	13–26	17–31	21–35	24–37	25–39	26–40	24–37	21–33	16–28	11–23

Israel's Calendar(s)

Israel officially operates on two separate systems for determining day, month, and year: the Jewish calendar, dating from some 5,750 years ago, and the Gregorian calendar, used in most countries. Recognized, but unofficial, are even more calendars, such as the Julian (Julius Caesar) calendar, which runs 13 days behind the Gregorian; and the Muslim era, which counts the years from A.D. 622, when the Prophet Muhammad led the Hegira from Mecca to Medina. These calendars disagree not only about dates but also about whether time is measured by the sun, the moon, or a combination of the two and when the year should start and end. (We know of at least three Christmases in Israel.)

THE WEEKLY HOLIDAY SCHEDULE Israel is a confusing place when it comes to the weekly holiday schedule. Jews stop work at midafternoon on Friday; some Muslims stop at sundown on Thursday (although many shops remain open on Fri); most Christians are off all day on Sunday. In Tel Aviv, buses stop running between late Friday afternoon until Saturday after sundown, although small private minibuses cover some of the main routes. In Jerusalem, buses run only in the Arab neighborhoods on Saturday; in Haifa, there's partial bus service on Saturday. In Eilat, there is no public transport on Shabbat. Throughout the country, some shops open just as others are closing for a holiday.

On Saturday, almost all shops throughout the country are closed (except in Israel's Arab communities, including cafes and Arab or Christian establishments in Jerusalem's Old City), as are nearly all transportation stops (only Haifa has limited municipal bus service at this time, and only taxis or small sherut companies operate in or between cities). Gas stations are mostly open on Shabbat because few are located in religious neighborhoods. Most admission-free museums are ordinarily open for part of Shabbat. Precise start and end times for the duration of Shabbat, which vary according to the time of sunset, are listed in Friday newspapers or can be found online (just search "shabbat times" or check www.chabad.org).

There is a growing list of exceptions: In Tel Aviv, many restaurants, cafes, clubs, and theaters close on Friday afternoon for a few hours but reopen on Friday night; Haifa has always had a quiet alternative Friday nightlife; and in Jerusalem, a number of cinemas and non-kosher restaurants remain open; recently the pub area around Jerusalem's Russian Compound has begun to boom, and Friday nights are busy.

Most Israelis are not Sabbath-observant and love to travel on their day off, so if you drive on Saturday, you'll find the roads to beaches and parks quite busy. The streets to and within religious areas will be empty, though, and possibly blocked with boulders. Some ultra-Orthodox neighborhoods in Jerusalem and Bnei Brak, near Tel Aviv, have official permission to close their streets to traffic. Don't drive in these areas—you can be stoned and your vehicle damaged, and you will have no help from the police.

HOLIDAYS If awards were given for having the maximum number of holidays a year, Israel would win. Israeli holidays will affect your visit in several important ways. First, hotels and campsites fill to capacity, and rates rise by as much as 20%. Next, transportation and restaurant service may be curtailed or completely suspended, and places of entertainment may be closed. On the other hand, a holiday is a special occasion, and you won't want to miss the events that may take place. To keep your wits amid all these openings and closings read the following information carefully.

Israel Calendar of Holidays & Events

Here's a general guide to when holidays and festivals occur in Israel. Keep in mind that a Jewish holiday that generally falls in March may some years fall on a late date in February, because Jews follow a lunar-based year. Note also that not all Jewish holidays are subject to Sabbath-like prohibitions and closings. Holidays when things close down are indicated by an asterisk (*). ***Note: The celebration of each holiday commences at sundown on the evening before the date listed and ends at sundown of the last day shown.***

For updated information about holidays, special events, and festivals, check with your nearest IGTO office. In North America, call the Israel Tourism Information Center at ✆ **888/77-ISRAEL** (477-235) or visit www.goisrael.com.

JANUARY/FEBRUARY

Israeli Arbor Day (Tu b'Shevat): Thousands of singing and dancing schoolchildren traipse off to plant trees all over the country. Synagogues and some restaurants have special Tu b'Shevat dinners featuring dried fruits.

MARCH

Purim (Feast of Lots): Celebrating how Queen Esther saved her people from persecution in 5th c. B.C. Persia, this is a fun holiday when kids and grown-ups alike dress up in costumes, have parties, parade in the streets, give food baskets, eat *hamantaschen* (triangular cookies with sweet fillings), drink, and make merry. In Jerusalem and Safed, Purim is celebrated 1 day later than in the rest of the country.

APRIL

Passover (Pesach)*: The commemoration of the ancient Israelites' Exodus from Egypt. Because the Israelites left in haste, before the bread in their ovens could rise, no bread, beer, or other foods containing leavening are obtainable for 7 days (8 days outside Israel). Some restaurants simply shut down for this period, while others (in cities such as Tel Aviv) may ignore Passover's food restrictions entirely. The first night of the holiday is devoted to a Seder, a family meal and ritual recalling the Exodus of the ancient Israelites from Egypt. (***Note:*** In the Diaspora, the Seder is held on both the first and second nights of Passover; however, inside Israel, the Seder is held only on the first night.) Many hotels and restaurants offer special Seders for tourists. The first and last days of this holiday are Sabbath-like affairs, which means the country more or less closes down. During the days of Passover week, many shops, museums, and services operate on reduced schedules. As schools are closed, Israelis travel during this week, and it is a busy week for domestic tourism. Accommodations and flights during this period should be booked well in advance, so expect peak rates.

Holocaust Memorial Day (Yom Ha-Shoah)*: This marks the moment in 1945 when concentration camps were liberated and the Holocaust ended. It also marks the Warsaw Ghetto Uprising in 1943. All places of entertainment are closed. As the day begins (like all Jewish days, at nightfall), most restaurants are closed, although public transportation continues, and most shops and businesses are open. At 10am on Yom Ha-Shoah, a siren sounds throughout Israel, and a period of silence is observed in memory of the six million Jews who perished. A memorial ceremony is held at Yad Vashem in Jerusalem.

MAY/JUNE

Memorial Day*: One week after Yom Ha-Shoah, the nation remembers its fallen soldiers. Restaurants and places of public

A man blows a shofar to mark Passover at the Western Wall.

entertainment are closed, but transportation companies operate, and most shops are open. Again, at 11am, a siren sounds, and a period of silence is observed. Throughout the country, memorial services are held.

Independence Day: The day after Memorial Day, Israel commemorates the day in 1948 when the British Mandate ended and the State of Israel was proclaimed. The evening that starts the holiday is celebrated with municipal street parties and fireworks, while the next day many meet in parks and backyards for barbeque lunches.

Jacob's Ladder Country, Folk, and Blues Festival (hosted at Kibbutz Kfar Blum): This longstanding festival is held in the Galilee for a weekend in May or June. Global types of folk music are performed live, from Bluegrass to bagpipes. For information, call ✆ **04/685-0403** or visit www.jlfestival.com.

Lag b'Omer: This celebratory ending of a 33-day mourning period is observed by the religious and secular alike. Observant Hassidim visit the tomb of the mystical Rabbi Shimon Bar Yochai in the Galilee's Mount Meron, to sing and dance around bonfires. Elsewhere around the country (and especially along the coastline), children and youngsters light bonfires into the wee hours of the night.

Shavuot (Pentecost)*: A summer harvest celebration that also marks the receipt of the Ten Commandments, this holiday is observed through both religious learning and agricultural celebrations. Children often dress in white, wear flower crowns, and tote baskets full of fresh produce to mark Shavuot, while farms may host tractor rides and other events. Dairy foods, such as blintzes and cheesecakes, are traditionally prepared. At synagogues as well as at the Western Wall, the Torah is studied throughout the night.

Abu Gosh Music Festival: This 3-day festival is held in the Arab-Israeli village of Abu Gosh, in the hills west of Jerusalem. Classical and religious music is performed in the village's two churches; there are also street performances and arts and crafts. It's held each year at Shavuot and Succot. For more information, visit agfestival.co.il/home.

Israel and Jerusalem Festivals of the Performing Arts: In late spring, two festivals featuring extraordinary music groups and theater and dance companies come from all over the world to perform. Exact dates at www.goisrael.com.

White Nights: This is Tel Aviv's annual late-June, all-nighters' festival, featuring rock concerts, free architectural tours, parties at local bars, dancing on the beach, art-gallery receptions, outdoor videos, and special dinner deals. Look for detailed information on the Tel Aviv municipality website (www.tel-aviv.gov.il/en).

Tel Aviv Gay Pride Month: The crowning event of this month-long celebration of Tel Aviv's LGBTQIA community is a big, colorful parade, usually marching along the boardwalk. Expect dozens of events and thousands of visitors from Israel and abroad. Visit www.lgbtqcenter.org.il for more information.

JULY/AUGUST

Israeli Folkdance Festival (Karmiel, in the Galilee): Jewish ethnic dancers come from around the world for this festival. Early July. www.karmielfestival.co.il.

Tel Aviv's Gay Pride celebration is one of the largest in the world.

Jerusalem Film Festival: Increasingly prestigious, with offerings from around the globe, this festival takes place at the Jerusalem Cinémathèque. For more information, call ✆ **02/565-4333** or visit www.jff.org.il.

Jerusalem Arts and Crafts Festival (Hutzot Hayotzer): Held in the Sultan's Pool in the valley outside the western walls of the Old City, the contemporary Israeli craft booths are not usually of a high level, but the large International Craft Section is excellent. Performances by Israeli musicians take place every night. Late July or early August.

Ramadan: During the holy month of Ramadan, Muslims do not eat or drink during daylight hours, but at night many parties are held. Most places serving food in Arab communities are closed during the day; Islamic sites and mosques are closed to non-Muslims during the entire month.

Eid Al Fitr: The biggest holiday in the Islamic year is celebrated the day Ramadan ends and for 2 or 3 days immediately following. On Eid Al Fitr, most Muslim-owned shops are closed.

Tisha b'Av: The fast day on the 9th day of the Jewish month of Av is a time set aside to remember the destruction of the First and Second Temples, which by ominous coincidence were destroyed on the same calendar day in the years 586 B.C. and A.D. 70. Entertainment facilities and many restaurants are closed.

SEPTEMBER/OCTOBER

The Jerusalem International Chamber Music Festival: Held at the YMCA Concert Hall and produced by the Jerusalem Symphony Orchestra, this festival offers an array of internationally famous musicians performing classical chamber music. For information, check out jcmf.org.il/?p=home. ✆ **02/625-0444.**

Rosh Hashanah (Jewish New Year)*: The start of the High Holy Days is a 2-day religious holiday, during which families typically gather for a festive meal and synagogue services are held. Traditional foods eaten on Rosh Hashanah include a round challah, apples and honey, and pomegranates. Almost everything in the Jewish sectors close.

Yom Kippur (Day of Atonement)*: On the 10th day of the Jewish year, the High Holy Days culminate in the most solemn of Jewish holidays. Places of worship are crowded, but the large synagogues reserve seats for tourists, and some of the larger hotels organize their own services. Yom Kippur is a fast day, but hotel dining rooms may still serve guests who wish to eat. Expect to stay put if visiting during Yom Kippur since everything comes to a standstill; roads close to vehicular traffic (except for emergencies, of course) and even TV and radio stations suspend broadcasting.

Succot (Feast of Tabernacles)*: This 7-day holiday recalls how Moses and the children of Israel dwelled in "booths" (or "succot") as they left Egypt to wander in the desert. Observant families have meals and services in specially built, highly decorated yet simple huts located in gardens or on balconies. Many restaurants also build succot in the outdoor parts of their establishments, to make available to diners. Succot is also a harvest festival and thus an agricultural and kibbutz favorite. On the first and last days of Succot, Sabbath-like restrictions are observed.

Simchat Torah*: As Succot ends, Jews rejoice as they complete the yearly cycle of reading the Torah (the first five books of the Bible); street festivities in Jerusalem and Tel Aviv mark this day. Cantors read the final verses of the Torah in synagogues around the country and then immediately start again.

Eid Al Adha: The second-biggest Islamic holiday commemorates Abraham's near-sacrifice of his son. Animals are sacrificed, big family feasts are held, children receive gifts and new clothes, many shops in Arab neighborhoods are closed, and mosques are closed to tourists.

NOVEMBER

Olive Festival: In recent years, both Jewish and Arab communities in the Galilee have come to mark the November olive-harvest period with at least a dozen local festivals of traditional foods, music, crafts, and dance. Check with the Nazareth and Akko tourist information offices for the best options.

Red Sea Jazz Festival (Eilat): This acclaimed international jazz festival is held in Eilat. Visit www.redseajazz.co.il for information.

DECEMBER

Hanukkah: Celebrates the victory of the Maccabees over Syrian Greeks and the consequent rededication of the Temple in 164 B.C. For 8 days, this history-based holiday is marked by the nightly lighting of the eight-branch menorah. Look out for traditional Hanukkah jelly doughnuts (or their contemporary versions, which include anything from butterscotch and Belgian chocolate to pistachio crème) in bakeries across the country.

International Choir Concerts: These take place in Bethlehem on Christmas Eve (December 24). The Christian Information Centre (www.cicts.org/en) inside Jaffa Gate has information about these programs and security conditions in Bethlehem.

Liturgica (Jerusalem): A week of choral music organized by the Jerusalem Symphony Orchestra in late December. For program information, visit www.jso.co.il.

SETTLING INTO JERUSALEM

By Elianna Bar-El

4

Planning your trip to Jerusalem needn't cause you undue *tsuris* (that's the Yiddish word for "stress"). This chapter covers the best ways to navigate the city and introduces you to the city's most authentic and evocative restaurants and hotels, places that truly wouldn't exist outside the Holy Land. With these suggestions in hand, the practical issues involved in your stay should go smoothly and allow you to concentrate on sightseeing (covered in chapter 5), which is really the reason you've come to Israel. But having a nice place to stay and great meals surely adds to the overall experience.

ORIENTATION

Arriving

BY PLANE Ben-Gurion Airport is the country's international arrivals center. It's a 45-minute drive west of Jerusalem and a 25-minute drive in the opposite direction to Tel Aviv. There are a number of options to get from Ben-Gurion into Jerusalem.

Sherut A popular, reasonably priced way to get to Jerusalem from Ben-Gurion Airport is by these 8- to 10-passenger vans with a fixed per-person rate (NIS 66, baggage included). The sherut stand, run by **Nesher Tours,** is to the left as you exit the arrivals area of the terminal building, between gates 02 and 03. Confirm that the destination of the van is Jerusalem, give your luggage to the driver, and climb in. When all the seats are claimed, the van will take off. For no additional charge, the driver must take you from the airport to the doorstep of the hotel or residential address of your choice anywhere in Jerusalem. If your hotel is in the Old City, a sherut will generally take you *near* but not *inside* the Jaffa Gate or Damascus Gate. Depending on conditions, sheruts may not serve addresses deep inside East Jerusalem.

Sherut from Jerusalem to Ben-Gurion Airport For the return trip to the airport, your hotel will be glad to make an appointment for **Nesher Tours** to pick you up (let the hotel know about 2 days before your departure or you can contact them directly, at their website www.neshertours.co.il or by calling © **02/625-7227**). The company picks up passengers round-the-clock, 7 days a week. Be sure to specify **sherut** rather than a **special,** which means a much more expensive private taxi. ***Note:*** If you need transportation to the airport on the Sabbath, you must make your reservation by Thursday—although sheruts run during Shabbat, the Nesher office is closed on Shabbat and is not available for reservations in person or by phone. If you are with a group of three or four people, it is more cost effective to take a private taxi.

Private Taxi The fixed-price rate for a **private taxi** is NIS 280, with the rate going up to NIS 320 on the Sabbath, holidays starting at 4pm on Fridays (or the eves of holidays) and weekday nights after 9pm. If you happen to have three or four people in your party (standard taxis take only up to four passengers, and the fourth passenger is at the driver's discretion), the cost for this most convenient option is really little more than that of a sherut. Agree on a definite price ahead of time. Taxi drivers do not expect tips, but if you have a number of bags, the driver may add around NIS 5 per bag. If your driver doesn't charge extra for help with luggage, offer a tip of NIS 10.

Rental Car All major car-rental companies have offices at Ben-Gurion Airport. However, traffic, road construction, and parking problems make having a rental car in Jerusalem more hindrance than help.

BY TRAIN On weekdays, trains run every 30 minutes between Tel Aviv and Jerusalem's Malha Station, on the far western edge of the city. From there, you must take a municipal bus into the center of town. Trains are slower and less frequent than buses, but the route is a bit more scenic. Officially the trip takes 1½ hours; the fare from Tel Aviv to Jerusalem is NIS 24, with discounts for senior citizens, students, and children up to age 10; kids under 10 are free. For current schedules and fares, visit www.rail.co.il/en.

BY BUS There is direct, scheduled bus service from most major cities to Jerusalem. Between Tel Aviv and Jerusalem, buses leave every 12 to 25 minutes or as soon as they are full; the trip takes 1 hour, and the fare is NIS 18 for a one-way fare and NIS 30 both ways. Most buses arrive and depart from Jerusalem's **Central Bus Station,** at the western entrance to the city, right on Jaffa Road. From there, you can easily pick up municipal buses to all parts of West Jerusalem. We recommend you purchase a **Citypass Rav-Kav** card, which admits the bearer to the country and city's railways and Egged buses. You may purchase these at any Light Rail stop, at the central bus station, at the Pa'amon Center in the center of Jerusalem, or simply download the app and use that.

To Bethlehem, West Bank: Arab-owned buses run (as far as the Crossing Point from Jerusalem into Bethlehem) from a bus station across the street and a block east of the Damascus Gate. At press time, bus no. 22 went to the Bethlehem crossing. Returning from Bethlehem, you can request to be let off near Jaffa Gate or the New Gate (if you are staying in West Jerusalem). Fare is NIS 6.

BY CAR Route 1 (Hwy. 1) is the main road to Jerusalem from Tel Aviv and Ben-Gurion Airport; it runs right into Jaffa Road, the main street in downtown West Jerusalem. You know you've reached the western entrance to the city when you go under the **Chords Bridge,** a structure shaped like a white harp in the sky, over which the Jerusalem Light Railroad passes. Signs at the city entrance direct you to the downtown center, via a slightly circuitous route, as private cars are barred from most of Jaffa Road. If you're going to hotels on Herzl Boulevard, or points in the extreme western part of the city, follow signs for Herzl Boulevard/Government Center. Highway 443 from Tel Aviv runs parallel to and north of Route 1 and leads to the northern part of Jerusalem. Parts of it traverse territory lined by high cement security walls, so you don't see much of the landscape. If you're coming from the coast north of Tel Aviv, this is the fastest route.

From the Sea of Galilee, the Dead Sea, or Eilat and the Negev: The most direct way is via Route 90, which follows the Jordan Valley. From Route 90, turn onto Route 1 just south of Jericho and make the steep ascent up to Jerusalem. At the edge of the city, follow signs to the "Centre." This route takes you to the northern walls of the Old City, approaching Damascus Gate. Keep right if you're heading for the center of West Jerusalem, and left for East Jerusalem.

Warning: Parking is difficult in Jerusalem. So, if you can avoid it, don't keep your rental car during your visit to Jerusalem. Many hotels have limited or no parking facilities, and it's far easier to get around town using public transportation or taxis. The Old City is only accessible by foot.

If you *must* have a car with you, note that there are parking garages in downtown Jerusalem, outside Jaffa Gate on Mamilla Street, and on Mamilla Street under the David Citadel Hotel. Metered streets and resident-parking-only streets are scattered throughout the center of town; there are also non-meter streets, where you must purchase a ticket in advance from a kiosk or sidewalk ticket machine and display it with the appropriate time marked. Parking is free after 7pm and during the Sabbath.

Visitor Information

A **Ministry of Tourism** information desk (✆ **03/975-4260**) is located in the arrivals hall of Ben-Gurion International Airport and available 24/7. The staff provides city maps and brochures (which you must buy) and answers questions.

In the Old City, the **Jaffa Gate Tourist Office** lies just inside Jaffa Gate, a few steps down on the left (✆ **02/627-1422;** Sun–Thurs 8:30am–5pm). This office sells maps and booklets, but a shelf offers free maps and tourist brochures as well. Look for the Jerusalem Menus booklets, with its discount coupons. A recorded self-guided walking tour of the Old City is available for

Jerusalem's cityscape encompasses both the contemporary and the ancient, sometimes in a very abrupt fashion.

free for smartphones or with a recorder that can be rented for NIS 50/day plus security deposit.

The **Christian Information Centre,** at the far end of the square inside Jaffa Gate (www.cicts.org; ✆ **02/627-2692;** Mon–Fri 9am–5pm, Sat 9am–noon), offers all kinds of useful information about tours, Christian hospices, group tours to Bethlehem (on the West Bank), and religious services.

The **Ministry of Tourism** site is www.goisrael.com, and the **Municipality of Jerusalem** site is www.jerusalem.muni.il. Both offer information on special events, festivals, and activities going on in the city year-round.

PUBLICATIONS The print version of the ***International New York Times*** contains the entire daily English-language edition of ***Haaretz,*** Israel's most respected, and decidedly left-of-center, newspaper (www.haaretz.com). The Friday *Haaretz* contains a detailed weekend section on events in Jerusalem and throughout the country. *The Jerusalem Post* (www.jpost.com) has a daily listing of city events, but the Friday (weekend) edition is your best bet. Another source of information is the free monthly *Events in the Jerusalem Region,* prepared by the Tourist Information Office and available at various tourist office locations and in many hotel lobbies.

GETTING connected IN JERUSALEM

Downtown West Jerusalem's Ben Yehuda–Jaffa Road–King George Street triangle is a free Wi-Fi hotspot, expanding outward in all directions for several blocks and filled with Wi-Fi–friendly cafes, restaurants, and small hotels. Cafes, indoors and out, welcome anything that connects. Same with the **German Colony**'s many eateries along its main drag, Emek Refaim Street, and at Safra Square next to the Jerusalem City Hall. All hotels, of course, have Wi-Fi.

Inside the Walled City of Jerusalem, wireless connections (including cellphones) are not great. You can make long distance calls in the center of the Old City above the venerable **Abu Assab Orange and Carrot Juice Shop,** 172 Suq Khan es-Zeit St. (the main thoroughfare running from Damascus Gate south; ✆ **02/628-2486**). It is open daily 9am to 10pm. It serves as a travel agency for outgoing trips to Turkey and Egypt, plus serves freshly squeezed orange, grapefruit, and carrot juice (the best in town). You can even get your laundry done here, killing three birds with one stone.

City Layout

To get around Jerusalem easily, it helps to understand how the city has grown. In the mid-1800s, Jerusalem was still a walled medieval city—a tortuous maze of semi-ruins with sewage running down the streets. After the mid–19th century, Christian pilgrims and Zionist settlers began to create neighborhoods outside the city walls. From 1948 to 1967, Jerusalem was further divided when modern West Jerusalem remained under Israeli jurisdiction while the Old City and downtown East Jerusalem became part of the Kingdom of Jordan. Although the city has been united under Israeli control since 1967, Jerusalem is still three different cities in one: the Old City, the newer Israeli city of West Jerusalem, and the newer Arab city of East Jerusalem.

Due east of the Old City, the Kidron Valley lies between ancient Jerusalem and the long ridge known as the Mount of Olives (*Et-Tur* in Arabic). On the slopes of the mount is the Garden of Gethsemane. Farther down the valley, south of the Old City walls, is the Arabic town of Silwan, where the earliest settlement of Jerusalem developed more than 5,000 years ago. This is where the Jerusalem of King David was located in ancient times; today, it is a densely inhabited East Jerusalem neighborhood (find more details on the neighborhood below).

The Neighborhoods in Brief

THE OLD CITY

The Old City is easily defined: It is the area still enclosed within the grand walls built by the Ottoman Turkish Sultan Suleiman the Magnificent in 1538. The Old City is divided into four quarters: the **Muslim Quarter,** the **Christian Quarter,** the **Armenian Quarter,** and the **Jewish Quarter.** Seven gates provide access through the massive walls; two of these are important for visitors. The **Jaffa Gate** (*Sha'ar Yafo* in Hebrew, *Bab el-Khalil* in Arabic), at the end of Jaffa Road *(Derech Yafo)*, offers the main access to the Old City from West Jerusalem. **Damascus Gate**

(*Sha'ar Shechem* in Hebrew, *Bab el-Amud* in Arabic) offers the main access from East Jerusalem (if you get lost in the Old City's labyrinthine alleys, just ask for either gate).

The great Jewish, Christian, and Muslim holy sites are mostly found in the Old City. Except in the Jewish Quarter, the dominating influence here is Arab: The food is Arabic, the language is Arabic, and customs are Eastern.

WEST JERUSALEM

Extending far to the south and west, and encroaching on the east of the Old City, this modern section of Jerusalem includes residential, commercial, and industrial developments punctuated by high-rise hotels and office blocks. The "New City" (as it's sometimes called) includes the Knesset and the government precinct on the western edge of town; one of Hebrew University's two large campuses; the Israel Museum; and, in a distant western area beyond the neighborhood called Ein Kerem, the Hadassah Medical Center. Broad avenues twist and turn along the tops of the Judean Hills to connect West Jerusalem's outlying quarters with the century-old downtown area.

Downtown West Jerusalem is centered on Zion Square *(Kikar Ziyon),* where Jaffa Road intersects with Ben Yehuda Street. A few short blocks west of Zion Square is King George V Avenue (known as King George St., or *Rehov Ha-Melech George*), which joins Ben Yehuda Street and Jaffa Road to form a **Downtown Triangle.** Many of the hotels, restaurants, and businesses of interest are in or near this triangle. **Ben Yehuda Street** is now a bustling pedestrian mall filled with souvenir, jewelry, and Judaica shops; cafes; and places to grab a quick snack. In the evening, especially in good weather, Ben Yehuda becomes a mecca for younger travelers and young Israelis. A quainter pedestrian mall network, centering on **Yoel Salomon Street,** runs off Zion Square at the foot of Ben Yehuda Street. This area is known as **Nahalat Shiva.** Its renovation has transformed Jerusalem's evening ambience from that of a quiet mountain town to a lively, Mediterranean-style city where people like to stroll and rendezvous in cafes. This small enclave of old West Jerusalem is being preserved, but other 19th-century neighborhoods in West Jerusalem are slated for demolition and will be replaced by large office blocks. Many of Nahlat Shiva's most charming cafes and eateries have moved to the multistory **Mamilla Shopping Mall** that leads up to the Jaffa Gate. In South Jerusalem, the areas around the **Cinémathèque** and the renovated Ottoman-era **First Train Station in Abu Tor** as well as the gentrified **German Colony** neighborhood are also filled with cafes and dining spots, some of which are open during Shabbat.

EAST JERUSALEM

Not as modern and sprawling as its western counterpart, downtown East Jerusalem is nevertheless a bustling modern cityscape lying north of the Old City. Its compact business, commercial, and hotel district starts right along the Old City's north wall on **Sultan Suleiman Street,** which runs from Damascus Gate to Herod's Gate and then downhill to the Rockefeller Museum. **Nablus Road** (*Derech Shechem* in Hebrew) runs northeast from Damascus Gate to the American Colony Hotel; **Saladin Street** (*Sallah ad-Din* in Arabic), the area's chief shopping thoroughfare, starts at Herod's Gate and meets Nablus Road near the American Colony Hotel. The triangle formed by these streets encloses the heart of downtown East Jerusalem.

GETTING AROUND

BY BUS All buses in Israel require a **Rav-Kav** smartcard (www.ravkavonline.co.il) for payment. You can typically buy one and add money to it at any small kiosk or supermarket (*makolet* in Hebrew), or you can download the app on your phone and scan it once you board the bus. For more information,

A Transportation Advisory

When considering public transportation in Israel, always remember that the security situation in the country is complex and unpredictable. Always follow the news and bear in mind that even when the situation is one of calm, the U.S. government prohibits its employees from using public and intercity buses throughout Israel and the West Bank. If you do take a bus in Jerusalem make sure you know your route well *before* stepping on board and be aware of your surroundings at all times. If you are exploring the Old City on foot and need to get to a major site outside of it, such as Yad Vashem, we recommend taking a taxi.

use the **Moovit** app to conveniently access bus schedules in real-time and according to your scheduling needs. Most bus drivers speak English. A single full-fare city bus ticket costs NIS 5.90. ***Tip:*** Be aware that you may occasionally be asked to produce proof that you've paid, otherwise it is all based on the honor system.

Using the Jerusalem Light Rail

With its space age, shining silver cars, and its clanging bells reminiscent of San Francisco's antique cable cars, the **Jerusalem Light Rail** is a great way to see and get around the city. The route glides from the outer southwestern neighborhoods of the city; then along Downtown Jerusalem's main thoroughfare, Jaffa Road; then near the Old City's Damascus Gate; and then northeastward with stops in the Palestinian neighborhoods of Shuafat and Beit Hanina. Finally, it travels to the extreme northeastern Israeli neighborhood of Pisgat Ze'ev. The Light Rail line intersects with bus lines that take you to all other areas of the city.

Despite armed guards, who are posted at many stops, it is advised to remain alert while riding the Light Rail, especially while passing through Palestinian neighborhoods, like those in East Jerusalem, and Bethlehem in the West Bank. Stay informed about the current security situation in Jerusalem by checking the many English media outlets, or inquire at your hotel's front desk before going for a trip.

Trains arrive at frequent intervals. Digital signs on each train alternately flash the direction of the train and the name of each stop. Either use a Rav-Kav (smartcard or app) or buy a ticket from the automated machines at each Light Rail stop and enter the next train. Once aboard the train, you must immediately validate your ticket on the validation machine. From the time validated on your ticket, you have 90 minutes during which you can use your ticket to transfer to any connecting bus line along the Light Rail's route. Inspectors make random checks of passengers. Failure to be in possession of a time-validated ticket results in a fine, and pleading ignorance is no excuse. The

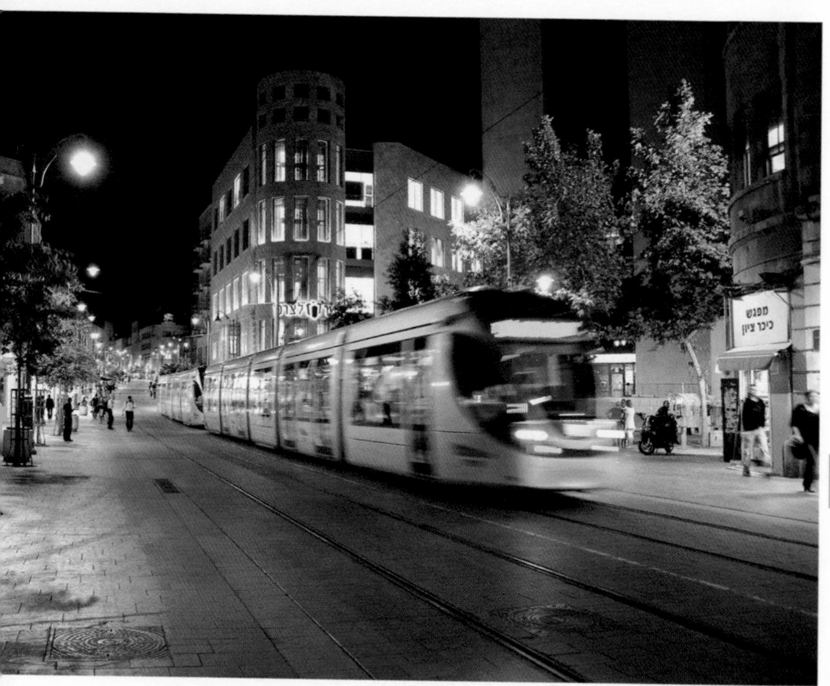

Jerusalem's Light Rail.

single fare on the Light Rail is NIS 10.90 (just like the bus), and discounts are available when purchasing multi-trip tickets.

BY TAXI Private taxis take you throughout the city and charge higher night and Shabbat rates. The standard initial rate is NIS 13. By law, the meter (*ha-sha-on*) must be turned on, and you will be given a printed receipt (*ka-ba-lah*) at your destination, but when taxi drivers see a foreigner, many ask for a set price before starting. Except during the most terrible rush-hour traffic jam, you'll always do better with the meter. (But on a rainy Friday night, if the driver claims his meter is broken, you may not want to argue.) In central Jerusalem, a daytime ride should not be much more than NIS 30 to NIS 40, higher after 9pm and on Shabbat. Taxi drivers do not expect tips; at most, if your driver claims to have no change, round off the fare to the nearest shekel. Your driver may charge extra if he assists you in dragging baggage into or out of a building. If he doesn't charge for this, a tip of a few shekels is a nice courtesy.

ON FOOT Central Jerusalem and the Old City are compact and easy to walk. However, it's hard to get to museums and the Knesset area at the western side of town on foot because distances are far, and pedestrian facilities along access roads are not good. If in doubt about how to get to where you want to go, we advise taking a taxi.

[FastFACTS] JERUSALEM

Area Code The telephone area code is **02.**

Consulates See chapter 11.

Currency Exchange Banking hours are typically 8:30am to noon or 12:30pm Sunday through Friday and on Sunday, Tuesday, and Thursday from 4 to 5pm. **Money-changers,** which are legal, can be found in the Old City, inside Damascus and Jaffa gates; they are generally open daily from 9am to 5 or 6pm. In West Jerusalem, **Change Point,** a convenient money-changing office, has branches on the Ben-Yehuda Mall near Zion Square that are open Sunday through Thursday from 9am to 8pm and on Friday from 9am to 1pm.

You can also change currency at almost any **Post Office** branch, usually for much better conditions than at banks or money-changers.

Conveniently, **ATMs** connected to the major international networks can be found almost everywhere, with a large concentration at Zion Square and on the Ben-Yehuda Mall. You must use ATMs with the Cirrus, Sum, PLUS, or other international connection networks indicated or ones specifically indicating that foreign ATM cards can be used.

Drugstores *The Jerusalem Post* lists under "General Assistance" the names and addresses of duty pharmacies that stay open nights and on Shabbat.

Emergencies To call the **police,** dial ✆ **100.** Dial ✆ **101** for Magen David Adom (Red Shield of David), Israel's emergency first-aid ambulance service. Magen David Adom has a clinic in Romema, near the Central Bus Station, and a **mobile intensive-care unit** (✆ **02/652-3133**) on call 24 hours a day. For medical emergencies requiring hospitalization, dial ✆ **102.**

Events Information For details on special performances and events in Jerusalem, call the **city hot line** (✆ **02/531-4600,** wait for prompt and press 3) or visit **www.jerusalem.muni.il**.

Hospitals Hospital emergency rooms are open daily, 24 hours. Bring your passport and a means to pay the fees. In central Jerusalem: **Bikur Holim Hospital** (✆ **02/646-4111**), Strauss Street near Jaffa Road.

At the western edge of the city: **Sha'arei Tzedek Hospital,** Sderot Herzl, Bayit VeGan (✆ **02/655-5111**). **Hadassah Hospital,** Ein Kerem (✆ **02/677-7111**). For information on possible Blue Cross–Blue Shield coverage at Hadassah Hospital, Ein Kerem, call ✆ **02/677-6029.**

Luggage & Storage Lockers Bags are best stored at your hotel. Be prepared for a security check before storing.

Post Office Jerusalem's Central Post Office (✆ **1-700-500-171**) is at 23 Jaffa Rd., near the intersection with Shlomzion HaMalka Street. General hours for all services are Sunday to Thursday from 7am to 7pm; limited services (telephone and telegraph) are available nights and on Shabbat. East Jerusalem's post office is opposite Herod's Gate at the corner of Saladin Ibn Sina and Sultan Suleiman streets.

The Old City's post office is a few steps from Jaffa Gate, past the Citadel of David and next to the gate of the Christ Church Anglican Hospice.

Religious Services The **Christian Information Centre** (✆ **02/627-2692**), inside Jaffa Gate on Omar Ibn El-Khattab Square, has a list of all Christian services. The center is open Monday through Saturday from 8:30am to 1pm, closed Sunday and holidays. *This Week in Jerusalem,* available free at major hotels, lists Reform, Conservative, and Orthodox Jewish synagogues. Because of security regulations, which vary according to the level of warnings from week to week, independent Muslim tourists who do not have Israeli IDs or advance security clearance may not be allowed into the Al Aqsa compound on Friday (when only Muslims are allowed onto the Temple Mount for Friday prayers) unless they are with an official group.

Safety Jerusalem is a low-crime city, but be aware of pickpockets in the crowd crushes of the Old City. Political demonstrations in West Jerusalem are passionate but usually safe. Avoid demonstrations in East Jerusalem or in the Old City. Keep alert at all times. Get away from and report any unattended or suspicious objects immediately.

Telephones Information is ✆ **144.**

Toilets In the Old City, signs reading WC or OO indicate public restrooms. In West Jerusalem, restaurants and cafes are your best option.

WHERE TO STAY

Moderately priced hotels are in short supply, especially in Jerusalem and especially during holiday periods. So when are the important, rate-raising holidays? Jerusalem's hotels are busiest at Passover and Easter, in September or October during the Jewish high holidays (Rosh Hashanah, Yom Kippur, Succot, and Simchat Torah), and at Christmas. Many hotels also consider July and August to be high season.

The Old City

The advantage to staying in the Old City is that you feel the rhythms and hear the sounds of this extraordinary (and largely car-free) place—the calls to

alternative ACCOMMODATIONS

Bed-and-breakfast accommodations in a private home or apartment are an interesting alternative to hotel stays. To find them, head to **Airbnb**—these types of digs are available all over Jerusalem. Prices are considerably lower than for hotels, and hosts are usually long-time Jerusalemites with lovely, spacious (by Israeli standards) homes and a genuine interest in meeting visitors from abroad. Unique places with private entrances, gardens, views, and especially nice decor, or accommodations for families, can be on the pricier end.

Christian hospices or guesthouses are also a good option. Jerusalem abounds with them, and guests of all faiths are welcome. Guesthouses were originally built to accommodate the pilgrims who began to arrive in great numbers in the 1880s. Many are housed in 19th-century complexes with evocative Jerusalem architecture and style. The atmosphere is, of course, sedate; and better hospices are like extremely well-run small hotels, with comfortable private rooms with bathrooms. Depending on denomination, decor may include a crucifix over the bed, a Byzantine-style icon, or a framed photo of the pope.

St. George's Pilgrim Guest House (65 Nablus Rd; www.stgeorgesguesthouse.org; ✆ **02/628-3302**) offers single rooms with private bath for $100 per night and $140 for a double, with breakfast and service included. A small studio or private flat is available for long-term rates (monthly). For other choices, the **Christian Information Center** (www.cicts.org/en/guesthouses-jerusalem) offers extensive listings of guesthouses and hospices with available accommodations.

Tip: Unmarried couples might run into trouble sharing a room at Christian guesthouses. It varies from place to place, but keep this in mind. You might be able to fudge separate last names on passports, but no visible wedding ring means no double room.

ATTRACTIONS ●

Al Aqsa Mosque 34
Bethseda Pool 44
The Burnt House 38
Cardo Maximus 21
Church of All Nations 48
Church of the Holy Sepulchre 10
Church of St. Anne 45
Coenaculum 28
Davidson Exhibition Center 32
Dome of the Rock 42
Dormition Abbey 27
The Garden Tomb 2
Gate of the Chain 41
Gihon Spring 31
Hurva Synagogue 22
Islamic Museum 35
King David's Tomb 29
Old Yishuv Court Museum 24
Petra Hotel 16
Pool of Hezekiah 12
Pool of Shiloah 30
Ramban Synagogue 22
Robinson's Arch 36
Sephardic synagogues 23
Solomon's Stables 33
St. James Cathedral 19
St. Stephen's Church 46
Tiferet Yisrael Synagogue 37
Tomb of the Virgin 47
Tourist Office 14
Tower of David Museum of the History of Jerusalem 17
Western Wall 40
Zedekiah's Cave 3

ACCOMMODATIONS ●

Al Hashimi Hotel 6
Austrian Hospice 4
Dan Boutique Hotel 25
Gloria Hotel 13
New Imperial Hotel 15
St. Mark's Lutheran Guest House 20

DINING ●

Abu Assab 5
Abu Shukri 43
Adom 26
Amigo Emil 8
Armenian Tavern 18
Between the Arches 39
Family Restaurant 7
Hamarakla 1
Jaffar Sweets 9
Papa Andreas 11
Piccolino 1

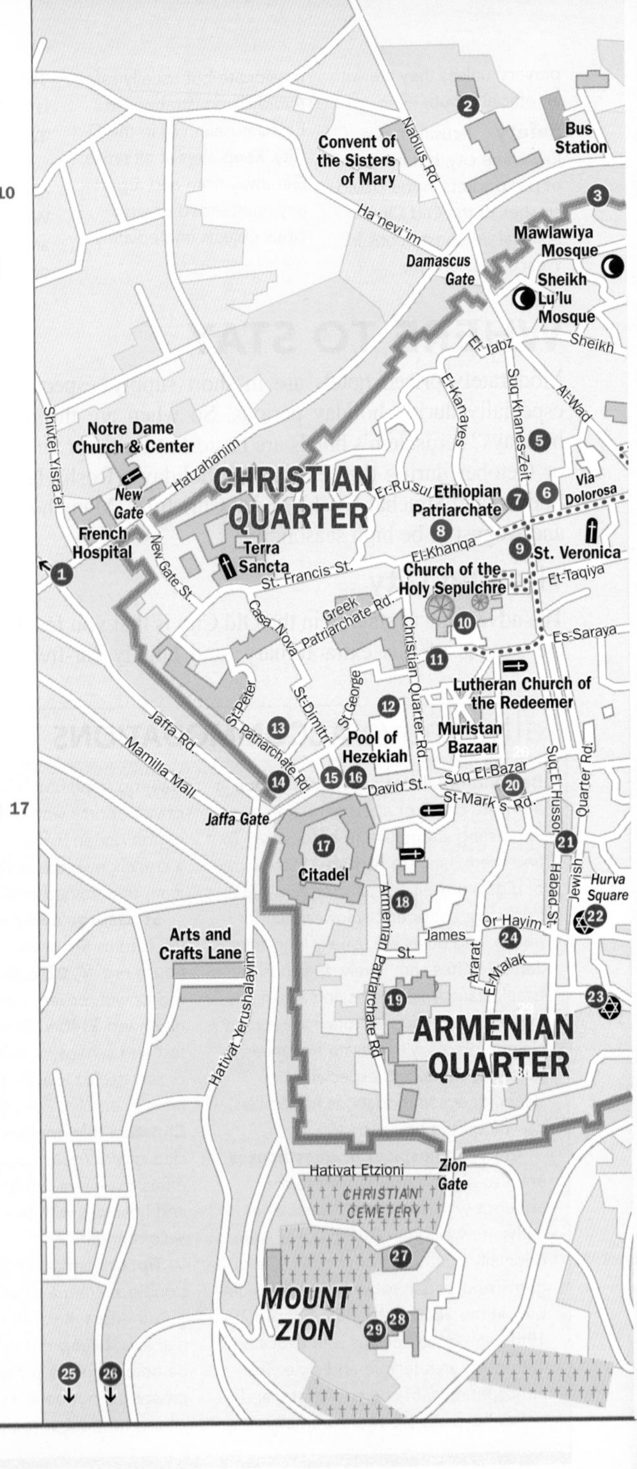

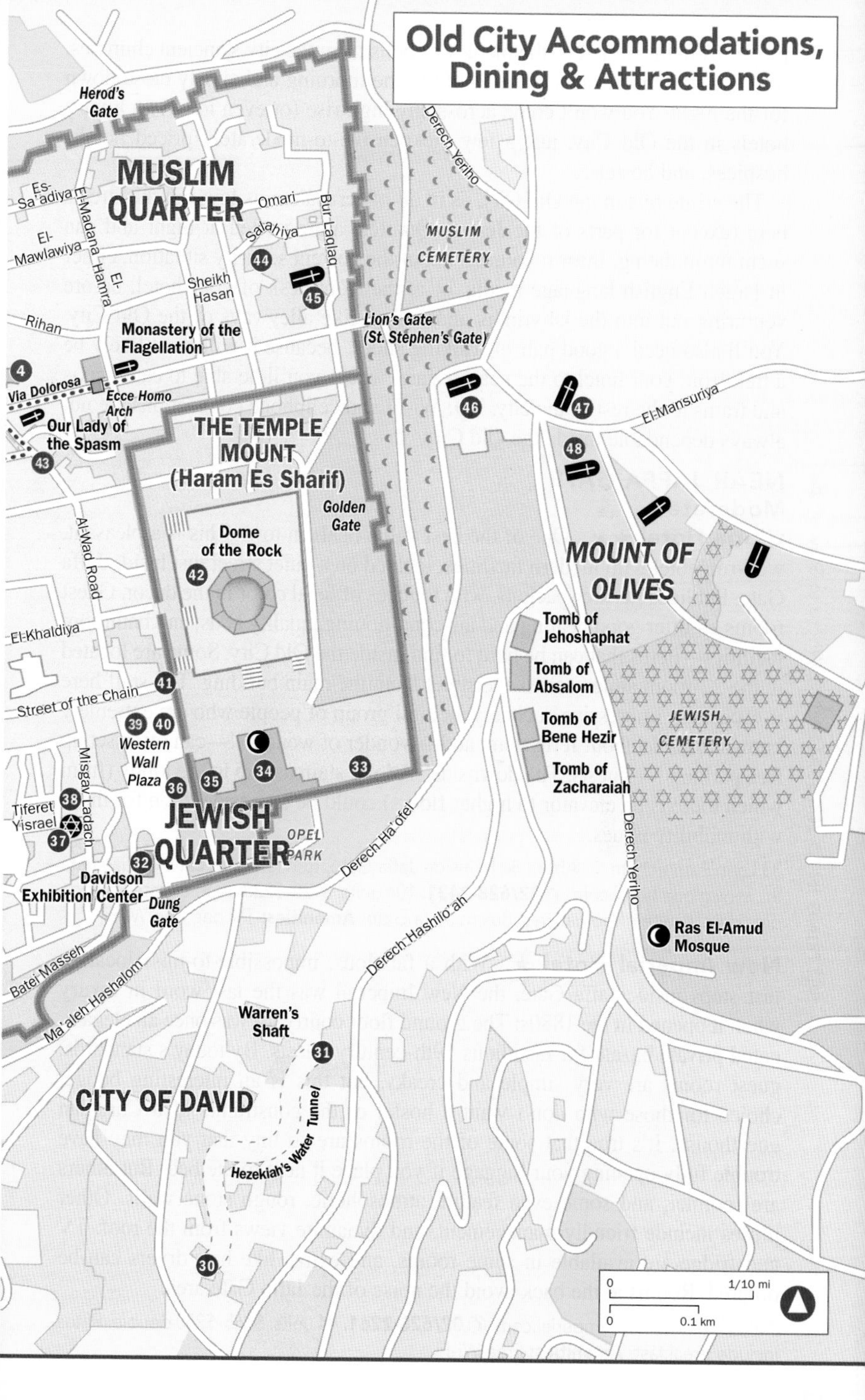
Old City Accommodations, Dining & Attractions
Herod's Gate
MUSLIM QUARTER
Es-Sa'adiya
El-Madana Hamra
El-Mawlawiya
Omari
Salahiya
Bur Laqlaq
Sheikh Hasan
Rihan
Monastery of the Flagellation
Lion's Gate (St. Stephen's Gate)
Derech Yeriho
MUSLIM CEMETERY
Via Dolorosa
Ecce Homo Arch
Our Lady of the Spasm
THE TEMPLE MOUNT (Haram Es Sharif)
Golden Gate
Dome of the Rock
Al-Wad Road
El-Khaldiya
El-Mansuriya
MOUNT OF OLIVES
Tomb of Jehoshaphat
Tomb of Absalom
Tomb of Bene Hezir
Tomb of Zacharaiah
JEWISH CEMETERY
Street of the Chain
Western Wall Plaza
Misgav Ladach
Tiferet Yisrael
JEWISH QUARTER
OPEL PARK
Derech Ha'ofel
Davidson Exhibition Center
Dung Gate
Derech Hashilo'ah
Ras El-Amud Mosque
Batei Masseh
Ma'aleh Hashalom
Warren's Shaft
CITY OF DAVID
Hezekiah's Water Tunnel
0
1/10 mi
0
0.1 km
4
30
31
32
33
34
35
36
37
38
39
40
41
42
43
44
45
46
47
48

prayer from the minarets, the medley of bells from the city's ancient churches. You'll watch the bazaars come to life in the morning and slowly close down for the night. You won't come across any high-rise (or even low-rise) luxury hotels in the Old City, just a few inexpensive-to-moderately priced hotels, hospices, and hostels.

The crime rate in the Old City, as in all of Jerusalem, is low, but the streets here (except for parts of the Jewish Quarter) are deserted at night and can seem intimidating. Inform yourself about the current security situation, either in Israeli English language media, or at the front desk of your hotel, before venturing out into the labyrinths and casbah-like alleyways of the Old City. You'll also need a good pair of walking shoes, because it will most likely be a trek from your hotel to the nearest gate, where you'll be able to catch taxis and trams to the rest of the city. ***Tip:*** Wi-Fi and cellphone connections are not always dependable inside the Old City.

NEAR JAFFA GATE

Moderate

Gloria Hotel ★★ One of the best value deals in town, this is a pleasant, well-run hotel with modern facilities, located on a quiet street just inside Jaffa Gate. Public areas are spacious, with touches of local color in the decor. Guest rooms all offer good heating and air-conditioning, quality beds, and bathroom facilities—items that can be hard to find inside the Old City. Some are located in the 22-room annex across the street from the main building. The staff here is especially impressive, a cheery, helpful group of people who are extremely knowledgeable about Jerusalem, and—wonder of wonders!—can often set up free parking for guests. The downside? A long staircase up to the lobby (from which there is an elevator to higher floors) could be a consideration for those with mobility issues.

33 Latin Patriarchate St. About 80 ft. inside Jaffa Gate, turn left onto Latin Patriarchate St. www.gloria-hotel.com. ✆ **02/628-2431.** 104 units. $125–$220 double. Rates include breakfast. Limited free parking. Bus to Jaffa Gate. **Amenities:** TV; bar; free Wi-Fi.

New Imperial Hotel ★ With a fabulous, impossible-to-miss location just steps inside Jaffa Gate, the New Imperial was the last word in luxury when it opened in the 1880s: The ground floor courtyard was once an elegant, gated private bazaar for fastidious 19th-century guests. By today's standards, guest rooms are very simple and creaky, but this is an interesting budget choice for those who don't want a hostel or the constraints of a Christian guesthouse. It's true that some of the rooms are so tiny that you may have trouble fully opening your luggage if you place it next to the bed. But others are roomier, and some even feature atmospheric, rough stone walls. Other pluses include friendly management, and dynamite views from the roof. TV and fridge are available in some rooms, and extras like hair dryers can be ordered. Rooms at the back avoid the noise of the Jaffa Gate area.

Jaffa Gate. www.newimperial.com. ✆ **02/628-2261.** 44 units. $165–$250 double. Rates include breakfast. **Amenities:** Free Wi-Fi.

With its rough stone walls, its traditional painted arch decorations, and its furnishings, the Gloria Hotel gives visitors an authentic taste of Jerusalem for a reasonable price.

Saint Mark's Lutheran Guest House ★★ This tranquil, atmospheric enclave, a 5-minute walk from Jaffa Gate, is hidden behind a lovely walled garden and features terraces that overlook the Dome of the Rock and the rooftops of the Old City's bazaars. So yes, it's in a splendid location (made even better by being off a quiet street). Who cares that many of the rooms are closet-size (some are larger; ask to move if you're unhappy), are decorated with mass-produced motel furniture, and have tiny bathrooms with showers only? This still counts as one of the best bargains in the city. An unusually generous breakfast is served in a lovely, stone-walled dining hall and included in the nightly rate. Visitors of all backgrounds are welcome, so don't worry if you're not Lutheran, or even Christian. Two quirks you should know about: The guesthouse, unlike most in the city, quotes its prices in euros. And Saint Mark's lies up an obscure staircase street off the David Street bazaar, so phone for directions before arrival. If you're traveling with a lot of luggage, it may be wise to arrange for a baggage porter to meet you at Jaffa Gate.

St. Mark's Rd. www.guesthouse-jerusalem.com. ✆ **02/626-8888.** 30 units. $160–$175 double. Rates include breakfast. Any bus to Jaffa Gate. **Amenities:** Lounge; garden; guest kitchen; free Wi-Fi.

NEAR DAMASCUS GATE

Inexpensive

Al Hashimi Hotel and Hostel ★ A traditional-style Middle Eastern inn built some 500 years ago, the Al Hashimi is set around a handsome interior atrium. It boasts spectacular views eastward toward the Dome of the Rock and the rooftops of the Old City, especially from its panoramic terrace. In fact, we've met guests who spent more time on that lovely terrace than they did in their guest rooms. That may be because this is a terrifically social inn, one that attracts both Muslim and non-Muslim guests (it's in the Muslim Quarter), people of all ages and nationalities, and has a staff savvy and friendly enough to make sure that everyone gets acquainted. The other reason for all the terrace time may be the ultra-compact (read: tiny) size of most of the guest rooms. In its defense, rooms are kept spotlessly clean and boast quality mattresses and decent showers (in the small attached bathrooms). Spacious VIP rooms can be secured for higher rates. With any size room, make sure you're facing away from the bazaar, as it can get quite noisy. Three things to take into consideration: If you have heavy baggage, phone ahead from Damascus Gate so that a porter can be arranged. Alcohol is not allowed on the premises, and unmarried couples are not allowed to room together here.

73 Suq Khan es Zeit. www.hashimihotel.com. ✆ **02/628-4410** or 054-813-0822 for reservations. 40 units plus dorm beds. $90–$130 double. Rates include breakfast. **Amenities:** Free Wi-Fi.

Austrian Hospice ★ Ever dreamed of sleeping in a convent? If so, there's no better place to give it a try than in Jerusalem. Okay, so the Austrian Hospice of the Holy Family is not exactly a convent, but its history is nearer to one than most other lodgings in the Holy City. The hospice was founded in 1857 and was also the residence of the Austrian Consul in Jerusalem. Its role as a center for pilgrims was interrupted by the world wars but was restored to Austrian ownership in the 1980s. Today the Austrian Hospice offers both traditional guest rooms and dormitory-style accommodation. Prices are far below what you'll pay at Jerusalem's bigger and better-known hotels and best of all, the location in the heart of the Old City puts you almost literally at the doorstep of some of Israel's most famous historical and religious sights. There's also a Viennese cafe on the premises—bring on the Sacher torte!

37 Via Dolorosa St. www.austrianhospice.com. ✆ **02/626-5800.** $90–$180 double. Rates include breakfast or half board. **Amenities:** Free Wi-Fi.

The Viennese cafe at the Austrian Hospice.

West Jerusalem

ZION SQUARE, JAFFA ROAD & BEN-YEHUDA MALL

Step out of your hotel and it's a short walk to the Old City and the heart of the New City's downtown shopping-and-restaurant district. The area is noisy, and in summer, discos add to the roar of traffic.

Expensive

Orient by Isrotel ★★ Location is the reason you pick the Orient. While it's about a third of a mile (1km) from here to the Old City, the Orient occupies a very appealing spot in the German Colony, in the vibrant and fun Mishkenot Sha'ananim neighborhood, which was the first community to be built outside the Old City walls. On one side of the hotel is the boutique and restaurant mecca known as the First Station Complex (it was once Jerusalem's first train station) and on the other side is the culturally diverse Liberty Bell Park. You can also *see* the Old City from the hotel, and gazing at the views, especially from one of the sunbeds surrounding the Orient's glam rooftop pool, is another big lure. The hotel is set in a historic 1883 building, and part of the exclusive Isrotel collection, which means rooms are quite cushy (excellent bedding, elegant if corporate-looking decor) and the on-site spa is state of the art, with saunas, Turkish baths, and a menu of 70+ treatments.

> **Avoiding the VAT on Hotel Rooms**
>
> Hotel bills paid in foreign currency or with foreign credit cards by non-Israelis are not subject to the 17% VAT; if possible, always pay for your room and meals charged to your room with a credit card. If you pay in shekels, the VAT may be added to your bill. A few B&Bs and small hotels may post a shekel price list. If they do, ask whether paying in foreign currency will allow them to eliminate your VAT.

3 Emek Refaim St. www.isrotel.com/isrotel-hotels/jerusalem/orient. ✆ **02/569-9090.** 243 units. $398–$745 double. Rates include breakfast. Street pay parking. Light Rail to Hatachana **Amenities:** Airport shuttle; restaurants; spa & hammam; business lounge; rooftop pool; fitness room; free Wi-Fi.

Moderate

Arthur Hotel ★★ Modeled after the Harmony (see below), and a member of the same Atlas chain of boutique hotels, the Arthur offers similar services and amenities and is also located on a pedestrian-only street that offers no direct car or taxi access. Guests who arrive with a car can park for NIS 60 per day in a nearby parking lot and then walk over. It is also possible to call once you arrive and have your baggage picked up and shuttled over to the Arthur by golf cart. A rear-facing room helps minimize street noise.

13 Dorot Rishomim St. Hotel is off Ben Yehuda Pedestrian Mall. www.atlas.co.il. ✆ **02/623-9999.** 58 units. $230–$385 double. Rates include breakfast. Paid parking. **Amenities:** Airport shuttle available; free Wi-Fi.

Harmony Hotel ★★ In the past few years, Israel's moderate-range Atlas Hotel chain has developed new standards for style, up-to-the-minute amenities, helpful staff, and all kinds of guest-pampering extras, such as free late-afternoon happy hours with snacks and refreshments. Its Harmony Hotel is a wildly popular property, located on a charming pedestrians-only street just off Zion Square. Public areas are pleasant and include a library stocked with coffee-table books. Guest rooms are not the largest but are sleek and chic, with zebra print chairs, fluffy white duvets, and, in the suites, actual working fireplaces. Double-glazed windows and summer air-conditioning help block out street noise in this busy area (ask for a rear-facing room). For religious guests, a special elevator is programmed to run on Shabbat.

6 Yoel Salomon St. www.atlas.co.il. ✆ **02/621-9999.** 59 units. $250–$375 double. Rates include breakfast. Limited pay parking. Light Rail to King George St. **Amenities:** Airport shuttle available; free Wi-Fi.

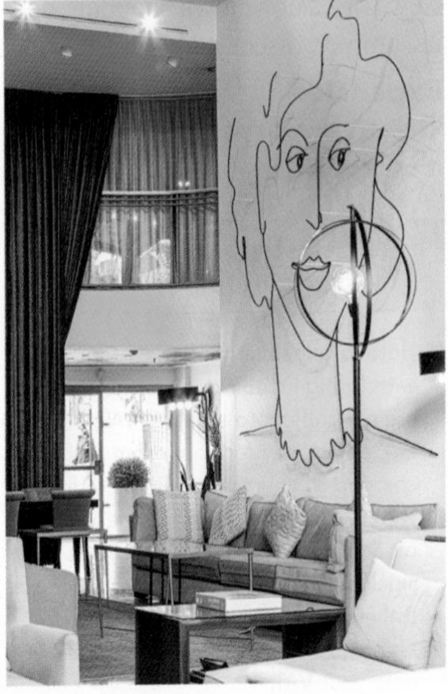

The handsome contemporary lobby at the Harmony Hotel.

Inexpensive

Abraham Hostel ★★★ The biblical Abraham wasn't just the founder of monotheism—he was the world's first backpacker, according to Maoz Innon, the irreverent owner of this funky, fun hostel/hotel. He hopes to extend "biblical hospitality" to his guests, and no, that doesn't have dirty connotations. What it means is that much is free here, from Wi-Fi to walking tours of the city to breakfast. It also means, we think, that the spirit of communalism that enlivened Israel's first kibbutzim is alive and well at the Abraham. Guests and staff cook up Shabbat dinners together and engage in passionate conversations in the Abraham's bar and numerous friendly lounges. Sound too touchy-feely? Guests don't have to partake of any of this. In fact, they don't even have to stay in dorm rooms here (despite the word "hostel" in the name). In addition to communal rooms, there are also sleek private doubles (with bendy wall lamps for reading in bed, high-quality linens, and lots of light). Group and family rooms also available. ***Note:*** The hostel doesn't only do beds; its brilliant "Hop On Hop Off Bus Routes," operated by the affiliated Abraham Tours (p. 386), lets guests travel at their own speed to many typically hard-to-access areas in Israel.

67 Hanevi'im St. at Davidka Sq. www.abrahamhostels.com/jerusalem. ✆ **02/650-2200.** 72 units. Dorm bed $22–$26; private double $66–$110. Rates include breakfast. Light Rail to Mahane Yehuda/Davidka Sq. **Amenities:** Bar; tour programs; billiards room; free Wi-Fi.

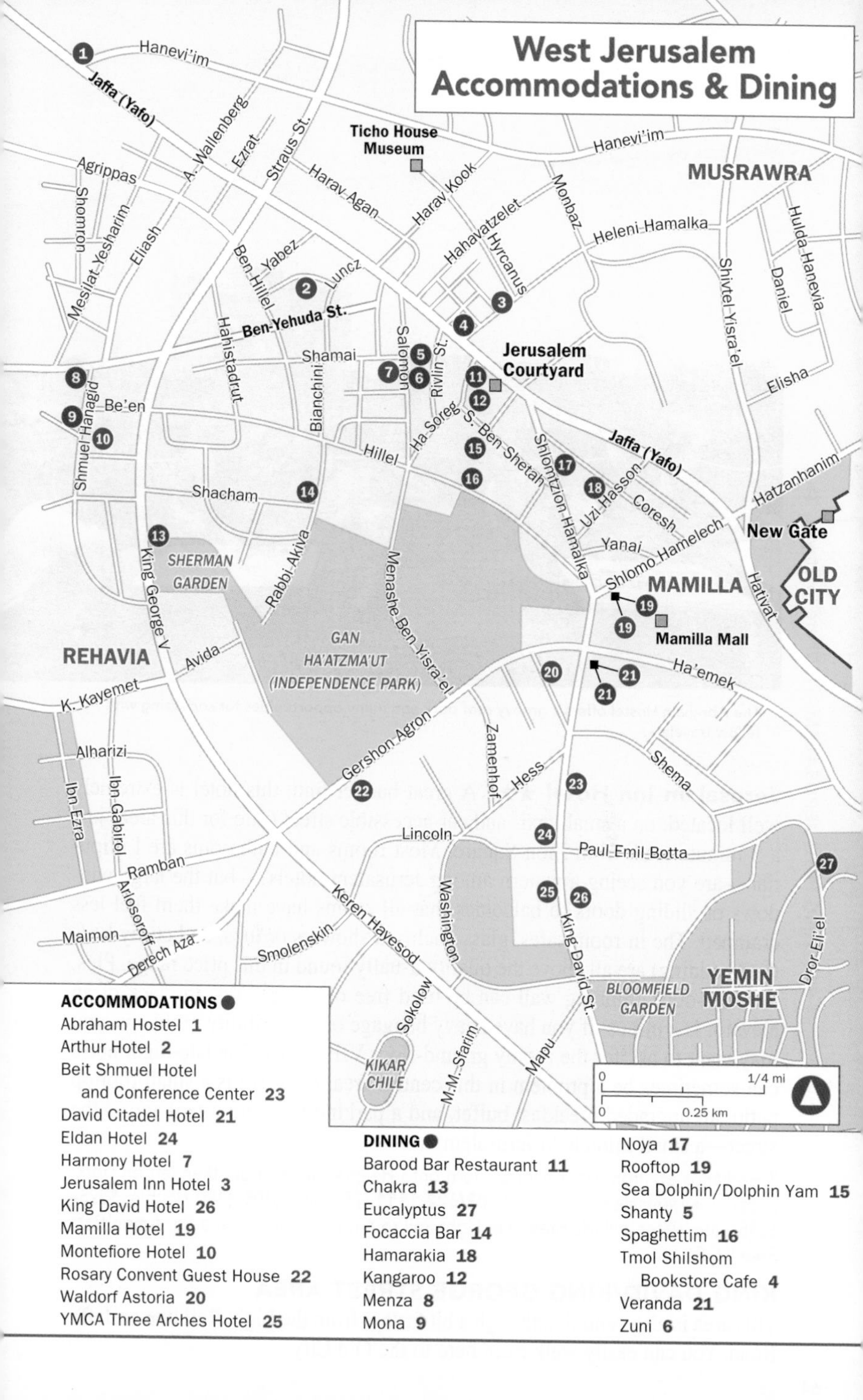
West Jerusalem
Accommodations & Dining
Hanevi'im
Jaffa (Yafo)
Agrippas
Shomron
Mesilat-Yesharim
Eliash
A. Wallenberg
Ezrat
Straus St.
Harav Agan
Ticho House Museum
Harav Kook
Hahavatzelet
Hyrcanus
Monbaz
Heleni-Hamalka
MUSRAWRA
Shivtei-Yisra'el
Daniel
Hulda-Hanevia
Elisha
Ben-Hillel
Yabez
Luncz
Ben-Yehuda St.
Hahistadrut
Shamai
Bianchini
Salomon
Rivlin St.
Jerusalem Courtyard
Shmuel-Hanagid
Be'en
Ha Soreg
S. Ben-Shetah
Hillel
Shlomtzion-Hamalka
Uzi-Hasson
Coresh
Hatzanhanim
New Gate
Shacham
Yanai
Shlomo Hamelech
MAMILLA
OLD CITY
Hativat
Mamilla Mall
King George V
SHERMAN GARDEN
Rabbi-Akiva
Menashe-Ben-Yisra'el
GAN HA'ATZMA'UT (INDEPENDENCE PARK)
REHAVIA
Avida
K. Kayemet
Ha'emek
Gershon Agron
Zamenhof
Shema
Alharizi
Ibn-Ezra
Ibn-Gabirol
Hess
Lincoln
Paul-Emil-Botta
Ramban
Arlosoroff
Washington
King David St.
Maimon
Derech Aza
Smolenskin
Keren Hayesod
Dror-Eli'el
YEMIN MOSHE
BLOOMFIELD GARDEN
Sokolow
M.M.-Sfarim
Mapu
KIKAR CHILE
0 1/4 mi
0 0.25 km
ACCOMMODATIONS
Abraham Hostel 1
Arthur Hotel 2
Beit Shmuel Hotel and Conference Center 23
David Citadel Hotel 21
Eldan Hotel 24
Harmony Hotel 7
Jerusalem Inn Hotel 3
King David Hotel 26
Mamilla Hotel 19
Montefiore Hotel 10
Rosary Convent Guest House 22
Waldorf Astoria 20
YMCA Three Arches Hotel 25
DINING
Barood Bar Restaurant 11
Chakra 13
Eucalyptus 27
Focaccia Bar 14
Hamarakia 18
Kangaroo 12
Menza 8
Mona 9
Noya 17
Rooftop 19
Sea Dolphin/Dolphin Yam 15
Shanty 5
Spaghettim 16
Tmol Shilshom Bookstore Cafe 4
Veranda 21
Zuni 6

The Abraham Hostel offers a groovy roof deck and many opportunities for socializing with fellow travelers.

Jerusalem Inn Hotel ★★ A great budget find, this hotel is extremely well located: on a small taxi- and car-accessible street (rare for this area) just a 3-minute walk from Zion Square. Most rooms and bathrooms are Lilliputian—are you seeing a pattern among Jerusalem hotels?—but the large windows or sliding doors to balconies that all rooms have make them feel less cramped. The in-room safes, glass-enclosed showers or tubs, and cushy beds (and bedding) are all above the quality usually found in this price range. Plus, the next-door climbing wall can be used free of charge. Yes, the lack of an elevator is a minus; if you have heavy baggage or accessibility problems, you may want to ask for the roomy ground-floor VIP rooms. The late-night noise can sometimes be a problem in this central area, but there is a small rooftop patio, an upgraded breakfast buffet, and a parking lot (with a fee) across the street—a small miracle in Jerusalem!

7 Horkanos St. (from Hanevi'im St., turn onto Helena HaMalka St., then left on Horkanos). www.jerusalem-inn.com. ✆ **02/622-1111.** 25 units. $105–$190 double; $225–$245 suite. Rates include breakfast. Light Rail to King George or Safra Sq. **Amenities:** Free Wi-Fi.

KING DAVID/KING GEORGE STREET AREA

This area is also central, although a bit farther from the Light Rail line on Jaffa Road. You can easily walk from here to the Old City.

family-friendly **HOTELS**

Traveling with kids in tow? Try the following hotels, which either offer savings for families or swell amenities for the little ones.

David Citadel Hotel ★★★ (see below) This is the luxury choice for families, as it boasts both a heated, outdoor pool (open year-round) and a whimsical children's playroom that your kids will find difficult to leave. The Citadel's super-size rooms are perfect for large groups, and the staff is particularly attentive to the needs of young guests.

King David ★★★ (p. 66) and **Dan Jerusalem ★** (p. 71) Members of the same chain, these hotels go out of their way to accommodate families with interactive kids' activities for all ages during the weekends, summer months, and holidays. The "DanyClub" is operated by an energetic team, and they even have a few areas dedicated to toddlers and infants.

Ramat Rachel ★ (p. 70) The Rachel not only offers a large swimming pool but also has playground facilities on the property, plus basketball and tennis courts. When school is out, the staff here offer specialized kids' activities.

Expensive

David Citadel Hotel ★★★ Feeling lucky? You will be when you check into this horseshoe-shaped hotel (designed by architect Moshe Safdie of Yad Vashem fame). It is filled with every luxury imaginable and lies just a short stroll from the Old City. Rooms are opulent in the extreme, large and bright

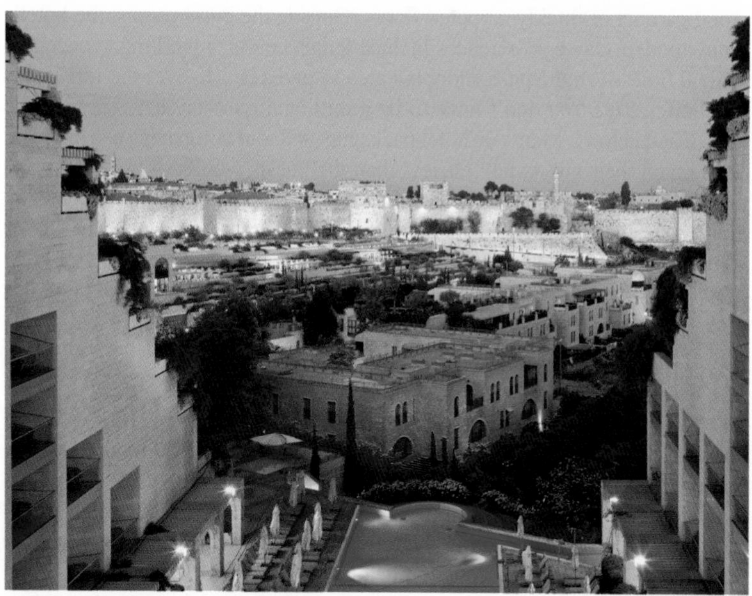

This guest room view highlights the David Citadel's striking architecture, its rooftop pool, and its unbeatable location.

and outfitted with Fendi furnishings and superbly comfortable beds swathed in Frette linens. Almost all have balconies, many with dramatic views. The pampering continues in the hotel's award-winning spa; at its many inventive restaurants (which include the fabulous **Seasons** and **Veranda**); and in each and every interaction with the staff, a group of *mensches* (Yiddish for "good people") who bend over backward to make sure that all requests are accommodated. This may sound like an adults-only type of place, but the Citadel is wonderfully family-friendly, thanks to those large rooms (with alcove rooms, for those sharing digs with their kids); the hotel's large, all-season, heated pool; and its dedicated, whimsical, and well-equipped playroom.

7 King David St. (at the corner of Mamilla St.). www.thedavidcitadel.com. ✆ **02/621-2121.** 384 units. $425–$850 double. Underground parking (fee). Light Rail: 1. **Amenities:** Restaurant; terrace cafe; bar; children's activities; concierge; health club; children's pool and heated outdoor pool; room service; sauna; spa; steam room; synagogue; free Wi-Fi.

King David Hotel ★★★ Built in 1930 during the British Mandate, the King David has outlasted the British Empire and continues to sail on, refined and majestic. Its Egyptian-esque Art Deco lobby still draws gawkers, as does its lushly gardened pool area, made famous in the film *Exodus* (it's where Paul Newman romanced Eva Marie Saint). For world leaders visiting the city, there's no other choice for digs. Surprisingly, though, the rooms are not in the least old-fashioned. In fact, a number of them were combined in the late 1990s to offer more space to guests (although some remain small). Today, all boast fine wood furnishings, handsome heavy draperies, luxe bed linens, and shiny wood parquet or thickly carpeted floors. Outside the guest rooms, the hotel's many modern-day conveniences include tennis courts, a working synagogue, a small fitness center/spa, a shopping arcade, and a lavish, over-the-top breakfast buffet. ***Tip:*** You don't have to be a millionaire to stay here (despite the rates listed below). Many air/hotel packagers and tour companies use the King David, and their guests pay far less than the guests who book with the hotel directly (although they're usually relegated to the smaller rooms or ones that don't have the iconic views of the Old City). Parent company Dan Hotels sometimes offers off-season discounts; check the website.

23 King David St. www.danhotels.com. ✆ **02/620-8888.** 233 units. $600–$740 double; $760–$1,060 deluxe double with Old City view. Rates include breakfast. Limited parking (fee). Light Rail or Bus: 18, 74, or 75. **Amenities:** Restaurant; cafe; gym and spa; outdoor pool; room service; sauna; synagogue; tennis court; free Wi-Fi.

Mamilla Hotel ★★★ The dynamic duo of Israeli architect Moshe Safdie and Italian designer Piero Lissoni were the masterminds behind this posh contemporary palace. Every detail of it either pleases the eye or calms the body, from the bedside walls of exposed Jerusalem Stone to the deep, cascading rectangular bathtubs within modular glassed-in bathrooms that frost over for privacy. Guests have access to the hotel's Akasha Holistic Wellbeing Center, which encompasses a gym with state-of-the-art equipment plus rooms

Old-school elegance at the King David Hotel.

dedicated to spin classes, Pilates, and Tai chi; and a spa offering Watsu pool hydro-treatments, special hammam treatments, and more. The hotel also has a top-notch restaurant on its roof (**The Rooftop ★★★**, see p. 82) and an appealing location, perched above the open-air Mamilla Alrov pedestrian mall. It's about a 15-minute walk to the Old City from here.

11 King Solomon St. www.mamillahotel.com. ✆ **02/548-2200.** 194 units. $530–$799. Rates include breakfast. Parking for a fee of NIS 50 per day. **Amenities:** Restaurant; cafe; bar; babysitting (book in advance); concierge; wellness center, including gym, hammam and indoor pool; free Wi-Fi.

Waldorf Astoria ★★★ One of the most magnificent buildings in Jerusalem, this hotel was originally built to be the city's treasury building in 1928-29 under the order of Jerusalem's Supreme Muslim Council (it was supervised by the infamous Mufti of Jerusalem). Its ornate facade and interior are a wonderful mélange of influences—Art Deco, Roman, Moorish, Arabic—all brought back to vibrant life in 2014, when the former owner finished a reported $150-million top-to-bottom renovation. Today, there's a subtle Ottoman-inspired theme that that runs throughout the hotel, and lots of luxury, from the size of all the guest rooms (huge); to heated marble bathroom floors and mirrors with built in TVs in the bathrooms; to heavenly and massive beds. Balcony rooms above the fourth floor have superb Old City and downtown views. More luxury awaits in the spa, the hotel's two gourmet restaurants, and in the **Kings Court,** where afternoon tea, creative cocktails, and sweet treats are served. There is also a tapas bar. ***Tip:*** Ask the concierge about having your luggage checked in at the hotel and delivered to the airport. The Waldorf Astoria is situated on the corner of King David and Agron streets, only a few minutes from Jaffa Gate and the Old City.

26-28 Gershon Agron St. (at the corner of Mamilla St.). www.hilton.com. ✆ **02/542-3333.** 222 units. $500–$950 double. Underground parking (fee). **Amenities:** Restaurants; terrace cafe; bar; concierge; health club; indoor pool; business center; free Wi-Fi.

Moderate

Eldan Hotel ★ This modern hotel is affiliated with Israel's largest car-rental company, which means you can get a small discount if you rent an Eldan vehicle; the Eldan Rental office is in the hotel, so pick-up and drop-off couldn't be easier. And just like a decent rental car, the hotel runs smoothly, although you'll likely forget what it looks like the moment you check out. That being said, it's superbly located (right across from the King David Hotel), clean, and comfortable and boasts tubs in most of the bathrooms, a nice perk. The refurbished fifth-floor rooms are quieter than rooms on lower floors.

24 King David St. www.eldanhotel.com. ✆ **02/567-9777.** 76 units. $180–$240 double. Rates include breakfast. Limited free parking. Light Rail or Bus: 18, 74, or 75. **Amenities:** Restaurant; bar; fitness room; room service; complimentary happy hour; free Wi-Fi.

Montefiore Hotel ★★ Not to be confused with the Tel Aviv hotel of the same name, this cheery property, built in the 1990s, has more of a Western vibe than others in its price category, for all the good and the bad that implies. Rooms are a hair larger than one usually gets at this price point and feature more color: navy blue rugs, happy bubble-patterned coverlets, toast-colored curtains. Rooms that face Shatz Street on higher floors tend to be the quietest picks, unless you get one near the squeaky elevator (ask to move if that happens). In late fall and winter, there are often fabulous room deals. The location is just right: on a pedestrian street a mere 1½ blocks from the intersection of King George Street and the Ben-Yehuda pedestrian mall. Because the hotel is on a pedestrian street, taxis can't drop you off at the door, but it's only a half-block downhill from Shmuel HaNagid Street. Call ahead for arrival info and possible help with baggage. Parking is difficult here.

7 Schatz St. www.smarthotels.co.il. ✆ **02/622-1111.** 48 units. $218–$240 double. Rates include breakfast. **Amenities:** Restaurant; free Wi-Fi.

YMCA Three Arches Hotel ★ When locals need to house visiting relatives and friends, this unpretentious yet historic property is the one they often pick. That may be partly because it's so famous: Completed in 1933 and designed by Arthur Loomis Harmon (architect of the Empire State Building), the building is a beauty, with a magnificent lobby that mixes Art Deco and

The lobby is more opulent than the rooms at the YMCA Three Arches.

Islamic-Byzantine touches, and a famed observation tower. Plus, guests have free access to the 1930s-style indoor swimming pool and modern fitness room. But their choice likely also has to do with the prices, which are usually more-than-reasonable for digs this well located (it's just across the street from the King David Hotel). So although the rooms are nothing to write home about—they tend to be small but clean and with adequate air-conditioning—most who stay here are pleased with the experience.

26 King David St. www.ymca3arches.com. ✆ **02/569-2692.** 56 units. $175–$250 double. Rates include breakfast. Limited free parking. Light Rail or Bus: 18, 74, or 75 to King David St. **Amenities:** Fitness room; library/lounge; indoor pool; room service; free Wi-Fi.

Inexpensive

Beit Shmuel Hotel and Conference Center ★ Designed by acclaimed architect Moshe Safdie (he also did the David Citadel Hotel and the Mamilla Hotel), this sprawling, contemporary cultural and educational center is run by the World Union for Progressive (Reform) Judaism. The complex boasts excellent views of the Old City and a network of terraces, gardens, and courtyards. At night, the college campus–like area bustles with activity—lectures, concerts, art exhibits, you name it. As for Beit Shmuel's hotel, it contains rooms with private bathrooms that can be arranged for two to four people; better rooms in the Guest House wing can handle up to six guests. Visitors of all faiths and ages are welcome. Phone ahead to make arrangements if you need wheelchair access. Reserve far in advance because this is a popular place to lodge.

6 Shama St. www.beitshmuel.co.il. ✆ **02/620-3555.** 69 units. $130–$165 double. Rates include breakfast. **Amenities:** Free Wi-Fi.

Rosary Convent Guest House and Hostel ★★ This hidden gem is centrally located in a quiet garden around the corner from the high-rise Jerusalem Leonardo Plaza Hotel and across the street from a SuperSol supermarket. Most of the rooms are airy, with high ceilings, heating, and air-conditioning, and roomy enough to fit three beds (there are no double beds here, just singles). Everything is spotless, homemade breads and jam grace the table at breakfast, and the Rosary Sisters are especially helpful to guests. The gate to the convent closes at 10pm, but you can arrange to be let in later.

14 Agron St. rosarysisters-gh.com. ✆ **02/625-8529** or 02/623-5581. 23 units, most w/ private bathroom. $130 double. Rates include breakfast. Cash only. **Amenities:** Free Wi-Fi.

FARTHER WEST: EIN KEREM

Moderate

Notre Dame de Sion Convent Guest House Ein Kerem ★★ Not to be confused with the Notre Dame de Sion Guest House in the Old City, this is one of the most special places to stay in the Jerusalem area. It's set in a walled convent with its own orchards and gardens in the charming village of Ein Kerem (birthplace of John the Baptist), a half-hour municipal bus ride from downtown Jerusalem. Not all guests are religious; many travelers come for the poetry and romance of the place. The convent itself is a lovely ensemble of atmospheric stone buildings; rooms are very simple but spotless, and many share a balcony, a huge plus in a setting this lovely.

23 Ha-Oren St., Ezor "D," Ein Kerem. www.notredamedesion.org/centres/ein-kerem-guest-house. ✆ **02/641-5738.** 34 units, 23 w/private bathroom, 8 w/shared bathroom. Sun–Thurs $200 double; Fri–Sat $250 double. Rates include breakfast. Light Rail or Bus 50 to Mount Herzl, then bus line 28 to Ein Kerem. **Amenities:** Chapel for meditation and prayer; gardens; free Wi-Fi.

South Jerusalem

South of the King David Street area, it's about a 30-minute walk or short bus ride from the city center. The area is convenient to the many cafes, shops, and restaurants in the German Colony. You are also close to the dramatic Cinémathèque complex and the renovated First Train Station in Abu Tor.

MODERATE

Dan Boutique Hotel ★★ The Dan Boutique has all the class and comfort that are the hallmarks of this hotel chain (think cushiony beds, decor in serene tans and taupes, well-trained staff, a generous breakfast buffet) but because of its original architecture, rooms come in a wide variety of sizes and arrangements, which can make it a good choice for families and large groups. The better rooms (some of which have balconies) are on floors five to eight; these include 14 roomy suites. The worst are the ground-floor rooms; they get a "lovely" view of the parking lot. Nearby bus stops take you all over the city. Look for off-season specials.

31 Hebron Rd. (just north of Havaselet St.). www.danhotels.com. ✆ **02/568-9999.** 126 units. $190–$225 double. Rates include breakfast. Limited free parking. **Amenities:** Cafe; bar; fitness center; synagogue; free Wi-Fi.

Ramat Rachel Hotel ★ The only kibbutz guest accommodations accessible via Jerusalem's city buses, the Ramat Rachel may be the top choice in the area for families with very active children. Along with an Olympic-size outdoor pool and an indoor pool for rainy days, the resort—and it's much more of a resort than a hotel—offers lit tennis and basketball courts and a playground, along with organized children's activities. There are refurbished, less-expensive older rooms in addition to 60 newer rooms; all are comfy by kibbutz standards, and some even have balconies with killer views of the desert and Bethlehem in the distance (the hotel is set on a hill). Meals are glatt kosher, and all hotel facilities are wheelchair accessible. The kibbutz is heavily booked in summer and Jewish holidays, and the pool is filled with locals on weekends. ***Note:*** The bus into town runs on schedule but is infrequent, so this is a better choice for travelers who have cars (there's ample free parking).

Ramat Rachel Hotel. www.ramatrachel.co.il. ✆ **888/669-5700** in the U.S., or 02/670-2555. 164 units. $145–$275 double. Rates include breakfast. Free parking. **Amenities:** Cafe; bar; airport transfers (fee); children's center; health club and spa; Jacuzzi; playground; Olympic pool and indoor heated pool; sauna; tennis and basketball courts; free Wi-Fi.

Saint Andrew's Church of Scotland Guest House ★★ The flag of St. Andrew's waves from the tower of this guesthouse, welcoming visitors. It's a cheery sight, as are the gardens that surround this hillside lodging; stand in their midst or on St. Andrew's sun porch, and you'll be treated to postcard-perfect views of Mount Zion and the Old City. St. Andrews offers spotless, guest rooms (bright white usually, with cool tile floors and top-quality beds), a lounge/library, and a dining room where guests can have free tea and coffee all day. The location is a block away from cafes and eateries at the Cinémathèque and the First Station complex as well as a few steps to buses all over town. Staff is congenial, and there's a ground-floor special-access room and free, gated parking for guests.

1 David Remez St. www.scotsguesthouse.com. ✆ **02/673-2401.** 23 units. $160–$220 double. Rates include breakfast. Free parking. **Amenities:** Lounge; free Wi-Fi.

INEXPENSIVE

Little House in Bakah ★ Not so "little," this extremely friendly hotel is set in a landmark, early-20th-century mansion in one of the city's outer neighborhoods. It gets a lot of repeat business thanks to its affordable rates and genial staff, who make guests feel like family. That familial ambience continues in the guest rooms, which are nowhere near luxurious but are tidy, comfortable, and pleasant, with art on the walls of the kind your great-aunt might pick. The house offers 13 singles (a rarity in Jerusalem) and an annex with family rooms and suites. Double rooms in the basement are less expensive but not too inviting. The location is on busy Derech Hebron (ask for a room in the back if you want quiet), with relatively frequent buses into the center of town. It's within walking distance to the beautiful streets and eateries of the German Colony; there's also an excellent on-site restaurant. If this popular place is full, the management also runs the **Little House in Rehavia.** Both are on the same website and offer similar accommodations. For reservations, be sure to specify which Little House you're asking for. Food is kosher mehadrin.

Hebron Rd. (at Yehuda St.). jerusalem-hotel.co.il/bakah. ✆ **02/673-7944.** 33 units. $90–$190 double. Rates include breakfast. Free on-street parking. Bus: 74 or 75. **Amenities:** Cafe/bar; limited room service; free Wi-Fi.

North Jerusalem

EXPENSIVE

Dan Jerusalem ★ If you're looking for a good deal at a major hotel and are willing to stay in a somewhat out-of-the-way neighborhood, head to the

Dan Jerusalem, nestled on the lower slopes of Mt. Scopus. Built in the 1980s, with an impressive contemporary design by an award-winning Israeli architect, the hotel was taken over by the Dan Hotel chain not long ago, which did extensive renovations of the 130 executive rooms in the King David Wing and a lighter update to most of the standard rooms. Pluses include sweeping views of the Old City in the distance, very good breakfasts, top service, a large pool and extensive sports facilities, and a free hotel shuttle service that runs to the Old City and West Jerusalem. The staff goes out of their way to accommodate families as well. But there are some downsides to staying here, such as the lack of interesting nearby streets for strolling around. The Light Rail station to downtown is 2 long blocks away; at night, most take taxis.

32 Lehi St. www.danhotels.com. ✆ **02/533-1234.** 500 units. $200–$300 double. Rates include breakfast. Free parking. Light Rail to Ammunition Hill. **Amenities:** Restaurant; cafe; bar; lit basketball, volleyball, and tennis courts; in-season children's activities; fitness center and spa (fee); playground; outdoor swimming pool; room service; free shuttle to downtown Jerusalem; synagogue; free Wi-Fi.

East Jerusalem & the East/West Jerusalem Seam

The atmosphere in East Jerusalem is Palestinian, and the genuine helpfulness and hospitality found in many of East Jerusalem's hotels are well known. As a rule, East Jerusalem hotels are somewhat less expensive than those in the western part of town. Be forewarned, however, that the area is relatively dead at night and that many of the cheaper East Jerusalem hotels, not listed here, can be run-down and smoky. For safety, you should also refrain from venturing into this part of the city while displaying recognizable Jewish symbols.

EXPENSIVE

American Colony Hotel ★★★ Few cities anywhere are as rich in history, so it should come as no surprise that Jerusalem's hotels have scintillating stories attached to them. The American Colony was originally constructed for a Turkish pasha and his harem of four wives and later became a commune or "colony" for a cult of messianic American and Swedish Christians (hence the name). It was transformed into a hotel in 1902 by Plato von Ustinov, grandfather of British film star Peter Ustinov. In 1917, when British troops arrived at the city during World War I, a white bed sheet from the hotel was used to signal Jerusalem's surrender. Famous past guests include Lawrence of Arabia, Bob Dylan, John Le Carré (who wrote a novel while staying here), and Winston Churchill, among others. But even if you didn't know the history, you could tell this was a storied place by gazing at the exquisite painted wooden ceilings, tracing the patterns on the colorful Armenian tile that coat the public areas, or walking through the walled courtyards. Those lucky enough to stay in one of the pasha rooms or suites in the original 19th-century building are surrounded by fine antiques. More affordable but still spacious (deluxe) rooms and smaller economy rooms are available in the newer, less-exotic wings. Within each room category there's variation, so try to see different

At the historic American Colony Hotel, the decor couldn't be more chic and contemporary.

rooms, if possible, before settling. If you decide *not* to stay here, consider coming by for the **Saturday luncheon buffet in the Arabesque Room** (p. 94; food is not kosher), a Jerusalem tradition. There is a pool in the hotel's famously stunning gardens.

1 Nablus Rd. www.americancolony.com. ✆ **02/627-9777.** 95 units. $275–$415 double; up to $850 for pasha rooms and suites in main building. Rates include breakfast. Limited free parking. **Amenities:** Restaurant; cafe; bar; babysitting (book in advance); concierge; fitness center; Jacuzzi and sauna; outdoor pool and children's pool; free Wi-Fi with most rates.

MODERATE

Jerusalem Hotel ★★ A special, boutique hotel, the Jerusalem is known as the affordable, more personal version of the legendary, nearby American Colony Hotel. Set in an old Jerusalem mansion with Middle Eastern architecture, exposed stone walls, and handcrafted furnishings, the hotel is located 1 long block from Damascus Gate. You enter through a walled, vine-covered garden restaurant that's heated in winter and is a rendezvous spot for Israelis, Palestinians, and in-the-know internationals. The restaurant is famous for live, traditional Arabic music on Friday nights, with diners and waiters often dancing in the aisles. Depending on conditions, the management can arrange tours to Bethlehem and the West Bank. Ask for a room away from the restaurant because it can get loud, but that's about the only negative as rooms are quite handsome, with colorful, exotic coverlets, heavy wood furnishings, exposed stone walls, and arched windows. This is a Christian-owned hotel, so alcohol is served.

Nablus Rd. (entrance at 4 Antar Ben-Shadad St. on a side street facing the north side of the Egged East Nablus Rd. Bus Station). www.jrshotel.com. ✆ **02/628-3282.** 15 units. $150–$235 double. Rates include breakfast. Light Rail to Damascus Gate. **Amenities:** Restaurant; free Wi-Fi.

St. George Hotel ★★ Originally built in the 1960s, the St. George was totally redesigned and everything—from the relatively spacious guest rooms to the rooftop terrace and pool, double-glazed windows, and free Wi-Fi—is new and, in the case of the decor, quite handsome. Alas, views could not be added to most of the rooms, but the vista from the rooftop terrace is breathtaking. Up there you'll also find the **Meejana Lounge** serving delicious traditional Arabic cuisine. When booking a room, ask for one in the back because they're quieter. Families may want to consider the generous, but not too pricey, mini-suites. The hotel is an easy walk to Damascus Gate.

6 Amir ibn al A'as St. (btw. Nablus Rd. and Saladin St.). www.stgeorgehoteljerusalem.com. ✆ **02/627-7232.** 130 units. $120–$250 double. Rates include breakfast. **Amenities:** Concierge; restaurants; rooftop pool and terrace; free Wi-Fi.

INEXPENSIVE

St. George's Cathedral Pilgrim Guesthouse ★ Centered around a green and tranquil English garden, this Anglican/Episcopal establishment is welcoming to all travelers. In fact, we'd say that the service is what makes St. George's special: The tireless staff dispense savvy travel and dining advice from morning until night, always with a smile. Guest rooms, as you might imagine, are somewhat monastic, but they can vary in shape and size, so ask to see a few before you check in. All have air-conditioning, thankfully. If you like quiet, try for a room away from the bar or the street. The cavelike lounge (open in the evenings until midnight) is an unusual extra and contributes to the congenial, mildly English ambience.

20 Nablus Rd. (at Saladin St.). www.stgeorgesguesthouse.org. ✆ **02/628-3302.** 24 units. $150–$180 double. Light Rail to Shivtei Israel. **Amenities:** Lounge; bar; free Wi-Fi.

WHERE TO EAT

Jerusalem has a huge selection of restaurants, dairy bars, lunch counters, snack shops, delicatessens, and cafes.

In the Old City and East Jerusalem, you'll find mostly Middle Eastern cuisine, including numerous snack stands and inexpensive Arab eateries. Pork is prohibited for Muslims and Jews, but you will find pork, shellfish, and alcohol (forbidden to Muslims) in East Jerusalem restaurants catering to tourists or Christian Jerusalemites. There are no kosher restaurants in East Jerusalem or in the Old City except in the Jewish Quarter. Most Old City restaurants open daily from late morning to 5 or 6pm.

Catching Restaurants at Their Best

Saturday night is big for dining out in Israel, but think twice before booking a top table at a kosher restaurant, because you won't find restaurants at their best. Many kosher restaurants prepare food on Thursday, when they receive their last batch of fresh fish and vegetables before the weekend, so their staff won't have to work on the Sabbath. If you're going to splurge at a top restaurant, do it midweek.

In West Jerusalem, the dining scene is quite different. There's an oversupply of French/Mediterranean restaurants overseen by talented, inventive chefs. These meals are not cheap, but almost all restaurants offer incredible business lunch specials from noon until 5 or 6pm that make them very affordable, at least at that time of day. You'll find pedestrian streets that are wall-to-wall eateries, but some of the best dining choices are in quiet, slightly out-of-the-way streets and in old Ottoman-era mansions surrounded by walled gardens. Almost every restaurant or cafe has a security guard at its entrance (and many add a small security charge that's worth the peace of mind).

The Old City

NEAR JAFFA GATE

Inexpensive

Armenian Tavern ★ ARMENIAN Specializing in tasty home-style Armenian dishes flavored with traditional spices and sauces, this restaurant can be hard to find. Make the effort. You descend a steep flight of stairs to an atmospheric Crusader-era room decorated with hand-painted Armenian tiles. Soft Greek and Armenian music adds to the atmosphere. Frankly, we could—and often do—make a meal of the appetizers here, particularly the small, traditional meat pies, salads, and soups (try the pepper salad and the cucumber-and-yogurt salad). Imported beer and a good selection of wine are served, and a $10 minimum order is required.

79 Armenian Orthodox Patriarchate Rd. (after entering Jaffa Gate, turn right at the Tower of David [Citadel]; continue straight; restaurant is on the right, down a flight of stairs). ✆ **02/627-3854.** Reservations necessary Fri–Sat evenings. Main courses NIS 40–NIS 85. Mon–Sat noon–10pm.

Papa Andreas ★ MIDDLE EASTERN We'll be frank: The magnificent views of the Dome of the Rock are why you choose this rooftop terrace restaurant—it's a truly memorable spot for a meal. As for the menu, it offers standard Middle Eastern cuisine as well as a few Western-style dishes, such as pizza and pasta. Service is friendly, and you can usually linger over tea and baklava in the twilight amid evening prayer calls. There's also a large indoor dining room, but we'd suggest eating elsewhere if it's too cold for the roof; you come here for the view. The restaurant and terrace require a climb up four long flights of stairs.

64 Aftimos St., Muristan Bazaar, Christian Quarter. ✆ **02/628-4433.** Reserve if you want a table with a great view. Main courses NIS 39–NIS 85. Daily 9am–9pm.

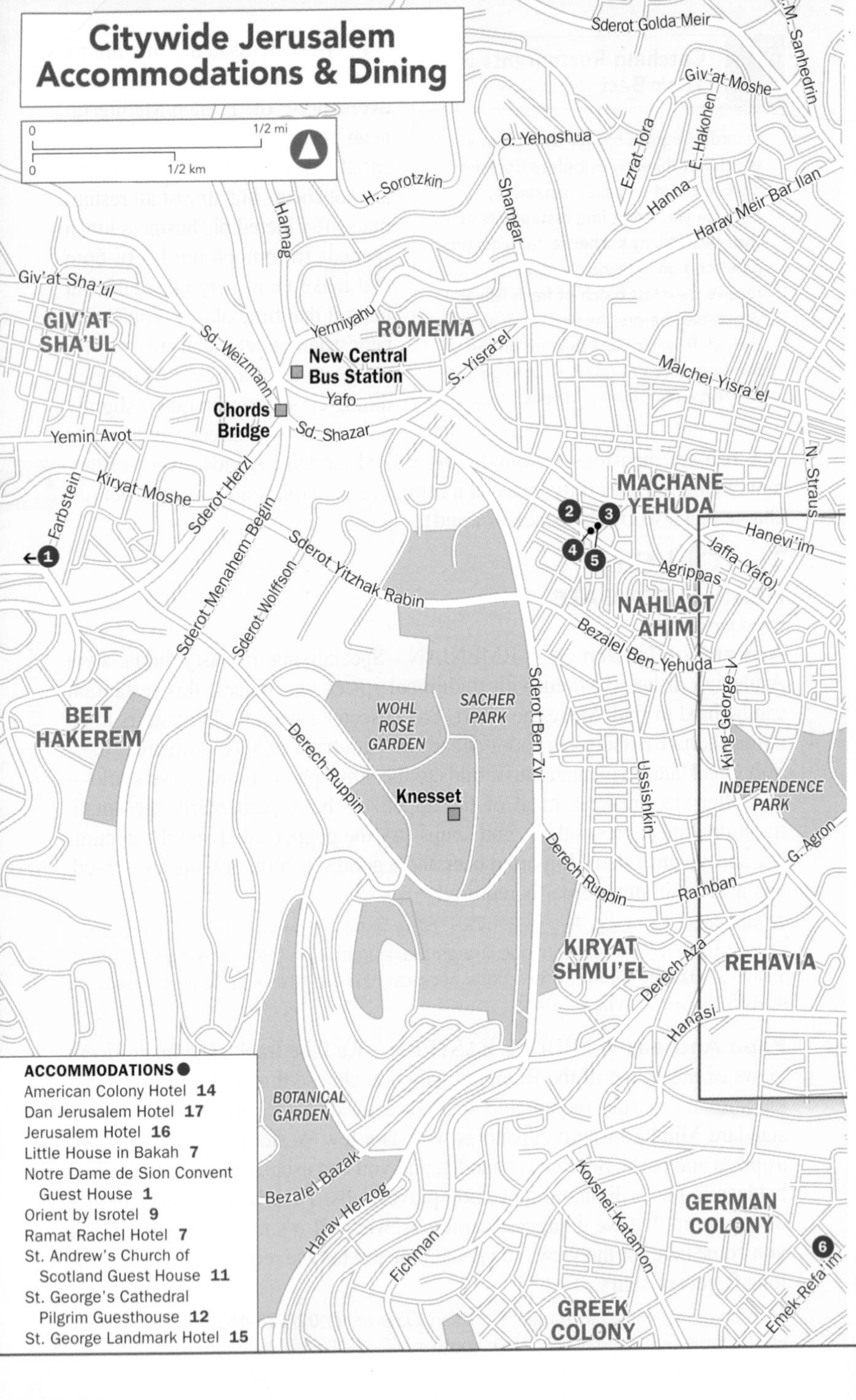

Citywide Jerusalem Accommodations & Dining
0
1/2 mi
0
1/2 km
Sderot Golda Meir
H.M. Sanhedrin
Giv'at Moshe
E. Hakohen
Ezrat Tora
O. Yehoshua
Hanna
Harav Meir Bar Ilan
H. Sorotzkin
Shamgar
Hamag
Giv'at Sha'ul
GIV'AT SHA'UL
Yermiyahu
ROMEMA
Sd. Weizmann
New Central Bus Station
S. Yisra'el
Malchei Yisra'el
Yafo
Chords Bridge
Sd. Shazar
Yemin Avot
N. Straus
MACHANE YEHUDA
Kiryat Moshe
Farbstein
Sderot Herzl
Sderot Menahem Begin
Sderot Yitzhak Rabin
Hanevi'im
Jaffa (Yafo)
Agrippas
NAHLAOT AHIM
Sderot Wolffson
Bezalel Ben Yehuda
Sderot Ben Zvi
SACHER PARK
WOHL ROSE GARDEN
BEIT HAKEREM
Derech Ruppin
King George V
Ussishkin
INDEPENDENCE PARK
Knesset
G. Agron
Derech Ruppin
Ramban
KIRYAT SHMU'EL
Derech Aza
REHAVIA
Hanasi
BOTANICAL GARDEN
Bezalel Bazak
Harav Herzog
Kovshei Katamon
GERMAN COLONY
Fichman
Emek Refa'im
GREEK COLONY
ACCOMMODATIONS
American Colony Hotel 14
Dan Jerusalem Hotel 17
Jerusalem Hotel 16
Little House in Bakah 7
Notre Dame de Sion Convent Guest House 1
Orient by Isrotel 9
Ramat Rachel Hotel 7
St. Andrew's Church of Scotland Guest House 11
St. George's Cathedral Pilgrim Guesthouse 12
St. George Landmark Hotel 15

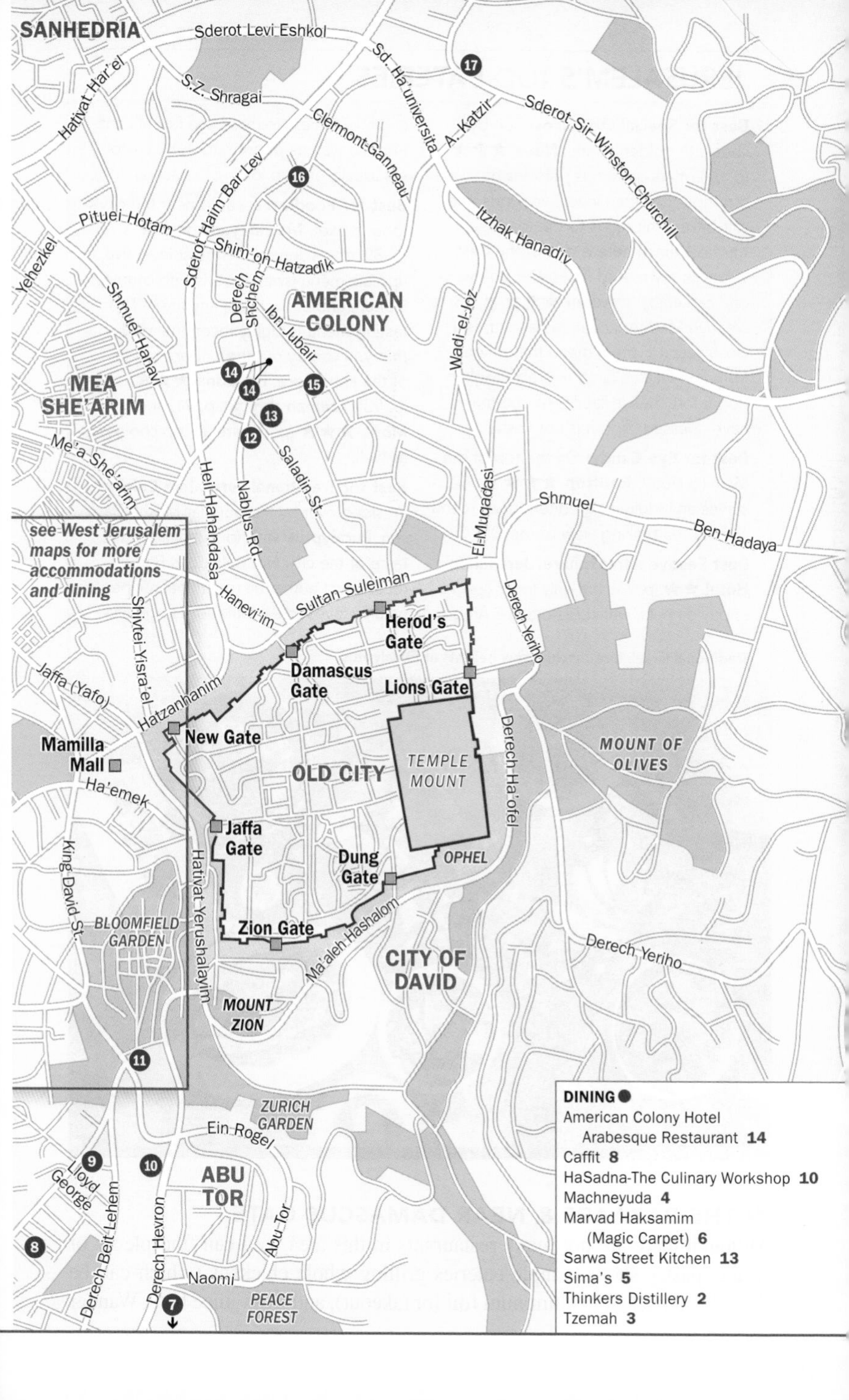

SANHEDRIA
Sderot Levi Eshkol
Hativat Har'el
S.Z. Shragai
Sd. Ha'universita
A. Katzir
Sderot Sir Winston Churchill
Clermont-Ganneau
Sderot Haim Bar Lev
Pituei Hotam
Shim'on Hatzadik
Itzhak Hanadiv
Yehezkel
Shmuel Hanavi
Derech Shchem
Ibn Jubair
AMERICAN COLONY
Wadi-el-Joz
MEA SHE'ARIM
Me'a She'arim
Heil Hahandasa
Nablus Rd.
Saladin St.
El-Muqadasi
Shmuel
Ben Hadaya
see West Jerusalem maps for more accommodations and dining
Shivtei Yisra'el
Hanevi'im
Sultan Suleiman
Herod's Gate
Derech Yeriho
Jaffa (Yafo)
Damascus Gate
Lions Gate
Hatzanhanim
New Gate
Mamilla Mall
MOUNT OF OLIVES
TEMPLE MOUNT
OLD CITY
Ha'emek
Derech Ha'ofel
Jaffa Gate
Hativat Yerushalayim
King David St.
Dung Gate
OPHEL
BLOOMFIELD GARDEN
Zion Gate
Ma'aleh Hashalom
Derech Yeriho
CITY OF DAVID
MOUNT ZION
ZURICH GARDEN
Ein Rogel
ABU TOR
Lloyd George
Derech Beit Lehem
Derech Hevron
Abu Tor
Naomi
PEACE FOREST
DINING
American Colony Hotel Arabesque Restaurant 14
Caffit 8
HaSadna-The Culinary Workshop 10
Machneyuda 4
Marvad Haksamim (Magic Carpet) 6
Sarwa Street Kitchen 13
Sima's 5
Thinkers Distillery 2
Tzemah 3

JERUSALEM'S top EATERIES

Best for Special Occasions: Run by a chef with golden hands, **Noya ★★★** (p. 88) offers generous portions of scrumptious, often inventive foods (the salt-baked chicken is to die for). The business lunch here is one of the best values in town. And it's kosher, so everyone can enjoy it. **Adom ★★★** (p. 93), a creative Mediterranean restaurant, is a close second with a menu that ranges from fine Galilee lamb to crab ravioli in Roquefort cheese sauce. As you may have guessed, Adom is not kosher.

Best for Eye Candy: On the top of the Mamilla Hotel, **Rooftop ★★★** (p. 82) serves an indulgent Mediterranean menu with a breathtaking view of the Old City.

Best Festive Atmosphere: Jerusalem Hotel ★★ (p. 73), but only for its special Friday dinners, which feature live Arabic and Middle Eastern music and lots of dancing (the waiters perform, but the customers usually end up joining the action, too).

Best for Foodies: Located near the city's food market, **Machneyuda ★★★** (p. 89) offers Jerusalem's most inventive, upscale menu (sweetbreads with chutney, labneh, and cornichons, anyone?). The tasting menu is highly recommended so that you can try out the brilliant range of the chefs here. **HaSadna ★★★** (p. 93), **Tzemah ★★★** (p. 91) and **Mona ★★★** (p. 81) are all top choices, as well.

Best for Traditional Jerusalem Cuisine: Presided over by the popular Moshe Basson, **Eucalyptus ★★** (p. 80) offers a true taste of the city. Not only does Basson reconstruct authentic traditional recipes, he also loves to explain them to guests.

Traditional Israeli fare reaches new heights at Eucalyptus.

IN THE BAZAARS & NEAR DAMASCUS GATE

Although there are not many restaurants in this area, you can find plenty of Arabic pastry shops, simple eateries grilling whole chickens (which can be carved and packed in aluminum foil for takeout), and fresh juice bars. Wander from Damascus Gate along Suq Khan es-Zeit Street, which bears to the right at the fork.

Inexpensive

Abu Assab Refreshments ★★ FRESH JUICES For decades, this little counter with three tiny tables has served up the best freshly squeezed orange, grapefruit, and carrot juice in town. You can't miss it in the main Suq Khan es-Zeit bazaar halfway from Damascus Gate to the Cardo. Cash only.

Suq Khan es-Zeit Bazaar. No phone. NIS 8–NIS 20. Sat–Thurs 9am–5pm; Fri 9am–3pm.

Abu Shukri ★★ HUMMUS There's only one Abu Shukri, although the hummus here is so famous that other places as far away as the town of Abu Ghosh (p. 174) in the hills West of Jerusalem have taken on the name, hoping to cash in on the legend. Abu Shukri has been immortalized in the pages of *The New York Times, Condé Nast Traveler,* and even *Playboy.* Decor is nonexistent, and it's a good idea to bring a supply of napkins, but the hummus is heavenly. It's served plain or with your choice of a dab of *ful* (brown beans), whole white garbanzo beans, or roasted pine nuts (a gourmet extra). You can also add a plate of chopped salad and falafel, grilled kabobs, or *kibbe* (fried cracked wheat dumpling stuffed with ground meat). Lots of pita to sop up your hummus is included in the price. Make sure to ask for it to be served heated: Cold pita is an insult to the meal. Sorry, cash only here.

63 Al Wad Rd. (near the 5th Station of the Cross, where the Via Dolorosa and Al Wad Rd. meet). ✆ **02/627-1538.** Main courses NIS 20–NIS 50. Daily 8am–3pm (sometimes later on Sat).

Amigo Emil ★★ INTERNATIONAL/ARABIC Located on the edge of the Christian Quarter, this spotless, pleasantly decorated place, set in an ancient structure, is a good choice for a tranquil break while exploring the bazaars. The menu is wide-ranging. You can order a fresh omelet, pasta, spicy chicken wings, an assortment of Middle Eastern salads, chicken breast stuffed with feta and herbs, or the highly recommended California/Arabic-style wraps and sandwiches. Great espresso is served, as are local treats, such as *karabij halab* (a crunchy biscuit with marshmallow cream made by the owner's family) or freshly squeezed tangerine juice. There's a wine and beer list, a bonus in the Old City. Major credit cards are accepted.

El Khanka St. Bazaar (left side as you go downhill; from David St., near Jaffa Gate, turn left onto Christian Quarter Rd.; at the end, turn left onto El Khanka). ✆ **02/628-8090.** Main courses NIS 32–NIS 70. Mon–Sat 11am–9:30pm.

Family Restaurant ★ MIDDLE EASTERN This spot, deep in the market, serves the best *shawarma* (seasoned meat cut from a spit) in the bazaar—you can order it in a pita sandwich or as a more expensive shawarma platter, or have it wrapped in flat, fluffy *laffa* bread. Whatever you choose, stay at the counter at the front of the restaurant while your shawarma is being prepared so that you can point out which of the wide range of salads and toppings you would like added to your order. We don't advise trying to eat a shawarma sandwich while walking in the crowded bazaar, so grab a table in the large, arched-ceiling dining room that dates from Crusader times. No alcoholic drinks. Cash only.

Suq Khan es-Zeit Bazaar (coming from the direction of Jaffa Gate, it will be on the right about 30m/98 ft. after the turn for Via Dolorosa). ✆ **02/628-3435.** Main courses NIS 30–NIS 45; shawarma sandwich NIS 20. Daily 9am–8pm.

Jaffar Sweets ★★ ARABIC PASTRY This is the top place in the Old City for sampling *kanafeh,* a rich traditional Middle Eastern dessert made of mildly sweet cheese, grains, and pistachios baked in a very light honey syrup. You'll see flat, orange-colored slices of *kanafeh* in Jaffar's window being cut on large pizzalike trays. Purchase a ticket at the cashier's counter for an order of *kanafeh,* take a seat at a table, and your order will soon be delivered. Decor is plain (think polished gray walls and Formica tables), but this is an authentic place filled with locals enjoying this much-loved treat. You can order takeout, but *kanafeh* is best fresh from the oven. Cash only.

Suq Khan es-Zeit Bazaar (from Damascus Gate, bear right at the fork in the road, and continue into the narrow bazaar; Jaffar is the 2nd large pastry shop with glass windows on the right). ✆ **02/628-3582.** Items NIS 14. Daily 9am–5pm.

THE JEWISH QUARTER

This part of the Old City is home to a number of kosher fast-food spots on Jewish Quarter Road, where you can have a bowl of soup (usually made from powder), a slice of kosher pizza, or a bagel at a shop at the Seven Arches, near the Burnt House. On Jewish Quarter Road you'll also find two (non-kosher) old-fashioned Arabic-style bread bakeries where you can buy warm, freshly baked pita and big sesame rolls, which are tasty to snack on as you explore the Old City. Ask the baker for a tiny, free package of *zaatar* (local spices) to flavor the bread in Middle Eastern style.

Inexpensive

Between The Arches ★ KOSHER DAIRY Many a weary traveler has rested their legs, and stopped a blood sugar crash, here. This simple eatery is situated right in front of the Wailing Wall, in a tavern dating back to the 13th century—an awe-inspiring structure. Less exciting? The food, which is standard fare: soups, salads, pasta, pizza, and filets of grilled fish. But it's slightly better than what you'll get elsewhere in this quarter. Slightly.

174 Hagai St. www.betweenarches.co.il. ✆ **053/941-9157.** Mains NIS 28–NIS 98. Open Sun–Thurs 9am–5pm.

West Jerusalem

AROUND MAMILLA MALL & JUST OUTSIDE JAFFA GATE

Moderate

Eucalyptus ★★ JERUSALEM HOME-STYLE Chef/owner Moshe Basson, who grew up on the southern edge of Jerusalem, has a stockpile of traditional family recipes and knows the wild herbs and plants that grow around the city like the back of his hand. His original little neighborhood eatery has

The staff at Eucalyptus have a real talent for making a meal feel like a party.

moved to this romantic, candle-lit spot in a picturesque enclave just outside the walls of the Old City. The menu includes an array of traditional soups, which you can sample in tiny espresso cups; local appetizers, such as stuffed sage leaves and figs stuffed with chicken in tamarind sauce (a favorite, and quite filling); or highly recommended medleys of small tapas-style salads and spreads. Main courses include such specialties as *ingria,* a sweet-and-sour meat and eggplant casserole, and *makluba,* a chicken/rice casserole served with great ceremony. When Moshe is present, he loves to explain the ingredients and preparation of his dishes, and hearing him do so is one of the delights of dining here. Traditional desserts (interesting but not lavish) are on offer, and complimentary shots of local *arak* (licorice liquor) are a regular toast to the table. There's indoor and outdoor seating, and reservations are recommended. 14 Hativat Yerushalayim, Artists' Colony Hutzot Hayotzer (outside Old City, across the road and downhill from Jaffa Gate). www.the-eucalyptus.com. ✆ **02/624-4331.** Reservations recommended. Main courses NIS 89–NIS 165; tasting menus NIS 327–NIS 477 per person, must request in advance. Sun–Thurs 6–11pm.

Mona ★★★ BISTRO This rustic, landmark restaurant inside the Jerusalem Artists' House has a cozy fireplace on cold winter nights and a well-stocked bar that attracts journalists, politicians, Jerusalem personalities, and savvy internationals. But it's not just the bar scene that draws crowds. Top-quality ingredients and a talented chef who puts out a consistently delicious menu are big draws, too. We partial to the mussels steeped in bonito butter and

The view doesn't get much better than at the aptly named The Rooftop restaurant.

the red tuna sashimi over labneh with chili oil—but all the dishes are expertly prepared and executed.

8 Shmuel Hanagid St. ✆ **02/622-2283.** Main course NIS 60–NIS 140. Open Sun–Fri 6–11pm; Sat 12:30–4pm and 6–11pm. Reservations recommended.

The Rooftop ★★★ MEDITERRANEAN It's a truism in travel that when a restaurant has spectacular views, its food won't match the eye candy. Not here! Perched above the strikingly contemporary **Mamilla Hotel** (see p. 66), The Rooftop's offerings are exquisite—creative, thoughtful food that more than competes with the panoramic, Old City views each table enjoys. From the roasted goose breast in maple caramel sauce and Valrhona chocolate "snow," to the lamp chops over an eggplant carpaccio with tehina and date honey, each dish tops the next. Get reservations well in advance because this restaurant is as popular with Israelis as it is with visitors.

Inside Mamilla Hotel, 11 Shlomo Hameleh St. www.mamillahotel.com/rooftop. ✆ **02/548-2222.** Main courses NIS 80–NIS 150. Open Sun–Thurs 6–11pm; Shabbat menus on Fri 6–11pm and Sat noon–11pm.

ZION SQUARE AREA: JAFFA ROAD, BEN-YEHUDA & YOEL SALOMON PEDESTRIAN MALLS

Moderate

Barood Bar Restaurant ★★ CONTINENTAL/SEPHARDIC Barood is a great choice for a Friday night or Saturday afternoon meal, when few West Jerusalem restaurants are open. Late on Friday and Saturday nights, it's also a pleasant, low-key bar for drinks and meeting people. There's occasional live

SABBATH dining

Kosher restaurants usually close by 2 or 3pm on Friday for Shabbat. The following non-kosher restaurants, described in detail in this chapter, have Friday evening or Saturday afternoon hours and provide a good variety of choices.

In downtown West Jerusalem: Barood (p. 82), Focaccia Bar (p. 84), the restaurant at the King David Street YMCA (p. 68), Spaghettim (p. 85), and Zuni (p. 87).

In South Jerusalem: Adom (p. 93)

In East Jerusalem: Restaurants are open on Shabbat.

music, and in good weather, tables are set up in the vine-covered Jerusalem Courtyard. As for the food, it's quite different from what you'll get at most other Israeli restaurants, featuring a daily changing menu of home-style choices, such as pork spareribs with a rosemary barbecue sauce, Balkan/Sephardic leek stew with meat and plums, or plates of crispy fried calamari.

Jerusalem Courtyard (enter through arch at 31 Jaffa Rd.). misadot.rol.co.il/images/sites/barood/eng.html. ✆ **02/625-9081.** Main courses NIS 60–NIS 125. Mon–Fri 5pm–1am; Sat 12:30pm–1am. Light Rail to Safra Sq.

Piccolino ★★★ VEGETARIAN/DAIRY/FISH The food at this restaurant is among the very best in Jerusalem. It's run by the same wonderful chef who once headed the team at the restaurant Little Jerusalem in the historic,

Pizza, pasta, and other classic Italian dishes are given creative makeovers at Piccolino.

much-loved home of Abraham and Anna Ticho (p. 148). You will always feel like one of their favored guests when you dine here, because every dish is prepared in a way that includes special, surprising twists. That's despite the fact that they seem, on the surface, to be fairly standard: salads, crepes and quiches, various sorts of pasta and fish. But the salads will be super-fresh, the pastas innovative, and the fruits of the sea perfectly prepared. Don't be shy about bringing kids, as there's a children's menu and various, spacious rooms to accommodate large groups, and a host of live musical performances in the afternoons and evenings (check the Piccolino website for the weekly schedule). Always call ahead for reservations.

12 Yoel Moshe Solomon St. www.piccolino.co.il/en. ✆ **02/624-4186.** Main courses NIS 45–NIS 98; light meals or brunch NIS 40–NIS 70. Sun–Thurs 10am–10pm; Fri 9am–2pm. Light Rail to King George St.

Inexpensive

Focaccia Bar ★★ ECLECTIC/MEDITERRANEAN A very popular place (especially on Shabbat) filled with travelers, families, and young Jerusalemites, Focaccia Bar serves pizzas and focaccias baked in a traditional brick *taboon* oven. But there's much more on the menu, ranging from heaping stir-fried salads laced with chicken or goose breast to excellent calamari or seafood pasta in a spicy Indian-style coconut sauce. The setting is a 19th-century Jerusalem stone cottage with a large dining garden (covered and heated in winter). Good wines and desserts round out the menu. Reservations are useful here, especially for Shabbat. ***Tip:*** A kosher version of Focaccia Bar with an inventive menu, in the German Colony at 35 Emek Refaim St. (✆ **02/538-7182**), offers a similar menu but is closed for Shabbat.

4 Rabbi Akiba St. (off Hillel St.). bar.focaccia.co. ✆ **02/625-6428.** Main courses NIS 40–NIS 80. Daily 10:30am–1am.

Kangaroo ★★ GEORGIAN/RUSSIAN Hidden on a quaint pedestrian street, this charming, family-run restaurant serves authentic, home-style Georgian cuisine. The food is rustic, hearty, and intricately spiced with complex sauces, laced with finely ground walnuts and herbs. The menu ranges from dumpling-filled soups to hefty meat pies and rich lamb stews that are especially great in winter. But an absolute must is *khachapuri,* a cheese-and-egg puff-pastry dish that's rich, delicate, and made on the spot. With a soup and salad, a *khachapuri* is a good choice for a lighter meal or lunch. There's an outdoor terrace for summer dining.

7 Nahalat Shiva St. (btw. Yoel Salomon and Rivlin sts.). ✆ **02/625-0618.** Main courses NIS 45–NIS 90. Mon–Sat 1–9pm. Light Rail to King George St.

Shanty ★★ INTERNATIONAL This intimate pub is loved by locals for its well-stocked bar and trendy, imaginative menu that interprets dishes from all over the world. It's a place where you can linger and talk over a slow meal of fabulous spiced sweet potato soup and pad Thai noodles, baby-back ribs, or a generous, lightly stir-fried Mediterranean salad loaded with herbs, spices, and chunks of succulent chicken. There's a wide range of tapas-like dishes

coffee & PEOPLE-WATCHING

Jerusalem's cafe life is thriving. All over town, you'll find happily caffeinated customers at bustling cafes, downing cup after cup, arguing, laughing, and living a life that's downright Parisian. The draw ain't just brewed beans: Customers at these places accompany their java with giant, eminently shareable salads as well as quiches, pasta dishes, soups, sandwiches, and rich desserts. ***Tip:*** If you *just* want coffee, make sure there are no minimum charges.

Here's where to go if you'd like to join the scene:

- A great cup of coffee can be found 2 blocks south of Ben-Yehuda Mall at **Aroma,** on the corner of Hillel and Rabbi Akiva streets. It's a busy counter with a few tables, but it's a Jerusalem institution, serving inexpensive sandwiches as well and open 7am to midnight every day. Other branches are at 43 Emek Refaim St. in the German Colony and 40 Jaffa St.
- **Cafe Rimmon,** at the lower end of Ben-Yehuda Mall, is an ideal spot for watching Jerusalem life pass by. Here, gaping is more important than imbibing.
- **Hillel Café** offers an abundance of sidewalk and indoor tables and is known for its excellent salads, sandwiches, quiches, and desserts. It's located in Jerusalem's free Wi-Fi access zone, so tables tend to be dotted with laptops.
- **Tmol Shilshom Bookstore Cafe** is located a block to the east, on the corner of Jaffa Road and Helene HaMalka Street, at 5 Yoel Salomon Mall (p. 166). Tmol Shilshom is a most atmospheric retreat. Its walls are lined with books, and its patrons seem unusually scholarly as they sip coffee, write letters, and read.
- **Eldorado** (128 Saladin St.) is East Jerusalem's trendiest coffee shop, owned by a family that has procured coffee for generations. People actually dress up to sip coffee here.

and appetizers and even a few desserts to accompany conversation. It's tricky to find but definitely worth the effort.

4 Nahalat Shiva. (On Yoel Salomon St., turn into the alleyway to the side of the Ceramics gallery at 11 Yoel Salomon. At the end of the alley, turn left into the courtyard. The security guard for Shanty, Mike's Place, and Tmol Shilshom Bookstore Cafe is at the end of the courtyard.). www.shantyres.co.il. ✆ **02/624-3434.** Main courses NIS 60–NIS 139. Daily 7pm–last customer.

Spaghettim ★ ITALIAN Serving spaghetti and pasta with all kinds of interesting tomato, olive oil, or cream-based sauces, this is an affordable choice that has the added benefit of being open on the Sabbath. Dishes are filled with generous amounts of fresh herbs and vegetables; but more unusual choices are also recommended, such as spaghetti and chicken in an Indian-style coriander sauce. The mint-filled panzanella salads and a loaf of freshly baked house bread (extra charge) are worthwhile additions to any meal. The restaurant is located in a spacious, contemporary room inside Beit Agron, the modern Journalists' Center. Whole-wheat pasta and non-pasta dishes are available for those who want a healthy choice.

Inside Beit Agron, 35 Hillel St. spaghettim.co.il. ✆ **02/623-5547.** Main courses NIS 45–NIS 100; 10% student discount. Daily noon–midnight.

street **MEALS**

Want to grab a quick bite on the run? Here are some suggestions:

Falafel You can find this dish almost everywhere, but we're partial to the **Yemenite falafel counter** on the corner of Agripas Street and the wide, uncovered pedestrian street of the Mahane Yehuda Market (on your right as you walk up Agripas St. from King George; it's the first broad market street past the covered market area). It serves well-spiced falafel and all kinds of salads, pickled vegetables, sauces, and condiments. For a bit extra, you can ask for your falafel to be wrapped inside a *laffa* (an enormous Iraqi pita) instead of a regular pita, which makes for a very filling meal. Best of all, you can carry your sandwich across Agripas Street and through one of the entrance portals to the old Nahalat neighborhood, where you'll find a small playground with benches. There, under the scrutiny of the local cats, you can sit down and enjoy your meal (but bring your own napkins!). For added flavor, slice a few little plum or cherry tomatoes from the market into your sandwich.

A second, and similarly nameless, choice sits on the corner of Agripas and King George streets, where you'll find a large and very busy **falafel and shawarma place**. Here you'll have to eat standing on the sidewalk like a typical Israeli (hopefully you've acquired the local skill of not dripping sauce all over yourself or having your sandwich land in the gutter). The falafels are solid, and turnover is fast, which ensures freshness. It's open until 10pm or later from Sunday to Thursday (until 2pm Fri).

Shawarma **Moshiko's,** at the lower end of the Ben-Yehuda Mall, makes Jerusalem's finest shawarma sandwiches, hands down. The quality of the meat is tops. Portions, spicing, and accompanying salads are excellent. And if you can nail down one of Moshiko's outdoor tables, you can people-watch while you nosh without running the risk of losing half your sandwich on the ground.

Prefer a bit more heat in your meat? The **Gate Cafe,** just inside the Damascus Gate on an upstairs covered terrace on the left, serves fabulous, extra-spicy **hand-built shawarma,** a kind of shawarma not made on a spit. It's different, authentic, and quite memorable.

Bagels You may be surprised to find that the doughy rounds we're used to in the United States taste far more

Tmol Shilshom Bookstore Cafe ★★ VEGETARIAN A Jerusalem institution, thick with atmosphere, this is one of the best vegetarian choices in town. It's also an unofficial social club, a place where people come during off-hours to sit and talk over coffee or a glass of wine. Many stay through dinner so they can order steaming bowls of soups, salads, a slice of hefty lasagna, or *shakshuka* (a spicy North-African Maghrebi home-style tomato-and-egg dish). The daily menu ranges from excellent filet of Denis from the Red Sea served on a bed of couscous to homemade bread with lox and cream cheese. Set in a 19th-century house with rooms lined with used books, the cafe hosts a lively program of readings and lectures in Hebrew and English on some nights, music on others. Check the monthly schedule of events.

5 Yoel Salomon St. (in rear courtyard of Yoel Salomon St.; enter from alley at 11 Yoel Salomon St., next to Ceramics Gallery; cafe is at far left and upstairs). www.tmol-shilshom.co.il. ✆ **02/623-2758.** Main courses NIS 55–NIS 100. Sun–Thurs 9am–11:30pm; Fri 8:30am–4pm; also open Sat after Shabbat.

breadlike in Israel. But that doesn't mean they're not tasty, especially those at **Bagel Cafe,** 54 Emek Refaim (www.bagelcafe.co.il; ✆ **02/587-7877;** Sun–Thurs 6:30am–10pm, Fri until 2:30pm). It sells a wide variety of freshly made bagels, ranging from onion and garlic to whole-wheat and cheese, for approximately NIS 5 each. As in the U.S., they can be "super-sized" with the addition of various types of cream cheeses, lox, and other fillings. In the Jewish Quarter of the Old City, you can pick up your bagels at a similar shop, set right beside the Seven Arches, near the Burnt House Museum.

Burekas (phyllo-dough pastries) The block of shops on Haneviim Street opposite Havatzelet Street includes a bakery with a sidewalk window counter where you can order flaky, fresh-from-the-oven, potato, spinach, or cheese *burekas,* as well as miniature cheese or fruit Danish-style pastries. You can find *burekas* throughout the city, but they're always more of a treat when fresh.

The **Mahane Yehuda Market** is another good place for freshly baked *burekas,* as is the **English Bakery,** on Jaffa Road opposite Zion Square.

Stuffed Breads The Middle Eastern answer to pizza, these piping hot breads are stuffed with savory cheeses and herbed vegetables. Tops for this treat is **Samboosak Bakery/Café** on Jaffa Road next to the Coffee Bean on the corner of Helene HaMalka Street.

Ice Cream & Frozen Yogurt

Ah, where should we start on this one? We think local chain **Golda** is the top choice, thanks to creative choices like salted bagel, limoncello, or watermelon and mint sorbet. It has locations across Jerusalem including in the outdoor Mamilla pedestrian mall, the Machne Yehuda Market and Malcha Mall. At the corner of Lunz and Ben Yehuda streets, there's another **popular place** (no name, but you won't be able to miss it) that offers a choice of 25 kinds of fruits, nuts, and chocolates that staff can whip into a fresh frozen yogurt for you on the spot. Finally, **Aldo Ice Cream,** 21 Ben Yehuda St., 40 Jaffa Rd., and 46 Emek Refaim St. in the German Colony, uses ingredients prepped in Italy but made fresh daily (without preservatives) in Israel. It's a chain, but a good one, with shops throughout Israel.

Zuni Restaurant/Café/Bar ★ FRENCH/INTERNATIONAL This stylish, pub-like space in the upstairs rooms of an old stone building on the Yoel Salomon pedestrian street is conveniently open 24/7. It's good for a late morning brunch, soup, coffee, sandwich, quiche, or a late evening talk and drink. After 5pm, more ambitious dishes are served, such as seafood risotto and a grilled breast of chicken with a green salad on the side. There's nothing too exotic, but the round-the-clock hours are unique.

15 Yoel Salomon St. www.zuni.co.il/lunch-dinner-en. ✆ **053/934-5582.** Main courses NIS 60–NIS 130. Daily 24-hr. Light Rail to Safra Sq.

OFF & ON SHLOMZION HAMALKA STREET

Shlomzion HaMalka Street, running south for 2 blocks from Jaffa Road to David Street, is lined with very stylish restaurants and bars. Restaurants here pride themselves on their friendly vibe. Late on Thursday, Friday, and Saturday nights, the establishments sometimes morph into a wall-to-wall party.

Expensive

Sea Dolphin (Dolphin Yam) ★★ FISH/SEAFOOD Top-quality fresh seafood is not the norm in Jerusalem, except at really expensive restaurants. Moderately priced Sea Dolphin is the exception to that rule, owned by a family that's been bringing fresh fish to Jerusalem for decades. Included in the price of your main course is a (bottomless) *mezze* of 10 Middle Eastern salads and appetizers, but there are also good seafood soups and seafood appetizers you can add a la carte. You can order your fish fried, baked, or grilled (your waiter will suggest which would be best for your choice). There's a selection of intriguing sauces, but you might ask for the sauce to be served on the side so you can savor a true taste of the sea. A few meat and vegetarian options are served, and there's a good selection of lunchtime specials.

9 Ben Shetah St. www.seadolphin.co.il. ✆ **02/623-2272.** Reservations recommended. Main courses NIS 90–NIS 150; lunch specials (Sun–Thurs noon–5pm) NIS 75–NIS 130. Daily noon–11pm. Light Rail to Safra Sq.

Moderate

Noya ★★★ CONTINENTAL/MODERN ISRAELI A triple threat, Noya is elegant, affordable, and kosher, which in this town is an unbeatable combination. It also offers a raft of well-prepared, sometimes unusual meat dishes, such as salt-baked chicken and entrecote steak stuffed with lamb. Vegetarians and those who eat fish are well taken care of too, with such options as stuffed sardines in olive and pepper sauce or root vegetable ravioli. And the focaccia here is legendary. If you're an early-bird type, the excellent lunch special is served all the way until 5pm, making it one of the best deals in town.

3 Shlomzion HaMalka St. (off Jaffa Rd.). www.noya-jerusalem.co.il. ✆ **077/230-7590.** Main courses NIS 60–NIS 190; complete lunch specials until 5pm NIS 60–NIS 80. Sun–Thurs noon–11pm. Must make reservations in advance.

Inexpensive

Hamarakia ★★ SOUP Loved by students, artists, musicians, and travelers of all stripes, the Hamarakia, with its attic-sale decor, looks like an eatery in San Francisco or New York's East Village. "Marak" means soup, and this little local institution started out as a soups-only eatery that has expanded over the years to include great *shakshuka* (a spicy Maghrebi tomato-and-egg dish) and a few other simple additions. Soups come with lots of bread and pesto; the choices

A silverware chandelier at fun and funky Hamarakia.

are all vegetarian and vary each night, but standards include sweet potato; lentil with wine; spicy Yemenite tomato, onion, and cheese; and tomato with anise. Teas, coffee, wines, and beer are served. There's often live music Monday and Wednesday nights after 10pm. The staff is mostly students and always helpful. Cash only.

4 Koresh St. (behind the Jaffa Rd. Central Post Office). ✆ **02/625-7797.** Soup and bread NIS 30; half-liter of wine NIS 20. Sun–Thurs noon–11:30pm, closed Fri, Sat 6pm–11:30pm. Light Rail to Safra Sq.

WEST OF KING GEORGE V AVENUE

Expensive

Chakra ★★★ ECLECTIC Chef Eran Peretz's mastery of wildly varied cooking techniques and his endless energy combine to give this sleek restaurant a menu that's inventive, cosmopolitan, and absolutely delicious (it also changes with the seasons). Expect scrumptious seafood dishes like black tiger shrimp in a chili sauce or wild sea bass filet with handmade gnocchi. The cauliflower crème agnolotti in garlic, butter, and lemon is a must-have, and the cocktail and wine list are as well-curated as the food choices. Chakra is usually busy and the atmosphere is festive. Come with friends so you can sample and share. Reservations are necessary because this is one of Israel's best restaurants at any price.

41 King George St. www.chakrarest.com. ✆ **02/625-2733.** Main courses NIS 82–NIS 240. Mon–Sat 6pm–midnight. Light Rail to King George St.

Moderate

Menza ★★ MEDITERRANEAN This neighborhood eatery earns major points for being open every day of the week and serving a wide-ranging, delicious menu. Staff is welcoming and upbeat, and the breakfasts, lunches, and dinners all have kid-friendly alternatives. Among the options here are a downright delectable corned beef sandwich, an array of omelets, a host of fresh and healthy Mediterranean salads, and a surprising variety of seafood dishes. This is *not* your typical Jerusalem fare.

10 Betsal'el St. www.menza.today. ✆ **02/625-5222.** Main courses NIS 28–NIS 104. Daily 10am–10pm. Bus: 18, 25, or 45.

AGRIPAS STREET & MAHANE YEHUDA MARKET

Walk a few blocks up Agripas Street, and you'll find yourself surrounded by no-frills restaurants and tiny spots serving generous portions of grilled meats, *shashlik* (chunks of meat on a skewer), and *kabobs* (ground meat on a skewer). Don't be afraid to try semi-nameless holes-in-the-wall. Any place that survives in this competitive market area has to be good!

Moderate

Machneyuda Restaurant ★★★ MODERN ISRAELI Named for the way locals pronounce Mahane Yehuda Market (and with a decor that purposefully looks like a market warehouse), this has consistently ranked as one of the hottest upscale restaurants in Jerusalem for over a decade. Today, the Machneyuda

Locals and visitors dining at Mahane Yehuda Market.

Group, helmed by founding (now-celeb) chef Assaf Granit, has opened sterling restaurants in Paris (Balagan) and London (The Palomar), but Jerusalem remains home-base, and you will often catch a glimpse of Granit in the kitchen. If you can't score a seat here, try Yudale, Dekel, or **Tzemah ★★★** (see review below); all stellar and all within steps from one another in the market. Be forewarned, Machneyuda is not the choice for an intimate, romantic meal (it's too loud and bustling for that). But if you're interested in modern Jerusalemite gastronomy, try to nab seats at the bar overlooking the kitchen so you can watch the chefs working, joking, and (often) dancing around at their stations. The menu is written on a board each day and always features what's freshest at the market, often in zany combinations. When we were last here, we were lucky enough to try bluefin tuna with watermelon, purple foie gras; sea bream on fresh buffalo yogurt with Swiss chard; and a special market stew that bubbled all day long until it was meltingly tender. Two notes: Portions are *not* huge, so most get both appetizer and entree. And although the restaurant is not kosher, it's closed until after Shabbat. Make reservations well in advance.

10 Beit Ya'acov St. www.machneyuda.co.il. ✆ **02/533-3442** or 053/809-4897. Main courses NIS 80–NIS 180. Sun–Thurs 12:30pm–midnight; Fri 11:30am–3:30pm; Sat after Shabbat to last customer.

Tzemah ★★★ VEGETARIAN Much justified praise has been bestowed upon celebrity chef and Jerusalemite Assaf Granit and his exceptional restaurants. Best known for his mothership, Machneyuda (see above), Tzemah is one of his most recent outings, and a love letter to the vegetable. He takes beetroot, okra, and eggplant to unbelievable heights. The presentation and balance of each dish is precise and impeccable. The tasting menu is recommended, but if you prefer to choose your dishes, don't miss the pumpkin steak in beurre noisette crumble; the *skordelia* with almonds, garlic, and tomato; or the nicely rhyming lychee ceviche. In fact, just do yourself a favor and order it all. When in Jerusalem...

1 Hadekel St. www.tzemahrest.com. ✆ **02/533-3444**. Mains NIS 44–NIS 72. Tasting menu NIS 220. Sun–Thurs 9am–11pm, Fri 9am–4:30pm, Sat 6:30–11pm.

Inexpensive

Sima's ★★ MIDDLE EASTERN Sima's is legendary throughout Israel for its fabulous seasoned *me'orav Yerushalmi* (Jerusalem mixed grill), an *a la plancha* combination of succulent pieces of lamb, chicken, and sweet breads served on a platter with French fries, salad, olives, and pickles. There's also a less-expensive (NIS 38) sandwich inside a large pita (order a small tomato salad on the side to add to the sandwich). When Sima's is busy, you must order a platter meal rather than a sandwich to qualify for table service. To our

A chef prepares plates at Machneyuda.

A vegetarian feast awaits at Tzemah.

mind, Sima's secret spice recipe is unequaled, but **Sami's,** its slightly less-legendary next-door competitor, has its own committed following. If Sima's is too crowded, don't feel too put out if you end up at Sami's.

82 Agripas St. www.simajerusalem.co.il. ✆ **02/623-3002.** Main courses NIS 40–NIS 70. Sun–Thurs 11am–midnight; Fri 11am–4pm; Sat 6pm–1am. Light Rail to Mahane Yehuda.

NEAR THE YMCA & KING DAVID HOTEL

Expensive

Veranda ★★ CONTEMPORARY MEDITERRANEAN Another meal with stunning Old City views (ask to sit on the terrace), Veranda isn't as accomplished as **Rooftop** ★★★ (p. 82), but it has very tasty, and often unusual, meat offerings, like a winter stew of legumes and lamb tongue. Its melt-in-your-mouth short ribs are another highlight. Carefully chosen boutique Israeli wines are offered by the glass and bottle. Service is intelligent and discrete, and the decor is soothingly understated. The restaurant is located at the David Citadel Hotel. Reservations are necessary.

In the David Citadel Hotel, 7 King David St. www.thedavidcitadel.com/veranda. ✆ **02/621-2582.** Main courses NIS 100–NIS 180. Sun–Wed 6–10:30pm; Thurs 6–11pm.

South Jerusalem

NEAR THE CINÉMATHÈQUE, FIRST TRAIN STATION & GERMAN COLONY

Moderate

Adom ★★★ FRENCH/MEDITERRANEAN Long a favorite non-kosher option, Adom occupies an upscale, designer location in the renovated Ottoman-era First Train Station. Its seasonally changing chef menu is among the best in town. Standouts to look for include a heavenly gnocchi with porcini and chestnuts; pasta and calamari in curry and apple sauce; seaweed risotto with calamari and split blue crab; and veal sweetbreads. In winter, the palate-warming chestnut soup appetizer reappears on the menu and must be tried. After 10pm, when Adom becomes more of a wine bar and pick-up spot, a menu of tapas-style dishes and half-portions becomes available. The cocktails are excellent, as are desserts.

4 Remez St. (in the First Train Station complex). www.adom.rest/en. ✆ **02/624-6242.** Reservations recommended. Main courses NIS 65–NIS 175. Sun–Thurs 12:30pm–midnight; Fri–Sat noon–midnight.

HaSadna-The Culinary Workshop ★★★ ISRAELI MEDITERRANEAN Another one of the wildly innovative dining establishments under the Machneyuda Group umbrella (see p. 89), this one was formed to find a meeting point between what they call "Oriental home cooking" and Israeli Mediterranean cuisine. That's a squishy concept, but note that what comes out of it is usually wildly delicious, whether it's a tuna sashimi with a lemongrass and yogurt "salsa"; smoked brisket (all the cured meats are top-notch here); or a splendid corn and seafood *piste.* The look of the place is artfully industrial, and there are a number of seating areas, but we recommend grabbing a spot underneath the Edison-bulbed orbs hanging in the bar since the bartenders delight in doling out shots of *arak* (the local liquor of choice). They'll also have primo recommendations for what to sink your teeth into first. The on-point advice comes in handy; without it, you just may end up ordering everything in sight.

28 Hebron Rd. (in the First Train Station complex). www.sdnrest.com. ✆ **02/567-2265.** Reservations recommended. Mains courses NIS 75–NIS 170. Sun–Thurs 6:30pm–1am; Sat 6:30–11pm.

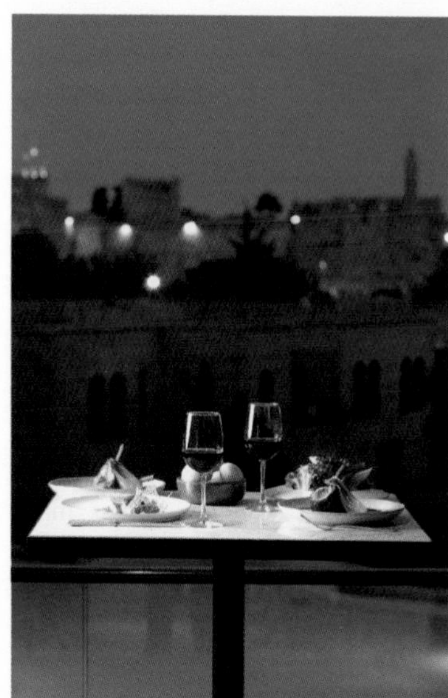

An elegant meal overlooking the Old City is on the menu at Veranda.

Inexpensive

Caffit ★ VEGETARIAN CAFE As the grandparent of the many dairy vegetarian eateries in the gentrified German Colony, Caffit has a panache that keeps locals, travelers, and Jerusalemites from other parts of town coming from early morning to after midnight. The excellent dairy menu is made up of hefty herbed salads, sweet potato pancakes with sour cream, quiches, pastas, and crepes as well as dinner courses, such as pan-fried fish. A selection of wines and alcohol is served. Caffit is such a Jerusalem institution that it was invited to open a branch (✆ **02/648-0003**) in Jerusalem's Botanical Gardens several years ago. Both offer the same menu.

36 Emek Refaim St. caffit.co.il/en. ✆ **02/563-5284** or 053/943-8321. Main courses NIS 40–NIS 100. Sun–Thurs 7:30am–midnight; Fri 7:30am–2:30pm; Sat after Shabbat–midnight

Marvad Haksamim (Magic Carpet) ★ ISRAELI This popular place has been serving up traditional home-style food in generous portions for great prices since 1948. They currently offer takeout food only, and what they serve makes no pretense to gourmet standards, but the wide-ranging menu comprises dishes that draw from Israel's multiethnic melting pot. Start with warm, flaky Yemenite *salouf,* a flatbread, served with traditional tomato puree dip, and then go on to a Kurdish dumpling soup, East European liver blintzes, a Viennese-style chicken schnitzel, a Middle Eastern plate of grilled lamb or chicken kabobs (the chicken is better), or a Moroccan couscous, all served with side orders of veggies, potatoes, pasta, or salad. All is available to take out.

1 Rachel Imenu St. Also at 16 King George St. www.marvad-rest.co.il. ✆ **053/934-5559.** Main courses NIS 45–NIS 90. Fri 8:30am–2pm. Takeout only and recommended to call and order in advance.

EAST JERUSALEM

Expensive

American Colony Hotel Arabesque Restaurant ★ CONTINENTAL/MIDDLE EASTERN The American Colony hotel, looking like a vision from *Masterpiece Theater,* has been used as the locale for numerous films. The generous half-Continental, half–Middle Eastern **Saturday luncheon buffet** at the hotel's Arabesque Room is a Jerusalem institution that offers non-guests the chance to experience the hotel's romantic, old-timey ambience without actually staying here. A delicious, fresh whole chilled salmon is often the centerpiece of this all-you-can-eat spread that stretches across many tables. For other meals, the Arabesque Restaurant can only be considered average. Reservations are needed for the Arabesque Room, especially for the Saturday buffet at 11:30am and 3pm.

1 Louis Vincent St. www.americancolony.com. ✆ **02/627-9777.** Main courses NIS 80–NIS 150; Sat buffet NIS 187. Daily 6:30–11am, 3–6pm, and 7–10:30pm.

Garden dining at the American Colony Hotel.

Inexpensive

Sarwa Street Kitchen ★★ PALESTINIAN This is the kind of chill, welcoming spot you always hope to land upon after a day of sightseeing. The menu features traditional Palestinian dishes with fresh side salads and *mujadara* (lentil stew). Tops on the menu: their famous *maqluba,* a classic Arabic rice dish. Special kudos to the gracious staff, and owners who cater to bibliophiles with their collection of take-one-leave-one books in the corner.

42 Salah Ad-din St ✆ **02/627-4626.** Entrees NIS 30–NIS 60. Open every day except for Fri, noon–10pm.

JERUSALEM NIGHTLIFE

Israel has long been known for the high quality of its musicians, and the diverse and dynamic waves of incoming immigrants has led to an even greater blend and output of talent. Classical music lovers will discover new and remarkable artists performing everywhere, from concert halls and clubs to street corners and pedestrian malls. Also watch for **English Theater productions** listed in the Friday editions of *The Jerusalem Post* and *Haaretz* newspapers.

Note: Jerusalem's main **ticket agency** is **Bimot,** 8 Shamai St. (www.bimot.co.il. ✆ **02/623-7000**).

Additional note: To find out what's going on in town, look in the Friday edition of *The Jerusalem Post, Haaretz,* and in the monthly ***Calendar of Events,*** which you can pick up free at the Tourist Information Office. If you have a student card, bring it; at times, you may be given a discount.

Performance Centers

Beit Shmuel/Center for Progressive Judaism ★ PERFORMING ARTS VENUE Performances here offer the best in contemporary and popular Israeli singers and musicians, ethnic music, readings and lectures, and dance and theater performances. In summer, concerts are held in the outdoor courtyard; always bring something warm to put on, because Jerusalem can get downright chilly at night. Shama'a St. (off King David St.). www.beitshmuel.co.il. ✆ **02/620-3455** or 02/620-3555. Bus: 18, 74, 75, Light Rail: 1.

Bible Lands Museum ★★★ PERFORMING ARTS VENUE Famous for a wide range of Saturday evening concerts, the Bible Lands Museum often includes wine and cheese in the admission price. You'll need a taxi to get here before buses start running. Museum Row, 25 Granot St. www.blmj.org. ✆ **02/561-1066.** Bus: 66, 14, 35.

Israel Museum ★★★ PERFORMING ARTS VENUE The museum is host to a wide range of concerts, performances, films, and cultural and international events. Museum Blvd. www.imj.org.il. ✆ **02/670-8811** for the box office. Bus: 7, 9, 14, 35, 66.

Jerusalem Performing Arts Center (Jerusalem Theatre) ★★★ PERFORMING ARTS VENUE Located near the corner of Chopin (in the Rehavia District near the president's house), this modern complex houses the Jerusalem Theater (Sherover Theater), Henry Crown Auditorium, and the smaller, more intimate Rebecca Crown Hall. Original Israeli plays and Hebrew translations of foreign classics and modern works are performed in the theater's main hall. The theater also hosts performances of the **Jerusalem Symphony Orchestra** and the **Israel Chamber Ensemble,** and the Israel Philharmonic performs here. From October through early June, the Henry Crown Auditorium hosts the free **Etnacha Concert Series,** produced by Israel Radio's classics station. 20 David Marcus St. www.jerusalem-theatre.co.il. ✆ **02/560-5755.** Bus: 15, 18, 74, 75.

Mount Zion Cultural Center ★ PERFORMING ARTS VENUE Saturday nights, after Shabbat, the center often hosts Klezmer music concerts and Hassidic-style dancing and music. starting around 8pm in winter, 9pm in summer. This section of Mount Zion houses yeshivas and Jewish outreach programs; many of the participants are students, but all are welcome. Call for information; prices vary by event. Outside Zion Gate (near King David's Tomb). ✆ **02/671-6841.** Bus: 18.

The Jerusalem Symphony Orchestra performs at the Jerusalem Performing Arts Center.

Targ (Ein Kerem Music Center) ★ PERFORMING ARTS VENUE Located in the rustic village of Ein Kerem, at the far western edge of Jerusalem, this center hosts Friday late-morning/early-afternoon concerts as well as other events. Allow at least 1½ hours by public transportation from downtown Jerusalem. 29 HaMa'ayan St. www.edentamir.org. ✆ **02/641-4250**. Bus: 50, 28 or 39.

Ticho House ★★ PERFORMING ARTS VENUE A block away from Zion Square, Ticho House maintains a busy schedule, including readings, events for children, and Friday morning concerts. 10 Ha Rav Agan St. www.imj.org.il/en/wings/arts/ticho-house. ✆ **02/624-5068.** Light Rail or any bus to Zion Sq.

Train Puppet Theater ★★ PERFORMING ARTS VENUE Jerusalem has become a center for puppetry, interestingly enough. Inventive performances are held here year-round, with an International Puppet Theater Festival in August. Many performances will be understandable to English-speaking children. Liberty Bell Park. www.traintheater.co.il. ✆ **02/561-8514.** Bus: 74, 75, or 18.

YMCA ★ PERFORMING ARTS VENUE Concerts and performances of Israeli music and folk dancing are held here throughout the year, usually on Monday, Thursday, and Saturday evenings. As there are no reserved seats, come early to nail down a spot. Always call to verify schedules and performances. 26 King David St. www.ymca3arches.com. ✆ **02/569-2692.** Bus: 13, 18, or 77.

More Entertainment

Night Spectacular Sound & Light Show ★★ LIGHT SHOW During the warmer months, a first-class sound-and-light show combined with multimedia presentations about the history of Jerusalem is featured in the Citadel of David at Jaffa Gate. Performances take place daily, but check on times and tickets in advance. Be prepared for the chill created by the stone fortress and the night breezes. In summer, there are also special night concerts and performances at various venues inside the Old City. Check with the Tourist Information Office for details. Take note, the Sound and Light Show is an impressive evening out in Jerusalem, but it can be difficult for children under 10 to follow or, frankly, enjoy. Jaffa Gate. www.tod.org.il. Adults NIS 65, ages 3–18 NIS 55.

Sultan's Pool ★★★ PERFORMING ARTS VENUE Major outdoor classical, rock, and jazz shows are held in this dramatic setting in warm weather; a typical month might include a live concert by local band Balkan Beat Box or a performance of the opera *Carmen.* This sprawling venue is also home to the annual arts and crafts festival, Hutzot Hayotzer, which typically takes place every August. In a valley beneath the Old City walls btw. Jaffa Gate and Mount Zion.

Clubs & Bars

Israelis (especially Jerusalemites) are not really a drinking people—an evening at a cafe over a meal or wine and snacks are more the local style. Try **Rivlin Street** (where some of the ever-changing bars offer small dance floors) or the neighboring **Salomon Street Mall,** in the heart of the cafe/pub scene near Zion Square.

BEST IN booze: A DISTILLERY TOUR

Thinkers Distillery is still an under-the-radar gem, but we think it's just a matter of time before it is a household name. Set in a nondescript building on Agripas Street, Thinkers was built, piece-by-piece, right before the pandemic hit. Owner and founder, Queens New York native Bennet Kaplan, thought of every detail, from its communal bar welcoming everyone in for a taste, to the encased glass room offering guests a peek into the process of Thinkers' spirits-in-the-making machinery. Jerusalemites and visitors from all over the world make a point to stop in for a shot and a bottle—or a full case. The house-made vodka, gin, and bourbon have already earned a number of global awards, and the handsome bottles make a wonderful gift. Owner Kaplan is often here, and his generous nature and extensive knowledge of the craft make him the ultimate guide...and drinking buddy. 88 Agripas St. www.thinkersdistillery.com. ✆ **050/809-2752.** Open Sun–Thurs 11am–7pm, Fri 11am–one hour before Shabbat starts; Saturdays after Shabbat by appointment only. Private and group tours can be booked Sun–Thurs.

The Abraham Hostel (p. 62) is as well known as a live music and bar venue (open to all) as it is as a place for lodgings.

The American Colony Hotel Bar in East Jerusalem is atmospheric, visited by locals and travelers in the know. You can also have drinks and tasty food at the hotel's garden **Courtyard Cafe/Bar.**

Barood ★★ This is a friendly, authentic little place with an amazingly well-stocked bar and excellent food (p. 82) ranging from Sephardic-style snacks to major meals. Live music some nights. Open Monday to Saturday 12:30pm to 1:30am. Jerusalem Courtyard, off 31 Jaffa Rd. ✆ **02/625-9081.**

Mike's Place ★★ A friendly expat hangout hosting live folk, jazz, and blues performances, or a range of televised sports events, every night, Mike's is a central spot that draws Americans, internationals, and Israelis for beer and wine, talk, music, and a well-worn pool table. Food is pub-style and kosher. Open Sunday to Thursday noon to 2am; Friday closed; Saturday 8pm to 3pm. 33 Jaffa Rd. (at the corner of Rivlin St.). www.mikesplacebars.com. ✆ **02/502-3439.**

Films

West Jerusalem shows the latest European and American films, almost always in the original language with Hebrew subtitles.

The Jerusalem Cinémathèque ★★★ (www.jer-cin.org.il; ✆ **02/565-4333**) offers a dramatic location and features nightly screenings of classics, the best of the current international scene, rarely shown international films, and the experimental and arcane. The Cinémathèque is located near the old railway station. Go to the traffic intersection between the railway station and Hebron Road. Walk down the slope to the northeast, toward the Old City, and soon you'll come to the Cinémathèque, built into the hillside below Hebron Road (bus no. 163, 18, or 78).

EXPLORING JERUSALEM

By Elianna Bar-El

Jerusalem has been a holy city for 3,000 years, far eclipsing the length of time that any other place has carried such a title. It is also a holy city for all three major religions of the Western world: Judaism, Christianity, and Islam. In the past 150 years, Jerusalem has slowly expanded from a mysterious, charismatic walled city in the Judean Mountains to a modern metropolis spread across the surrounding hills. It's a complicated place of exotic communities, ancient traditions and rivalries, plus the highest hopes and aspirations of humanity. There is no place on earth like it.

5

The city invites exploration. Jerusalem's sacred sites and dramatic vistas are filled with spirituality and meaning. In one day, you may find yourself wandering the Old City's bazaars; awestruck by the golden, shimmering Dome of the Rock on the Temple Mount; overwhelmed by the site of the Crucifixion; or by Yad Vashem, the memorial and museum dedicated to the six million Jews who fell victim to the Nazis. Later you'll stop in your tracks, mesmerized by the evening calls to prayer echoing through the streets of the Old City.

Although the ancient grandeur of Jerusalem long ago vanished in the ravages of warfare and time, the city's mystique has expanded far beyond anything that could have been dreamed in ancient times. The most awesome holy places of Judaism, Christianity, and Islam have come to dot the Old City and its nearby hills. During the centuries of the Crusades, Jerusalem was the shimmering vision that moved the armies of Europe and Islam. But for almost 700 years after the Crusades ended, the actual city of Jerusalem existed mostly as a shadowy, forgotten backwater, slowly falling into ruin and decay. Not until the 19th century did the city again begin to come alive and reemerge from behind its walls to spread across the surrounding hills.

During the years of the British Mandate (1918–48), the modern incarnation of Jerusalem developed as a religious center, tourist attraction, and university town in a remarkably beautiful mountain setting. Nineteen years of division by war, barbed wire, and minefields (1948–67) brought Jerusalem's gentle renaissance to a temporary halt. However, with the city's reunification in 1967, Teddy Kollek, the city's world-renowned former mayor, began a modern, ongoing crusade to make sure that Jerusalem would not merely exist or even thrive but would absolutely shine.

Jerusalem today is a busy place where the old and new mix and clash. A state-of-the-art light-rail tram glides from points all over the biblical Judean Hills and continues along the Old City walls and the middle of downtown West Jerusalem's main thoroughfare, Jaffa Road. New high-rise construction is going on everywhere.

The city is at a crossroads politically and socially as well as physically. Will it someday be a shared capital for Palestinians and Israelis? Will the religious Jewish community become the demographic and ruling majority in West Jerusalem, and, if so, what will happen to the museums, parks, entertainment, and cultural institutions created by the city's secular community over the past 50 years? Should developers be allowed a free hand to Manhattanize Jerusalem, or should limits be placed on the future growth of the city? Optimists

On Palm Sunday, thousands of palm-bearing worshippers make their way from the sanctuary of Bethphage to the Old City.

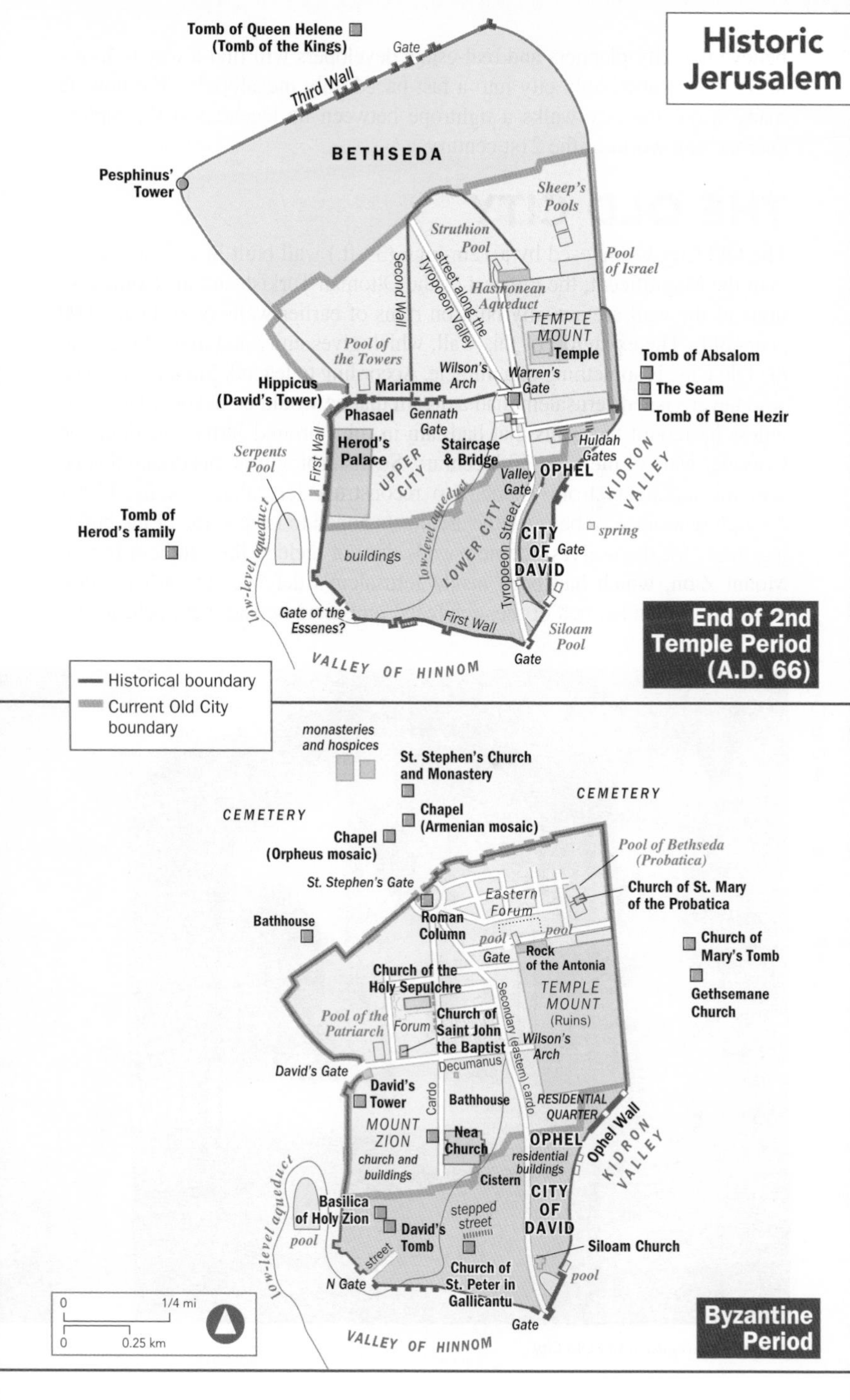
Historic Jerusalem
Tomb of Queen Helene (Tomb of the Kings)
Gate
Third Wall
BETHSEDA
Pesphinus' Tower
Sheep's Pools
Struthion Pool
Second Wall
street along the Tyropoeon Valley
Pool of Israel
Hasmonean Aqueduct
TEMPLE MOUNT
Temple
Pool of the Towers
Wilson's Arch
Warren's Gate
Tomb of Absalom
The Seam
Tomb of Bene Hezir
Hippicus (David's Tower)
Mariamme
Phasael
Gennath Gate
First Wall
Serpents Pool
Herod's Palace
UPPER CITY
Staircase & Bridge
Huldah Gates
OPHEL
KIDRON VALLEY
Valley Gate
Tomb of Herod's family
low-level aqueduct
buildings
LOWER CITY
Tyropoeon Street
CITY OF DAVID
Gate
spring
Gate of the Essenes?
First Wall
Siloam Pool
Gate
VALLEY OF HINNOM
End of 2nd Temple Period (A.D. 66)
Historical boundary
Current Old City boundary
monasteries and hospices
St. Stephen's Church and Monastery
CEMETERY
CEMETERY
Chapel (Armenian mosaic)
Chapel (Orpheus mosaic)
Pool of Bethseda (Probatica)
St. Stephen's Gate
Church of St. Mary of the Probatica
Eastern Forum
Bathhouse
Roman Column
pool
pool
Church of Mary's Tomb
Gate
Rock of the Antonia
Gethsemane Church
Church of the Holy Sepulchre
Secondary (eastern) cardo
TEMPLE MOUNT (Ruins)
Pool of the Patriarch
Forum
Church of Saint John the Baptist
Wilson's Arch
David's Gate
Decumanus
David's Tower
Cardo
Bathhouse
RESIDENTIAL QUARTER
Ophel Wall
MOUNT ZION
Nea Church
OPHEL
church and buildings
residential buildings
KIDRON VALLEY
Cistern
Basilica of Holy Zion
stepped street
CITY OF DAVID
pool
David's Tomb
Siloam Church
street
Church of St. Peter in Gallicantu
pool
N Gate
0 1/4 mi
0 0.25 km
Gate
VALLEY OF HINNOM
Byzantine Period

believe that city planners and real-estate developers will find a way to turn a mysterious walled holy city into a fast-paced holy megalopolis. For now, in many ways, the city walks a tightrope between its legend and the rapidly encroaching world of the 21st century.

THE OLD CITY

The Old City is enclosed by a 12m-high (39-ft.) wall built in 1538 by Suleiman the Magnificent, the greatest of the Ottoman Turkish sultans (some portions of the wall are actually built on ruins of earlier walls more than 2,000 years old). The existence of this wall, which gives unity and magnificence to the Old City, is something of a miracle. According to legend, Sultan Suleiman, who never visited Jerusalem, had a dream that he would be devoured by lions unless he rebuilt the walls that had lain in ruins around Jerusalem since the Crusader wars of the early 13th century. So disturbing was this dream that he sent his architects from Istanbul to reconstruct Jerusalem's walls. Either through ignorance or because the architects hoped to keep some of the building funds for themselves, the new walls did not include the southern part of Mount Zion, which had been inside Jerusalem's defenses in earlier times. When the sultan learned of the architects' omission, he had them beheaded.

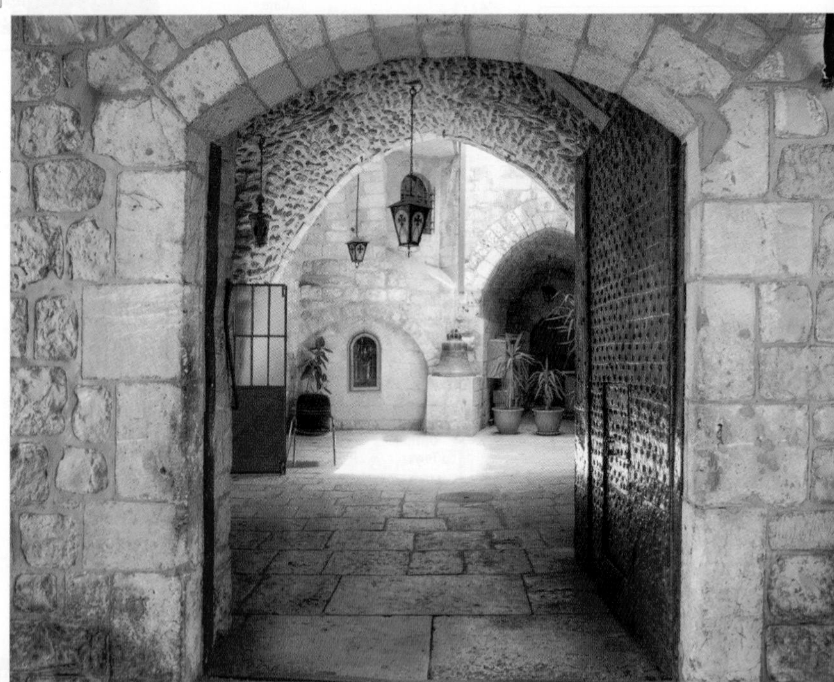

A serene courtyard in the Old City.

There are eight gates in the Old City fortress wall. The most famous are:

- **Jaffa Gate** (in Hebrew, Sha'ar Yafo; in Arabic, Bab al Khalil), the main entrance into the Old City from West Jerusalem and approached from a promenade that runs from the end of Jaffa Road along the Old City walls or via the new, multilevel Mamilla Shopping Mall.
- **Damascus Gate,** in the northern wall of the Old City, entered from Ha-Nevi'im Street or Nablus Road and the main entrance into the Old City from the Arab New City. Israelis call Damascus Gate Sha'ar Shechem; the Arabic name is Bab-el-Amud. On some maps it is also called Nablus Gate.
- **Dung Gate,** in the southern wall of the Old City, closest to the Western Wall and now accommodating taxis and buses.
- **Zion Gate,** in the southern wall of the Old City and leading directly to the Jewish Quarter. It bears the scars of the battle by Israeli forces to relieve the besieged Jewish Quarter in 1948.
- **The Lions' Gate** (St. Stephen's Gate), in the eastern wall of the Old City, which leads to the Mount of Olives.
- **Golden Gate,** or the Gate of Mercy, on the eastern side of the Old City and in ancient times the most magnificent of the city gates. According to tradition, this will be the gate through which the Messiah will enter Jerusalem; however, it has been walled up for many centuries.

The Old City itself is divided into five sections: the **Christian Quarter,** the **Armenian Quarter,** the **Muslim Quarter,** the **Jewish Quarter,** and **Temple Mount** (Mount Moriah), the latter including the Western (Wailing) Wall, the Dome of the Rock, and Al Aqsa Mosque. The Dome of the Rock and the Al Aqsa Mosque were built from A.D. 691 to 720, 600 years after the Temple was destroyed by Rome. Throughout the Islamic world, this complex is called **Haram esh Sharif,** or the Noble Sanctuary.

The Jaffa Gate ★

This is the traditional entrance into the Old City from the western part of the New City. The citadel tower, beside the Jaffa Gate, is known as the **Tower of David ★**, although historically this fortress was first developed 800 years after King David died. Three massive towers built by Herod on the foundations of Hasmonean fortifications originally stood on this spot. Just to the south, close to the protection of the garrison in the Jaffa Gate's tower, would have been Herod's palace. After the destruction of Jerusalem by the Romans in A.D. 70, the foundations of the towers guarding the Jaffa Gate were among the few structures not deliberately obliterated on orders from Rome. They were left standing to show there had once been a city that had been no push-over to subdue. Each of the subsequent rulers of Jerusalem, from Romans and Byzantines to Muslims, Crusaders, and Ottoman Turks, has rebuilt the fortifications beside Jaffa Gate, although none have come close to the scale of Herod's three towers. The Ottoman Turks built a mosque here, and its minaret still dominates the complex.

The **Tower of David Museum of the History of Jerusalem ★★**, Omar Ibn El Khattab Square (www.tod.org.il; ✆ **02/626-5333**), now fills the citadel, hosting well-chosen, often very exciting temporary art and history exhibits, performances, and tours. Although some of the permanent exhibits look like illustrations from a school textbook, they are useful teaching tools. The structure of the citadel itself, with its great views of the New and Old Cities, is fascinating. The courtyard of the citadel is also used for concerts and performances of plays by contemporary Israeli writers. The **Night Spectacular** narrates Jerusalem's history in 40 minutes and is presented in English and Hebrew. Bring warm clothes for evening performances. If special performances and events are scheduled, look for bundled admission packages to the museum, the performance, and the sound-and-light show. Admission is NIS 62 for adults and NIS 52 to the Night Spectacular; a combined ticket with the Tower of David Museum is NIS 80 for adults, NIS 70 for children. The museum is open Saturday through Thursday 9am to 4pm (9am–5pm in Aug) and Friday 9am to 2pm (9am–4pm in Aug). There are **guided tours in English** and **reservations** can be made in advance.

Segway-riding tourists enter the Jaffa Gate.

A breach in the city walls beside Jaffa Gate was made for the visit of Kaiser Wilhelm II of Germany and his entourage in 1898. Here, the leader of the British forces, General Allenby, liberating Palestine from Ottoman rule, entered Jerusalem in 1917. Today, this breach allows automobiles to enter the area of the Old City just inside the Jaffa Gate, and the **Tourist Information Office** is located here.

If you head straight into the **bazaar** (the *suq*) from the Jaffa Gate, you'll enter David Street, bustling with shops selling religious crafts, souvenirs, maps, and household items.

If your first destination is the **Church of the Holy Sepulchre,** proceed straight down David Street and take the first left, which is called Christian Quarter Road. Follow this road until you come to St. Helena's Road, a stepped bazaar on the right that will lead you down to the entrance to the church.

If the **Western Wall and the Temple Mount** are your first goal, continue straight along David Street. It makes a quick jog to the right and then to the left in the heart of the covered bazaar, where it changes its name to Street of the Chain (Silsila, in Arabic). Follow the street downhill as the bazaar continues. Eventually, turning right on a small side street marked Ha-Kotel leads to the Western Wall. Just to the right of the Western Wall, a long, curved ramp leads to the Mograbi Gate, the only gate non-Muslims can use to enter the Temple Mount.

Armenian Quarter ★

As you pass Omar Ibn El Khattab Square, just before you descend the steps into David Street, you'll see a road heading off to the right, past the moat and the Tower of David. This is the Armenian Patriarchate Road, leading into the Armenian Quarter, a walled world unto itself, centered around Armenian religious structures and home to much of Jerusalem's Armenian community. Around A.D. 300, Armenia became the first nation to adopt Christianity, predating Emperor Constantine's conversion of the Roman Empire by several decades. From that time, there has always been an Armenian presence in Jerusalem.

Follow the Armenian Patriarchate Road, look left for an entrance into the walled Armenian Quarter, and follow the signs.

Saint James Cathedral ★★ is the most important site in the Armenian Quarter. Entered through the Armenian Monastery on Armenian Patriarchate

A ceramicist hand-paints a piece in his store in the Armenian Quarter.

Road, it dates from the 11th and 12th centuries and is built on the site of earlier churches. It commemorates the place where James the Elder, son of Zebedee, was put to death by order of Herod Agrippa I in A.D. 44 (Acts 12:2). The cathedral also contains the tomb of James, the oldest brother of Jesus and first bishop of the Jerusalem Christian community. This James was the author of the Epistle of James and was stoned to death in A.D. 62. The cathedral, with its rich interior of hanging lamps, censers (for burning incense), and ceremonial objects, may be visited for services daily from 3 to 3:40pm. Additional services are held Monday through Friday and Sunday 6:30 to 7:30am, Saturday 6:30 to 9:30am.

Tip: The intricacies of the secluded Armenian Quarter are difficult to explore on your own. Aram Khatchadourian (Old City, Jerusalem; © **050/335-1859**), a licensed guide and member of Jerusalem's Armenian community, gives full- or half-day private walking tours of the quarters of the Old City.

The Jewish Quarter ★★★

Take a detour through the Jewish Quarter on your way to the Western Wall and Temple Mount. By doing so, you'll save an uphill walk, as the wall lies well below most of the quarter.

The Jewish Quarter lies directly west of the Temple Mount and sits on a higher hill than the Temple Mount itself. With the exception of the sacred Temple Mount, the entire original city of Jerusalem from the time of David (1000 B.C.) was outside the walls of the present Old City, just downhill and to the south. Over the centuries, ancient Jerusalem spread northward, up the slope. By the time of King Hezekiah, around 700 B.C., much of the uphill area now occupied by the Jewish Quarter had become a new addition to the city, surrounded by the Broad Wall. But the wall and its many towers were not strong enough to keep out Nebuchadnezzar of Babylon, who conquered and laid waste to Jerusalem in 586 B.C.

Jews returned to rebuild Jerusalem after the Babylonian Captivity, but it took centuries for the city to regain its former size. In the late Second Temple period, Jerusalem again expanded uphill, and the area that is now the Jewish Quarter was inhabited once more and developed into an aristocratic and priestly residential neighborhood. The main market street of Herodian Jerusalem developed at the bottom of the Tyropoeon (Cheesemakers') Valley, which separates the heights of the present Jewish Quarter from the Temple Mount. The market street continued northward to the Damascus Gate. For thousands of religious pilgrims to make their way to the Temple Mount without becoming entangled in the crush of the market, two massive pedestrian staircases and overpasses were constructed above the market street. By the A.D. 1st century, Jerusalem had expanded northward, beyond the present Old City's northern wall. A new, bustling Upper Market developed where the Suq Khan es-Zeit market leads toward the Damascus Gate. The original City of David, the oldest part of town, came to be known as the Lower City.

Jerusalem was again leveled in A.D. 70 by Roman armies (the remains of houses burned in that conflagration have been uncovered in what is now the Jewish Quarter); 65 years after the Romans destroyed Jerusalem, they (and later their Byzantine successors) rebuilt the city. You can visit several uncovered vestiges of Roman/Byzantine times in the Jewish Quarter, including the ruins of the gigantic **Nea Church** and the southern end of the city's colonnaded north-south thoroughfare, the **Cardo Maximus.** Jews were forbidden to reside in Jerusalem during the long Byzantine period, which began in A.D. 326, and many Jewish inhabitants of the area allied themselves with the then-pagan Persians, who conquered and occupied Jerusalem from A.D. 614 to 629. The Byzantines returned in A.D. 629, followed quickly by the Muslims, who conquered Jerusalem in A.D. 638. Under their more tolerant rule, a permanent Jewish community was reestablished in the northeast quadrant of the Old City, on the site of the present Muslim Quarter. The Crusaders conquered Jerusalem in 1099 and celebrated their triumph by massacring most of the city's Jewish population as well as thousands of Muslims and local Christians.

In 1267, after the Crusaders were driven from Jerusalem, a small Jewish community reestablished itself in the ruins of what is now the Jewish Quarter. This area has been the center of the Jewish community in the Old City ever since.

The Jewish Quarter's most recent destruction came during and after the 1948 war with Jordan, when all the synagogues and most other buildings in the quarter were severely damaged and over the next 2 decades fell into almost total ruin; many were systematically demolished. Since the Israeli conquest of the Old City during the 1967 war, the quarter has been rebuilt and revitalized. Although some original buildings have been carefully re-created, and many new structures were designed to blend in with them, the basic nature of the current Jewish Quarter is quite different from the impoverished, densely populated neighborhoods that existed here before 1948.

Following St. James Road (a left turn off Armenian Patriarchate Rd.) to where it becomes Or Hayim Street, you'll come to the **Old Yishuv Court Museum ★**, 6 Or Hayim St. (www.oyc.co.il; ✆ **02/627-6319**). This small museum displays artifacts and crafts typical of Ashkenazi and Sephardic communities in the Jewish Quarter from the middle of the 19th century to the end of Turkish rule in 1917. Admission is NIS 20, children NIS 10, and it's open Sunday to Thursday from 10am to 3pm, Friday 10am to 1pm.

The **Cardo Maximus ★** is a recently excavated A.D. 2nd- to 6th-century street that was Roman and Byzantine Jerusalem's main market and processional thoroughfare, once bordered by stately columns and lined with portico-shaded shops. The original street is said to have been laid out by the Roman emperor Hadrian (A.D. 117–38) when he rebuilt the city as Aelia Capitolina after the Bar Kochba Revolt of A.D. 132 to 135. In late Byzantine times, the Cardo was extended southward and served as the processional route between the **Holy Sepulchre** and the **Nea,** Jerusalem's two largest churches of that era.

The southern portion of the Cardo is open to the sky; the rest is beneath the modern buildings of the Jewish Quarter. At the end of Or Hayim Street, the Cardo's imposing columns, found by archaeologists, have been re-erected. As you walk northward along the reconstructed Cardo, where modern tourist shops have been installed, you can see on your right the walled-up facades of Crusader-era shops built into the arches. In this restored section, you can look down well-like structures that reveal how far above the original level of the land the city has risen in its constant rebuilding on the ruins of each wave of destruction. You'll also see fragments of the city's defensive walls dating from the First Temple period, around 700 B.C.

Parallel to the Cardo is the Jewish Quarter Road. Many Jewish Quarter buildings from other times are today recalled by only a single arch, doorway, or minaret. You can inspect the haunting arches, altar, apse, and ruined cloister from the once-lost **Crusader Church of Saint Mary of the Teutonic Knights ★** (A.D. 1128) on Misgav Ladach Street. If you enter the ruins, walk back to the apse, where the windows frame a wonderful view of the Temple Mount.

Across from the entrance to the church is a small covered square known as **Seven Arches.** In the pre-1948 Jewish Quarter, Seven Arches was the heart of a lively market packed with vegetable vendors and customers. To the west, you'll see the minaret from the **Omar Sidna Mosque,** and beside it is the rebuilt (2010) **Hurva Synagogue,** which was once the Great Synagogue of the Jewish Quarter. The name, meaning "ruin," recalls its difficult and unfortunate history. The original Hurva was built in the 17th century with Ottoman permission but was soon destroyed by Ottoman decree. In the 1850s, a new synagogue was authorized and built. Heavily damaged in the 1948 war, it was demolished after the Jordanians captured the Jewish Quarter. In the decades after 1967, when the Israelis recaptured the Old City, there were a number of movements and plans (including one by visionary American architect Louis Kahn) calling for a new Hurva Synagogue. From 1967 until 2010, the site of the Hurva was marked only by a simple arch, in memory of the Great Synagogue of Jerusalem. The new Hurva, with its landmark dome matching the arch of the original synagogue, is as close as possible to the design of the one destroyed in 1948.

The Hurva Synagogue in the Jewish Quarter.

Between the minaret and the Hurva is the **Ramban Synagogue** of Rabbi Moshe Ben-Nachman, who helped reconstitute the Jewish community of Jerusalem in 1267, after it had been obliterated by the Crusaders. You'll also want to take a look at the complex of **Four Sephardic synagogues ★** named for Rabbi Yochanan Ben-Zakkai, whose school, according to tradition, occupied this site during the Second Temple period. One of the four is named for the rabbi himself and another for Eliyahu Ha-Navi (Elijah the Prophet); the other two are the Central Synagogue and the Istanbuli Synagogue. During Muslim rule, no church or synagogue was allowed to exceed the height of the nearest mosque, so to gain headroom, the floors of these synagogues were laid well below ground level. The synagogues are open Sunday to Thursday from 9:30am to 3:45pm and Friday from 9:30am to 1pm.

The **Tiferet Israel (or Yisrael) Synagogue** (Ashkenazi, or Eastern European Jewish) was founded by Nisan Bek and inaugurated in 1865. Dedicated to the Hasidic Rabbi Israel Friedman of Ruzhin (the synagogue's name means "Glory of Israel"), it was destroyed after the War of Independence and was restored after 1967.

Moving eastward across the Jewish Quarter in the direction of the Western Wall, you can visit remnants of the neighborhood's elegant Herodian past.

The **Burnt House ★** (www.travelrova.co.il; ✆ **02/626-5906**) is a remnant of the destruction of Jerusalem by the Romans in A.D. 70. The wealthy Upper City, site of the present Jewish Quarter, held out for a despairing month after the Lower City and the Temple Mount fell. From these heights, the inhabitants of the Upper City stood on their roofs and watched with horror as the Temple went up in flames. When the Romans finally decided to storm the Upper City, they found little resistance; much of the population was dead or near death from disease and starvation. The Burnt House chillingly brings to light the day when the Romans burned the Upper City. In the 1970s, when archaeologists excavated what had been the kitchen or workroom of this building, they found the forearm bones of a young woman amid the debris. As diggers continued to excavate the area of the room that lay where the arm pointed, they uncovered a wooden spear, almost as if the young woman had been reaching for this weapon when she met her death. Most tantalizing of the household artifacts found on this site is a set of weights marked with the name "Bar Kathros," a priestly family mentioned in the Talmud (and also in an ancient folk song as one of the wealthy families that oppressed the poor). Historians know the House of Bar Kathros was responsible for the manufacture of incense for the Temple. The excavated house, now preserved beneath modern buildings, offers a brief slideshow about the site. The entrance to the house is marked on a modern door in Seven Arches off Misgav Ladach Road (ask if you have difficulty finding the door). The house is open Sunday to Thursday from 9am to 6pm. Admission is NIS 20 for adults and NIS 10 for children. Make reservations in advance online.

The Western Wall ★★★

This is known in Hebrew as the *Kotel Ha-Ma'aravi.* It was formerly called the "Wailing Wall" by European observers because for centuries, Jews came here to mourn the loss of their temple. It is the holiest of Jewish sites, a remnant of the monumental Herodian retaining wall that encloses and still supports the Temple Mount.

Orthodox Jewish men pray at the Western Wall.

For centuries, the Wall stood 18m (59 ft.) above the level of the earth and 27m (89 ft.) long, towering over a narrow alley 3.6m (12 ft.) wide that could accommodate only approximately a hundred densely packed worshippers. In 1967, immediately after the Six-Day War, the Israelis bulldozed the Moors Quarter facing the wall to create a plaza that could accommodate tens of thousands of pilgrims. They also made the wall about 2m (6½ ft.) higher by digging down when building the plaza and exposing two more tiers of the Wall's ashlars (squared stones) that had been buried by accumulated debris for centuries. At the southern end of the Wall, away from the area reserved for prayer and worship, archaeologists (since 1967) have uncovered spectacular remains from various periods.

At the prayer section of the Western Wall, grass grows out of the upper cracks. The lower cracks of the chalky, yellow-white blocks have been stuffed with thousands upon thousands of rolled up bits of paper containing prayers. Orthodox Jews can be seen standing at the wall, chanting and swaying. Visitors of all religions are welcome to approach the Wall and pray silently beside it (both Pope John Paul II and the Dalai Lama prayed here as pilgrims). Men who would like to go to the Wall must wear a hat or take a head covering; if you don't have a yarmulke, sun hat, or baseball cap, you can take one, at no cost, from a box beside the entrance to the prayer area. Women may borrow shawls and short-skirt coverings, but it is best to come with a longish skirt and long sleeves. Men and women each have their own private sections of the Wall, in keeping with Orthodox Jewish tradition. The section at the extreme right is reserved for women. On some days, you may encounter a number of beggars; giving charity at a time of pilgrimage is an ancient Jewish tradition, but many travelers choose to make a donation to an organized charity instead.

Services are held here daily; no photography or smoking is permitted on the Sabbath and some Jewish holidays.

The exposed lower courses of the Western Wall are composed of enormous rectangular *ashlars,* or carefully carved stones, each dressed only with the recessed borders typical of Herodian-era stonework. The sides of these monumental ashlars have been carved with such precision that they rest perfectly against and on top of each other, without mortar. Over the millennia, the fine straight lines and margins of some of the ashlars have eroded.

The Wall was built by King Herod just before the time of Jesus and is part of a structure that retains the western part of the Temple Mount and the vast, artificial ceremonial plaza Herod created on the Temple Mount itself. These retaining (as well as defensive) walls surround the western, southern, and eastern sides of the Temple Mount. The largest of the ashlars is 3.6m (12 ft.) high and 14m (46 ft.) long and weighs approximately 400 tons. According to Josephus, the Roman Jewish historian, construction of the walls took 11 years, during which time it rained in Jerusalem only at night so as not to interfere with the workers' progress.

In the right-hand corner of the women's prayer area, beside a protruding newer building, you can see an area of the Wall composed of small, rough stones. These stones block a fragment of a Herodian-era door to the Temple Mount, today called **Barclay's Gate** after the 19th-century American who first identified it. South of the earthen ramp leading up the Temple Mount, you'll see a fragment of large stonework protruding from the upper reaches of the Wall. This is **Robinson's Arch,** all that remains of a great stairway, set on arches, which passed over the busy market street at the foot of the Western Wall and led directly onto the southern side of the Temple Mount.

The Western Wall is actually much higher and longer than the portion you can readily see today. For an idea of how high the original construction was, and what the level of the earth was 2,000 years ago, enter the doorway located between the men's restrooms and the public telephones on the plaza's northern side. Both men and women can enter (on weekdays, by request) this dark passage of vaults, chambers, and pitfalls (now rendered safe by lamps, grates, and barriers). Inside, the continuation of the Wall is clearly visible. Shafts have been sunk along the Wall to show its true depth. The arches in this artificial cavern date from various eras, ranging from Herodian (37 B.C.–A.D. 70) to Crusader (1100–1244). The platform is behind a prayer room filled with Orthodox worshippers. The prayer room is off limits to women, except in the viewing area.

Several tours into excavated tunnels alongside the Western Wall can be arranged by making an appointment with the **Western Wall Heritage Foundation** (english.thekotel.org; ✆ **02/627-1333,** wait for the prompt in English, then press 2). Best of the bunch is the **Bridge Tunnel Tour ★★★**, which opened in 2022 and shows visitors the most recent excavations, including ones that have uncovered 2,000-year-old fragments of the First Temple. Don't bother with the underwhelming **Chain of Generations** tour. General admission is NIS 33 adults and NIS 25 children. Book ahead.

Temple Mount (Haram esh Sharif)—Dome of the Rock ★★★

Take the rising pathway to the right of the Western Wall, which leads to the Temple Mount, one of the most historic and sublime religious sites in the world. In the Islamic world, this is the Haram esh Sharif, the Noble Sanctuary, and one of its crowning architectural achievements. After David conquered Jerusalem, he purchased the flat rock at the top of Moriah from Araunah the Jebusite, who had used it as a threshing floor. Some historians theorize that the name Araunah, a dialect variation of the name Aaron, may indicate that Araunah was a Canaanite priest, and the site a Canaanite holy place. The Bible (2 Chron. 3) relates that "Solomon began to build the house of the Lord at Jerusalem on Mount Moriah." The more modest Second Temple (Solomon's was destroyed by Nebuchadnezzar in 586 B.C.) was originally built by returnees from the Babylonian Captivity between 525 and 515 B.C., and later, shortly before the time of Jesus, Herod enlarged and rebuilt it into the most massive religious complex in the eastern Roman Empire. The vast Temple Mount you see here is an artificially created, flat, stone-paved platform, about 12 hectares (30 acres) in area, built by Herod to accommodate vast numbers of pilgrims in ancient times. Herod's temple complex was destroyed by the Romans in A.D. 70. All structures on the Temple Mount today, including the Dome of the Rock and the Al Aqsa Mosque, are Islamic holy places and religious institutions built after the Muslim conquest of A.D. 638—but that doesn't mean things aren't complicated.

There is no charge to enter the Temple Mount compound. You must not, however, wear shorts or immodest dress in the compound. (If your outfit is too revealing, guards may provide you with long cotton wraps, or they may ask you to return another time.) Jewish prayer is forbidden at the entire site.

There is an admission fee to go inside the two mosques and the Islamic Museum, but they have been closed to non-Muslims since 2000. If the

Scheduling a Visit to the Temple Mount

Tourists can only visit the Temple Mount/Haram esh Sharif Sunday to Thursday 7:30 to 11am (10am in winter) and 1:30 to 2:30pm. Hours can change, so it is best to always check beforehand and arrive at least an hour ahead of closing time. Although visitors may walk around on the Temple Mount, take photographs, and enjoy the vistas, for now entry into the Dome of the Rock, the Al Aqsa Mosque, and the Islamic Museum is not permitted. The Temple Mount is always closed to non-Muslims on Friday and Saturday and is either totally closed or, depending on circumstances, open for very limited hours during the entire holy month of Ramadan. Non-Muslims may not bring prayer books or engage in public or private prayer on the Temple Mount.

buildings are again open to foreign visitors, we highly recommend that you invest in the combined admission ticket, which may be purchased from a stone kiosk between Al Aqsa and the Dome of the Rock. Admissions change with the security conditions of the area. It is best to check once on the premises what is the current status.

Al Aqsa Mosque ★★, the third-holiest place of prayer in the world for Muslims (after Mecca and Medina), is the first large edifice you'll come to. Completed in approximately A.D. 720, it is among the oldest mosques in existence and also among the most beautiful—a vast broad basilica originally nine naves wide (it was rebuilt somewhat smaller after the Crusades). It was in front of the graceful porticos of the Al Aqsa that King Abdullah I of Jordan was assassinated in 1951 by gunmen who believed he was attempting to create a basis for eventual peace in the area. He died here in the presence of his then-15-year-old grandson, the late King Hussein of Jordan.

Note: Although at press time the interiors of Al Aqsa and the Dome of the Rock were **closed** to visitors—it's likely you'll have to be content with exterior views—the following information is provided in case they are reopened.

A mosque is a sacred enclosure open to air and light (as opposed to the dark interiors of pagan-era temples). Because a mosque is a sacred precinct, you must remove your shoes before entering. This tradition is very ancient, going back to the time when Moses, approaching the Burning Bush in the Sinai,

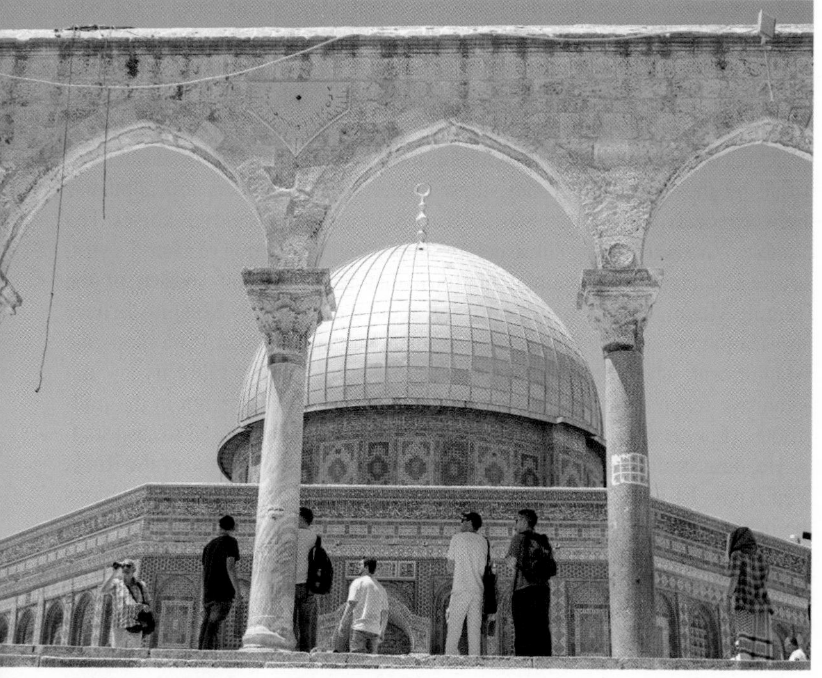

A look at the outside of the Dome of the Rock.

heard the voice of God telling him to take off his shoes. You must also leave handbags and cameras outside, so you might want to come with a partner who can watch these things for you. Try to stash your wallet and identification papers in a pocket.

After passing through the portico, you will enter a broad, open hall with chandeliers, its floor covered with Oriental rugs. The mosque's lofty ceilings, supported by a forest of varied columns, are embellished with early Islamic and Byzantine design. Up front, past rows of great marble pillars, is a wood-partitioned platform reserved for the Jordanian royal family. The extraordinary wooden-stair pulpit of the Al Aqsa Mosque, one of Islam's great artistic treasures for more than 7 centuries, was commissioned by Saladin for the rededication of Al Aqsa as a mosque after the Crusader occupation. Originally built by master artisans from Syria, it was destroyed when a mentally disturbed Australian tourist set fire to Al Aqsa in 1969, and it has been painstakingly reconstructed by craftspeople retrained in techniques that have not been used for hundreds of years. A separate women's prayer chamber, in blue, is at the right. As you enter Al Aqsa, you face south, in the direction of Mecca. **Mihrabs,** or prayer niches on the southern wall, remind worshipers of the *qibla,* or direction they must face during prayers, which are performed five times a day. Unlike most churches and synagogues, mosques contain no pews or chairs. Visitors are invited to view the architecture and design details of the building; however, they are requested not to engage in any prayers.

Leave Al Aqsa, reclaim your shoes and belongings, and turn right. You will only be permitted to walk to the end of the building, but at the far end of the vast pavement is a corner in the city walls. Some say this is the "pinnacle of the Temple" where Satan took Jesus to tempt him (Matt. 4:5). In the distance, you can get a marvelous view of the Mount of Olives and the Kidron Valley.

A stairway leads to the so-called **Solomon's Stables,** perhaps first misidentified by the Crusaders. Today, these subterranean chambers are popularly believed to have been the stables for King Solomon's thousands of horses. The "stables" are actually the substructure supporting this portion of Herod's vast, artificially created ceremonial platform that is the present surface of the Temple Mount. To add to the confusion about the site, many Muslims believe the "Solomon" referred to is the Ottoman Sultan Suleiman (Solomon) the Magnificent, who rebuilt the walls that surround the present Old City and did extensive repair work on the Dome of the Rock during his reign in the mid-1500s. (For security reasons, this area will most likely be closed to visitors.)

Heading straight across Temple Mount Plaza toward the Dome of the Rock, you'll pass **El-Kas,** the fountain where Muslims perform their ritual ablutions before entering the holy places. It is equipped with a circular row of pink marble seats, each of which has a faucet. The fountain is not for use by non-Muslims.

The exterior walls of the dazzling **Dome of the Rock ★★★** are covered with a facade of Persian blue tiles, originally installed by the Ottoman Sultan

Suleiman the Magnificent in the mid–16th century. In 1994, under the auspices of Jordan's King Hussein, the great dome was completely reconstructed and re-gilded with 80kg (176 lb.) of 24-karat gold. The Dome of the Rock is reached by climbing the broad ceremonial stairs that lead to a decorative archway and a raised center portion of the Temple Mount complex. The Dome of the Rock's interior is every bit as lavish and intricate as the outside. Plush carpets line the floor, and stained-glass windows line the upper ceiling.

Everything in this beautiful Muslim sanctuary, built in A.D. 691, centers on the rock that occupies the middle of the shrine. According to Islamic tradition, this rock is the spot from which the Prophet Muhammad ascended to view paradise during the Night Journey described in the 17th Sura of the Koran. Tradition holds that when the Prophet rose, the rock tried to follow, and although it failed, the cave beneath the rock was formed. Footprints of Muhammad are pointed out on the rock.

Next to the rock, a few strands of the Prophet Muhammad's hair are kept in a latticework wooden cabinet. A stairway leads under the rock to a cave-like chamber; according to tradition, this is the Well of the Souls, where it is said the souls of all the dead are gathered. Glass partitions have been erected to stop pilgrims from eroding the sacred rock—for centuries, it was chipped away by the faithful who wanted to bring home a memento.

Jewish tradition holds that on this rock occurred the supreme act of faith that stands at the foundation of the Jewish religion: Abraham's near-sacrifice of Isaac. Genesis 22 relates how Abraham, in approximately 1800 B.C., followed God's instructions to go to Moriah and sacrifice Isaac, his beloved son. At the final moment, the voice of God intervened and ordered Abraham to lower his knife. Approximately 900 years later, around 960 B.C., the Temple of Solomon was constructed either on or beside this rock. For the next millennium, the First and Second Temples were located on this site.

From the flat courtyard surrounding the two mosques, you have a wonderful view. To the south are the **Valley of Jehoshaphat** (Valley of Kidron) and the **UN Government House** (Mount of Contempt) on the hill. To the east are the lower slopes of the **Mount of Olives;** the **Russian Magdalene Church,** with its many onion-shaped golden domes; and the **Tomb of the Virgin.** Midway up the Mount of Olives is a large, modern, white structure with many levels of arcades that seem built into the side of the slope. This is the vast **Mormon Center,** constructed in the 1980s and considered to be one of the most beautiful examples of contemporary architecture in Jerusalem. On the crest of the Mount of Olives, above the Church of Mary Magdalene, you'll see the high-steepled **Russian Monastery** and the **Dome of the Ascension,** marking the site from which Jesus is traditionally believed to have ascended to heaven. Farther to the right and a bit downhill is the gray, tear-shaped dome of Dominus Flevit, which commemorates the spot where Jesus wept as he saw a vision of Jerusalem in ruins. Indeed, from the time of the city's destruction in A.D. 70 until the building of the Dome of the Rock in A.D. 691, Jews traditionally stood near this spot and viewed the actual ruins of the Temple Mount. To the right, on the southern crest of the ridge, is the modern Seven Arches Hotel, built during Jordanian times on the ancient Jewish cemetery of the Mount of Olives.

Your combined entrance ticket also admits you to the **Islamic Museum,** in the southwest corner of the Temple Mount complex, to the right of the Al Aqsa Mosque. The museum is filled with architectural details, including capitals and carved stonework from earlier structures on the Temple Mount as well as ornamental details from earlier periods of the Al Aqsa Mosque's existence.

Dung Gate, Silwan (the City of David) & the Jerusalem Archaeological Park ★★

The gate in the city wall near the Temple Mount is Dung Gate, which leads downhill to the Arab neighborhood of Silwan, the site of Jerusalem and the ancient City of David as it existed around 1000 B.C. Until the medieval era, Silwan was encompassed within the walls of Jerusalem; only when the walls of the city shrank to their present configuration and the city wall separated Silwan from the rest of the city was the Dung Gate built. For centuries, the gate was just a small doorway in the wall, but in recent years it has been widened to accommodate cars and buses. Jerusalemites claim that the gate is named for the debris from each consecutive destruction of Jerusalem that was dumped out into the valley below. Silwan today is as crowded as in ancient times—its houses now climb the sides of a steep cliff at the edge of the Mount of Olives. Silwan is where the original settlement of Jerusalem developed in prehistoric times beside the **Gihon Spring.** Its streets are where the prophets walked and the events of First Temple Jerusalem took place.

By the 2nd century B.C., the growing city of Jerusalem was expanding uphill and northward onto the site of the present Old City. The newer Upper City was the more affluent part of town; the older Lower City was densely populated and poor. In the centuries after the Roman destruction of Jerusalem in A.D. 70, the population of Jerusalem had so greatly decreased and the technology of warfare had progressed to such a point that the original City of David was no longer militarily defensible. It was left outside the walls of the city and by medieval times had sunk to the status of a small, sporadically settled village known as Silwan. So completely forgotten was the site of the original city that until late in the 19th century, most historians and visitors believed the Jerusalem of the First Temple period had been located on the site of the present Old City.

Since the 1950s, extensive archaeological excavations have been made of the area; however, dramatic claims that specific sites and structures from the time of David and Solomon have been identified require further academic assessment.

In Silwan you can visit the underground water tunnel and the collection **Pool of Siloam** (in Hebrew, Shiloah) built by King Hezekiah in 701 B.C. (and rediscovered in the late 19th c.). This remarkable structure hid Jerusalem's water supply from the Assyrians and saved the city from destruction.

At the southern end of Silwan (which takes its Arabic name from the biblical pool of Siloam), just beyond where the walls of old Jerusalem would have been, are ancient overgrown gardens of pomegranates and figs still watered by the **Gihon Spring.** These gardens, originating in prehistoric times, most likely occupy the site of the gardens of the kings of Judah and may be the site of the walled gardens that inspired the Song of Songs. It was to a tent beside the Gihon Spring that David initially brought the Ark of the Covenant, the pivotal first step in Jerusalem's transformation into a holy city. Here the ark rested until the Temple of Solomon was built to house it. The Bible also records that King David was buried inside this city; if so, his tomb should be somewhere in Silwan rather than at the site on Mount Zion that has been venerated since at least medieval times. Normally, under Judaic law, burials are not permitted within the walls of a city, but the Bible records that an exception was apparently made for King David. Archaeologists are still searching for evidence of the Davidic burial site, but the Lower City was extensively quarried for building stone in the centuries after the Roman destruction, and the true location of David's tomb, legendary for its powers, remains one of Jerusalem's mysteries.

You can enter daily from 9am to 5pm for free and follow the paths along the steep hillside past the excavation site. However, under current political conditions, it is best to visit this area with an organized tour. **Sandeman's Tours** (www.newjerusalemtours.com) offers a variety of escorted Old City walking tours, including a free introductory 2-hour tour; ask at the tourist office for information. **Archaeological Seminars Ltd.** (www.digforaday.com; ✆ **03/915-0080**) and **SPNI** (Society for the Protection of Nature in Israel; www.natureisrael.org; ✆ **03-638-8653**) also lead very good guided tours. See "Organized Tours," later in this chapter, for more information.

THE JERUSALEM ARCHAEOLOGICAL PARK

The Southern Wall of the Temple Mount and the Davidson Center ★★ HISTORIC SITE The Jerusalem Archaeological Park just outside the southern wall of the Temple Mount offers an opportunity to explore the monumental ruins of the Herodian Temple Complex and later Byzantine/Islamic structures that have been uncovered here during the past 3 decades.

When the Temple was in existence (before A.D. 70), the southern wall of the Temple Mount was the main route for approaching the Temple. A wide staircase, mentioned in Talmudic writings, ended in a broad esplanade, which was wide enough to provide access to the two sets of gates that once existed, fragments of which can still be seen. From the gates, pilgrims would have

The Jerusalem Archaeological Park traces the bones of the city as it probably looked during the time of King David.

proceeded through tunnels that dramatically emerged onto the surface of the sacred enclosure not far from the Temple building itself. Visitors to the park can now stand on the Broad Stairs (the gates are blocked by later construction, but traces are still visible) and walk on the Herodian market street that ran along the western side of the Temple Mount. They can also explore the ruins of Herodian-era shops along the market street (they were part of the complex, and rents may have gone toward the upkeep of the Temple Mount) and see where the great staircase to the Temple Mount once stood, supported by a series of arches that spanned the market street below. The excavations have also uncovered Byzantine-era structures that once stood beside the partly destroyed southern wall of the Temple Mount and the impressive walls of early Islamic palaces (ca. A.D. 8th c.) that took their place.

The Davidson Exhibition Center ★ CULTURAL COMPLEX This attraction offers a chance to take a virtual tour of the Temple Mount, as archaeologists believe it might have appeared to a pilgrim in Herodian times (late 1st c. B.C. until the Roman destruction of Jerusalem in A.D. 70). Located in the ruins of an early-8th-century Islamic palace uncovered by archaeologists at the foot of the Temple Mount, the Davidson Center contains a small

THE hidden WALL

For centuries, the small stretch of the Western Wall of the Temple Mount used for Jewish prayers was the only part of the Herodian Temple Mount complex that non-Muslims could actually approach and touch. The once-important southern wall of the Temple Mount was largely hidden by accumulated earth and debris and by later buildings that rose and fell with each successive wave of history. Now excavations have made the southern wall and extreme southern part of the Western Wall accessible all the way down to the Herodian street level. At a quiet time of day, when no tour groups are trudging through, you can sit in the shade of an ancient doorway and contemplate the charisma and enormity of the Herodian ashlars. Wild capers grow out of the monumental walls. If you look up near the extreme southern end of the Western Wall where the level of earth would have been centuries ago, you can see a large ashlar on which, probably in the Byzantine era, archaeologists believe a Jewish pilgrim to the ruined Temple Mount carved the Hebrew words from Isaiah 66:14: "And when you see this, your heart shall rejoice, and your bones shall flourish like an herb." For 1,500 years, this visitor's message lay hidden and forgotten in the earth.

museum with artifacts found at the site as well as videos and computer information on the Temple Mount's history. The video and digital re-creation of the Herodian Temple Mount are interesting, but there are a number of anachronistic and questionable details (see if you can spot them). There are 1-hour audio tours of the center (which is already relatively self-explanatory) and of the archaeological park (worthwhile for those who want to understand all the intricate details). Private guides can be booked in advance, but a map and the recorded audio tour of the site, available at the Davidson Center, are sufficient for most visitors.

Entrance from near inside of Dung Gate. www.travelrova.co.il. ✆ **02/626-5906.** NIS 30 adults; NIS 15 students, children, and seniors. Sun–Thurs 10am–6pm; Fri 9am–3pm; closed Sat and Jewish holidays.

The Muslim & Christian Quarters

Church of Saint Anne and the Pools of Bethesda ★★ CHURCH Sixty meters (197 ft.) inside the Lion's Gate, on your right, is a wooden doorway leading to a hidden garden enclave where you'll find this beautiful 12th-century Crusader church, erected in honor of the birthplace of Anne (Hannah), the mother of Mary. It is built next to the Bethesda Pool, the site where Jesus is believed to have healed a paralytic. The pool would have been used by Herodian-era Jewish pilgrims for ritual purification before entering the northern gate of the nearby Temple Mount. The ruins of a small Crusader-era church can be seen amid the excavations of the ancient pool.

As the Church of St. Anne is just a few hundred feet east of the Sanctuaries of the Flagellation and the Condemnation, at the beginning of the Via Dolorosa, you might want to visit it before following the Stations of the Cross. Saint Anne's acoustics, designed for Gregorian chant, are so perfect that the church is virtually a musical instrument to be played by the human voice. Pilgrim groups come to sing in the church throughout the day, and you, too, are welcome to prepare a song of any religion—only religious songs are permitted. The church's acoustics are most amazing when used by a soprano- or a tenor-range solo voice. ***Tip:*** If you want to try the acoustics, "Amazing Grace," sung with pauses between the lines to allow for the echo, will sound truly powerful in this 900-year-old church; so will "Silent Night."

Lion's Gate (Saint Stephen's Gate). Admission NIS 10. Mon–Sat 8am–noon and 2–5pm (until 6pm in summer).

VIA DOLOROSA ★★

This is the **Way of the Cross,** traditionally believed to be the route followed by Jesus from the Praetorium (the Roman Judgment Hall) to Calvary, which was the scene of the Crucifixion. Over the centuries, millions of pilgrims have come here to walk the way that Jesus took to his death. Each Friday at 3pm, priests lead a procession for pilgrims along Via Dolorosa (starting at the First Station of the Cross in the Monastery of the Flagellation at the tower of Antonia, not far from the Lion's Gate). Large wooden crosses are carried by some of those in the procession and prayers are said at each of the 14 Stations of the Cross. The Via Dolorosa begins in the Muslim Quarter, in the northeast corner of the Old City, and winds its way to the Church of the Holy Sepulchre in the Christian Quarter.

The **Sanctuary of the Condemnation (✆ 02/627-0444)**, where Jesus was scourged and judged, marks the first Station of the Cross. It's open daily from 7am to 6pm. As you leave the sanctuary to follow the Via Dolorosa, keep in mind that each Station of the Cross is marked by a small sign or a number engraved in the stone above the spot. Paving stones on the Via Dolorosa itself have been set in a semicircular pattern to mark those stations directly on the street. Other stations are behind closed doors; knock and a guardian, monk, or nun will probably be there to open up for you. There's a restroom opposite Station 3.

The following is a quick guide to the Stations of the Cross:

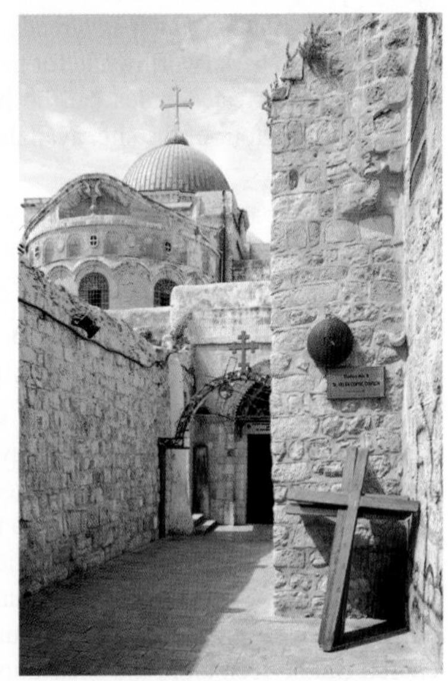

The Ninth Station of the Cross along Via Dolorosa.

Station 1: Jesus is condemned to death. **Station 2:** Jesus receives the cross (at the foot of the Antonia). **Station 3:** Jesus falls for the first time (Polish biblical-archaeological museum). **Station 4:** Jesus meets his mother in the watching crowd. **Station 5:** Simon the Cyrene helps Jesus carry the cross. **Station 6:** A woman named Veronica wipes Jesus's face; his image remains on her cloth. **Station 7:** Jesus falls for the second time (at bazaar crossroads). **Station 8:** Jesus consoles the women of Jerusalem. **Station 9:** Jesus falls for the third time (Coptic Monastery).

The five remaining Stations of the Cross are inside the Church of the Holy Sepulchre (see below). **Station 10:** Jesus is stripped of his garments. **Station 11:** Jesus is nailed to the cross. **Station 12:** Jesus dies on the cross. **Station 13:** Jesus is taken down from the cross and given to Mary. **Station 14:** Jesus is laid in the chamber of the sepulcher and from there is resurrected.

Church of the Holy Sepulchre ★★★ CHURCH After the Roman emperor Constantine converted to Christianity and made it the religion of Rome in A.D. 326, his mother, Queen Helena, made a pilgrimage to the Holy Land and located what was believed to be the tomb from which Jesus rose. According to tradition, further excavation near the tomb uncovered the True Cross, revered as the most sacred relic of the Christian world until it was

A choir sings for worshippers at the Church of the Holy Sepulchre.

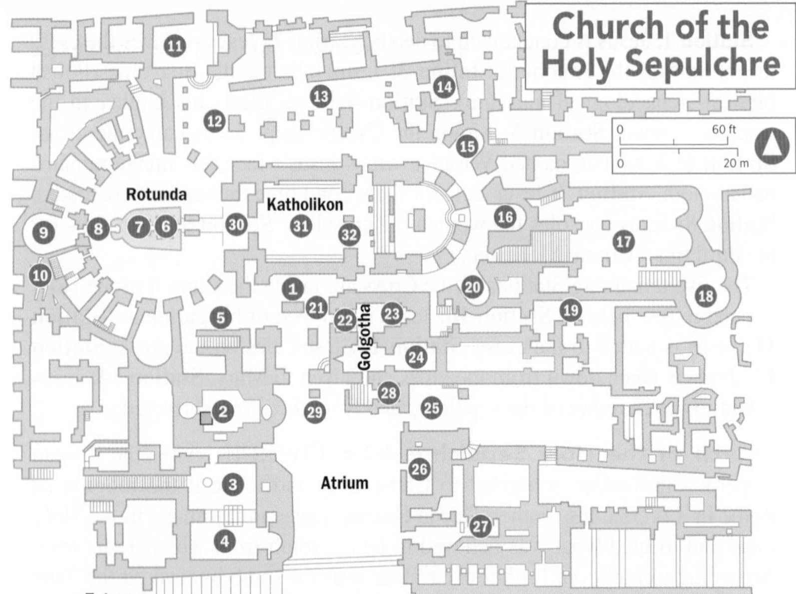

1 Stone of Unction
2 Chapel of Forty Martyrs and bell-tower
3 St. John's Chapel and Baptistery
4 St. James's Chapel
5 Place of the Three Marys (Armenian Orthodox)
6 Angel's Chapel
7 Holy Sepulcher
8 Coptic Chapel
9 Jacobite Chapel (Syrian Orthodox)
10 Tomb of Joseph of Arimathea (Abyssinian)
11 Franciscan Chapel (R.C.)
12 Altar of Mary Magdalene (R.C.)
13 Arches of the Virgin
14 Christ's Prison (Greek Orthodox chapel)
15 Chapel of Longinus (Greek Orthodox)
16 Chapel of Parting of Raiment (Armenian Orthodox)
17 St. Helen's Chapel (Armenian Orthodox)
18 Chapel of Discovery of Cross (R.C.)
19 Medieval cloister
20 Chapel of the Mocking
21 Chapel of Adam (Greek Orthodox)
22 Site of tombs of Godfrey of Bouillon and Baldwin I
23 Altar of Crucifixion and Stabat Mater Altar (Greek Orthodox)
24 Altar of the Nailing to the Cross (R.C.)
25 St. Michael's Chapel
26 St. John's Chapel (Armenian Orthodox)
27 Chapel of Abraham
28 Chapel of the Agony of the Virgin and Chapel of St. Mary of Egypt
29 Tomb of Philippe d'Aubigny
30 Latin Choir (R.C.)
31 Navel of the World
32 Greek Choir

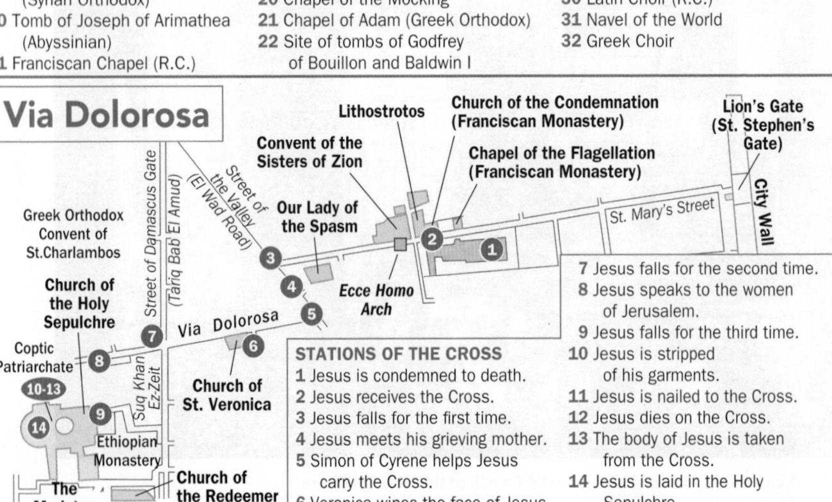

carried off by the Persians in A.D. 614. It was over this tomb that Constantine began the construction of the first Holy Sepulchre Church around A.D. 328, a complex of classical structures that was enlarged 200 years later by the Byzantine emperor Justinian. Fire, earthquake, a 7th-century Persian invasion, and an 11th-century Muslim caliph destroyed much of the great, classical church, but the Crusaders rebuilt it in the 12th century—a mixture of Byzantine remnants and medieval Frankish reconstruction that was far less grand than the original. In 1997, the renovated interior of the great dome covering the sepulcher was unveiled. It is bright, fresh, and, to some visitors, a bit incompatible with the antiquity of the place. Its design motifs had to be neutral, avoiding incorporating any of the special artistic traditions of the six rival branches of Christianity that control different areas of the building.

The church is divided among the six oldest Christian sects: Roman Catholic, Armenian Orthodox, Greek Orthodox, Egyptian Coptic, Ethiopian, and Syrian Orthodox. Each denomination has its own space—right down to lines drawn down the middle of floors and pillars—and its own schedule of rights to be in other areas of the church at specific times. The decor, partitioned and changed every few feet, is a mixture of Byzantine and Frankish Crusader styles. As the Protestant Reformation developed more than a thousand years after the building of the church, there is no specifically Protestant section.

You can observe the final Stations of the Cross inside the church—the marble slab at the entrance is the Stone of Unction, where the body of Jesus was prepared for burial; the site of Calvary is on the second floor; and the early-19th-century marble tomb edifice encloses the actual cave of the sepulcher.

If you're in Jerusalem during Easter Week, you can attend many of the fascinating services based on ancient Eastern church traditions that are held at the church. Most notable are the Service of the Holy Fire, the dramatic pageant called the Washing of the Feet, and the exotic midnight Ethiopian procession on the part of the church under Ethiopian jurisdiction—the roof. Admission inside the church at this time is by invitation only, but the ceremonies can be viewed outside on closed circuit TV. Entry to the church is free, and modest dress is required.

Lutheran Church of the Redeemer ★ CHURCH Kaiser Wilhelm II of Germany made a pilgrimage to Jerusalem in 1898 to dedicate the Church of the Redeemer, a Protestant church just outside the gates to the Church of the Holy Sepulchre. Ottoman-Turkish permission to allow construction of a Protestant church at such a prestigious location symbolized the growing alliance between Germany and the Ottoman Empire, one that would continue through World War I. The church has become a **venue for concerts** and performances of organ music; **the view** from the tower (no elevator, and a steep climb of more than 200 steps) is exceptional.

Btw. Muristan Bazaar and Suq Khan es-Zeit Bazaar. www.church-of-the-redeemer-jerusalem.info. ✆ **02/626-6800.** Admission to tower NIS 5. Tues–Sat 10am–4pm.

DAMASCUS GATE & THE BAZAARS ★

The Damascus Gate, the largest and most magnificent of all the entrances to the Old City, is the main route into the Old City from East Jerusalem. Once you are inside the gate, cafes, shops, and market stalls line a wide-stepped entrance street going downhill. Whether you take **El-Wad Road** (the Valley Road) to the left or **Suq Khan es-Zeit** (the Market of the Inn of the Olive Oil) to the right, the way becomes very narrow and confusing. Unlike the markets near the Jaffa Gate, which cater primarily to tourists, this part of the bazaar is an authentic market used by the people of East Jerusalem. You'll see stalls of spices and coffees, craft shops, bread bakeries, shops selling sneakers and children's wear, tiny one-chair barber establishments, and more.

Suq Khan es-Zeit eventually becomes the covered **Suq El Attarin,** or Bazaar of the Spices, now mostly a clothing bazaar. In other centuries, this covered market was lined with open sacks of cumin, cocoa, sesame, pepper, sumac, saffron, and all kinds of beans, dried herbs, medicines, and vegetables. Parallel and to the right of this central market street is the covered Suq El-Lahamin (the Butchers' Bazaar).

If you continue walking straight, eventually Suq El Attarin will cross David Street, and soon thereafter it becomes the excavated and renovated Cardo (the

The Damascus Gate has been in use since the 10th century. Beneath the current gate are the remains of a more ancient one, dating to the era of the Roman Emperor Hadrian.

main street of Roman and Byzantine Jerusalem), which runs through the restored Jewish Quarter. Here you will find modern, Jewish-owned tourist shops. The area, incidentally, is well patrolled by police officers.

THE OLD CITY RAMPARTS ★★

A good place to explore is the walk on the **Old City Ramparts.** You can enter the wall route at Jaffa Gate. The views are thrilling, but an entire circuit of the walls (about 4km/2½ miles) is no longer permitted, because part of the route skirts the Temple Mount. Underneath the present Damascus Gate, the Roman-era gate, to the left and below, has been excavated. Within this classical, triple-arched gate (which may have been extant in Jesus's time) there's a small museum (closed at press time) displaying laser reconstructions of the original gate; the museum is worth a quick visit if it's open.

Note: It's not a great idea for anyone to walk alone on the ramparts at any time of day. The ramparts are at times patrolled by groups of unruly local kids and unsavory illegal "guides." The circuit involves many ancient, irregular stone stairs, and although some have guardrails, this is *not* a place for young children or anyone not sure-footed.

The entry ticket costs NIS 25 for adults, NIS 12 for children and is good for 2 days (3 days if you buy on Fri). The ramparts are open Saturday to Thursday from 9am to 5pm.

STREET OF THE CHAIN ★

Perpendicular to the Suq El Attarin–Cardo market is the Street of the Chain, which runs gently downhill to the **Gate of the Chain,** the most important entrance to the Haram esh Sharif (Temple Mount). This was the great residential street of medieval Islamic Jerusalem. It starts out as a typical market passageway, but as you get closer to the Haram, you'll begin to notice (hidden behind shop displays) monumental, richly ornamented doorways of Mamluk period mansions and buildings decorated with carved stonework in "stalactite" patterns over the entryways. You can only surmise this area's affluent past; like much of the Old City, the neighborhood is overcrowded and has not yet benefited from preservation and renovation programs.

Mount Zion ★★

This important location can be easily spotted as you approach the walls of the Old City from the west or the south. The building with a round, squat tower is the Dormition Abbey, and near this site is King David's Tomb, with the Room of the Last Supper (Coenaculum) above it. To reach **King David's Tomb** from inside the Old City, walk out Zion Gate, proceed down a narrow alley bounded by high stone walls, and turn left. Although this place has been venerated as the site of David's burial, the tradition can only be traced back to early medieval times; many believe the tomb would have been located in the ancient City of David, south of the present Old City. The building is open

Schindler's Grave on Mt. Zion

Thanks to the making of the film *Schindler's List*, the story of Oskar Schindler, a German businessman who fervently worked to save the lives of Jewish slave laborers during the Holocaust, has become world famous. His final resting place, arranged by those who owed their lives to him, is in a graveyard on Mount Zion. Exit the Zion Gate, turn left, cross the road, and continue downhill around to the right to a Catholic cemetery (many of the graves have Arabic inscriptions). The grave of the often puzzling but heroic Oskar Schindler is in the lower tier, marked by the many stones that visitors leave on it (a Jewish tradition).

daily, including the Sabbath, from 8am to 5pm and until 2pm on Friday. Men should cover their heads; modest dress and headscarves are advisable for women.

Near King David's Tomb (in fact, in the same building) are a doorway and flight of stairs leading to the **Coenaculum (Upper Room) ★**, where Jesus sat with his disciples to celebrate the Passover Seder, the Last Supper. Again, the room's authenticity is based on many centuries of veneration; however, some question this tradition. It is open daily from 8:30am to 4pm.

Close by is the graceful **Dormition Abbey ★** (✆ **02/565-5330**), completed in 1910 by the German Benedictine Order on the spot where, according to tradition, Mary fell asleep before her burial and assumption into heaven. Inside the church, you'll find an elaborate golden mosaic, a crypt containing interesting religious artwork, and a statue of Mary surrounded by chapels donated by various countries. From the tower of the church, there's a fabulous panoramic view. It's open Monday to Saturday 9am to 5:30pm and Sundays 11:30am to 5:30pm (admission is free; check www.dormitio.net for schedules of services). The Dormition Abbey at times is a dramatic venue for public concerts.

The Dormition Abbey on Mount Zion.

AN EASY WALKING TOUR OF THE OLD CITY

Start: **The Jaffa Gate**

Finish: **The tour has two options: The first takes you to the Jewish Quarter and the Western Wall, the second to an unusual Christian enclave on the roof of the Church of the Holy Sepulchre.**

Best Times: **Sunday to Wednesday 8am to 3pm**

Worst Times: **Shabbat, Muslim holidays, Friday, or after 3pm when the Dome of the Rock is closed**

This meandering walk gets you to some major sites, offbeat vista points, and authentic eateries, but the Old City is a vast, intricate set of experiences, as unplanned and exotic as the 4,000-year history of Jerusalem itself. One way to enjoy the texture of this sublime hodgepodge is simply to plunge in and wander, chancing upon hummus parlors and holy sites, ancient bakeries and antique Bedouin embroideries. Learn a bit of Jerusalem's history and local lore as you move along.

The first part of the walk takes you to the Cardo, where the walk divides into two possible options. Begin at:

1 Jaffa Gate

Before you enter Jaffa Gate, which is the traditional entrance to the city for visitors from the West, check out the stones from many eras that make up the present Old City wall, which was erected by order of the Ottoman-Turkish sultan Suleiman the Magnificent in 1538. Some stones have been dressed with carefully cut flat borders surrounding a raised, flat central area (the boss) in the style of King Herod's stonecutters and probably date from 2,000 years ago. You will see this style again in the monumental stones of the Western Wall, which Herod constructed to surround the original Jerusalem Temple site. You'll notice other kinds of stones with flat borders and rougher raised bosses. These are in the pre-Herodian style of the Hasmoneans (the Maccabees), who were the last Jewish rulers of Jerusalem until modern times. You'll also see rough ashlars of the Byzantine era as well as the virtually undressed stones of Crusader and medieval times. In each of the upper corners of the closed decorative archway to the left of the Jaffa Gate, notice stones carefully carved into a leaf design, which are believed to have come from a long-destroyed Crusader church. The walls of Jerusalem, like the city itself, are composed of stones used again and again, just as many of the legends and traditions of the city reappear and are reassembled by each successive civilization.

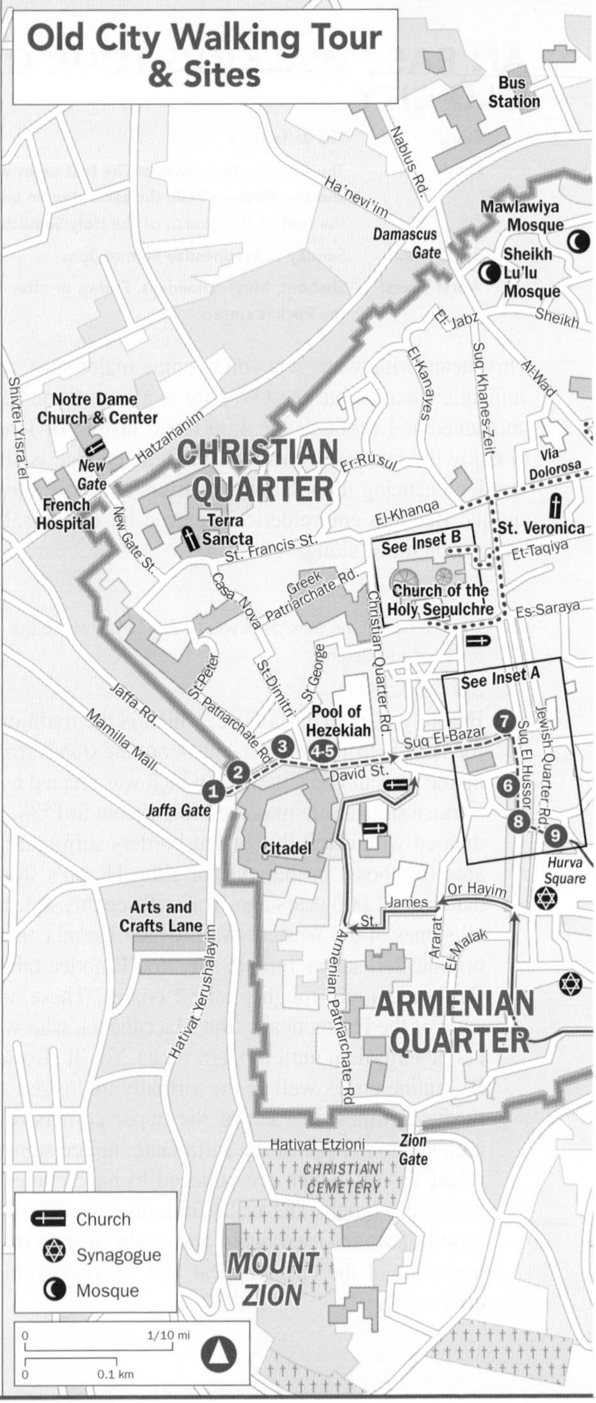

Old City Walking Tour & Sites

1 The Jaffa Gate
2 Government Tourist Information Office (GTIO)
3 New Imperial Hotel
4 The Petra Hotel
5 The view from the Petra Hotel roof
6 Suq El Hussor
7 Stone rooftop
8 Cardo

1st Option: The Jewish Quarter

9 Hurva Synagogue
10 Herodian Quarter Excavations
11 Crusader Church of St. Mary
12 Western Wall
13 Archeological excavations at the southern foot of the Temple Mount
14 Southern Wall of the Old City

2nd Option: The Bazaars & the Church of the Holy Sepulchre

9 Suq El Attarin Bazaar
10 Suq Khan Es Zeit
11 Ethiopian Compound and Monastery
12 Crafts shop
13 Ethiopian Chapel
14 Chapel of the Archangel Michael
15 Church of the Holy Sepulchre

Bus Station
Nablus Rd.
Ha'nevi'im
Damascus Gate
Mawlawiya Mosque
Sheikh Lu'lu Mosque
Sheikh
El-Jabz
El-Kanayes
Suq Khanes-Zeit
Al-Wad
Shivtei Yisra'el
Notre Dame Church & Center
Hatzahanim
New Gate
CHRISTIAN QUARTER
Er-Rusul
Via Dolorosa
French Hospital
New Gate St.
Terra Sancta
St. Francis St.
El-Khanqa
See Inset B
St. Veronica
Et-Taqiya
Casa Nova
Greek Patriarchate Rd.
Christian Quarter Rd.
Church of the Holy Sepulchre
Es-Saraya
St-Peter
St-Dimitri
St-George
See Inset A
Jaffa Rd.
Mamilla Mall
St. Patriarchate Rd.
Pool of Hezekiah
Suq El-Bazar
Suq El Hussor
Jewish Quarter Rd.
David St.
Jaffa Gate
Citadel
Hurva Square
Or Hayim
James St.
Arts and Crafts Lane
Ararat
El-Malak
Armenian Patriarchate Rd
Hativat Yerushalayim
ARMENIAN QUARTER
Hativat Etzioni
Zion Gate
CHRISTIAN CEMETERY
MOUNT ZION

Church
Synagogue
Mosque

0 1/10 mi
0 0.1 km

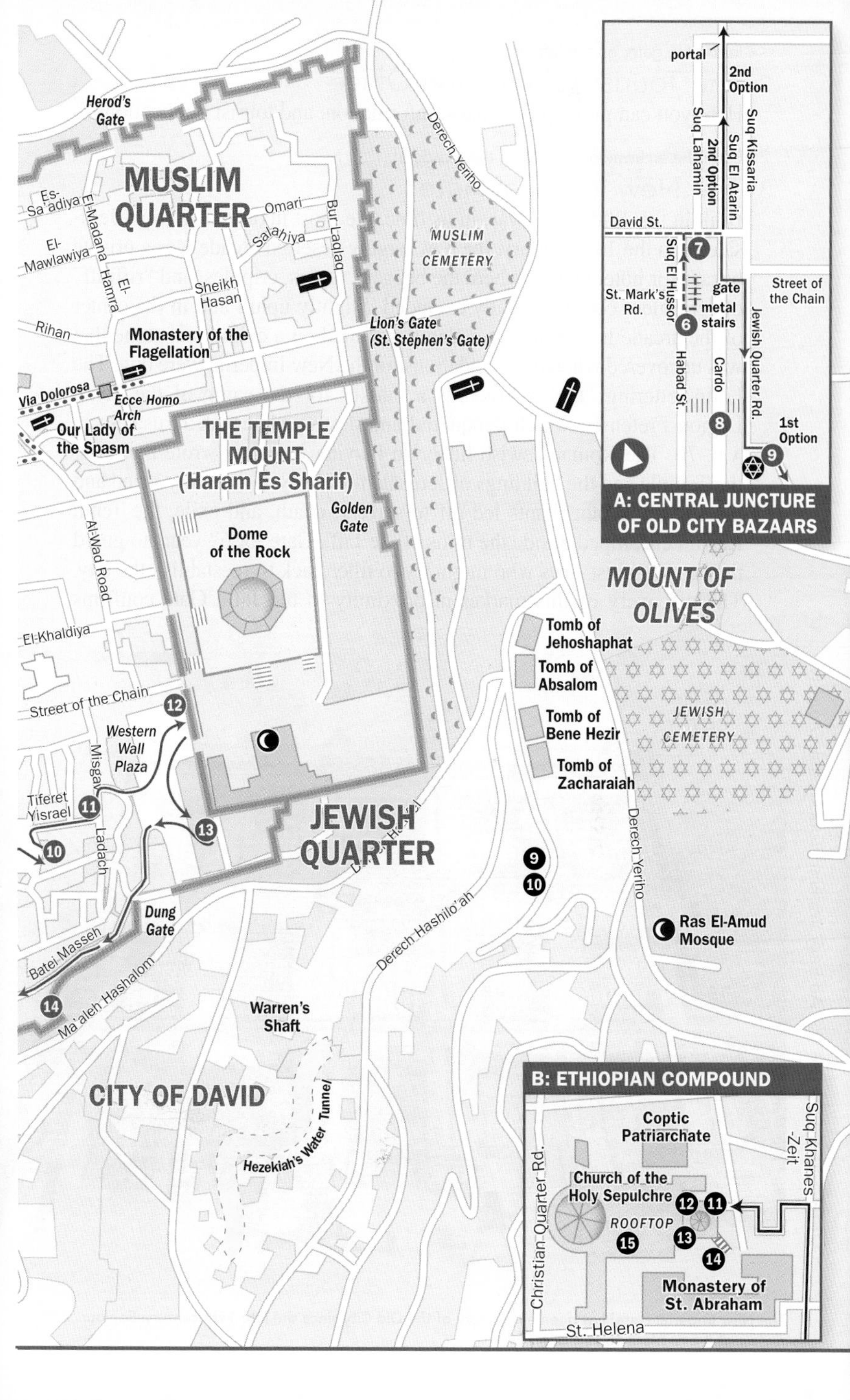

Herod's Gate
MUSLIM QUARTER
Es-Sa'adiya
El-Madana
El-Mawlawiya
Hamra
El-
Omari
Salahiya
Bur Laqlaq
Sheikh Hasan
Rihan
Monastery of the Flagellation
Via Dolorosa
Ecce Homo Arch
Our Lady of the Spasm
Derech Yeriho
MUSLIM CEMETERY
Lion's Gate (St. Stephen's Gate)
THE TEMPLE MOUNT (Haram Es Sharif)
Golden Gate
Dome of the Rock
Al-Wad Road
El-Khaldiya
Street of the Chain
Western Wall Plaza
Misgav
Tiferet Yisrael
Ladach
JEWISH QUARTER
Dung Gate
Batei Masseh
Ma'aleh Hashalom
Derech Hashilo'ah
Warren's Shaft
CITY OF DAVID
Hezekiah's Water Tunnel
MOUNT OF OLIVES
Tomb of Jehoshaphat
Tomb of Absalom
Tomb of Bene Hezir
Tomb of Zacharaiah
JEWISH CEMETERY
Derech Yeriho
Ras El-Amud Mosque
A: CENTRAL JUNCTURE OF OLD CITY BAZAARS
portal
2nd Option
Suq Lahamin
2nd Option
Suq El Atarin
Suq Kissaria
David St.
Suq El Hussor
gate
metal stairs
St. Mark's Rd.
Street of the Chain
Habad St.
Cardo
Jewish Quarter Rd.
1st Option
B: ETHIOPIAN COMPOUND
Coptic Patriarchate
Church of the Holy Sepulchre
ROOFTOP
Christian Quarter Rd.
Suq Khanes -Zeit
Monastery of St. Abraham
St. Helena

Inside the gate, on the left, is:

2 The Tourist Information Office

Here you can pick up free maps, information, and tourist publications.

Enter the archway on the left to the arcade of:

3 The New Imperial Hotel

Built in the 1880s, this was, in its time, the most luxurious hotel in Jerusalem. In the 19th century, the now largely deserted arcade was a private bazaar for hotel guests, where the beggars, lepers, cripples, and "riffraff" of Jerusalem could be neatly excluded. Slightly uphill and in the center of the arcade is a broken streetlamp mounted on a cylindrical stone that was uncovered when the foundations for the New Imperial were dug. The Latin lettering "LEG X" records a marker for the camp of the Tenth Legion Fretensis, which conquered and destroyed Jewish Jerusalem in A.D. 70. The Roman Jewish historian Flavius Josephus wrote that after the Temple and the buildings of Jerusalem were systematically razed and the surviving inhabitants led off to slavery, death, and exile, the Tenth Legion encamped beside the ruins of the Jaffa Gate for 62 years to guard the ruins against Jews who might try to filter back to reestablish the city. The discovery of this marker in proximity to the Jaffa Gate confirms

The New Imperial Hotel has been a landmark of the Old City since the late 19th century. See our review of it as a place to stay on p. 58.

Josephus's account. The once-elegant New Imperial, as it drifted into seediness, became a spot for romantic assignations during the British Mandate period. Characters played by Humphrey Bogart and Ingrid Bergman would have felt right at home.

Next door is the:

4 Petra Hotel

The first modern hotel built in the Old City in the 1870s, the once-elegant Petra, now reduced to the status of a hostel, is popular with backpackers. Herman Melville and Mark Twain may have stayed in an earlier structure on this site (the old Mediterranean Hotel) during their visits to what was then a decrepit warren of ruins filled with lice-covered beggars and crazed religious fanatics. Neither Melville nor Twain found Jerusalem a pleasant place to stay.

Enter at the far right as you face the building, climb the stairs to the second-floor lobby of the Petra, and ask the person at the desk for permission to see:

5 The View from the Petra Hotel's Roof

Be sure to show this book at the desk in the lobby on the second floor and ask for permission to see the roof. Admission is about NIS 10 per person. From the lobby, climb two more long flights of stairs and emerge from the creaky wooden attic stairs onto the roof with its strange series of curved stone domes. Turn left, go up a few steps, turn left again, and you will face one of the Old City's great panoramas—perfectly aligned, with the golden Dome of the Rock (site of the First and Second Temples) in the exact center of the vista, with the roofline of the city spread out below you. This is where photographers come for postcard views.

As you look eastward toward the Temple Mount, you'll see the Mount of Olives across the horizon behind the Dome of the Rock. In ancient times, this now-barren ridge was a natural olive grove, and its cultivation was one of the sources of ancient Jerusalem's wealth. The green area of the ridge, just behind the Dome of the Rock, is the Garden of Gethsemane (Gethsemane is the anglicized version of the Hebrew word for "olive press"), where Jesus was arrested after the Last Supper. This is the western side of the Mount of Olives ridge. On the eastern side, out of view, is the site of the village of Bethany where Lazarus, who was raised from the dead by Jesus, and his sisters, Mary and Martha, lived. Jesus may have been making his way to their house after the Passover dinner at the time of his arrest.

The Dome of the Rock was built in A.D. 691. According to legend, the saintly warrior Omar Ibn El Khattab, who conquered Jerusalem for Islam in A.D. 638, was greeted by Sophronius, the Christian archbishop, at the Jaffa Gate. Sophronius surrendered the city peacefully to Omar and then offered to lead the new ruler on a tour of his conquest. The first thing Omar Ibn El Khattab asked to see was "the Mosque of Suleiman," or the place where Solomon's Temple had once stood. The vast ceremonial platform surrounding the site of the ancient Jewish temple was one of the few architectural landmarks of Herodian Jerusalem that the Romans had found too difficult to eradicate when they destroyed the city in A.D. 70. Three hundred years later, as Christianity triumphed over Roman paganism, the Temple Mount was one of the places in the city left purposely in ruins (perhaps symbolically) by the Byzantine Christians. By the time of the Muslim conquest, the Temple Mount had become the garbage dump for Jerusalem and the surrounding area. Omar Ibn El Khattab was so saddened by the sight of the ancient holy place defiled and in ruins that he removed his cloak and used it to carry away debris. Sophronius prudently followed Omar's example. Later, Muslim authorities ordered the most beautiful building possible to be placed over the Temple Mount's sacred rock. The silver-domed Al Aqsa Mosque, on the southern edge of the Temple Mount, also commemorates this event.

Just below the Petra's roof is a large, empty, rectangular area, the Pool of Hezekiah, misnamed centuries ago for the Judean king whose hidden water system saved ancient Jerusalem from Assyrian onslaught in 701 B.C.; the pool is actually a disused reservoir for a water system constructed in Herodian and Roman times. To the north, you'll see the great silver dome of the Church of the Holy Sepulchre, built over the site venerated for almost 2,000 years as the place of Jesus's crucifixion and entombment. In the far distance, beyond the walls of the Old City, on the northern part of the Mount of Olives, the small modern city is the complex of the Hebrew University and Hadassah Hospital on Mount Scopus. To your right (south), inside the walls of the Old City, are the domes of the Armenian Cathedral of Saint James, the roofs of the Armenian and Jewish quarters of the Old City; to the south, beyond the hill of Abu Tor (believed to have been the Hill of Evil Counsel, the site of the Blood Acre purchased for a potters' field with Judas Iscariot's 30 pieces of silver) lies Bethlehem, the birthplace of King David and Jesus.

Leave the Petra Hotel and continue down David Street to:

6 Suq El Hussor

This former basket bazaar, which once sold the big, traylike olive-twig baskets older Palestinian women sometimes still balance on their heads, filled with grapes, fruits, and vegetables, is now a small covered street of ordinary shops, but it leads to a great view.

About 18m (59 ft.) on the left side of Suq El Hussor, you'll notice an open metal staircase. Climb up the staircase, and you'll be on:

7 The Stone Rooftop of the Covered Markets

Here you'll discover a different world above the bustling labyrinths of the bazaars. The broad rooftop area straight ahead covers the exact center of the Old City, where the four quarters meet. At the right time of day, if you listen carefully, you will hear the unmistakable sound of a game of billiards emanating from the large dome on your right; this dome, at the very heart of the Holy City, covers a billiard parlor. In Crusader times, this large structure housed the city's *bourse* or exchange. From this rooftop, you can clearly see the architectural distinctions among the four quarters of the walled city: the orange-tile–roofed Christian Quarter to the northwest; the dome-roofed Muslim Quarter with its many television antennas to the northeast; the new stonework of the Jewish Quarter to the southeast, rebuilt by the Israelis after they reoccupied the Old City in 1967 (this area is devoid of antennas; its inhabitants receive cable); and, to the southwest, the older stone buildings of the Armenian Quarter. Again, through the maze of TV antennas, you get an interesting chance to photograph the lavish Dome of the Rock.

Descend the metal staircase and backtrack on Suq El Hussor to David Street. Turn right onto David Street. The next right on David Street leads to:

8 The Cardo

The restored and renovated section of Roman and Byzantine Jerusalem's main market street is now filled with stylish modern shops.

At this point you have two choices for the rest of your tour.

THE FIRST OPTION: THE JEWISH QUARTER You could easily wander the streets of this beautifully reconstructed area for a number of hours.

Walk south on the Jewish Quarter Road to the:

9 Hurva Synagogue

This site was home to the Jewish Quarter's main synagogue from the 16th to the mid–20th centuries, but it has been destroyed a number of times since its original construction. Most recently, it was blown up during the Jordanian occupation of the Old City after the War of Independence in 1948. In 2010, it was rebuilt almost exactly as it stood before it was destroyed. For more on this site, see p. 110.

TAKE A BREAK

A slice of kosher pizza, a falafel, a light meal, and a wonderful Arabic sesame bread fresh from the bakery oven (with a packet of local spices) are available on the section of the Jewish Quarter Road beyond the Hurva Synagogue.

Walk across the square behind the synagogue, and you'll see signs for the:

10 Herodian Quarter

The present Jewish Quarter, on a hill opposite the Temple Mount, was the aristocratic residential part of Jerusalem in Herodian times. During the 1970s, intensive archaeological excavations were carried out here while the Jewish Quarter was being rebuilt. The ruins of large mansions were found with facilities for *mikveh* (ritual baths) and with mosaic floors ornamented by simple geometric designs (in strict keeping with the Mosaic commandment against graven images).

Take Tiferet Israel Street, which runs from the northeastern corner of the big square to the end, where you will come upon the:

11 Crusader Church of Saint Mary

In the extensive ruins of this Crusader-era church, once hidden beneath buildings from later times, explore the ruined cloister and the basilica, with a view of the Temple Mount and the Mount of Olives framed in the window of the central apse. See p. 110.

Turn right at the church and make a left to the great staircase, which descends down to the:

12 Western Wall

The Herodian retaining wall for the western side of the Temple Mount was built by Herod the Great more than 2,000 years ago. It's a remnant of the outer courtyard of the Jerusalem Temple and the holiest place of prayer in Jewish tradition. See p. 112.

Between the Western Wall and the Dung Gate, you can enter the area of:

13 Archaeological Excavations

Set at the southern foot of the Temple Mount, these excavations are accessed through the Davidson Exhibition Center (p. 120), which shows video programs depicting what the Jerusalem Temple would have been like in the years before its destruction in A.D. 70. Self-guided audio tours take you to various points along the southwestern and southern walls of the Temple Mount, where you can study the grandeur of this structure away from the crowds at prayer at the Western Wall.

From the excavations, take the road inside the city wall uphill to the:

14 Southern Wall of the Old City

Here you'll find a lovely view into the valley below, which was the site of the original City of David 3,000 years ago.

You will see a parking lot inside the city walls; cross it and turn right into a pathway that becomes Habad Road; follow Habad Road to the far end. Or Hayim Street is a left turn off Habad Road; continue uphill until the road ends at the Armenian Patriarchate Road. A right turn onto this road gets you back to the square inside the Jaffa Gate. Alternatively, at the edge of the parking lot at the end of Habad Road is a stop for Bus 38, which takes you back to West Jerusalem's New City.

SECOND OPTION: THE BAZAARS & THE CHURCH OF THE HOLY SEPULCHRE This walk begins at the intersection of David Street and the Cardo.

Turn left into the narrow, covered:

9 Suq El Attarin Bazaar

The Spice Market was covered during the time of the Crusaders, who perhaps could not bear the blazing summer sun of the region. It's actually an additional segment of the Cardo, once the great Roman north-south market and ceremonial street. The Roman Cardo, originally broad and

An iconic view of the Western Wall with the Dome of the Rock behind it.

colonnaded, evolved over centuries into the present warren of narrow, parallel bazaars including the Butcher's Bazaar, with its dangling skinned sheep heads and gutters of blood, parallel just to the left). Suq El Attarin becomes Suq Khan es-Zeit and runs all the way north to the Damascus Gate. El Attarin is now mostly populated by clothing and sneaker shops.

Follow this covered market street until you exit from the covered portion, through a nondescript portal, and continue straight ahead. The next section of the street, no longer roofed over but covered by shop awnings, is:

10 Suq Khan es-Zeit (the Market of the Inn of the Olive Oil)

Probably since Herodian-Jewish times, this area has been a major food market—the Frankish Crusaders called this the *Malcuisinat,* or the Street of Bad Cookery, unhappy with the many Middle Eastern specialties sold here. You will notice pastry shops displaying mysteriously radiant mountains of baklava arranged on top of glowing lightbulbs and flashlights; the peanut baklava filling is sometimes dyed green to approximate the costlier pistachio. There are also chewy rolled pancakes filled with nuts or sweet cheese, served in a honey syrup; other shops sell dried fruits or dark globs of fruit- and nut-filled nougat. There are also hibachis cooking

A popular bakery in Suq Khan es-Zeit.

Armenian clergymen hold Mass in the Chapel of Saint Helena.

kabobs, *shashliks,* and rotisserie chicken to go. Any of these places are good bets for snacks.

TAKE A BREAK

Abu Assab Refreshments ★★ (p. 79), a busy Old City landmark, sells fresh orange, grapefruit, and carrot juice and is the least expensive and best of its kind in town. It's a good place to stave off dehydration and fill up on vitamins, and you can order the juices straight or in any combination.

A short way along the same side of the street is a stone staircase. Climb the staircase to the top, turn left, follow the lane to the end, turn right, and follow the street around through the Coptic Convent and onto the:

11 Ethiopian Compound & Monastery

It's located on the Church of the Holy Sepulchre's roof with the protruding dome in the center. Through slits in the windows of the dome, you will be able to glimpse the **Chapel of Saint Helena** inside the Holy Sepulchre Church below; you'll even be able to smell the church incense and, at times, hear services and prayers.

The Ethiopians use this roof area each year on the Saturday midnight eve of Easter Sunday for one of the city's most exotic religious processions.

The Ethiopian patriarch, with a great ceremonial African umbrella, circumambulates the dome, followed by monks beating ancient drums—so large that they must be carried by two men—and by chanting white-robed pilgrims. The procession then retires to a leopard-skin tent (nowadays made of canvas in a leopard-skin pattern) to chant and pray through the night. This very moving ceremony is open to the public, and many Jerusalemites make it a point to attend each year.

The Ethiopian compound is spread across the sprawling segments of the roof of the Church of the Holy Sepulchre. Note that on this ancient roof entire trees and gardens grow, among them the olive trees (or offshoots of olive trees) in which Abraham supposedly found the ram he offered in sacrifice after God freed him from the commandment to sacrifice his son, Isaac. Beside the expanse of the roof surrounding the dome are the living quarters of the tiny, walled, fortress-like monastery. Visitors may not enter this monastery compound, but you can look into the lane at the entrance to the monastery: The low, round-walled buildings and trees offer a distinctly African feeling. For centuries, the Church of the Holy Sepulchre has been divided among the six oldest factions of Christianity, and in the most recent division, the Ethiopian Church, with roots dating from the A.D. 4th century, got the roof. Both Ethiopian monks and a lay community have inhabited this location for centuries (you can often smell the wonderful spicy cooking of the communal kitchen). Note the church bells hanging in the ruined Gothic arches of the Crusader-era church structure to the right and above the tiny main street.

To the left of the doorway into the monastery lane, you will find the community's well, with a shaft running down through the Holy Sepulchre Church (running water has obviated the need for the well, but the Ethiopians still have the right to a certain amount of water from it each day).

Opposite the well is a small, sometimes open door leading to a:

12 Crafts Shop

It's usually closed, but at times you can find Ethiopian crafts and hand-painted icons for sale.

From this door, continue around the corner to the large, ancient wooden door leading to the:

13 Ethiopian Chapel

This structure was probably built in medieval times. Here, if a monk is in attendance, you will be shown crucifix-shaped holy books written in ancient Ge'ez (the sacred language of Ethiopia), and you will have time to take in the paintings (unfortunately done by European religious painters rather than traditional Ethiopian religious artists) that depict the Queen of Sheba visiting King Solomon in approximately 940 B.C. Charmingly, the

Monks celebrate the Eucharist at the Ethiopian Chapel of the Church of the Holy Sepulchre.

artist decided to depict an anachronistic group of 18th-century Polish Hasidic Jews among King Solomon's entourage. The royal Ethiopian family is said to have descended from the traditionally believed union of the queen and King Solomon (one of the emperor of Ethiopia's titles was "the Lion of Judah"), and in 1935, when Emperor Haile Selassie was forced to flee Mussolini's invasion of his country, he took up residence in Jerusalem, "the land of my fathers." There is a tray for contributions at the back of the chapel.

Continue to the rear of the chapel and down the staircase to the:

14 Chapel of the Archangel Michael

In this ancient chapel, with its carved and inlaid wood paneling, the community of Ethiopian monks gathers in late afternoon for prayers (around 4pm in winter; 5pm during daylight saving time, depending on how long sunlight is). Visitors are allowed to sit on the bench in the rear of the chapel outside the wrought iron fence and listen to the traditional Ethiopian chanting, which is extremely beautiful.

The ancient wooden door of the chapel leads outside to the main entrance plaza in front of the:

15 Church of the Holy Sepulchre

Now that you've seen the roof, you are ready to journey through the very special interior. (See p. 123 for a detailed description of the church.) After visiting the church, make your way back through the bazaars to David Street and the Jaffa Gate.

WEST JERUSALEM ATTRACTIONS

Museums

The Bible Lands Museum ★★ MUSEUM This is a museum for people who appreciate beauty. Just next to the Israel Museum, the Bible Lands Museum concentrates on archaeological treasures from Middle Eastern areas beyond the land of Israel. It was founded by Dr. and Mrs. Elie Borowski, who donated their world-famous collection of ancient Near Eastern artifacts. In the words of Dr. Borowski, a noted Near Eastern scholar and consultant to museums, "Each of the objects [in the museum] has its time in history, its location in space, its meaning in religion and daily life, and last but not least, its beauty and artistry."

The collection's treasures include priceless **Assyrian ivories** from Nimrud (ca. 800 B.C.), with an iconic, delicately carved winged griffin grazing on foliage; the A.D. 4th-century **sarcophagus of Julia Latronilla,** decorated with elaborately sculpted depictions of scenes from the life of Jesus (among the earliest known representations of Jesus); and more simple, charming objects, such as an Egyptian cosmetics container in the shape of a swimming girl (ca. 1550 B.C.). The Bible Lands Museum also houses mysterious objects, like an A.D. 1st-century Roman painted linen shroud with the ethereal image of a woman covering its length (think: the controversial Holy Shroud of Turin). A fascinating gallery is devoted to cylinder seals and scarabs; lively, kid-friendly computer/video programs explore these minute works of art and offer detailed explanations. There are also constant visiting exhibitions.

21 Shmuel Stefan Wise St. (beside the Israel Museum). www.blmj.org/en. ✆ **02/561-1066.** Admission NIS 44; students and children NIS 22. Child admission is free on Wed & Sat. Sun–Tues and Thurs 10am–5pm; Wed 10am–9pm; Fri & Sat 10am–2pm. Closed holidays. English tours daily 11:30am. Call ahead for a schedule of additional English-language tours. Bus: 66, 14, or 35.

Israel Museum ★★★ MUSEUM Israel's national museum would be a treasure-trove even if it *didn't* house the Dead Sea Scrolls. But because they are the main reason people visit, we'll start our discussion with those ancient scrolls, which are 1,000 years older than the oldest previously known copies of the Hebrew Bible. Located in an area titled **the Shrine of the Book,** the exhibit that houses them not only displays pieces of the scrolls, with translation and fascinating commentary on the passages shown, but tells the story of their discovery. And what a story it is! They were discovered by chance in 1947 by Bedouin shepherds in a cave near the Dead Sea, where they were apparently hidden in advance of the Roman invasion of A.D. 67. They contain the only surviving biblical scrolls from the time when the Temple still stood in Jerusalem, plus so-called extra-biblical writings that didn't make it into the canon.

The Shrine of the Book also exhibits some of the fascinating, precious personal possessions hidden in the Dead Sea caves by refugees who did not survive to retrieve them. Archaeologist Yigal Yadin's beautifully photographed book *Bar Kochba* brings the stories behind these discoveries to life. ***Tip:*** In collaboration with Google, the museum has made a number of the Dead Sea Scrolls in its collection available in their entirety on the Israel Museum website, providing an amazing opportunity for readers of Hebrew as well as a chance for others to examine the innate beauty and restrained grace of this sacred world heritage treasure in its most ancient form.

The museum holds far more than these precious scrolls (although they are, arguably, the "Mona Lisa" of the place), so don't just see the scrolls and bolt! You'll want to dedicate a good half-day to touring here.

A historic Hebrew language scroll from Germany, on display at the Israel Museum.

The museum is divided into five main sections: The vast **Archaeology Wing** contains the world's largest and most dramatic display of Israeli archaeological finds. The **Judaica Wing** displays the world's most comprehensive, dazzling collection of Jewish cultural and religious objects, gathered from communities ranging from the Caribbean and Italy to Russia, Morocco, Iran, and India. The pavilions of the **Fine Arts Complex** house carefully chosen collections of Impressionist and 20th-century art as well as galleries of beautifully displayed Primitive, pre-Columbian, and Asian art. The 20-acre **Billy Rose Sculpture Garden,** designed by Japanese-American artist Isamu Noguchi, displays a 100-piece collection of works by Israeli and international artists ranging from Rodin to Picasso to Henry Moore. Near the sculpture garden, a very popular, intricate **Scale Model of Herodian Jerusalem,** created in the 1960s and constantly updated according to archaeological finds, is nestled against the landscape of the Jerusalem hills; elsewhere, other works of art and archaeological treasures dot the museum's grounds.

Also not to be missed: the **ancient mosaic floors of Israeli synagogues, churches, and villas,** filled with stories and messages about the cultural and religious worlds of their creators; the indoor **"Synagogue Route,"** lined with intact interiors of synagogues transported from their original sites in places as varied as Cochin, India and the Italian Veneto; the wall of exotic antique Hanukkah menorahs from all over the world; or the costumes, furnishings, and **model rooms of Jewish homes in various countries.**

And beyond the permanent exhibits, there's an ever-changing array of exciting temporary exhibits. The museum also hosts programs of international and Israeli concerts, dance performances, theater, and film. Check them out—they're often the hottest tickets in Jerusalem!

There's so much to see in the museum that you should plan a visit of many hours. Look into a special discount "return visit" ticket so that you can come back another day. Fortunately, the museum contains a stylish cafe and a more elegant, expensive restaurant called **Modern,** featuring a daytime menu of contemporary Israeli food. Both choices make meals in the museum a pleasure. All food services are kosher. A large, imaginative **museum shop** featuring well-designed reproduction items is filled with good ideas for gifts and special mementos. Parents should know that a lively, innovative **Children's Wing** is available and engages both kids and their parents, often with interactive exhibits of ancient through modern art.

Ruppin St. www.imj.org.il. ✆ **02/670-8811.** Admission NIS 54, students NIS 39, children NIS 27; ages 5–17 are free on Tues & Sat. Sat–Mon and Wed–Thurs 10am–5pm; Tues 4–9pm; Fri and holiday eves 10am–2pm; call for special hours on certain holidays. The cafe and restaurant are closed on Shabbat. Bus: 7, 9, 14, 35, or 66.

L. A. Mayer Memorial Museum of Islamic Art ★ MUSEUM Even those who know nothing about Islamic art will find themselves moved by this extraordinary collection of ceramics, illuminated manuscripts, jewelry, textiles, carpets, and artwork. It truly is eye candy of the first degree. As well, the museum is world famous for its gallery of clocks, including the Salomons collection of antique and Breguet watches from Paris. Be sure to save time for the changing exhibits of contemporary Islamic art, which often features the work of local artists. Only parts of the museum's inventory are on display at any one time, but the museum is always a worthwhile stop.

2 Ha-Palmach St. www.islamicart.co.il. ✆ **02/566-1291.** Admission NIS 44, discounts for children and students. Mon–Wed 10am–3pm; Thurs 10am–7pm; Fri 10am–2pm; Sat 10am–4pm. Bus: 13.

The Wolfson Museum of Jewish Art ★ MUSEUM Hidden on an upper floor of Heichal Shlomo, this museum displays a changing array of exceptional Jewish ceremonial objects, drawn from the famous Wolfson Collection of Judaica. The museum's antique Hanukkah menorahs, Kiddush cups, and scribal arts are on display and are a worthwhile quick stop. The collection also includes works of contemporary Judaica by such craftspeople as Oded Davidson and Danny Azoulay, whose workshops can be visited in downtown Jerusalem.

In Heichal Shlomo, 58 King George St. ✆ **02/623-7908.** Admission NIS 20. Sun–Thurs, 9am–3pm, by appointment only. Bus: 18, 74, 75; Light Rail 1.

Memorials

Mount Herzl ★★ CEMETERY Mount Herzl is the cemetery for Israel's most heroic war dead and for many of its leading citizens, including Golda Meir, Levi Eshkol, and Yitzhak Rabin. But the memorial that, arguably, draws the most visitors is that of Theodor Herzl, who envisioned and worked for the founding of Israel until his death in 1904. A large, black monolith marks Herzl's interment, and the on-site **Herzl Museum** (www.herzl.org.il; ✆ **02/632-1515**) explores the life and work of the founder of modern Zionism with an inventive new 1-hour video production. It also contains a replica of Herzl's Vienna study with his own library and furniture.

Accessed on Herzl Blvd. in the Bet Ha-Kerem section. Park and cemetery free; museum NIS 30, children 6–18 NIS 24. Sun–Thurs 8:30am–6pm; Fri 8:30am–1:30pm. Reservations required. Light Rail to Mt Herzl (final stop) and buses: 10, 16, 20, 23, 24, 26, 26a, 27, 27a, 28, 28a, 29, 33, 35, 39 or 150 to Mt. Herzl.

Yad Vashem Memorial and Holocaust Museum ★★★ MEMORIAL/MUSEUM A biblical verse was the inspiration for the name of Israel's most heartrending memorial: "And to them I will give within my temple and its walls a memorial and a name better than sons and daughters; I will give them an everlasting name that will not be cut off." The words "Yad Vashem" are the "memorial" and "name" of that verse. This intensely affecting monument and museum of the Holocaust is an effort to create a place and a name for those six million Jewish lives who fell victim to the Nazis—lives that were allowed no place of refuge on earth and whose persecutors hoped to erase even the memory of their existence.

The Hall of Names at Yad Vashem commemorates those souls lost in the Holocaust.

The memorial campus is vast, spreading across a hill overlooking mountains on the edge of Jerusalem, and with a number of different memorials. ***Important:*** All visits to the Holocaust Museum, for individuals and groups, must be reserved via Yad Vashem's online reservation portal and it is recommended to do so several days in advance: https://forms.yadvashem.org/reservations.

Start your visit with the modern **Holocaust Museum;** it fills a long, tunnel-like structure, an agonized trail of personal possessions, diaries, photographs, and videos of Holocaust victims. Audio testimonies of survivors help reveal the history of the Holocaust on a very personal level (this museum replaced a smaller, simpler exhibit originally built in the 1960s).

Next, head to the large, empty, tomblike **Hall of Remembrance,** with an eternal flame shedding light on a stone floor containing plaques with the names of the many death camps and places of murder; and the moving **Avenue of the Righteous Among the Nations,** planted with trees in tribute to each individual Gentile who helped save Jewish lives. Many of these heroes and their families suffered torture and death at the hands of the Nazis. Among those honored here are the courageous friends who tried to save the family of Anne Frank, as well as thousands of others in every corner of Europe who acted with equal bravery and humanity.

Yad Vashem's **Hall of Names** should be your next stop. It collects and preserves more than three million pages of testimony about the actions that were undertaken against the Jewish people during World War II, as well as the names, photographs, and personal stories of thousands of Holocaust victims. Visitors to Yad Vashem are asked to contribute any information they may have so that every possible victim may be remembered. Other memorials include the **Valley of the Destroyed Communities,** commemorating over 5,000 Jewish communities that were wiped from the face of the earth; and a haunting memorial to more than 1.5 million murdered **Children of the Holocaust.** In addition, there are research archives, an education center, and temporary exhibits.

After the Western Wall, Yad Vashem is the most visited site in the country. It demands a good amount of time to see (a minimum of 2 hr.) and is not recommended for young children.

On Har Ha-Zikaron. www.yadvashem.org.il. ✆ **02/644-3400.** Free admission. Headsets for self-guided tours can be rented for NIS 30 per person and are recommended. Open Sun–Thurs 9am–5pm, Fri & holiday eves 9am–2pm; archives and library Sun–Thurs 9am–5pm. Closed Sat and Jewish holidays. Must make reservations in advance. Light Rail to Mt Herzl (final stop) and various buses: 10, 16, 20, 23, 24, 26, 26a, 27, 27a, 28, 28a, 29, 33, 35, 39 or 150 to Mt. Herzl. Free shuttle from Mt. Herzl goes to Yad Vashem. Car park at Yad Vashem available for a fee of NIS 28.

Churches & Monasteries

Rehov Ha-Nevi'im (Street of the Prophets) was the "Christian street" of 19th-century West Jerusalem, and still has a variety of churches and missionary societies. From Zion Square in the heart of downtown Jerusalem, cross Jaffa Road and go up the hill on Ha-Rav Kook Street. Opposite the intersection of Ha-Rav Kook and Ha-Nevi'im streets is the entrance to the narrow, high-walled **Ethiopia Street,** with its 19th-century stone mansions. Here you'll find the splendid **Abyssinian (Ethiopian) Church.** The elegant building with the Lion of Judah carved into the gate above the courtyard is the spiritual home of the Coptic Ethiopian clergy. The lion symbolizes the meeting of the Queen of Sheba (an Ethiopian empress) and King Solomon, from whom she received the emblem, according to legend. The interior of the century-old circular church is filled with a wonderful array of icons and paintings; although none are in the Ethiopian tradition, many were chosen for their charm and native beauty. Bungalows for clergy and pilgrims from Ethiopia surround the church enclave.

Notre Dame de France, built in 1887, is at Tzahal Square, just opposite New Gate in the Old City walls. The monumental buildings of the complex, on the old border between East and West Jerusalem, were badly damaged during heavy fighting in the 1948 war. Part of the complex, restored in the 1970s, contains a restaurant, a hotel, and a Roman Catholic pilgrimage center.

Saint Andrew's Church of Scotland, its interior decorated with Armenian tiles, was built by the people of Scotland in 1929 and was dedicated by General Allenby, whose army liberated Jerusalem from the Ottoman Empire in 1917. This Presbyterian Church is situated on a scenic hilltop near Abu Tor and the old Jerusalem railroad station.

The **Russian Orthodox Holy Trinity Cathedral** is just off Jaffa Road. This white, multi-domed architectural gem in the Renaissance style was constructed after the Crimean War for pilgrims of the Russian Orthodox faith.

The **Monastery of the Cross,** in the Valley of the Cross outside Rehavia, was built in the 11th century and is now maintained by the Greek Orthodox Church. According to tradition, this medieval, atmospheric monastery is located on the spot where the tree stood from which the True Cross was made. The monastery is open Monday to Friday from 9am to 4pm. Admission is NIS 5. Bus 9 or 17.

There are also a number of interesting churches and monasteries in Ein Kerem (p. 155), and in Abu Ghosh (p. 174).

More Attractions

Beit Ticho (Ticho House) ★ HISTORIC SITE Loved by Jerusalemites for both its beauty and its history, Ticho House was built in 1880 as a private villa for the Aga Rashid Nashashibi. Around 1924, it became the home of artist Anna Ticho and her husband, Dr. Abraham Ticho, a legendary ophthalmologist who maintained his surgery there. The building today is a downtown branch of the Israel Museum. There's a permanent exhibit of Anna Ticho's controlled, powerful charcoals and drawings of the wild Israeli landscape, as

Two Dreams Restored

Israel's older branch of Hadassah Hospital is on Mount Scopus, overlooking Jerusalem's Old City. The Mt. Scopus branch, opened in 1938 in an ultramodern building designed by Erich Mendelssohn, was funded by the contributions of Hadassah members throughout the world. It was the pride of the Jewish community during the British Mandate and the embodiment of a dream to bring quality medical care to all in Jerusalem "without regard to nationality or religion." By chance, at the time of the cease-fire at the end of Israel's War of Independence in 1948, the Hadassah Hospital on Mount Scopus became a small, Israeli-held military bastion in the middle of Jordanian-controlled East Jerusalem, protected by international agreement but cut off from Israeli-held West Jerusalem.

A new Hadassah Hospital was built in Ein Kerem at the far western edge of Jerusalem, where it would be relatively safe in case fighting broke out again. Marc Chagall created 12 jewel-like stained-glass windows depicting the Twelve Tribes of Israel for the synagogue of the new Hadassah in Ein Kerem—windows so special he claimed he dreamed them while he worked. Ironically, when the Six-Day War erupted in 1967, one of the first places hit by Jordanian bombardment was the new hospital. When Chagall learned that his windows had been shattered, he promised to return and make them "more beautiful than ever." He more than succeeded.

Today, the original Hadassah on Mount Scopus is again open, and both Hadassah hospitals serve all the people of Jerusalem.

well as visiting exhibitions arranged by the museum. Upstairs, Dr. Ticho's consulting office is preserved, filled with his international collection of antique Hanukkiahs. Especially moving are the notes to Dr. Ticho, preserved under glass on his desk, from members of the Arab, Jewish, and British communities after he was seriously wounded during the political unrest of 1929. When the Tichos were alive, their home was a center for meetings, discussions, and private concerts. In that tradition, Ticho House hosts poetry and fiction readings, intimate theater and music performances, and a morning concert series. We highly recommend taking a stroll through the gardens here.

10 HaRav Agan St., near Zion Sq. www.imj.org.il. ✆ **02/645-3746.** Free admission. Light Rail to Zion Sq.

Chagall Windows at Hadassah Ein Kerem Medical Center ★★ LANDMARK One of the largest medical centers in the Middle East, the Hadassah Hebrew University Medical Center stands on a hill several miles from downtown Jerusalem. The center contains a medical school, nursing school, hospital, dental and pharmacy schools, and various laboratory buildings. The hospital's synagogue contains Marc Chagall's 12 stained-glass windows depicting the blessings that Jacob, on his deathbed, bestowed to each of his 12 sons (Gen. 49:1–27). The sons of Jacob became the founders of the Twelve Tribes of Israel. Call for information on bus routes to Hadassah, for

It took Chagall 2 years to create the stained glass for the Hadassah Hospital's synagogue. His assistant, Charles Marq, developed a special process that allowed Chagall to stain each pane with up to three colors (rather than just one, as in traditional stained glass).

holiday visiting hours, complete tours of the medical center, or for the short tour of the Chagall windows.

Abbell Synagogue, Kalman Ya'acov Man St., Ein Kerem. www.hadassah.org.il. ✆ **02/677-7109.** Admission and tour of Chagall windows NIS 25, children under 10 are free. Sun–Thurs 8:30am–4pm. Bus: 19 or 27 from Jaffa Rd.; 19 from Jaffa Gate, Agron St., King George V Ave., or Bezalel St.

Hansen House Center for Design, Media and Technology ★ ARTS CENTER Originally designed by German architect Conrad Schick, the Hansen House served as a storied leper asylum in the 19th century. In 2009, the impressive historical building was taken over by the Jerusalem Municipality and has since been turned into an interdisciplinary cultural arts center for design, media, and technology. It now houses a historical exhibition of its deep origins, a movie theatre, a fabrication laboratory (Hansen Fablab), and a pastoral garden that was expertly conserved and maintained with the rest of the compound. The Mamuta Art & Media Center and the Erev Rav Culture and Society Journal host dynamic events and exhibits that are open to the public. There is also the delicious on-site Ofaimm Cafe, which serves organic dairy dishes straight from their farm and strong coffee.

14 Gdalyahu Alon St. www.hansen.co.il. ✆ **02/579-3702.** Mon–Thurs 10am–6pm; Fri 10am–2pm; Sat 10am–4pm. Bus: 18, 78.

Hebrew University, Givat Ram Campus ★ CULTURAL INSTITUTION Located on two Jerusalem campuses with more than 23,500 students, Hebrew University is one of Israel's most dramatic accomplishments. Built to replace the university's original campus, which was cut off from West Jerusalem from 1948 to 1967, the Givat Ram campus now functions in tandem with the Mount Scopus campus, which was reclaimed in 1967 during the Six-Day War.

Outsiders visit here for the spectacular architecture, particularly of the Belgium House Faculty Club, La Maison de France, the physics building, and the huge Jewish National and University Library (partly inspired by Le Corbusier's Villa Savoye in Poissy, France) at the far end of the promenade. And don't miss the mushroom-shaped synagogue behind the library and the futuristic gym. The synagogue, with its dome supported by eight arches, was designed by Heinz Rau (one of the designers of Brasilia) and the Israeli architect David Reznik; Reznik's imprint dots the city—he designed the Dan Jerusalem Hotel and co-designed the Mormon Center on Mount Scopus.

You can stop for lunch in the cafeteria of the administration building, or at the cafeteria in the Jewish National and University Library, which contains a vast stained-glass window depicting images of Jewish mysticism.

Givat Ram campus (West Jerusalem). new.huji.ac.il. ✆ **02/588-2222.** Free university tours Sun–Thurs 11am from Visitors Center in the Sherman Building. Bus: 9, 24, or 28 to modern Givat Ram campus.

Jerusalem Artists' House and Old Bezalel Academy of Arts and Design ★ COMMERCIAL GALLERY This Turkish-era mansion, hidden in a walled garden, was an early home of Jerusalem's famous Bezalel Art School. Inside holds exhibition rooms and a gallery where the works of more than 500 select artists are sold (if you buy, they'll pack and ship your purchases). Note the beautifully carved outside doors, the crenellated roof, and dome, all icons of this Jerusalem landmark. This is also home to the decadent and charming **Mona** ★★★ restaurant (see p. 81).

12 Shmuel Ha-Nagid St. ✆ **02/625-3653.** Free admission. Mon–Thurs 10am–6pm; Sat 11am–2pm. Bus: 18, 74, 75, Light Rail 1.

The Knesset (Parliament) ★★ LANDMARK This modern landmark—called by some West Jerusalem's Acropolis, by others an airport terminal without a runway—houses magnificent mosaics and tapestries by Chagall, as well as Knesset sessions that run the gamut from funereal to the rowdiest in the democratic world. Visitors are allowed to watch the proceedings, so call ahead to check the parliamentary schedule. The entryway, a grillwork of hammered metal, is the work of Israeli sculptor David Polombo, who did the dramatic doors at Yad Vashem. ***Important note:*** **You must have your passport with you,** and you will be subject to a careful security search when you enter, so it is recommended to arrive at least 30 minutes in advance.

Outside the Knesset are the Wohl Rose Garden, and a large, seven-branched menorah (the symbol of the State of Israel), given as a gift from the British

The Knesset in session.

Parliament to the people of Israel in 1956. ***Tip:*** The Knesset may not be the mother of parliaments, but it now has a dress code for visitors: no sandals, sleeveless T-shirts, T-shirts with political slogans, shorts, or bare midriffs. Ben-Gurion himself would not have passed muster on certain days.

Government Quarter—Kiryat Ben-Gurion, Kaplan St. main.knesset.gov.il/en. ✆ **02/675-3337.** Free guided tours Sun and Tues at noon. Closed Jewish holidays. Bus: 15, 66.

Russian Compound ★ HISTORIC SITE Once, this 19th-century series of structures surrounding the beautiful Russian Orthodox Holy Trinity Cathedral was the world's largest "hotel"; it could accommodate 10,000 Russian pilgrims at one time (until World War I, Russians composed the largest block of pilgrims in the Holy Land). Today, this neglected but architecturally striking enclave serves as a prison. Around the back, near the entrance to the prison, a low iron fence surrounds a monumental Herodian-era column, abandoned in the process of being carved directly from bedrock—it apparently cracked, and its size has led to speculation that it may have been meant to adorn the Temple complex. Sadly, much of the charming Russian-style neighborhood around the prison is being demolished to make way for office blocks.

Off Jaffa Rd. (near Zion Sq.).

Sanhedrin Tombs ★ CEMETERY Go up Shmuel Ha-Navi, off Shivtei Israel Street, to northeast Jerusalem's beautiful public gardens of Sanhedria. Here are the Tombs of the Sanhedrin or the Tombs of the Judges, where the judges of ancient Israel's "Supreme Court" (during the A.D. 1st c., before the Romans destroyed Jerusalem and banned Jewish residence in the area) are buried. The three-story burial catacomb is intricately carved from rock.

Sanhedria. Free admission. Gardens daily 9am–4 or 5pm; tombs Sun–Fri 9am–4 or 5pm. Bus: 2 from Jaffa Gate or 3, 68, 67.

Supreme Court Building ★ LANDMARK The Supreme Court Building, opened in 1992, has an unusual and pleasing contemporary design that incorporates traditional Middle Eastern motifs of domes, arches, and passageways, all set up to create interesting interplays of shadow and light. Call for the current schedule of English tours, which highlight the building's architecture and the traditions of the court.

Next to Knesset. supreme.court.gov.il. ✆ **02/675-9612.** Sun–Thurs 8:30am–2:30pm; free tours in English on Thurs at noon. Bus: 6, 50,15, 66.

YMCA ★★ LANDMARK The YMCA was built in the early 1930s with funds donated by James Jarvie, an American philanthropist. Designed by the architectural firm that did New York City's Empire State Building, the building is an interesting mixture of Art Deco, Byzantine, and Islamic styles. On the first floor you'll find a replica of the London room in which the YMCA was founded in 1844. The 46m (151-ft.) **YMCA Tower** (Mon–Sat 8am–8pm, NIS 20 per person with a minimum of two people at a time) offers one of the most dramatic panoramas of the city. Notice the six-winged bas-relief seraph that ornaments the center of the tower's facade; the tower also houses the only carillon in the Middle East. Concerts played on the tower bells, especially at midnight on New Year's Eve, are one of the city's little-known pleasures. Built by Christian, Jewish, and Muslim workers and artisans, the YMCA is a meeting place for all the city's communities. The complex includes a swimming pool, sports facilities, lecture and concert halls, a gymnasium, and one of the best-located, reasonably priced hotels in Jerusalem, with deluxe and standard rooms including breakfast (p. 68).

24 King David St. www.ymca3arches.com. ✆ **02/569-2695.** There is a one-day pass for NIS 95 to use the public facilities if you are not staying at the Three Arches Hotel. Bus: 13, 18, or 77.

Other West Jerusalem Neighborhoods Worth a Visit

YEMIN MOSHE ★

In the 1850s, British philanthropist Sir Moses Montefiore, with the help of Judah Touro from New Orleans, built the nucleus of this residential quarter, the first outside the walls of the Old City, in an effort to bring indigent Jews from the Old City into a more healthful environment. The project included a now-famous windmill for grinding flour. Despite its magnificent view and graceful architecture, the neighborhood remained poor for more than a century.

Today, Yemin Moshe is a picturesque, beautifully restored neighborhood—an architectural treasure and one of the most elegant addresses in town. There are no shops, but the views are spectacular. It's a fascinating place for an early evening or winter afternoon stroll (don't attempt it at noon in summer unless you enjoy heat-stroke). ***Note:*** The steep pedestrian-street staircases of Yemin Moshe may make visiting here a bit difficult for some.

Down one of the first flights of stairs is the **Yemin Moshe Windmill,** which houses an exhibit room dedicated to Sir Moses Montefiore, a famed 19th-century Jewish philanthropist and proto-Zionist. It's open Sunday to Thursday from 9am to 4pm, and until 1pm on Friday. Admission is free. Below the windmill is the original row of **old stone buildings (Mishkenot Sha'ananim),** the first Jewish houses built outside the walls of the Old City since ancient times. Ornamented by Victorian ironwork porches, the buildings are now used as residences by visiting artists and diplomats.

A **replica of the Liberty Bell in Philadelphia** stands in the center of Jerusalem's **Liberty Bell Garden,** across King David Street from the windmill. You may wonder why a copy of the Liberty Bell is the centerpiece of a Jerusalem park. The words inscribed on the American original were spoken by one of Jerusalem's most famous inhabitants, the Prophet Isaiah, more than 2,500 years before the Declaration of Independence: "Proclaim liberty throughout the land, and to all the inhabitants thereof." It was with these words that Israel's independence was announced in 1948.

MEA SHEARIM ★★

This area, a few blocks north of Jaffa Road, is populated by Hasidic and ultra-Orthodox Jews of East European origin. It is a world unto itself, and a visit here is like going back in time to an era of religious Eastern European Jewry that existed before the Holocaust. A number of residents here speak only Yiddish in conversation, as Hebrew is considered too sacred for daily use. Some don't even recognize the laws of the Israeli government, believing that no State of Israel can exist before the coming of the Messiah.

Architecturally, Mea Shearim has the feel of an 18th-century Polish neighborhood, even more so because of the traditional dress and lifestyle of its residents. Visitors to this area are requested to dress modestly (no shorts, short skirts, uncovered arms or shoulders for women; slacks for men). Men and women are advised not to walk in close proximity (certainly not hand in hand), and visitors are advised to stow away cameras and to be very discreet in taking photographs. No inhabitant of Mea Shearim will voluntarily pose for snapshots, and there have been incidents in which improperly dressed visitors have been spat upon or stoned.

GERMAN COLONY & BAKA ★

About 1.6km (1 mile) south of downtown West Jerusalem, these two picturesque neighborhoods are filled with gardens. For many years after 1948, the old cottages and mansions (built at the start of the 20th c. by German Protestants and affluent Arabic families) housed Israelis from places such as Kurdistan and Morocco, but more recently, members of Jerusalem's American, British, and Latin American immigrant communities have been moving in. **Emek Refaim Street** (a southern continuation of King David St.) is the German Colony's main artery and is lined with shops and eateries; a walk down **Yehoshua Ben Nun Street,** which runs parallel to Emek Refaim 1 block to the west beginning at **Rachel Imenu Street,** gives you a better idea of the neighborhood's interesting old residential buildings. For those who like architecture, the quiet back streets of this neighborhood are good places to meander by bike or on foot.

REHAVIA-TALBEYEH ★

A turn to the west from King George V Avenue, at either the Jewish Agency compound or the Kings Hotel, will bring you into Jerusalem's most prosperous residential section. Rehavia's glory is its collection of 1930s International Style apartment buildings and houses made of Jerusalem stone, many of which are, sadly, being razed in order to build high-rises. Talbeyeh, just to the south, is filled with elaborate villas and mansions built mainly by Jerusalem's Arab Christian community in the 1920s and 1930s. Abandoned when their original owners fled in 1948, these houses are now inhabited by Israelis. **Hovei Zion Street** is lined with examples of these gracious homes.

Sights in the area include the **prime minister's residence,** at the corner of Balfour and Smolenskin, at the southern edge of Rehavia. And in Kiryat Shmuel, is **Bet HaNassi,** the residence of the president of Israel. You can look through the gates, but except for receptions, neither building is open to the public.

EIN KEREM ★

This ancient village, in a deep valley at the western edge of Jerusalem, is traditionally regarded as the birthplace of John the Baptist. Now incorporated into Jerusalem, you can reach it in less than 30 minutes by bus no. 19 from King George Street or Jaffa Road. The lanes and gardens of Ein Kerem (Well of the Vineyard) are lovely; the old Arabic-style houses have been grabbed up and renovated by some of the city's most successful and famous inhabitants; and high above the area, on the crest of the mountains, is the vast Hadassah–Ein Kerem Medical Center (not accessible from Ein Kerem itself). Ein Kerem contains a number of 19th-century European churches, convents, and monasteries. Most important is the **Church of Saint John** in the center of town, marking John the Baptist's birthplace (daily 6am–noon and 2–5pm); on request you can see the grotto beneath the church with its Byzantine mosaic. On Ma'ayan Street you'll find the **Church of the Visitation** (daily 8–11:45am and 2–5pm), commemorating the visit of Mary to her cousin Elizabeth, the mother of John the Baptist. It was often depicted in medieval and early Renaissance paintings as a scene in which the two expectant women touch each other's stomachs, and according to legend, the two infants jumped for joy inside their mothers' wombs when Mary and Elizabeth met. Below the Youth Hostel off Ma'ayan Street is a mosque and minaret marking the well from which Mary drew water; farther along the ridge is the Russian Convent, known as the **Moscobiyah,** a fascinating enclave of 40 Jerusalem stone buildings scattered among a wooded area of pines and cypresses. The nuns live in small, ocher-painted houses reminiscent of wooden cottages in Russia. They are open to visitors 9am to 1pm and 3pm to 6pm daily. The bus schedule to return to Jerusalem should be posted at the bus stop in the center of Ein Kerem; you may have to wait in downtown Jerusalem for up to 30 minutes until the infrequent bus no. 19 to Ein Kerem picks you up.

EAST JERUSALEM ATTRACTIONS

You can probably cover the major sights of East Jerusalem in a half-day. **Saladin Street** leading northward from the Old City walls is a modern thoroughfare of clothing shops, appliance stores, and restaurants.

The Garden Tomb ★ RELIGIOUS SITE This 1st-century tomb, discovered in 1867, resembles the biblical description of the tomb of Jesus. In 1883, the very "Kiplingesque" General Gordon (later to die in the siege of Khartoum) visited Jerusalem on his way to Egypt, and in a fit of pique over the exclusion of Protestant services from the Church of the Holy Sepulchre, had a vision that this site outside the Damascus Gate was the real tomb of Jesus. The tomb was finally excavated in 1891, and whether it is the correct place or not, it did meet some of the specifications: close to the site of the Crucifixion,

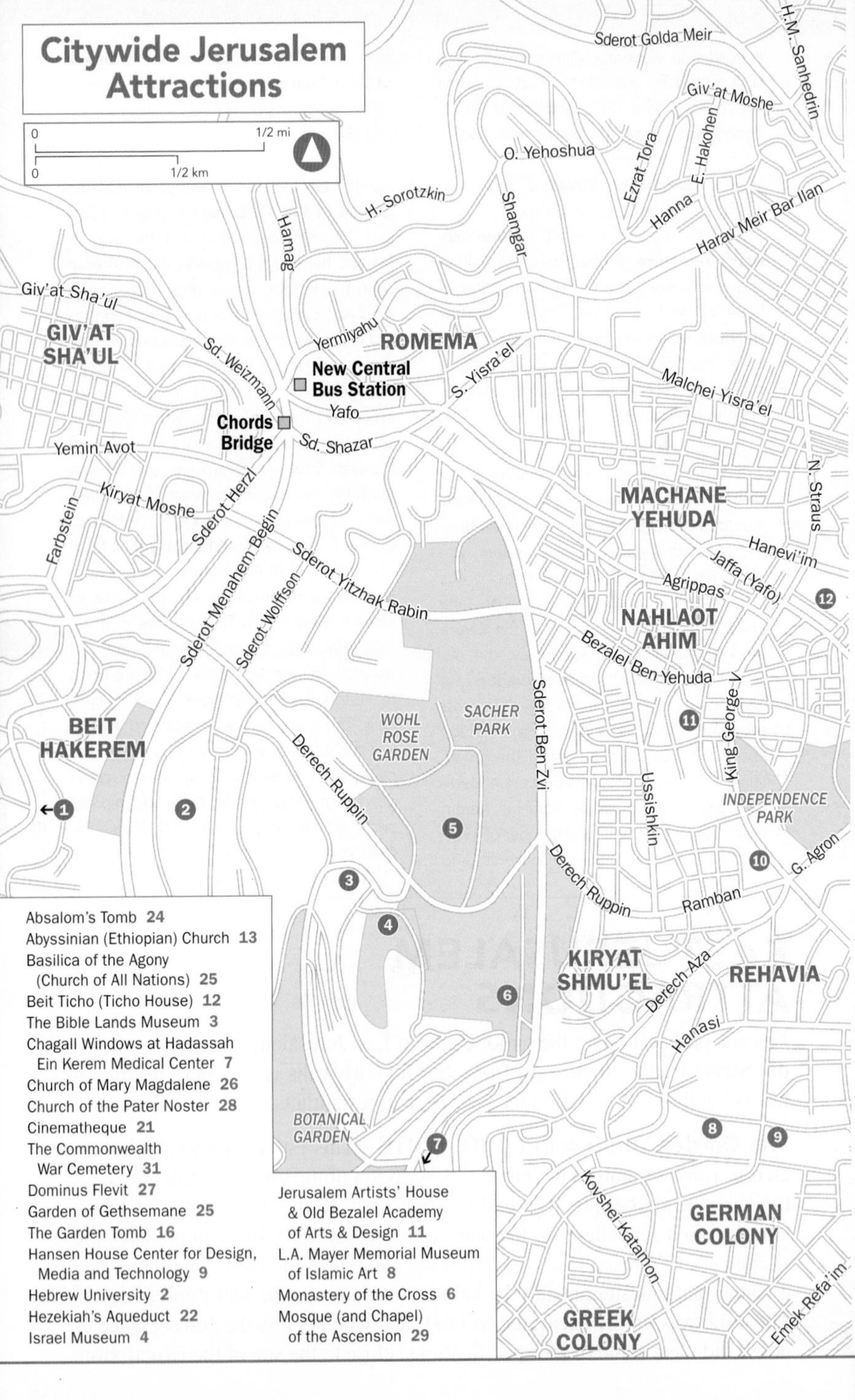

Citywide Jerusalem Attractions
0
1/2 mi
0
1/2 km
Sderot Golda Meir
H.M. Sanhedrin
Giv'at Moshe
E. Hakohen
Ezrat Tora
O. Yehoshua
H. Sorotzkin
Hamag
Shamgar
Hanna
Harav Meir Bar Ilan
Giv'at Sha'ul
GIV'AT SHA'UL
Sd. Weizmann
Yermiyahu
ROMEMA
New Central Bus Station
S. Yisra'el
Malchei Yisra'el
Yafo
Chords Bridge
Sd. Shazar
Yemin Avot
Kiryat Moshe
Sderot Herzl
Farbstein
Sderot Menahem Begin
Sderot Yitzhak Rabin
Sderot Wolffson
MACHANE YEHUDA
N. Straus
Hanevi'im
Jaffa (Yafo)
Agrippas
NAHLAOT AHIM
Bezalel Ben Yehuda
King George V
BEIT HAKEREM
WOHL ROSE GARDEN
SACHER PARK
Sderot Ben Zvi
Derech Ruppin
Ussishkin
INDEPENDENCE PARK
G. Agron
Ramban
Derech Ruppin
KIRYAT SHMU'EL
Derech Aza
REHAVIA
Hanasi
BOTANICAL GARDEN
Kovshei Katamon
GERMAN COLONY
GREEK COLONY
Emek Refa'im
Absalom's Tomb 24
Abyssinian (Ethiopian) Church 13
Basilica of the Agony (Church of All Nations) 25
Beit Ticho (Ticho House) 12
The Bible Lands Museum 3
Chagall Windows at Hadassah Ein Kerem Medical Center 7
Church of Mary Magdalene 26
Church of the Pater Noster 28
Cinematheque 21
The Commonwealth War Cemetery 31
Dominus Flevit 27
Garden of Gethsemane 25
The Garden Tomb 16
Hansen House Center for Design, Media and Technology 9
Hebrew University 2
Hezekiah's Aqueduct 22
Israel Museum 4
Jerusalem Artists' House & Old Bezalel Academy of Arts & Design 11
L.A. Mayer Memorial Museum of Islamic Art 8
Monastery of the Cross 6
Mosque (and Chapel) of the Ascension 29

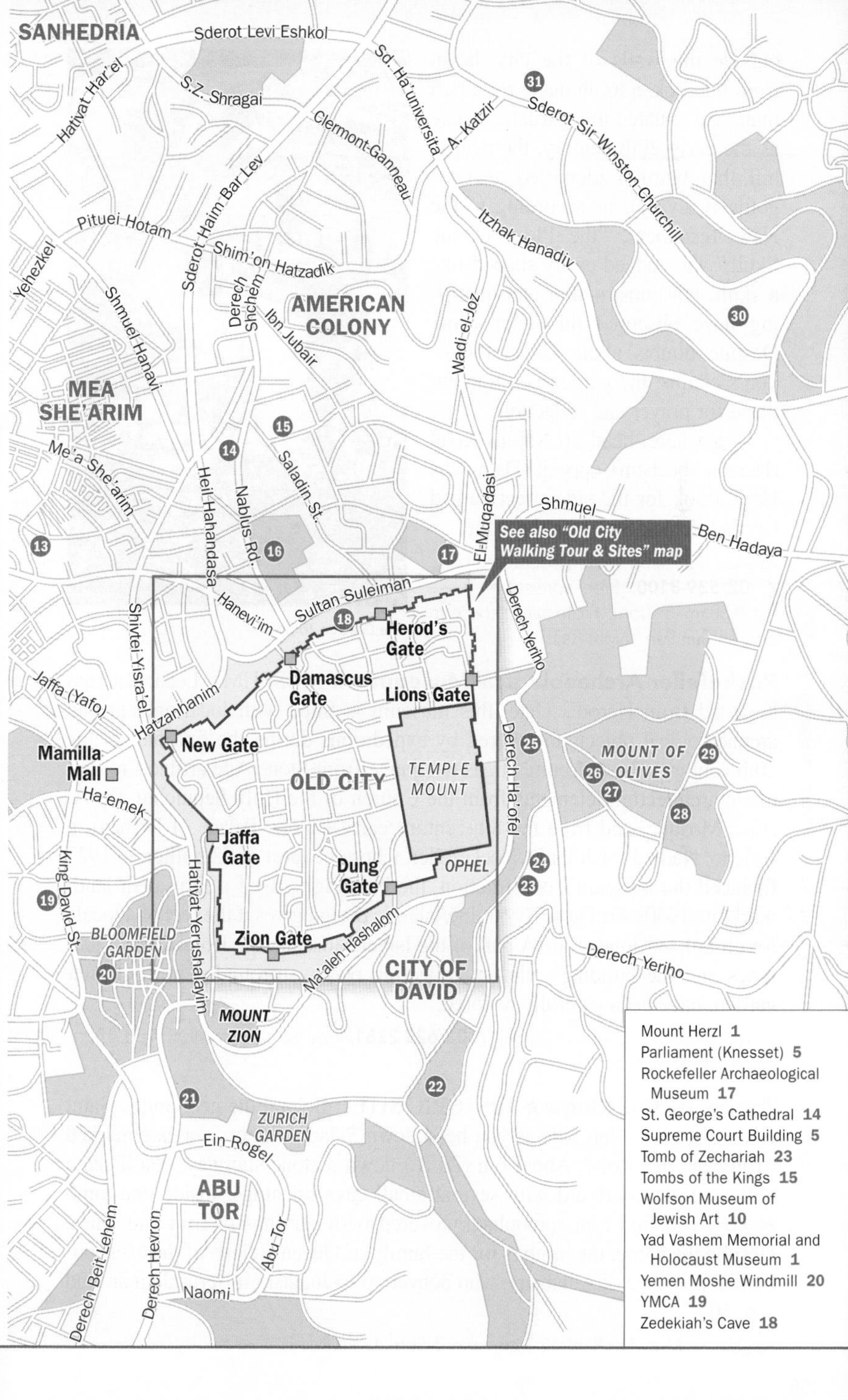

SANHEDRIA
Sderot Levi Eshkol
Hativat Har'el
S.Z. Shragai
Sd. Ha'universita
A. Katzir
Sderot Sir Winston Churchill
Clermont-Ganneau
Sderot Haim Bar Lev
Pituei Hotam
Shim'on Hatzadik
Itzhak Hanadiv
Yehezkel
Shmuel Hanavi
Derech Shchem
Ibn Jubair
AMERICAN COLONY
Wadi-el-Joz
MEA SHE'ARIM
Me'a She'arim
Heil Hahandasa
Nablus Rd.
Saladin St.
El-Muqadasi
Shmuel Ben Hadaya
See also "Old City Walking Tour & Sites" map
Hanevi'im
Sultan Suleiman
Herod's Gate
Damascus Gate
Lions Gate
Derech Yeriho
Shivtei Yisra'el
Jaffa (Yafo)
Hatzanhanim
New Gate
Mamilla Mall
Ha'emek
OLD CITY
TEMPLE MOUNT
Derech Ha'ofel
MOUNT OF OLIVES
Jaffa Gate
Dung Gate
OPHEL
King David St.
Hativat Yerushalayim
BLOOMFIELD GARDEN
Zion Gate
Ma'aleh Hashalom
CITY OF DAVID
Derech Yeriho
MOUNT ZION
ZURICH GARDEN
Ein Rogel
ABU TOR
Derech Beit Lehem
Derech Hevron
Abu Tor
Naomi
13 14 15 16 17 18 19 20 21 22 23 24 25 26 27 28 29 30 31
Mount Herzl 1
Parliament (Knesset) 5
Rockefeller Archaeological Museum 17
St. George's Cathedral 14
Supreme Court Building 5
Tomb of Zechariah 23
Tombs of the Kings 15
Wolfson Museum of Jewish Art 10
Yad Vashem Memorial and Holocaust Museum 1
Yemen Moshe Windmill 20
YMCA 19
Zedekiah's Cave 18

outside the walls of the city, hewn from the rock, a tomb made for a rich man, and situated in a garden. As late as the early 20th century, the nearby hill that Gordon identified as Golgotha (Calvary), or according to the New Testament, "the Place of the Skull," was indeed eerily shaped like a skull, but construction and quarrying have obscured this impression. Despite doubts about General Gordon's claims, the garden is a tranquil place for prayer and reflection.

To get here, head up Nablus Road (Derech Shechem), opposite Damascus Gate. Look for the side street named Conrad Schick Street on the right.

Conrad Schick St. www.gardentomb.com. ✆ **02/539-8100.** Free admission. Tues–Sat 8:30am–5:30pm; Protestant service in English Sun 9am. Light Rail 1.

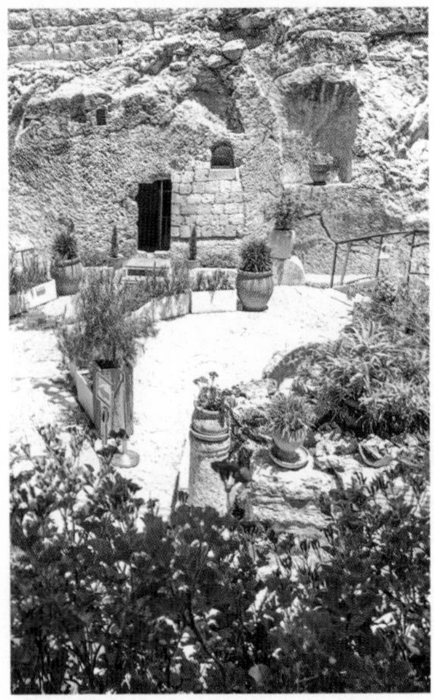

The Garden Tomb.

Rockefeller Archaeological Museum ★★ MUSEUM Located across the road from Herod's Gate, this museum is filled with local ancient and archaeological objects uncovered by expeditions during the first half of the 20th century. The museum's treasures range from Stone Age artifacts to dramatic architectural elements from the Church of the Holy Sepulchre, the Al Aqsa Mosque, and from the 8th-century early Islamic Palace of Hisham in Jericho. Named for John D. Rockefeller, whose bequest of $2 million in 1927 financed the museum's construction, the building is itself a Jerusalem landmark; its 1930s Art Deco/Byzantine/Islamic design gives it the feel of a locale for an Indiana Jones film. A part of the Israel Museum, the Rockefeller's galleries and the building's elegant reflecting pools, surrounded by a cloister garden, have been carefully restored.

Sultan Suleiman St. www.imj.org.il. ✆ **02/628-2251.** Free admission. Mon, Wed, Thurs, Sat 10am–3pm. Bus: 1, 3, or 66.

Tombs of the Kings ★ HISTORIC SITE Behind the neo-Gothic Saint George's, on the left side as you head down Saladin Street, is a gate marked "Tombeau des Rois." About 6m (20 ft.) down a stone stairway, you'll see a hollowed-out courtyard with several small cave openings. Inside one tomb visitors will find four sarcophagi, covered with carvings of fruit and vines. Despite the name, the tomb is for the family of Queen Helena of the Mesopotamian province of Adiabene, who converted to Judaism in Jerusalem around A.D. 50.

Saladin St. Mon–Sat 8am–12:30pm and 2–5pm. Light Rail 1.

Zedekiah's Cave ★ HISTORIC SITE Follow the Old City walls to the east of Damascus Gate, and you'll soon come to the entrance leading under the walls into Zedekiah's Cave, or Solomon's Quarries, which tradition calls the source of the stones for Solomon's Temple. Because of this, the cave is of special importance to the worldwide **Order of Masons,** which claims spiritual descent from the original builders of the First Temple. Jewish and Muslim legends claim secret tunnels in the caves extend to the Sinai Desert and Jericho. The quarries got their name because King Zedekiah was supposed to have fled from the Babylonians through these tunnels in 587 B.C., only to be later captured near Jericho. An illuminated path leads you far back into the caves under the Old City. ***Note:*** The cave is often closed during regular hours. Do not enter unless a guard selling official admission tickets is at the gate.

Near the Damascus Gate. ✆ **02/627-7550,** press 2. At press time closed for renovations. Call for updated information.

Mount Scopus, Mount of Olives & Valley of Kidron ★★

The northern half of the long, high Mount of Olives ridge just east of the Old City is called **Mount Scopus**—Har Hatsofim, which means "Mount of Observation." It was here that the Roman armies of Titus and Vespasian camped in A.D. 70 and observed the city under siege as they planned their final attack. The southern part of the ridge is the Mount of Olives. The deep Valley of Kidron/Valley of Jehoshaphat separates the ridge from the Old City. Traditionally, many believe this will be the site of the Last Judgment.

For Hebrew University Mount Scopus campus, take bus no. 4A, 9, or 28 from downtown West Jerusalem. Other parts of the Mount of Olives are best reached by foot from the Old City's Lion's Gate, or by taxi.

The Commonwealth War Cemetery ★ CEMETERY At the northern end of Mount Scopus is the final resting place for 2,472 Christian and Jewish soldiers who died fighting in the British Army during World War I. A memorial also honors 1,000 Muslim and Hindu soldiers, buried in separate graveyards in South Jerusalem. Open Monday through Saturday, 10am to 4pm. Bus 19, 66.

About 90m (295 ft.) from the crest of the ridge is **Mount Scopus Hadassah Hospital;** at the crest is **Hebrew University on Mount Scopus,** which opened in 1925, and is now one of the largest institutions of higher learning in the Middle East. The university is mostly housed in a modern, fortress-like mega-complex designed by David Reznik. The design reflects the university's past experience, when from 1948 to 1967 it was a besieged Israeli enclave surrounded by then-Jordanian-controlled territory. From the Harry S. Truman Institute (a pink stone building), there's a sweeping view of both the New and Old cities. Tours are conducted Sunday to Friday at 11am from the Sherman Building.

The road skirting the ridge of the Mount of Olives proceeds past the high-towered Augusta Victoria Hospital, the Arab village of Et-Tur, the Mount of

THE PEOPLE'S princess

Among the thousands of people who have found their final resting place on the Mount of Olives, one of the most recent and unusual is Princess Alice of Greece, mother of Prince Philip, Duke of Edinburgh, and mother-in-law of the late Queen Elizabeth II. Born in Windsor Castle in 1885, the great-granddaughter of Queen Victoria, Princess Alice at an early age was diagnosed as being almost entirely deaf. Carefully trained in lip reading, she was fluent in both English and French; later in life she also mastered Greek.

In 1903, Princess Alice married Prince Andrew, son of King George of Greece, and devoted her life to helping others. During the 1912 Balkan War, she worked as a nurse close to the battlefront, caring for sick and wounded Greek soldiers. During this time, both the princess and King George stayed in the home of the family of Haim Cohen, in the northern Greek city of Trikala, near the war zone. Alice was fascinated by the family's warmth and traditions. The friendship continued when Cohen later became a member of the Greek Parliament. By the late 1930s, the Greek royal family was no longer in power, but Princess Alice remained in Athens, wearing the habit of a nun as she became increasingly committed to a life of religion and charitable work.

In 1943, during the Nazi occupation of Greece, Princess Alice learned that the widows and children of Haim Cohen were desperately trying to escape deportation to the death camps in Poland. At the risk of her life, and with the help of two servants, Princess Alice hid her Jewish friends on the grounds of the royal palace in Athens for 13 months until Greece was liberated. Princess Alice died at Buckingham Palace in 1969, and in 1988, in accordance with her dying wish, was reinterred at the **Church of Saint Mary Magdalene** on the Mount of Olives. In 1994, Prince Philip and his sister, Princess Sophie, traveled to Jerusalem to receive Yad Vashem's Medal of Honor of Righteous Among the Nations, awarded to their late mother. A tree in memory of Princess Alice has been planted at Yad Vashem.

Olives, the Jewish Cemetery, and the Seven Arches Hotel. The **best views** of Jerusalem are from Hebrew University on Mount Scopus, or from the Jewish graveyard on the Mount of Olives, and the Seven Arches Hotel. For optimum viewing and photographing, come in the morning, when the sun is behind you.

Central Part of the Mount of Olives ★★ Here you'll find six churches and one of the oldest Jewish cemeteries in the world. It was this cemetery that religious Jews had in mind when they came to die in the Holy Land through the start of the 20th century. Start down the path on the right, and you'll come to the Tombs of the Prophets, believed to be the burial place of Haggai, Malachi, and Zechariah, but identified by archaeologists as tombs of prominent and noble families from the time of the Hasmoneans (Maccabees) in the 1st century B.C.

Farther up the road, on the southern fringe of Et-Tur, stands the **Mosque (and Chapel) of the Ascension** (ring the doorbell for admission), marking the spot where Jesus ascended to heaven. Interestingly, this Christian shrine is under Muslim control. Muslims revere Jesus as a prophet. However, they do not believe Jesus to be the son of God, nor do they believe that Jesus died on the cross.

Just a few steps away is the **Church of the Pater Noster** that was built on the traditional spot where Jesus instructed his disciples in the Lord's Prayer. Tiles along the walls of the church are inscribed with the Lord's Prayer in 44 languages. The Carmelite Convent and Basilica of the Sacred Heart are on the adjoining hill. From up here you can see a cluster of churches on the lower slopes of the Mount of Olives. All can be reached either from here or from the road paralleling the fortress wall, diagonally opposite Saint Stephen's Gate (Lion's Gate).

If you head down the path to the right of the Tomb of the Prophets, you'll come to **Dominus Flevit** (daily 8am–noon and 2:30–5pm), which is a relatively contemporary Franciscan church that marks the spot where Jesus wept over his vision of the future destruction of Jerusalem. Next, the Russian Orthodox **Church of Saint Mary Magdalene,** with its Muscovite-style onion-shaped domes of gold, was built in 1888 by Czar Alexander III (Tues and Thurs 10–11:30am).

There's much to see and do on the Mount of Olives, but be sure to leave time to enjoy the panoramic views you get from the summit of Jerusalem.

The Roman Catholic **Garden of Gethsemane** (Apr–Oct daily 8:30am–noon and 3pm–sunset; in winter daily 8:30am–noon and 2pm–sunset) adjoins the **Basilica of the Agony (Church of All Nations);** it's in the courtyard where Jesus is believed to have prayed before his arrest. The church's gold mosaic facade (which shines gloriously in late-afternoon sun) shows God looking down from heaven over Jesus and the peoples of the world. The church was built by people from 16 different nations in 1924. Next door, past beautifully tended gardens of ancient olive trees and bougainvillea, is the **Tomb of the Virgin,** which is a deep underground chamber housing the tomb of Mary. The tomb is open Monday through Saturday 8am to noon and 2:30 to 5:30pm.

Kidron Valley ★ The Valley of Kidron is between the Mount of Olives and the Old City walls. It runs south, between Mount Ophel (where David built his city) and the Mount of Contempt. Just under the wall here, roughly in front of Al Aqsa Mosque, are two tombs: **Absalom's Tomb** and the **Tomb of Zechariah.** At one time, religious Jews would throw stones at Absalom's tomb (Kever Avshalom) in condemnation of Absalom, who rebelled against his father, King David. Modern scholars attribute Absalom's Tomb and its neighboring structures to Herodian times—they're Jerusalem's only relatively intact structures from before the Roman destruction in A.D. 70.

The Valley of Kidron is also known as the Valley of Jehoshaphat. The Book of Joel records that the last judgments will be rendered here.

About 180m (591 ft.) down the valley is the **Fountain of the Virgin,** in the Arab neighborhood of Silwan. Water from the spring (the Gihon) anointed Solomon king and served as the only water source for ancient Jerusalem. During the Assyrian invasion that wiped out the northern Kingdom of Israel (8th c. B.C.), Jerusalem's King Hezekiah constructed an aqueduct through which the waters of the Gihon could be diverted and hidden inside the city, an extraordinary engineering feat at the time. Today, no one knows exactly how the tunnel diggers, working from each end of the project, were able to link up deep inside the city's bedrock. This tunnel saved ancient Jerusalem and the surrounding Kingdom of Judah from oblivion and changed the course of world history. **Hezekiah's Aqueduct** is still there, underneath the ruins of a church commemorating the spot where Mary once drew water to wash the clothes of Jesus. It's about 480m (1,575 ft.) long, and the depth of the water is from .5 to 1m (1⅔ ft.–3⅓ ft.). The walk (currently in escorted tour groups only) takes about 40 minutes; take a flashlight or a candle and a bag to keep valuables dry with you. You can walk through from Sunday to Thursday between 8:30am and 3pm, on Friday and holiday eves until 1pm. Entrance is free, but give the caretaker a tip. It is best to visit Silwan and Hezekiah's tunnel with a tour group (see "Organized Tours," below, for information). Beside the **Gihon Spring** lie the ruins of the oldest part of Jerusalem: The City of David (see "Dung Gate, Silwan & the Jerusalem Archaeological Park," p. 118).

ESPECIALLY FOR KIDS

The **Train Puppet Theater** in Liberty Bell Park offers programs (in Hebrew, but nonetheless interesting) for children and hosts an International Puppet Theater Festival every August. During the high holidays, Purim, and Hanukkah they host various performances. Call ✆ **02/561-8514** or go to www.traintheater.co.il for information, or check the listings in Friday's *Jerusalem Post.* Also see "Jerusalem After Dark," later in this chapter. The **Israel Museum**'s lively **Children's Wing** has extremely engaging exhibits, many of them hands-on, including workshops in recycled materials. Also on site: a library of children's books you can sit and read together. See "Museums," earlier in this chapter.

Gottesman Family Aquarium ★ AQUARIUM The only aquarium in the world that focuses on the preservation of Israel's aquatic habitats, the Gottesman Family Aquarium is located near the Biblical Zoo, making it a possible two-in-one-day visit for families; just be aware, it would be a packed day! Also note, the aquarium is 1.5 km (about a mile) from the zoo's entrance gate, so visitors can either drive or walk along the access road that begins at the end of the zoo's parking area (buses only reach as far as the zoo's main entrance). Exhibits at the aquarium showcase marine life from the Mediterranean Sea, the Red Sea, and the Sea of Galilee in an impressive 7,000 square meter space with tanks holding more than 2.5 million liters of seawater space. Thousands of fish, sharks, sea stars, jellyfish, turtles and many other magnificent creatures from around the world are housed here, split between dozens of aquariums of various sizes. Be sure to visit the exceptional Butterfly Pavilion on the premises, a hot and humid oasis that's a magical simulation of a rainforest; visitors get a peek into the lives of butterflies in all their stages of life.

1 Aharon Shulov St. www.israel-aquarium.org.il. ✆ **073/339-9000.** Admission adults NIS 57, children ages 3–18 NIS 47. Sun–Thurs 9am–6pm; Fri and holiday eves 9am–4pm; Sat and holidays 9am–6pm. Tickets must be booked in advance online. Bus: 17, 26A, 33, 517.

The Time Elevator ★ TOUR This is a 30-minute, multimedia, semi-virtual-reality history of Jerusalem, presented in an auditorium refitted with special chairs and a floor that provides special motion effects. It's not good for younger children or those who get motion sickness. The presentation itself is interesting, especially for children. The show is repeated about every 40 minutes.

Located in the Mamilla Mall, Alrov Mamilla Ave, indoor complex. www.time-elevator.co.il. ✆ **02/624-8381,** ext. 0. Admission NIS 54 per person, 5 and up. Sun–Tues 10am–5:20pm; Fri 10am–2pm. Advance reservations required. Bus 13 or Light Rail 1.

The Tisch Family Zoological Gardens ★ ZOO A beautifully landscaped site at the western edge of the city, the Tisch Zoo boasts a state-of-the-art open design that blends into the surrounding countryside. Emphasis is on creatures mentioned in the Bible or native to Israel, but there are also many animals, large and small, from the far corners of the world (the giraffe herds are world famous). Kids enjoy the friendly waterfowl and the camel encampment (camel- and pony-ride facilities are planned). There is a refreshment facility on the grounds. The zoo is at its best late in the day or in cooler weather, when the animals are most active. Prepare for a 10-minute walk from the bus stop. A zoo train takes you through the high points of the park, but accompanying explanations are generally in Hebrew. The zoo train does not operate on Shabbat. Admission ends an hour before closing time.

Manahat, Jerusalem. www.jerusalemzoo.org.il. ✆ **02/675-0111.** Admission NIS 63 adults, NIS 49 children 3–18, free for kids under 3 years old. Sun–Thurs 9am–6pm, Fri 9am–4pm, Sat and holidays 9am–6pm. Bus: 17, 26A, 33, 517.

ORGANIZED TOURS

As a general rule of thumb, make certain that your tour guide is officially licensed by the Ministry of Tourism. The licensing process is an extremely rigorous one, so those who get one are usually quite well-versed in Israeli history. Also, on any guided tour that includes holy places, you must dress modestly. This means no shorts (men or women), no sleeveless shirts or blouses, and women should have a head covering handy.

Families enjoying the "Dig for a Day" program of Archaeological Seminars Ltd.

GUIDED WALKING TOURS Free, and usually quite interesting, walking tours of the Old City are offered by **Sandeman's New Jerusalem Tours** (www.newjerusalemtours.com). They leave from in front of the **Tourist Information Office** at Jaffa Gate daily at 11am and 2pm. Since the guides are relying entirely on tips for payment, they do their best to present their information in a compelling fashion. The 2-hour tour covers all four Old City quarters, with a relatively limited amount of time spent in each.

For a more in-depth tour, various local operators run programs that emphasize the city's history and archaeology. Most of these are 3-hour excursions in small groups with other visitors—but remember, you'd need a long, very full day to really get an idea of all the city's quarters and traditions. **Archaeological Seminars Ltd.** will guide you through the Jewish Quarter, Temple Mount, the Temple Mount excavations, the City of David (Ophel), or the Christian and Muslim quarters of the Old City. Tours run Sunday to Thursday and cost NIS 28 for adults, NIS 14 for children. For information on schedules, various itineraries, and the chance to "Dig for a Day" at an archaeological site, consult their website or call (www.digforaday.com; ✆ **03/915-0080**).

For other tours, see our suggestions on p. 119.

OUTDOOR PURSUITS & SPORTS

JOGGING Jerusalem, with its many hills, is not the easiest place for unplanned jogging. The Tayelet (Promenade) in southern Jerusalem, overlooking the entire city, offers traffic-free pathways and a dramatic site (bus no. 8). The roads and pathways in the Bloomfield Gardens, just above Yemin Moshe, are also good options. Jogging in these places at night is not advised.

SWIMMING In summer, reserving a hotel with a pool can be a good investment. However, there are public pools across the city (***Note:*** They get *packed* on especially scorching days). One of the most reasonably priced, if you're going for more than a quick dip, is the vast country club pool at **Ramat Rachel Hotel** (✆ **02/670-2555**). It's open from 6am to 9pm in summer only. If you decide to go by taxi, or have limited time, an in-town pool at a hotel would be a better choice.

The more expensive option is to pay the visitors' rate to use a pool at one of the city's hotels. In central Jerusalem, the **Inbal Hotel** (✆ **02/675-6666**) has a covered pool open year-round. The **David Citadel Hotel** (✆ **02/621-1111**) has a large, heated outdoor pool open year-round, with direct water access from indoors. Prices are higher Friday and Saturday. Most hotel pools are open 10am to 6pm, and many fall under the chilly shadows of surrounding buildings, especially in late afternoon.

THE SHOPPING SCENE

Jewelry, Judaica, and local Israeli crafts and art objects are the most worthwhile buys in Jerusalem. Many shops in the Ben-Yehuda area, as well as in the Jewish Quarter of the Old City, sell modern menorahs, mezuzahs, dreidels, candleholders, and embroidered yarmulkes, as well as objects for Passover, Succot, Shabbat, and synagogue services. ***Tip:*** It is recommended to try to bargain a bit at most tourist shops in West Jerusalem.

Many of our listings are for places where you can find handmade items and purchase them directly from the artisans who make them. Merchants are generally cooperative about packing your purchases securely for shipping or for the plane ride home.

Shopping A to Z

ART

Israel Museum Gift Shops ★★ An exciting selection of posters is on sale here. Also, check out reproductions of Anna Ticho's charcoal and pen-and-ink landscapes, Shalom of Safed's vibrant primitive paintings, and high-quality reproductions of Judaica and antiquities at reasonable prices. Ruppin St. ✆ **02/670-8811.** A smaller Israel Museum Gift Shop is in downtown Jerusalem at Beit Ticho (p. 148).

Jerusalem Artists' House Gallery ★ This cooperative gallery, sponsored by the Jerusalem Municipality and the Israeli government, represents more than 500 juried Israeli artists, ranging from the famous and established to the newest and most promising. The staff of the Artists' House can put you in touch with any artist whose work interests you and will arrange for the shipping of your purchase. Open Sunday to Thursday 10am to 1pm and 4 to 7pm, Friday 10am to 1pm, and Saturday 11am to 2pm. 12 Shmuel Ha-Nagid St. ✆ **02/625-2636.**

BOOKSTORES

Most bookstores carrying a selection of books in English are within 2 blocks of Zion Square. Look for the well-stocked **Steimatzky** chain, with its main branch at 39 Jaffa Road (at Zion Square). It sells a good selection of new and remaindered English- and foreign-language periodicals, books, and guidebooks to various regions of the country. Prices are reasonable to high, but look for interesting remainder tables.

For used books, **Sefer Ve Sefel Bookshop** (4 Yavetz St., upstairs; ✆ **02/624-8237**) has the largest selection of English-language fiction in town, and current guidebooks. The **Book Gallery/Books on Schatz** (6 Schatz St., off King George St., a block south of Hillel St.) is extremely well stocked, with vast subterranean browsing rooms; a few armchairs encourage reading while you browse. **Clal Center Bookstore** (97 Jaffa Rd.) has a good, interesting stock of quality used English books. **Tmol Shilshom Bookstore Café** (in a rear courtyard off 5 Yoel Salomon St.; ✆ **02/623-2758**) has a small, eclectic collection of new and used books and magazines and remains open until midnight; it's mainly a cafe/restaurant with a wonderful program of readings and live music. The **Bookshelf** (2 Jewish Quarter Rd.; ✆ **02/627-3889**), in the Jewish Quarter of the Old City, has especially helpful management. **Stein Books** (52 King George St.; ✆ **02/624-7877**) specializes in Jewish studies.

> **Shopping Rules**
>
> You'll find attention-grabbing items in Judaica and tourist shops all over the Ben-Yehuda Mall area and in Mea Shearim (p. 154). Remember that bargaining (or politely asking for a discount) has become customary in most of these shops, and that prices for identical and nearly identical items can vary greatly from store to store. For this reason, many of Jerusalem's tourist/Judaica stores display signs that say in Hebrew, if not English: NO REFUNDS, RETURNS, OR EXCHANGES. So, comparison-shop before making a purchase: Once you buy it, it's yours.

The **American Colony Hotel Bookshop,** at the American Colony Hotel, stocks works by many Middle Eastern writers and hosts publishing parties and talks by Palestinian, Israeli, and international writers.

CERAMICS

The outer walls of the Dome of the Rock are covered with turquoise and cobalt-blue ceramic tiles in the Persian tradition. Two world-famous Armenian pottery workshops, the Karakashian family's **Jerusalem Pottery** and the Balian family's **Palestinian Armenian Pottery,** listed below, were brought to Jerusalem at the start of the British Mandate in order to maintain the Dome of the Rock's lavish facade. Their traditional Anatolian hand-painted ceramics have come to be regarded as a national treasure: They've had exhibitions in Israeli and world museums, and in 2004 the State of Israel honored them with a series of commemorative postage stamps.

Darian Armenian Ceramics ★★ ArAman Darian, who emigrated from the former Soviet Armenia, where he studied traditional calligraphy and design, is a relative newcomer to the field of Armenian ceramics. Here you'll find soup tureens, cups and plates, tiles, and lamp bases, all hand-painted in the Armenian tradition but with new color combinations and graceful designs that are uniquely Darian's. He'll also design to your specifications. Open Sunday to Thursday 10am to 6pm and Friday 10am to 3pm. 12 Shlomzion HaMalka St. ✆ **02/623-4802.**

Jerusalem Pottery ★★ Near the sixth Station of the Cross (p. 123) in the Old City, this shop, run by the renowned Karakashian family, is notable for individual plates and tiles decorated with lovely traditional bird, animal, and floral designs, as well as for its interpretations of ancient Jewish and Christian motifs. Standards of craftsmanship are the highest, with careful hand painting (tile designs are incised) and vibrant colors. There's also a selection of plates, cups, and even ceramic mezuzah cases for doorposts. Jerusalem Pottery is open Monday to Saturday from 9:30am to 5pm; always call to check. 15 Via Dolorosa. www.jerusalempottery.biz. ✆ **02/626-1587.**

Palestinian Armenian Pottery ★★ This workshop's chief artist, Marie Balian, is famous for her rich, multi-tile ceramic panels, which are hand-painted visions of Persian gardens, desert oases, and Middle Eastern motifs. In 1992, the Smithsonian Museum in Washington, D.C., mounted *Views of Paradise,* a special exhibit of 22 of Balian's creations; her panels also adorn the Succot Patio at the house of the President of Israel. Palestinian Armenian Pottery produces a steady stream of traditional plates, bowls, teapots, pitchers, name and address tiles, and smaller panels. Monday to Saturday from 9am to 4pm; call ahead and check on hours. 14 Nablus Rd. www.armenianceramics.com. ✆ **02/628-2826.**

CHOCOLATE

Sweet 'N Karem ★ For handmade chocolates (and ice cream), this little gem, run by Ofer and Sima (who taught themselves), is reason enough to come out and explore the already charming western fringe neighborhood of Ein Kerem (p. 155). In addition to being rich and filled with exotic ingredients, the chocolates here are all certified kosher. Open daily 9am to 6pm. At the crossroads in the center of Ein Kerem. ✆ **050/202-4481.** Bus: 17.

CRAFTS

8 Ceramists Altogether ★★ For contemporary handmade ceramics, this pottery cooperative in West Jerusalem will give you a good idea of the current Israeli ceramics scene. Look for beautiful ceramic Hanukkah menorahs and Passover Seder plates as well as functional and decorative pottery made by the cooperative's artists. 11 Yoel Salomon Mall. ✆ **02/624-7250.**

Cadim Gallery ★★★ This cooperative gallery displays the work of award-winning potters and a range of excellent functional pottery and inventive Judaica by some of the country's best ceramists. 4 Yoel Salomon Mall. ✆ **02/623-4869.**

Guild of Ceramists ★★ EE Eleven ceramists are represented in this cooperative shop at the Hillel Street end of the Yoel Salomon Mall. Among other things, many of these artisans will custom design tiles. 27 Salomon St. ✆ **02/624-4065.**

House of Quality ★★ Across the street from and midway between the Mount Zion Hotel and the Cinémathèque, this conglomeration of craft workshops offers all sorts of delights. Keep an eye out for the witty, unique ceramic Judaica of Gaia Smith and the silver creations of Oded Davidson, but all of the craftspeople at this center are of very high caliber. Craftspeople are in their workshops at varying times. Just around the corner, in Saint Andrew's Guest House, you can also visit **Sunbula,** which sells traditional Palestinian crafts and embroidery. Hours vary for each individual artist's studio. 12 Hebron Rd. No phone. Bus: 4, 5, 6, 7, 8, 18, 21, or 48 and walk to Hebron Rd.

FOOD

Machane Yehuda Produce Market ★★★ One of the great traditional food markets left in the Western world, Machane Yehuda is labyrinths and caves filled with mountains of edible wonders: luscious Israeli tangerines, grapes, tomatoes, and freshly picked basil; polished eggplants; hundreds of varieties of olives; freshly baked breads and pastries; ladies plucking chickens; and dozens of tiny holes-in-the-wall serving authentic market snacks. It's also becoming dotted with great little fashion boutiques, gourmet food shops,

There's an astonishing variety of food at the Machane Yehuda Produce Market.

and both simple and expensive eateries. Sunday to Thursday early morning to dusk; Friday early morning to early afternoon. Closed only for Shabbat and holidays. Btw. Jaffa Rd. and Agripas St. Light Rail: Machane Yehuda.

GIFTS

Lifeline for the Old ★ This shop sells toys, needlework, clothing, jewelry, Judaica, and crafts handmade by Jerusalem's senior citizens, and is a source of pleasure for both craftspeople and customers. Sales and donations keep this remarkable institution afloat. The workshops, which help provide a meaningful creative outlet for Jerusalem's elderly, can be visited Sunday to Thursday from 8:30am to 11:30pm. Prices are very reasonable, and the items are guaranteed to charm. Open Sunday to Thursday 9am to 4pm and Friday 9 to 11am. 14 Shivtei Israel St. ✆ **02/628-7829.**

GLASS

Nekker Glass Company ★★ This workshop, near the Mirrer Yeshiva on the northern fringe of Mea Shearim, revived the ancient glassblowing traditions that began in this part of the world more than 2,000 years ago. The Nekker family arrived in Jerusalem from Baghdad in the early 1950s and set up a small glass factory with both Arab and Jewish glassblowers who now create designs and techniques from ancient times. They have even developed ways to reproduce soft, ancient patinas in a variety of colors. At Nekker's tiny workshop, you can watch the glassblowers creating delicate, affordable objects. The stock is on sale for a fraction of what it costs in retail shops. A special line of museum reproductions based on the shapes and patinas of delicate Roman glass is a bit higher in price. Staff will pack your purchases securely for travel. Call ahead to be sure it's open. 6 Bet Israel St. ✆ **02/582-9683.**

JEWELRY

Hedya Jewelers and the Sarah Einstein Collection ★★ Here you'll find jewelry, often made from small, exquisite component pieces of antique objects such as Yemenite wedding necklaces or Persian headdresses. Hedya's own custom-made jewelry, Hands of Fatima, and Judaica are exquisite. Special orders are welcome. 23 Hillel St. (in the passageway btw. Hillel and Shamai sts.). ✆ **02/622-1151.**

Ophir ★★★ For a half-century, Jerusalemites and visitors have been fans of this shop's delicate jewelry designs that echo Victorian, Edwardian, Art

Deco, and Middle Eastern styles, all created by the owner, Avraham Lor. Prices are extremely reasonable, and Lor's stock is augmented by many unusual antique and semi-antique items. Much of the jewelry collection is still to be seen in the tiny "back-room" workshop. Open Sunday, Monday, Wednesday, and Thursday 9am to 1pm and 4 to 7pm and Tuesday and Friday 9am to 1pm only. 38 Jaffa Rd. www.ophir-jewelry.com. ✆ **02/624-9078.**

Exquisite jewelry on offer at Ophir.

JUDAICA

Archie Granot, Papercuts ★★ Traditional Jewish papercuts began to develop as a folk art in Europe and North Africa. In many homes it was the custom to hang a delicately cut piece of paper (called a *mizrach,* from the Hebrew word for "east") on the eastern wall of a room, to indicate the direction of Jerusalem. Archie Granot has raised this folk tradition to new levels with his extraordinary multi-layer contemporary designs. Prices can range from a few hundred to several thousand dollars. Granot's works are in the collections of the Israel Museum, the Victoria and Albert Museum, the Jewish Museum of New York, and the Philadelphia Museum of Jewish Art. 1 Agron St. www.archiegranot.com. ✆ **02/625-2210.**

Danny Azoulay ★★ A highly skilled craftsperson who came to Israel from Morocco as a small child, Danny Azoulay specializes in porcelain and fine ceramic Judaica, and his tiny shop is filled with hand-painted Hanukkah

THE ART OF bargaining

If you find something you like, you must bargain for it. The main rules are to be courteous and keep your cool. Appear politely unsure the object is something you really want. It often helps if you're with a friend who pretends you're late for a bus or an appointment—you might even pretend to walk away. If a merchant doesn't come down on his price, don't panic and pay full price. On the other hand, never back a merchant into a corner: Never argue: "$25? I saw the same thing on Ben Yehuda Street for $5!" This leaves the merchant no honorable alternative but to say, "Okay, go to Ben Yehuda Street!" The chance is that you'll find the same thing or something similar close by; if not, if you leave gracefully, you can always come back and try again. Much depends on how badly the merchant needs to convert some of his stock to cash on the day of your visit. If nothing else, after a few hours of browsing and bargaining, you'll have a new appreciation for the intricacies of the Middle East peace process.

Those in the market for a *ketubbot* (marriage contract) head to Danny Azoulay. The boutique works with the top calligraphers and scribal artists in the business.

menorahs, charity boxes laced with brass or silver designs, mezuzahs, spice boxes, and dreidels. The shop also sells illuminated manuscripts and *ketubbot* (marriage contracts) by some of **Israel's finest scribal** artists, such as **Amalya Nini Goldstein.** 5 Yoel Salomon St. ketubahazoulayart.com. ✆ **02/623-3918.**

Judaicut ★ In this small shop, you can find a selection of papercuts, calligraphy, and *ketubbot* (marriage contracts) by leading Israeli calligraphers and artists. Prices are reasonable. Special orders can be commissioned. 21 Yoel Salomon St. judaicut.com. ✆ **02/623-3634.**

THE OLD CITY MARKETS

A major attraction for visitors, the Old City markets have many shops offering such local products as olive-wood chess and nativity sets, rosaries, carved camels, boxes, and olive-wood Christmas tree ornaments—a great buy at about two for NIS 16. You'll also find heavy, hand-blown, bubble-filled glassware from Hebron, inlaid wooden boxes from Egypt and Syria, mother-of-pearl objects from Jordan, dramatic Palestinian embroidery, new and inexpensive imitations of antique Bedouin, Yemenite, and Bedouin-style jewelry, and locally made leather goods. ***Tip:*** The markets are filled with all kinds of Arabic desserts, spices, and snacks, all of which should be part of the Old City experience!

Old tribal Bedouin flat-weave rugs and weavings can be found in a few shops in the Arab bazaar around the Christian Quarter Road. In older, more expensive pieces, look for bold diamond patterns and rich, subdued reds, browns, yellows, and oranges made from natural dyes of henna, pomegranate, saffron bark, and leaves from desert plants. Newer pieces tend to bright reds and other hard colors, but are still attractive. The shop of **Mr. Maazen Kaysi** (no sign), with a plate-glass show window and a recessed entrance on the right side of the Christian Quarter Road (just past the first pedestrian street turning on the right as you come from David St.), has the finest and largest selection of Bedouin weavings and other rugs. The shops dealing in **ancient antiquities** are fascinating, but unless you're an expert, judge any object you may want to purchase in terms of its decorative value rather than its alleged age or rarity.

In the Jewish Quarter of the Old City, a good shop for **old objects and Judaica** is **Mansour Saidian** (sign may say Old City Antiques), opposite the Mizrachi Bank on the corner of Tiferet Israel Street. There's always a selection of real 19th-century European and Iranian kiddush cups and old menorahs stashed away among the cases of newer objects and jewelry. These treasures are often a bargain.

PALESTINIAN EMBROIDERY

Antique Palestinian embroidered robes (among the world's great still-existing national costumes) hang from the doors of many shops in the Old City bazaar. Red, rose, and scarlet on hand-woven black cloth are the preferred colors, stemming from a tradition that goes back almost 3,000 years to the centuries when the prophets warned against women who sewed with scarlet threads of vanity. Many embroidery designs can be traced back to patterns introduced by the Crusaders. Prices for a caftan will range into the hundreds of dollars. The shop of **Maher Natsheh** (10 Christian Quarter Rd.) is noted for antique and old textiles.

In addition, the following two church-supported nonprofit shops offer a dazzling array of **freshly made, exotic new embroideries** all done by specially trained women who are working to support their families. Quality is assured, and prices at these shops are extremely fair.

Melia ★ Melia offers many beautiful traditional pieces, as well as some imaginative decorative items. In addition to the classic divan pillowcases, there are embroidered mirror frames as well as designer-embroidered women's jackets and embroidered T-shirts. Also on sale: Western-style tablecloths and embroideries. Arab Orthodox Society Art and Training Center, Frere's St., inside the New Gate, Old City. © **02/628-1377.**

Sunbula ★★ This nonprofit shop sells a magnificent collection of densely embroidered divan pillowcases, wall hangings, and shawls, all alive with traditional motifs and colors. Many superb pieces are less than NIS 600. Other good buys here include heavy woven Bedouin tent rugs, embroidered linen tablecloths and napkins, and a good selection of inexpensive handmade crafts and gift items. Custom-tailored jackets and other fashion items can be ordered. Open Monday to Saturday from 9am to 6pm and Sunday from 11am to 1pm. The shop is in the Saint Andrew's complex, on a hill between the train station and the Cinémathèque, and is close to the **House of Quality ★★** (p. 168), with its many artists' studios. Saint Andrews Guest House, King David and Remez sts. www.sunbula.org. © **02/672-1707.**

PHOTOGRAPHS

A number of venerable, family-run photography studios on Al Khanka Street in the Old City have gone through their archives and are now selling fascinating, often very beautiful reprints of views of Jerusalem (and the entire region)

wineries IN THE HILL COUNTRY

West of Jerusalem are a number of interesting small wineries. The **Latrun Monastery** (✆ **08/922-0065**) is a gardened enclave founded by Trappist monks in 1890 just where the Judean hills begin to rise from the coastal plain 20km (12 miles) west of Jerusalem. A shop at the entrance gate sells Domaine de Latrun wines, liqueurs, and spirits as well as honey and olive oil produced at the monastery. Visitors are welcome to explore the gardens, vineyards, and orchards. From Hwy. 1, the Tel Aviv–Jerusalem Highway, get off at the Latrun interchange. Follow Hwy. 3 briefly in the direction of Ashkelon, and you'll come to the Latrun Monastery, opposite the large Armored Forces Monument. Open 8:30am to 5:30pm every day except Sunday.

The **Soreq Winery** (www.soreq.co.il; ✆ **08/945-0844**) is a non-kosher, boutique winery located 30 minutes south of Tel Aviv at Kibbutz Nachshon. Opened in 1994, it produces cabernet sauvignons, chardonnays, and merlots. Call ahead to arrange a private tour of the winery and vineyards. You can buy wine and cheese at the winery shop, and there is a seating area on the premises. From Hwy. 1, exit at the Latrun interchange. Take Hwy. 3 south toward Ashkelon for approximately 9km (5⅔ miles). The winery is located 2km (1¼ miles) after the Nachshon interchange. Open every day from 8am to 4pm, tours only on Fridays.

The **Tzora Winery** (www.tzoravineyards.com; ✆ **02/990-8261**) is a boutique winery with a rising reputation for cabernet sauvignon, sauvignon blanc, and chardonnay wines. It is located on Kibbutz Tzora in the mountains between Beit Shemesh and Jerusalem, and they will arrange private tours if you call ahead. There is a wine and cheese store and picnic area on the premises. From Hwy. 1 exit at the Beit Shemesh (Sha'ar Hagai) interchange and take Rte. 38 south toward Beit Shemesh. From Rte. 38 (about 8km/5 miles from Hwy. 1) take Rte. 3835 to Kibbutz Tzora. Wine tasting and workshops are by appointment only; call to book.

The **Cremesan Winery** is run by members of the Italian Salesian monastic order. The beautiful winery can be visited (when security allows) daily at Beit Jala, near Bethlehem on the West Bank. You can also purchase the Italian-style wines produced at Beit Jala at the **Bet Jamal Monastery** (✆ **02/991-7671**), inside Israel, near the town of Beit Shemesh from Monday to Saturday 8:30am to 5pm. There are picnic tables overlooking a fine view behind the monastery, where you may visit until dusk. This lovely place is located 2km (1¼ miles) south of Beit Shemesh (left turn off Rte. 38).

from the first half of the 20th century. Kevork Kahvedjian, of **Elia Photo Service** (14 Al Khanka St.), has published a striking book, *Jerusalem Through My Father's Eyes,* containing over a half-century of his father's photographic work at the Elia Studio. A few doors down, you'll find the **Varouj Photography Studio,** also selling remarkable matted reproductions of Old Jerusalem scenes from their archives for about NIS 80, many taken with an eye for the poetry of Old Jerusalem. To get to Al Khanka Street, enter Jaffa Gate and continue straight on David Street into the bazaar. At Christian Quarter Road, turn left and continue to the end. Turn right (downhill) onto Al Khanka Street at the end of Christian Quarter Road. The shops with antique photo collections for sale are all on the right side of the street.

Vision Gallery ★★ Neil Folberg, noted for his landscapes and photographs of the Jewish world, is the owner of this world-class gallery that handles the works of international contemporary photographers. Wonderful temporary exhibits and vintage photographs of the Middle East and of Jewish subjects are also featured. Prices begin at NIS 400 and continue to hundreds and thousands of dollars. Israel's other gallery of note specializing in photography is the **Silver Print Gallery** in Ein Hod. 18 Rivlin St. www.visiongallery.com. ✆ **02/622-2253.**

SHOES & SANDALS

Khalifa Shoes ★★★ This shop is packed with Naot Teva footwear (the Birkenstock-like sandals and shoes of Israel), as well as with international brands known for comfort, such as Clarke's and Ecco. If you need great walking shoes, this is the place. 44 Jaffa Rd. (corner of Rav Kook St., opposite Zion Sq.). ✆ **02/625-7027.**

Sharabati Shops ★ With two locations in the Old City bazaar near Jaffa Gate, the Sharabati family stocks the largest collection of very reasonably priced, stylish leather sandals (as well as walking and sport sandals) in the market and is known for fair, unexaggerated opening prices. A second branch is on Christian Quarter Road, in the third store on the left from the intersection with David Street. On the left side of David St. as you descend the steps into the bazaar, midway btw. the Petra Hotel and Christian Quarter Rd. No phone.

SIDE TRIPS OUTSIDE JERUSALEM

Kennedy Memorial ★ MEMORIAL Eleven kilometers (6¾ miles) from downtown Jerusalem, in the same general direction of Hadassah Medical Center, Yad Kennedy is reached by following the winding mountain roads past the Aminadav Moshav. Opened in May 1966, the 18m-high (59-ft.) memorial to President John F. Kennedy is designed in the shape of a cut tree trunk, symbolizing a life cut short. The mountaintop memorial is encircled by 51 columns, each bearing the emblem of a state of the Union, plus the District of Columbia. The view from the parking lot is breathtaking—a never-ending succession of mountains and valleys. The monument and adjoining picnic grounds are part of the John F. Kennedy Peace Forest.

Abu Ghosh ★ HISTORIC SITE The Israeli-Arab town of Abu Ghosh (biblical Kiriath Yearim), 13km (8 miles) west of Jerusalem, can easily be reached from Jerusalem by car. Abu Ghosh is one of the few Arab villages that decided to side with Israel in the 1948 War of Independence. Israelis love to flock to Abu Ghosh on Saturday to enjoy hummus and other Arabic-style foods at the town's numerous restaurants. A number of hummus places call themselves "Abu Shukri"; most are good, but have no connection to the *real*

excursions TO BETHLEHEM

Note: At press time the governments of most Western countries are advising their citizens not to travel in the West Bank.

That being said, in recent years, more and more travelers have ventured into Bethlehem, especially on Christian-organized tour groups for visits to the holy sites in the center of town. For those who decide to visit Bethlehem, we advise reading the news and getting background on what's going on. Political conditions can change from day to day. **The Christian Information Centre** www.cicts.org/en inside Jerusalem's Jaffa Gate is a good place to get up-to-date advice on political conditions and information about possible organized tours or pilgrimage groups, as well as information about how to use public transportation, or arrange for a private taxi or guide to facilitate your excursion. Travelers from Israel into the Palestinian Authority must be in possession of their foreign passports and show them at the checkpoints that separate Israel from the West Bank. Remember: You cannot drive an Israeli rental car into the West Bank.

The highlight of a visit to Bethlehem, the **Basilica of the Nativity** marking the birthplace of Jesus, was built by order of the Roman Emperor Constantine in A.D. 326. It's the oldest surviving church in the Holy Land, a wondrous place scented with incense and decorated with Byzantine art. It was spared the general destruction of churches during the Persian Invasion of A.D. 614, because it was adorned by images of the Magi, whom the Persian soldiers recognized as fellow Persians.

A tour of Bethlehem should also take in the churches and chapels adjacent to the Basilica; the nearby **Milk Grotto Church;** the two possible sites of the **Shepherds' Field;** and **Manger Square,** in front of the Church, with its cafes and shops filled with olive-wood items and souvenirs. The **Visitor Information Office** (www.visit-palestine.com; ✆ **02/277-6832**) is in the Peace Center on Manger Square (open every Mon–Thurs and Sat from 8:30am–3pm; Fri and Sun closed). It offers maps and information about museums and sites in Bethlehem.

8km (5 miles) south of Jerusalem, in the Palestinian Authority/West Bank. Transportation: Public buses do go between Jerusalem (from the bus station near the Jaffa Gate, cost is about NIS 7) and Bethlehem, but they don't drop passengers near the Church of the Nativity, meaning you'll have to take a taxi from the drop-off point to the historic sites. For this reason, many travelers opt for a tour. Recommended tour companies include Egged Tours (www.eggedtours.com), Viator (www.viator.com), and City Discovery (www.veltra.com). Prices vary according to length of tour and inclusions and range from half- to full-day offerings, which include highlights in Jerusalem.

Abu Shukri in Jerusalem's Old City. On the other hand, Abu Ghosh's **Lebanese Restaurant** is the best of the wall-to-wall dining choices in town and serves some of the most fabulous lamb in Israel.

Abu Ghosh's great treasure is the 12th-century **Crusader Church of the Resurrection**, now under the guardianship of the Lazarist fathers. Like the Crusader Church of Saint Anne in Jerusalem's Old City, the Church of the Resurrection was designed to create marvelous acoustics for Gregorian chants, but it's less heavily restored and more atmospheric. It is built over an

Pilgrims pray in the Christmas Cave at the Basilica of the Nativity in Bethlehem.

ancient cistern and well that was in use from early Canaanite times. It's open Monday to Wednesday and Friday and Saturday from 8:30 to 11:30am and 2:30 to 5:30pm. The 20th-century **Church of Notre Dame of the Ark,** built on the site of a Byzantine church, marks the last place the Ark of the Covenant rested before it was brought to Jerusalem by King David. It's open daily from 8:30 to 11:30am and 2:30 to 5:30pm.

Neot Kedumim Biblical Landscape Reserve ★★ NATURE RESERVE Located in between Jerusalem and Tel Aviv on Rte. 443 (www.neot-kedumim.org.il; ✆ **08/977-0777**), Neot Kedumim is a living museum of the farming, harvesting, and shepherding techniques of ancient times, laid out across 250 hectares (618 acres) of land carefully planted with flora of the biblical period. An explanatory text brings the landscape vividly to life. Expert guides explain references to nature in Judeo-Christian scriptures; you'll find an olive press and a *succa* (harvesters' shelter), and see how ancient ink was made from resin, ground pomegranates, and oak gallnuts. It is NIS 25 for ages 3 and up, and the opening hours are Sunday to Thursday 8:30am to 4pm and Friday and holiday eves from 8:30am to1pm. Telephone for driving or bus instructions. Private guided tours in English are available, though must be reserved ahead. There are also self-guided tours; trails are wheelchair-accessible, and electric carts and wheelchairs are available on advance reservation.

Soreq Stalactite Cave/Avshalom Nature Reserve ★ NATURE RESERVE Located 20km (12 miles) west of Jerusalem, along the road out of Ein Kerem toward Bar Giora (www.parks.org.il; ✆ **02/991-1117**), this nature reserve, with its unusual, delicate, and varied stalactites, is a favorite excursion for tour groups. Set in the limestone region, the caves are full of incredible formations. The scenery along the road from Ein Kerem to the moshav of Nes Harim, 1.6km (1 mile) from the caves, is by itself quite beautiful; admission to the park is NIS 28 (children NIS 14) and includes a lecture with slides and a tour. ***Note:*** English-language tours are generally scheduled for early in the morning. Exploring the Soreq Cave entails climbing down (and up) 140 steps. The cave is NOT wheelchair accessible. Direct service is by tour bus only. Open daily from 8am to 4pm, on Fridays until 3pm.

6 THE DEAD SEA & MASADA

By Elianna Bar-El

Israel has many dramatic sights. But these two—one an unparalleled natural wonder, the other the site of extraordinary courage and tragedy—may well top the list. Conveniently, they can be experienced via easy day trips from Jerusalem, either separately or in tandem.

THE DEAD SEA ★★★

The Dead Sea, so dense with salt and other minerals that it's impossible to sink when immersed in its waters, is the lowest point by far on the face of the earth. It's also the most otherworldly body of water on the planet.

The southern part of the Dead Sea, where travelers can experience the floating phenomenon, can have a metallic sheen in soft daylight, while in noon sunlight, it can be sky blue with mirage-like white "saltbergs" floating on its surface. The northern coast (along Hwy. 1) is rugged and beautiful. At Ein Gedi and the spa hotel strip at Ein Bokek, the water is the most dense and helpful for skin diseases such as psoriasis. These were Cleopatra's chosen waters for her beauty needs, and today the water and the mud are said to be cleansing and healing for the skin and scalp, improving skin texture and even working miraculous wonders on various skin ailments.

Essentials

GETTING THERE

BY TOUR BUS Public transport is difficult and infrequent, especially in the blazing summer weather. Both **Egged** (www.eggedtours.com) and **United Bus Tours** (www.unitedtours.co.il) run affordable half-day and full-day tours to Masada and the Dead Sea including pick up from Tel Aviv and Jerusalem, usually allowing time for a quick dip and brief stops along the way at interesting sites and vista points. **United Bus Tours** offers tours in English, French, Spanish, and German. Although convenient, just note that the tour buses can spend a big chunk of time collecting passengers at various hotels and drop-off points in Jerusalem before heading out. **Abraham Tours** (abrahamtours.com), run by Jerusalem's Abraham Hostel, also operates daily bus tours to the area; check with them

The mud at the Dead Sea is thought to have healing properties.

about middle-of-the-night departures for hikers who want to climb to the top of Masada in the cool, pre-dawn hours and catch the sunrise (a cable car carries non-climbing visitors up to Masada after 8am).

BY CAR A **rental car** allows you to explore at your leisure and make an overnight trip. There are parking lots at Ein Gedi Beach and at all historic sites and nature reserves along the way. From Jerusalem take Hwy. 1 east to its intersection with Hwy. 90. Turn right (south) onto Hwy. 90 (the main road along the coast of the Dead Sea) and continue following the signs to Qumran, Ein Gedi, and Masada. Hwy. 1 from the heights of Jerusalem to the Dead Sea (1,200 feet below sea level) is a steady 4,000-foot downhill run. Along the way, you'll pass black goat hair Bedouin tent encampments, and a sign noting that you've passed sea level.

DEAD SEA safety

The waters of the Dead Sea, though purportedly healing, will burn open cuts and scrapes on your skin. It is most important not to let the water touch your eyes. Don't even think about plunging underwater. Backstroke is the way to go—the buoyancy of the Dead Sea is amazing, and most of your body will stay above the water level. If you get water in your eyes, shower with fresh water immediately.

WHAT TO SEE & DO

Visitors come here, primarily, to look, float, and heal. The Dead Sea contains the highest mineral content of any waters in the world: 300 grams per liter. As you bathe in the Dead Sea, you'll also be breathing the dense air of the below-sea-level atmosphere, which contains over 10% more oxygen than at sea level. This is helpful for people with respiratory problems and heart disease. In addition, bromides evaporating into the air from the Dead Sea contribute to a relaxed feeling of well-being. Don't be put off by the smell—that sour scent is, in fact, good for you! Many tired and anxious people come here for at least a week in order to unwind. The dense atmosphere also filters out harmful sun rays—psoriasis sufferers can stay out in the sun a bit longer without burning. Large tour groups and long-term residents fill the area's rows of high-rise, all-inclusive hotels and spas, therapeutic colonies that don't really feel like the rest of Israel.

Note: Because the Dead Sea is drying up and water levels are falling, many of the Dead Sea spa hotels that once enjoyed beach fronts now find themselves as much as a quarter of a mile or more from the water line. Sinkholes caused by the falling underground water table have become a recent danger around the region. Do not venture into areas that are barricaded off or marked as dangerous.

The Good Samaritan Inn ★ HISTORIC SITE Located 20km (13 miles) east of Jerusalem, just off Hwy. 1, this caravan stop and inn houses a collection of ancient mosaic floors from synagogues, churches, and Roman-era edifices, transported from excavations throughout Israel and reassembled here. The

Mosaics from archaeological sites across Israel are displayed at the Museum of the Good Samaritan.

Museum of the Good Samaritan houses one of the world's largest collections of mosaics. Tradition holds that this is the site of the New Testament's parable of the Good Samaritan, who helped an injured traveler ignored by others on the Jerusalem-Jericho Road. Among the floors on display is one from a synagogue of Samaritans, who follow a Torah-based religion, but in ancient times were rivals of their Jewish neighbors. In Byzantine times, Samaritans numbered at least several hundred thousand. The present-day Samaritan community numbers only several hundred.

Hwy. 1, 20km (13 miles) east of Jerusalem. ✆ **02/500-6261.** Admission free. Apr–Sept 8am–5pm; Oct–Mar 8am–4pm (closes one hour earlier on Fri and eves of holidays).

Qumran ★ HISTORIC SITE According to some archaeologists, the ruins of Qumran may have been a trading post; others believe that at the time of the First Jewish Revolt against Rome (A.D. 66–73) it was a communal settlement of the Essenes, an ascetic Jewish sect that may have influenced the earliest Christians. The Dead Sea Scrolls (the oldest existing copies of Jewish Holy Scriptures, plus other hitherto unknown extra Biblical writings) were discovered in 1947 in caves overlooking Qumran, leading many to believe the scrolls may have been written by Essene scribes. Others believe the scrolls may have been brought from libraries in Jerusalem and hidden in the caves in advance of the Roman destruction of Jerusalem in A.D. 70. Check out the stone platforms in the ruins of Qumran's "Scriptorium," where some scholars postulate scribes labored over the scrolls. Others feel these low structures could not possibly have been writing tables for normal size human beings. A video and brochures at the modern, air-conditioned Visitor's Center and cafe explain the mysteries of the site.

Rte. 90 (13km/8 miles south of junction with Hwy. 1). http://en.parks.org.il. ✆ **02/994-2235.** Admission NIS 29. Daily 8am–4pm (to 5pm in summer), Fri until 3pm.

WHERE TO STAY & DINE

The in-house hotel restaurants offer the best possibilities for a major meal. Many visitors staying here hotel-hop to try out the different lunch or dinner buffets; they're all vast, and you're sure to find something interesting. Prices range from NIS 100 to NIS 200. In the shopping mall at Ein Bokek, there are a number of cafes and restaurants where you can get inexpensive meals and light snacks. None of the choices, however, are standouts. There's a frantically busy McDonald's and the typical mall chain fare.

Expensive

Herbert Samuel Hod Dead Sea ★★ None of the hotels in the Dead Sea area come up to international five-star standards. Having a built-in clientele, here to "test the waters," they don't have to try that hard. That being said, this one likely comes the closest, with its location right on its own beach, its lovely pool areas, top-notch spa, and better-than-usual dining options. Rooms are large and very clean, with a somewhat Scandinavian look (lots of blond wood), and boast huge windows, comfortable beds, and free Wi-Fi in public areas. Search online for a discount, as the hotel often offers special deals that drop it into the moderate category.

Ein Bokek, 86930. www.herbertsamuel.com. ✆ **08/668-8222.** 211 units. $300–$450 double. Rates include breakfast. Free parking. **Amenities:** Restaurant; bar; fitness center; several pools, including a pool with water from the Dead Sea and sulfur pools; room service; spa; salon; free loaner bikes; free Wi-Fi in public areas.

The beach at the Herbert Samuel Hod Dead Sea hotel.

Moderate

Kibbutz Ein Gedi Resort Hotel ★★★ Dramatically located on a hill overlooking the Dead Sea, this kibbutz and its low-rise accommodations are set amid the exotic plantings of the only internationally registered botanical garden in which people live. For visitors to this Eden, boasting over 900 plants, including the otherworldly Baobab, it's hard to believe that before 1949 there was nothing but barren rock here. This location, a 20-minute drive from Masada, makes a good base for those who want to climb Masada at dawn, explore the region at their own leisure, or just enjoy the beauty of the place with its gorgeous swimming pools.

There are four kinds of accommodations at a wide range of prices set over a sprawling shared community on the grounds of the kibbutz. Standard rooms are basic, but set amid wonderful gardens and air-conditioned. Upgraded boutique rooms and new mini-suites and deluxe-plus rooms are more luxurious; some offer decks that overlook dramatic vistas. Highlights include a pampering spa, Olympic-size outdoor pool (with cocktail bar and snack kiosk) and a well-organized schedule of daily and nightly activities, including desert excursions, live music, circus performances for kids, and ceramics and shibori workshops (by appointment, inquire at the reservation desk). A supermarket is accessible on-site.

Note: It's possible to arrive here using public transport, as the kibbutz provides a shuttle down to the public beach, but a car is essential in order to explore the area. Ein Gedi is heavily booked by groups, so reserve far in advance. This is a kibbutz community, so service is very family-friendly and community-driven, if frill-free.

Ein Gedi Guest House. www.ein-gedi.co.il. ✆ **08-659-4222.** From $245 double; $360 mini-suite for 2. Rates include half-board. **Amenities:** Kibbutz dining room; desert excursions; botanical garden; 2 pools (indoor, outdoor); massage; Dead Sea Synergy Spa & Wellness Center; tennis courts; mini-golf; handicap-accessible rooms; free Wi-Fi.

Inexpensive

Badolina ★★ Those looking for basic accommodations, but with a fun bent, will find their place here. Badolina has a Burning Man vibe, with glamping tents and trailers to rent, and an outdoor resto/bar where seemingly everyone knows each other…or is getting to know each other. You can rent or bring your own tent for a minimal fee and use the facilities. Be aware that no tents have private bathrooms. The campground and recreational center are just below the Ein Gedi Kibbutz (you can't miss it on the drive up the hill).

Badolina Ein Gedi Glamping. badolina.co.il. ✆ **052/331-3113.** Private cabins, bungalows, tents, parking spots for trailers and caravans for rent; clean shared bathrooms. From $20 and up.

Ein Gedi ★

Hwy. 90, 33km (21 miles) south of Qumran.

There is no modern town at Ein Gedi. The area is spread out along a 5-mile stretch of Hwy. 90 alongside the Dead Sea. It includes a **Nature Reserve,** an IYHA Association Youth Hostel, a **public beach** with lifeguards and showers, and **Kibbutz Ein Gedi.** Kibbutz Ein Gedi (see above) is the most beautiful place to stay in the area and contains a sprawling Resort Guest House and impressive botanical gardens.

This remote, canyon oasis near the Dead Sea has attracted small bands of people since prehistoric times. More than 5,000 years ago, an unknown Chalcolithic people built a sanctuary amid the waterfalls and springs here—a cache of their mysterious, elegantly wrought sacred vessels, copper wands, crowns, and scepters were discovered in the 1960s by Israeli archaeologists searching for hidden Dead Sea Scrolls (from 150 B.C.–A.D. 135) amid the crevasses of inaccessible cliffside caves. According to the Bible, it was to the isolated canyons of Ein Gedi that the young David fled from the paranoid King Saul around 1000 B.C.; here David had the chance to kill his pursuer, but he would not lay a hand on his king, the anointed of God. The Song of Songs rhapsodizes over the exotic herbs and spices grown in Ein Gedi's rarefied atmosphere and soil. From approximately the 6th century B.C. until the A.D. late 8th century, Ein Gedi was famous throughout the ancient world for priceless incense, lotions, and perfumes. Ein Gedi's plants and formulas were carefully guarded by the Ein Gedi community until its demise in early Islamic times. Indeed, an inscription in the mosaic floor of the Byzantine-era synagogue discovered at Ein Gedi warns members of the community not to divulge the "secret of the town" to outsiders. After more than 1,000 years of complete desolation, the region was resettled in 1949 by a group of kibbutzniks who were amazed at how trees and plantings thrive at Ein Gedi. **Kibbutz Ein Gedi** is now lushly planted with 900 species of trees and shrubs from all over the world, and is the only internationally recognized botanical garden in which people live.

Ein Gedi Nature Reserve ★★ NATURE RESERVE Spectacular waterfalls and hiking trails are within the **Ein Gedi Reserve's Nachal David and**

Nachal Arugot canyons. Maps and suggested trail routes are available at the entrance; more-detailed maps and trail advice for hikes of several hours through these two neighboring canyon systems are available at the SPNI Center, near the hostel and the Nachal David entry gate. Follow the trail and the signposts, winding through tall pines and palm trees up and into the desert hills. You proceed between slits in the rock formations, under canopies of papyrus reeds, and after about 10 minutes of steady climbing, you'll hear the wonderful sound of rushing water. In another 5 minutes, your appetite whetted, you arrive at what is surely one of the wonders of the Judean desert—the **Nachal David–Ein Gedi waterfalls,** hidden in an oasis of vegetation that hangs in a canyon wall. A second trail involving a 30-minute climb takes you to the **Shulamit Spring** and then to the **Dodim Cave** at the top of the falls.

A 20- to 30-minute walk to the left brings you to the fenced-in ruins of a **Chalcolithic sanctuary** dating from about 3000 B.C. Mysterious copper wands and crowns, probably belonging to this sanctuary and hidden in nearby caves for more than 5,000 years, are displayed in the antiquities section of the Israel Museum.

Another walk leads to the ruins of Byzantine-era Ein Gedi's synagogue, with its marvelously intact mosaic floor. The reserve is open from 8am to 4pm; in summer until 5pm. You must make arrangements with the Nature Reserves Authority if you plan to do any of the 5- to 6-hour hikes into the depths of the *nachal* (canyon) systems, especially if you plan to go beyond the **Hidden Falls.** Always carry at least 5 liters (5⅓ qt.) of water with you if you're planning a major hike in summer. From autumn to spring, it is important to be aware of the possibility of flash floods caused by rain in distant places. No food or cigarettes are allowed on the grounds. Parts of the Reserve and the Antiquities Park are wheelchair accessible. Admission to the reserve is NIS 28 (adults) NIS 14 (kids) with discounts for groups and includes admission to the Antiquities Park (see below), but a reservation must be made in advance online or by phone (en.parks.org.il; ✆ **08/658-4285**). There is a snack kiosk at the entrance. ***Tip:*** Ein Gedi is impossibly hot midday in the summer. Worse yet, during school holidays, it is overrun by school groups. Not recommended with strollers, although the initial hikes are doable with a baby carrier. Sturdy shoes highly recommended.

At the **Ein Gedi Antiquities National Park** are the ruins of **Ancient Ein Gedi ★**, one of Israel's most important archaeological sites. From the times of the First and Second Temples until the end of the Byzantine era, Ein Gedi was a largely Jewish outpost famous throughout the ancient world for its production of rare spices; fragrant, intoxicating balsam oil; and priceless myrrh. Perhaps Ein Gedi was permitted to survive the tumultuous decades of wars and rebellions against Rome because its secret formulas for spice and incense production were not only beyond value, but also irreplaceable. At Ein Gedi, the **mosaic floor** of an A.D. 6th-century synagogue has been uncovered. If you visit other mosaic synagogue floors discovered in the Jordan Valley and the Galilee, you'll find that a number of Byzantine-era synagogues (at Bet Alpha, Hammat Tiberias, and Zippori) contain a depiction of the zodiac as the

One of the many waterfalls at the Ein Gedi Nature Reserve.

centerpiece of their mosaic floors. Some scholars believe the zodiac was meant to represent the orderly patterns of God's universe. At Ein Gedi, in place of a zodiac circle, the mosaic floor is dominated by a central circle design of peacock chicks and adult birds, perhaps illustrating continuing patterns of birth and growth through which divine presence is revealed. It may be that the Jewish community at Ein Gedi, less influenced by outside cultures than the Jewish communities farther north, was reluctant to employ pagan motifs in the ornamentation of its synagogue.

The extraordinary personal papers, letters, and possessions found in the Dead Sea caves and dating from the Second Jewish Revolt against Rome (A.D. 135) belonged to Jewish inhabitants of Ein Gedi who attempted to escape the Roman armies by hiding in the region's almost inaccessible caves. Esteemed archaeologist Yigael Yadin's book *Bar-Kokhba* details these dramatic finds.

Hwy. 90 (33km/21 miles south of Qumran). www.parks.org.il. ✆ **08/917-0586** or 08/658-4285. Admission NIS 14 adults, NIS 7 children. Sat–Thurs 8am–4pm; Fri 8am–3pm.

MASADA ★★★

It's a tradition for Israelis to make the ascent to the top of Masada at least once—this is the scene of one of the most heroic and tragic incidents in Jewish history. Few non-Jews outside Israel had heard of Masada until its story was dramatized in a book and a subsequent television miniseries in 1981. The story of a small garrison that defied the Roman army, as the historian Flavius Josephus recorded and perhaps embellished, is worth retelling.

King Herod had built a magnificent palace complex and fortress atop this nearly inaccessible desert mountain plateau around 30 B.C. Underground cisterns ensured the fortress a lavish water supply for the palace's baths and gardens. Most impressive was Herod's personal winter villa, the extraordinary hanging palace on the northern tip of Masada, calculated to catch breathtaking vistas of the Dead Sea as well as refreshing breezes from the north. He furnished the luxurious place with every comfort as well as storehouses of food and arms, protecting the almost inaccessible location with impregnable walls. The audaciousness of such an undertaking tells much about Herod's personality. After Herod's death in 4 B.C., a small Roman garrison occupied the mount. However,

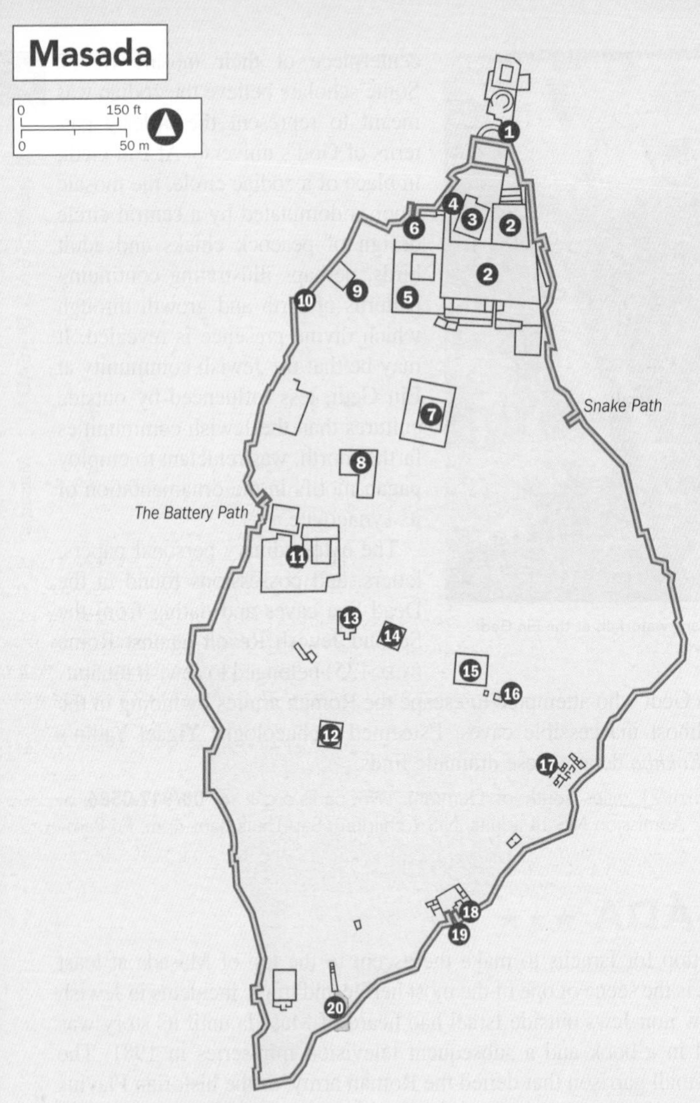

Administration building **5**
Bath house **3**
Byzantine chapel **8**
Byzantine structure, apartments **7**
Herod's three-tiered palace **1**
"Lots" found here **4**
Mikveh **18**
Mosaic workshop **16**
Scrolls found here **10**
Small palace **14**
Small palace **15**
Southern water gate **19**
Storerooms **2**
Swimming pool **13**
Synagogue **9**
Underground cistern **20**
Water gate **6**
Western palace **11**
Zealot's Quarters **12, 17**

during the Jewish Revolt against Rome in A.D. 66, a small band of Jewish zealots attacked and overtook the almost unattended fortress. They brought their families, lived off the vast storehouses of food, and used the arsenal of arms to defend themselves. They even raided the surrounding countryside.

Finally, in A.D. 73, three years after the fall of Jerusalem and the end of the First Jewish Revolt, the Romans decided to put an end to this last pocket of Jewish resistance. They built a siege ramp up to the mountaintop, using captured Jews as slave laborers, knowing the defenders of Masada could not bring themselves to attack or harm their enslaved countrymen. After an onslaught using siege engines, flaming torches, rock bombardments, and battering rams, Masada was still in Jewish hands. But with 10,000 Roman troops camped on the hillside and daily bombardments smashing at the walls, it became only a question of when the 900 defenders would succumb. Flaming torches thrown at the fort's wall were whipped by a wind into the midst of the defenders, and the garrison's gates caught fire. The Romans, seeing that Masada was practically defenseless, decided to wait until dawn and take it over in their own good time.

That final night, the 900 men, women, and children who inhabited Masada held a desperate meeting. Their leader, Eliezer Ben-Yair, in a dramatic speech (as reported by the historian Flavius Josephus who, of course, was not actually present), persuaded his followers to accept death bravely, on their own terms. In the darkness at Masada nearly 2,000 years ago, a great mass suicide

An aerial view shows just how extensive the ruins of Masada are.

INTO THE negev

Israel's Negev region is the dusty, desert expanse that fills most of the southern triangle formed with the busy city of Beersheba in the north with Eilat at its southernmost point. No less a figure than State of Israel founding father David Ben-Gurion (and the country's first prime minister) saw in this generally stark, foreboding landscape great potential and indeed viewed its development, inasmuch as nature can allow it, as something of an imperative. He made his retirement home at Sde Boker, a kibbutz in the Negev, and is buried there along with his wife Paula.

Today the Negev draws Israelis who go on nature hikes through the desert and travelers who seek a measure of solitude away from Israel's bustling cities and mostly developed coast. But by no means does that mean you have to rough it. In fact, the Negev is home to two of the most spectacular hotels to open in Israel in recent years. The first is the luxe **Beresheet Resort ★★★**, Hebrew for "genesis" (1 Beresheet Rd.; http://isrotelexclusivecollection.com; ✆ **08/659-8000;** doubles from $350–$700), which is located in the otherwise nondescript Mitzpe Ramon, about 2 hours south of the Dead Sea. It's on the edge of the Makhtesh Ramon, the world's biggest crater formed from natural erosion. A geological highlight of the Negev, the crater is worth a detour even if you don't stay at the hotel. That said, it's highly recommended that you do. Beresheet aspires to eco-sensitivity—after you park and arrive, the only way to get around is by electric golf cart or on foot. There are upwards of 111 rooms and suites located in different areas throughout the property; 42 have their own swimming pools. The restaurant features organic cuisine and a decor that, thanks to floor-to-ceiling glass walls, opens up to the desert views. Activity options abound, including camel rides, rappelling, jeep tours, cycling trips, and even hot-air balloon rides.

The other hotel in this otherworldly location is **Six Senses Shaharut ★★★** (Hevel Eilot, Negev Desert; http://sixsenses.com/en/resorts/shaharut; ✆ **08/615-0050;** doubles from $850–$950, more for villas) which opened to much fanfare in August of 2021. Nestled in a remote earth-toned expanse of sand dunes and mountains, it offers sprawling views in all directions (including of neighboring Jordan). Wood, stone, and adobe structures blend into the environment and hold 60 glam suites; an on-site garden

occurred. Ten men were chosen as executioners. Members of families lay side by side and bared their throats. After all the families had been killed, one of the ten executioners was chosen to kill the other nine; he then ran himself through on his own sword. Two women and five children survived, hiding in one of the caves on the plateau. The Romans, who had expected to fight their way in, were triply astonished at the eerie silence and the orderly groups of bodies where they had expected to encounter battle. Josephus recorded the "calm courage of [the defenders'] resolution . . . and utter contempt of death." So ended the Jewish resistance against Rome. Like almost everything in Israel, the meaning of Masada has become a matter of controversy, with some contending that glorification of a political stand that resulted in mass suicide is not good for the national psyche.

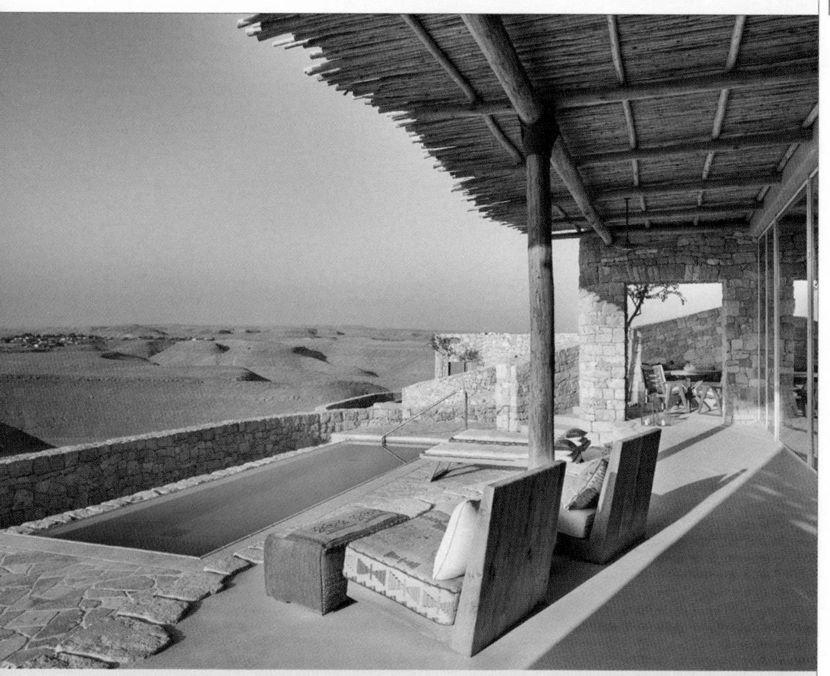

A desert view from one of the cushy suites at the Six Senses Shaharut Masada.

feeds the two restaurants. Camels will greet you during check-in, and these dromedaries can also be rented for a trek, as one of the many add-on experiences on offer. ***Note:*** Small children are not allowed, just ages 12 and up.

For more on the Negev region, visit www.goisrael.com.

The Visitor Center & Climbing the Ascent

Masada is now a UNESCO World Heritage Site, and a new, air-conditioned, state-of-the-art visitor complex has been set up at the entrance to the park. You'll find a very useful history video and a model of ancient Masada, a small snack bar, and a souvenir shop. It doesn't fit in with the isolation and antiquity of Masada, but the cool air and the chance to stock up on bottled water is most welcome. There's also **Yigael Yadin Masada Museum** (www.parks.org.il; ✆ **08/658-4207,** press 2 for operator; admission NIS 20; Open daily 8am–5pm, Fri until 4pm). Portable multi-lingual audio guides to the museum and Masada itself can be rented at the museum for NIS 20. Admission includes a pamphlet with a map detailing the Masada site. A combined ticket of the museum and Masada is NIS 31.

The cable-car ride up to Masada is an adventure in and of itself.

From the parking lot at the foot of **Masada National Park** you've got two choices—climb on foot or ride the cable car that carries you almost to the summit. If you climb, especially in the summer months, be sure to start (literally) at the crack of dawn, before the spectacular heat. On days when the heat is too great, park rangers ban climbing, so get to Masada before dawn if you are determined to make the climb.

Climbers also have two choices: the route from the Dead Sea side or the Roman siege ramp originally built in A.D. 73 on the side of the mountain facing in the direction of Arad (this Roman ramp path is only accessible by car from Arad). The route from the Dead Sea side requires approximately 40 minutes to an hour; it's called the **Snake Path** because of the steep, hairpin curves. The Snake Path opens approximately an hour before sunrise (so climbers can catch the stunning vista) and closes at 3:30pm. Most visitors are happy to use the cable car to ascend and descend. ***Note:*** **Special-access pathways** have been created on top of Masada for those with disabilities, and special arrangements can be made to help transport those with special needs to the top. Call for information and special help in advance.

The **Sound and Light Show,** lasting 50 minutes, is usually given Tuesday and Thursday evenings at an outdoor theater on the Arad (western) side of Masada. The theater is not accessible from Hwy. 90, which runs along the

Dead Sea, so allow 45 minutes to get there by car (your hotel will give you the best directions). For exact time schedules and reservations, go to the website. **Admission** is NIS 50 per adult, NIS 40 per child. A historical narrative is given in Hebrew, but simultaneous translations are available for free.

Masada National Park. www.parks.org.il. ✆ **08/658-4207.** Cable cars operate Sun–Thurs 8am–4pm, Fri and eves of holidays (including Sat) 8am–2pm. The cable car will deposit you steps from the fortress top.

Where to Stay

Masada Guest House and Youth Hostel ★★ This architecturally impressive youth hostel is a great budget base for exploring the region, and it is right at the foot of Masada, so those who wish to climb to the top in the pre-dawn don't have to drive or bus in from Jerusalem in the middle of the night. It's often mobbed with student groups, but the management tries to keep them in wings away from private guests. There are doubles and family rooms, all with fridge, TV, and a private bath/shower; terraces overlook the desert and a refreshing swimming pool. Towels, sheets, soap, and shampoo are provided. Full or half-board and even picnic meals can be arranged; meals are kosher. A synagogue is also on the premises.

Rte. 90 at Masada National Park. www.iyha.org.il/Eng/masada-hostel. ✆ **02/594-5623,** or 1-599/510-511 in Israel. 88 units, all w/private shower. $120–$175 double. Rates include breakfast. Free parking. **Amenities:** Basketball court; pool open from March through October; free Wi-Fi. Egged bus no. 444 from Jerusalem-Eilat/Eilat-Jerusalem; ask driver for special stop at Masada Hostel.

Masada's Different Types of Entry Fees

Entrance with combination ticket and cable car round trip: Adult: NIS 77; child: NIS 45.
Eastern side (entrance and climb Snake Path): Adult: NIS 31; child: NIS 17.
Entrance with combination ticket and cable car one way: Adult: NIS 59; child: NIS 31.
Cable car one-way: Adult NIS 28; child NIS 14.
Cable-car round trip: Adult NIS 46; child NIS 28.

7 THE GALILEE

By Karen Chernick

The Galilee, encompassing much of Northern Israel, is an inviting network of forested hills, olive groves, kibbutzim, and Israeli Arab towns and villages. At this region's eastern edge is Israel's greatest natural treasure: the Sea of Galilee, a 2½-hour drive north of Jerusalem. This magical, turquoise body of water is a jewel-like, freshwater lake, set amid a circle of mountains, and surrounded by dramatic Old and New Testament sites.

Organized bus tours can take you through the highlights of this region, but, if possible, the Galilee is the place to bring a rental car so you can free-wheel and explore, perhaps visit boutique wineries, and stay for a few days at a kibbutz guesthouse or a country lodge. Beyond the circuit around the Sea of Galilee, some of the area's highlights include:

Safed (Zefat): A mountain city 33km (20-mile) drive northeast of the Sea of Galilee, this has been a center for Jewish scholarship and mysticism since the 15th century; the old city is filled with quaint lanes and artists' homes.

Nazareth: The village of Jesus's youth, Nazareth is now a modern city and important center for Israel's Arab community. It's the site of the basilica that marks the Annunciation. The re-created Nazareth Biblical Village is a worthwhile attraction. Nearby are Zippori, the vast ruins of a Roman Jewish city, traditionally the home of Mary's family, and Mt. Tabor, a place of mystery since prehistoric times (with views across Israel to Mt. Carmel) and site of the Transfiguration of Jesus.

Bar'am National Park: A beautiful drive 40km (25 miles) northwest of Safed, where well-preserved ruins of the Bar'am synagogue from the A.D. 3rd and 4th centuries stand amid the remnants of a Maronite Christian village ordered evacuated by Israeli forces during the 1948 War of Independence.

GETTING AROUND You can approach the Galilee from the southeast on the road that runs northward up the Jordan Valley, or there are two good central routes for entering the Galilee from the west: One is from Haifa to Akko and east to Safed, then down to the Sea of Galilee. The other is due east from Haifa to Nazareth and straight across to Tiberias. An offshoot of the Haifa-Nazareth road is a route that detours down through the Jordan Valley, south of the Sea of Galilee; at the Jordan Valley, turn north. In summer, the Jordan Valley, which is far below sea level, can be oppressively hot. Give yourself time to enjoy the beaches of the Sea of Galilee, which can be paradisiacal.

The Galilee is filled with so many places of natural beauty and historical interest that it's worth it to rent a car, at least for a few days of travel. Buses connect the major cities, but don't always run frequently, and public transport to places in the countryside is poor to nonexistent.

NAZARETH ★

40km (25 miles) SE of Haifa

Nazareth is where Jesus grew up, and today it is the main city in the southern Galilee. In biblical times it was just a tiny hamlet, scarcely recorded on maps or mentioned in historical works. Modern Nazareth, by contrast, is a bustling city, filled with industry and new construction. Only recently, with the restoration of Ottoman-era mansions and markets in its old city, has Nazareth become more than a brief stop where visitors can check out the churches and shrines marking the life of Jesus.

The population of Nazareth is approximately 35% to 40% Christian and 60% to 65% Muslim. Along with Jerusalem, it's the headquarters of the Christian mission movement in Israel, with more than 40 churches, convents, monasteries, orphanages, and private parochial schools. Nazareth's very name is used by Arabs and Israelis to designate Christians. Just as Jesus was also known as the Nazarene, in Arabic, Christians are called *Nasara,* and in Hebrew *Notzrim.* Nazareth has always been the cultural and political center for the more moderate Arabic community in northern Israel. The city abounds with musicians, writers, filmmakers, local artists, small concerts, and poetry readings.

The old town's crop of interesting, atmospheric guest houses, cafes, and eateries can help introduce you to Nazareth's unique spirit. English is widely spoken, but the first language of most inhabitants of Nazareth is Arabic.

Essentials

GETTING THERE & AROUND

BY CAR Nazareth is in the center of the lower Galilee, set in the largest and most fertile valley in Israel, the Yizreel Valley, often called simply Ha-Emek ("the valley"); it lies between the Galilee mountains to the north and the Samaria range to the south, midway between Haifa and Tiberias. From Tiberias, take Rte. 77, and turn south onto Rte. 754 near Kana, which will take you into Nazareth. From Haifa, take Rte. 75.

Warning: Nazareth has a "bypass," a road that circles the town, which explains the confusing signs that point in opposite directions for the same

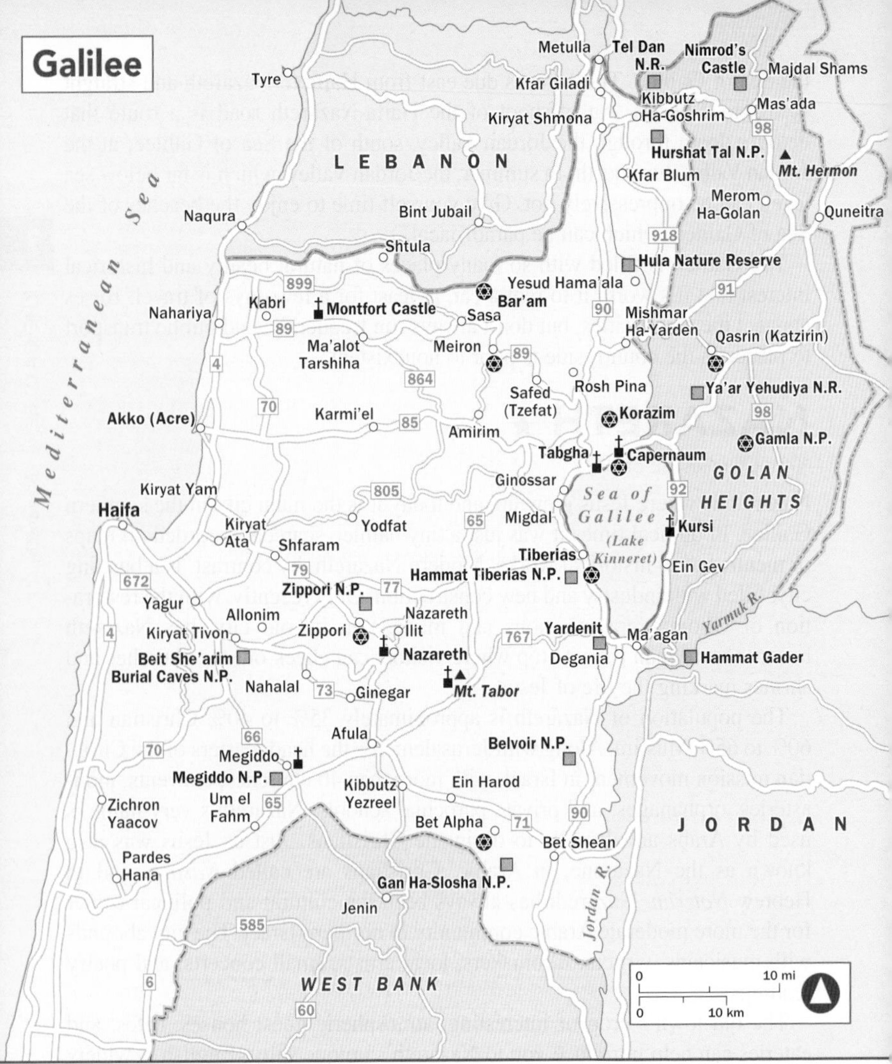

destination. One of these destinations is **Nazareth Elit** (or Nazerat Illit—meaning Upper Nazareth), the new, modern, mostly Jewish area to the north. It's a separate municipality.

For Nazareth itself, you'll want to go down Pope Paul VI Street and into the center of Nazareth, then follow the signs to the Basilica of the Annunciation, Nazareth's principal religious monument off Pope Paul VI Street on Casa Nova Street (also known as Bishara or Annunciation St.).

BY BUS Major cities offer bus service to Nazareth, though there isn't a central bus station: Intercity buses stop at Pope Paul VI Street near Bank Hapoalim. **Egged Information** (www.egged.co.il) is just across from the bank, open daily 6am to 6pm, and is best to approach for the most convenient bus route for your destination. Buses to Haifa or Tiberias depart approximately every half hour. **Nazareth Municipal Buses** get you up the steep hill to the Salesian and Nazareth Illit neighborhoods. The website for the **Jesus Trail** organization (www.jesustrail.com) provides the best information on travel to and from Nazareth. Abraham Hostels in Jerusalem and Tel Aviv (www.abrahamtours.com) also run **minibus shuttles** to Nazareth (a more private, direct option costing just a few dollars more each direction).

ORIENTATION

CITY LAYOUT Use the basilica's huge cupola, topped by a beacon, as your landmark—everything you'll need is within sight of the basilica. There are very few street signs, and building numbers are often in Arabic. Remember that it's downhill to the basilica and the center of town from most points in the city. The main roadway downhill into Nazareth (and uphill out of it) is separated into a right-hand roadway, clogged with cars parking, unloading, and waiting; and a central, less-gridlocked roadway for (we hope) moving traffic.

Casa Nova Street is the approach to the basilica, and on it you'll find restaurants, cafes, hotels, hospices, and the Tourist Information Office.

To get a feel for old Nazareth, turn into the narrow alleys that wind up and back into the terraced limestone ridges, and wander through the narrow cobbled streets of the Arab Market. Keep in mind that Nazareth is completely closed on Sunday and in full swing on Saturday. Interesting eateries, venues for small concerts, readings, and theatrical performances are opening in the beautiful, freshly restored old mansions off the main streets of the town center.

VISITOR INFORMATION The website of the **Nazareth Tourism Association Information Office** (www.visitnazareth.co.il/en) is filled with excellent information on places of interest, walks, shopping, and food. The **Fauzi Azar Inn** (p. 198) gives free walking tours of the Old City (Mon–Fri at 9:30am and Sat at 12:30pm) and is a helpful one-stop shop for maps and information about the area.

What to See & Do

There are four major things for tourists to do in Nazareth: Shop in the market, visit the New Testament sites, enjoy the many Arabic restaurants and sweet shops in the city, and visit the fascinating "Nazareth Village," a re-creation of what life was like in the tiny hamlet of Nazareth at the time of Jesus.

New Testament Sites ★★ The **Basilica of the Annunciation ★★** is located on Casa Nova Street, on the spot where, according to Christian tradition, the Angel Gabriel appeared before Mary, to announce she would bear a child. The present Basilica of the Annunciation, completed in 1966, was built over earlier structures dating from 1730 to 1877. Unlike most Christian

Mass is celebrated at the Greek Orthodox Church of the Annunciation.

shrines in Israel, this basilica has a bold, modern design. Around the nave, on the walls, are murals that were created by artists from around the world. Note the Japanese mural of the Madonna and Child on the left (north) wall—Mary's robe is made entirely of Japanese seed pearls. Summer hours are daily from 8am to 6pm. Holy Masses are held in the Grotto of the Annunciation daily at 6:30am and 7am on Sunday. Walk out the north-side door to reach the other religious sites.

The **Church of Saint Joseph ★** is 90m (295 ft.) away, set on the site believed to have been occupied by Joseph's carpentry workshop. Open daily 7am to 6pm.

On the main street in the bazaar is the **Greek Catholic "Synagogue" Church ★**, believed to be the site of the ancient Nazareth synagogue that Jesus frequented. Farther along the road is the **Franciscan Mensa Christi Church ★**, believed to occupy the spot where Jesus ate with his disciples after the Resurrection.

Mary's Well ★, with its source inside the **Greek Orthodox Church of the Annunciation,** is another important holy site. The church was built at the end of the 17th century over the remains of three earlier churches. At the church entrance, on the archway above the stone staircase leading down to the well, is a mural depicting the Angel Gabriel appearing to Mary.

Walking the Jesus Trail ★★★

For millions of modern travelers, walking in the footsteps of Jesus has meant taking a few steps from a tour bus to the Church of the Annunciation or to the banks of the Jordan River.

But thanks to a collaborative effort of local Christians, Muslims, and Jews—headed by the dynamic Maoz Inon and Suraida Nassar—that method of touring is changing. The group has mapped a careful, 65km (40-mile) itinerary (mainly downhill from Nazareth) of the routes Jesus would have taken as he crisscrossed the Galilee on foot from Nazareth to Zippori, Kana, and down to the Sea of Galilee. Along the way, visitors pass olive groves, ancient springs, historic sites, and ruins. Yes, modern towns and their outskirts are also passed (there's no way to avoid them), but they don't account for the majority of the trail.

The route can be hiked by independent walkers or done with organized tours. Included are places to camp, overnight lodgings, and places to eat and buy supplies. Participants can hike as much or as little of the trail as they like. An optional return route to Nazareth includes the ethereal Mount Tabor.

For more information, go to www.jesustrail.com or pick up a complimentary guidebook at Fauzi Azar Inn (see p. 198).

Our Lady of Fright Chapel ★, sometimes called the Tremore, is on a wooded hill south of the center opposite the Galilee Hotel. It commemorates the spot where Mary watched while the people of Nazareth attempted to throw Jesus over the Precipice.

Nazareth Village ★★ This extraordinary re-creation of houses, farms, workshops, oil and wine presses, and terraced fields as they existed in the time of Jesus could easily have been embarrassingly hokey. It's not (we promise) because everything seen here is based on knowledge gleaned from archaeological digs in the area. Every structure in the "village" has been built in the same dimensions, and with the same materials and techniques, used 2,000 years ago. The same goes for the ancient costumes the cast members here wear as they perform traditional labors, such as plowing, wine and olive oil pressing, cooking, and weaving. The re-creation is designed to help visitors understand the environment in which

A re-enactor at Nazareth Village demonstrates how wool was turned to yarn in biblical times.

Jesus found material for his teachings and parables. Guided tours include readings from the New Testament at various points along the way, but the village should be of interest to visitors of all faiths, as it carefully delineates the nature and customs of the Jewish community that existed in Nazareth 2,000 years ago. Especially fascinating is the re-creation of a very modest A.D. 1st-century synagogue that would have existed in a Galilean village while the Temple at Jerusalem was still standing. For an additional charge, it may be possible to arrange to attend a 1st-century vegetarian meal, served in a Bedouin tent. The men, women, and children "inhabiting" the village are both Christian and Muslim residents of modern-day Nazareth.

Beside the YMCA in downtown Nazareth. www.nazarethvillage.com. ✆ **04/645-6042.** NIS 50 adults, NIS 30 children, NIS 40 students and seniors. Additional charge for meals. Mon–Sat 9am–5pm. Hours are flexible, and you must call ahead to schedule a mandatory tour (included with admission). Additional evening tours offered Christmas, Easter, and in summer.

Where to Stay

Fauzi Azar Inn ★★★ The Fauzi Azar Inn, one of our two top picks in Nazareth, is now a member of the Abraham Hostels group, but is both a guesthouse and a hostel—so there are accommodations here for people in all price ranges and group sizes. The inn is set in a splendid 200-year-old Nazareth

Fauzi Azar Inn was created from a 2-centuries-old Ottoman mansion and fosters a genuine sense of community among its guests.

mansion, replete with high, hand-painted ceilings; Ottoman arches; splendid Turkish marble floors; and a lovely garden. The private rooms have simple but clean wooden furnishings, and the dorm rooms have the usual hostel bunkbeds. But one comes here more for the overall ambience than the decor. Included in the price of the stay is a free tour, during which the very moving history of the inn is detailed and Nazareth is explored including a visit to a, you guessed it, modern-day carpenter. Other freebies include use of the communal kitchen (where cooking classes occasionally take place) and breakfast. Check the website for instructions on finding the inn, which is tucked behind a tiny door in Nazareth's Old City.

Old City, Nazareth Center. www.abrahamhostels.com/nazareth. ✆ **04/602-0469** or 054/432-2328. 14 units, most w/shared bathrooms. Private double NIS 240–NIS 513; dorm bed NIS 105. **Amenities:** Guest kitchen; patio; free tour; free Wi-Fi.

Michel House ★★★ Exceptionally warm hospitality combined with an unbeatable location (just steps from the city's major churches) make this our other top choice. The digs are quite pleasant too, eight guest rooms, many with view-rich private terraces, set in an 18th-century mansion on a narrow street in the old city. The first mayor of Nazareth built the place, but today it has such modern conveniences as strong air-conditioning and comfy mattresses. Each day starts with a homemade breakfast of cheeses, omelets, and different local salads, often prepared by the gregarious Michel himself.

Old City, Nazareth Center. www.michel-house.com. ✆ **04/657-7947.** 8 units. $170–$190 double. Rates include breakfast. **Amenities:** Free Wi-Fi.

Villa Nazareth Hotel ★ Another centrally located choice, the Villa Nazareth Hotel was a school in a former life. Today it offers simple but comfortable accommodations, with such appreciated extras as good air-conditioning, mini-fridges in all the rooms, and hair dryers. The generous breakfast spread—which includes everything from olives, salads, and falafel to yogurt and dates—is one of the highlights here, and can be enjoyed in the outdoor courtyard.

Mary's Well Square, Nazareth. www.villa-nazareth.co.il. ✆ **04/600-0569.** 18 units. 42 private double NIS 470–NIS 800 (breakfast included). **Amenities:** Parking, restaurant, bar, handicapped accessible; free Wi-Fi.

NEAR NAZARETH: ZIPPORI

Two thousand years ago, Zippori (Sepphoris) was a thriving city and Nazareth a humble village less than 6km (3¾ miles) away. Now those roles are reversed, and Zippori is a cooperative agricultural village and the site of a fascinating archaeological park. If you have a car, this is a placid, convenient place from which to explore.

Zippori Village Guesthouses ★★ Built by husband-and-wife American expats Mitch and Suzy Pilcer, this collection of rustic cottages are set in a lush garden. Each contains a bedroom, a small living room with fireplace, a

Every guest gets their own charming villa at Zippori Village Guesthouses.

sofa bed, a Jacuzzi, and a fully equipped kosher *halavi* kitchenette (non-meat only). A loft area, reached by ladder, adds more sleeping space. A re-created crusader castle is available for night rent, too, but is usually reserved for groups (it sleeps 18). The nonchemical, freshwater swimming pool is a definite plus, especially in summer. The management offers good touring advice (Mitch is a tour guide), and wonderful kosher breakfasts can be ordered, left each morning beside your door. You need a rental car in order to consider a stay here. Nearby are the ruins of Zippori, country walks, and even donkey rides for children.

Moshav Zippori. www.zippori.com. ✆ **04/646-4749** or 053/782-9568. 7 cottages. Sun–Thurs NIS 500, Fri–Sat NIS 650. Breakfast is extra. Discounts for large families and long-term stays. **Amenities:** Barbecue/picnic area; pool; free Wi-Fi.

Where to Eat

There are lots of places on Pope Paul VI Street and Casa Nova Street near the basilica where you can grab a falafel, a shawarma, or a mezze of Arabic salads, grilled meats, and fresh pita bread. All have been around forever, and serve tasty (if predictable) fare. There's also no shortage of charming cafes and bakeries inside Nazareth's old city. For something really special and different, try:

Luna Bistro ★★★ CONTEMPORARY NAZARENE CUISINE Yes, Luna is located in a shopping mall, but if you can get past its unfortunate location, this is truly one of the top restaurants in town. (The terrace offers unparalleled evening views of the old city, so the address has its benefits.) Serving excellent renditions of traditional Galilean salads, meat dishes, and mezze, this woman-owned restaurant has something delicious for everyone at the table: vegan *maqluba* (a one-pot rice and vegetable dish that is dramatically turned upside-down from individually portioned pots, tableside), *shushbarak* (lamp dumplings in a yogurt sauce), and a kids' menu. For dessert don't skip the *halva knafeh,* a pastry made with delicate and toasted *kataifi* noodles, which is Luna's signature take on this sweet treat usually made with cheese.

Big Fashion Mall, 53 Tawfiq Ziad St. www.luna.rest.co.il. ✆ **04/888-8626.** Main courses NIS 61–NIS 104. Open daily from 11:30am–10pm. Reservations recommended. Ample parking available at the shopping mall.

Attractions near Nazareth

Beit She'arim National Park ★ Somewhat reminiscent of the Sanhedrin Tombs in Jerusalem, these catacombs are located on the main road from Haifa that heads toward Afula (the principal town of the Jordan Valley).

In the late 2nd and early 3rd centuries, the town of Beit She'arim was the home of the Supreme Religious Council, the Sanhedrin, as well as headquarters of the famous Rabbi Yehuda Ha-Nasi (Judah the Prince), the compiler of the Mishnah. Many learned and famous Jews were laid to rest in this, the town's cemetery, a network of caves beneath a tranquil grove of cypress and olive trees. Over the centuries, however, the tombs were destroyed and the caves looted. The town was abandoned, and earth and rock covered the entrances to the catacombs as if they had never existed. They were unearthed in 1926 but only fully explored after the War of Independence.

A sarcophagus in the underground tombs at Beit She'arim National Park.

Enter the burial chambers through an opening in the rock or a stone door. Inside you'll see sarcophagi carved with rams' horns and lions' heads, menorahs, and other examples of Roman-era Jewish folk art. We think catacomb 20 is the most interesting, with its legible inscriptions, carvings, and interesting relics.

The entire site here is well tended, with a parking lot, visitor facilities, and an outdoor cafe. To better understand

sweet TREATS

Several stores in Nazareth are named **Mahroum's Sweets**—pass them by! They "borrowed" the name because the concoctions at the original store—at Pope Paul VI and El-Bishara Streets near the Basilica of the Annunciation—are so delectable, they've become a necessary late afternoon stop for tourists and locals alike. If you're like us, you'll start drooling just at the sight of the shop windows, which are filled with Israel's best baklava, Turkish delight *(majoun)* with nuts, and *Esh el-Bulbul* ("Nightingale's Nest," a nest of shredded wheat filled with nuts laced with honey). Dessert and Turkish coffee cost about NIS 30 or less. Trust us, the calories (and cost) are worth it. Mahroum's is open daily from 7am to 9pm.

what you'll be seeing, take in the introductory film before heading down into the catacombs.

Off Rte. 75 and Rte. 722, near HaTishbi Junction. en.parks.org.il. Admission NIS 22 adults, NIS 9 children. Sat–Thurs 8am–5pm (to 4pm in winter); Fri 8am–4pm (to 3pm in winter).

Mount Tabor (or Tavor) ★★ Like the summit of Mount Carmel, near Haifa, where the Prophet Elijah challenged the Canaanite prophets of Baal,

Atop Mount Tabor, the Basilica of the Transfiguration has views that stretch for miles.

the summit of Mount Tabor is believed to have been a Canaanite "high place," or altar, from at least the 2nd millennium B.C. The defeat of the Canaanites at such a prominent sanctuary (the mountain stands 540m or 1,772 ft. above sea level, making it the tallest of the Lower Galilee Mountains) must have had a stunning psychological effect.

Mount Tabor certainly played a crucial role in the life of Jesus Christ. Just 9.6km (6 miles) southeast of Nazareth, it must have been a dominant feature of the landscape Jesus knew in his childhood. At the summit stands the **Basilica of the Transfiguration,** which marks the traditional site where Jesus was transfigured as he spoke to Moses and Elijah in the presence of three of his disciples (Luke 9:28–36). The current Basilica was built in the 1920s over the ruins of long-destroyed Crusader and Byzantine churches (visitors can still go into the grottoes of the Crusader church). Also on the mount is the **Church of Elias** (Elijah), built in 1911 by the Greek Orthodox community. From here on a clear day you can see the Sea of Galilee, Mount Hermon, the Mediterranean Sea, and the Yizreel Valley. At this dramatic mountain, in the period of the Judges (ca. 1150 B.C.), the Prophet Deborah and her general, Barak, led the Israelite tribes to victory over the Canaanite general Sisera of Hazor (Judges 4:12–16).

At the base of the mountain, in the Arabic **village of Shibli,** you'll find the modest but charming **Center of Bedouin Heritage** (**© 04/676-7875**). It's open Saturday to Thursday from 9am to 5pm; admission is NIS 12; Shibli also hosts a number of Bedouin-style restaurants, good for an afternoon break.

Another spot for a break in the area is **Beit HaMarzipan** (**Marzipan House;** www.nuthouse.co.il) in nearby Kfar Tabor. Using ground almonds grown in the village, the center offers workshops on sculpting marzipan into different shapes—a fun activity for kids who might need some respite from trekking between historic sites. Beit HaMarzipan is open from Sunday to Thursday from 9am to 5pm, and on Fridays from 9am to 4pm.

Mount Tabor is accessible from Nazareth by Egged Bus, private car, or taxi. Although it looks close, the way is circuitous. If you are driving or walking, the road up Mount Tabor becomes increasingly steep the higher you ascend, with absolutely hair-raising hairpin turns. Beware of vehicles in front of you conking out and rolling downhill. The descent can seem even more horrific, but the view from the summit is magnificent.

Tel Megiddo (Armageddon) National Park ★ In the Old Testament, the name Megiddo appears in a number of places, mostly in relation to war. In the New Testament, the book of Revelation names Armageddon (a corruption of the Hebrew *Har Megiddo*—Mount Megiddo) as the place where the last great battle will be fought when the forces of good triumph over the forces of evil.

Which shouldn't be surprising as this UNESCO World Heritage site has always been a place of blood and swords, a crucial fortress, thanks to its strategic position on the major route leading from Egypt to Syria and Mesopotamia.

Archaeologists have uncovered the remains of cities of more than 20 distinct historical periods on this *tel* (Hebrew for an archaeological mound or hill), dating from 4000 B.C. to after A.D. 500.

In fact, Megiddo has been a place of battle continuing right down into the 20th century. General Allenby launched his attack against the Turks from the Megiddo Pass in 1917, and in 1948 the Israeli forces used the fortress site as a base of operations against entrenched Arab armies.

As you enter the Megiddo National Park there is a **museum** with detailed information about the excavations, the artifacts found there, the biblical and historical references relating to its past, and a model of the site as it now exists. Many more artifacts discovered here have been removed, and may now be found in Jerusalem's Israel and Rockefeller museums.

You can walk among the ruins, including what may be a **palace** from the time of King Solomon, **King Ahab's "Chariot City,"** and what some archaeologists call **stables** with a capacity for almost 500 horses (other archaeologists claim that the structures are not stables, though exactly what they were is a matter of controversy). There is also a large **grain silo** from the reign of Jeroboam Ben Joash, king of Israel in the 8th century B.C., and a building some attribute to the time of King David (1006 B.C.–970 B.C.). On strata way down below the later buildings, you can see excavated ruins of temples 5,000 and 6,000 years old, constructed during the Chalcolithic period.

Most amazing of all is the **water tunnel** ★★ dating from the reign of King Ahab in the 9th century B.C. You enter it by walking 183 steps 36 meters (118 ft.) down into a large pit in the earth (the collection pool inside the city walls), from which you can walk along the tunnel extending 65 meters (213 ft.) to a spring located outside the city, which was camouflaged by a wall covered with earth, designed to assure a constant supply of fresh water to the city even when it was under siege. (Read "The Psalm of the Hoopoe," in James Michener's *The Source,* to learn how tunnelers, digging from both ends, managed to meet underground using simple engineering techniques.) ***Note:*** The water tunnel is wheelchair-accessible with advance arrangement by phone. It closes 30 minutes before the rest of the park.

20km (12 miles) from Haifa. ✆ **04/659-0316.** Admission NIS 28 adults, NIS 14 children. Apr–Sept Sat–Thurs 8am–5pm, Fri 8am–4pm; Oct–Mar Sat–Thurs 8am–4pm, Fri 8am–3pm. Located just north of junction of Rte. 65 and Rte. 66.

Zippori (Sepphoris) National Park ★★ Now a small *moshav,* or cooperative agricultural community, the ancient city of Sepphoris dates from the era of the Maccabees in the 2nd century B.C. An enormous period of expansion and building that started in the A.D. 1st century turned the city into "the ornament of the Galilee," according to Flavius Josephus, the famed 1st-century Romano-Jewish scholar.

With its worldly, mixed population of Hellenistic pagans and Jews, it's interesting to speculate about the influence of Zippori on Jesus, who grew up in what was then the small village of Nazareth, a mere 6.5km (4 miles) away.

According to some traditions, Zippori was **the birthplace of Mary.** As a city requiring the services of many skilled carpenters and builders, Zippori may have been a place often visited by Jesus; the landscapes and vistas around Zippori, unlike those of modern, urbanized Nazareth, may still resemble the countryside Jesus knew. The Crusaders built a church in Zippori, the ruins of which can still be seen, dedicated to Saint Anne and Saint Joachim, the parents of Mary. Another tradition, however, holds that although the home of Mary's family was in Zippori, Mary was born in Jerusalem.

A Roman theater at Zippori National Park.

The Jewish community in Zippori grew rapidly after the Bar Kochba revolt of A.D. 135, when thousands of refugees from Judea migrated into the Galilee. By the late 2nd century, Zippori was the seat of the Sanhedrin and the home of many great rabbinical sages, including Yehuda Ha-Nasi, who codified the Mishnah. During the Talmudic era, the city contained numerous synagogues; in 1993, archaeologists uncovered a **mosaic synagogue floor ★** from the A.D. 5th century, decorated with an elaborate zodiac design and inscriptions in Hebrew, Aramaic, and Greek.

Other impressive finds in Zippori are the ruins of a 4,000-seat Roman amphitheater and a vast, late Roman–era Dionysian mosaic floor of a villa that includes the **"Mona Lisa of the Galilee" ★★**, a hauntingly beautiful depiction of a young woman that is one of the greatest examples of ancient mosaic portraiture ever discovered. There is also an intricate mosaic depiction of Nile landscapes, including the famous Nilometer. In other parts of the excavations, you'll find a Crusader fortress and church. A computer/multimedia program has been set up to help bring the site to life for visitors. By prior reservation, a vehicle for those with disabilities can be ordered without charge.

6.5km (4 miles) northwest of Nazareth, on Rte. 79. en.parks.org.il. ✆ **04/656-8272.** Admission NIS 28 adults, NIS 14 children. Sat–Thurs 8am–5pm (in winter to 4pm); Fri 8am–4pm (in winter to 3pm). Last admission an hour before closing. No public transportation.

TIBERIAS ★

330km (205 miles) N of Jerusalem; 116km (72 miles) E of Haifa

For centuries, what little industry existed in Tiberias was built around pilgrimage and veneration of ancient tombs, some with very dubious traditions.

Today Tiberias is bustling, thanks to its new incarnation as a center for discos, party boats, fish restaurants, and international tour groups. The beaches are full during the hot weather months and pubs and restaurants along the Waterfront Promenade pound with techno and heavy metal on summer evenings.

At the same time, many large and small hotels in Tiberias have come to cater especially to a religious Jewish clientele, giving the city a decidedly split personality.

Little of the town's splendid history is immediately visible, though it is interesting for those who seek it out. The ancient city of Tiberias was built in A.D. 18 by Herod Antipas (son of Herod the Great), and named in honor of the Roman emperor Tiberias. With its natural hot springs and mild, far-below-sea-level climate (warm in winter; brutally hot in summer), it became one of the most elegant winter resorts in this part of the ancient world. Classical writers describe a city adorned with colonnaded streets, impressive Roman baths and temples made of imported white marble, and broad marble steps leading into the waters of the lake. Ancient and Byzantine/Talmudic-era Tiberias was larger and more spread out than the modern city; many archaeological sites are outside its present boundaries, and most have not yet been excavated.

For more than a century after its founding, rabbis condemned Tiberias as a place of pagan cults and immoral activities; worse yet, it was built on a cemetery, making it forbidden to Jews as a place to live. But the healing powers

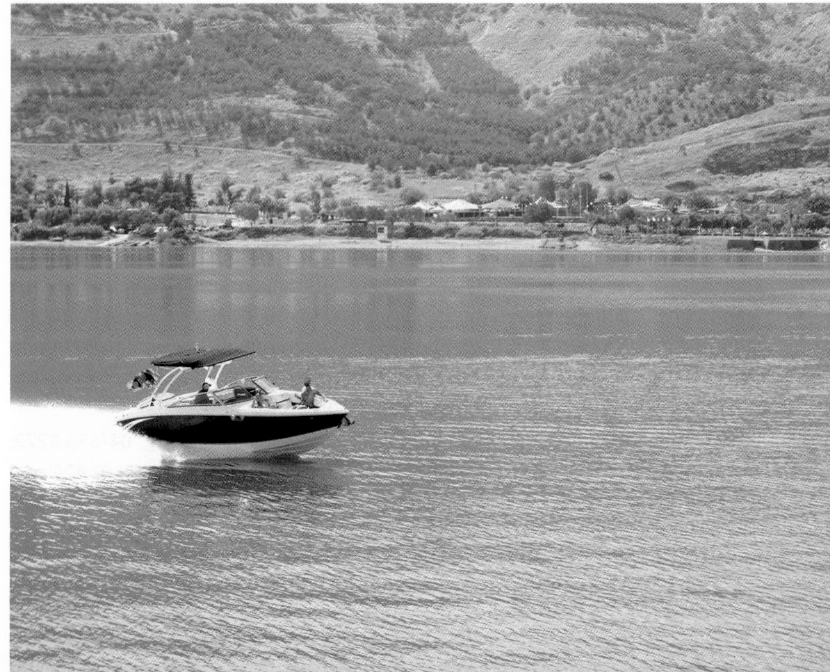

Tiberias is one of Israel's holiest cities, but today many come just to party on Lake Kinneret.

of the hot springs caused the rabbinical prohibition to be rescinded, and by the late Roman era, many of the rabbinical leaders themselves were enjoying the restorative powers of the hot springs.

In the centuries after the Temple of Jerusalem had been destroyed, Tiberias developed into a new major center for Jewish learning. It was here that the Mishnah was completed in the A.D. 2nd and 3rd centuries, at the direction of Rabbi Yehuda Ha-Nasi, "Judah the Prince." Here the Jerusalem Talmud was compiled in the A.D. 4th century, and the standardized rules for vowel and punctuation grammar were introduced into the Hebrew language by the scribes of Tiberias. Mystics, academicians, and men believed to have magic powers have been drawn to Tiberias throughout its history. Both the town and the towering scholarship declined after the A.D. 5th century due to the many wars fought here by the Persians, Arabs, Crusaders, and Turks. A medieval Arab historian recorded that the residents of the town led a life of decadence—dancing, feasting, playing the flute, running around naked in the summer heat, and swatting green flies, the eternal plague of the region until modern times.

Tiberias lies on one of the earth's major geological fault lines, the Syrian/African Rift, and in 1837 the city was virtually destroyed by an earthquake. A few portions of the city's medieval walls and older buildings, composed of volcanic rock called black basalt, survived that catastrophe, but almost nothing else of medieval or ancient Tiberias can be seen today outside of the archaeological sites open to the public.

It is this rift that has given shape to the mountains and valleys, and it is the reason why you can stand at the Sea of Galilee, 210m (689 ft.) below sea level, and look up toward the north and see Mount Hermon towering 2,700m (8,858 ft.) above sea level. It's also the reason for the earthquakes and volcanic eruptions over the eons, as well as the mineral hot springs around the shores of Lake Kinneret and the Dead Sea.

Another interesting feature of the low-lying Syrian/African Rift is that it forms an incredible highway for bird migration between Europe and Africa. Two of Israel's major wildlife reserves—Hula Valley in the north, Hai Bar in the south—serve as stopping-off points for the birds on their long journey, and are popular with bird-watchers and nature lovers.

Tiberias is considered one of Israel's four "Holy Cities" (along with Jerusalem, Hebron, and Safed) and though visitors do still come here to visit the tombs of ancient sages, many simply come to party. In recent years, Tiberias has become a favored base for visiting the Sea of Galilee. It's a place of pounding discos, mass volume tourist hotels (both for secular and religious Jews; quite a split personality this town has!), spas, and boardwalk strolling.

GETTING THERE There is direct bus service from all of Israel's major cities. If you're driving yourself, from Jerusalem via the Jordan Valley, it's a 2½-hour drive; from Haifa, 1 hour and 20 minutes. Four main roads lead to Tiberias and the Sea of Galilee: from Safed, from the Jordan Valley, via Mount Tabor, and from Nazareth.

WHEN TO VISIT Because Tiberias is so far below sea level, the climate is mild in the fall, winter, and spring, but torrid when Tiberias is busiest in July and August.

SPECIAL EVENTS The **Ein Gev Music Festival** takes place at Kibbutz Ein Gev in spring during Passover Week. Israeli folk dance and song festivals are organized along the waterfront in summer; ask the Tiberias Tourist Information Office, Ha-Banim Street, Tiberias (www.visit-tiberias.com; ✆ **04/672-5666**) for details. It's open Sunday to Thursday from 8am to 3:45pm.

ORIENTATION Tiberias (pop. 45,000) spreads out along the Kinneret shore and climbs the hillside to the west. The very center of Tiberias is **Kikar Ha-Atzma'ut,** or Independence Square, in the Old City. Surrounding Ha-Atzma'ut Square is what little is left of historic Tiberias.

Tiberias's main street changes names as it winds through the city. As it descends from the mountains to the lake it's called Ha-Nitzahon Road; in the residential district of Kiryat Shmuel up on the hillside it becomes Yehuda Ha-Nasi Street; and as it descends to approach the Old City its name changes to Elhadeff (or El-Hadeff or Alhadif) Street. After passing Ha-Atzma'ut Square, it becomes Ha-Banim Street, and this name serves it all the way to the southern limits of the city. South of the Old City about 1.5km (1 mile) is the section called **Hammat,** or **Tiberias Hot Springs.** Ruins of an ancient resort center and synagogue, a national park, a museum, and the Tomb of Rabbi Meir Baal Haness are located near the springs.

North of the Old City, Gdud Barak Road skirts past several beaches on its way to the newly excavated site of **Magdala** (where Mary Magdalene came from), **Tabgha** (where the miracle of the loaves and fishes took place), the **Mount of Beatitudes** (where Jesus preached the Sermon on the Mount), and **Capernaum** (Kfar Nahum), a fishing community that was the hometown of Peter and the center for Jesus' ministry.

Getting Around

There are several places where you can rent a **bicycle** in town, such as the **Astoria Galilee Hotel** (www.astoria.co.il). You can rent a car at any of the major rent-a-car companies with offices in Tiberias. Many of them are located in the block of Elhadeff Street north of Ha-Yarden Street. If you plan to pick up a rental car in Tiberias, it's a good idea to reserve online in advance.

What to See & Do

The main city on the Sea of Galilee, Tiberias has a split personality. **Ha Galil Street** is reminiscent of a tree-shaded main street in any small American town—it's lined with small shops serving the population from the surrounding countryside. If the old basalt-rock buildings, with their second-story balconies, were renovated, the street could be charming. A block to the east is the other main street, **Ha-Banim Street,** passing high-rises, mega hotels, and the *Midrehov,* or Pedestrian Mall, leading to the **Waterfront Promenade,** packed with tourists during the summer and Jewish holidays, throbbing at night with wall-to-wall discos, pubs, cafes, and restaurants. The Waterfront Promenade has a magnificent view across the lake. Ninety meters (295 ft.) to the left are the remains of a **Crusader fort,** jutting up in black basalt stone from the water.

Tiberias's Jewish Tombs ★ Important places of veneration for religious pilgrims over the centuries, the tombs of the city of Tiberias are varied and many. Arguably the most notable is the famed **Rambam's (Maimonides's) Tomb** (it's located off Yochanan Ben-Zakkai Street). Rabbi Moses Ben-Maimon, known both as Maimonides and the Rambam, was the greatest Jewish theologian of the Middle Ages. A Sephardic Jew, he was born in Cordova, Spain, but lived most of his life in Morocco and Egypt, where he was an Aristotelian philosopher, a physician (he served as personal physician to Saladin, at his royal court in Egypt), and a leading scientist and astronomer. His principal work was *The Guide for the Perplexed.* Although he didn't live in Tiberias, according to legend, as he was dying, the great Maimonides had himself strapped to a donkey and was carried northward from Egypt, toward the Holy Land, where he hoped to be buried. The inhabitants of Tiberias found his body and buried him in their city. The philosopher, who died in 1204, is now honored by a newly restored mausoleum and gardens.

Nearby is the **tomb of Rabbi Yochanan Ben-Zakkai,** founder of the Yavne Academy in the years following the destruction of Jerusalem in A.D. 70 (the Yavneh Academy was central to keeping Judaism alive in the decades after Jerusalem's destruction). And on a hillside just west of town is the **memorial to Rabbi Akiva,** a cave in which, according to tradition, he was buried. This great sage compiled the commentaries of the Mishnah before the Romans tortured him to death at Caesarea around A.D. 135 for his role in supporting the Bar Kochba revolt.

The tomb of **Rabbi Meir Baal Haness** (Meir, Master of Miracles; he also lived in the time of the Mishnas), on the hill above the hot springs, is considered one of Israel's holiest sites; pilgrims visit in search of medical cures and help with personal problems. Rabbi Meir is remembered in a white building that has two tombs. The Sephardic tomb, with the shallow dome, was built around 1873 and is believed to contain the actual grave, close to the interior western wall of the synagogue; the building with the

Jewish pilgrims at the burial site of Rabbi Yochanan Ben-Zakkai.

This splendid mosaic from the A.D. 4th century once graced the floor of the synagogue of Hamat Tiberius. It's protected by a national park of that same name.

steeper dome is the Ashkenazi synagogue, erected about 1900. Tradition has it that Rabbi Meir was brought here after his death but had willed that he be buried standing up, so that when the Messiah came he could simply walk out to greet him.

Tiberias is home to other tombs in varying states of neglect, and strong pilgrimage traditions have developed over the centuries. A marble structure beside a modern apartment building, the **Tomb of the Matriarchs** is believed, according to some traditions, to be the final resting place of a number of biblical women, including Jacob's third and fourth wives, Bilhah and Zilpah; Yocheved (the mother of Moses); Zipporah (Moses' wife); Elisheva (wife of Aaron); and Avigail (one of the wives of King David).

Free admission. Open 24/7. Direct bus service to Tiberias from all major cities. The Central Bus Station is on Ha-Yardem Street, 2 blocks inland from Ha-Atzma'ut Square.

Hamat Tiberias National Park ★★ **Hamat Tiberias** contains the ruins of one of Israel's most magnificent ancient synagogues, as befits a town that would have hosted wealthy visitors from distant Jewish communities (it was a famous spa resort for centuries and was founded well before Tiberias in the A.D. 1st century). Most spectacular is the Hamat Tiberias synagogue's well-preserved **mosaic calendar floor ★★** (A.D. 4th c.), which depicts the zodiac cycle and, in its outer corners, four women representing the seasons of the year. At the center of the zodiac, the sun god Helios rides on a chariot through the heavens. Beyond the zodiac, a separate mosaic panel depicts traditional Jewish symbols, including the Ark of the Covenant flanked by two ceremonial menorahs. The famous naïve-style zodiac floor of the Bet Alpha synagogue (which served a Byzantine-era farming village in the Jordan Valley) may have drawn on this very sophisticated mosaic for inspiration.

Entrance to the ruins is through the **Ernest Lehman/Hammam Suleiman Museum,** which inventories information on regional history and the curative powers of the hot springs. ***Warning:*** Be aware that the open water flowing through the gardens around the ruins comes directly from the hot springs and will scald you. Up the hill from the baths is the **Tomb of Rabbi Meir Baal Haness** (Rabbi Meir, Master of Miracles), a disciple of Rabbi Akiva and one of the great sages who helped to compile the Mishnah in the A.D. 2nd century. en.parks.org.il. ✆ **04/672-5287.** Admission NIS 14 adults, half-price children. Sat–Thurs 8am–5pm (4pm in winter); Fri 8am–4pm (3pm in winter). Parts of the park and museum are wheelchair accessible.

CRUISES & FERRIES

Lido Cruises Sailing Company (www.lido.co.il; ✆ **04/671-0800**) operates a ferry that runs between Lido Beach in the northern part of town and Kibbutz Ginosar, toward the northeastern corner of the lake, for NIS 32 round-trip; bicycles are free to take onboard, but there's no discount if you only travel one-way. Departures often depend on a minimum number of passengers. Lido Cruises Sailing Company also offers rides on evening party boats, and water-ski and sailboard rental. Boats leave from the docks at the parking lot for the Pagoda and the Decks Restaurants, just off Gdud Barak Street, a short walk north of downtown Tiberias.

Holyland Sailing Tiberias Marina (www.jesusboats.com; ✆ **04/672-3006**) offers more of a pleasure cruise, with 45-minute sails on the lake in smaller boats modeled after the design of a Roman-era boat (known locally as "the Jesus Boat,") found in archaeological excavations at Kibbutz Ginosar,

Dancing on the Waters

In good weather, the Lido Cruises Sailing Company sends out evening party boats to cruise the Sea of Galilee in the moonlight or under the stars. On board, the boats are filled with Israeli Arabs, Jews, and a smattering of tourists dancing in the wind to traditional Arabic tunes, pop Israeli music, international hits, and even a waltz or two. It's happy pandemonium: Everyone dances with everyone—Galilee Arabs with Jews from Jerusalem and Tel Aviv; men with men for traditional Arabic *debkas;* women with women for the Macarena; everyone together for golden oldies or the latest on the Israeli hit parade. It's NIS 55 to join in this vision of a deliriously happy, peaceful Middle East for an hour; and it's free with a voucher you get when you dine at Decks, the best restaurant in Tiberias.

north of Tiberias. Pricing depends on whether you're joining a group or chartering a private boat. All passengers receive a pilgrim certificate.

ORGANIZED TOURS

The **Society for Protection of Nature in Israel** (SPNI; www.aspni.org) offers well-curated walks and hikes in the Jordan and Jezreel valleys, as well as the Galilee, exploring the flora, fauna, and geology of the area. The society's tours are mostly in English; when they aren't, there are usually others taking the tour who can translate.

SPORTS & OUTDOOR ACTIVITIES

Watersports are offered on and around the lake, including water-skiing, water parachuting, sailboarding, giant waterslides, kayak trips, and more. Check at your hotel or at the Tiberias Tourist Information Office for information.

BEACHES The gardened **Blue Beach** (www.bluefun.co.il), with a large swimming area, charges NIS 50 to NIS 60 for the use of its lake facilities and a beach-chair rental. Open daily (in season) 9am to 5pm. We'd say it's worth it. The NIS 45 fee at **Quiet Beach** (✆ **04/670-0800**) includes a noisy children's pool (ironically), and is open daily (in season) from 9:30am to 5:30pm. The **Gai Beach** (www.gaiwaterpark.co.il) 1km (⅔ mile) south of town, beyond the Galei Kinneret Hotel, has an elaborate water park and a fine beach with all the requisite facilities; it charges a NIS 119 admission fee. Due to drought conditions, the coastline is often far from the beach, and pollution has become a serious problem, from time to time, at all the area beaches.

HORSEBACK RIDING In the countryside around the lake, you can join groups for trail riding; call **Vered HaGalil Guest Farm** (www.veredhagalil.co.il; ✆ **04/693-5785;** p. 215). Vered HaGalil offers beautiful (and beautifully tended) horses for everything from guided trail rides to 15-minute pony rides for kids.

Where to Stay

Tiberias has everything from hostels to megahotels geared toward tour groups, with a few religious guesthouses, as well. You should note that most hotels in Tiberias have kosher kitchens and that several especially cater to the Orthodox and have glatt kosher certification (see p. 38 for an explanation of kashrut). On summer and holiday nights, the noise level from discos and party boats can make sleep difficult. Small hotels and kibbutz accommodations in the countryside around the lake can be a good option if you have a car; they also offer a better sense of the Galilee's beauty. The Tiberias Tourism Information Office gives out lists of rooms to rent in private homes.

DOWNTOWN TIBERIAS

Expensive

Galei Kinneret ★★ Originally opened in 1946, the Galei Kinneret overlooks the serene, freshwater Sea of Galilee and harkens back, in its ambience, to the golden days of the city. We can thank the hotel's original CEO, Lotte

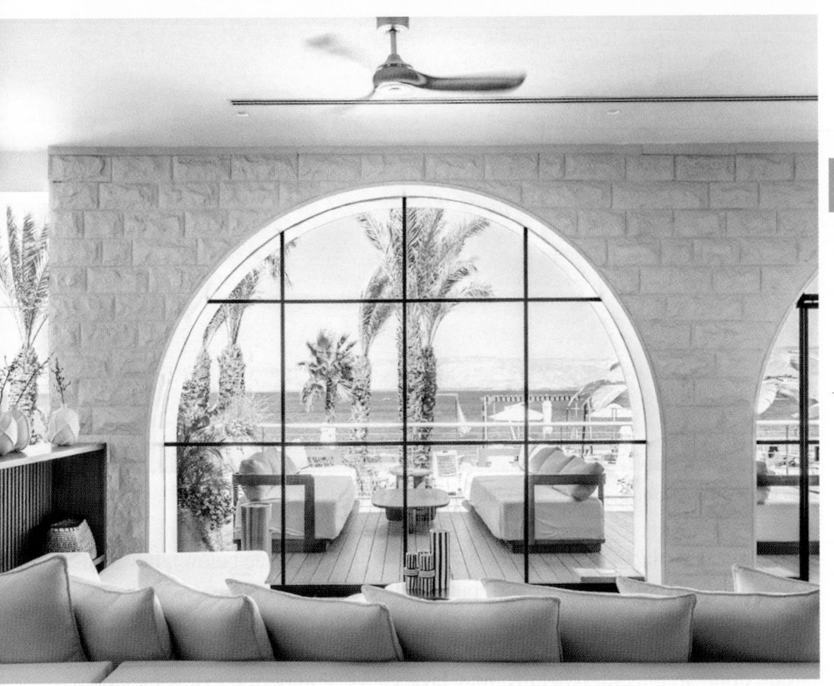

A serene indoor/outdoor lounge at the Galei Kinneret.

Eisenberg, for its good looks. Partnering with the Africa Palestine Company and architect Aharon Kempinski, Lotte oversaw the luxury hotel's creation from the ground up and filled it with antiques, works of art, and delightful treasures from all over the world. The guest rooms were recently refurbished and feature sinuously elegant wooden furnishings, chaise lounges, and rain showers. All rooms face either the Sea of Galilee or surrounding mountains, some with balconies, and a few with Jacuzzis on those balconies. Guests are treated to private boat excursions and have access to a private, manicured beach beneath the citrus cliffs of the Golan Heights, where sun beds and a food truck await (open 9am–4pm). The on-site restaurant, named as a tribute to the hotel's first lady, is a gluttonous culinary experience with famed chef Assaf Granit (of Machneyuda and Tzemah in Jerusalem) calling all the delicious shots. Granit's extensive menu pulls from the Tiberian food heritage with salads highlighting local produce, wines of the region, and a number of reimagined classics, like sweetbreads with an almond tahini, or Tunisian Cigar with mackerel.

1 Eliezer Kaplan St. www.galei-kinneret.com. ✆ **04/670-7070.** $250–$475 double. Rates include breakfast. Free parking. **Amenities:** Spa; pool; fitness center; restaurant; private beach; synagogue; free Wi-Fi.

The Scots Hotel ★★ Set in an expansive walled garden, this hotel, composed of 19th-century stone buildings in the heart of downtown Tiberias is one

Lush landscaping surrounds the historic buildings of the Scots Hotel.

of the loveliest places to stay in town—most of the time (see below). It's affiliated with the Church of Scotland, but travelers of all religions are welcome. Room categories include the modern standard ("unique") rooms and the more expensive "antique" rooms that offer atmospheric arched ceilings and exposed basalt-stone architectural details, plus lake views. Pampering extras include a fine spa with massage services, a very nice swimming pool, private beach, an in-house program of evening performances and activities, a friendly staff, and truly excellent meals. That last perk is important, as "room only" rates are not available here; rates always include two meals. ***Warning:*** When booked by tour groups, the tranquility of the location can be lost, and the room rates become unusually high, but this is a wonderful base from which to tour the region when it's not jam-packed. Dining facilities are not kosher.

1 Gdud Barak St. www.scotshotels.co.il. ✆ **04/671-0710.** 66 units. From $390–$550 (half board, which means two meals included). Thurs–Sat minimum 2-night stay sometimes required. Limited free parking. **Amenities:** Restaurant; bar; private beach; spa; pool; free Wi-Fi.

ACCOMODATIONS AROUND THE LAKE

Expensive

The Setai Sea of Galilee ★★ This manicured resort right on the lake not only has magnificent water views, but every guest also gets their own bit of splash with either a lap pool or a Jacuzzi set on the terrace of their private villa. The water features continue inside these swank, bright guest digs, with rainfall showers and tubs big enough for two. The hotel's spa, set in its own building, is the largest such facility in Israel and offers a broad range of massages and beauty treatments. The extravagant breakfast buffet is a highlight, included for all guests.

Tzeelon Beach. www.thesetaihotels.com. ✆ **03/526-3332.** 158 units. $490–$720 double; higher rates may apply on weekends. Rates include breakfast. Free parking. **Amenities:** Restaurant; spa; business center; fitness center; free Wi-Fi.

Moderate

Kibbutz Ein Gev Resort Village ★★ This kibbutz resort is a great base for exploring the region as it boasts one of the most beautiful beaches on the lake. In fact, that may be its downfall as a lodging because you'll be tempted to stay put—the warm waters and splendid views of the Galilee hills and the Golan Heights invite lingering. Consider doing that over dinner: the kibbutz is home to its own famous restaurant specializing in fresh St. Peter's fish, and it features the same lovely views. Accommodations range from simple five-person family bungalow units to basic, modern motel-style doubles, all with fridge or kitchenettes and set amid pleasant gardens. There's a minimart on the grounds, and a hearty kibbutz-style dinner buffet available with advance reservation or with a half-board plan.

Kibbutz Ein Gev. www.eingev.com. ✆ **04/665-9800.** 166 units. $175–$220 double; higher rates may apply Fri–Sat, Jewish holidays, and July 15–Aug 31 and for apartments and villas. Rates include breakfast. Free parking. The Holiday Village is 1.6km (1 mile) south of Ein Gev Kibbutz. **Amenities:** Restaurant; beach; massage; synagogue; free Wi-Fi.

Vered HaGalil Guest Farm ★★★ Located a mile north of the Sea of Galilee, with sweeping vistas of the lake, this is one of Israel's hidden secrets: a relaxing retreat of rustic cabins, and more expensive cottages and suites with separate bedrooms (many with kitchenettes and Jacuzzis), all set among

Even if you don't stay at the Vered HaGalil Guest Farm, you can participate in one of their top-notch horseback riding programs.

gardens. Vered HaGalil is famous for its beautiful horses and riding programs (open to non-guests). A short drive or hike takes you to the fascinating ruins of Korazim, a Roman-era Jewish village abandoned in early Islamic times, with many of its houses still standing, and with an impressive synagogue adorned with finely carved details in stone as the town's centerpiece. The staff offers personal, helpful attention. A pool and a country-style restaurant make this a good base to come home to after a day's touring. The restaurant features a star chef, but does not carry kosher certification. However, breakfasts are composed of dairy kosher products, on kosher kitchenware.

Korazim. www.veredhagalil.com. ✆ **04/693-5785.** 31 units. Cabin: $135–$170 double; Cottage/Studio: $170–$200; Suite: $210–$226. Rates are higher for Jewish holidays and July–Aug. Rates include breakfast. Free parking. Located at the Korazim-Almagor crossroad, 3.5km (2¼ miles) past the turnoff to the Mount of the Beatitudes. **Amenities:** Restaurant; bar; playgrounds; equestrian stables; horseshoes; seasonal outdoor pool; spa; free Wi-Fi.

Inexpensive

Selina Kinneret ★★ Part of an international chain of hip hostels that all have a co-working focus, the Selina Kinneret has an enviable lakeshore location, meaning its young guests can do their (included) morning yoga class on the sands. That's just one of the many activities at the Selina; it also hosts live music, craft markets, kids' classes, nightly beach parties by a bonfire, and other events. Guests have a choice of dorm accommodations, or private rooms with what we'd call a flea market aesthetic (a mix of found furnishings, plus brightly colored walls and curtains). A fresh Israeli breakfast is included with both options, and the hotel is trying to attract families, so it can provide baby beds, highchairs, and other gear, for an additional fee. Overall: a good, reasonably priced option—although it will be louder than many other lakeside spots.

Migdal. www.selina.com/israel/kinneret. $102–$170 double with private bathroom, $32–$50 dorm bed. Rate includes breakfast. **Amenities:** Pool; cafe; bar; communal kitchen; free parking; free Wi-Fi.

Where to Eat

In addition to the choices in Tiberias, travelers who have use of a car should dine at some of the delightful restaurants in the countryside and on the shore around Kinneret; see "Country Dining Around the Sea of Galilee," below. And even if you're not staying at the Galei Kinneret, be sure to treat yourself to a meal at their on-site restaurants, **Lotte,** one of the best in the region (see p. 212).

ON THE WATERFRONT

The specialty in Tiberias is St. Peter's fish, so-called because it is the very fish that swam in the Sea of Galilee when Jesus called Peter away from his nets to become a "fisher of men." It's a white fish that's indigenous to the Sea of Galilee, and its taste resembles that of bass. The main place in Tiberias to try the fish is along the **Waterfront Promenade** in the Old City.

Three of the large, attractive waterfront restaurants have the same management, the same menu, the same prices, and the same delicious food. These are the **Nof Kinneret** (✆ **04/672-0310**), the **Galei Gil** (www.8033040.rest.co.il; ✆ **04/672-0699**), and the **Roast on Fire** (✆ **04/672-0310**). The indoor decor is different in each restaurant, although outdoor dining on the boardwalk is virtually the same, so stroll along and see which you like the best; if the weather is good, you'll likely want to eat by the water. All three restaurants offer their fish fried, charcoal-grilled, or in a special sauce. Plan to spend about NIS 75 for something simple to NIS 140 for a large (more than a pound) serving of St. Peter's fish, French fries, salad, and pita bread. In summer, these places may be open 24 hours on weekends.

DOWNTOWN

A bit away from the crush of the Waterfront Promenade, around Ha Galil and Ha-Banim streets, you'll find restaurants that are less tourist-oriented. The north end of Ha Galil Street and Ha-Yarden Street next to Shimon Park is **"Falafel Row."** The lineup starts right outside Ha-Atzma'ut Square and stretches up toward the bus station. Quality and fixings can vary, but the cost should be about NIS 20 for falafel to go. The best falafel and shawarma stands offer a big selection of salads to tuck inside your pita, and fry falafel balls to order.

NORTH OF DOWNTOWN—THE LIDO COMPLEX

Just about a 5-minute walk up Gdud Barak Street from the downtown promenade are three lively yet romantic restaurants, each of which serve top-notch fare. They're worth the stroll, but offer free parking for those who don't want to hoof it.

Decks ★★★ KOSHER BARBECUE Set on a long, curving deck that seems to float over the surface of the Sea of Galilee, Decks is famous for exquisite meats, poultry, and fish barbecued over fires that combine citrus wood, olive wood, and American hickory. That mix gives them a unique (and memorable) smokiness. Specialties, not always written on the menu, may include boneless shoulder of lamb, priced according to weight and of gourmet quality; moist, juicy salmon and tuna, cooked in a traditional charcoal oven brought from the coast of Dalmatia; and carpaccio of Mediterranean tuna. Dinner comes with a voucher for one of the Lido Sailing Company's daytime or evening party boats—a fun experience, with local partygoers sometimes dancing on the waters.

Gdud Barak St. Tiberias. www.decks.co.il. Main courses NIS 70–NIS 150. Sun–Thurs noon–11pm; Sat after Shabbat until 11:30pm.

The Pagoda ★★ KOSHER CHINESE/THAI The Pagoda also offers a deck overlooking the water (with spectacular views), but here both the fare and the building are Asian. In fact, the airy pavilion extending over the water was designed by Chinese architects who used feng shui principles to make the best use of the lovely site. Recommended dishes include the spicy Thai chicken coconut soup and the light, healthful steamed Thai dishes, including delicate fresh fish and vegetables. On the Sabbath, the Pagoda opens its non-kosher affiliate, the charming **House Restaurant,** just across Gdud Barak Street (Fri 1pm–midnight, Sat 1–4:30pm). The menu, prices, and phone number are the same as the Pagoda's—the one difference is that it operates on Shabbat (and is the best choice in town for Friday night and Saturday dining).

Gdud Barak St. ✆ **04/672-5513.** Reservations recommended. Main courses NIS 55–NIS 115. Sushi fixed menu for 2 NIS 85–NIS 110. Sun–Thurs 12:30–3pm and 6pm–midnight.

COUNTRY DINING AROUND THE SEA OF GALILEE

Tiberias can become very hectic in the evening, especially during the summer. If you have a car, a drive out into the countryside for dinner can be very pleasant. Beyond those mentioned below, the restaurant at the Ein Gev Kibbutz serves excellent St. Peter's fish (see p. 215).

Magdalena ★★★ CREATIVE GALILEAN CUISINE Magdalena has become a favorite among Israeli travelers, and for good reason. In an area where the dining options can be hit or miss, the dishes here are memorably delicious. We're talking Galilean fare but with a contemporary twist, like tabouleh with candied pumpkin and labneh; lamb-stuffed Levantine pasta in a yogurt sauce perfumed with saffron; or classic grilled meats and fish with sides such as *freekeh* (toasted wheat salad) or truffled potato puree. If you're hungry and feel like a culinary splurge, opt for the eight-course tasting menu (priced at NIS 349 per person). A la carte options available, too.

Migdal. www.magdalena.co.il. ✆ **073/702-7299.** Reservations recommended. Main courses NIS 110–NIS 185. Daily 12:30–4:30pm and 6–9:30pm.

Rutenberg ★★★ MEDITERRANEAN If you're visiting Israel, you likely were inspired to come, at least partially, by the long and storied history of the country. Does that curiosity extend to culinary history? If so, make a pilgrimage to Rutenberg, a restaurant that pays homage to the 1,000-plus-year food story of the Jordan Valley. That means some of the dishes served in the course of this tasting menu event will be derived from recently translated recipes nearly a millennium old. Other dishes experiment with traditional preservation and fermentation techniques, and all make use of produce grown at the restaurant's garden or at nearby farms and wineries. The evening starts with a cocktail hour in the restaurant's garden, after which no more than 20 people (always in either couples or foursomes) sit down in the century-old building that holds Rutenberg for a 3-hour-long meal. If that's too much of a time commitment for you, lunch is shorter and cheaper (see below). ***Note:*** Rutenberg can accommodate special diets, so make your limitations known in advance.

Old Gesher. www.rutenberg.co.il/en. ✆ **04/675-2237.** Dinner NIS 325 per person, lunch NIS 125. Open Mon–Fri for lunch and dinner. Reservations strongly recommended for lunch, required for dinner.

Chef Yizhar Sahar gathers herbs for that day's meal at Rutenberg.

Tiberias After Dark

Tiberias bustles after dark, as prodigiously as it does in the daytime. That's particularly true in summer when performers of all types (both local and foreign) make appearances at the **Bet Gabriel Amphitheater** ★★★ and the majestic **Sherover Promenade** ★★, both on the southern tip of the Sea of Galilee (across from the Tzemach Junction). With parklike grounds, a snack bar/restaurant, and stunning vistas of the lake, it's a memorable venue for concerts. Check with the Tiberias Tourist Information Office for a schedule of performances.

Folklore events are often scheduled at hotels, and everyone is welcome to attend. For details, contact the tourist office at the end of the Ha-Banim Street Pedestrian Mall.

There are also many late-night pubs, cafes, bars, and restaurants. Good places for a quiet drink with live music include the **Leonardo Plaza** and the **Jordan River** hotels at the southern end of the Old City. **Big Ben,** on the Pedestrian Mall, has a more traditional indoor pub as well as a terrace; the crowd is a bit older and less rowdy. Many of the hotels (and even the hostels) around town have nice bars and pubs where you can relax and enjoy a drink and conversation with fellow travelers.

There are plenty of opportunities to go dancing, as well. The most unusual is the summer **disco dancing** on the boat operated by the Kinneret Sailing Company on the Sea of Galilee; call © **04/665-9800,** or stop by its office at the Waterfront Promenade, for information. An evening **disco cruise** also leaves from the Lido Kinneret Beach (Lido Kinneret Cruises; © **04/672-1538**) at varying times.

Day Trips

Hot Springs of Tiberias ★ Located 1.6km (1 mile) south of Tiberias, these thermal baths have been famous for their curative powers for more than 3,000 years. They are probably among the earliest-known thermal baths in the world, noted by Josephus, Pliny, church historians, and many Arabic writers. Some biblical commentators have surmised that Jesus cured the sick here. There's a local legend that Solomon got demons to heal his kingdom's ailing people at this site, tricking them into perpetually stoking the fires in the earth below to heat up the water.

The hot springs contain high amounts of sulfuric and hydrochloric acid, and calcium salts, and over the centuries they've reportedly cured skin problems and such ailments as rheumatism, arthritis, and gynecological disorders. They continue to have a following: Pharmacies across Israel keep supplies of mineral salts from these springs.

For those who want to try them in person, several treatments are available, including mineral bubble bath, physiotherapy, therapeutic massage, inhalation, and mud baths. There's an inexpensive restaurant on site. The older Hot Springs building is segregated by sex; the newer building is a bit spiffier. ***Note:*** Bring a bathing suit and towel.

To gain a better understanding of the waters, check out the **museum** next to the springs. While visiting the springs, you can also spend some time exploring the ancient ruins of Hammat.

Hot Springs of Tiberias (Hamei Tyeria), Eliezer Kablan Blvd., Tiberias. ✆ **04/672-8500.** Admission to the mineral pools NIS 72 Sun–Thurs, NIS 83 Fri–Sat; discounts for children. Sun–Mon and Wed 8am–10pm; Tues and Thurs 8:30am–8pm; Fri 8am–4pm; Sat 8:30am–8pm.

AROUND THE SEA OF GALILEE ★★★

The Arabic and Aramaic poets called it "the Bride," "the Handmaiden of the Hills," and "the Silver Woman." The ancient Hebrews called it "the Harp," in honor of the soothing harplike sounds of its waves, and because it roughly resembles the shape of an ancient harp. That's the name that stuck, with Israelis still calling the Sea of Galilee Kinnor, or Kinneret (both words for harp in Hebrew), as it is popularly known. According to one lexicographer, an ancient sage wrote: "God created the seven seas, but the Kinneret is His pride and joy." It's a marvelous lake, its surface constantly changing during the day. In summer, the Sea of Galilee's waters are sparkling and almost bathtub-warm; if you find a tranquil, beautiful beach for a swim, you'll emerge from the lake feeling refreshed, soothed, and cleansed.

Some 210m (689 ft.) below sea level, the Sea of Galilee is 21km (13 miles) long from the place where the Jordan flows in at the north to where it empties out in the south. It was here that Jesus preached to the crowds and fed them by multiplying the bread and fishes; it is also where he restored the sick and maimed. Today, parts of the sea are filled with speedboats and water-skiers; other parts are as serene and mysterious as in ancient times.

Kinneret's waters are a vast reservoir of sardine, mullet, catfish, and the unusual combfish. They are the same fish once caught by the disciples, and they are caught in the same manner today, though some of the kibbutzim have developed careful methods of farming fish.

Touring the Area

To tour the Sea of Galilee, head north, starting a circle that will bring you back to Tiberias before heading into the Upper Galilee region. There is no regular bus route that completely circles the lake, so you'll have to depend on a tour bus, rental car, bicycle, or boat.

MAGDALA (MIGDAL) ★

Just more than 3km (1¾ miles) north of Tiberias along the lakeside road, you'll come to the newly excavated ruin of the New Testament village of Magdala, the birthplace of Mary Magdalene. This is one of the most active archaeological digs in Israel. Fresh discoveries are being made almost daily amid the lovely scenery. The town stretched right down by the water's edge. On the hill just to the south of old Magdala, along the far (west) side of the highway, you can still see the sarcophagi (stone coffins) carved out of the rocks in the place that was Magdala's cemetery. The modern town of Migdal, founded in the 20th century, is about 1.6km (1 mile) to the north of the site of ancient Magdala.

THE GINOSAR VALLEY ★

A little farther on, about 10km (6¼ miles) north of Tiberias, you'll find yourself in a lush valley with many banana trees. These are part of the agriculture of **Kibbutz Nof Ginosar,** one of the larger kibbutzim, with a vast and busy kibbutz hotel. In the kibbutz, you'll find the multimedia **Yigal Alon Museum of the Galilee** (✆ **04/672-7700**). More a learning experience about the area than a museum, it offers only one genuine antiquity, **a Galilee fishing boat from approximately the A.D. 1st century,** preserved in the muddy sediment of the lake floor and revealed in the 1980s when, because of drought, the lake receded to record-low levels. The boat is touted by some guides as "the Jesus boat." Although it may be typical of fishing boats from the time of Jesus, there is, of course, no evidence that ties it to any specific persons. Still, it's an amazing discovery, and of special interest to pilgrim groups. The wooden frame of the boat is preserved in a climate-controlled boathouse structure. The museum is open Sunday to Thursday 8:30am to 5:30pm, Friday from 8:30am to 3:30pm; closed Saturdays.

TABGHA ★★

14km (8⅔ miles) N of Tiberias.

To reach Tabgha, where Jesus miraculously multiplied the loaves and fishes, proceed northward along the shoreline from Migdal, passing Minya, a 7th-century Arabian palace that is one of the most ancient and holy Muslim prayer sites. It's open daily from 8am to 4pm.

At Tabgha, you'll find the beautifully restored **Benedictine monastery** and the **Church of the Multiplication of the Loaves and Fishes ★★** (✆ **04/672-1061**). When the ancient church ruins, hidden for 1,300 years, were excavated, the **mosaic basilica floor** of a Byzantine-era church that once stood on this site was found. The floor is one of the most lyrical and skillfully made ever discovered in Israel. The section of the floor in front of the ancient altar is starkly unadorned, rather primitive, and interesting mainly for what it depicts: two fish and a humble basket filled with loaves of bread. In contrast, the main section of the mosaic is a skillfully executed, colorful tapestry of all the birds that once thrived in this area: swans, cranes, ducks, wild geese, and storks. The mosaic artist has captured the liveliness, humor, and grace of these creatures with a style rarely seen in this art form. The Nilometer, used to measure the flood levels of the Nile and famous throughout the ancient world, is also represented, leading some to speculate that the talented mosaic designer might have been Egyptian.

Be sure to read the history of this church posted just inside the entrance, in the church's courtyard. The early Judeo-Christians of nearby Capernaum (Kfar Nahum) venerated a large rock, upon which Jesus is said to have placed

A congregation prays at the Church of the Multiplication of the Loaves and Fishes in Tabgha.

the bread and fish when he fed the 5,000. The rock, a natural **dolmen,** is believed by historians to have been a sacred place since prehistoric times, and was used as the altar in a Byzantine church erected over the spot in about A.D. 350. The church is open Monday to Saturday from 8:30am to 5pm and on Sunday only for Mass; modest dress required. Admission is free, but donations are accepted. There's a bookstore and souvenir shop on site.

Just east of the Multiplication Church is the **Heptapegon** ("Seven Springs" in Greek), also called the **Church of the Primacy of Saint Peter ★**, or Mensa Christi. It was here on the shores of Galilee that Jesus is believed to have appeared to his disciples after his crucifixion and resurrection. Peter and the others were in a boat on the lake, fishing, but with no luck. When Jesus appeared, he told them to cast their nets again. They did, and couldn't haul in the nets because they were so heavy with fish. As the disciples sat with their master having dinner, Jesus is said to have conferred the leadership of the movement on Peter. The theory of Peter's primacy, and the tradition of that primacy's being passed from one generation of disciples to the next, is the basis for the legitimacy of the Roman pontiff as leader of Christendom.

The black basalt church rests on the foundations of earlier churches. Within is a flat rock called **Mensa Christi,** or "Christ's Table," where Jesus dined that evening with his disciples. Outside the church, you can still see the stone steps said to be the place where Jesus stood when he appeared, calling out to the disciples; on the beach are seven large stones, which may once have supported a little fishing wharf.

To reach Heptapegon, you must leave the Multiplication Church, return to the highway, turn right, and climb the hill to a separate entrance. This Greek Orthodox church is open daily from 8:30am to 4:45pm; admission is free.

If it's not too hot, you can easily walk to nearby Capernaum (3km/1¾ miles) and even to the Mount of the Beatitudes (see below).

MOUNT OF THE BEATITUDES ★★★

8km (5 miles) N of Ginosar; 3km (1¾ miles) N of Capernaum

Just beyond Tabgha, on a high hill, is the famous Mount of the Beatitudes, now the site of an Italian convent. Here Jesus preached the **Sermon on the Mount**—the site, though beautiful in itself, bears a special feeling of spirituality. As you stand on the hill, the acoustics often seem crystal-clear; you can imagine the listening crowds and the words of Jesus reverberating over the countryside. There are many good views of the Sea of Galilee and its surroundings, but the vista from this place is among the most magnificent. One odd fact about this church is the inscription on the sanctuary, which informs you that the entire project was built by Mussolini in 1937.

The dome of the basilica surrounded by gallery columns at the top of the Mount of Beatitudes.

The domed church building itself is open daily from 8:30 to 11:30am and 2:30 to 4:40pm. Admission is free, but the fee per car is NIS 10. If you go by bus from Tiberias, ask the driver to let you off at the closest stop, which is 1km (⅔ mile) from the church. There are benches along the way to rest on as you make the climb.

CAPERNAUM (KFAR NAHUM) ★★

Known in biblical times as the village of Nahum, this is a lakeside town where Jesus preached and his disciples Peter and Andrew made their homes. During the lifetime of Jesus, in the A.D. 1st century, Kfar Nahum was a prosperous fishing community, port, and waystation on the main trade route from Israel's Mediterranean coast to Damascus. It even had its own Customs House and was probably the most cosmopolitan of the lakeside towns until the founding of Tiberias in the mid–1st century. The town was abandoned around A.D. 700 and never reconstituted.

Today, you'll find a modern Franciscan monastery, which was built on the abandoned site in 1894, as well as ancient excavations spanning 6 centuries. Among the most impressive are the ruins of **a 3rd- or 4th-century synagogue** built on the site of an even earlier synagogue—perhaps one that Jesus would have prayed in (Peter's house was nearby; see below). It's built of imported white limestone rather than native black basalt. The ruins include tall columns, marble steps, shattered statuary, a doorway facing south to Jerusalem, and many ancient Jewish symbols: carved seven-branched menorahs, palm branches, and rams' horns. Again, this structure is not the actual synagogue in which Jesus taught, since it dates from several centuries after his time, but it clearly stands on the traditional location of the town's main synagogue. It is interesting to speculate on what the proximity of St. Peter's house to the synagogue might tell us about the position of his family in Capernaum's Jewish community. The excavations of basalt stone in the garden lead toward the sea, where you can still glimpse the remains of a small-boat basin with steps leading to the water. Admission is NIS 10. The site is open daily from 8:30am to 4:15pm.

Nearby are several houses of the period and the excavated remains of a 5th-century octagonal church built over the ruins of the traditional site of **St. Peter's house,** in which Jesus would have stayed. Byzantine architects frequently built domed octagonal structures over places of special veneration (the octagonal Dome of the Rock in Jerusalem, built by early Muslim rulers in A.D. 691 but designed by Byzantine architects, is an example of this type of structure). Other finds include an ancient olive press and a 2nd-century marble milestone on the Via Maris (Coastal Rd.), the Roman route from Egypt to Lebanon (an inland fork of the Via Maris passed through this district en route to Damascus). It was in Kfar Nahum that Jesus began to gather his disciples around him, saying, "Follow me, and I will make you fishers of men."

Where to Eat

St. Peter's Restaurant ★ MIDDLE EASTERN Restaurants on the northern shore of the Sea of Galilee are few and far between, but this one overlooking the water is one of the better ones. The menu isn't extensive—it's mostly fish filets, fried shrimp, and grilled meat—but what they do serve they make well. Lunch only.

Hof Amnun. st-peters-restaurant.business.site. ✆ **52/534-8878.** Complete meals NIS 55–NIS 95. Daily 11:30am–3:30pm.

KORAZIM ★★

For a thousand years, the ruins of this village lay hidden under an ocean of impassable thistles until the land was cleared in the late 20th century. It's a hauntingly evocative site that gives the visitor a feeling for what a Jewish community in the Galilee was like 1,500 years ago. According to the New Testament, Korazim was one of the towns chastised by Jesus.

The centerpiece of this village is a large A.D. 4th- to 5th-century synagogue made of local black basalt, heavily ornamented with carved grapevines, birds,

Remains of a synagogue in the ancient town of Korazim.

animals, and images of people harvesting the bounty of the land. You can also visit lightly reconstructed streets, houses, and a ritual bath attached to the synagogue, which was apparently destroyed either by earthquake or during civil unrest in the 7th century. A ceremonial chair carved from basalt, which served as the seat of honor for the synagogue, is especially interesting.

The national park office here (en.parks.org.il; ✆ **04/693-4982**) is open from 5am to 4pm; in summer to 5pm. Admission to the site is NIS 22 for adults and NIS 9 for children. The park is located at the Korazim-Almagor crossroad, between Tiberias and Rosh Pina. Nearby is the beautiful guest farm and dude ranch Vered HaGalil Guest Farm (p. 215).

KURSI ★

17km (11 miles) from Tiberias; 7km (4⅓ miles) N of Ein Gev

Kursi is on the eastern shore; according to the gospels, it is the "country of the Gergesenes" (or Gadarenes), where Jesus cast the demons out of a man who was possessed and into a herd of swine, which then plunged into the lake and drowned. For many years, speculation existed about the exact location of Kursi (also called Gergasa) and about what kind of religious structure might have been built here in commemoration of the casting out of the demons. After the Six-Day War, a bulldozer clearing the way for a new road happened to uncover the ruins of a Byzantine church complex, complete with a monastery (perhaps the largest ever built in the Holy Land), dating from the 5th to the 7th centuries. The monastery apparently contained hostel facilities for the thousands of pilgrims who came to the Galilee during Byzantine times.

Over the decades since 1967, a large basilica with an intricate mosaic floor has been uncovered, as well as a cave chapel that may have marked the place (according to the Gospel of Mark, a tomb) where Jesus encountered the possessed man. Most remarkable among the discoveries is the underground crypt where more than 30 skeletons were found, all of middle-aged men, except for one child. There is a snack counter and a place to buy votive candles.

The national park at Kursi (✆ **04/673-1983**) is open daily from 8am to 4pm (until 5pm in summer); admission is NIS 15 for adults and NIS 7 for children.

KIBBUTZ EIN GEV ★★

12km (7½ miles) N of Tzemach Junction; 7km (4⅓ miles) S of Kursi

About two-thirds of the way south along the lake's eastern shore is **Kibbutz Ein Gev,** one of the loveliest places in Israel. Nestled between the hills of Golan and the lakefront, Ein Gev was founded in 1937 by German, Austrian, and Czechoslovakian refugees. (It was former Jerusalem Mayor Teddy Kollek's kibbutz.)

These days Ein Gev has a 5,000-seat auditorium, which has presented some of the world's greatest musicians at its annual music festival. A free mini-train tour of the kibbutz is available for visitors (ask at the office next to the Ein Gev restaurant). On the hillsides are tiers of vineyards, and elsewhere on the grounds are a banana plantation and date groves. Fishing is another big industry here; Ein Gev is home to the country's largest restaurant, serving St. Peter's fish straight from the Sea of Galilee. The kibbutz also offers accommodations at Ein Gev Resort Village (p. 215).

Not far from the auditorium, in a garden, is a bronze statue by the Israeli sculptress Hanna Orloff, depicting a woman holding a child aloft, in memory of a young mother-to-be from the kibbutz who was killed in the 1948 battle

BED & BREAKFASTS in the galilee

One of the great pleasures of visiting the Galilee is getting closer to the people and history of the region. You do this by skipping hotels in favor of these alternative accommodations:

- **The Kibbutz Country Lodgings.** These are the less-expensive list of kibbutz accommodations compiled by the **Kibbutz Hotel Chain office** (www.booking-kibbutz.com). They're less fancy than those in the more upmarket Kibbutz Hotels, but they're adequate, often in beautiful locations, and give you a closer look at kibbutz life than the more insulated Kibbutz Hotels. At some kibbutzim, the rooms are in special guest buildings; in others, you get an empty kibbutz member's room or apartment that has been especially set up for visitors. ***Tip:*** There are often special deals for visitors, so do ask before booking.
- **Accommodations in Israel—B&Bs, Country Lodging, Rural & Agro Tourism** (www.zimmeril.com). This is the preeminent source for rural tourism across a wide spectrum of accommodations types. You might find yourself staying in a private home, with the family on site (and serving you delicious breakfasts each morning), at a kibbutz, or in a fancy B&B. Check the site for options.
- **Hostels in Israel** (www.hostels-israel.com). This is a network of over 30 very good, unusual hostels throughout Israel, including the Galilee and the Golan Heights.

All tourist information offices in major cities (including those in Tiberias, Haifa, and Safed) now are equipped with computers that let you access the current lists of bed-and-breakfast facilities available throughout the Galilee. You can telephone for reservations ahead of time, or play things by ear when you arrive in Israel.

for Ein Gev. This settlement bore the brunt of heavy attacks in the 1948 war, and its position at the foot of the Golan Heights, below heavy Syrian military emplacements, made it a perennial target. From 1949 to 1967, Ein Gev kibbutz members depended on an endless maze of slit trenches throughout the grounds, as well as concrete underground shelters.

You can get to Ein Gev from Tiberias by bus no. 22. Farther south along the lake is a campsite, at **Kibbutz Ha-On,** with its **ostrich farm** and moderately priced Holiday Village and bed-and-breakfast accommodations; continue south along the shoreline and you'll come to **Ma'agan,** with its Holiday Village. Ma'agan is very near the junction for the road to the hot-spring resort of Hammat Gader. (Ask at the Tiberias Tourist Information Office or at the Tzemach Junction for information on other campsites around the lake and in the vicinity.)

HAMAT GADER ★

The **hot springs of Hamat Gader** (✆ **04/665-9999**), east of the southern tip of the Sea of Galilee, are a favorite Israeli spa and day trip for visitors to the Galilee. Nestled in the valley of the Yarmouk River, this dramatic site has been inhabited for almost 4,500 years.

The Roman city here was first constructed in the A.D. 3rd century, restored and beautified in the 7th century, and destroyed by an earthquake around 900. The **ruins of the Roman spa city** are extensive and significant, and several important parts (the baths, the theater) have been excavated and beautifully restored. The still-apparent elegance of the Oval Hall, the Hall of Fountains, and the Hall of Pillars in the Spring Area point to the magnificence of this Roman resort in ancient times. Don't miss the wonderful lions on the mosaic synagogue floor (A.D. 5th c.). The ruins are set up as a **self-guided tour** (ask at the park office about guided tours of the park).

The spa was known as El-Hamma to the Arabs and Turks, and the site is dominated by the minaret of a mosque that has fallen into disuse and been disfigured by graffiti.

For present-day hot springs fans, there are modern swimming pools, hot pools, hot sulfur springs, and baths for medical therapy and beauty treatments. Just to keep you tranquil as you relax in the baths, there is also an **alligator farm in a jungle setting** with elevated walkways. For the kids, the park has trampolines and water slides. You will also find showers, changing rooms, a bar, and a Thai restaurant. Admission Sunday to Wednesday NIS 108; Thursday through Saturday, and holidays NIS 118. There is free entry for children up to one meter (3 ft.) in height. Bring a towel and bathing suit. Residents of the area as well as visitors come in droves (especially after work), often bringing picnics. The many clay oil lamps found here may indicate the ancient inhabitants of the area enjoyed night bathing after a long day of work.

The springs can be reached by bus from Tiberias. Bus schedules vary according to season, so check with the bus station for a morning departure and afternoon returns. Hamat Gader is 22km (14 miles) southeast of Tiberias.

river jordan **BAPTISMS**

A mass baptism in the Jordan River.

Kibbutz Kinneret, just west of Degania, has established a spot where Christian pilgrims can immerse themselves in the waters of Jordan in safety and tranquility. The baptismal spot, called **Yardenit** (www.yardenit.com; ✆ **04/675-9111**), is 180m (591 ft.) west of the lakeshore highway (follow the signs). The river seems to flow peacefully, but its currents can be dangerous, so no swimming is allowed. The area set aside for baptisms is sheltered, and there are guide railings leading into the water. Snack and souvenir stands provide refreshment and sustenance (no charge for the baptismal dip). A special lift has been installed to enable visitors with disabilities to enter the water with a minimum amount of difficulty. It's open Saturday to Thursday 8am to 5pm and Friday 8am to 4pm; the last baptism is 1 hour before closing. Baptisms are performed free of charge, but are only allowed while wearing special white robes that cost $10 to rent or $25 to purchase.

You'll find Hamat Gader's pools open Sundays to Wednesdays, and Saturdays, from 9am to 5pm; Thursday and Friday 9am to 10pm. Hours are subject to change (check www.hamat-gader.com). Antiquities and children's activities close at 4pm. As if the ruins, hot springs, and alligator farm were not enough, there are three restaurants on the premises, including poolside dining and an Israeli grill called **The Pan.**

KIBBUTZ DEGANIA ★

Located at the very southern tip of the Sea of Galilee, Degania is the country's very first kibbutz, founded in 1909 by young Russian Jewish pioneers. Without any real experience in farming, this handful of self-made peasants left city jobs to fight malarial swamps and Bedouin and local marauders. Much of the philosophical basis of kibbutz life was first formulated in this Jordan Valley settlement by its leader, A. D. Gordon. Gordon believed that a return to the soil and the honesty of manual work were the necessary ingredients for creating a new spirit in people. Although never a member of the kibbutz, he farmed until his death at age 74. A natural history museum on Degania's grounds, **Beit Gordon** (www.beitgordon.co.il; ✆ **04/675-0040**), contains a library and exhibition of the area's archaeology, flora, and fauna.

Degania grew so quickly that its citizens soon branched out to other settlements. The father of Moshe Dayan, the famous commander (with the eye patch) of the Sinai Campaign, left Degania to help establish Nahalal, Israel's largest *moshav* (cooperative settlement). Eventually, some of the Degania members split with the original Degania over political and philosophical issues (especially about the nature of the Stalinist-era USSR). They broke away from Degania, establishing their own kibbutz right next door, and called it simply Degania B. The older Degania is now called Degania A.

Outside the entrance to Degania, there's a small tank—a reminder of the battle the inhabitants of Degania waged against Syrian tanks in 1948 (the members fought them off with Molotov cocktails). Today, both Degania A and B are thriving.

SAFED (ZEFAT) ★★

36km (22 miles) NW of Tiberias; 74km (46 miles) E of Haifa

The medieval, mystical town of Safed (Zefat, Zfat, Tsfat, Tzfat) lies about 40 minutes northeast of Tiberias. Beginning in the 15th century, Safed was known for its Jewish scholars and visionary mystics. At 837m (2,746 ft.), it's Israel's highest town.

For a while in the 1950s and 1960s, the town became Israel's major summer mountain resort, attracting secular and religious vacationers who enjoyed Safed's quant side streets, artists' galleries, and cool nights. Today Safed is once again very religiously oriented, and it can be a problematic stay for visitors due to limited parking, restaurants, and accommodations. But the beauty of Safed's mountain location and its history as a center for Jewish mysticism and Kabbalah combine to create a special aura to the town and make it memorable if you give it time and a bit of effort.

Safed's known history began in A.D. 66, during the time of the First Jewish Revolt against Rome, when the rebel Jewish commander, Flavius Josephus (who later went over to the Romans and became a noted historian), started building a citadel on the mountaintop in the center of Safed. In 1140, the Crusaders again built a fortress on this peak, the ruins of which can be seen

The Artists' Quarter of Safed.

today. But whatever early communities existed here in those centuries were small and unimportant.

During the 16th century, the Ottoman Turks chose the town of Safed for the provincial capital, and it became the primary government, economic, and spiritual center for the entire Galilee region. It was during this period that Sephardic Jews from Spain came here. Having escaped the horrors of Spain under the Inquisition, many of these Jewish scholars and intellectuals launched into a complex and mystical interpretation of the Hebrew scriptures called Kabbalah. The town became a great center of learning, with a score of synagogues and religious schools. The first printing press in the East was introduced here during this period of scholarship and mysticism, and in 1578 the first Hebrew book—a commentary on the Scroll of Esther—was printed. During this golden age of Safed, less-mystical groups of Ashkenazi Jews were also attracted to Safed, and the entire community and its rabbinical scholars became renowned and revered throughout the Jewish world. At its height, the Jewish community numbered about 10,000, but by the 18th century, Safed was in serious decline.

In 1837, the entire town was leveled by a powerful earthquake, after which both the Jewish and Muslim communities of Safed struggled in increasing poverty. The wave of anti-Jewish rioting that swept British Mandate Palestine in 1929 was particularly severe in Safed, where the Jewish population was mainly elderly and religious. During the 1948 War for Israel's Independence, control of the strategic heights of Safed was crucial to control of the Galilee. Although outnumbered, Israeli forces held the town, and the large Arab population of Safed fled amid panic and rumors. Since then, the center of Safed (pop. 30,000) has had three parts to its personality—a rather outdated resort town, an artists' colony in the abandoned Arab neighborhood, and the long-established religious community. Until the 1970s, Safed, with its cool nights, was a favorite summer resort, but as Israelis became more international in their vacation habits, Safed's tourism industry withered, and the once-vibrant Artists' Quarter is now relatively quiet—all the better for those who decide to explore the town.

Essentials

GETTING THERE **By Bus** Buses run between Safed and Tiberias, Tel Aviv, and Jerusalem. Check Egged Bus Lines for schedules, www.egged.co.il.

By Car Follow the main but winding roads from Tiberias, Haifa, and Akko.

GETTING AROUND Most city buses, such as nos. 1, 13, 14, or 3, go from the center to the hotels on Mount Canaan.

VISITOR INFORMATION The **Safed/Hazor/Rosh Pina Tourism Association Office** is unfortunately not in Safed, but in the Galilee Mall at the entrance to Rosh Pina (✆ **1-800/323-223** or 04/680-1465, open Sun–Thurs 8am–4pm). In Safed itself, you'll find the **Tzfat Tourist Information Center,** 27 Alkabetz St. (✆ **04/692-4427**). This useful office is run by a private Jewish outreach organization, Livnot U'Lehibanot, and offers a short film on the history of Safed, as well as maps, books, local events, and lists of bed-and-breakfast options and private guides.

July and August are the most popular months because of Safed's cool climate. In the winter, it can be windy and as much as 20° cooler than Tiberias. Year-round, especially at night, Safed is usually the coldest city in the country.

CITY LAYOUT Safed is built on hilltops. The main part of town is compactly clustered atop one hill, while South Safed occupies another hilltop to the south, and Canaan perches on a hillside across the valley to the east. Although you may find occasion to go to Mount Canaan (a few hotels are there), you'll spend most of your time in the center of Safed. Jerusalem Street (Rechov Yerushalayim) is a circular street that girdles the hill, passing through the commercial street, the Artists' Quarter, and residential sections before beginning its circle again. Walking the circle should take only 15 minutes, and it is a good way to see most of Safed.

The **Egged Bus Station** (✆ **04/692-1122**) is at the lowest point on Jerusalem Street's circle through town, where it intersects with Derech Jabotinsky. Walk up to Jerusalem Street from the bus station and go right, and after 360m (1,881 ft.) you will come to the tourism office. But if you come up from the bus station and go left, you'll be headed toward the commercial district. In any case, once you find Jerusalem Street you can't get lost in Safed.

What to See & Do

While there is much to see in Safed, a traveler unfamiliar with the city's crooked streets and unimpressive doorways may unknowingly pass some of the city's best sites. Consider getting a **guided tour** with a travel company, such as **Pomegranate Travel** (www.pomegranate-travel.com), or leading yourself on a self-guided tour. These are available free of charge through the Safed Israel website (www.safed-home.com/selfguidedtoursofsafed.html). Note that modest dress is required when touring the religious quarter of Safed.

THE SYNAGOGUES

During Safed's golden age in the 16th century, some of the synagogues here were devoted to the study of the Kabbalah, a mystical interpretation of the Bible and other sacred writings in which every single letter and symbol in holy writ has deep, hidden significance. Hebrew words, numbers, and the names of God have mystical powers in themselves, and can be used to ward off evil and to perform miracles.

Kabbalists believed that the system originated with Abraham and was handed down by word of mouth from ancient times. Historians of religion dispute this, however, saying that Kabbalism arose only in the 600s; it continued to be a thriving belief until the 1700s. Kabbalism was, in a way, a reaction to the heavy formalism of rabbinical Judaism. It allowed for more latitude in the interpretation of holy writ and gained great popularity in the 1100s. The most significant Kabbalist text is the Zohar, a mystical commentary on the Pentateuch (the first five books of the Hebrew scriptures). For an interesting, fictionalized interpretation of what Safed was like at the height of its glory as a Jewish religious center, we recommend the chapter "The Saintly Men of Safed" in James Michener's novel ***The Source.***

It's not easy to describe exactly where the various synagogues are—the religious quarter has few street names and is really a collection of alleyways and courtyards. Ask for *"kiryat batei knesset,"* the synagogue section.

Among the most famous old synagogues here is the one named for the scholarly 16th-century **Rabbi Joseph Caro,** author of the Shulchan Aruch (the Set Table), which is the standard codification of practical Jewish law. Nearby is another named in honor of **Rabbi Moshe (Moses) Alsheich** (a renowned biblical commentator) and the only fully intact synagogue to survive the 1837 earthquake. Just a few steps away is the synagogue of **Rabbi Isaac Abuhav,** a sage of the 1400s; it contains an ancient Torah scroll said to have been written by the rabbi himself. Nearby is another, dedicated to **Rabbi Yosef Bena'a,** a famous 12th-century liturgical poet also called Ha-Lavan (the White).

The synagogue quarter has two houses of worship dedicated to the greatest of the Kabbalist scholars, **Rabbi Isaac Luria** (known as Ha'Ari, or "the Lion," an acronym for Adoneinu Rabbeinu Yitzchak, "Our Master Teacher Isaac"). Although Luria lived, studied, and taught in Safed for only 2½ years at the end of his life (he died here at the age of 38), his work changed the face of Judaism forever. The fortress-like Sephardic synagogue, graced by fine

A rabbi reads Torah during morning prayers in Safed.

carved-wood doors, is built where the rabbi studied and prayed, at the edge of the cemetery. The **Ashkenazi Ha'Ari Synagogue** is closer to Jerusalem Street, at a spot where the rabbi is said to have come to welcome the Sabbath with his followers. Rabbi Luria was the author of the "Kabbalat Shabbat" (Receiving the Sabbath), the liturgical arrangement of prayers recited at the start of the Sabbath in normative Judaism.

The original building, constructed after Rabbi Luria's death, was destroyed by an earthquake in 1852 and later restored. Its ark, done in the 1800s, is especially notable. If you come with an official guide, you will get a better sense of how every nook and cranny has a story and sometimes a supernatural occurrence connected with it.

At the end of the synagogue area is a **cemetery** containing the sky-blue tombs of many famous religious leaders; they're the ones with rocks placed upon them as symbols of love, respect, and remembrance. There is also a military cemetery, and nearby is a third cemetery containing the graves of Israelis who served with the underground Stern Gang and Irgun groups at the time of the British Mandate. Buried here are those executed by the British in Acre prison, including Dov Gruner, who is one of the best known of the underground fighters.

Another holy site is the **Cave of Shem and Eber** (or Ever), the son and grandson of Noah. This cave, located just off Ha-Palmach Street near where the Ha-Palmach stone overpass crosses Jerusalem Street, is said to be the place where Shem and Eber lived, studied, and were buried. Legend also has it that Jacob spent 14 years here studying before he went to the house of Laban, and that here he immersed himself in a ritual purifying bath before he wrestled with the angel. Today, there is a synagogue opposite the cave; if the cave is locked, you can ask the caretaker of the synagogue to open it for you.

20TH-CENTURY MEMORIALS

Going down the hill from Jerusalem Street, in the area between the synagogues and the Artists' Quarter, is a straight stairway: **Olei Ha-Gardom.** Stand at the top of this stairway, where it intersects with Jerusalem Street, and you're within sight of a lot of Safed's 20th-century historical landmarks.

Olei Ha-Gardom was the dividing line between Safed's Jewish and Arab quarters until 1948; that's why all the synagogues are clustered on the right-hand side as you're facing down the stairway. The present Artists' Quarter is in what used to be the Arab section. Look up toward the citadel, and you'll see a small opening in the fortress from which a direct line of machine-gun fire could be sent straight down the stairway, a British attempt to keep an uneasy peace between the two communities. The same day the British withdrew, the Arab and Jewish factions went to war. Look at the walls of the old police station, and you'll see it's pocked with bullet holes from the fighting.

Down Jerusalem Street from this intersection you can also see a war memorial, with a tablet describing how the fighting favored first the Arabs, then the Jews. Poised on a stone mount is a Davidka (little David), one of those homemade Jewish mortars that, though not too accurate or damaging, made a terrific noise and gave the impression of being much more dangerous than it actually was. At the top of the hill, in the beautiful hilltop park, are the ruins of a Crusader fortress (unfortunately not well-maintained at present) from which you can enjoy a fine view of Mount Meron, Mount Tabor, the Sea of Galilee, and a smattering of tiny hill villages and settlements. A war memorial commemorates the Israelis who were killed pushing the Arabs back from the heights.

The **Artists' Quarter ★★** is the area down the hill from Jerusalem Street between the Olei Ha-Gardom stairway facing the police station and the stone overpass that crosses Jerusalem Street. Here you will find picturesque houses, tiny streets, manicured gardens, and outdoor art displays. Many artists have galleries in their homes, and the homes themselves are often so charming and atmospheric that some owners charge a small admission.

Ascent Institute of Safed ★ This can be a rather intense place and is specifically designed for Jewish visitors who want to renew and expand their attachment to Judaism. But even if you don't sign up for a course or stay here, it's worth checking out Ascent's program of events, concerts, and lectures, many of which are open to all travelers.

2 Ha'Ari St., Old Safed. www.ascentofsafed.com. ✆ **04/692-1364.**

General Exhibition ★ While many of the houses in the artists' colony may be closed in winter, the General Exhibition, which shows a wide range of work by many Safed artists, is open year-round. The galleries display everything from paintings to ceramics to silk. You can purchase objects here, or get in touch with artists whose work you find interesting. Next door is the New Immigrant Artists Exhibition.

Old Mosque, Artists' Quarter. www.safed.co.il/general-exhibition-art-gallery.html. ✆ **04/692-0087.** May–Sept Sun–Thurs 10am–6pm), Fri–Sat 10am–2pm; Oct–Apr Sun–Thurs 10am–5pm, Fri–Sat 10am–2pm. Head downhill from the intersection of Jerusalem and Arlozorov sts.

Hameiri House ★ Located down the hill in south Safed, Hameiri House is the **Museum and Institute for the Heritage of Safed.** It's housed in a historic 16th-century edifice, the restoration of which was done over a 27-year period, completed in 1985. Artifacts and documents portray the history of Safed's Jewish community; photographs and videos of elderly residents are interesting, especially if a translator is available.

Old City. ✆ **04/697-1307.** Admission NIS 16. Sun–Thurs 8:30am–2:30pm; Fri 8:30am–1:30pm.

Museum of Printing Art ★ Safed was the site of the first Hebrew press in Israel, which was set up in 1576 and published Israel's first Hebrew book a year later. Here you can see a copy of the first newspaper printed in Israel (1863); a copy of *The Palestine Post* of May 16, 1948, announcing the birth of the State of Israel; a centuries-old Kabbalistic text printed in Safed; examples of modern Israeli graphics; and many other things.

Corner of Arieh Merzer and Arieh Alwail sts. ✆ **04/692-0947.** Free admission. Sun–Thurs 10am–noon and 4–6pm; Fri–Sat 10am–noon.

Where to Stay

Artists' Colony Inn ★★★ This lovely, carefully restored boutique inn is one of the most delightful places to overnight in Israel. Each room is different, but they share a design aesthetic that blends the ancient "bones" of the house—stone walls, arched ceilings and windows—with handsome modern furnishings and splashes of deep jewel-like color, either on the bed's throw or on one wall of the room (just enough to give the rooms life, but not so much that they look gaudy). Run by owners Bernay and Jeff Katz—they have a special gift for hospitality—the nightly rate includes a truly gourmet breakfast and tea and snacks throughout the day. The Inn helps you feel the magic of Safed's mysterious, sometimes elusive atmosphere. On Shabbat, when restaurants are closed in Safed, a wonderful country brunch can be ordered. Jeff is a licensed guide and so a wonderful source for what to see and do in town. Call ahead for directions and help with baggage; parking is difficult and somewhat far away. Children from 11 years of age are welcome.

9 Simtat Yud Zayin, Safed. www.theartistscolonyinn.com. ✆ **04/604-1101.** 4 units. $196–$275 double (varies by season), less for solo travelers. Rates include breakfast. **Amenities:** On-site library; snacks throughout the day; free Wi-Fi.

The Way Inn ★★ This B&B offers 10 distinctive guest rooms set in a picturesque Ottoman-era house in Safed's charming Artists' Quarter. Rooms

The bedrooms at the Way Inn are all joyfully colorful.

have been nicely renovated and offer a kitchenette, air-conditioning, TV, and modern bathroom. Breakfasts are excellent—owners Genine and Rony Bar El are great cooks, have a vegetarian and fish (non-meat) catering business, and are helpful with touring information. The only downside: As a B&B is in the Old City, there's no adjacent parking.

23 Yud Zayin St., Artists' Quarter. www.thewayinn.co.il. ✆ **073/775-0045.** 10 suites. NIS 544–NIS 666 double. Rate includes breakfast. No credit cards. **Amenities:** Roof terrace; spa and hammam; free Wi-Fi.

OUTSIDE SAFED

Amirim ★★ Founded in 1958 by a group of self-described "nature freaks," Amirim is a vegetarian *moshav* (cooperative village) in a peaceful forested area with magnificent vistas. Most of the *moshav* families rent out comfy guest rooms; for those who want more privacy, there are also a number of private cabins that are in great demand. Each unit is different, but has similarly woodsy decor (the look is log cabin–esque, with knotty walls, comfy furnishings, and in some cases, such niceties as Jacuzzi tubs and private terraces). On site are a number of exclusively meat-free restaurants (and they're serious about the vegetarianism here; you can be expelled from your cabin if you use your kitchen or outdoor grill to cook meat). For vegans and vegetarians this is the unusual spot where they can eat everything on every menu, although higher quality plant-based dishes can be found in Israel's big cities.

Rte. 886, 4km (2½ miles) north of junction with Rte. 89. www.amirim-home.co.il. Cabins $165–$260, less for rooms in private homes. Rates include breakfast. **Amenities:** Massage and beauty treatments; pool; free Wi-Fi in some units.

Where to Eat

The first thing you'll notice about Safed is its multitude of kosher sandwich, snack, and falafel shops along Jerusalem Street (the main downtown road), open day and night, except for the Sabbath, when the whole town is closed up tight. That being said, Safed is not a great place for fine dining, but if you have a car, there are good choices in nearby Rosh Pina and in the surrounding countryside.

NEAR SAFED

These choices are possible lunch or dinner excursions from Safed, but can also be reached from such places as Rosh Pina, Vered HaGalil, or even Akko, Nahariya, Tiberias, or Haifa. Besides the opportunity to enjoy unusual meals, these restaurants offer a chance to explore remoter parts of the countryside. One favorite is **Bait 77** (www.bait77.com; ✆ **04/698-0984**) in Amirim, a vegetarian bakery that has tasty pastries in the morning and pizzas at dusk (and after).

Bat Ya'ar Ranch Steak House ★★ STEAKS This steakhouse and horse ranch, set in the rugged, wooded hills, will make you think a chunk of Wyoming somehow fell from the sky and landed in the Galilee. A good map or careful instructions from the restaurant and strong bright lights on your car are necessary to get here. And when you see a series of rough wooden buildings, set near a beautiful viewpoint, stop: That's the restaurant! Grilled steaks, chicken, and burgers are served with fries or baked potato and salad in a rugged, cowboy-style room. In recent years they've also made concessions to vegans, adding plant-based kebab and veggie burgers to the menu. The quality is top-notch, and the fresh air and panoramas will invite a pre- or post-dinner stroll. There's a playground for children on the grounds. It's out of character for Safed (or even for the Middle East), but Israel is filled with surprises. Reservations necessary.

Biriya Forest 5km (3 miles) northwest of Safed. www.batyaar.co.il/restaurant. ✆ **04/692-1788.** The restaurant is not kosher, but kosher food can be arranged in advance for groups. Main courses NIS 69–NIS 165. Daily 11am–10:30pm.

Safed After Dark

Summer is the time for most of Safed's musical events. About eight chamber music concerts are held throughout the year, mostly in the summer, as well as a summer musical workshop. The **Klezmer Festival of East European Jewish Music** is the highlight of the summer programs. Check with the tourist office for the weekly scene. For piano concerts, check out **Hemdat Yamim** (✆ **04/698-9085**) on the Acre-Safed highway, which usually has concerts every Monday and Saturday evening during the summer. The **Yigal Alon Cultural Center and Theatre,** on Jerusalem Street in Safed (✆ **04/697-1990**), has everything from Shakespeare to ballet and popular folk dancing. It's named for the man who led the forces that liberated Safed in the 1948 war.

Day Trips

MERON ★

Eight kilometers (5 miles) west of Safed is the town of Meron, a holy place for religious Jews for 1,700 years. When Judea fell to the Romans after the Second Revolt against Rome in A.D. 135, the mountainous northern Galilee took on many refugees. One early Meron inhabitant, a 2nd-century Talmudist named **Shimon Bar Yochai,** was ultimately forced to hide in a cave in Peqiin, a village some distance from Meron. There, according to legend, he wrote the mystical Zohar ("Book of Splendor"), which is central to the Kabbalist belief.

Meron is the scene of considerable pageantry during the holiday of **Lag b'Omer,** which occurs in the spring just 3½ weeks after Passover. Thousands of orthodox Jews pour into Safed, and there follows a torchlight parade to Meron with singing and dancing. They burn candles on top of Rabbi Shimon's tomb and light a great bonfire into which some, overcome by emotion, throw their clothes. In the morning, after the all-night festivities, 3-year-old boys are given their first haircuts, and the cut hair is thrown into the fire.

There still exists Meron's **ruined ancient stone synagogue** of restrained but impressive architectural design from the A.D. 3rd century, as well as **Rabbi Shimon's tomb** and a rock called the **Messiah's Chair.** Reputedly, on the day the Messiah arrives, he will sit right here while Elijah blows the trumpet to

Rabbi Elimelech Biderman during a grand "tische" celebration in Meron with his Hasidic followers.

announce his coming. **Mount Meron,** the highest peak in the Galilee at 878m (2,881 ft.), dominates the rugged countryside, with vistas that sweep virtually across northern Israel. The local **SPNI Field School** (✆ **04/698-0022**) offers trail maps and information about a number of hikes through the beautiful, wooded Meron Nature Reserve.

SASA & THE BAR'AM SYNAGOGUE ★★★

In the northern foothills of Mount Meron 16km (10 miles) northwest of Safed.

In 1949, American and Canadian settlers built Kibbutz Sasa atop a 900m-high (2,953-ft.) hill and persevered despite many problems, including a polio epidemic. The thriving kibbutz is now the center of an area of forest reservations.

Just 5km (3 miles) to the north, the A.D. 3rd- to 4th-century **Bar'am Synagogue ★★★**, which served a small, rural community, is probably the best preserved and most beautiful of all the ancient synagogues in Israel. Its location, in the wild mountains near the Lebanese border, is breathtaking.

According to some scholars, the synagogue may have been in use through early medieval times. In the style of early Galilee synagogues, the building faces south, toward Jerusalem. Beautifully carved clusters of grapes ornamenting the main entrance testify to the town's abundant vineyards and orchards. At some point the design of the synagogue was changed and the main entrance walled over with large ashlars that can be seen in a 19th-century

The evocative ruins of the Bar'am Synagogue.

engraving of the ruined site, made from an early photograph. Archaeologists theorize that over the centuries, it became customary for worshipers to face both the Ark of the Torah and Jerusalem while praying, and the central doorway, on the southern wall of the synagogue, was walled over in order to build a Torah shrine. By the late 19th century, the ashlars walling the entrance, as well as other chunks of the synagogue, had been carried off by locals for reuse in other buildings.

The **National Park at Bar'am** (en.parks.org.il; ✆ **04/698-9301**) is open daily from 8am to 4pm (until 5pm in summer); admission is NIS 14. The park is wheelchair accessible.

Just a 5-minute drive from Baram National Park is an unmissable culinary destination, especially if the weather is hot. **Buza** (Arabic for "ice cream"; www.buzaisrael.co.il) is one of the country's best fresh ice cream makers, with shops sprinkled throughout the country from the Galilee to Tel Aviv. It also started as a collaboration between two friends—one Muslim, one Jewish. You'll find flavors here that exist nowhere else, such as Turkish coffee with cardamom, and *knafeh* (goat cheese) with figs. Buza's Kibbutz Sasa location is its main factory, and offers tours (which must be arranged in advance). Regardless of whether you're taking a tour, the shop is open and slinging scoops daily from 11am to 6pm.

The ruins of the Maronite (Christian) Arab village of **Birim** surround the cleared areas around the synagogue. As noncombatants cooperating with Israeli forces during the 1948 War of Independence, the residents of Birim had quartered Israeli troops in their homes. Late in the war, the people of Birim were told by the Israeli army to evacuate their town for what was promised would be a short time during a possible enemy offensive. They were never allowed to return, despite a ruling by the Israeli Supreme Court in the early 1950s upholding the villagers' rights to their homes. Since then, the former inhabitants of Birim, who all possess Israeli citizenship and are now scattered throughout the Galilee, have maintained an unending legal struggle to reclaim their village.

Past the synagogue, you can follow a path to the left and uphill to the **Church of Birim,** still maintained by the people of the village for weddings and funerals. If you climb the rather difficult stairs onto the roof of the church, you will be rewarded with a dramatic panorama of countryside so intensely loved by two peoples. Arabic graffiti on the church walls promise that the members of the congregation will return.

ROSH PINA ★★

27km (16 miles) NW of Tiberias; 75km (46 miles) E of Haifa

Only 2km east of Safed lies Rosh Pina. This quaint town, nestled onto the eastern slopes of Mount Canaan, was originally established by 18 local Jews from Safed under the name of Gei Oni ("Valley of My Strength") in 1878.

An aerial view of the lovely town of Rosh Pina.

Only 4 years later, after most of its residents had already abandoned the young settlement due to years of drought, Jewish immigrants from Romania joined the remaining three families and eventually renamed the village Rosh Pina (Hebrew for "cornerstone"). In 1883, Rosh Pina became the first Jewish settlement in the Land of Israel to be financially supported by Baron Edmond James de Rothschild.

Rosh Pina consists of only a handful of streets, and the village's Old Town at its southwestern tip is actually made up of only three short cobblestone roads, one of which has been turned into a pedestrian zone. From here, you can explore the quiet alleys lined with beautiful old stone houses, some of which have not been altered since they were originally built, and discover the many art galleries selling everything from paintings to jewelry. On a different historical note, the first Jew who was hanged by the British Mandatory Authorities, Shlomo Ben-Yosef, is buried in the town.

Even though the "mother of the Galilee settlements" turned into a flop for its early farmers and wasn't well known to many Israelis until the 1980s, today Rosh Pina has developed into a thriving artists' colony and draws tourists from all over the world.

Essentials

GETTING THERE **By Bus** Buses run between Rosh Pina and Tiberias, Haifa, Tel Aviv, and Jerusalem. Check Egged Bus Lines for schedules, www.egged.co.il.

By Car Follow the main but winding roads from Tiberias, Haifa, and Akko.

GETTING AROUND Most city buses, such as nos. 1, 13, 14, or 3, go from the center to the hotels on Mount Canaan.

VISITOR INFORMATION The **Safed/Hazor/Rosh Pina Tourism Association Office** is located in the Galilee Mall at the entrance to Rosh Pina (© **1-800/323-223** or 04/680-1465; open Sun–Thurs 8am–4pm).

CITY LAYOUT Just like nearby Safed, Rosh Pina is built on hilltops. The old part of the town is condensed into no more than three streets at the top of the hill, while the newer neighborhoods sprawl across the hillside to the north and east. Ma'ale Gei Oni Street, an homage to the original name of the early settlement that preceded Rosh Pina, runs from the Rosh Pina shopping center at the foot of the hill, all the way to the Old Town—called The Pioneers Restoration Site—where its name changes to HaKhalutsim Street.

What to See & Do

Rosh Pina is small but well worth a visit, and most of it can be seen in a few hours and without the need for a car. If you came to Rosh Pina by bus, you will arrive at the Central Bus Station which, as in many Israeli cities, is located at the town's main shopping center. From here, head up the hill on Ma'ale Gei Oni Street until it changes into HaKhalutsim Street. Follow it until you reach the **HaBaron Garden** located at the heart of Rosh Pina's Old Town. This public park was unveiled in 1886 by Baron Edmund de Rothschild. Take a stroll among the olive and almond trees planted on the hillside and take in the stunning view of the valley below. At the heart of the HaBaron Garden are three cobbled alleys, Ma'ale Binyamin St., HaNadiv St., and HaRishonim St. This is where the first residents came to settle in Rosh Pina.

Just a few steps south of Professor Mer's House (see below) stands the **Old Synagogue** ★ of Rosh Pina. Its interior has remained virtually unchanged since it was built in the mid-1880s. The dark timber brought over from Romania has aged beautifully, and its painted ceilings dance with palm trees and biblical motifs. The roof of the synagogue is actually made from the wood of the fishing boats the Romanian immigrants brought with them in the belief they could find fish in the small streams near Rosh Pina. The doors of the synagogue usually remain locked, but ask a nearby local and you might find someone with a key.

Most of the town's art galleries, as well as a few very good eateries, can be found at The Pioneers Restoration Site.

Professor Mer's House ★ HISTORIC SITE This home once belonged to Professor Gideon Mer, one of the leading experts on malaria in the 1930s. It is here that Mer carried out his groundbreaking work in his efforts to combat the disease. The British rulers of Mandate Palestine were so impressed with Mer's work that they sent him to Burma to fight a rampant malaria epidemic there. The house, which has been turned into a humble museum, gives you a glimpse into the early days of Rosh Pina.

HaRishonim St. ✆ **04/693-6603.** Admission NIS 15. Sun–Thurs 8:30am–5pm; Fri–Sat 8:30am–1pm.

Where to Stay & Eat

Mizpe Hayamim Spa Hotel ★★★ This colonial-style hotel has made it its mission to pamper every guest. About half of the rooms are suites with their own hot tubs. The hotel's lavish spa features a range of treatments ranging from olive-branch massages to rubdowns with wildflower oils. All rooms are equipped with mountain views and a corner where you can make yourself coffee, or tea with fresh herbs picked from the hotel's own organic garden. There are two restaurants, one specializing in vegetarian cuisine. Local artists work on site and a gallery sells artworks, plus a ground floor delicatessen offers homemade breads, cheese, and other gourmet products.

Off Rte. 8900 (from the Rosh Pina shopping center, drive toward Rte. 90 and turn right onto Rte. 8900 at the first roundabout). www.mizpe-hayamim.com. ✆ **04/699-4555.** 97 units. $360–$590 double. Rates include half-board (two meals). Free parking. **Amenities:** Free Wi-Fi.

Pina Barosh ★★ This boutique, family-run property was established in 1876 by the owner's great-grandfather and once housed livestock, which you would never guess given the beautifully arranged stained glass windows, wooden furniture, and handwoven rugs. Pina Barosh is run by members of the Friedman family who operate a hotel, wine bar, and great rustic restaurant on the premises (see below). Seven different rooms spread across Rosh Pina offering luxurious accommodation and panoramic views across the Hula Valley, Golan Heights, and on a clear day, even Mount Hermon. The various accommodations include rooms, cottages, and villas. Separate rural wood houses in the town's center offer a private swimming pool, and a renovated stone house at the entrance to Rosh Pina, called Wadi Roshi Pina, includes a family unit. Ask the owners about tours around the vineyards of the Galilee and Golan Heights.

HaKhalutsim 8. www.pinabarosh.com/engRooms.htm. ✆ **04/693-6582.** 7 units. NIS 600–NIS 950 double. Rates include breakfast at Shiri Bistro. Free parking. **Amenities:** Restaurant; wine bar; free Wi-Fi.

Shiri Bistro & Wine Bar ★★★ Run by the owners of **Pina Barosh,** this French bistro is named after the chef Shiri Friedman, who trained with noted chef Bernard Loiseau in France. Not only does the bistro offer stunning views and superb rustic bistro fare (with some exceptionally tasty salads), but also the chance to sample some of the rarer Israeli boutique wines. At least 250 Galilee and Golan wines are available. The menu is large and blends French cuisine with local ingredients, creating a unique flavor you won't find anywhere else. Reserve a table on the spacious outdoor covered terrace, overlooking the breathtaking Hula Valley and Golan Heights.

HaKhalutsim 8. www.pinabarosh.com/engbistro.htm. ✆ **04/693-6582.** Main courses NIS 45–NIS 200. Daily 8:30am–11pm.

TEL AVIV

By Shira Rubin

8

Tel Aviv has become one of the hottest travel destinations on the planet, with rave reviews from travel magazines, TV pundits, and good old-fashioned word of mouth. "Best for Style," "Best Urban Beaches," "Best LGBTQ Destination," "Best Foodie Scene," and "Best Nightlife"—these are just a few of the accolades heaped on the city. While it lacks the white stone architecture of Jerusalem, the ancient ruins of Caesarea, or the breathtaking landscapes of the Negev Desert, this seafront metropolis more than makes up for it with a pulsing, youthful, effortlessly cool culture scene—many times hidden in plain sight behind uniformly drab, white buildings. Tel Aviv is, in many ways, the ultimate Mediterranean vacation hotspot, with miles and miles of sparkling beaches, nearly yearlong sunshine, constantly upgrading eating haunts and a seriously laid-back vibe.

That is not to say that it's similar to Los Angeles, Barcelona, or any other warm-climate international city—an excuse visitors sometimes give for skipping the city in favor of more time in Jerusalem. Tel Aviv, which boasts its own fascinating history, shouldn't be missed. The city was founded in 1909 and designed entirely by the Scottish urban planner Sir Patrick Geddes along the sand dunes of the Mediterranean. Tel Aviv has (many residents would say blessedly) no holy sites, and until its founding, it had no history. But its founders hoped that on this swath of sandy tabula rasa, intentionally unadorned buildings would pave the way to a truly modern, wholly Israeli culture in which human interactions, rather than opulent architecture, would form the city's social glue.

Today, Tel Aviv is Israel's cultural and economic hub, known by many nicknames. It's called "The White City," in reference to its vast trove of original Bauhaus architecture. By Israelis, it's dubbed, with, pride, disdain, or sometimes both, as "The Bubble," because of its hopping cafe culture, world-renowned art scene, vibrant LGBTQ community, and distinct internationalism that separates it so dramatically from the rest of the country. Tel Avivians love their rooftop tapas bars, all-night dance clubs and matkot paddleball beach sessions. In summer, the heat and humidity can put New

Orleans to shame, but a short walk or bus ride can always get you to the refreshing waters of the Mediterranean.

Home to the Israeli stock exchange, Tel Aviv is where the country does most of its global business deals. Glass skyscrapers dot the city's landscape, and many more are under construction. But Tel Avivians love to relax and play. In the 1980s, the city's beaches were smartly renewed, and they are now among the pristine and most easily accessible urban beaches in the world. That is most true during the "winter" months, when the temperatures often hover in the 70s and Israelis think it's too cold for a dip—meaning you'll have the whole beach to yourselves.

The 1990s saw the construction of an opera house, new performing-arts centers, and the development of a rarefied luxury restaurant scene. In 2018, the promenade and the iconic fountain at Dizengoff Square got a face-lift, and, at the time of publication, long-awaited construction has begun for a light rail running throughout the city that will serve as a highly anticipated alternative for the often traffic-clogged streets.

Tel Avivians are also busy appreciating, preserving, and upcycling once neglected landmarks. The formerly derelict **Tel Aviv Port,** at the northern end of the city, is now the hottest spot in town, packed with inventive eateries, a rarified farmer's market, nightclubs, and shops overlooking the sea. With a

Tel Aviv's sinuous boardwalk (*tayelet* in Hebrew) winds its way past beaches with different identities, from pick-up scenes to family strands to ones that are popular with the LGBTQ community.

wave of newly built luxury hotels and restaurants, the neighborhood of **Historic Jaffa,** at Tel Aviv's southern end, is a romantic enclave of medieval buildings, cobblestone streets, and flea markets boasting innovative Israeli and Palestinian chef restaurants. It's great for evening strolling, and it's loved by visitors and Israelis alike.

Elsewhere in Tel Aviv, you'll see the delightful 1930s and early 1940s **Bauhaus/International Style** buildings forged by German refugee architects, designers and intellectuals who sought shelter, and saw an opportunity to create a dazzling metropolis—based on clean, functional lines—out of the Tel Aviv sands. In the 1930s, Tel Aviv was not a sleek, perfectly planned utopia. Many of the photographed buildings admired by the outside world were filled with old-fashioned workshops. In summer, the broad, futuristic streets (designed by architects whose hearts were still in pre-1933 Berlin) sweltered under the sun and blocked whatever evening breezes might blow in from the sea.

But by the beginning of World War II, Tel Aviv had blossomed into a garden of white concrete, flat-topped architectural wonders—the curvilinear balconies and rounded corners of Tel Aviv's building boom were featured in architectural journals throughout the world. And after Israeli independence in 1948, the Tel Aviv landscape changed irrevocably, first by refugee camps and temporary housing for the hundreds of thousands of Holocaust survivors who poured into the country, and, in the subsequent years, with vast housing projects that sought to jumpstart the lives of the new arrivals. During the austere 1950s, Tel Aviv, although a young city, was run-down, especially around its downtown center. The beach, one of Tel Aviv's strong points, piled up with garbage. The ultra-modern buildings of the 1930s and early 1940s, constructed of sand bricks, began to crumble. The city offered little in the way of museums, hotels, or restaurants, and word was out that Tel Aviv was a hot, humid, concrete heap, ungainly and uninteresting.

In the past 50 years, however, Tel Aviv has been undergoing a carefully nurtured revolution. The beach, only a few blocks from anywhere in the city center, has made a spectacular comeback. Israeli chefs, many of whom have exported their restaurants to resounding acclaim in cities like London, Paris and New York, have put Tel Aviv on the culinary map, showcasing an Israeli culinary tradition obsessed with fresh produce and bold spices. Innovative, lively museums abound, as well as an intimate, highly regarded art gallery scene.

Tel Aviv now incorporates the once-separate city of Jaffa, which *does* have a history going back thousands of years (its port is among the oldest in the world, and the Prophet Jonah lived here before his encounter with the whale). If you climb the hill of Old Jaffa and look northward toward Tel Aviv's shoreline, you'll see an amazing achievement for a metropolis that's just over 100 years old.

BEST TEL AVIV EXPERIENCES

Exploring Old Jaffa

Wander the picturesque byways overlooking the sea, explore galleries and antique shops, and dine at one of Jaffa's atmospheric restaurants. By day, there's the **Jaffa Flea Market ★★★** (p. 308), which is full of vintage clothes and furniture, unique homeware shops, tons of casual but chic eateries, and lots of trendy cocktail bars.

Joining the Israeli Food Revolution

Tel Aviv is the beating heart of Israel's culinary scene. Dine here, and you'll understand why Israeli chefs have been conquering London, New York, and Los Angeles. Even—or especially—street snacks and mid-range eateries, Tel Aviv is a world-class gourmand's paradise. Good restaurants are everywhere, and there are several special zones, like the Tel Aviv Port, the Carmel Market, and the Jaffa Flea Market, where they are virtually wall-to-wall.

Museum Hopping

Each one is lively and imaginative, starting with the **ANU Museum of the Jewish People ★★★** (p. 257), the sprawling **Eretz Israel Museum ★★★** (p. 259), and the daring **Tel Aviv Museum of Art ★★** (p. 262). South of Tel

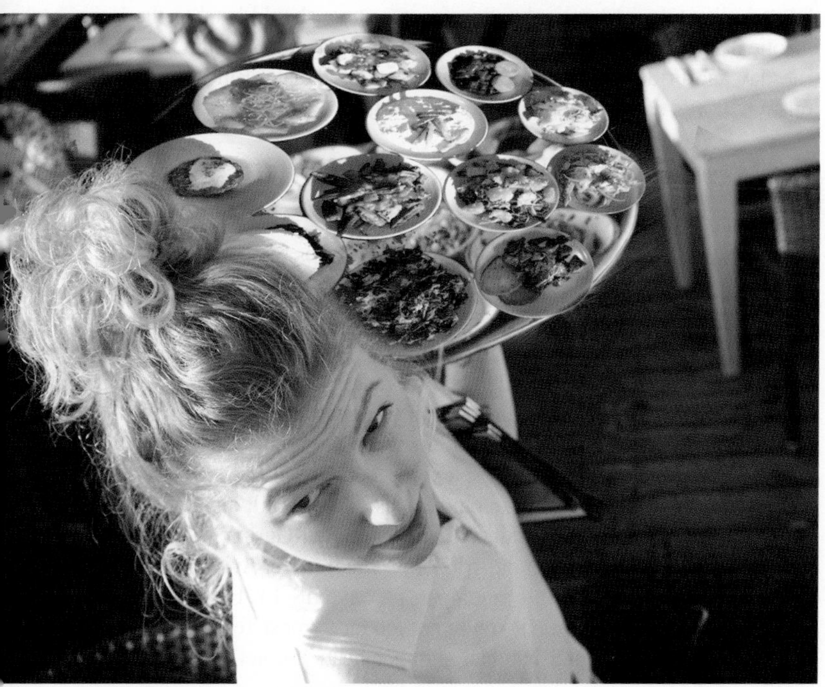

A waitress's tray is overloaded with tasty dishes at the popular Manta Ray restaurant.

Aviv are the uber-modern **Design Museum Holon ★★★**, whose spiraled, multicolored facade is an award-winning exhibit in itself, as well as the **Children's Museum ★★★** of Holon (p. 263), which hosts the interactive "Dialogue in the Dark" exhibit that offers a glimpse into living life as a blind person, under the care of blind guides.

Relaxing

Superb shorefronts, from Jaffa in the south to Mezizim Beach in the north, encourage locals to chill out, swim, people-watch, snooze under an umbrella, or join in a no-holds-barred game of paddleball, known in Hebrew as "matkot"—revered as an Israeli national pastime. When the weather permits, EllaYoga (at the Tel Aviv Port and with a second location at the Sarona Market) hosts a free Friday morning yoga class on the deck in front of the Padani jewelry store, allowing you to gaze at the sparkling water as you lean into your downward-facing dog. Kikar Kedumim in Old Jaffa, Gordon Pool, Elifelet Park in Florentin, and several other parks host similar yoga and exercise classes at sunset.

Shopping

Brash, original designer clothes make Tel Aviv a shopaholics mecca; you'll find the best selection on **Dizengoff Boulevard** and trendy boutiques in the picturesque neighborhood of **Neve Tzedek.** Those who want to experience the Tel Aviv lifestyle, and enjoy hunting for treasures, should head to the large, chaotic daily flea market in Old Jaffa, open every day but Saturday; and to the Tuesday and Friday craft bazaar on the streets of Nahalat Binyamin; and the Tel Aviv Port's daily organic Farmer's Market.

ESSENTIALS

Arriving

BY PLANE Flights arrive at Ben-Gurion International Airport on the outskirts of the city, which without traffic is about 15 minutes from the center of the city. From Sunday to Thursday from 6am to 9pm, and on Friday from 6am to various times depending on the start time of Shabbat (Fri sundown to Sat sundown), there is a fixed daytime **taxi fare** ranging from NIS 110 to NIS 190 from Ben-Gurion to Tel Aviv, in addition to a starting fee of NIS 11 and a surcharge of NIS 5. This fare includes one suitcase per passenger; additional suitcases are NIS 4 each. ***Note:*** Most taxis accept only cash, so it's a good idea to stop at the airport ATM to take out shekels if you didn't already exchange your currency. **Trains** (www.rail.co.il/en) leave Ben-Gurion Airport for the Savidor Merkaz Train Station on Arlozorov Street in Tel Aviv roughly every 20 to 30 minutes from 6am to midnight. Fare is NIS 13. From there you'll need to take a local bus or taxi. You're not too far to most Tel Aviv hotels, but with baggage, jet lag, and habitual summer heat, it's not walkable. ***Note:***

Check the train schedule ahead of time because there are often delays or changes. Once you arrive, be aware that the Arlozorov Train Station is a magnet for taxis looking to cash in on exhausted, unknowing tourists arriving from Ben-Gurion Airport. Always insist that your driver use the meter.

BY TRAIN The **Tel Aviv Savidor Central Railway Station** stands at the intersection of several major arteries—Namir Road, Arlozorov Street, and the Ayalon Highway. From here, municipal buses will take you throughout the city. For Israel Railways information, schedules, and fares to points in Israel, go to www.rail.co.il/en.

BY BUS From the **New Central Bus Station** (in a southern part of town) take bus or sherut no. 4, which runs along Allenby Road and then up Ben Yehuda Street. As you ride along Ben Yehuda, you'll be parallel to, and a block away from, Ha-Yarkon Street, where most of the beachfront hotels are located. Ask the driver for the stop closest to your hotel. For the more inland Dizengoff Square area, take the no. 5 bus or sherut. For all bus line and real-time arrival information, use Google Maps or download the Moovit app to your phone.

BY SHERUT Ten-passenger vans from Jerusalem, Haifa, and other cities around the country drop passengers off just outside the main door of the vast Tel Aviv Central Bus Station and leave for the return trip as soon as they're full. Sheruts cost a few shekels more than buses do, but are less of a hassle than wending your way through the labyrinthine, six-story bus station. They also operate on Shabbat, when most public transportation is closed.

BY CAR Major highways connect Jerusalem, Haifa, and Ashkelon with Tel Aviv.

Visitor Information

Tel Aviv's two main **Tourist Information Offices** are located at 46 Herbert Samuel Promenade (✆ **03/516-6317;** open Sun–Thurs 9:30am–5:30pm and Fri 9am–1pm) and at 2 Marzouk and Azar St., at the Clock Tower in Jaffa (✆ **03/516-6188;** open Sun–Thurs 9:30am–6:30pm, Fri–Sat 9:30am–4pm). There's a smaller, pop-up tourist information office nearby, in Jaffa at David Raziel Street and Yefet Street (✆ **03/681-4466;** open Fri–Sat 9:30am–4pm), as well as at Rothschild Boulevard 11 (✆ **03/516-6188;** open Sat–Thurs 9am–9pm, Fri 9am–4pm), and, during the summer months of April to October, an information truck stationed at Frishman Beach (open Sat–Thurs 10am–6pm, Fri 10am–5pm). You can buy and load your Rav-Kav, a smart rechargeable card for contactless bus payment, at any of the offices, as well as receive free maps, brochures, city guides, and discount coupon books for Tel Aviv and sites all over Israel. Note that Rav-Kavs are now also available as a phone app.

Online, **Time Out Tel Aviv** (www.timeout.com/israel/tel-aviv) offers lots of good information about independent tours, travel tips, and reviews of attractions, hotels, and dining.

City Layout

Tel Aviv and Jaffa (Yaffo in Hebrew and Yaffa in Arabic) together form a large urban area. But the part of Tel Aviv–Jaffa visitors focus on is the seafront section, extending east only to the thoroughfare of Ibn Gvirol Street. This is a 6km-long (3¾-mile) strip at least 1km (⅔ mile) wide, but only certain sections are of interest to visitors—the rest of the turf is mostly residential or commercial.

MAIN ARTERIES & STREETS

Tel Aviv's big streets mostly run north and south, roughly parallel to the sea. **Herbert Samuel Street** is right along the beach. It starts near the Dan Hotel and runs south to Jaffa, with a promenade running alongside it—great for strolling, biking, or jogging.

Hayarkon Street is a half-block inland and runs from the northern tip of Tel Aviv down to the border with Jaffa; it is dotted with hotels of all sizes and prices. At the northern tip of Hayarkon, you'll find the **Tel Aviv Port,** filled with trendy cafes, pubs, clubs, and restaurants overlooking the sea. **Ben Yehuda Street** is the next block inland. The streets between Hayarkon and Ben Yehuda from the Dan Hotel southward are thick with good restaurants and small hotels.

The Tel Aviv skyline.

The Tel Aviv Port Promenade at sunset.

At its southern end, Ben Yehuda curves into **Allenby Street,** which continues southwest. Allenby is an old-fashioned, chintzy shopping drag. Off Allenby you'll find the **Carmel Market,** Tel Aviv's roaring outdoor labyrinth where fabulous fruits and vegetables (as well as a million other things) are sold, and where, if you don't mind putting up with a little bit of grit, you can chow down on everything from Venezuelan arepas to ceviche-stuffed pitas. The **Nahalat Binyamin network of pedestrian streets,** filled with shops, cafes, and a busy Tuesday and Friday crafts fair, is right off Allenby next to the Carmel Market; farther south you'll find the quaint, narrow streets of **Neve Tzedek.**

Perpendicular to Allenby, inland from the Carmel Market, is **King George Street,** lined with bakeries, eateries, and small shops connecting to the next big north-south thoroughfare, **Dizengoff Street.** Here you'll find the big Dizengoff Center Shopping Mall at Dizengoff and King George streets, plus lots of fast-food places up to and north of **Dizengoff Square,** crowned by the iconic, recently renovated "Fire and Water" fountain, and plenty of shaded space for picnic-goers.

Ibn Gvirol is the most inland of the major north-south streets. At its northern end is **Rabin Square,** the site where Israeli Prime Minister Itzhak Rabin was assassinated in 1995. Today it is marked by a small memorial and encircled with a lotus flower–filled pond and the country's largest public protest

Getting Connected in Tel Aviv

Tel Aviv is one of the most Web-connected places on earth. More than 80 locations across the city offer free, high-speed Wi-Fi connection. With a robust startup and freelance community, cafes are often full of patrons typing away on their laptops.

site. Farther south, you'll find the **Golda Meir/Tel Aviv Center for Performing Arts** and the **Tel Aviv Museum of Art,** the **Culture Palace** (Heichal Hatarbut in Hebrew), the city's largest concert hall, and the **Tel Aviv Cinémathèque** at the very end of Ibn Gvirol. All are lined with lots of excellent places to eat.

Getting Around

BY BUS **Bus no. 4 and Sherut no. 4** from the **New Central Bus Station** to the center of Tel Aviv go northward to Allenby Street and on to Ben Yehuda Street; on Ben Yehuda, you will be running parallel to and a block inland from the many hotels on Hayarkon Street.

Bus no. 5 and Sherut no. 5 from the **New Central Bus Station** go to Heichal Hatarbut, Dizengoff Square, and Dizengoff Street. **Bus no. 54** runs from **the New Central Bus Station to Jaffa.** Ask to get off at the Clock Tower Square on Yefet Street.

Note: You'll need to either purchase a Rav-Kav, a smart card that you load ahead of time and which can be used on buses and trains, or use the Rav-Kav app (ravkavonline.co.il/en/download), which allows you to scan a QR code on the bus to pay your fare, or to load more cash onto your card. Rav-Kavs can be bought at Tourism Information Centers, at the airport, train stations, kiosks, and at many local businesses. For a list of places where you can purchase and charge your card, go to ravkavonline.co.il/en/store/service-stations.

Standard bus fare is NIS 5.5. You can transfer on buses within the city for up to 90 minutes from the time you first swiped your card. Kids under 5 ride for free. An unlimited day pass that allows you to travel throughout Tel Aviv and its suburbs costs NIS 13. But if you prefer to pay as you go, it's worth it to pre-load money onto the card or app ahead of time, as you'll get more value for your cash; for example, for NIS 50 you get NIS 62.50 that you can use for bus fare; NIS 100 translates into NIS 125. You should always check Google Maps or Moovit before heading out, as bus lines can change due to road work or special city events.

To get to **Jaffa** from central Tel Aviv, take bus nos. 10, 14, or 18, heading southward. Buses no. 10 and no. 13 run along the beach and take you to Jaffa's Clock Tower on Yefet Street, close to Old Jaffa and the flea market. Bus nos. 14 and 18, which you can pick up on King George Street near Dizengoff Street, runs through Jaffa on Yefet Street. If you're walking (30–45 min., depending on your starting point), simply head south along the Tel Aviv Waterfront Promenade, which runs into Jaffa. If you're going northward, you can catch bus no. 289 from Ibn Gvirol to get to the ANU Diaspora Museum of Jewish History and Tel Aviv University.

As part of an effort to modernize and liberalize a transportation system historically dominated by the ultra-Orthodox establishment, which opposes travel on Shabbat, Tel Aviv's mayor in 2019 began a system of 19-passenger minibuses that run on Shabbat, with more than 500 stops throughout Tel Aviv and nearby cities. It's called Busofash, meaning "bus on the weekend" in Hebrew. They look like large tour buses and are clearly labeled. The buses run roughly every half hour, though be sure to check whatever transportation app you're using, as they're known to run off-schedule. Bus no. 706 starts at the central Israeli town of Ramat Hasharon, continues through the Tel Aviv University area, then into northern and central Tel Aviv, the Tel Aviv suburb of Givatayim, then south toward Jaffa. Bus no. 707 connects Ramat Aviv to Tel Aviv and Jaffa. Bus no. 705 runs along Yefet Street into southern Jaffa. Bus no. 708 will bring you to the tech hub of Ramat HaHayal, where you can dine at the bustling **Shuk Tsafon** food market or watch a concert at the **Zappa Live Music** bar. At the time of publication, the Shabbat bus service was still in its extended launch phase and free of charge (for political reasons, it will likely remain free for some time). For a map of the lines and updated information, visit the City Hall's Shabbat bus service website: busofash.co.il/home-en.

Before heading out on any day of the week, check the **Moovit app** (moovit app.com) for suggested routes, arrival times, and changes due to light rail construction and other circumstances that could affect your journey.

BY TAXI/SHERUT WITHIN TEL AVIV Ten-passenger vans run along the bus nos. 4 and 5 lines. They run on a reduced schedule on Shabbat. If a van comes along, by all means take it rather than wait for the bus. Most take Rav-Kavs. Prices are slightly higher than bus fares on weekdays and another several shekels higher on Shabbat.

It's almost impossible to hail a taxi from the street, especially during rush hour or at night. Instead, head to a hotel and enlist the help of a doorman, or order a taxi through the **Gettaxi** app. You have the right to demand that the meter (*ha-sha*-on) be used, but many drivers will try to negotiate a fixed non-metered fare to your destination, which (especially if they're speaking in English) will likely not be to your advantage. By law, the meter must be used, so if your driver refuses, feel free to get out of the car and catch another cab. There are legal surcharges above the metered fare on Shabbat and after 9pm. If you use the meter, ask for a receipt (ka-*ba*-lah).

BY TRAIN For train schedules go to **www.rail.co.il/en**. The best train station for those staying in central Tel Aviv is Savidor Merkaz Station, located at the eastern end of Arlozorov Street. If your hotel is in the northern part of Tel Aviv, it might be closer to get off at the Tel Aviv University Station. There is train service up the coast to Nahariya; south to Beersheba; a rail link to Ben Gurion Airport; and a new, high-speed train to the central Yitzhak Navon Station in Jerusalem that is also a wonderful way to beat the chronic, ever-growing traffic jams. Israel Railways is undergoing revival and expansion, and the trains are becoming more and more pleasant to use.

Scooters have become a popular way to zip around the city, and many rental ones include helmets.

BY SCOOTER/BIKE Tel Aviv is outfitted with more than 500 miles of convenient bike paths, providing an extremely convenient and time-saving solution to getting around quickly and largely independently of traffic jams. For bikes, download the **Tel-o-Fun app** on your phone, and pick up and return a bike at any one of the city's 200 parking stations.

There are even more reserved parking spots for electronic scooters—a white outline on the side of the street, probably already packed with other scooters—where you can use **Bird, Lime, Wind, Dott, Tier,** and a number of other operators. Wear a helmet (many vehicles already have one attached), as there has been a rise in accidents involving scooters, especially in areas in south Tel Aviv and Jaffa where bike paths are less common.

ON FOOT If you can spare the time, and if it's not sweltering hot, Tel Aviv is a fabulous walking city, with people-watching and landscape changes that vary from block to block. Walking from the Port in the northern part of the city to the Port in Jaffa in the southern part of the city takes around an hour and a half. Abraham's Hostel offers fabulous walking tours in Jaffa's Old City (on Tues and Sun) and around the graffiti'd walls and street art of hipster-packed Florentin (on Thurs and Sat) for around NIS 100 per person.

[FastFACTS] TEL AVIV

Currency Exchange There are a number of internationally connected ATMs in the hotel district along Hayarkon and Ben Yehuda streets, as well as scattered elsewhere in the city. Most banks also have ATMS outside their branches. Check with your hotel desk about which is the closest. In addition, you can use the currency exchange offices along Hayarkon and Ben Yehuda streets. They usually have exchange rates comparable to the banks.

Doctors & Dentists You can get a list of English-speaking doctors and dentists from your embassy and often from your hotel's front desk. For **Tel Aviv Doctor,** a private, expensive, but very convenient service for travelers on Basel Street, call ✆ **054/941-4243.** The **Tel Aviv Dental Clinic** offers emergency dental care, 24/7 at 1 Zeitlin St., near Rabin Square (✆ **03/691-5159**).

Drugstores The Superpharm at 4 Shaul Hamelech St. is open throughout the week, 24 hours. For a list of on-duty pharmacies open on Shabbat (Fri sunset to Sat sunset, website in Hebrew only), ask your hotel or go to **www.tel-aviv.gov.il/Residents/HealthandSocial/Pages/Pharmacies.aspx**.

Emergencies For police, dial ✆ **100.** In medical emergencies, dial ✆ **101** for Magen David Adom (Red Shield of David), Israel's emergency first-aid service and ambulance. For fire, dial ✆ **102.**

Hospitals **Ichilov Hospital** (✆ **03/697-4000**) has an emergency room, dental clinic, and Malam Traveler's Clinic for immunizations. **Bikur Rofeh,** an emergency health clinic at 90 Yigal Alon St., accepts all forms of travel insurance and can be reached at ✆ **03/627-2350.**

Post Office There are branches of **Israel Post,** the country's postal service, in different locations throughout Tel Aviv. One close to the beach area is at 61 Hayarkon St. Another branch is at 170 Ibn Gvirol St. Hours are usually Sundays, Tuesdays, and Thursdays from 8am to noon and 3:30 to 6:30pm, Wednesdays from 8:30am to 12:30pm, and on Fridays from 8am to noon. Most branches require you to make an appointment before arriving, which you can do at the post office website (israelpost.co.il), on the app, or by calling ✆ **171.** Israelis, especially tech-adverse elderly, use the post office for everything from sending and receiving packages to paying their electric bills and city taxes, so be prepared to wait.

Safety Israel's largest metropolitan area has less crime than most cities its size, but there is still enough that you must observe the normal precautions. Don't walk in deserted areas, especially the beaches, after dark. Terrorism is always a concern. Get away from and report any unattended bags or packages to a police officer or any other passerby.

EXPLORING TEL AVIV

ANU Museum of the Jewish People ★★★ MUSEUM Formerly the Beit Hatfutsot Museum, this impressive museum was revamped and rebranded in 2021 to place itself in the center of some of the most intriguing and controversial questions to face the Jewish people in Israel and in the diaspora. Over three floors of original artwork, interactive digital displays and historical artifacts, this museum looks at the fate of the Jewish people from the time they left the Holy Land some 2,500 years ago until their return after World War II and its struggles, in the world in which a Jewish state does exist, to continue to grapple with its own, numerous identity crises. A recent $100-million renovation tripled the museum in size, and added a number of fascinating artifacts, including the

Historic dress on display at the ANU Museum of the Jewish People.

guitar Leonard Cohen played at his final concert in Israel in 2009, a lace collar worn by U.S. Supreme Court Justice Ruth Bader Ginsburg, and a 15th-century Book of Esther scroll from pre-Inquisition Spain. Eleven of the replicas of ancient synagogues remain from the previous museum, but "ANU"—or "us," in Hebrew—also includes exhibits on cuisine, music, and culture that testify to the vastly global, and even "non-religious" characteristics that make up the Jewish experience.

In addition, visitors are invited to search a vast digital database containing more than 5 million individuals and thousands of genealogies of Jewish families, including photos, music, and other artifacts from all over the world. If your family hasn't done it yet, you'll have the option to register your own family tree, and potentially trigger connections with other registered users.

15 Klausner St. near the Tel Aviv University campus. www.anumuseum.org.il. ✆ **03/745-7808.** Admission NIS 52. Sun–Thurs 10am–5pm; Fri 9am–2pm. Closed Sat and Jewish holidays. Bus: 10, 8, 289, 49.

In the 1930s, a group of young Jewish architects, trained in Germany's Bauhaus School, moved here and built some 4,000 buildings across the country in that style. Tel Aviv has the largest concentration, including this beaut.

Bauhaus Center ★★ GALLERY Tel Avivians now understand the rich Bauhaus/International Style heritage of their city, and this gallery/boutique is dedicated to the architectural design and decor of these movements. The center is famous for its tours of Tel Aviv's Bauhaus treasures. Call for tour information/reservation.

77 Dizengoff St. www.bauhaus-center.com. ✆ **03/522-0249.** Free admission. Sun–Thurs 10am–7pm; Fri 10am–2:30pm; Sat closed. Tours (NIS 80) given Fri 10am from Bauhaus Center. Bus: 2, 8, 39, 172.

Ben-Gurion House ★ HISTORIC SITE The house and personal items remain as they were when Paula and David Ben-Gurion lived here. Ben-Gurion was Israel's first Prime Minister, and his impressive personal library, comprising some 20,000 books, bears witness to his knowledge and scholarship. The building itself is an interesting example of Bauhaus/International design. Most of the signs in the house are in Hebrew, but this will not detract much from your visit. In the bedroom, note a blocked-in window used as a bomb shelter.

17 Ben-Gurion Blvd. www.bg-house.org. ✆ **03/522-1010.** Free admission. Sun and Tues–Thurs 9am–4pm; Mon 9am–7pm; Fri 9am–1pm; Sat 11am–3pm. Bus: 4 or 5.

Eretz Israel Museum ★★★ MUSEUM At the heart of the fascinating Eretz Israel (or state of Israel) Museum is an actual archaeological site. Called **Tel Qasile,** it contains 12 layers of settlement, meaning visitors can view an excavated Canaanite temple and enter a reconstructed house from the pre-Israelite era—approximately 1100 B.C.! But this dig is just the beginning of the wonders of this university-like campus, which has eight other pavilions dedicated to a variety of intriguing subjects. The **Glass Pavilion** houses a rare collection of vessels, some dating back to 1500 B.C.; it's one of the largest collections of ancient glass in the world. The **Ethnography pavilion** displays Judaica, folk-crafts, costumes, and an exquisite collection of antique Hanukkah menorahs from across the world. **The Nechustan Pavilion** explores the topics of mining and metallurgy during the biblical era. **"The Man and His Work Center"** is set up like a bazaar in which the tools of the trade from ancient industries such as weaving, olive-pressing, glassblowing, pottery-making, and basketry are on display. There's also a garden of ancient mosaic floors from all over Israel. Covering the contemporary world are the **Lasky Planetarium** offering Hebrew-language shows of astronomy, and visiting exhibits of works by contemporary artisans. The Museum Gift shop is top-notch, featuring inventive gifts special to the Holy Land, as well as beautiful items of contemporary design. There's also a good cafe on the premises.

2 Chaim Levanon St., Ramat Aviv. www.eretzmuseum.org.il. ✆ **03/641-5244.** Admission NIS 67, children under 18 free; museum and planetarium NIS 84. Sun, Mon, Wed 10am–4pm; Tues, Thurs 10am–8pm; Fri 10am–2pm; Sat 10am–6pm. Bus: 13, 7, 24, 25, 45, 127, 126, 171, 270, 271; Rail: Tel Aviv University station.

A young woman poses with artifacts on display at the Eretz Israel Museum.

Haganah Museum ★ MUSEUM Before the establishment of the State of Israel, the Haganah ("Defense" in Hebrew) was the provisional organization that provided for the protection of the Jewish community in Mandate Palestine. It was the forerunner of the Israeli Defense Forces. This museum, located in the architecturally preserved house of one of Haganah's founders, traces the history of Haganah, from the earliest defensive watch towers guarding 19th-century farms, to the struggle for independence in the 1940s and its development as Israel's modern army. There is brief background information in English. It is especially interesting when troops of young Israeli soldiers are brought through on educational tours.

23 Rothschild Blvd, near Allenby St. museums.mod.gov.il/sites/Hahagana. ✆ **03/560-8624.** Admission for adults NIS 20. Discounts for students and children. Sun–Thurs 8:30am–4:30pm. Bus: 48, 129, 172.

Museum of the History of Tel Aviv–Jaffa ★ MUSEUM Tel Aviv's carefully restored old City Hall, built in 1927, now houses displays of historical photographs, documents, and a video that tell the story of Tel Aviv's early decades.

27 Bialik St. ✆ **03/517-3052.** Free admission. Mon–Thurs 9am–5pm; Fri–Sat 10am–4pm. Bus: 4.

Rubin Museum (Reuven House) ★ ART MUSEUM One of Israel's most popular and acclaimed artists, Reuven Rubin (1893–1974) painted the landscape of Mandate Palestine and the young Israeli State. Today, the modernist home of the artist, dating from 1930, houses a collection of his work, a gallery for temporary exhibits of modern Israeli art, and a multimedia presentation of Rubin's life. On the top floor, Rubin's studio and living space have been kept as he left them.

14 Bialik St. www.rubinmuseum.org.il. ✆ **03/525-5961.** Admission NIS 20, free for children. Discounts for students. Mon, Wed, Thurs, Fri 10am–3pm; Tues 10am–8pm; Sat 11am–2pm. Bus: 4, 172.

Safari Ramat Gan (Zoological Center) ★★ ZOO Founded in the 1970s, this park southeast of Tel Aviv is a wide-open plain (100 hectares/247 acres) where African and Asian animals roam free. The park has been so successful with breeding hippos, elephants, giraffes, and other animals that it exports several species all over the world. For obvious reasons, visitors must remain in closed vehicles while traversing the 8km (5-mile) trail, but there is another walking path that traverses an open-air zoo as well. You'll have the opportunity to see lions, rhinos, gazelles, impalas, zebras, ostriches, storks, and much more. The on-site veterinary hospital treats more than 4,000 animals every year. There's also a monkey enclosure, as well as an aviary and reptile area. The lion area closes an hour before the rest of the park. Across

The critters at Safari Ramat Gan are at their liveliest on the morning tours.

the street is the Ramat Gan National Park (free admission), with even more animals. ***Note:*** We consider this a three star attraction for those traveling with children.

Ramat Gan. www.safari.co.il. ✆ **03/632-0222.** Admission NIS 78 online, NIS 89 if you buy at the park the day of. Open from around 9am–sunset, though check the website for the opening hours, as they change every few months. Visitors may remain in the park for 2 hr. after the last entrance hour. Closed on Holocaust Memorial Day, Israel Memorial Day, Yom Kippur Eve, and Yom Kippur. Bus: 33 (from Reading Bus Terminal), 31 (from Carmelit Bus Terminal, via Central Bus Station), 63 (from Carmelit via Dizengoff Center, Azrieli), 55 (Reading Bus Terminal, via Arlozorov Station), and 56 (Reading Bus Terminal, via Azrieli). ***Note:*** The bus drops you off at the entrance gate that's about a 10-min. walk from the actual park.

Tel Aviv Museum of Art ★★ ART MUSEUM Housing the world's largest permanent collection of Israeli art, the Tel Aviv Museum of Art is also famed for its 20th-century Russian art holdings, its strong collections of pieces from all the modernist movements, and choice works of international Impressionism and Expressionism. Always energetic and lively, the museum's Israeli art wing showcases the rich, diverse, and often contradictory puzzle that is the Israeli artistic canon, and the often tortured connection between Israel's art scene and Israel's constant state of war. The Museum Shop sells items of elegant, modern design and original Israeli artwork. There are also plenty of activities for kids, like performances and workshops for toddlers and

Architect Preston Scott Cohen's origami-like building for the Tel Aviv Museum of Art includes an 80-foot-tall spiraling, central atrium called "Lightfall" that refracts sunlight into many of the galleries.

DESIGN MUSEUM & CHILDREN'S MUSEUM in holon

Technically speaking a separate municipality, the town of Holon is essentially a southern exurb of Tel Aviv and home to two top museums. The remarkable **Design Museum Holon ★★★** (8 Pinhas Eilon St.; www.dmh.org.il; ✆ **073/215-51515;** Admission NIS 45, Mon, Wed 10am–6pm; Tues 10am–8pm; Thurs 10am—6pm; Fri 10am–2pm; Sat 10am–8pm) makes its home in an unusual building by acclaimed architect Ron Arad and is distinguished by a series of intertwined, curving metal loops colored a deep burnished orange. There's a permanent collection of design works created in Israel from the 1930s to 2000, and a contemporary design collection from 2000 onwards. Give yourself at least three hours so you don't feel rushed.

If you have children in tow, the innovative **Israel Children's Museum ★★★** (214 Jerusalem St.; www.childrensmuseum.org.il; NIS 68 admission; Sun–Thurs 9am–8pm, Fri 9am–1:30pm, Sat 9:30am–2pm) should be on your itinerary. It requires advance reservations because its exhibits are actually pretty intense experiences that will show your child (and you) what it's like to live as a person without sight or without hearing.

Those are the marquee exhibits, but there's also fun to be had at ones about the Beatles, the life cycle of butterflies, and other topics.

To get to Holon by bus from Tel Aviv, take bus 73 from the Carmelit station or Allenby St., or take bus 71 from the Azrieli Mall or Arlozorov St.

A skateboarder poses with the ribbon-like appendages of Design Museum Holon.

older children, which can be a lifesaver if the weather's too hot or too rainy to enjoy Tel Aviv's mostly outdoor offerings.

27 Shaul Ha-Melekh Blvd. www.tamuseum.org.il/en. ✆ **03/607-7020.** Admission NIS 45. Discounts for students. Children up to 18 free. Mon, Wed, and Sat 10am–6pm; Tues and Thurs 10am–9pm; Fri 10am–2pm. Bus: 9, 55, 2, 8, 36.

Jaffa ★★★

Now an integrated part of the sprawling Tel Aviv–Jaffa municipality, Jaffa has a long and colorful history, dating from biblical times. This is the port, the Bible tells us, where King Solomon's ally, the Phoenician King Hiram of Tyre, landed cedars of Lebanon for the construction of Solomon's Temple. From here Jonah embarked for his adventure with the whale. The Greeks were here too, and they fostered the legend that a poor maiden named Andromeda, chained to a rock and on the verge of being sacrificed to a sea monster, was rescued by Perseus on his winged white horse. Today, visitors are shown this rock, a tourist attraction since ancient times.

But that's just the beginning of Jaffa's history. The Crusaders also came this way. And Richard the Lionhearted built a citadel here that was promptly snatched away by Saladin's brother, who slaughtered 20,000 Christians in the process. Napoleon passed through 600 years or so later; a few Jewish settlers came in the 1890s; and Allenby routed the Turks from the port in 1917.

One Jewish legend has it that all the sunken treasure in the world flows toward Jaffa, and that in King Solomon's day the sea offered a rich bounty, accounting for the king's wealth. Today, Jaffa still shows traces of its romantic and mysterious past. The city is built into a kind of amphitheater on the side of a hill. The old section of the city has become the starlit patio of Tel Aviv, providing an exceptional view, fine restaurants, and the most beautifully restored Old City in Israel. The flea market district, near the Clock Tower, is chock-full of charming restaurants and bars that spill out into the street.

Tel Aviv'a Ha-Yarkon Street runs into Jaffa's Yefet Street where the landmark limestone **Clock Tower** and the large Turkish mosque, Mahmoudiya (1812), remind you of the city's continuing Arab community.

A STROLL AROUND OLD JAFFA ★★★

The reclamation of Old Jaffa—only a short time ago it was a slumlike area of war ruins and crumbling Turkish palaces—has proven to be one of the most imaginative projects in Israel.

Jaffa's port and Old Town from the water.

Yefet Street near the landmark **Clock Tower** is the place to start exploring. This limestone column was built by a Jew in 1896 to honor the Ottoman ruler of Palestine. Today, it features a commemorative plaque for the Israelis killed in the 1948 battle for the city of Jaffa.

On the west side of Yefet Street is the vast 19th-century **Mahmoudiya Mosque.** Although closed to the public, you can peek past its impressive gates to see a glimpse of the courtyard and hear the calls to prayer that drift over the neighborhood five times a day.

On the east side of Yefet Street (as you walk south), you'll find the street-side counters of **Abulafia's bakery,** famous throughout Israel for its freshly baked snacks. Just beyond Abulafia's are the streets leading eastward into Jaffa's motley but always interesting **Flea Market and Covered Bazaars,** selling everything from old jeans and British Mandate era detritus to old Persian tiles and reproductions of antique Hanukkah menorahs.

Judaica on display at the Jaffa Flea Market.

To your right, as you walk south on Yefet Street, is an uphill road that leads to the beautifully gardened hill of Old Jaffa, with its stunning views of the Tel Aviv coastline. At the summit is the open space of **Kikar Kedumim,** the central plaza, and at one side of it, the **Franciscan Monastery of Saint Peter,** which was built above a medieval citadel. The church commemorates the visit of St. Peter to Jaffa, and the raising from the dead of Tabitha. Opposite the church is an excavation area, surrounded by a fence, where you can inspect remnants of a **3rd-century** B.C. **catacomb.** Facing the catacomb is a hilltop garden, **Gan Ha-Pisgah,** atop which, surrounded by trees, is a white monument depicting scenes from the Bible: the conquest of Jericho, the near-sacrifice of Isaac, and Jacob's dream.

Past the church gardens, on the sea side of the hill, you can wander through Old Jaffa for a superb all-encompassing view of Tel Aviv and the Mediterranean coastline. Incidentally, **Andromeda's Rock** is traditionally the most prominent of those blackened stones jutting up from the floor of the bay. The view is brilliant in the morning sunlight and magical at sunset and into the dark of the evening.

Returning to Kikar Kedumim, you enter the restored maze of Old Jaffa's picturesque, cobblestone market streets, filled with Crusader-era architecture, eateries, artists' studios, galleries, antiques, and souvenir shops. For those interested in art and interior design, the **Ilana Goor Museum** (www.ilanagoormuseum.org; ✆ **03/683-7676**) is a delightful stop. It's a beautifully renovated mansion/gallery of one of Israel's most successful sculptors who also specializes in furniture and jewelry design. Over the centuries, this building has been put to many uses, including a long stint as a caravansary for 19th-century Jewish pilgrims. Now each room is like a page out of a fancy architecture magazine, filled with Goor's own works and her private collection of art. In the summer months, the rooftop sculpture garden hosts jazz concerts and other cultural events, with the added bonus of sweeping views of the city and the sea. The admission fee is rather steep (NIS 45), but the building is intriguing architecturally, and there are often temporary exhibits of Israeli artists. It's open Sunday to Thursday from 10am to 4pm and Friday and Saturday from 10am to 3pm.

A short (.5km/⅓-mile) stroll south of Old Jaffa brings you to the old port area of Jaffa Harbor, which hosts a few lovely fish restaurants and the fantastic **Na Lagaat,** meaning "please touch" in Hebrew (www.nalagaat.org.il/en; ✆ **03/633-0808**), a culture and arts center where the deaf-blind community put on stunning plays (tickets around NIS 40) and host dinners in the dark at the kosher restaurant, **BlackOut** (NIS 155 for a three-course fish meal). All proceeds feed back into the organization, which employs some 100 members of the deaf, blind, and deaf-blind community.

"Jaffa Tales" at the Old Jaffa Visitor's Center ★★ MUSEUM When history meets multimedia exhibits at visitors' centers, the results are often tacky. Not here. This site is literally cool, occupying as it does a cavernous

Old Jaffa Visitor's Center.

space underneath Old Jaffa's central Kedumim Square (Kikar Kedumim). Inside there are historical artifacts plucked from the town's millennia of history, glass walkways over an archaeological site, and a fine sound-and-light show.

Kedumim Sq. www.oldjaffa.co.il. ✆ **052/622-9200.** Admission is NIS 35, reservations required. Sun–Thurs and Sat 9am–5pm, Fri 9am–2pm.

Simon's House ★ RELIGIOUS SITE Christian tradition places the house of Simon the Tanner (venerated by Christian pilgrims for centuries) next to the lighthouse of the port, at the site of a small mosque. Acts 10 recalls St. Peter's visit to Simon's house in "Joppa."

8 Shimon Ha-Burskai St. Visitors can walk to the entrance of the house, but the house itself is closed to the public. To get here, walk south through Kikar Kedumim, the main square of restored Old Jaffa. At the end of the square, turn right to the steps.

ORGANIZED TOURS & SPECIAL EVENTS

ORGANIZED & SELF-GUIDED TOURS Want to see Tel Aviv on foot? Enlist the help of the **Tel Aviv Tourist Information Office** (46 Herbert Samuel St.; ✆ **03/516-6188**) which gives out municipal maps with four **"Orange" self-guided walking tours ★★★** of Tel Aviv marked on the map. Signs along the routes mark the way as you go. Some of the routes are too long to undertake on a sweltering summer day, but if you break them up into smaller units, they are a solid itinerary of what to see in different neighborhoods. ***Tip:*** Most Atlas chain hotels lend you free bikes for touring.

The tourist office also coordinates free walking tours of the Sarona Complex and its Templar history (Tues at 11am) and of the **Bauhaus Architecture of the White City** (Sat at 11am). There are often free tours during holidays like Rosh Hashanah and Yom Kippur, as well as on some Shabbat evenings. Always check with the tourist office for times, dates, and starting points at visit.tel-aviv.gov.il/see-do/whats-on, or email tourism@mail.tel-aviv.gov.il.

The **Tel Aviv Greeter ★★** (www.telavivgreeter.com) organization offers free tours (no tips accepted) from enthusiastic Tel Aviv residents. Reservations preferred 2 weeks in advance.

Another good source of guided tours is the **Society for the Protection of Nature in Israel (SPNI),** 2 Hanegev St. Call ✆ **03/638-8653** for information on the society's English-language walking tours in the Tel Aviv area. These are highly recommended group tours highlighting the area's natural flora and fauna (often on relatively easy hiking trails) that individuals can join. Tours cost around NIS 55 per person and there are occasionally free Saturday walking tours. Go to the American Friends of SPNI website (www.aspni.org) and reserve as far in advance as possible. Most tours are given in Hebrew, but in many cases the guide can give you a brief English translation.

Boat Tours around the Jaffa Port (depending on demand and weather) run every day and start from NIS 30 per person for a half hour trip. Call **Kef** (✆ **052/863-3266**) for schedules and reservations.

SPECIAL/FREE EVENTS **Hof Hatupim,** or Beach of the Drums, located at the southern end of the waterfront, hosts a Friday afternoon drumming session, enjoyed by everyone from toddlers to 83-year-old hippies. There's Israeli folk dancing at the esplanade opposite the volleyball nets on Gordon Beach every Saturday morning at 11, and 7 to 11pm during the hottest summer months. The nearby Gordon Pool, the EllaYoga Studio at the Tel Aviv Port, and other public parks offer free yoga and exercise classes at sunset or sunrise, depending on the season and the weather. There is also music and dancing at other points along the beach on evenings throughout the week; free concerts are held in Yarkon Park and in Old Jaffa during the summer. Check with Tel Aviv Tourist Information (see above).

Nahalat Binyamin Pedestrian Mall has an active, colorful outdoor **Craft Bazaar** and street performers every Tuesday and Friday from 10am to 5pm. Take bus no. 4.

OUTDOOR PURSUITS & SPORTS

BEACHES Tel Aviv's seashore is within walking distance of most of the city. A promenade runs the entire length of the beach. Most beaches have free showers and facilities for changing, as well as beach umbrellas and chaises for a small fee. The cleanest beaches, with the best swimming, are behind the Dan and Sheraton hotels (Frishman–Gordon sts.) northward to the Hilton hotel. The **Hilton Beach** is especially **gay friendly,** but also hosts a mix of families

Crowds enjoy the beach in Tel Aviv.

and surfers, and allows dogs. **Alma Beach** and **Givat Aliyah Beach** also allow dogs to play. Farther north, the **Nordau Beach is reserved for religious Jews,** with visitors segregated by sex according to alternate days of the week, starting with women on Sundays, though many secular people like to take advantage of the spot on Saturdays, when religious Jews do not swim.

Warning: Swimming at Israel's Mediterranean beaches can be dangerous. The problem is riptides and whirlpools that even a strong swimmer can't fight. It's safe, however, to swim at beaches where guards are stationed. Pay attention to the safety symbols along the beaches in the form of small flags. Black flags mean absolutely no swimming, red warns you to be especially cautious, and white indicates that the water's fine. Tel Aviv's city beaches are protected in many places by a system of breakwaters and are the safest in the area.

BOATS Small motorboats, pedal boats, and rowboats can be rented by the hour, daily, from 10am to 5pm on the lake at **Hayarkon Park** (© **03/642-0541**) at the northern end of the city. Motorboats are NIS 180 per hour; rowboats NIS 120 per hour; pedal boats are NIS 145 per hour. **Danit Tours** (danit.co.il. © **052/340-0128**) does party and group boat tours from the Tel Aviv Marina. Call for information and see if you can join a group ride into the sea.

CYCLING Tel Aviv is relatively flat and, in that respect, more bicycle-friendly than the mountainous cities of Jerusalem and Haifa. Drivers, however, are NOT bicycle-friendly (though new bicycle lanes through much of the city make the activity far safer than it used to be). The **Tel Aviv Municipality** offers a public network of blue rental bikes called **Tel-o-Fun** with computerized pick up and return stations at strategic locations throughout the city, similar to those in many European cities. You pay by credit card through the app.

Tip: The Tel-o-Fun Bikes are designed to promote short 30-minute rental periods to encourage Tel Avivians to get from place to place without using cars or buses. Rental rates are reasonable for the first 20 minutes, but become increasingly steep the longer you keep the bike. Worse yet, readers report problems getting the computerized rental machines to unlock or return your bike. Meanwhile, the rental rate keeps ticking away and your credit card gets billed while you fight with the machine. Maps with pick-up and drop-off stations can be picked up at City Hall.

For longer periods of leisurely biking, you would do better to rent a bike from one of the offices listed below, or, if you're a guest at one of the **Atlas Hotels,** reserve one of their free on-loan bikes. Serious cyclers should check ahead with the **Israeli Cycling Federation,** 6 Shitrit St., Tel Aviv (www.israelcycling.org.il; © **03/649-0459**). For bike rentals, try **Cycle,** 147 Ben Yehuda St. (© **03/529-3037**), and **O-Fun,** 197 Dizengoff St. (© **03/544-2292**); rates run approximately NIS 75 per day from the time you rent until the day's closing time for the shop.

JOGGING The long beachfront promenade, running several miles from the northern end of Jaffa to the Tal hotel, provides an excellent stretch for urban jogging, without the inconvenience of cross streets and traffic lights. It's

Kite surfers get a spectacular view of the city's skyline.

busy, which adds an element of safety, and you can stop for a dip in the sea or cool off at the public drinking fountains and showers that dot the beaches.

WATER SPORTS Tel Aviv Beach, midway between Mograbi Square and Jaffa, is designated for surfboarding, kayaking, windsailing, and kiteboarding. Contact **Hilton Bay TLV Surf Academy** (www.surfacademy.co.il; ✆ **052/500-0204;** info@surfacademy.co.il) for equipment rental and lessons.

If your hotel has no pool and you want to swim a few laps, or on the days when Tel Aviv's sea become a soup of stinging jellyfish in July and August, check out the historic, beautiful, and renovated **Gordon Pool,** 14 Perry Eliezar St. (off Ha-Yarkon St., btw. the Tel Aviv Marina and the Carlton Hotel; ✆ **03/762-3300**), which is filled, even in the steaming summer, with delightfully chilly sea water. Admission is NIS 69 Sunday to Friday, NIS 79 on Saturday. Children under 2 are free; Discounts for students and pensioners. (Sun 1:30pm–9pm; Mon–Thurs 6am–9pm; Fri 6am–7pm; Sat 7am–6pm.) Call ahead for the most updated hours and rates.

WHERE TO STAY

Many of Tel Aviv's hotels are comparatively high in price and modern in amenities and design, in keeping with a city barely more than 100 years old. The larger, internationally branded hotels are generally located along the beach and often have pools and in-house restaurants. Smaller, boutique hotels, many of which are located in restored heritage buildings, boast the advantage of providing a more immersive, neighborhood feel. A number of chic, luxury boutique hotels are located on and around the tree-lined Rothschild Avenue.

The Dizengoff Square area, which is further inland, is another hotel hub, especially for smaller boutique hotels.

Tel Aviv can be a very noisy city. In the more expensive, high-rise hotels, upper floors are quieter. If you're looking for a moderate or budget hotel, don't take a room facing a main street unless it has air-conditioning and soundproof windows. By international standards, many "deluxe" hotels are barely that, and many hotels claiming to be five-star properties are four stars at best.

Central Beach Hotels

Tel Aviv's *Tayelet,* or seaside promenade, runs parallel to Hayarkon Street on one side and the Mediterranean on the other. The major hotel chains are all right off the sea and have either direct access to the beach or are across a small but busy road. Because of the summer heat and humidity, a hotel with a pool can be a good investment. For a long block north of the Renaissance Hotel near Gordon Beach, Hayarkon becomes a wider thoroughfare with divider barriers, meaning guests staying in moderate hotels on the inland side of the street can't just dash across the road and down to the beach. Skyscraper, residential building demolitions, and light rail construction are everywhere, and accompanying noise is a daytime fact of life.

EXPENSIVE

Carlton Hotel Tel Aviv ★★ This seafront hotel first opened in 1981 and benefits from one of the best locations in Tel Aviv, a stretch of the seaside promenade with no roadway in front of it. Walk out the door and the beach is practically right there. Don't be deceived by the Carlton's hulking concrete

private ROOMS & APARTMENTS

For Tel Aviv stays of longer than a few days, consider renting a short-term furnished apartment. Airbnb (or VRBO.com) is the obvious choice, but pay close attention to the reviews, as—similar to Israeli hotels—price does not necessarily reflect the level of quality. For a great selection of apartments with the highest standards of cleanliness and the best, most responsive service, a company called **TLV2GO** (www.tlv2go.com; ✆ **073/797-1118;** email info@tlv2go.com) is highly recommended. The company is based in the heart of Tel Aviv and rents dozens of apartments in locations around the city, with an emphasis on luxury. They don't charge broker's fees or commissions and will help you find the place that's right for your particular needs (e.g., if you want to be close to the beach, they will do their best to see that you are; or if you want to bring your pets).

If you're looking for only high-end accommodation options, you can also try the **Plum Guide,** a bespoke service that lists hundreds of unique homes throughout Tel Aviv. They have categories like pet-friendly, large groups, or pool, to help you find a place that perfectly suits your needs. Peruse their gorgeously designed apartments at www.plumguide.com/tel-aviv, or call ✆ **03/376-3289.** Email: guests@plumguide.com.

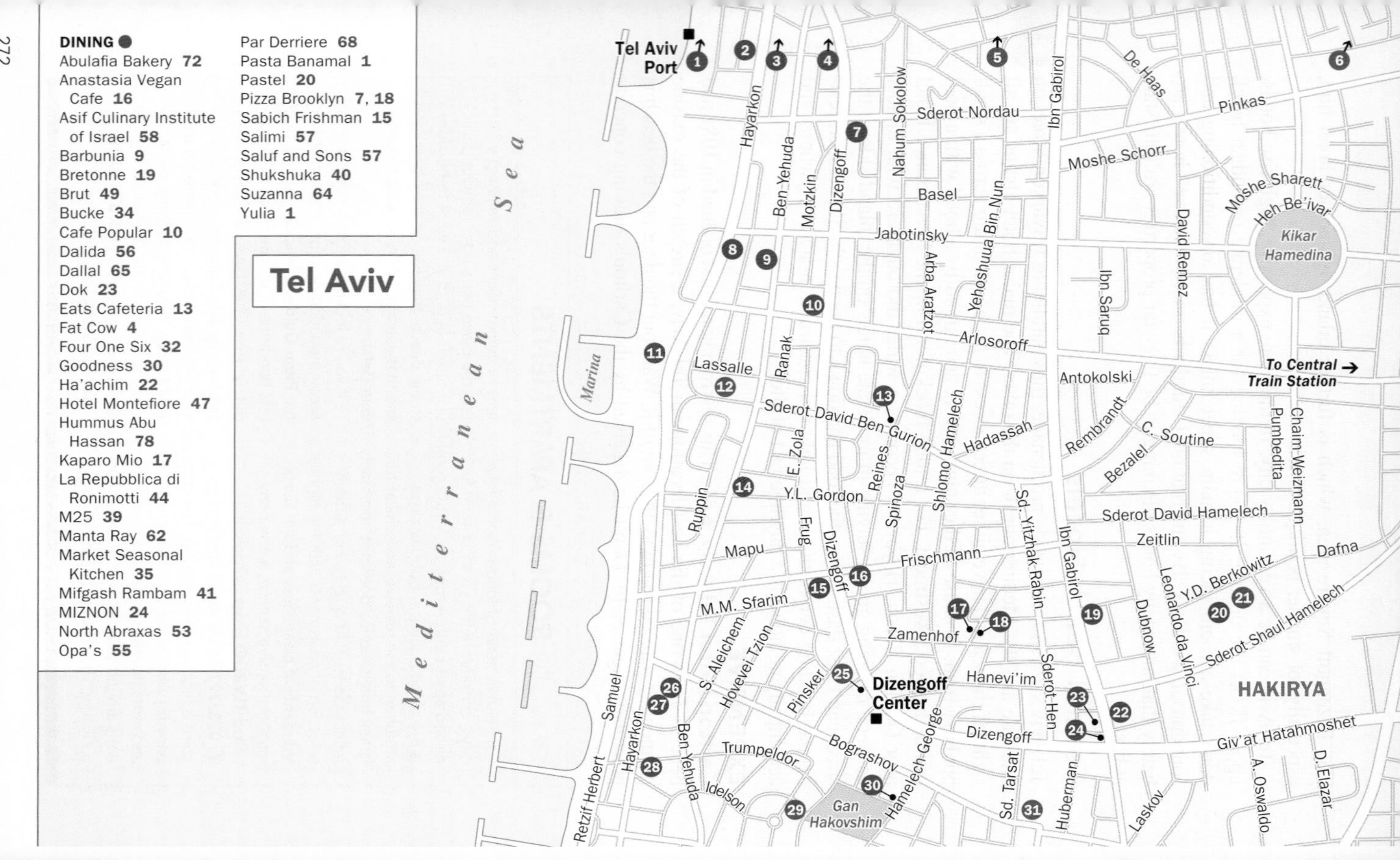
Tel Aviv
DINING
Abulafia Bakery 72
Anastasia Vegan Cafe 16
Asif Culinary Institute of Israel 58
Barbunia 9
Bretonne 19
Brut 49
Bucke 34
Cafe Popular 10
Dalida 56
Dallal 65
Dok 23
Eats Cafeteria 13
Fat Cow 4
Four One Six 32
Goodness 30
Ha'achim 22
Hotel Montefiore 47
Hummus Abu Hassan 78
Kaparo Mio 17
La Repubblica di Ronimotti 44
M25 39
Manta Ray 62
Market Seasonal Kitchen 35
Mifgash Rambam 41
MIZNON 24
North Abraxas 53
Opa's 55
Par Derriere 68
Pasta Banamal 1
Pastel 20
Pizza Brooklyn 7, 18
Sabich Frishman 15
Salimi 57
Saluf and Sons 57
Shukshuka 40
Suzanna 64
Yulia 1
Mediterranean Sea
Marina
Tel Aviv Port
Dizengoff Center
HAKIRYA
Kikar Hamedina
Gan Hakovshim
To Central Train Station
Hayarkon
Ben Yehuda
Dizengoff
Ibn Gabirol
Sderot Nordau
Nahum Sokolow
Pinkas
De Haas
Moshe Schorr
Moshe Sharett
Heh Be'ivar
Basel
Motzkin
Jabotinsky
Yehoshuua Bin Nun
Arba Aratzot
David Remez
Ibn Saruq
Arlosoroff
Antokolski
Lassalle
Ranak
Sderot David Ben Gurion
Shlomo Hamelech
Hadassah
Rembrandt
C. Soutine
Bezalel
Pumbedita
Chaim Weizmann
E. Zola
Reines
Spinoza
Y.L. Gordon
Ruppin
Frug
Sd. Yitzhak Rabin
Sderot David Hamelech
Zeitlin
Mapu
Frischmann
Dafna
Y.D. Berkowitz
M.M. Sfarim
Dubnow
Leonardo da Vinci
Sderot Shaul Hamelech
Zamenhof
S. Aleichem
Hovevei Tzion
Pinsker
Hanevi'im
Sderot Hen
Samuel
Retzif Herbert
Trumpeldor
Bograshov
Hamelech George
Idelson
Sd. Tarsat
Huberman
Laskov
Giv'at Hatahmoshet
A. Oswaldo
D. Elazar

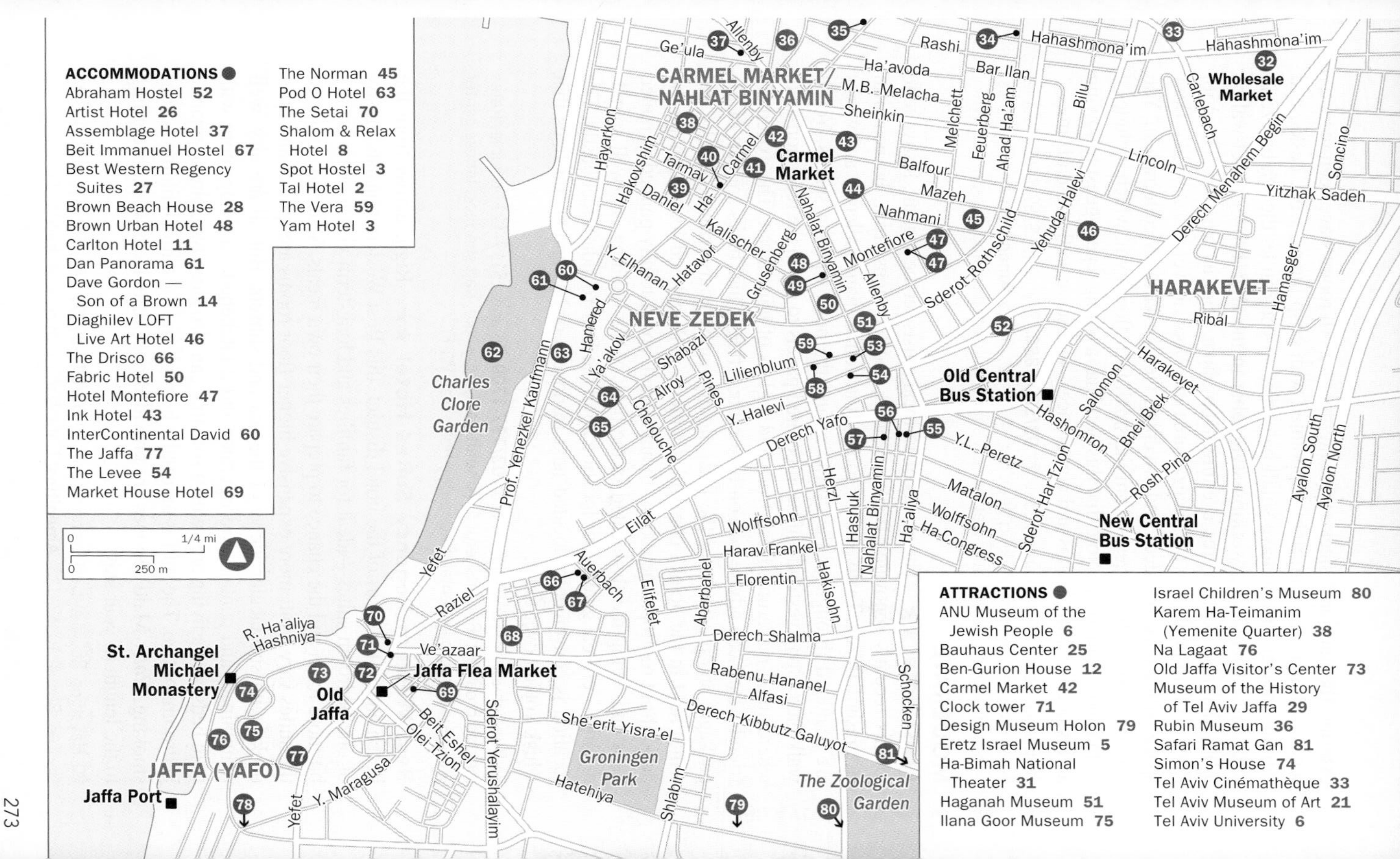
ACCOMMODATIONS
Abraham Hostel 52
Artist Hotel 26
Assemblage Hotel 37
Beit Immanuel Hostel 67
Best Western Regency Suites 27
Brown Beach House 28
Brown Urban Hotel 48
Carlton Hotel 11
Dan Panorama 61
Dave Gordon — Son of a Brown 14
Diaghilev LOFT Live Art Hotel 46
The Drisco 66
Fabric Hotel 50
Hotel Montefiore 47
Ink Hotel 43
InterContinental David 60
The Jaffa 77
The Levee 54
Market House Hotel 69
The Norman 45
Pod O Hotel 63
The Setai 70
Shalom & Relax Hotel 8
Spot Hostel 3
Tal Hotel 2
The Vera 59
Yam Hotel 3
ATTRACTIONS
ANU Museum of the Jewish People 6
Bauhaus Center 25
Ben-Gurion House 12
Carmel Market 42
Clock tower 71
Design Museum Holon 79
Eretz Israel Museum 5
Ha-Bimah National Theater 31
Haganah Museum 51
Ilana Goor Museum 75
Israel Children's Museum 80
Karem Ha-Teimanim (Yemenite Quarter) 38
Na Lagaat 76
Old Jaffa Visitor's Center 73
Museum of the History of Tel Aviv Jaffa 29
Rubin Museum 36
Safari Ramat Gan 81
Simon's House 74
Tel Aviv Cinémathèque 33
Tel Aviv Museum of Art 21
Tel Aviv University 6
0 1/4 mi
0 250 m
CARMEL MARKET/ NAHLAT BINYAMIN
Carmel Market
Wholesale Market
NEVE ZEDEK
HARAKEVET
Old Central Bus Station
New Central Bus Station
Charles Clore Garden
Jaffa Flea Market
Old Jaffa
St. Archangel Michael Monastery
JAFFA (YAFO)
Jaffa Port
Groningen Park
The Zoological Garden
Ge'ula
Allenby
Rashi
Hahashmona'im
Ha'avoda
Bar Ilan
M.B. Melacha
Sheinkin
Melchett
Feuerberg
Ahad Ha'am
Bilu
Carlebach
Hayarkon
Hakovshim
Tarmav
Daniel
Ha-Carmel
Balfour
Lincoln
Derech Menahem Begin
Soncino
Yitzhak Sadeh
Mazeh
Nahmani
Yehuda Halevi
Kalischer
Y. Elhanan
Hatavor
Grusenberg
Nahalat Binyamin
Montefiore
Sderot Rothschild
Hamasger
Ribal
Hamered
Ya'akov
Shabazi
Alroy
Pines
Lilienblum
Y. Halevi
Chelouche
Derech Yafo
Harakevet
Salomon
Hashomron
Bnei Brek
Rosh Pina
Y.L. Peretz
Prof. Yehezkel Kaufmann
Herzl
Hashuk
Ha'aliya
Matalon
Wolffsohn
Ha-Congress
Sderot Har Tzion
Ayalon South
Ayalon North
Eilat
Harav Frankel
Hakisohn
Florentin
Yefet
Raziel
Auerbach
Elifelet
Abarbanel
Derech Shalma
R. Ha'aliya Hashniya
Ve'azaar
Rabenu Hananel
Alfasi
Schocken
Derech Kibbutz Galuyot
She'erit Yisra'el
Beit Eshel
Olei Tzion
Sderot Yerushalayim
Hatehiya
Shlabim
Y. Maragusa

exterior; the interior is sleek and contemporary. All rooms have been recently renovated and are comfortably appointed with crisp linens, work desks, and rainfall showers; many have small balconies so you can let the sea breeze in with ease. There's a coworking-style table in the chic, brown panel-walled lobby that also hosts a free evening happy hour from its bar/cafe. The 15th floor rooftop pool, like the Jacuzzi area one floor above, is a Zen-like floor space with a gorgeous deck and sweeping views over the Mediterranean. You can also take in those views from the small fifth-floor gym, which includes a sauna and steam room. Note that this hotel has a strong repeat-guest following and is popular with groups and conferences, so reserve well ahead of time.

10 Eliezer Peri St. www.carlton.co.il. ✆ **03/520-1880.** 270 units. $259–$460 double. Rates include breakfast. Parking (fee). Bus: 4, 10, 62, or 115. **Amenities:** 2 lounge/bars; coworking space; health club; wet and dry sauna; outdoor pool and Jacuzzi; free Wi-Fi.

MODERATE

Artist Hotel ★★ The works of 15 local artists set the vibrant, festive tone to this recently renovated boutique hotel, located steps from the beautiful Bograshov Beach. Twelve of the rooms function as living galleries, and works are scattered throughout the corridors and the hotel's public spaces. You'll walk past a long vestibule of neon-colored panels to get to the reception area, where small macarons, fresh fruit, and a glass of wine await. The extremely friendly staff can advise you on bike routes (free loaner bikes are part of the package) and preside over the free, nightly happy hours (simple snacks and wine) held in the hotel's cheerful, flamingo pink–colored lounge, or on the decked-out rooftop. The rooms, though small, are tastefully painted in muted hues and, being mostly located in the back of the building, are well soundproofed—critical given your location amid the Ben Yehuda Street bustle. The location is conveniently located next to dozens of bus and sherut lines that whisk you all over town.

35 Ben Yehuda St. www.atlas.co.il. ✆ **03/797-1700.** 56 units. $119–$217 double. Rates include breakfast. Bus or sherut 4. **Amenities:** Lobby cafe; bar; sundeck; fitness center and sauna; free bike rental; free happy hour; free Wi-Fi.

Best Western Regency Suites Hotel ★★ Right across from the beach and in the heart of the hotel district, this Best Western consists mostly of one-bedroom suites—ideal for families and long-term visitors who want a bit more room and the chance to prepare their own meals. Size and set ups of the suites vary a bit; more expensive higher-floor rooms are quieter and offer decks with spectacular views of the sea and sunsets. But all are airy, well maintained, and contain a refrigerator and a kitchenette, a living room with twin beds, and a living area with a sofa that can also sleep two, plus a separate bedroom for two. The staff is unusually helpful, and the entire building is nonsmoking. ***Note:*** Maid services are provided once or twice a week, according to the length of your stay.

80 Hayarkon St. www.bestwestern.com. ✆ **03/517-3939.** 33 units. $160–$230 suite double. Bus: 4, 10, 62, 115. **Amenities:** Cafe; bar; room service; free Wi-Fi.

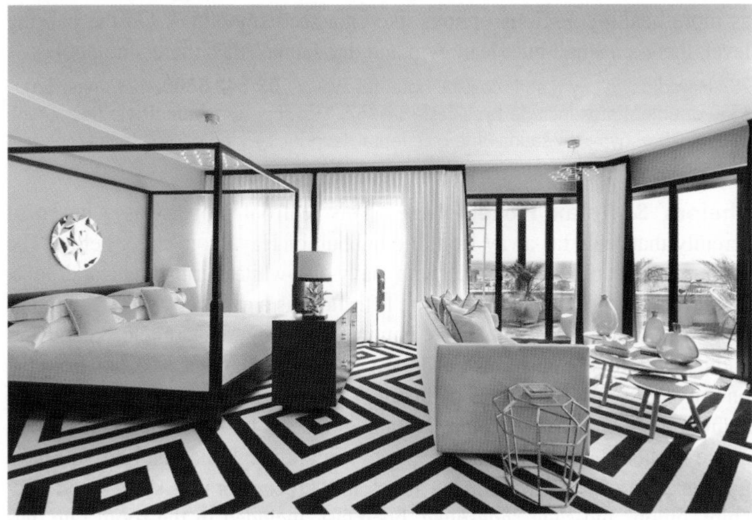
The movie set–like penthouse suite at the Brown Beach Hotel.

Brown Beach House Hotel ★★ The Brown Beach House Hotel is the slightly edgier sister of the older, but ever-trendy, Brown Urban Hotel. As you might guess, it's also closer to the beach—across busy Hayarkon Street, but the spacious, quirkily appointed rooms are well-insulated from traffic noise. Most feature wide sun terraces with comfy furniture so you can soak up views. Inside, decor is a well-executed reimagining of 1950s retro summer resorts, so expect bold colors and a bit of a Miami Beach vibe, which extends to the aptly named Flamingo Bar & Lounge, where an illuminated pink flamingo oversees a boisterous crowd of local night owls. Kosher breakfasts included in the rate.

64 Hayarkon St. www.browntlv.com. ✆ **03/760-5000.** 52 units $165–$325 double; suites from $380. Rates include breakfast. Bus: 4, 10; sherut 4. **Amenities:** Bar/cafe; fitness room; spa; Jacuzzi; kids' club; free bike rental; free Wi-Fi.

North Tel Aviv

MODERATE

Tal Hotel ★ A stalwart in the Tel Aviv tourism scene, the Tal is a long-time favorite choice for tour groups (so it can feel crowded). But it does occupy a prime location between the beach and the Tel Aviv Port, which guests can explore with a complimentary bike. The decor is contemporary, if unimaginative: a vertical green wall at the entrance and pleasant blue palettes in the rooms (all recently renovated). The lobby bar hosts a happy hour every evening, serving cava and *burekas* (pastries). The breakfast buffet, included in the room rate, offers the standard fare of eggs, waffles, and assorted salad, as well as more health-conscious options like chia seed smoothies. On the parking level, there's a small but clean gym and dry sauna. Alas, there's no pool.

287 Hayarkon St. www.atlas.co.il/tal-hotel-tel-aviv. ✆ **03/542-5500.** 123 units. $200–$350 double. Rates include breakfast. Bus: 62, 115; sherut 4. **Amenities:** Restaurant; free mini bar; gym; dry sauna; free bike rental; laundry; parking garage (extra fee); free Wi-Fi.

Shalom & Relax Hotel ★★★ This seafront property is a haven of serenity that feels far away from the hubbub of Hayarkon Street below. The rooms are beach house–chic, with navy-and-white furnishings and luxe, incredibly comfortable beds. On the fifth floor is a decadent roof deck, complete with wooden rocking chairs, hammocks, sitting pods (enclosed couches padded with lots of cushions), and, best of all, free massage sessions from the on-duty masseuse. For more pampering, you can book a longer massage or splurge on a "Spa Guest Room," which includes a hot tub. The kitchen hosts a free kosher, dairy happy hour every evening, though the hotel doesn't have a *kashrut* certificate. With menu items like green morning shakes and zucchini, onion, and sage *shakshuka,* breakfast, included in the room rate, has plenty of options for vegans, vegetarians, and any visitor looking to sample an elevated version of the world-renowned Israeli breakfast. Location is primo, too, across the road from Independence Park from where it's an easy stroll to Hilton Beach.

216 Hayarkon St. www.atlas.co.il/shalom-hotel-tel-aviv. ✆ **03/762-5400.** 50 units. $161–$297 double. Rates include breakfast. Bus: 4, 10. **Amenities:** Restaurant; bar; loaner Rav-Kav cards; free bike rental; Jacuzzi; room service; sauna; free Wi-Fi.

The, yes, relaxing roof deck of the Shalom & Relax Hotel.

Simple but spotless and comfy room at the Yam Hotel.

Yam Hotel ★★ The small, family-friendly Yam hotel (Beach Hotel in Hebrew) has a definite surfer vibe, with boards hanging on the wall, chalk-boards with the temperature and wave conditions, and abundant indoor and outdoor areas to hang. The downstairs lobby is adorned with blue couches and colorful, mismatched pillows that make a great setting for the nightly, free-of-charge happy hour. The rooms are compact but comfortable, with sea view balconies for rooms on floors 3 to 7. Less than 5 minutes' walk in either direction are the Tel Aviv Port, the Mezizim Beach, and some of the city's best restaurants. The extremely informative, mostly young and friendly staff will send you out with a beach bag stuffed with towels, water bottles, and snacks.

16 Yordei Hasira St. www.atlas.co.il/yam-hotel-tel-aviv. ✆ **03/545-5000.** 42 units. $148–$231 double. Bus: 8, 129, 172. **Amenities:** Free bike rental; free happy hour; loaner Rav-Kav cards; free Wi-Fi.

INEXPENSIVE

Spot Hostel ★ This massive, container-like structure, smack dab in the middle of Hayarkon Park and steps from the Tel Aviv Port, is proof that the hostel movement is still alive and kicking. With options that include single-person pods, family rooms, and classic 12-bed, mixed gender dormitories, the Spot is more of a travel hub than any one category of accommodation. Its spacious lobby-level restaurant serves complimentary breakfast as well as a full menu throughout the day, both to hostel guests and to the many locals who appreciate its convenient location and ample sitting space. The front desk staff can advise on a number of activities oriented to young, single travelers, like pub crawls, bikes tours, music performances, or beer-making workshops on the premises if you feel like staying in. The beds have curtains, though the rooms lack windows and can get extremely humid, especially during the summer months.

3 Hataarucha. www.thespothostel.com. ✆ **03/790-7477.** 80 units. $96–$130 double, less for hostel beds. Bus: 4, 10. **Amenities:** Restaurant; bar; games room; free Wi-Fi.

Dizengoff Square & Ben Yehuda Street

This area is a good choice for a winter visits, when the weather is milder and you can bear the 5-minute walk to the closest beach. This area, which has exploded with boutique hotels in the past few years, is also a culinary hotspot.

MODERATE

The Dave Gordon—Son of a Brown ★★ This budget hotel, located in a preserved Bauhaus building, boasts a central location and bordello-inspired aesthetic that sets it apart from most of the other properties in the Brown Hotel chain. We're talking flea market furnishings, blood red walls, and abundant spots to schmooze. It also has convenient access to both Gordon Beach and the many bustling bars of Dizengoff Street. The rooms, like the rest of the hotel, are '70s-style vintage, and range from a "Solo Room" to the most extravagant "Foxy Superior Room," which is on the fourth floor (no elevator, though the staff is happy to help you with your luggage) and includes a complimentary minibar and a freestanding tub. All rates include breakfast. Guests are greeted with a glass of cold beer on arrival, and invited to enjoy the complimentary coffee, popcorn and snacks served 24/7 on the leafy outdoor patio.

17 Gordon St. www.brownhotels.com/dave. ✆ **03/757-9000.** 35 units. $151–265 for double. Bus: 4, 10. **Amenities:** Rooftop terrace; free coffee and snacks; free beer at check-in; free Wi-Fi.

Southern Tel Aviv

Across a divided thoroughfare from the sea (but a 2-block walk to a guarded swimming beach), two high-rise hotels, the Dan Panorama and the David InterContinental, tower over a rapidly gentrifying stretch between Tel Aviv and Jaffa, approximately 2.4km (1½ miles) south of the main Hayarkon Street hotel district. **Old Jaffa** is a 15-minute walk along the seaside promenade, and the bustling The **Carmel Market** (from which you can reach the restaurants and cafes of the trendy **Nahalat Binyamin, Neve Zedek,** and **Rothschild St.** areas) is a 5-minute walk across a shabby, but perfectly safe, park. Further inland, the new boutique hotels offer Tel Aviv chic, though in summer, they lack the city's beach ambience.

EXPENSIVE

Hotel Montefiore ★★ The best-known boutique hotel in Tel Aviv is a fun, cool place to stay. There's no lobby—the legendary eponymous Franco-Vietnamese restaurant that occupies the ground floor *is* the lobby and is a preferred haunt for the Tel Aviv glitterati. But upstairs, there are 12 luxuriously appointed guest rooms that feature high ceilings, dark hardwood floors, tall windows, cheeky photography by Israeli artists, and unusually large selections of books arrayed in floor-to-ceiling libraries. Minibars have French press coffee makers, and mineral water is provided in a glass decanter, never plastic. The swank vibe extends to the black marble bathrooms, with rainfall showers and fragrant custom amenities. The Eclectic-style building that houses all of this dates from 1922 and has been respectfully restored, but the overall flavor is more playful than patrician. Breakfast, included in the rate, is a classy but relaxed affair—no buffet, rather a lovely a-la-carte menu that covers all the bases and then some. If the rooms here are a bit beyond your price range, don't miss the opportunity for a meal at the **Montefiore Restaurant ★★★**. Whether you book a table for breakfast, lunch, dinner, or high tea, you'll be treating yourself to some of the best food in Tel Aviv (full review on p. 293).

36 Montefiore St. www.hotelmontefiore.co.il. ✆ **03/564-6100.** 12 units $379–$500 double. Rates include breakfast. Bus or sherut 4. **Amenities:** Bar; restaurant; free access to nearby gym; free Wi-Fi.

InterContinental David Tel Aviv ★★★ Coming here is like walking into a business-class airline cabin: For a while at least, you can blissfully forget about the rest of the plane. Unlike most of the hotels along Tel Aviv's seafront, this one is of more recent construction, meaning that, despite its large size, the rooms are spacious and quiet, and most come with stunning sea views. Even standard rooms exude refined luxury, and from gleaming bathroom fixtures to work stations, nothing ever feels worn out or dated—the same can't be said for all the city's luxe seafront addresses.

The hotel is just south of Tel Aviv's central beach area, but it's less than a 10-minute walk, and there's a fine stretch of beach literally across the street. Moreover, this end of the sea promenade puts you within easy walking distance of Carmel Market, Neve Tzedek, and Jaffa. That said, because of the array and quality of services on offer, this is also a great hotel to simply linger at the beginning or end of your trip. The pool lounge area is arguably the biggest and best in Tel Aviv. You can nosh away in the Atrium Lobby Bar, casual Jaffa Court restaurant, or the gourmet Nomi Bistro (all dining at the hotel is kosher). The InterContinental David has deservedly earned a reputation as a hotel with some of the finest service anywhere: From parking attendants to guest relations, affability prevails, and it seems there is no guest request—whether it's a hot restaurant tip or bucket of ice in the middle of the night—that can't be met.

12 Kaufman St. www.intercontinental.com/telaviv. ✆ **03/795-1111.** 555 units. $385–$515 double. Rates include breakfast. Parking (for a fee). Bus: 4, 10. **Amenities:** 3 restaurants; bar; gym; spa; wet and dry sauna; outdoor pool; 24-hour room service; free Wi-Fi; gift shop.

Lobby in the uber-chic Levee hotel.

The Levee ★★★ In this palatial, white, neoclassical villa, dating to 1913, guests have the rare privilege of serenity and ample space just a stone's throw from Neve Tzedek, Tel Aviv's posh artist and designer's district (the hottest bars, restaurants, and shopping in town are here). The Levee, named after its location on Yehuda Halevi Street, was originally known as the Gurevitch House. It was part of Ahuzat Beit, Tel Aviv's first settled neighborhood, which was marked as a UNESCO World Heritage Site in 2003. The hotel's 8-year restoration added two floors and an uber contemporary, steel-floored penthouse overlooking the bustling neighborhood below. The Levee has eight spacious suites of one or two bedrooms apiece, which have such niceties as private gardens, state-of-the-art kitchen appliances, washing machine and dryer, Molton Brown toiletries, and smart, mostly European imported furnishings. There's no spa, in-house gym, or breakfast service, but the Levee turns those problems into perks: guests get passes to the nearby Icon Fitness center and breakfast at Herzl 16, a trendy local restaurant. Stays require a minimum of 2 nights' reservation.

16 Yehuda Halevi St. www.leveetlv.com. ✆ **03/771-4421.** 8 units. $547–$630. Rates include breakfast. Min. 2 nights. Bus or sherut 4. **Amenities:** Washing machine and dryer; full kitchen; free valet parking; Netflix and cable; gym access; free Wi-Fi.

The Norman ★★★ Tucked in a quiet street in the UNESCO-listed "White City," a district dotted with character-heavy Bauhaus, Modernist, and Eclectic-style buildings, this widely lauded boutique hotel has set the standard for Tel Aviv luxury since it opened in 2014. The hotel is composed of two gorgeously restored buildings from the 1920s—one light yellow, the other pale blue—connected by a citrus garden and terrace as reminiscent of Beverly

Hills as the south of France. Staff is polite but reserved, mostly eager to respect guests' privacy, having hosted many international luminaries. The modern art on the whitewashed walls, the ground floor Library Bar—offering choice wines sourced from across Israel—and the contemporary Israeli restaurant, **Alena,** all exude a feel of relaxed elegance. Breakfast, included in the rate, offers specialties like roasted eggplant, home-cured okra and vegan *malabi,* a Middle Eastern rose water–infused rice pudding, along with the more standard fare. The rooftop infinity pool has a lifeguard who can shake a mean cocktail. Rooms are on the smaller side, but are outfitted with deliciously comfortable beds and impeccably decorated with vintage pieces. The infinity showers offer surround-sound speakers and artisanal bath amenities concocted by a local perfumer. Note that the beach is about 20 minutes away by foot.

23-25 Nahmani St. www.thenorman.com. ✆ **03/543-5555.** 50 units $615–$1,000 double. Rates include breakfast. Bus: 24, 25, 125, 18, 82. **Amenities:** Rooftop deck and pool; spa; gym; bar; rooftop yoga classes (for a fee); gourmet restaurant; free Wi-Fi.

MODERATE

Assemblage Hotel ★★ This boutique hotel packs a lot into a relatively compact space: a bar and cafe, an art gallery, a decadent spa, and, most importantly, well-appointed rooms that allow you to get a breather after a day of exploring one of Tel Aviv's most dynamic neighborhoods. The Assemblage has successfully meshed its architectural heritage—the building served as the Jewish National Fund offices in the 1920s—with quirky art and colorful decor accents, making it a fun, accessible property that does not skimp on service. Most rooms are on the smaller side and for that reason are best for single travelers and couples. But all come with fully equipped kitchenettes, including a small fridge and a Nespresso coffee machine. Keep in mind that there are no elevators, so it's best to request a room on one of the lower floors if you don't want a workout every time you go in and out of the room. The leafy courtyard cafe and bar is one of its hidden gems, and is beloved by locals (and their babies and their dogs), who appreciate the vegan and gluten-free options, the long list of reinvented Israeli tapas, and the all-around unpretentious vibe. The cafe's wine list is also fantastic, and pairs particularly well with the courtyard's frequent hosting of jazz sessions, lectures on contemporary Israeli art, and other cultural events. The Assemblage is conveniently located 5 minutes from the **Carmel Market** (see p. 307). It is another 5 minutes' walk from the beach.

48 Allenby St. www.assemblageboutiquehotel.com/en. ✆ **077/706-6760.** 20 units. $165–$190 double. Bus: 18, 25, 125. **Amenities:** Restaurant; bar; art gallery; courtyard; rooftop terrace; free yoga classes; free Wi-Fi.

Brown Urban Hotel ★★ Welcome to the grandfather of Tel Aviv's trendy hotel movement, a place so hip that its rooftop terrace—boasting a bar, fabulous city views, and a Jacuzzi—attracts more locals than guests. The lobby can be a scene, too, with its vintage-chic rocking chairs, pop-up souvenir design stand, and faded, blown-up Playboy magazine covers as decoration. As for the rooms, they're tight at just 10¼ sq. m (110 sq. ft.) for the cheapest standard ones, but so well-designed—chocolate walls, plush beds, rainfall showers in black marble bathrooms—that most guests don't mind the squeeze. More expensive "Relax" rooms include their own double Jacuzzi tubs. Deluxe rooms are larger and can accommodate two adults plus two children. Housed in a former, decidedly unsexy office building, the hotel's location draws its coolness from the endless clusters of fabulous restaurants and cocktail bars in its immediate vicinity. You're also always within about 10 minutes' walk from the nearest beach. Though the hotel doesn't have a restaurant, guests are given a voucher for breakfast for use at a number of local restaurants.

25 Kalisher St. www.brownhotels.com/tlv/design. ✆ **03/717-0200.** 30 units. $183–$235 double. Rates include breakfast. Parking (fee). Bus: 4, 129, 172. **Amenities:** Bar; fitness room (outside hotel); free yoga classes; rooftop deck; spa; Jacuzzi; loaner bikes; free Wi-Fi.

Diaghilev LOFT Live Art Hotel ★ Named for the famous Russian art critic and ballet impresario Sergei Diaghilev, this boutique hotel has cannily channeled both the great man's superb sense of style and his delight in the innovative. All of the one- and two-bedroom suites are soundproofed and decorated with striking original art (all for sale), and set up, purposefully, to promote restorative sleep. That means no blinking TV lights, glowing clocks, or other sources of light once you've gone to bed. The separate living areas make this a good choice for families who want room to spread out. Note that the smallest suites accommodate two people, with an option for an extra person for a charge; the largest are for up to four people, or six for an extra charge. Though the beach is not near, you're within walking distance of all the best markets, Rothschild Boulevard, and the picturesque neighborhood of Neve Tzedek.

56 Mazeh St. www.diaghilev.co.il. ✆ **03/545-3131.** 54 suites. $180–$230 suites; $260–$300 family suites. Parking (fee). Bus: 74, 189, 289. **Amenities:** Free Wi-Fi.

Fabric Hotel ★★ If you're feeling homesick for Brooklyn, or, more accurately, for the global concept today known as "Brooklyn," look no further than the Fabric Hotel. Opened in 2018 in a repurposed sewing factory, it gives homage to its roots, and to the once working-class boulevard on Nahalat Binyamin on which it's located, with room decor that features exposed wooden walls, stylishly mismatched furniture, and retro-style light fixtures. The "quadruple room" cleverly makes space for the kiddos, with bunk beds that come with their own curtains. Its indoor-outdoor lobby bar, called "Bushwick," serves as a coffee shop during the day and becomes a hopping bar at night, replete with a DJ. Staff is mostly young, and always friendly and attentive, and can help you join a rooftop yoga class, map out a biking tour with one of their free rentals, or wander to some of the best restaurants within walking distance (the hotel has a prime location in one of Tel Aviv's most lively and historically significant neighborhoods, just a 10-minute stroll from Aviv Beach).

28 Nahalat Binyamin. www.atlas.co.il/fabric-hotel-tel-aviv. ✆ **03/567-8000.** 42 units. $180–$230 double. Bus: 4, 129, 172. **Amenities:** Bar; restaurant; free bike rental; rooftop terrace; free Wi-Fi.

The bar at the Ink Hotel.

Ink Hotel ★★ In 2021, the finishing touches were put on this 52-room boutique hotel, transforming a building that in the 1950s served as a public library and bookstore and then, for decades later, as a Yiddish cultural center. Renowned local Tel Aviv architect Yoav Messer designed The Ink's facade to resemble a stack of weighty books piled at one's bedside. Most importantly, the hotel is proudly green: Natural light is used to reduce electricity consumption; smart insulation optimizes temperatures. The building is located on a quaint, low-key side street that feels far from the tourist bustle, though it's there if you want it. The compact rooms come with minibars, Nespresso coffee machines, and TVs hooked up to streaming sites, but the jewel in this hotel's crown is the lush rooftop pool deck. The beach is about 10 minutes away by foot, and the fashionable Sheinkin Street, one block over, has a many trendy cafes and shops.

14 Brenner St. www.inkhotel.com. ✆ **03/503-0088.** 52 units. Double from $234–$340. Rates include breakfast. Bus: 4, 172, 129. **Amenities:** Restaurant; bar; rooftop splashing pool; spa; parking; free Wi-Fi.

The Vera ★★★ This relative newcomer on the boutique hotel scene, is in, our opinion, also among the best. In the middle of hectic Lillenblum Street—in what was a maternity hospital a century ago, then an office building in the 1950s—the Vera is a five-story building with an unassuming exterior. But step inside the lobby and you'll find an open bar offering some of the best local wines, which you can take up to the rooftop, with stunning views of the city at night and free yoga and Pilates classes in the morning. The hotel produces an in-house magazine highlighting some of the most compelling people and trends in the city. The friendly staff are awash with tips for the shopping and foodie hotspots, located just outside the hotel's doors. Throughout the hotel,

Some of the guest rooms at The Vera have sitting tubs.

the decor is an equal balance between clean black, white, beige, and grey industrial palettes, wooden framed beds and bespoke designed furniture, all of which create an ambience of softness and comfort. The smaller rooms are bunker-esque, but, with their clever use of natural hues and strategic furniture placement, don't feel small. All rooms have extremely comfortable beds fitted with Egyptian sheets, and offer bowls of local fruit and aloe vera plants, which you're welcome to use in case you spent too much time at the beach. The artisanal, 100% organic bath products from the Israeli company Arugot are a real indulgence, as are the rain showers and the sleek, freestanding, egg-shaped bathtubs included in some of the larger rooms.

27 Lilienblum St. www.theverahotel.com. ✆ **03/778-3800.** 37 units; $250–$315 double. Rates include breakfast. Bus: 4, 129, 172. **Amenities:** Parking; free bike rental; free yoga and Pilates classes; spa; rooftop deck; free lobby wine and snacks; free Wi-Fi.

INEXPENSIVE

Abraham Hostel Tel Aviv ★★★ In an increasingly segregated Israel, Abraham Hostel has uniquely succeeded in building cross-cultural bridges through budget travel. Along with providing lodgings, the hostel hosts some of the city's most joyous, thoughtful concerts and cultural events, many featuring Arab-Jewish initiatives. If you plan to stay, know that there are more than just shared accommodations here; the Abraham has a variety of options, from dormitory-style digs to private rooms and suites. The edgy location in south Tel Aviv is about 20 minutes from the beach, but is close to the hopping bars and eateries of the hipster-packed Florentin district, and a 2-minute walk to the iconic Rothschild Blvd. The Abraham Hotel Tours company offers great tours through Tel Aviv and other fascinating destinations, including the **"Jesus Trail"** tour (see p. 197). You'll find Abraham hostels in all of Israel's tourist areas. ***Tip:*** If you'll be in Tel Aviv for a week or more, ask about long-stay discounts.

21 Levontin St. www.abrahamhostels.com/tel-aviv. ✆ **074/701-0772.** 250 dorm beds, 150 private rooms. From $42 per person for dorm-style lodging; from $116 per person for private room w/bath; private double suite w/bath from $174. Rates include breakfast. Bus: 5, 19, 25, 125. **Amenities:** Lounge; bar; guest kitchen; restaurant; rooftop; yoga classes; free Wi-Fi.

Two guests in the lobby of the Abraham Hostel Tel Aviv.

Pod O Hotel ★ Opened in 2021, this Japanese-style pod hotel is a solution for travelers wanting a step up from the hostel experience. The pods vary in size, with some allowing you to stand up and others only to lay down, though all come with some storage space and USB plugs to charge your devices. The showers and gender separated bathrooms are shared. If you can, spring for the sea view rooms, which make the expertly designed, cream-colored pods feel deceptively roomy. Guests spend most of their time in the common space balcony directly overlooking the Mediterranean. It's tastefully adorned with a vertical green garden and boho-style hanging lights. One of the O's highlights is its easy access both to the picturesque neighborhood of Neve Tzedek and to the cobblestoned alleyways of Old Jaffa.

2 Kaufmann St. www.theopodhotel.com. ✆ **077/756-5350.** 119 capsules. From $57 for single-person pods. Bus: 10, 18. **Amenities:** Outdoor terrace; vending machines; free Wi-Fi.

Jaffa

EXPENSIVE

The Drisco ★★★ In 1886, this hotel was founded by the Drisco brothers, two Christians from Maine, who were among a few dozen messianic Americans who planned to colonize the Holy Land in preparation for the second coming of Jesus Christ. Unfit for the mission, the brothers soon sold the hotel to a Templar hotelier, who renamed it the "Jerusalem Hotel," and it became one of the most prestigious Holy Land hotels, hosting Christian pilgrims docking at the Jaffa port on their way to Jerusalem. Mark Twain wrote part of

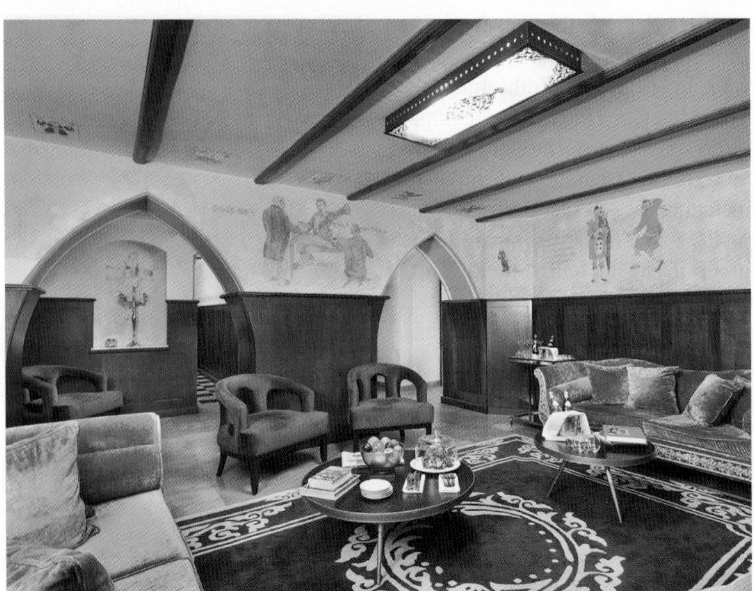

Nineteenth-century hand-painted murals adorn a lounge at the Drisco.

his satirical tourism novel *The Innocents Abroad* here. During the Second World War, as Templers were deported from Mandate Palestine, the British military seized the hotel and converted it into military headquarters. In 1958, a decade after the state of Israel was established, it housed Jewish refugees.

The Drisco sat neglected for decades before a 12-year restoration project painstakingly reconstructed the building's Ottoman arches, hand-painted interior murals, and marble columns. Today, the hotel is among the classiest properties in town. The rooms have hardwood floors, teardrop-shaped hanging lamps, stream-ready TVs, Nespresso machines, and subtle, Ottoman-style patterned walls. Beyond the standard amenities, all minibars are stocked with complimentary Israeli chocolates and Israeli juice. Some rooms boast balcony space, and the third-floor Premium rooms enjoy a coveted view of the city and sea. The in-house restaurant, **George and John,** cheekily named after the Drisco brothers, is where the hotel's spectacular breakfast (included in the room rate) is served; it feels like dining in the colonial era. You'll do well to make a reservation if you want to eat here on the weekends, as Tel Aviv's foodies amass at this restaurant, which serves innovative food inspired by Ottoman feasts.

6 Auerbach St. www.thedrisco.com. 42 units. ✆ **03/741-0000.** $510–$570 double. Bus: 25, 125, 18, 44, 40. **Amenities:** Restaurant; bar; gym; rooftop; happy hour; free Wi-Fi.

The Jaffa ★★ The Jaffa has done a remarkable job preserving a 19th-century Neo-Renaissance hospital and monastery. Arched colonnades, stained glass windows, Arabesque trellises, and stone-hewn walls are expertly balanced against a smattering of modern artwork and a newly built, clean-lined wing that features a tree-shaded courtyard. The rooms vary in size, but all have cavernous ceilings, high reaching windows, and neutrally hued, platform beds. There are backgammon—"sheshbesh" in Hebrew—sets out in each room, lending a colonial-style elegance. But modern comforts—like TVs built into the mirrors—are in line with this property's devotion to mixing the new with the old. The hotel's slickly modern **Golda's Restaurant** serves Israeli fare and Jewish-style deli favorites under the cream-colored arches; onsite are also cocktail bars and a laid-back rooftop pool area (also attended by a bartender) that overlooks the Jaffa Port and sea on one end, and the city on the other. While children are always welcome, this spot, with its hushed interior and numerous bars, has a distinctly adult flair. If you have Marriott points saved up, this hotel, part of the brand's Luxury Collection, is a worthy splurge.

2 Louis Pasteur St. www.marriott.com/hotels/travel/tlvlc-the-jaffa-a-luxury-collection-hotel-tel-aviv. ✆ **03/504-2000.** 120 units. $600–$790 double. Bus: 10, 14, 18, 44. **Amenities:** Rooftop pool; full spa; gym; restaurant; deli; free bikes; free Wi-Fi.

The Setai ★★ Housed in a renovated Crusader fortress, this hotel is dripping with ancient history. The subterranean spa and gym were carved around Crusader-era walls, and the rooms stand where there was once an Ottoman prison. Exposed archways and preserved stone and ceramic antiquities will encircle you as you wander through this sprawling, almost museum-like space. The rooms are a mix of Ottoman-style decor and modern amenities: delicately patterned light fixtures give a romantic hue and balance to the deep red Turkish rugs, complemented by minibars, flatscreen TVs, and other modern amenities built into the stone walls. If your budget allows, opt for the Premium Plus room with a sea view and balcony looking out onto the 4,000-year-old Jaffa Port. And don't miss out on morning laps at the rooftop infinity pool, overlooking the serene waters.

Though The Setai is a site in itself, its location, at the very entrance to Jaffa, is also a major draw. It is straight across from the iconic Clock Tower (see p. 264). It is also 5 minutes' walk from the bustling Port, where you can feast on fresh fish against the backdrop of the lapping waves of the Mediterranean.

22 David Raziel St. www.thesetaihotels.com/en-us/hotels/tel-aviv. ✆ **03/601-6000.** 120 units. $434–$515 double. Bus: 14, 18, 10, 44, 54. **Amenities:** Infinity rooftop pool; restaurant; cocktail bar; full spa with dry and wet sauna, treatments; gym; free Wi-Fi.

MODERATE

Market House Hotel ★★ The atmosphere of the Jaffa Flea Market is something unique in the world, and if you want to be in the beating heart of it all, you can do no better than this boutique hotel. One of its finest attributes is the glass-floored lobby, giving a peek down to the remnants of a Byzantine chapel; it does double duty as the breakfast room (extra fee, but very good food). Upstairs, the guest rooms are not huge, but they are very nicely appointed and come with wooden parquet floors and light, airy bathrooms. Ask for a room with a balcony for views of the market and, if you want a sea view that's nothing less than stunning, request room 401. This hotel is extremely popular, so don't leave your booking until the last minute.

5–7 Beit Eshel St. www.atlas.co.il/market-house-hotel-tel-aviv-israel. ✆ **03/797-4000.** 44 units. $211–$318 double. Bus: 10, 14, 18, 44, 54. **Amenities:** Restaurant; free bike rentals; free happy hour; free Wi-Fi.

INEXPENSIVE

Beit Immanuel Hostel ★ Located in a neighborhood of businesses and factories in the American Colony on the Tel Aviv–Jaffa border, this historic hostel is operated by a congregation of Christians and Messianic Jews, but guests of all persuasions are welcome. The guesthouse, located about 5 minutes' walk from the beach and another 10 minutes' walk from Old Jaffa, offers basic, well-maintained, air-conditioned private rooms with bathrooms, some outfitted for groups up to eight, and some with sun-drenched balconies. Street-facing rooms can be noisy, and many rooms are up several steep flights of stairs. Toiletries are not provided. The staff is helpful, and though the reception closes at 11pm, arrangements can be made for both late night or early morning arrivals and departures. Breakfast, included in the rate and served in the lush garden, is a special pleasure; and a coffee and tea station is available throughout the day.

8 Auerbach St. www.cmj-israel.org/beit-immanuel. ✆ **03/682-1459.** $85 single room with bath; $125 double with bath. Rates include breakfast. Parking (fee). Bus: 10, 25, 125, 44, 54. **Amenities:** Garden; free Wi-Fi in lobby.

WHERE TO EAT

On the Seaside Promenade

The seaside promenade is loaded with lovely seafood and fish restaurants, but there are also tons of culinary gems in romantic Old Jaffa and in more inland, though still easily accessible, parts of Tel Aviv.

From early in the morning until late at night, people come to Yulia's to feast on seafood.

MODERATE

Yulia ★★ SEAFOOD This seafront fish and seafood haunt near the Tel Aviv Port is a good option if you're hoping to feel the sea mist on your face as you feast on its fresh bounty. There's an indoor dining area with a fully stocked bar, but when the weather's fine (which is most of the year), opt for a table on the covered veranda or the outdoor terrace, which at night is especially romantic, with string lights and a soundtrack of the crashing waves. The highly attentive waitstaff can help you choose from their long list of Israeli wines and newer-to-the-scene Israeli whiskeys. Yulia is beloved by locals for its fantastic breakfast, served until noon with the late-night partiers in mind. Tucking into the "Fishermen's breakfast," a vast smorgasbord including white fish ceviche, cured roe, fresh breads, and locally sourced olives, is an ideal start to the day.

1 Yordei Hasira St. (adjacent to Mezizim Beach). www.yuliatlv.co.il. ✆ **077/231-1871.** Bus: 4, 10, 62, 115. Main courses NIS 60–NIS 140. Sun–Fri 8:30am–11pm, Sat 8am–11pm.

INEXPENSIVE

Pasta Banamal ★★★ MEDITERRANEAN A bustling, family-friendly pasta stand at the northern corner of the Tel Aviv Port Market, Pasta Banamal is a pint-size spot serving up some of the city's most reasonably priced, deliciously homemade pastas and salads, all based on what's available that day in the surrounding market. The brainchild of a local Israeli chef who's known for perfecting the art of street food, this casual eatery prides itself on its simplicity and family atmosphere—replete with the chef's kids manning the cash register during the summer and holiday breaks. The changing menu is written on a chalkboard above the open kitchen, but standouts includes the beetroot pasta topped with sage butter and blue cheese, and the light but still substantial Tunisian salad served with a hard-boiled egg, tuna, and pickled lemon—both of which pair well with a glass of the house wine. Outside of the lunch and dinner rush hour, you're welcome to pick something up from one of the other vendors in the market and request the chef to cook it into your dish. Seating is limited to about 10 barstools that wrap around the *basta* (market stall) where you can watch the cooks prepare your meal, as well as wooden picnic tables outside that belong to the whole market complex.

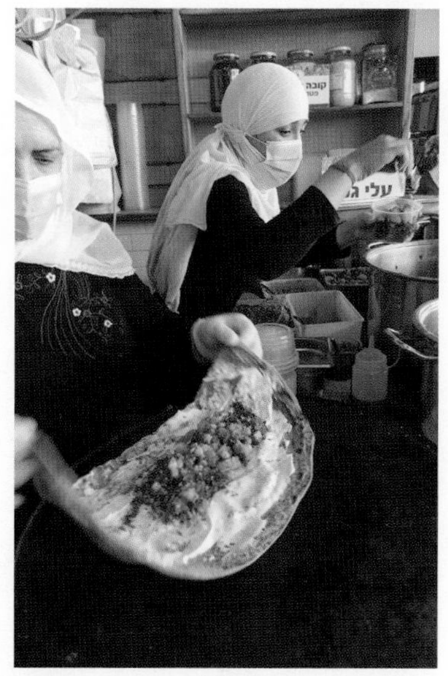

Chefs at the street food powerhouse Pasta Banamal.

Northern part of the Tel Aviv Port Market. ✆ **054/795-0473.** Main courses NIS 40–NIS 60. Sun 9am–4pm, Mon–Thurs 9am–8pm (in the summer as late as 10pm), Fri 7am–3pm (in the summer as late as 5pm, depending on the hour of the sunset), Sat 9am–8pm. Bus: 4, 10, 62, 115.

Along Ben Yehuda Street

MODERATE

Barbunia ★★ SEAFOOD Few places in Tel Aviv, or the world for that matter, can boast that for *years* a line of hungry customers has snaked out the door and down the street, most every day of the week. The reason? The freshest of

vegan **RESTAURANTS**

Tel Aviv is a foodie town par excellence, where the locals dish on their latest restaurant finds with almost as much relish as they do when actually chowing down. The most recent culinary craze is for vegan restaurants, and somehow it's fitting: after all, with hot, humid weather several months out of the year, lighter fare just makes sense. Even the most famous, most classic restaurants are now offering vegetarian or fully vegan alternative menus, but check out some of the insider addresses below for recommended hot spots.

Anastasia Vegan Café ★ (p. 291) was the first vegan cafe in Israel, and it is still known for its delicious breakfast with loads of tasty dips, good salads, healthy shakes, and incredible cakes.

54 Frishman St. www.anastasiatlv.co.il. ✆ **03/529-0095.** Sun–Thurs 9am–10pm, Fri 9am–4pm, Sat 10am–4pm. Bus: 24, 48, 3, 25, 125.

Four One Six ★★★ is a hip, dimly lit bistro restaurant that stands out as a special-occasions destination for vegans and their non-vegan friends. Any of the items on the impressive cocktail list (many based on gluten-free Stoli) go well with homemade signature dishes like the soy-based *labneh*, topped with sumac, chile, and sumac; or the Korean oyster mushroom skewers.

16 HaArba'a St. www.416tlv.com. ✆ **03/775-5060.** Daily noon–11pm. Bus: 62, 115, 63, 238, 2, 8.

Goodness ★★ is where you go to sample all the Israeli classics—*schnitzel, shawarma, shakshuka, kibbeh*—but vegan. They've somehow perfected the difficult task of making vegan cheese actually "cheesy" in texture and taste, and have a long menu of other fun, junk-food type dishes, like Sloppy Joe sandwiches or chicken nuggets, that are well complemented by the restaurants' raucous, joyous vibe.

41 King George St. www.goodness.co.il. ✆ **055/973-5792.** Sun–Fri 11am–11pm, Sat noon–11pm. Bus: 4, 125, 72, 172, 129, 61, 62, 115.

Market Seasonal Kitchen ★★ is a vegan salad bar and restaurant that opened in 2015, offering seasonal, homemade vegan comfort food such as stews, soups, sandwiches, and salads. Saturday's opening time is 1 hour after Shabbat.

31 King George St. and 140 Dizengoff St. ✆ **03/552-5808.** Sun–Mon noon–11pm, Tues–Thurs noon–9pm, Fri noon–3:30pm, closed Sat. Bus: 4, 62, 115, 61, 129, 172.

Opa's ★★★ low-key, monochrome cream decor is almost as impressive as its plant-based food, both of which strongly exude an elegant, minimalist ethos. As the antidote to the city's hippie vegan joints, Opa is a sophisticated chef restaurant where you'll sample dishes sourced from a farm just outside of Tel Aviv. Favorites include a salad dressed with fermented macadamia milk and, for dessert, a decadent Gianduja chocolate-hazelnut ganache.

8 Ha-Khalutzim St. www.opatlv.co.il. ✆ **052/583-8242.** Mon–Thurs 7pm–11pm, Fri noon–3pm. Bus: 4, 129, 172.

seafood, expertly and simply cooked. The menu offers two categories of fixed-price dinners. Each comes with an all-you-can-eat medley of Middle Eastern appetizers, chilled seltzer, and your choice of a main course from a daily list of fish or shrimp that can be ordered either grilled or fried and served with garlic, lemon, and butter. Tablecloths are sheets of packing paper, and no substitutions are permitted (or needed). Service is friendly, through reservations are not taken.

163 Ben Yehuda St. ✆ **053/942-4941.** Fixed-price meals NIS 90–NIS 110. Daily noon–midnight. Bus: 4, 10, 55.

On & Around Dizengoff Street

MODERATE

Anastasia ★★ VEGAN In 2014, two friends, an architect and a restaurateur, decided to open Tel Aviv's first vegan cafe with the hope that the city would learn to love the power of the plant. Turns out they were right. Since it took up residence in a Bauhaus-style building just minutes from Dizengoff Square, Anastasia has received award after award for its restorative shakes, its vegan versions of the typically egg-based Israeli breakfast, and its varied Indian- and Asian-inspired dishes. Especially beloved is the soba salad, topped with cauliflower, kale, cashew cream, and a spicy almond crumble; as is the vegan cheese plate, which includes a vegan labneh and feta. If you come outside of the lunch rush hour, grab a spot at the comfortable veranda couches, where the staff will be happy to have you linger for as long as you wish. You can take home the cafe's legendary cheesecake, sweet potato quiche, and other homemade vegan products from the mini grocery store, or, if you're planning to head to the southern end of town, pop by the deli at Yad Harutzim 15 for more options.

Super fresh salad at Anastasia.

54 Frishman St. www.anastasiatlv.co.il. ✆ **03/529-0095.** Mains NIS 44–NIS 69. Sun–Thurs 9am–10pm, Fri 9am–4pm, Sat 10am–4pm. Bus: 24, 48, 3, 25, 125.

Café Popular ★★ ISRAELI Israeli celebrity chef Avi Bitton recently opened this hopping bar-restaurant on the ground and basement floors of a central boutique hotel. The evening menu offers creative dishes balancing traditional and modern Israeli cuisine, like beef tartare served with hot chili harissa and pickled lemon aioli; or seared grouper fish on a bed of zaatar spiced risotto. But Café Popular is most famous for its decadent Saturday and Sunday brunch, with its never-ending rounds of small, beautifully prepared tapas dishes, like scrambled eggs with truffle cream, meat-topped masabacha hummus, and tangy fish ceviche. The decor is also fun, with graffiti-style wall murals done by Tel Aviv artist Andre Missing. Make sure to make a reservation because Popular, as its name suggests, gets packed pretty much every day.

197 Dizengoff St. www.cafepopular.co.il. ✆ **03/555-2020.** Mains NIS 62–NIS 178, Brunch NIS 138 per person. Sun–Thurs 6–11:30pm, Fri–Sat. 9:30am–2:30pm, 6–11:30pm. Bus: 4, 8, 10, 172.

Eats Cafeteria ★★ ISRAELI Eats Cafeteria is located in a restored heritage building known as Beit Hanna, or Hanna's House, named after the feminist political leader Hanna Chizik, who in the 1930s and 1940s trained women to work as farmers in preparation for the establishment of the state. Today, the house is a cafe-gym-wellness complex that is especially convenient for mothers, who can take a yoga or Pilates class and leave the babies with a babysitter downstairs. You'll order at the counter, where you'll be tempted by some of the tastiest homemade cookies and *chalva* and tahina chocolate brownies in town. It doesn't take a workout to appreciate Eats' colorful lunchbox options, filled to the brim with salads like pistachio couscous or cabbage with Caesar dressing. Take a seat on the outdoor, palm tree–shaded patio, where lectures, movie screenings, and other cultural events are often held after dark.

1 Adam Hacohen St. (on Ben Gurion Blvd.). www.eatscafeteria.com. ✆ **03/602-7888.** Main courses NIS 24–NIS 48. Sun–Thurs 7am–9pm, Fri 8am–4pm, Sat 9am–8pm. Bus: 5, 61, 66.

Kapara Mio ★★ ITALIAN This spot, which evolved out of a pop up during the Covid lockdowns, serves up some of the best homemade, Roman-style pasta in the city. The setting is simple: red-and-white checkered paper tablecloths on a handful of streetside tables. The menu is short and to the point, including a few fresh, acidic salads, classic Italian snacks like arancini, and a robust list of pastas made from local ingredients and lots of technical expertise. Favorites include the spaghetti Alla Norma, which uses locally sourced eggplant, olive oil, and ricotta cheese; and the incredibly creamy butter and sage ravioli. The chef, Bentzi Arbel, loves to add new dishes based on market availability or spontaneous inspiration. Kapara Mio intentionally (to the dismay of many of its fans) does not take reservations in order to keep it from being stuffy or too formal. But if you want to avoid waiting, you can come during lunch hours or before the nightly dinner rush that starts around 8pm.

105 King George St. ✆ **054/428-9765.** Mains NIS 60–NIS 72. Sun–Thurs noon–11:30pm, Sat. 6–11:30pm. Closed Fri. Bus: 48, 8, 56, 289.

INEXPENSIVE

Sabich Frishman ★★★ ISRAELI The menu at Sabich Frishman is simple: sabich or falafel. *Sabich* is a pillowy pita sandwich stuffed with fried eggplant, hardboiled eggs, and nutty tahini sauce. The dish is a mini history lesson: It had been a popular Shabbat morning meal among the Jewish community of Iraq and has had a massive revival, especially in recent years. The other side of the shop offers perfectly fried falafel. The condiments are an attraction in their own right and, again, an insight into the diverse, wonderfully harmonious forces that make up Israeli cuisine: Yemenite zhug spice, brilliantly colored pickles, and a tangy mango sauce known as "amba." Eating here cane be a messy experience, and the barstool seating at long black communal tables is not the most elegant, but that's part of the fun.

42 Frishman St. ✆ **054/795-5945.** Sabich NIS 29, falafel NIS 21. Sun–Thurs 10am–11pm, Fri 10am–4:30pm. Bus: 5, 8, 172.

Dining at the Port

The old Tel Aviv Port used to be a derelict strip of warehouses and garages along the northern stretch of Tel Aviv's beachfront. It's now booming with restaurants, shops, and bars, all linked by a boardwalk promenade. The Port, or the Namal in Hebrew, is bustling through the wee hours, and there are snack and bakery counters, bars, food markets, and other restaurants for every need and interest.

The easiest way to get there is simply to follow the seaside promenade as it continues north from Hilton Beach (about a 10-min. walk). Note that on weekends Tel Aviv Port is a favorite with Israeli families who come from other towns to catch the sea breeze; you'll have a calmer experience if you visit during the week.

Yemenite Quarter, Carmel Market & Levinsky Market

This area, which has undergone a massive rejuvenation since 2010, contains some of the best restaurants in town. These include the colorful and culinarily rich Carmel and Levinsky Market, as well as a grid of little streets off Allenby Street known as the Yemenite Quarter (Karem Ha-Teimanim in Hebrew). Built at the beginning of the 20th century, this is one of the oldest parts of the city, and its tangled streets harbor lots of scrumptious, tiny eateries that draws on the Yemenite, Iranian, Turkish, and Greek history of the neighborhood.

EXPENSIVE

Hotel Montefiore ★★★ CONTEMPORARY ISRAELI This iconic culinary institution located on the ground floor of a century-old boutique hotel of the same name serves modern French brasserie dishes made with local Israeli ingredients and Vietnamese touches. There are few greater pleasures than sitting at the restaurant's handsome wooden bar and enjoying a glass of fine Israeli wine. The artisanal cocktails, built around fragrant Israeli herbs and bitters, are equally delightful. All dishes here are executed with care and creativity, but some standouts include the thinly sliced raw albacore with yuzu sauce, the shrimp noodle salad, and the shredded lamb served with spongy pancakes and tangy sauces. The decor is classy: clean white walls, black slatted wooden blinds, and silver serving trays that make you feel like you're a world away from the Tel Aviv hubbub just outside the doors. Reservations are strongly suggested because this place gets busy most every night.

36 Montefiore St. www.hotelmontefiore.co.il. ✆ **03/564-6100.** Reservations recommended. Main Courses NIS 62–NIS 196. Daily noon–midnight. Bus: 4, 5, 38, 172.

MODERATE

Brut ★★★ ISRAELI/WINE BAR Located on Nahalat Binyamin, Tel Aviv's garment district and a stone's throw from the Carmel Market, Brut is an excellent "wine bistro" that gives a Levantine twist on French and Italian small plates. You'll be seated at just a handful of barstools at the open kitchen, where a knowledgeable and professional staff can give you all the information

kid-friendly RESTAURANTS

If your child has a sophisticated palate, feel comfortable taking them to most every restaurant in this chapter; Israel is a famously pro-kid country where even many of the pricier places will be happy to host young ones and provide them with entertainment like coloring books and crayons. This box really is geared towards the picky eaters among the younger set, which is easy in a country where restaurants serving schnitzel, fries, burgers, and pizzas are found every few streets. Try any one of the spots below and you're sure to find at least two or three dishes that will satisfy even the most spice-averse of youngsters:

Barbunia ★★ (see p. 289). No frills and near the hotel district, it offers fresh fish and relatively speedy service. The latter is always a blessing when traveling with impatient youngsters—just get there early at dinnertime to avoid the line.

Bretonne ★★ (p. 300). The kiddos will fall in love with this unassuming street food spot, serving up piping hot buckwheat crepes, made right in front of your eyes. The lamb bacon and cheddar cheese crepe is a popular savory option, as is the decadent, "Chubby Hubby" crepe, stuffed with peanut butter, chocolate, and pretzel pieces.

Fat Cow ★★. This chill burger spot focuses on its butcher-quality cut, grilled to perfection (though there are a few other options, like tasty chicken fingers and a remarkably good Caesar salad). It's great for a tasty, quick meal less than 10 minutes from Mezizim Beach. The interior is diner-style, and the outside your typical mix of bar stools and low tables, with an all-around focus on comfort.

265 Dizengoff St. www.fatcow.co.il. ✆ **03/773-2591.** Fri–Wed noon–midnight, Thurs noon–1am. Bus: 4, 10, 62, 115.

Pizza Brooklyn ★★. With two branches—on King George 88, near Dizengoff Center, and on Dizengoff 276, in the Old North, you'll find the perfect midway between gourmet and casual. The pies range from basic but delicious Margherita to more creative versions, like Hawaiian with corned beef. More info: www.brooklynpizza.co.il.

on dishes like entrecôte kebabs or calamari with lamb jus and challah croutons. The menu is constantly changing so as to stay up to date with hyperseasonal produce calendar of the region as well as of the wine labels that they import from small-scale vineyards in Piedmont and Bourgogne. Recently, Brut has been experimenting with vegan dishes, like vegan *kubeniya* (a Syrian tartare), accentuated with smoky freekeh—a Palestinian green wheat—imported from the northern West Bank. Desserts, like Turkish candied pumpkin or Italian lemon meringue, are truly exciting. This is a perfect choice for a romantic, intimate dinner, but it's a favorite among locals, so make reservations far in advance.

36 Nahalat Binyamin St. www.brutwinebar.com. ✆ **03/510-2923.** Reservations recommended. Main dishes NIS 62–140. Tues–Fri 7pm–midnight. Bus: 4, 10, 129, 172.

Dalida ★★★ ISRAELI/MIDDLE EASTERN/FRENCH Our favorite way to dine at this candlelit, handsome bistro is to get an array of small plates, as the recipes span the globe from Tehran to Paris and beyond. Some favorites include the spicy feta brulée, and a spread of bone marrow and Jerusalem artichoke cream served with brioche. Brunch is also top-notch, with two prix fix menus offering standout dishes like the smoky Lebanese eggplant salad and zaatar- and sumac-slathered labneh cheese balls. Dalida's prices are slightly higher than simpler spots in the Levinsky Market, but if you come for happy hour (Sun–Thurs 6–7:30pm), everything on the menu is discounted by 30%. Even if you can't make the happy hour, this gourmet spot is well worth the splurge.

7 Zvulun. en.dalidatlv.co.il. ✆ **03/536-9627.** Reservations recommended. Main dishes NIS 62–NIS 140. Tues–Fri 7pm–midnight. Bus: 4, 10, 129, 172.

North Abraxas ★★ CONTEMPORARY ISRAELI Eyal Shani is Israel's far more eccentric and innovative answer to Gordon Ramsay, and the Israeli media enjoys dishing on this power chef's business dealings almost as much as Israelis enjoy tucking into his always creative, always locally sourced culinary offerings. From wine-marinated lamb shawarma to roasted calamari on a bed of tomato foam and yogurt (Shani famously waxes nostalgic about tomatoes), North Abraxas takes simple food to such tasty heights you'll want to come back for more. Another Shani eccentricity: Many of the dishes are served on sheets of plain brown paper instead of plates. Desserts tend to be of the sticky, messy kind but they're great; bananas smothered in house-made *dulce de leche* and cookie crumbles is one example. The formula has been so successful that it has spurred copy restaurants in New York, Vienna, and Singapore, but (and Shani himself will agree), there's nothing like Israeli produce. Note that this is a very social, noisy spot, though kids are always more than welcome.

40 Lilienblum St. www.northabraxas.com. ✆ **03/516-6660.** Reservations recommended. Main Courses NIS 52–NIS 114. Daily noon–4pm, 6–11:30pm. Bus: 4, 129, 172, 25, 125.

At North Abraxas, chef/owner Eyal Shani eschews plates in favor of servings on brown paper.

INEXPENSIVE

M25 ★★ ISRAELI GRILL This carnivore's paradise serves up quintessential Israeli staples in a former market stall just off the main street of the crowded Carmel Market. It's named after its location: 25 meters from the high-end butcher that supplies its dishes—the first clue as to how seriously these people take their meat. The tables and chairs are wooden and some of the few items of decoration are the meat smoker and the fridge displaying the many choice cuts of meat used for popular dishes, from the hefty *arayes* appetizer, a crunchy toasted pita stuffed with charred minced lamb, to the perfectly smoked shawarma, served on a bed of tahini, and virtually any cut of meat you can imagine. To get to this restaurant you need to cross through the market side alley, behind the many stalls, so be aware that you might need to step over a good amount of trash, like pieces of discarded raw meat or fish, which for some only adds to this place's authentic and gritty charm but for others might be unappetizing. For a more sanitized experience, you can visit M25's Ramat Aviv outpost, located at 15 Brodetsky Street, not far from the swanky Ramat Aviv Mall.

30 HaCarmel St. m25meat.co.il. ✆ **03/558-0425.** Main dishes NIS 44–NIS 85. Mon–Thurs noon–11pm, Fri 11am–4:30pm. Bus: 4, 10, 129, 172.

Mifgash Rambam ★★★ ISRAELI/SHWARMA No hyperbole, Mifgash Rambam serves the best shawarma in Tel Aviv, and possibly all of Israel. The smoked, thinly sliced strips of lamb and beef are deeply seasoned here and never too fatty. The pickled onions, mango amba sauce, lemony tahini, and (in an unusual move) tzatziki are fantastic complements to the sumptuous meat. Mifgash Rambam also sells a tasty chicken version, and a sabich-shawarma sandwich, which combines shawarma with the classic hardboiled egg-eggplant-tahini sandwich—come with a big appetite for that one. Mifgash Rambam opens most days at 11am and closes when the meat runs out.

3 Rambam St. Shawarma NIS 45. Sun–Thurs 11am–midnight, Fri 11am–4pm. Closed Sat. Bus: 4, 48, 25, 125.

Salimi ★ JEWISH-IRANIAN The foods of Israel's immigrants from Yemen, Iraq, and other countries in the Middle East used to be relegated to "workers' restaurants," frequented by men who toiled in the area and sought a cheap and filling meal. Today, these historic eating establishments, when they still exist, are enjoyed by workers and hipsters alike. The family-owned Iranian soul food spot Salimi, in the center of the colorful Levinsky Market, is among the last standing. Here, austere lighting and plain white walls only reinforce the focus on hearty, high-quality food cooked in a traditional Iranian oven at the end of the dining area. The clientele is a steady, loyal stream of local families mixed with newer and younger residents, all of whom patiently (a rarity in Israel) wait for a table for the generous portions of kosher chicken kebabs with fluffy saffron rice, or the legendary *Gondi,* an herb-enriched Persian soup filled with chickpea and chicken meatballs. The waitresses come off as overly caring Jewish mothers, often lovingly suggesting ways to help you fatten up if you're so inclined ("You're skin and bones!" is a refrain often heard).

80 Nahalat Binyamin St. ✆ **03/518-8377.** Main dishes NIS 30–NIS 65. Sun–Thurs noon–6pm, Fri 8am–4pm. Closed Sat. Bus: 4, 129, 172, 25, 125.

Saluf and Sons ★★★ YEMENITE For decades, Yemenite cuisine was only available in Yemenite homes, never Israeli restaurants (those served almost exclusively Levantine and European foods). But times have changed,

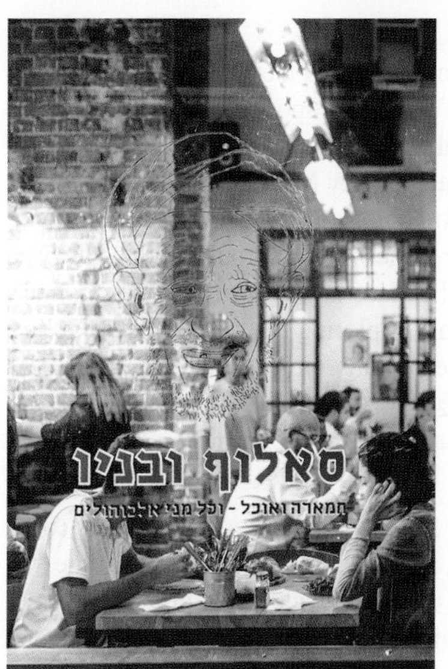

Looking in the window to Saluf and Sons.

and modern, more culturally expansive Tel Aviv has been rejoicing in the Yemeni moment, which has given a platform to food, music, and dress from the country that once hosted one of the region's largest Jewish populations. There's no better place to experience that than at Saluf and Sons, a festive hole-in-the-wall just a few steps from Levinsky Market. This restaurant, in typical Yemenite style, is cozy and inviting. Grab a spot at the heavy wooden communal table and tuck into a bowl of nutritious Yemeni meat soup or a plate of rolled *malawach,* a flaky savory pastry sandwich stuffed with tomato puree, nutty tahini, and a hardboiled egg, along with spicy dips. The portions of homecooked soul food are large, and the waiters are known to offer diners a free shot (or two) of *arak,* a Middle Eastern anise-based liqueur, to keep the party going.

80 Nahalat Binyamin St. www.salufandsons.co.il. ✆ **03/522-1344.** Main dishes NIS 50–NIS 60. Sun–Thurs 11am–10pm, Fri 10am–4pm. Closed Sat. Bus: 4, 129, 172, 25, 125.

Shukshuka ★★★ ISRAELI/NORTH AFRICAN Come to Shukshuka for some of the city's best iterations of Israeli Shabbat breakfast classic, which is a spicy yet comforting tomato stew, often served topped with a fried egg. This unassuming, crowded, and joyful food stall turns out several unique versions of the signature dish, including a "Spanish" shakshuka, with sausages, spinach, and chickpeas, and another "Italian" iteration, delicately complemented with goat cheese and basil. The small menu also offers lots of delicious accompaniments for your shakshuka main, including tangy tomato salad, homemade hummus, and dangerously potent arak lemonade. The service can be a little slow, especially when the lunch and dinner rush reach a peak, but still, feasting at one of the wooden stools at the blue and white Moroccan tiled bar, watching the market crowds, is a unique Tel Aviv pleasure.

41 HaCarmel St. Shakshuka dishes NIS 39–NIS 45. Sun, Mon 10am–4pm, Tues–Thurs 10am–11pm, Fri 8am–4pm, Sat 11:30am–4pm. Bus: 4, 48, 25, 125.

Neve Tzedek

After decades of neglect, this neighborhood, the oldest in the city, is coming alive with galleries, boutiques, cafes, and the Suzanne Dallal Center for Dance and Theater, the centerpiece for the revival of the area.

EXPENSIVE

Dallal ★ MEDITERRANEAN Dallal, on one of Neve Tzedek's charming alleyways, is among the neighborhood's prettiest spots. It's set among three restored houses and within them are both interior and al fresco dining options. The kitchen turns out reliably tasty contemporary Mediterranean fare such as tzatziki fish kebabs with roasted tomato chunks, and white fish sashimi with Japanese plum and aromatic herbs. For the less adventurous, there's always a nice range of fresh salads and pastas. The place has its own bakery, too, making Dallal a good breakfast option before exploring the rest of the neighborhood. Reservations are recommended, especially on weekends.

10 Shabazi St. www.dallal.co.il. ✆ **03/510-9292.** Main courses and light meals NIS 60–NIS 178. Mon–Thurs 5pm–12:30am; Fri–Sat 9am–5pm, 6pm–12:30am. Bus: 4, 10, 129, 172.

INEXPENSIVE

Suzanna ★ MEDITERRANEAN A lovely spot that's a favorite with dancers from the nearby performance center, Suzanna is perfect for a quick bite (we especially recommend their soups and wonderful salads). If you want something more substantial, the delicious puff filo pastries filled with chicken and almonds or with hearty liver are a great starter. For a main course, try the chicken stuffed with couscous and dried fruits, lamb kebabs, or the classic *hraymeh,* a spicy fish stew with chickpeas and tangy tomato sauce. You can also just stop in for coffee, dessert, brioche, or a lovely glass of wine, with a side of primo people watching. The discounted prix fixe lunch menu is served daily until the early evening. Meals and drinks are served indoors in the garden or on the roof patio late into the night.

9 Shabazi St. www.suzanatlv.co.il. ✆ **03/944-3060.** Main courses and light meals NIS 50–NIS 83. Daily 11am–midnight. Bus: 4, 10, 129, 172.

On & Around Ibn Gvirol Street, Habima & the Tel Aviv Museum of Art

Ibn Gvirol Street runs through Tel Aviv's center of culture, from the Cinémathèque northward toward Shderot Shaul Ha Melech, where you'll find the Tel Aviv Museum of Art and the fantastic Cameri Theater, and finishing at the green, activity-packed Hayarkon Park. This street is lined with many great choices for everything from post-theater fine dining to young and experimental street food joints.

EXPENSIVE

Pastel ★★ CONTEMPORARY ISRAELI Chef Gal Ben Moshe has recently remade this clean-lined, overwhelmingly white restaurant into one of the most interesting laboratories for modern Israeli cuisine. The menu showcases creative, thoroughly fun reinterpretations of dishes originating around the Levant (Syria, Lebanon, Galilee) region. Like *shish barak,* meat dumplings that are traditionally served in yogurt stew, but here are filled with Egyptian style *molokhia*—a leafy green vegetable stew—and served with sunflower cream and fermented mushrooms. The grouper fish coupled with sour, not-yet ripened grapes, known as *khursum,* is equally intriguing and delicious. When the weather's nice, opt for a seat on the outdoor terrace, which overlooks the Tel Aviv Museum sculpture garden.

27 Shaul Hamelech Boulevard. www.pastel-tlv.com. ✆ **03/644-7441.** Starters NIS 28–NIS 84; mains NIS 86–NIS 186. Daily noon–3:30pm, 6–11pm. Bus: 8, 9, 149.

MODERATE

Asif Culinary Institute of Israel ★★★ CONTEMPORARY ISRAELI Asif is a cafe, a museum, and a nonprofit organization dedicated to Israeli cuisine, supported by Michael Solomon, Naama Shefi, and a long list of other Israeli culinary stars. It's a space to take stock of the country's rich culinary past and present, a concept that many Israelis only consider once they eat at Israeli restaurants abroad. Dishes on offer express a great respect both for the Israeli kibbutz, where much of the national, mostly vegetarian cuisine was developed in the early years of the state; as well as for the cuisine of the Middle East, from which millions of immigrants arrived from the 1950s onward. Offerings are modern without being pretentious, and include authentic versions of dishes like the *kubaneh,* a traditional Yemenite Shabbat morning bread, smoked mackerel. and preserved lemon Tunisian sandwich; and Jerusalem *kugel,* a classic Ashkenazi egg noodle casserole.

While you wait for your order, wander around the gallery on the ground floor, the rooftop farm growing hyssop and other local herbs, or flip through Israeli cookbooks on a second floor library that overlooks the restaurant. The portions are generous, but you can also stop by the in-house deli before you go to pick up special spice mixes or cheeses and honeys sourced from Jewish and Arab agricultural communities throughout Israel.

28 Lilienblum St. asif.org/cafe. ✆ **03/375-2727.** Mains NIS 52–NIS 108. Sun–Thurs 9am–5pm, Friday 9am–3pm. Closed Sat. Bus: 25, 125, 48, 172.

Dok ★★★ CONTEMPORARY ISRAELI Named after brothers and owners Asaf and Yotam Doktor, this tiny, revelatory restaurant on a busy main street is easy to miss if you're not looking for it. It's a culinary lab as much as an eatery, where the owners experiment with purely local ingredients including specialty alcohols (for unique cocktails) and ice creams churned from the house-fermented butter or from the Israeli "Gili" corn. Even more experimental dishes have included (in the recent past) bresaola buried in ash around a month before being served, and charcoal grilled sardines wrapped in fresh vine leaves and topped with green almond salsa. This restaurant's second greatest achievement is that, despite the parade of rave reviews, the vibe, staff, and clientele are still wholly down to earth. Located amid a row of unpretentious, artisan-focused restaurants and shops on Ibn Gvirol Street, Dok has an understated ambience and a surprisingly tiny size, with a bar, a few tables inside, and a few more street side (the bathroom is off-site).

27 Ibn Gvirol St. ✆ **03/609-8118.** Tapas-style dishes NIS 40–NIS 80. Sat–Thurs 6pm–midnight. Closed Fri. Bus: 5, 26, 74, 189, 289.

Ha'achim ★★★ CONTEMPORARY ISRAELI/GRILL "Ha'achim" (The Brothers) is the predecessor to the more experimental "Dok," (see above) by the Doktor brothers, and is similarly beloved. This location, on the vast patio outside the Zionist Organization of America (ZOA) building, which also houses a comedy club and a theater, is a fantastic option if you're craving an expertly executed *fattoush* salad, homemade hummus, or charcoal grilled fish or meat. The *safayeh*—grilled pita sandwich stuffed with lamb or with spinach—is outstanding. If you're staying at an Airbnb or hotel without breakfast, this is a fabulous choice to start your morning. They have delicious *shakshuka,* an originally Moroccan dish that involves eggs in a skillet of spicy, fragrant tomato sauce. They also have a small deli where you can take home pastries, cheeses, local wines, and other specialties.

26 Ibn Gvirol St. www.haachim.co.il. ✆ **03/691-7171.** Mains NIS 32–NIS 84. Daily noon–midnight. Bus: 26, 126, 74, 189, 289.

INEXPENSIVE

Bretonne ★★ FRENCH Named after the northwestern district of France, Bretonne serves up a dizzying array of savory and sweet (mostly) buckwheat crepes that make for a substantial but casual meal. These include Middle Eastern versions of the classics, like the eggplant and *labneh* crepe, which is also stuffed with potatoes, tahini, and a healthy dash of spice. The dessert crepe menu is just as extensive, with standouts including the "Bretonnella," filled with homemade chocolate, and the salted caramel crepe, paired with crème fraiche and sliced almonds. This self-service street food spot has hefty wooden tables where patrons can seat themselves. The joint stays open late to cater to bar-goers with the munchies. ***Note:*** There's a second branch at 22 Washington Avenue in the neighborhood of Florentin.

52 Ibn Gvirol St. www.bretonne.co.il. ✆ **03/635-8221.** Main courses NIS 35–NIS 45. Sun–Thurs 10am–1am, Fri 10am–5pm, Sat 11am–1am. Bus: 25, 125, 26, 126, 189, 289.

Bucke ★★★ ISRAELI This vibrant Tel Aviv cafe, a stone's throw from Habima Theater, is renowned for food that's reasonably priced and healthy, with a strong emphasis on fresh vegetables. Vegetarians, vegans, and carnivores alike rave about the fresh and beautifully spiced salads, leafy sandwiches, freshly squeezed juices, and house-made cookies. We're fans of the indulgent *burekas,* a flaky Israeli pastry paired with tart *labneh* cheese, tomatoes, pickles, and a hardboiled egg. With mismatched chairs, communal wooden tables, and plenty of leafy greenery, the vibe is laid-back and oasis-like. ***Note:*** There's a second, usually much quieter branch at 40 Yehuda Hamaccabi in the Old North neighborhood, and a third, called Hamaniya (or "Sunflower") on 37 Basel St.

91 Ahad Ha'am St. www.bucke-cafe.com. ✆ **054/700-8808.** Mains NIS 46–NIS 62. Sun–Thurs 7am–10pm, Fri 7am–4pm. Bus: 3, 74, 126, 289.

MIZNON ★★★ CONTEMPORARY ISRAELI Celebrity chef Eyal Shani's *Miznon,* or "the buffet," celebrates the elegant simplicity of the pita.

In this rarefied hole-in-the-wall, though, you'll get an elevated sandwich like you've never tasted it before. The menu is short and to the point, featuring expertly executed classics like a meat stew cooked overnight and a silkily soft eggplant ratatouille, as well as several other dishes more frequently served as complete plates—and for triple the price. The first hint of the kind of experience Miznon offers is in the menu's verbiage, for which Shani is (in)famous, classified into categories like the "Secrets of the Universe in a Pita." He harbors a borderline fetish for Israeli produce and is known to wax poetic about the juices of a tomato or the curves of a cauliflower, which he roasts whole with a drizzle of olive oil and salt. You'll order at the counter, which is raucous thanks to a soundtrack of American hip-hop and the bellows of staff alternately screaming for a patron to receive their order or inviting them to join in a free shot. Be careful not to fill up on the pita with tahini and other dips available for free at the bar, as you'll want to save room for the hefty and satisfying mains. Miznon has opened up branches around the world, but the Tel Aviv branches at 23 Ibn Gvirol St., 30 King George St., and another at 1 Hanehoshet St. take pride in the fact that they're the originals.

23 Ibn Gvirol St. www.miznon.com. ✆ **03/716-8977.** Main courses NIS 39–NIS 48. Sun–Thurs noon–11:30pm, Fri noon–6pm, Sat 1pm–1am. Bus: 126, 189, 289.

By Alma Beach North of Jaffa

EXPENSIVE

Manta Ray ★★ SEAFOOD/MODERN ISRAELI With a pavilion open to the sea on a quiet stretch of beach where Tel Aviv becomes Jaffa, this is a great

Enjoying seafood at the beachfront Manta Ray.

place to watch the rolling waves by day, or take in the sunset while you dine. Start with a selection of small appetizers brought around by your waiter (the fish and seafood tapas are best—make sure to have the dishes explained to you before you choose the ones that you like). Stars among main courses include jumbo shrimp in a smoked bonito stock and the glorious seafood plate. A seafront table is essential, but remember, everybody else wants one, too. Booking ahead of time is essential.

Alma Beach, near Dan Panorama Hotel. www.mantaray.co.il. ✆ **03/517-4773.** Main courses NIS 115–NIS 185. Daily 9am–midnight. Bus: 10, 18.

Scallop elegantly plated at The Drisco.

Jaffa

In addition to the restaurants below, you can get splendid, if pricey, feasts at the restaurants associated with **The Drisco Hotel** (see p. 285) and **The Jaffa Hotel** (p. 286).

MODERATE

Par Derriere ★ PAN-EUROPEAN The brainchild of a Parisian expat, this romantic wine bar and bistro's secret weapon is its lush outdoor garden—be sure to ask to be seated there. As for the fare, the wine list is constantly changing but it usually features bottles from boutique French vineyards. And the vino pairs well with a pan-European menu of gourmet pizza, cheese platters, mussels mariniere, and grilled fish, meats, and burgers. Brunch, served in a leisurely fashion on Fridays and Saturdays until 4pm, is a big draw, with fun and filling dishes like steak and eggs, or a full English breakfast. The restaurant is a particular favorite of Tel Aviv's arts and culture communities.

7 Bat Ami St. www.parderriere.co.il. ✆ **03/629-2111.** Main courses NIS 57–NIS 134. Sun–Thurs 5pm–1am, Fri–Sat 11am–1am. Bus: 10, 25, 125.

INEXPENSIVE

Hummus Abu Hassan ★★★ HUMMUS A beloved Jaffa hole in the wall, Abu Hassan has for decades drawn a steady stable of loyal customers: Jews and Arabs, working-class people and tourists, all of whom are eager to sample one of the oldest hummus joints in Israel. The restaurant was founded by Ali Karawan, aka Abu Hassan, who started selling his hummus out of a cart in the Ajami neighborhood of Jaffa in the 1950s, before eventually settling in the location on Dolphin Street in the 1970s. Abu Hassan opens his doors every day but Saturday, and closes when the hummus runs out. Usually around lunchtime, lines go outside the door, as the clientele jostle to grab a spot at one

TEL AVIV'S ice cream SCENE

Tel Aviv, a city that is hot most of the year, has, unsurprisingly, some really great ice cream options. Among the most unique is **Buza,** an ice cream parlor that is named after the Arabic word for "ice cream," which is typically made according to techniques (pounding and stretching, rather than churning) that were honed over centuries in Syria. Launched by a Jewish-Israeli kibbutznik and a famed Arab-Israeli chef, Buza won a UN award for promoting coexistence, bringing together Jews and Arabs with a shared love of unique, locally inspired flavors. The incredibly creamy and chewy texture is simply in a different league from what Americans and Europeans know as "ice cream." Buza is located on 91 HaHashmonaim St. and in four other locations throughout northern Israel.

The chain known as **Golda** also keeps Tel Avivians cool and happy through the hotter months from dozens of branches, by serving European-style ice creams in often unique flavors (pistachio with white chocolate, limoncello). Our favorite outlets of that chain are at Tel Aviv Port, on Rothschild Boulevard, and at 9 Yehieli St., in the Neve Tzedek neighborhood. Golda's branches are open daily, generally from 8 or 9am to midnight.

For homemade Italian gelati, our favorite is **Arte Italian Ice Cream,** 11 Nahalat Binyamin; they also make sorbets and refreshing granitas, many of which are vegan.

of the coveted shared tables serviced by friendly but remarkably efficient waiters, who prioritize getting people in and out over the usual niceties. There's no written menu, as most diners here know what they've come for: either hummus *masabacha* (topped with chickpeas), *ful* (topped with fava beans), or *labneh* (a strained, tart Middle Eastern yogurt); or the in-house specialty known as "The Holy Trinity," *masabacha* and *ful* all in one plate, which goes excellently with the sliced raw onion and the garlic-lemony condiments on each table.

1 Hadolphin St. ✆ **03/682-0387.** Main courses 23 NIS. Sun–Fri 8am–until the hummus runs out. Bus: 10, 14, 18.

SHOPPING

Shops in Tel Aviv are typically open from 10am until 7pm, Sunday through Thursday. On Fridays, everything shuts down earlier, around 4pm, and on Saturdays, almost all shops are closed for Shabbat. You can find some open here and there on Shabazi Street in Neve Tzedek.

Shopping Streets

From north to south, Tel Aviv is filled to bursting with sweet shopping enclaves. Each neighborhood pocket has independent Israeli boutiques, local brands, secondhand shops, jewelry designers, and more. While there are massive malls with ice-cold air-conditioners blasting into big-box chains like Zara, H&M, and Mango, the more singular and interesting shops will be found on the streets (and that goes for the cool people-watching as well).

You may want to start on **Allenby Street,** not so much for its shops (which mostly hawk basics like tank tops and flip flops), but because it's a transportation hub, and just a 10- to 15-minute stroll from better shopping streets like **Nahalat Binyamin,** known for crafts stores and vintage shops; the boho **Sheinkin,** which has trendy, independent boutiques; and **King George,** a long stretch with varied merchandise, from alternative shops selling hippie/festival garb to others selling sneakers and comics. Other notable shopping destinations include **Shabazi Street** in **Neve Tzedek** for French brands, art galleries, and jewelry; **Masaryk Square** and **Levontin Street** for independent Israeli designers; and **Basel Compound,** which has a number of adorable shops for kids' shoes, clothes, and toys. Heading up and down **Dizengoff Street** you will find numerous shops by Israeli designers, plenty of housewares, cute shoe shops, and cafes and ice cream stops for when you need to take a retail break. Then there is also **Tel Aviv Port,** filled with a mix of kids' shops and activewear outlets, and **HaMedina Square,** best known for its temples of luxury brands like Gucci and Dior. Depending on where you lay your head for the night, any of these areas across the city offer an eclectic mix of shopping, strong coffee, great eats, and the distinct vibrancy of Tel Aviv.

Shopping A to Z

BOOKSTORES

If you're looking for English reading material—anything ranging from memoirs to spirituality to comics, and especially fiction—**Halper's Quality Used Books ★★★** (87 Allenby St.; halpers-books.business.site; ✆ **03/629-9710**) is the mother lode, with at least a quarter of a mile of used, reasonably priced books on its packed shelves! They also have extensive options for kids.

For a great selection of brand new books with thoughtful English sections, head to **HaMigdalor ★★★** (18 Mikveh Israel St.; hamigdalor.co.il; ✆ **03/686-8225**), and **Sipur Pashut ★★★** (36 Shabazi St.; sipurpashut.com; ✆ **03/5107040**), which are both independent booksellers in fun shopping neighborhoods.

There is also the very reliable and well-stocked **Steimatsky ★★** (109 Dizengoff St.; www.steimatzky.co.il; ✆ **077/269-9932**) chain with branches across the country.

CLOTHING

Israeli designers both create and follow local fashion trends, and today those veer towards a very clean, but nuanced, aesthetic. They tend to make basics and statement pieces from natural, breathable, and lightweight fabrics to offset the extremely hot temperatures that Israelis dress for during the majority of the year. Think cotton, linen, and silks in monochromatic tones that are then heightened by artful jewelry, shoes, and other fun accessories.

Alembika ★★ Designer Hagar Alembik-Hazofe is on a mission to make women who aren't petites feel comfortable in their own skin. To that end, she creates clothing that flatters medium and plus-size figures, often with chicly asymmetrical hems, slimming silhouettes, and subtle draping. These wonderfully sophisticated looks are quite comfortable to move around in. 87 Ibn Gvirol St. alembika.co.il. ✆ **03/522-0091.**

Ata ★★★ One of the first Israeli workwear brands (it was established in 1934), Ata had a major comeback in 2016 with gender-fluid, covetable denim jumpsuits and fun prints. Today, Ata is a mainstay in most Tel Avivians' closets, in much the same way as Everlane or Uniqlo is in the United States—the looks are similar. 93 Allenby St. atawear.co.il. ✆ **03/906-0223.**

Aviva Zilberman ★★★ Elegance sans the effort: that's Zilberman's aesthetic, which means clothing that's sleek and chic, but with a ruffle here, or a well-placed slit there, that shows that this designer's basics are anything but basic. Items for sale run the gamut from cocktail attire to sweatshirts; there's also a nice selection of menswear. The boutique itself is a welcoming place, peddling signature fragrances and floral bouquets alongside the duds. 23 Melchett St. avivazilberman.com. ✆ **03/641-1682.**

Comme Il Faut ★★★ Comme Il Faut consistently champions new local designers, selling artful clothing, accessories, and housewares that are by turns whimsical, kooky, or drop-dead-chic. Tel Aviv Port. comme-il-faut.com. ✆ **03/602-0521.**

Kedem Sasson ★★ This designer has been known for his sculptural, avant-garde garments for decades. They are on the pricier side, but they are statement pieces that last forever. 144 Herzl St. www.kedem-sasson.com. ✆ **03/517-0339.**

Maskit ★★★ Israel's first fashion house was founded by the legendary Ruth Dayan in 1954, and its items graced the racks of Bergdorf's and Neiman Marcus for decades. Audrey Hepburn and a stream of other Hollywood starlets all fell in love with the heritage brand's signature "Desert Coat." Maskit reinvented itself in 2014 and has since become a must-stop shop not only for its luxury, special event garments, but also for a peek into the archives of this historic brand. 14 Hatzorfim St. Jaffa. www.maskit.com. ✆ **03/688-4004.**

Numero 13 ★★★ A boho festival chick's dream, this spacious store is brimming with elaborate prints, silks, tassels, and embroidered caftans—but it is not for the bargain shopper. Almost all the brands are imported from France, and the quality, cuts, and fabrics are exquisite and pricey. 13 Shabazi St. www.numero13tlv.com. ✆ **03/634-8066.**

Shahar Avnet ★★ Flouncy and effervescent, Avnet's frocks have been worn by Beyonce, Zendaya, and Camila Cabello—so yes, this shop *can* make you look like a rock star. Avnet's mix of over-the-top tulle, wild colors, and specialty embroidery make each dress a stand-out. 26 Sheinkin St. www.shahar-avnet.com. ✆ **052/881-1084.**

Tres ★★ This sun-dappled boutique was named for a trio of young designer/owners who joined together after fashion school to form a label

Israel's iconic Maskit fashion house.

("Tres" is Spanish for three). Their clothing is aimed at women like themselves: urban, young, practical, but with an appreciation for fashion and whimsy. Many of their well-tailored pieces have floral motifs, or very feminine ruching. Along with the Tres label, the shop carries a well-curated selection of other Israeli designers. 58 Ahad Ha'am St. www.trestlv.com. ✆ **073/743-7277.**

SECONDHAND & VINTAGE CLOTHING

Aderet ★★★ Owner Ophira Oberweger has a great eye for fashion and a lot of empathy for her customers, meaning her prices are unusually reasonable. She and her fun-loving staff are a colorful cast of characters, but with a serious mission: to make the world a greener place by recycling clothing. 53 Bograshov St. www.aderet-store.com. ✆ **03/620-3854.**

Chelsy True Closet ★★ Great customer service, fair prices, color-coded racks, and good vibes make this two-story, secondhand/vintage store a treasure trove of goodies. Truly, this family-owned store is one of the best spots in town to snag a deal. But think carefully before you buy because they don't take returns. 22 Mikve Yisrael St. www.chelsy.co.il. ✆ **03/654-9940.**

Kassima ★★ Kassima is a blink-and-you'll-miss-it, closet-size boutique that keeps odd hours but is worth going out of your way for. Proprietor Avishai Pais has a keen eye for details and hand-selects each and every piece—from vintage Gottex and Maskit to Dior and Missoni. (Wed–Fri noon–7pm). 23 Nahalat Binyamin St. @vintage_kassima on Instagram.

Seekers ★★ You come here for a well-curated collection of vintage Levi's, '60s and '70s maxi dresses, and a host of shoes, jewelry. and accessories from a range of eras. 13 Barzilai St. seekersvintage.com. ✆ **050/350-0286.**

JEWELRY & CRAFTS

Beyond these two stores, the **Nahalat Binyamin Arts and Crafts Market ★★** (see p. 308) is also a top spot for crafts.

Chomer Tov Ceramic Co-op ★★★ You'll find decorative and functional items—glass jewelry, unique Judaica, artworks and more—in this lively, contemporary ceramics gallery showcasing the work of 12 artists. It's in the heart of quaint, eccentric Neve Tzedek, not far from the Suzanne Dellal Dance Center. 30 Shabazi St. chomertov.co.il. ✆ **03/516-6229.**

The Dizengoff Center Young Designers' Bazaar ★★ On the lower level of the Dizengoff Center Shopping Mall is a weekly market for clothing and accessories created by up-and-coming Israeli designers (mostly students who have recently graduated from the Shenkar School of Design). The goods are primarily for women. There are fitting rooms. Thursdays 2pm to 8pm and Fridays 10am to 3pm. 50 Dizengoff. dizengof-center.co.il. ✆ **03/621-2400** or 050/883-3449. Bus: 5.

MARKETS

Bezalel Market ★ Just off King George Street, this market is a haphazard mix of merchants selling items of the kind that are there one day and gone the next. We're talking overstock items, or goods with minor defects imported from India and China. They're usually sold in heaps, but if you like to dig, there may be gems to find. Bezalel St.

Carmel Market (Shuk Ha-Carmel) ★★★ At the intersection of Allenby, Nahalat Binyamin, King George, and Sheinkin streets, you enter a gigantic, throbbing, open-air, food-plus-everything-else market filled with sights and sounds. Here vendors hawk pistachios and guavas, sun hats and fresh hummus, the catch of the day in one aisle, memorial candles in the next, and more and more and more. Don't rush through. You want to stop and talk because here the vendors are as interesting as the goods. Yes, it's a crazily chaotic place, but at the Carmel market, the heart of the city beats. A must-see experience. Open Sunday to Thursday from 8am until dark and on Friday from 8am to 4pm. Bus: 4.

Dizengoff Center Food Fair ★★ On the Dizengoff Center Shopping Mall's lower level, the fair is a great place to pick up cakes, pastries, ethnic specialties, and comfort food. Meals to eat on the spot average NIS 30 to NIS 60. You'll meet interesting local chefs here, both professional and amateur. The fair takes place Thursdays from noon to 8pm and Fridays from 10am to 4pm. 50 Dizengoff St. dizengof-center.co.il. ✆ **03/621-2400.** Bus: 5.

Jaffa Flea Market (Shuk HaPishpishim) ★★★ Merchandise varies, but copper, brass, old Persian tiles, kilim rugs, and jewelry are always to be found in these covered bazaar streets, as well as Judaica items, old family-photo albums, and tons of used jeans and clothing from India. Bargaining is the order of the day, so feel free to indulge in lengthy haggling. Combine the market with an exploration of Old Jaffa and a leisurely lunch. The flea market is open Sunday to Thursday from 10am to around 5pm and Friday from 10am to 3pm. Take bus no. 10 from Ben Yehuda St. in Tel Aviv to the Clock Tower in Old Jaffa. Market area is 1 block east.

Nahalat Binyamin Arts and Crafts Market ★★ This large outdoor fair takes over the streets of the Nahalat Binyamin Pedestrian Mall (btw. Allenby St. and the Carmel Market) on Tuesdays and Fridays, often with street performers and Druze ladies making freshly baked, delicious bread in various corners. The cobblestone street is filled with local merchants selling handcrafted works from stained-glass Judaica to intricate jewelry, and photography. The area is lined with eateries (some of the best in the city) in all price ranges, as well as fab 1920s Tel Aviv architecture—all of which make it more than just another street fair. It is open Tuesday 10am to 5pm and Friday 10am to 3pm. Magen David Sq. (Allenby St., across from start of King George St., at the edge of the Carmel Market). Bus or sherut: 4.

Tel Aviv Port Organic Farmer's Market ★ Here you can buy everything from homemade cookies and cakes to fresh produce, street food, and great coffee—all with a stunning view of the port. The port itself is a fun shopping destination with a range of outdoor fitness apparel, kids' clothes, and local chains. The farmer's market is open Monday to Thursday from 9am to 9pm, Friday from 9am to 3pm, and Saturday from 9am to 7pm. Tel Aviv Port, at northern edge of Tel Aviv. Bus: 4 or 5; sherut: 4 (which runs on Sat).

MUSEUM SHOPS

MUZA Eretz Israel Museum Shop ★★ Without a doubt, this is one of the best museum shops in the country, with expertly selected modern Judaica, crafts, toys, children's books, jewelry, replicas, and other gift options. It's open Sunday through Wednesday 10am to 6pm; Tuesday & Thursday 10am to 8pm; Friday 10am to 2pm; and Saturday 10am to 6pm. Eretz Israel Museum, 2 Chaim Levanon St., Ramat Aviv. www.muzashop.biz. ✆ **072/394-4055.**

Artful objects at the MUZA Eretz Israel Museum Shop.

Nahalat Binyamin Street market
in the old city of Jaffa.

TEL AVIV & JAFFA AFTER DARK

No matter what season, Tel Aviv throbs with activity after sundown. Strollers are out on the boulevards, people-watchers crowd the cafes, clubs are hopping, and restaurants are packed. Wednesday, Thursday, Friday, and Saturday are the big nights out; Sunday and weekday nights are slightly quieter.

To find out what's going on in the city, pick up a free copy of *Time Out Israel,* available at many hotels, or visit www.timeout.co.il. Another great resource for event info is Tel Aviv municipality English-language site visit. tel-aviv.gov.il.

In addition to the listings below, **Park Hayarkon** (✆ **03/642-2828**), at the northern edge of Tel Aviv, hosts large outdoor concerts with international headliners like Justin Bieber; the Park's **Wohl Amphitheater** (✆ **03/641-8275**) also hosts large concerts.

The Performing Arts

While Jerusalem has many cultural offerings, Tel Aviv is the true performance center of Israel. The Heichal Hatarbut Auditorium is the home of the Israel Philharmonic; the Israel Ballet and the more contemporary Gaga Center in Neve Tzedek are also centered in Tel Aviv.

CONCERTS, OPERA & DANCE

Bet Lessin ★ A multi-use venue, this theater hosts contemporary plays in Hebrew, jazz groups, and contemporary and folk musicians. 101 Dizengoff St. www.lessin.co.il. ✆ **03/725-5333.**

Israel Philharmonic Orchestra ★★ The Heichal Hatarbut, which can seat around 3,000 concertgoers, houses this prestigious orchestra, which was founded in 1936 by Bronislaw Huberman at a time when Jews were being dismissed from orchestras in Europe. Concerts are also given at the Smolarz Auditorium in Tel Aviv University and in other towns, carrying on a tradition that began during the War of Independence when it played just behind the lines for the troops near Jerusalem and Beersheba. The orchestra is on vacation from August until the end of the Jewish high holidays in the fall. 1 Huberman St. www.ipo.co.il. ✆ **03/621-1777.**

The Israeli Opera ★★★ Housed in the architecturally controversial **Golda Meir/Tel Aviv Center for the Performing Arts,** the Israeli Opera is the country's cultural gem, performing a lively program of classic and modern opera. Historically, the company drew heavily on the talent of immigrants from the former Soviet Union; today, it often features the children and grandchildren of those folks. The Tel Aviv Center for the Performing Arts hosts classical, jazz, and popular concerts. 19 Shaul Ha Melekh St. www.israel-opera.co.il. Box office for all events. ✆ **03/692-7777.**

Dancers in performance at the Suzanne Dellal Center for Dance and Theater.

Suzanne Dellal Center for Dance and Theater ★★★ This complex, built in postmodern style, is the venue for visiting dance groups as well as for Israel's contemporary Bat Sheva Dance Company and the Inbal Dance Theater, which often draws upon Israel's ethnic traditions for its style. It also hosts the world-renowned Gaga Center, which puts on both performances and offers classes for all ages and levels. The Dellal Center is at the heart of the revival of the once old, quaint, now unmistakably posh Neve Tzedek neighborhood. 5 Yehieli St. www.suzannedellal.org.il. Box office ✆ **03/510-5656.**

Tzavta ★ This club specializes in Israeli music, both folk and popular, as well as theater productions. 30 Ibn Gvirol St. www.tzavta.co.il. ✆ **03/695-0156.**

THEATER

Cameri Theater ★ This theater presents both repertory classics and new Israeli plays in Hebrew. 19 Shaul Hamelech Ave. www.cameri.co.il. ✆ **053/531-1150.**

HaBima National Theater ★ Founded in Moscow in 1918 by the renowned Stanislavski and moved to British Mandate Palestine in 1928, the Ha-Bimah National Theater is the nation's first and best-known repertory theater. While performances are in Hebrew, some productions offer simultaneous translations. 2 Tarsat Ave. www.habima.co.il. ✆ **03/629-5555.**

The Club Scene

Tel Aviv and Jaffa are the nightlife centers of Israel. Their clubs have been the breeding ground for almost all Israeli singers who have gone on to international careers. The scene changes so frequently that only a few long-term stalwarts are listed here. The monthly English edition of *Time Out Israel* (free in most major hotels) will have the best list of what's current and popular. Nothing much starts before midnight, and most places are open daily.

CLUBS & DANCE BARS

Barby ★★ You need to come early to get a good spot, but this large Tel Aviv music venue is unique in that it's still conducive to allowing a connection between artists and audiences. The drinks are expensive, even for Israel, but the bands are great, and the bouncers actually enforce the ban on indoor smoking. 52 Kibbutz Galuyot Rd. www.barby.co.il. ✆ **03/518-8123.**

HaOman 17 ★ This is the country's iconic megaclub with top Israeli and international DJs and major parties Thursday, Friday, and Saturday nights after 1am. 88 Abarbanel St. www.haoman17.com. ✆ **03/681-3636.**

Kuli Alma ★★ This intimate Tel Aviv bar/club is composed of a few separate rooms, each playing different music and offering different vibes. There's a small cover charge and age minimum to keep the crowds under control some nights, and the lines to get in can be a bit long on the weekends, but Kuli Alma is a near guarantee for a fun night out. 10 Mikveh Israel St. www.kulialma.com. ✆ **03/656-5155.**

Levontin 7 ★★★ This is the hole-in-the-wall to visit if you're looking to get a taste of Tel Aviv's bustling indie music scene. The upstairs bar is chill, the underground stage hosts consistently memorable shows, and there's an adjacent, fabulous vegan pizza place for when you need a refuel from dancing. 7 Levontin St. www.levontin7.com. ✆ **03/560-5084.**

BARS, PUBS & WINE BARS

Jajo Wine Bar ★ Upscale and atmospheric, this wine bar is a fixture of the Neve Tzedek neighborhood. Mon–Thurs 5pm–midnight; Fri 4–11pm; Sat 5pm–midnight. 44 Shabazi St. ✆ **03/510-0620.**

La Otra ★★ What's a Mexican-Caribbean themed bar and restaurant doing in a Middle Eastern city like Tel Aviv? Well, when the nosh and cocktails are this good, does it really matter? We like La Otra because it's a trendy, original spot that's also close the beach. 66 Hayarkon St. www.laotratlv.com. ✆ **073/264-9464.** Sun–Wed 6pm–midnight; Thurs–Sat 6pm–1am.

Minzar ★★ Just off the Carmel Market, this mostly al fresco, thoroughly casual Tel Aviv institution, dating back to 1992, has cheap beer, delicious gastropub-style food, and a wonderful, welcoming atmosphere. Sat–Thurs 8am–4am; Wed 8am–midnight; Thurs and Fri 24 hours. 60 Allenby St. ✆ **03/517-3015.**

The Prince ★★ Its entrance is anything but royal, to say the least—and don't bother looking for a sign—but it's worth venturing into this historic building and hiking up two flights of stairs to get a taste of hipster Tel Aviv. Nibbles are served, but it's the fairly priced libations in an urban al fresco setting that packs them in nightly to this institution, open 'til the wee hours. 18 Nahalat Binyamin St. ✆ **058-606-1818.**

Shpagat ★★ This cafe in the city's former garment district becomes a hopping gay bar after sunset, when the music gets more festive, the cocktails start flowing, and the LGBTQ flock to occupy the coveted spots on the terraced seating area. 21 years and older. Every Wednesday is lesbian night, though it's usually a mix. Sun–Wed 10am–2am; Thurs 10am–3am; Fri 10am–5pm, 10pm–3am; Sat 8pm–2am. 43 Nahalat Binyamin St.

Film

Israeli films (which typically include English subtitles) punch way above their weight on the international scene, so try to fit in a cinema visit if you can. For English-language films, which are not dubbed (as they are in some countries in Europe), you can sit back and enjoy.

Tel Aviv Cinémathèque ★★ Located near the Habima Theater, the Cinémathèque offers a changing program of three or four films each day, ranging from international classics to rarely seen, experimental films. It also hosts an annual International Film Festival in the spring as well as special festivals of Israeli films throughout the year. 5 HaArba'a St. www.cinema.co.il. **✆ 03/606-0800.**

DAY TRIPS FROM TEL AVIV

Sorek Stream Nature Reserve & Palmachim Beach ★

Just 30 minutes south of Tel Aviv, two beautiful nature parks offer respite from the hustle and bustle of the big city. Whether you want a romantic hike along the tranquil Sorek River estuary or to spend a day with the entire family at one of Israel's most pristine beaches, these two unique destinations, just minutes apart, will offer you a full day of bliss in nature. Just be sure to bring a hat and plenty of water with you, as you can't count on shade and the burning Israeli summer sun will quickly bring you to your knees.

SOREK STREAM NATURE RESERVE

Not unlike many Israeli rivers before it, the Sorek is a river of once ill-repute. The 70km-long (43½-mile) stream, which originates in the Jerusalem Mountains and winds its way to the Mediterranean Sea, was once notorious for carrying the wastewaters of Jerusalem and other cities along its path. But an upstream waste-water purification plant means that clean water flows through the riverbed today. You enter the reserve through the Tzanchanim Grove (Paratrooper's Grove), a pastoral eucalyptus grove planted in the 1950s and named for the paratroopers who regularly train in the nearby dunes—don't be alarmed when you spot Israeli soldiers popping up in the woods. Past the gravel parking lot and picnic tables, a paved path splits at the eastern end of the grove. The path to your right will lead you upstream to Nabi Rubin, the shrine of the Prophet Reuben, before circling back to the parking lot. Be aware that the route along Nabi Rubin will add around 2.5km (1½ miles) to your trek. Alternatively, you can turn to the left and follow the more popular path passing under a small overpass to head directly towards the estuary.

The wheelchair-accessible path, which snakes alongside the Sorek River, will take you through the rich fauna and wildlife of the reserve and toward the so-called Eeh HaTzavim (Tortoise Island). Stop along the way to cross the stone dam to the other side of the river or gaze at the fish splashing about around the stones. Continue down the path until you reach a small clearing with numerous picnic tables giving you a chance to rest and enjoy a small snack you hopefully brought. Stand on the northern edge of the clearing, and you might be able to catch a glimpse of the Caspian turtles sunbathing on the banks of Tortoise Island. This small artificial island was built by the Nature and Parks Authority in 2002 in an effort to restore the population of Caspian turtles that was once abundant in all of Israel's coastal rivers.

From Tortoise Island, a path marked with short white poles continues into the dunes and toward Tatzpit HaCormoranim (Cormorant Lookout) before descending to a stunning natural beach. The clear-cut path and thick vegetation give way to dunes, small bushes, and grapevines growing from the sand. Make your way toward the big dune to the west and keep your eyes open for the wild boars that roam the area. Once you are at the top of the dunes, you have reached the Cormorant Lookout. From here, you can enjoy a fantastic view of the natural beach below and the Sorek Stream with its eucalyptus trees to your right. Carefully make your way down the footpath which will lead you past a small cave, nicknamed The Dwarves' Cave, and onto the stunning natural beach. Reminder, there are no lifeguards watching over this stretch of coast and riptides can always lurk, so be extra careful.

Make sure to climb the calcareous sandstone ridge at the southern tip of the beach to get a stunning view from the Sorek Estuary all the way to Palmachim Beach to the south. When you are ready to return, simply retrace your steps up the dune to the Cormorant Lookout and follow the path.

PALMACHIM BEACH

Just a few minutes past the Tzanchanim Grove lies Palmachim Beach itself. The pristine beach was declared a national park in 2014 after years of lobbying by various groups who wanted to prevent the beach from being turned into a holiday resort. Thanks to their relentless efforts, Palmachim Beach remains one of the last untouched beaches on Israel's Mediterranean coastline. Palmachim is not a large beach, and doesn't offer many facilities beyond a lifeguard (in season), a few sun shelters and public toilets. However, the lack of development is exactly what makes it one of the most beautiful beaches in Israel. As opposed to the hustle and bustle of the beaches of Tel Aviv, Palmachim truly offers a chance to relax and simply enjoy a quiet day in the sun. The only noise breaking the tranquility will be infrequent flyovers of helicopters en route to the nearby Palmachim airbase, which always makes for a spectacle for the children. The beach is bounded by some low cliffs to the south and boasts some great views of Tel Aviv to the north. Be sure to bring food and drink with you as there won't be any opportunities to purchase these here. Palmachim is reachable by bus, but we recommend renting a car for the day or simply taking a taxi to the entrance of the beach. Entrance to the park is NIS 10 in the winter, NIS 30 in the summer.

GETTING THERE

To get to Nahal Sorek from Tel Aviv, drive south on Rte. 20 until you reach Rte. 431 to Rishon LeZion/Jerusalem. Follow Rte. 44 until take a right on 3, then follow signs to the Nahal. Be aware that the road is fairly narrow and windy through the countryside. Palmachim Beach is another half hour drive on Rte. 4311, where, at the end, you will see a sign to the left to the Tzanchanim Grove. Keep driving straight to reach the car park of Palmachim Beach.

THE NORTHERN COASTAL PLAIN

By Elianna Bar-El

9

Like the rest of the country, the Northern Coastal Plain (*Mishor HaHof* in Hebrew) combines the old and the new in a uniquely Israeli way. Neon and chrome shopping malls and golden beaches exist side by side with biblical, Roman, and Crusader sites. The vast archaeological ruins of **Caesarea,** washed by Mediterranean waves and dotted with wonderful places to dine, is one of the most romantic ancient sites in Israel. Further north, **Haifa** (Israel's third major metropolis) provides a strategically smart base from which to explore the northern coast and the Western Galilee. Just north of Haifa, the medieval walled seaport of **Akko** (Acre), a UNESCO World Heritage Site, is one of Israel's unassuming treasures.

CAESAREA ★★

40km (25 miles) north of Tel Aviv

Caesarea was the culminating vision of Herod the Great (ruled 37 B.C.–4 B.C.), who created a new, spectacular classical Roman city by the sea to rival Alexandria as the greatest metropolis of the Eastern Mediterranean. Since it had no natural port, he built a vast artificial harbor. On the empty sands, he constructed theaters facing the sea, temples, hippodromes, palaces, colonnaded avenues, and markets. A thousand years later, the city was reborn as a Crusader fortress, but after the Crusades, the ruins of the city were covered by sand and forgotten.

Today, the romantic ruins by the sea have become one of Israel's most photogenic and lively archaeological sites, dotted with great eateries smack dab in the middle of the ruins. Nearby glittering beaches and wineries, plus the artists' village of **Ein Hod,** make this a pleasing road trip from Tel Aviv.

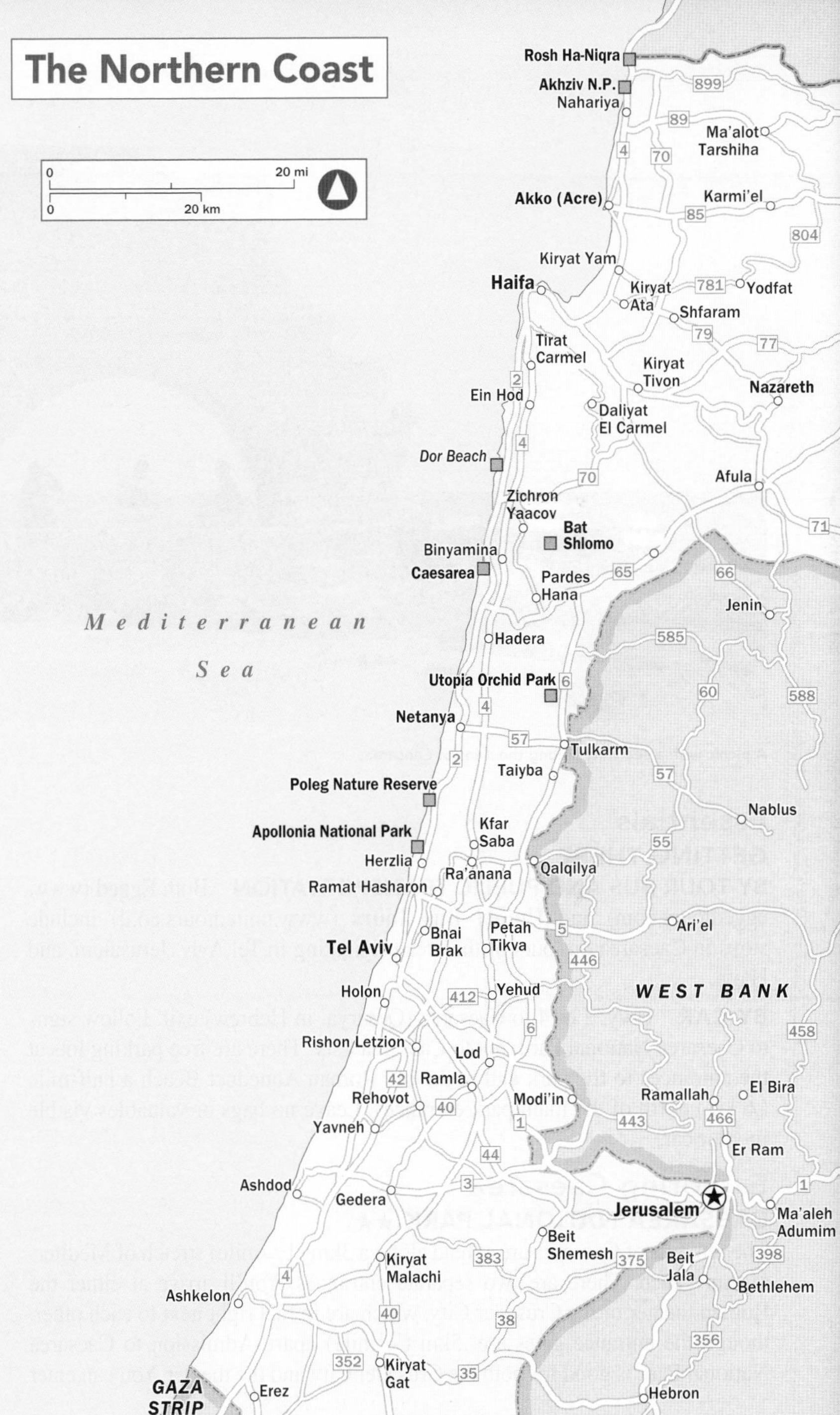

The Northern Coast
0
20 mi
0
20 km
Rosh Ha-Niqra
Akhziv N.P.
Nahariya
899
89
Ma'alot
Tarshiha
4
70
Akko (Acre)
Karmi'el
85
804
Kiryat Yam
Haifa
Kiryat
Ata
781
Yodfat
Shfaram
79
77
Tirat
Carmel
Kiryat
Tivon
2
Nazareth
Ein Hod
Daliyat
El Carmel
4
Dor Beach
70
Afula
Zichron
Yaacov
Bat
Shlomo
71
Binyamina
Caesarea
65
66
Pardes
Hana
Jenin
Mediterranean
Sea
Hadera
585
Utopia Orchid Park
6
60
588
4
Netanya
57
Tulkarm
2
Taiyba
57
Poleg Nature Reserve
Nablus
Kfar
Saba
Apollonia National Park
55
Herzlia
Ra'anana
Qalqilya
Ramat Hasharon
Petah
Tikva
5
Ari'el
Bnai
Brak
Tel Aviv
446
Holon
412
Yehud
WEST BANK
6
458
Rishon Letzion
Lod
42
Ramla
Rehovot
40
Modi'in
Ramallah
El Bira
Yavneh
1
443
466
Er Ram
44
Ashdod
3
Gedera
1
Jerusalem
Ma'aleh
Adumim
Beit
Shemesh
Kiryat
Malachi
383
375
Beit
Jala
398
Bethlehem
4
Ashkelon
40
38
356
352
Kiryat
Gat
35
GAZA
STRIP
Erez
Hebron

A picnic with a sea view among the ruins of Caesarea.

Essentials

GETTING THERE

BY TOUR BUS AND PUBLIC TRANSPORTATION Both **Egged** (www.eggedtours.com) and **United Bus Tours** (www.unitedtours.co.il) include stops in Caesarea on tours of the area originating in Tel Aviv, Jerusalem, and Haifa.

BY CAR Hwy. 2 or 4 to Caesarea (Qesarya, in Hebrew) exit. Follow signs to Caesarea National Park, not to Caesarea City. There are free parking lots at the entrances to the park and at the old Roman Aqueduct Beach a half-mile (.6 km) north of the main park entrances. Leave no bags or valuables visible in your car.

Exploring Caesarea

CAESAREA NATIONAL PARK ★★

The remains of Caesarea are spread along a 3km (1¾-mile) stretch of Mediterranean beach. There are two separate entrances: You'll arrive at either the Roman theater or the Crusader City, which are in fact right next to each other, though the entrance gates are .5km (⅓ mile) apart. Admission to Caesarea National Park is good for both the Crusader City and the theater. You can enter the city for free after 5pm closing time to stroll the ruins or visit the restaurants that have sprung up inside the park, but special exhibits are closed at night.

At the admission gates, get a map showing the details of the cities that have risen at this site, both on land and in the water—the cities and harbors of Straton's Tower (the earliest settlement at the site of Caesarea), as well as the Herodian, Roman, Byzantine, and Crusader incarnations of Caesarea. There is also an excellent, inventive audiovisual presentation that brings the site to life, re-creating what Caesarea would have looked like at different times in its history.

The excavations you see today are only a very small part of what's actually here, waiting to be discovered; new finds are constantly being unearthed. In recent years, ruins of a massive temple dedicated to Roman gods were uncovered and attributed to King Herod. Other highlights include the **Roman Theater,** constructed in the time of Jesus and used today to host summer performances. Test the acoustics by sitting in the stands and listening to someone speak on stage or clap hands.

You enter the **Crusader City** on a bridge across the deep moat, then through a gatehouse with Gothic vaulting. Emerging, you'll find yourself in the large fortified town, which covered a mere fraction of the great Herodian/Roman city. Especially noteworthy are the foundations of the **Crusader Church of Saint Paul** (1100s), down toward the sea, near the little Turkish minaret (1800s). The citadel, next to the group of shops, was badly damaged by an earthquake in 1837, as was most of the Crusader City.

The **Port of Sebastos,** a dockside part of the Crusader Port, extends from the Crusader City into the sea, but King Herod's Harbor at Caesarea, completed in 10 B.C. and also named Sebastos, extended at least three times as far as what you see today. It curved around to the right, where a separate northern breakwater extended to meet it, roughly where the northern Crusader fortification walls meet the sea. The breakwater was also a wide platform with room for large quantities of cargo, housing for sailors, a lighthouse, *colossi* (gigantic statues), and two large towers guarding the entrance gates to the harbor. The harbor could be closed off by a chain stretched between the two towers, preventing ships from entering.

The Roman Theater at Caesarea.

Herod's Harbor was one of the largest harbors of the Roman world, mentioned by historian Flavius Josephus as an especially amazing feat of engineering because it was a total creation—built without the usual benefit of a topographical feature such as a bay or cove. Historians did not find the harbor until 1960, when a combination of aerial photography and underwater archaeological explorations revealed the ruins sunken offshore. Historians and archaeologists believe that the harbor structure probably sank vertically downward as a result of an earthquake.

The excavation of the underwater ruins is an important international project. At the **Old Caesarea Diving Center** in the Old City (www.caesarea-diving.com; ✆ **04/626-5898**), at the site of the ancient harbor, you can take a private guided dive with equipment supplied starting at NIS 340. It is NIS 170 per person if you are in a group. Take note, you must be certified and bring your documents to show in person. If you haven't been diving in the last 6 months, you will be required to take a refresher dive, and all bookings must be made in advance. Snorkeling tours can also be arranged. The dive explores ruins of the ancient harbor and passes by ancient shipwrecks, classical statues, and fragments of a once-great lighthouse. Reserve ahead, although dives can't be guaranteed if sea conditions aren't good.

Tel Aviv–Haifa highway. www.parks.org.il/reserve-park/caesarea-national-park. ✆ **04/626-7080.** Admission (including the Roman Theater and Crusader City) NIS 39 adults, NIS 24 children; save your ticket for the interactive audiovisual presentation. Open Sat–Thurs 8am–5pm, Fri 8am–4pm (summer); Sat–Thurs 8am–4pm, Fri 8am–3pm (winter). Entrance fee for those going to the Diving Center is NIS 14. Must book dive in advance.

THE BYZANTINE STREET

Fifty meters (164 ft.) east of the Crusader city entrance, behind the little snack shop, is the Byzantine Street, or Street of Statues, which is actually part of a forum. The statues depict an emperor and other dignitaries.

THE HIPPODROME

Head east from either the Byzantine Street or the Roman Theater to reach the ruined hippodrome, in the fields between the two access roads. Measuring 72×288m (236×945 ft.), the hippodrome could seat some 20,000 people. Some of the monuments in the hippodrome may have been brought from Aswan in Egypt—expense was no object when Herod built for Caesar.

THE NEW CITY

Largely residential, the modern city of Caesarea is notable for its very worthwhile art museum, the **Ralli Museum ★**, located on Rothschild Boulevard (www.rallimuseums.com; ✆ **04/626-1013;** Mon–Tues and Thurs–Sat 10:30am–5pm. Free). The museum contains a large collection of works by Latin American and Spanish artists (including artists of Sephardic origin); is housed in a spacious, beautifully designed new building; and is one of Israel's unexpected and little-publicized surprises. The gems of the collection include sculptures by Dalí and Rodin, but the works of Latin American surrealists, representing artists from Mexico to Uruguay, are also powerful and impressive.

APOLLONIA: a secret site

Israel is packed with so many iconic sites, from the holy places of Jerusalem to the impressive archaeological grounds of Caesarea, that it's easy to overlook some lesser known gems. One that you shouldn't miss—especially if you're going to be traveling between Tel Aviv and Haifa—is Apollonia, sometimes called Arsuf. Situated some 15km (9⅓ miles) north of Tel Aviv and just past the commercial glitz of Herzliya Pituach, Apollonia is part of a small national park whose main attraction is a 13th-century clifftop Crusader fortress overlooking the Mediterranean Sea. Of course, it's mostly in ruins (dating from A.D. 1241–1265, plus an even older Roman villa), but the setting is spectacular.

The site was first settled by the Phoenicians as early as the 6th century B.C. and was renamed Apollonia in the Hellenistic period. Long before it was taken by Muslims in A.D. 640, it had become an important stop in Roman times between Jaffa and Caesarea, and in A.D. 1101 Apollonia fell into the hands of the Crusaders, led by Baldwin I of Jerusalem. Characteristically for Mediterranean towns of the time, other sieges followed and the site traded hands between the Knights Hospitaller, the Mamluks, and others. Today the ruins can be explored via either of two paths, one of which follows the cliff, and the view of the coast from the lookout point is especially memorable.

From coastal road No. 2, at the Kfar Shmaryahu junction, turn toward Herzliya Pituach. Follow the brown INPA (Israel Nature and Parks Authority) signs all the way to the site (you'll be going east). At the second traffic circle, turn right onto Wingate Street which leads to the park entrance. Hours are April to September 8am to 5pm, Fridays until 4pm, October to March 8am to 4pm, Fridays until 3pm. Admission fee is NIS 22 adults, NIS 9 children. www.parks.org.il.

Where to Stay

Dan Caesarea ★★ If you can't unwind at the Dan Caesarea, you may need medication. Set amid acres of lush gardens, the Dan boasts a vast swimming pool and is right next to Israel's top golf course. Horseback riding, fishing, diving, bicycling, and other local activities can be easily arranged through the front desk. There is also a full program of summertime in-hotel sports, including kids' basketball. The staff is attentive. And as for the hotel itself, the building is low-rise, 1980s modern, but rooms are spacious and comfy (large enough for an extra child), with terraces that take in wonderful views.

1 Rothschild St. www.danhotels.com. ✆ **04/626-9111,** 03/740-8966. 116 units. $270–$358 double. Rates include breakfast. Free parking. **Amenities:** Restaurant; cafe; babysitting (reserve in advance); children's activities (in season); health club; Jacuzzi; outdoor pool; room service; sauna; lit tennis court; free Wi-Fi.

Where to Eat

Restaurants in Caesarea are excellent and stay open after the archaeological park closes at 5pm. Be aware that these eateries will *not* validate the entrance fee or parking fees, and you will have to pay an entrance fee if you arrive while the park is open. Reservations are recommended for all locations.

a side trip TO ZICHRON YA'ACOV

Situated on a mountain ridge overlooking the Mediterranean Sea some 70km (43½ miles) north of Tel Aviv and 35km (21¾ miles) south of Haifa, Zichron Ya'acov is the heart of Israel's central wine country and home of the famous Carmel Winery, which was established in 1892, as well as other fine vino makers, such as the **Bat Shlomo Winery** (see below) and the **Tishbi Winery** in the gentle hills between Zichron and nearby Binyamina. Worth a side trip any time of year, the best time to visit may be August and September when the vineyards are heavy with grapes and tastings seem especially timely. Check www.carmelwines.co.il and www.tishbi.com for updated wine tasting information.

The winery success stories today are in contrast to the tough times of the pioneers who came to the area in 1882, who relied on the generosity of the Baron Edmund de Rothschild—after whose father Zichron is named. In 1886 the Baron brought a wine press to the town and the tradition of winemaking here began. Rothschild's dying wish in Paris in 1934 was to be buried in the Holy Land; and 20 years later he was reinterred in a tomb set amid lush grounds in nearby Ramat Hanadiv (www.ramat-hanadiv.org.il). The village of Zichron itself is a very pleasant place to stroll for its galleries, shops, and ice cream parlors. For dining, get reservations at the Tishbi Winery complex for a delicious lunch at their pastoral restaurant (great for groups and families), followed (or preceded by) a wine and chocolate tasting.

If you're hoping to stay in the area, you have two excellent, if pricey, options. The first is **Bat Shlomo Farmhouse & Winery ★★★** (thefarmhouse.co.il; ✆ **054/860-1889;** double from $700 including half board). Named for Baron de Rothschild's mother, the resort is actually a small village, one that's been brought back to vibrant life by Farmhouse owner and proprietor Elie

Crusaders ★★ MEDITERRANEAN There's little to find fault with at this kosher, beachside eatery. The fish is super-fresh and expertly prepared in hearty portions (there's also a smattering of meat dishes for those who don't like fish); service is efficient; and like so many of the restaurants here, the views can't be beat. Ask for one of the outdoor tables.

Old Caesarea Park. www.hazalbanim.co.il. ✆ **04/636-1931** or 04/636-1679. Main courses NIS 130–NIS 220. Sun–Thurs 11am–11pm. Fri open until 1 hour before Shabbat.

Hellena ★★★ MEDITERRANEAN A destination in its own right, this is one of Israel's finest gourmet restaurants. At its helm is the remarkable Amos Sion. His exciting contemporary menu takes inspiration from the cuisines of North Africa, the Mediterranean, and the Middle East. You might find yourself dining on shrimp and scallops in *arak* sauce with Kalamata olives, or lamb and veal "cigars" on a bed of sheep yogurt. If it's on the menu, the local and dry-aged entrecote or the chimichurri-glazed grilled octopus are over-the-top delish. Desserts are light and elegant; the wine list is excellent; and the view of the sunset over the sea is simply the cherry on top of the experience.

Old Caesarea Park. hellena.co.il. ✆ **04/610-1018.** Reservations recommended. Main courses NIS 90–NIS 140; group tasting menu NIS 260 per person. Sun–Sat noon–11pm.

Wurtman. His vineyards produce award-winning varietals, but he's also known for championing social enterprises within the intimate community. As for the Farmhouse itself, it was originally built in 1889, but now features sleek, mid-century modern–esque furnishings, rainfall showers, and other contemporary luxuries. Guests wake up to guided yoga and meditation sessions and then head to the communal dining table where a private chef has prepared wholesome, regional fare pulled straight from the farm's gardens. Bicycle tours, Watsu massage therapy in the saltwater pool, private cooking workshops, and in-depth wine tastings all take place on the grounds. A truly gracious staff make a stay in the villa impeccable.

Another highly recommended lodging in the area, and one that is exceptionally family-friendly, is the **Elma Arts Complex Luxury Hotel ★★★** (www.elma-hotel.com; ✆ **04/630-0111;** double from $300, including breakfast). This is another compound, with its spacious guest rooms and common areas occupying a sprawling landscape with splendid sea views. Centered around a now completely restored one-time sanitarium, it's the brainchild of arts patron Lily Elstein, a descendant of Zichron Ya'acov's founders. The main building is a concrete Brutalist style building, but the interiors feature lighter, modernist clean lines and natural walnut furnishings. With 750m (2,460 ft.) of gallery space there is contemporary art literally everywhere, plus an indulgent spa, and indoor and outdoor pools. If you don't stay the night, still consider stopping in for a peek at the extensive art collection and lunch at the Oratorio restaurant, which offers a seriously delicious Mediterranean buffet and its own kids' section. The cultural events and live music performances hosted at Elma's on-site performance art center The Cube are also renowned (see the website's rotating calendar).

HAIFA ★★★

Some compare Haifa, beautifully situated on a hill overlooking a broad bay, to San Francisco or Naples. Israel's third-largest metropolitan area (pop. 300,000) and the capital of the north, Haifa is very different from either Jerusalem or Tel Aviv, and it is a pleasure to visit for both its physical beauty and lifestyle. In a society unlike any other in the Middle East, Jews and Arabs live and work side by side; 25% of Haifa's population is either Muslim or Christian.

Haifa is also an excellent base for exploring northern Israel. You won't need to rent a car since many organized day tours originate in Haifa; or you can use public transportation to explore Akko or even Safed on your own. In the evenings, the city offers restaurants, films, concerts, and urban strolling to keep you busy.

You won't be the first to visit, of course. The prophet Elijah knew this territory well—from the top of Mount Carmel he won a major victory over 450 priests of Baal during the reign of King Ahab and his notorious Phoenician wife, Jezebel. In late biblical times, the Phoenician port of Zalemona thrived here, with predominantly Greek settlers, and the Jewish agricultural village of

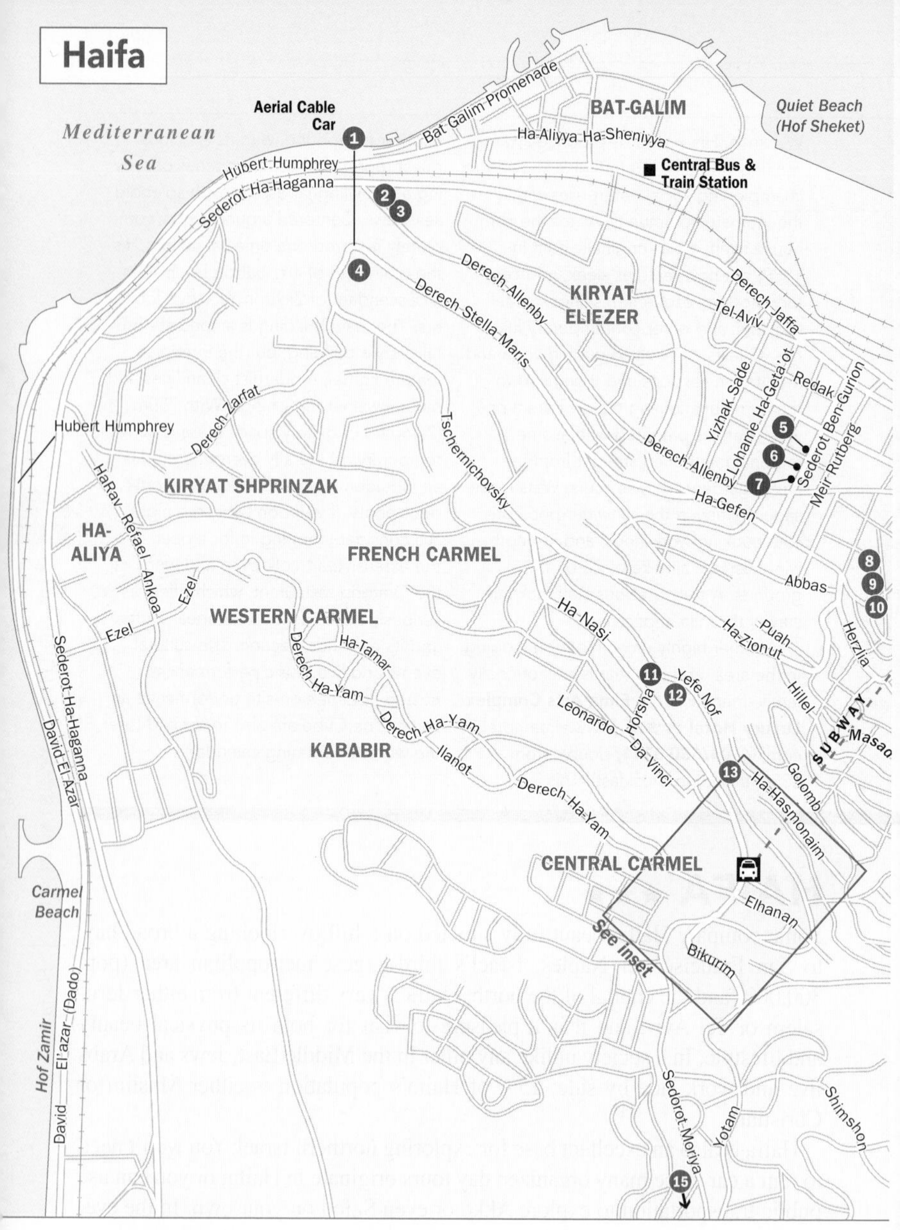

ATTRACTIONS ●

Aerial Cable Car 1
Baha'i Shrine & Gardens 9
Clandestine Immigration and Naval Museum 2
The Haifa Museum of Art 10
Haifa University & The Hecht Museum 15
Israel Museum of Science, Technology, and Space 22
Mané-Katz Museum 13
Mitzpoor Ha-Shalom (Peace View Park) 8
National Maritime Museum 3
Stella Maris Lighthouse, Church & Carmelite Monastery 4
Technion-Israel Institute of Technology 25
Tikotin Museum of Japanese Art 12

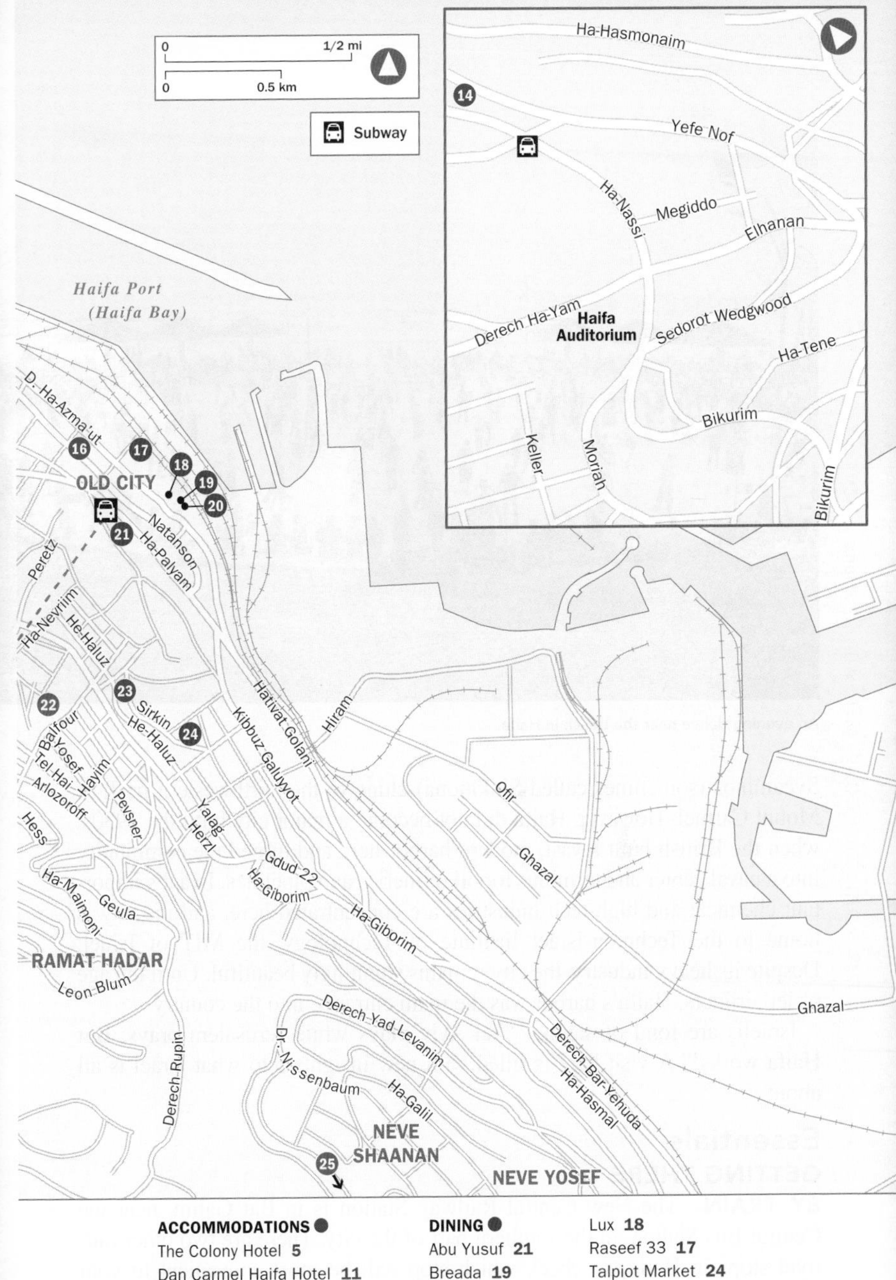

ACCOMMODATIONS
The Colony Hotel **5**
Dan Carmel Haifa Hotel **11**
Dan Panorama **14**
Loui Hotel **23**
Port Inn Guest House **16**

DINING
Abu Yusuf **21**
Breada **19**
Douzan **6**
Fattoush **7**
Fattoush Bar & Gallery **20**
Lux **18**
Raseef 33 **17**
Talpiot Market **24**

An evening dance near the beach in Haifa.

Sycaminos (sometimes called Shikmona) clung to the northwestern peak of Mount Carmel. However, Haifa did not become a major city until the 1930s, when the British built a vast, modern harbor here and turned the community into a naval center and terminus for oil refineries and pipelines. Israel's important chemical and high-tech industries are concentrated here, and the city is home to the Technion-Israel Institute of Technology, the MIT of Israel. Despite its heavy industry, the city remains stunningly beautiful. Until the age of jet airliners, Haifa's harbor was the main entrance into the country.

Israelis are fond of saying: "Tel Aviv plays while Jerusalem prays. But Haifa works!" A visit here is filled with new insights into what Israel is all about.

Essentials

GETTING THERE

BY TRAIN The New Central Railway Station is in Bat Galim, near the Central Bus Station, in the southern part of the city. There are two other railroad stops in Haifa, so check which stop will be most convenient to your hotel. Train information is available by calling ✆ **08/683-1222** (press 4 for English), or visit www.rail.co.il. Note that there is train service to Haifa directly to and from Ben-Gurion Airport (Terminal 3), as well as from central Tel Aviv.

BY BUS The **Egged Bus Terminal** (www.egged.co.il; ✆ **03/694-8888**), with intercity buses to and from all points in Israel, is next to the Central Railway Station in Bat Galim. From here, you'll have to take a taxi or city bus to either of our recommended hotel districts in the German Colony or Central Carmel. You will then need a **Rav-Kav** (card or app) in order to pay for any public transportation within Haifa (bus/train/Metronit/Carmelit/Rachbalit). You can purchase the card at the "Hof HaCarmel" Central Bus Station or download the app. If you go with the physical Rav-Kav card, you will need to charge it with money at any kiosk or supermarket and then scan the card once on the bus.

BY CARMELIT The **Carmelit** (www.carmelithaifa.com; ✆ **04/837-6861**) is an underground railway. It moves from Carmel Center, through Hadar, to downtown Haifa. It costs NIS 6.60 for a single ticket or NIS 15 for a daily ticket.

BY CAR Major highway networks connect Haifa with Tel Aviv, Jerusalem, and the Galilee. The main routes are Hwy. 2 and Hwy. 4 along the coast.

VISITOR INFORMATION

The **Haifa Information and Visitors Center,** 48 Ben-Gurion Blvd. (www.visit-haifa.org; ✆ **04/853-5606,** press 7 for English; Sun–Thurs 8am–5pm, Fri 8am–noon), is located on the main street of the German Colony neighborhood far from most hotels, but it's well organized and worth visiting.

The Carmelit, Haifa's impressive light rail system, zips commuters up and down the city's steep hills.

Orientation

Think of Haifa as a city built on three levels. Whether you come by bus or train, you will arrive on the lower (or port) level of the city, dominated by Haifa's shipping and transportation hub. This lower level also contains the **German Colony** that's centered around Ben-Gurion Boulevard, with trendy restaurants and small hotels leading up to the dramatic Bahá'i Center. The second level is **Hadar,** a downtown business area that's home to many of Haifa's architectural, cultural, and historical landmarks including Haifa Theater, Madatech—the National Science Museum, Talpiot Market, and Masada Street. It is also close to the famous Wadi Nisnas neighborhood, which is home to a distinctly mixed Jewish, Arab and Christian community. Since 1993, the annual "Holiday of the Holidays" festival during December celebrates Christmas, Ramadan, and Hanukkah and showcases the multiculturalism of the neighborhood and Haifa. It's not to be missed if you happen to be visiting during that timeframe.

At the top of the Carmel Range, with panoramic views, is the **Central Carmel District,** a verdant residential neighborhood with its own busy commercial center built around Ha-Nasi Boulevard. Here you'll find numerous hotels, restaurants, small museums, and two of Haifa's brightest cultural beacons: Haifa Auditorium and Bet Rothschild (with the adjacent Haifa Cinémathèque).

Note: Because Haifa is built up the side of a mountain, its main streets are sinuous switchbacks, curving and recurving like spaghetti to accommodate the steep slopes of Mount Carmel. If you're driving, the streets are always bewildering, and you will find it hard to orient yourself. Just remember: In Haifa, the two directions are up or down. About the only straight road in Haifa is underground—the Carmelit Subway that connects each level and climbs like an escalator, directly up the slopes of the Carmel.

Getting Around

BY SUBWAY The **Carmelit** (www.carmelithaifa.com; ✆ **04/837-6861**) is a fast and efficient means of getting up and down Haifa's various levels. Its lower terminal station is located on Jaffa Road, a few blocks north of the port entrance and not far from the old (Merkaz) central railway station. The Carmelit's upper terminal is at the Carmel Center.

Pulled on a long cable up and down the steep hill, the Carmelit resembles a sort of scale-model Métro. From bottom to the top, the stops are:

1. Paris Square (Kikar Paris, lower terminus, port area)
2. Solel Boneh (Hassan Shukri St.)
3. Ha-Nevi'im (Hadar business district, tourist center)
4. Masada (Masada St.)
5. Eliezer Golomb (Eliezer Golomb St.)
6. Gan Ha-Em (Central Carmel business district, upper terminus).

When you take the Carmelit, don't panic—the incline is so great that the floors of the cars break into escalator-like steps. The Carmelit operates Sunday through Thursday from 6am to midnight, Friday from 6am to 3pm, and resumes service on Saturday from 30 minutes after the end of Shabbat until midnight, and Saturday 8pm to midnight. On-site machines have English as well as Hebrew instructions. The fare is NIS 6.60.

BY BUS Most fares to places inside Haifa itself are NIS 6.60. Haifa's municipal buses operate from 5am to 11:30pm Sunday through Thursday; on Friday, bus service halts around 4:30pm; there's limited Saturday service from 9am to midnight on some lines. For info on buses inside Haifa visit www.egged.co.il.

BY RACHBALIT This is the newest cable car in Haifa. It runs between the Mifratz Transport Terminal, the Israel Institute of Technology campus, and the campus of the University of Haifa. Stops include:

1. Merkazit Mifratz (adjacent to the Cinemall shopping mall)
2. Check post (industrial area and shopping district)
3. Dori Road (Neve Shaanan neighborhood)
4. Central Technion
5. Upper Technion
6. The University of Haifa (and the Hecht Museum)

Haifa's cable cars are another fun way to get around.

It operates within the same framework as all public transport in Haifa (hours and fare) but not on Shabbat.

BY METRONIT This rapid transit system in Haifa has three lines: 1 (Red Line), 2 (Blue Line), 3 (Green Line). You can only pay with the aforementioned Rav-Kav card, and it must be charged with money either at the Metronit's stations or the central bus station. For more details: metronit.co.il; ✆ **1-700/700-181.**

Exploring Haifa

Beyond Haifa's sightseeing listed below, beachcombing can be considered a star activity. Haifa's great beaches, just south of town, are perfect for a late afternoon swim in summer, followed by fresh seafood at one of the beachside pubs. Allow time to watch the sun sink into the sea.

The Bahá'i Shrine and Gardens ★★★ LANDMARK Haifa's most impressive attraction is the splendid Bahá'i Shrine and Gardens, reached from Zionism (Ha-Zionut) Avenue. The immaculate, majestic Bahá'i gardens—with their stone peacocks and eagles and delicately manicured cypress trees—are a restful, aesthetic memorial to the founders of the Bahá'i faith.

Haifa is the international headquarters for Bahá'i, which began in Persia in the mid–19th century in a bloodbath of persecution. Bahá'is believe in the unity of all religions and see all religious leaders—Christ, Buddha, Muhammad, Moses—as messengers of God sent at different times in history with doctrines varying to fit changing social needs but bringing substantially the same message. The most recent of these heavenly teachers, according to Bahá'is, was Bahá'u'lláh. He was exiled by the Turkish authorities to Acre, wrote his doctrines there, and died a peaceful death in Bahjí House just north of Acre. See "Akko (Acre)," p. 338, for more information.

A downhill look at the extraordinary Bahá'i Shrine and Gardens.

In the Haifa gardens, the huge domed **shrine** entombs the remains of the Bab, the Bahá'u'lláh's herald. The tomb is a sight to see, with ornamental gold work and flowers in almost every nook and cranny. The Bab's remains, incidentally, were hidden for years after he died a martyr's death in front of a firing squad. Eventually, however, his followers secretly carried his remains to the Holy Land.

On a higher hilltop stands the Corinthian-style **Bahá'i International Archives** building, modeled after the Parthenon, and the **Universal House of Justice,** with 58 marble columns and hanging gardens behind. These are business buildings, not open to tourists. They, and the shrine of the tomb of the Bab, all face toward Acre, the burial place of Bahá'u'lláh.

The beautiful grounds are a geometric cascade of hanging gardens and terraces down to Ben-Gurion Boulevard—a gift of visual pleasure to the city that gave the Bahá'i religion its home. In addition to tourists, you'll see pilgrims who have come from all parts of the world to pay homage to the first leaders of this universal faith.

Off Ha-Zionut Ave. at Ben Gurion Blvd. ✆ **04/831-3131,** press 3 for English. Reservations for admission and official tour almost always required. Free admission. Guided tours by reservation only, online at www.ganbahai.org.il. Modest dress required. Use of strollers is prohibited. Shrine daily 9am–noon; gardens daily 9am–5pm. Bus: 3 Or 115 from Hadar; 27 from the port.

Clandestine Immigration and Naval Museum ★★ MUSEUM This museum tells the wrenching story of those who tried to escape from Nazi-occupied Europe and of the few Holocaust survivors who made it to safety. Throughout the time of the Holocaust, when Jews desperately needed a haven, admission to British Mandate Palestine was largely denied to them by the

The blockade-running ship *Af-Al-Pi Chen (Nevertheless)* is a major part of a visit to the Clandestine Naval and Immigration Museum.

British. Nevertheless, Jews fleeing from the Nazis during World War II, and Jewish escapees from displaced-persons camps after the war, constantly attempted to enter Palestine on rusty, unsafe, illegal vessels. One of these ships, the ***Struma,*** waited for months at sea for a country to accept the 765 refugees aboard until it was torpedoed and sank off Turkey in 1942. All but one on board perished. Other ships went down in Haifa harbor, with hundreds killed in sight of safety; still others, like the ***Exodus 1947*** (made famous by the Leon Uris book *Exodus* and the 1960 film), ran the British blockade only to have its passengers shipped to a Cyprus detention camp or returned to detention camps in Germany. The blockade-running vessel ***Af-Al-Pi Chen (Nevertheless)*** is now a part of the museum, commemorating all the ships that defied the British blockade.

204 Allenby Rd. www.shimur.org. ✆ **04/853-6249,** 072/279-8030. Admission NIS 20 adults; students and children NIS 15. Sun–Thurs 10am–4pm. Bus: 111.

Haifa Museum of Art ★★ ART MUSEUM The first branch of the Haifa Museum (the other two are the Tikotin Museum of Japanese Art and the National Maritime Museum) is home to a strong collection of contemporary painting, sculpture, and prints by Israeli and foreign artists, but with an emphasis on Israeli art. The museum is divided into five areas, each containing a different category of art or type of exhibit: emerging Israeli art, centering on artists who have never shown in a museum before; new mediums; a special presentation of installation art; "personal choice," containing an Israeli cultural figure's selection from the museum's collection with commentary; and a special visiting exhibition or headline exhibit from the museum's collection.

26 Shabtai Levi St. www.hma.org.il/eng. ✆ **04/852-3255.** Sun–Mon and Wed 11am–5pm; Tues and Thurs 4–8pm; Fri 10am–1pm; Sat 10am–4pm. Bus: 110, 111, 115, 3.

Haifa University and Hecht Museum ★★ CULTURAL INSTITUTION With a dramatic location on the Carmel heights and many buildings designed by Oscar Niemeyer (of Brasilia fame, the superfuturistic capital city of Brazil), Haifa University is dazzling and quintessentially "Haifa." The views from the 30th-floor observatory of the university's **Eshkol Tower** are not-to-be-missed, and the **Hecht Museum** contains an impressive collection of archaeological finds, as well as paintings by Impressionists and artists of the Jewish School of Paris.

Hecht Museum Haifa University, Mt Carmel. mushecht.haifa.ac.il. ✆ **04/824-0450.** Free admission. For a free guided tour of the campus, call in advance to reserve a spot. Rachbalit cable car: line 6.

Israel National Museum of Science, Technology and Space (Madatech) ★★ Museum This fun and interactive museum is catnip for kids of all ages—and curious adults. There are captivating science exhibits explaining optical illusions, a deep dive into Leonardo Da Vinci's prolific observations, a slew of rotating exhibits, and more.

25 Shmaryahu Levin St. www.madatech.org.il. ✆ **04/861-4444.** Mon–Wed & Fri 10am–3pm; Thurs & Sat 10am–5pm. NIS 89 per person 5+. Bus: 16, 24, 28, 37 from Bat Galim.

Statue of Archimedes in the bathtub at the Israel National Museum of Science, Technology and Space (Madatech).

Mané-Katz Museum ★ ART MUSEUM Located near the Dan Panorama hotel in Central Carmel, this was once the romantic mountaintop villa of French artist Mané-Katz. The museum now houses a collection of Mané-Katz's own work and personal art collection as well as interesting, well-curated visiting exhibits of contemporary art. The Mané-Katz Judaica collection is especially fine. ***Note:*** At press time, this museum was under renovation to make it more accessible for those with special needs. Call in advance or check online to make sure it's open before heading over.

89 Yefe Nof (Panorama Rd.). www.mkm.org.il. ✆ **04/603-0800,** press 2 for English. Admission for Mané-Katz collection is free.

Mitzpoor Ha-Shalom (Peace View Park) ★★ PARK The grounds of the Bahá'i gardens are split by Zionism Avenue. Farther up the hill is the lovely Mitzpoor Ha-Shalom (Peace View Park), also called the Ursula Malbin Sculpture Garden. Amid trees, flowers, and sloping lawns you'll find 18 bronze sculptures by Ursula Malbin of men, women, children, and animals at play. The view from here is magnificent—you can see all of Haifa's port area, Haifa Bay, Acre, Nahariya, and up to Rosh HaNikra at the Lebanese border, plus all the surrounding mountains.

Zionism Ave., at the corner of Shnayim Be-November St. Free admission.

National Maritime Museum ★★ This third branch of the Haifa Museum, near Bat Galim, encompasses 5,000 years of seafaring history in the Mediterranean and the Red Sea. These include archaeological collections of Mediterranean cultures from the beginning of history until the Islamic conquest in the 7th century. There are outstanding exhibitions of Greco-Roman culture, Coptic art, painted portraits from Fayum, coins from Caesarea and Acre, terra cottas of all periods, and finds from the Haifa area. The artifacts obtained through underwater archaeology are particularly impressive. The marvelous ethnology section of the Haifa Museum is also located here, but due to limited space, little of it is on display.

198 Allenby Rd. ✆ **04/603-0800.** Sat–Sun, Tues–Wed 10am–4pm; Thurs 10am–6pm; Fri 10am–2pm. Bus: 110, 112, 111 from Hadar.

Stella Maris Lighthouse, Church, and Carmelite Monastery ★★ CHURCH During the Crusades, groups of religious hermits began to inhabit the caves of the Carmel District in emulation of Elijah the Prophet, whose life was strongly identified with this mountain. These monastic hermits were organized into the Carmelite order, which spread throughout Europe. However, the founders on the Carmel range were exiled at the end of the Crusades. The present Carmelite monastery and basilica dates from 1836. With a magnificent view of the sea, the entire ensemble of buildings, including the lighthouse, is known as "Stella Maris." An earlier monastery complex on this site served as a hospital for Napoleon's soldiers during his unsuccessful siege of Acre in 1799. The pyramid in front of the church is a memorial to the many abandoned French soldiers who were slaughtered by the Turks after Napoleon's retreat.

The church is a beautiful structure, with Italian marble so vividly patterned that visitors mistakenly think the walls have been painted. Colorful paintings on the dome, done by Brother Luigi Poggi (1924–28), depict episodes from the Old Testament, the most dramatic being the scene of Elijah swept up in a chariot of fire; the statue of the Virgin Mary, carved from cedar of Lebanon, is also notable. The cave, situated below the altar, is believed to have been inhabited by Elijah. From Stella Maris, Haifa's little aerial cable car can take you down to the Bat Galim Beach Promenade, where you can walk in the Mediterranean or dine at waterfront eateries.

100 Stella Maris Rd. ✆ **04/833-7758.** Free admission. Daily 8:30am–noon and 3–6pm. Sunday church services, visiting hours after 10am. Modest dress required. Bus: 111, 112.

Technion ★ CULTURAL INSTITUTION The Technion-Israel Institute of Technology is Israel's version of MIT. Founded in 1912, the 120-hectare (297-acre) campus is a most impressive university complex, offering views of the city, the coastline clear to Lebanon, and the snow-topped Syrian mountains. The Coler-California Visitor Center greets visitors with a working robot and a free 20-minute video about the school, as well as high-tech multimedia touch-screen videos, Internet kiosks, and laser-disc productions. Grab a pamphlet for a self-guided campus tour.

Technion City. www.technion.ac.il. ✆ **04/829-3775.** Free admission, not suitable for young children. Visitor center hours Sun–Thurs 8am–3pm. Rachbalit cable car: 4, 5.

Tikotin Museum of Japanese Art ★★ ART MUSEUM As aficionados know, Israel plays host to one of the finest collections of Japanese art in the world. Collected originally by architect Felix Tikotin in the years prior to World War II, this exceptional museum owns some 7,000 traditional and modern works, from antique swords to painted screens to fine ceramics. The museum is located in a handsome, Japanese-inspired building (with sliding doors and a Zen garden) in Central Carmel.

89 Ha-Nassi Blvd. www.tmja.org.il. ✆ **04/603-0800.** Combined admission to Haifa Museum of Art, Tikotin Museum of Japanese Art, and National Maritime Museum NIS 35. Sun–Thurs 10am–7pm; Fri 10am–1pm; Sat 10am–3pm. Bus: 24, 28, 37, 115, 132 from Hadar. Carmelit: Gan Ha-Em Station.

Where to Stay

EXPENSIVE

Dan Carmel Haifa Hotel ★★ For more than 50 years, this has been Haifa's prestige hotel. Deluxe rooms on upper floors include indulgently luxurious bathrooms with sunken Jacuzzis and separate stall showers. Standard rooms are up to date, too. A large pool and good children's programs help make this a relaxing base, as does the location, near dozens of excellent restaurants (it's also just a 5-minute walk to the Gan Ha-Em Carmelit stop). Final perk: The dazzling views.

85–87 Ha-Nassi Blvd. www.danhotels.com. ✆ **04/830-3030.** 219 units. $340–$410 double. Rates include breakfast. Parking (fee). Carmelit: Gan Ha-Em. **Amenities:** Restaurants; cafe; bar; children's activities; spa; pool and children's pool; sauna; free Wi-Fi.

MODERATE

The Colony Hotel ★★ This boutique hotel is set in a stylish, restored 19th-century building on a picturesque pedestrian mall leading up to the dramatic Bahá'i Gardens and Center. Rooms vary, so ask to look around; those at the back of the hotel are significantly quieter. A roof deck, garden, and small in-house spa are quality perks. Rooms have fridges and TVs.

28 Ben-Gurion Blvd. www.colonyhaifa.com. ✆ **04/851-3344.** 39 units. $180–$255 double. Rates include breakfast. Carmelit: Paris Square. Free public parking. **Amenities:** Cafe; bar; spa; free Wi-Fi.

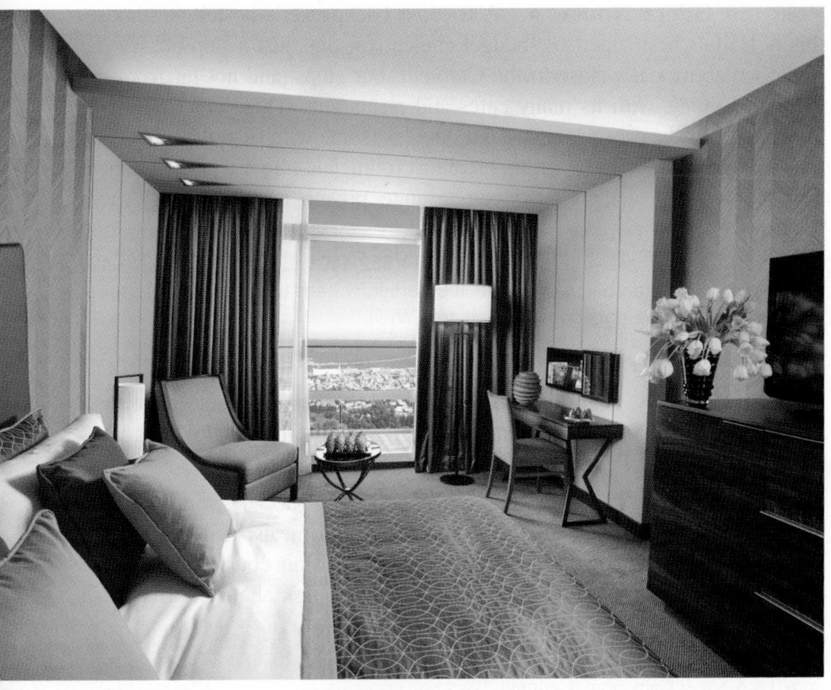

A view-blessed room at the Dan Carmel Hotel.

Dan Panorama ★ Located in a 1980s high-rise tower right at the Carmelit's Central Carmel subway stop, this is the most convenient place to stay in town, and its rooms offer tremendous views of the city. Other than that, it's bland-looking but efficient. The quality service and food here, along with the seasonal roof-level pool and proximity to the Central Carmel's bustling well-priced restaurant scene, make it a still-worthy pick.

107 Ha-Nassi Blvd. www.danhotels.com. ✆ **04/835-2222.** 267 units. $165–$250 double. Rates include breakfast. Parking (fee). Carmelit: Gan Ha-Em. **Amenities:** 2 restaurants; cafe; bar; concierge; outdoor pool and children's pool; sauna; free Wi-Fi.

INEXPENSIVE

Loui Hotel ★★ It's the little things that show someone cares when it comes to hotel stays. And at the Loui, those "tiny" items are myriad, including the good quality bedding (often done up in pretty floral coverlets); the inclusion of a fridge and kitchenette in each room; the pleasant roof deck; the way the staff seem eager to answer questions and help travelers; and the happy tchotchkes in the hallways—they give the place character. Small, too, are the prices, always a good thing. We consider the Loui a real find, especially for those who want to stay in the heart of the bustling downtown area (but well away from the noise).

35 HaHaluts. www.louihotels.com. ✆ **077/542-2909.** 18 units. $95 studio apartment. **Amenities:** Roof deck; free Wi-Fi.

Port Inn Guest House ★ A friendly backpacker's hostel/guesthouse, this is Haifa's best super low-budget choice (for digs just a step up, try the Loui; see above). It's close to the Carmelit, bus stops, and not far from the German Colony, with its many cafes and restaurants. There are well-maintained dorm beds, private singles and doubles (some with shared bathrooms), plus a garden terrace, a TV room, breakfast room, and free use of the kitchen. The helpful management also can arrange private apartment and room rentals.

34 Jaffa Rd. port-inn.haifa-hotels-il.com/en. ✆ **04/852-4401.** 12 units. NIS 300–NIS 400 doubles, also w/shared bathrooms; NIS 100 dormitory beds (male and female separated). **Amenities:** Lounge; guest kitchen; free Wi-Fi.

Where to Eat

Quite unexpectedly, Haifa has become a foodie scene in recent years, with trendy spots in the Port area, Central Carmel, and the German Colony's **Ben-Gurion Boulevard Pedestrian Promenade.**

Abu Yusuf ★★ ARABIC A Haifa landmark for decades, no-frills Abu Yusuf serves a menu of classic appetizers, grilled meats, and oven-baked dishes. The hummus here is particularly celebrated. Main courses include one trip to the buffet bar of 17 Middle Eastern salads. Ask about the fresh fish catch of the day.

1 Paris Square. ✆ **04/866-3723.** Main courses NIS 55–NIS 100. Sun–Thurs 7:30am–4pm; Fri & Sat 7:30am–5pm. Carmelit: Paris Sq.

Breada ★★ CAFE/SEAFOOD The fun-loving staff here know how to make customers smile, and they certainly can satiate most cravings. In the morning, they serve baked goods that are as Pinterest-worthy as they are delicious, like a buttery filo dough pastry shrouded in custard and topped with fresh kiwis. Come nighttime, the menu shifts to mouthwatering seafood dishes and vibrant mixed salads. Local, acclaimed street artists Broken Fingaz regularly shows their provocative artwork here.

6 HaNamal. ✆ **054/542-1618.** Entrees NIS 17–NIS 52. Sun–Mon, Fri 7am–2pm; Tues–Wed, Thurs 7am–2pm and 7pm–1am; Sat 8:30am–4pm. Bus: 2 from Bat Galim

Douzan ★ MODERN MIDDLE EASTERN With an eclectic menu that combines French and Arabic traditions, plus a good wine list, Douzan is a step above many of its compatriots in this restaurant-jammed part of town. Partially that has to do with the service, which is unusually warm and gracious (this is a family-owned place). And the food is always solid, particularly if you stick with the Middle Eastern specialties. Like **Fattoush** (see below), Douzan offers a terrace on the Ben-Gurion Pedestrian Mall with lovely vistas of the Bahá'i Center and Gardens stretching up Mt. Carmel.

35 Ben-Gurion Blvd. ✆ **053/944-3301.** Main courses and salads NIS 50–NIS 100. Daily 9am–after midnight.

Fattoush ★★★ MODERN MIDDLE EASTERN Two words: halvah ice cream. It's the reason it's so important to save room for dessert at Fattoush. Not that that's easy to do, as the food here is primo, whether you're trying the hummus with fried garlic and mushrooms or chowing down on the roasted eggplant with tahini. An excellent choice for vegetarians, Fattoush also shines when it comes to fish and meat dishes. And as with other restaurants on the Ben-Gurion Pedestrian Mall, the views are delightful. If you fall in love with this spot, come nighttime, check out **Fattoush Bar & Gallery** ★★★ (6 Hanamal St.; ✆ **04/881-3040;** daily 8:30pm–11pm), a vibrant complex of food, drinks, music, live performances, and an art gallery. The massive space spans two floors and offers an outdoor patio.

38 Ben-Gurion Blvd. ✆ **04/852-4930.** Main courses and salads NIS 55–NIS 100. Daily 7:30am–1am.

Lux ★★★ MODERN ARABIC-ISRAELI Try to get a seat at the long chef's counter, so that you can watch the culinary wizards here do their magic. It's the long centerpiece of this hip eatery, and you'll often see chef/owner Ala'a Musa (formerly of Akko's celebrated **El Marsa** ★★★, see p. 349), dotting plates with sauce, snipping fresh herbs over proteins, and overseeing the complex dance that goes into making each dish look artful and taste spectacular. Top dishes include ceviche with *labneh,* hot peppers, and pistachios; scallops set on a swirl of brown butter cauliflower creme with sage fries; and fried calamari and stuffed shrimp on a bed of lentils with tahini cream and pickled lemon sauce. It's a culinary/cultural experience that is not-to-be-missed.

13 HaNamal St. luxhaifa.co.il. ✆ **077/206-0970.** Entrees NIS 50–NIS 150. Open Mon–Thurs 5pm–midnight, Fri & Sat 12:30–4pm and 6pm–midnight.

Raseef 33 ★★★ CONTEMPORARY ARABIC This innovative new restaurant is the top choice at Haifa's port. Helmed by chef Hammoudi Oqla, it's named after the wharf that stood at the exact same point years ago. The menu is deeply influenced by Arab-Galilean cuisine, a type of cooking that flowers in the ethnically mixed Haifa neighborhood known as Wadi Nisnas. A piping-hot *taboon* oven is used for such dishes as Lebanese *arais,* which is grilled pita stuffed with ground lamb, pine nuts, roasted tomato, tahini, garlic confit, and *bharat.* The skewered shrimp smoked with fennel seeds and lime; and the *shushbarak* (meat dumplings in a goat yogurt stew), are other house specialties.

Haifa Port, 33 HaAtsmaut St. raseef33.co.il. ✆ **04/663-8071.** Mains NIS 60–NIS 160. Open Mon–Thurs 6pm–midnight, Fri–Sun noon–midnight.

Talpiot Market ★★★ You have a few choices for how to dine at Talpiot Market. You could simply graze. Along with fresh produce from farms in the Jezreel Valley, the Galilee, and the Shomron, the market hosts a vegan food shop, baked goods stalls, dried fruit and nut stands, and other types of stalls from which to cobble together a meal (there's even an on-site brewery, if you want a tipple). Or you could go to the top-notch small-plates restaurant on-site called **Talpiot** ★★ (talpiot.kitchen), which serves a range of classic and more creative seafood dishes (mussels marinara, fried calamari with ricotta, fish soup). Schedule in time, before or after your meal, to tour the historic, bustling market. Built in the International Style in the late 1930s it was inaugurated in April 1940. Local graffiti artists have created cool artworks on many of the metal shutters that roll down over the stalls in off hours. During the summer, there's often music, and other live performances, here during opening hours.

38 Sirkin St. in the Hadr HaCarmel neighborhood. Sun–Thurs 8am–5:30pm, Friday 7am–3:30pm.

Nightlife & Entertainment

Haifa was not known for its nightlife pre-pandemic, and, sadly, a number of its bars and clubs closed in 2020 and 2021, with few new ones taking their place. There are some options, however, for after dark fun. Concerts and performances at the **Haifa Auditorium** will be highlights, and there are often intriguing film programs at the **Cinémathèque,** and smaller folk and rock performances at **Haifa University.**

At the top of Hadar HaCarmel neighborhood, **Masada Street** is a vibrant hub, especially in the evenings. The population here is mostly young, and includes many students out to have a good time. You'll find cafes, bars, and specialty shops plus a number of architectural pearls, as the street retains its original character. The port area and the German Colony are also good options for those looking for low-key pubs and clubs.

AKKO (ACRE) ★★★

Akko's Old Walled City, a true architectural marvel (and a UNESCO World Heritage Site), has become one of Israel's new overnight destinations in recent

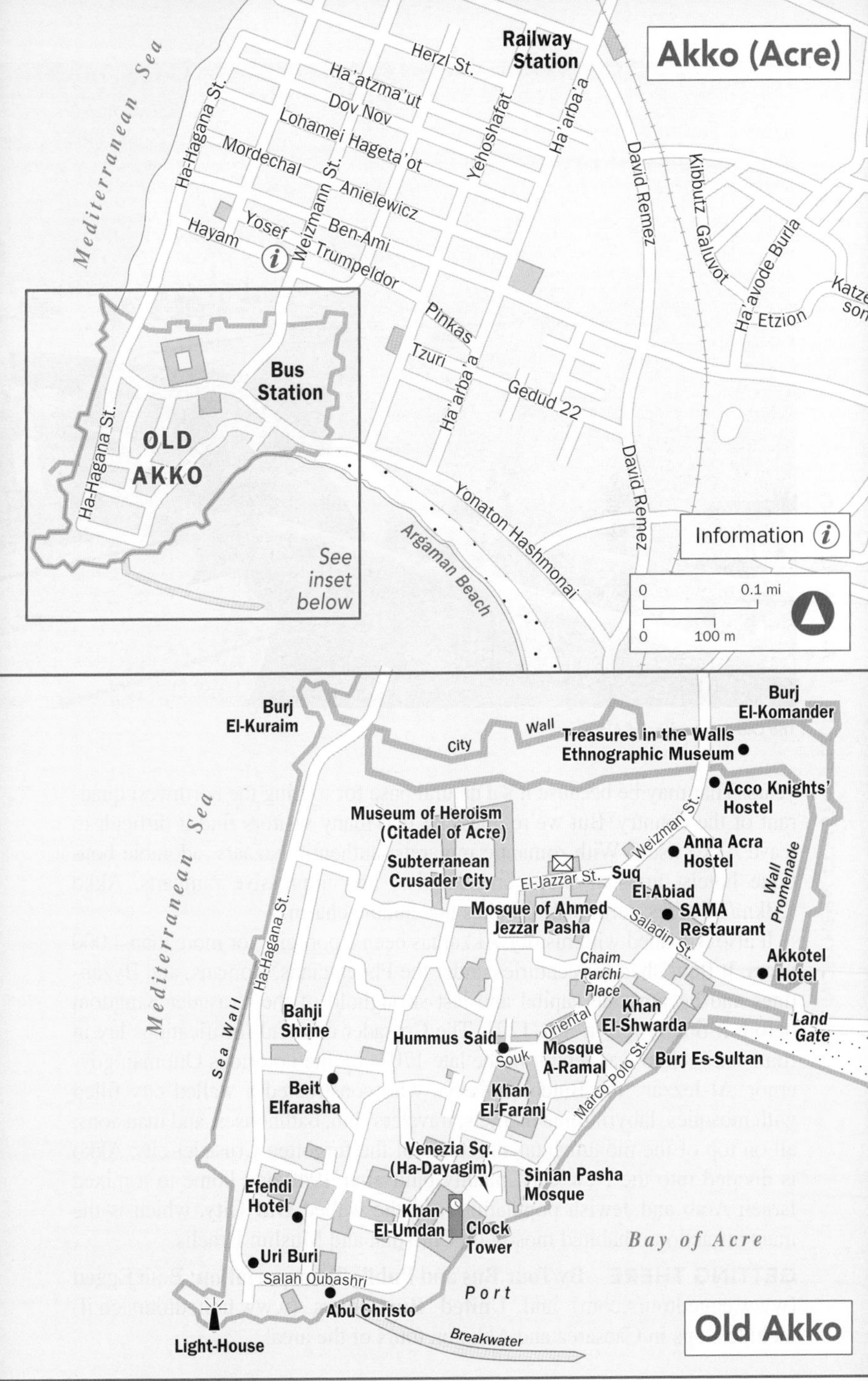

Akko (Acre)
Railway Station
Herzl St.
Ha'atzma'ut
Dov Nov
Lohamei Hageta'ot
Mordechal
Anielewicz
Ben-Ami
Yosef
Hayam
Trumpeldor
Weizmann St.
Ha-Hagana St.
Yehoshafat
Ha'arba'a
David Remez
Kibbutz Galuvot
Ha'avode Burla
Etzion
Katzenson
Pinkas
Tzuri
Gedud 22
Yonaton Hashmonai
Argaman Beach
Mediterranean Sea
Bus Station
OLD AKKO
See inset below
Information
0 0.1 mi
0 100 m
Burj El-Kuraim
Burj El-Komander
City Wall
Treasures in the Walls Ethnographic Museum
Acco Knights' Hostel
Museum of Heroism (Citadel of Acre)
Weizman St.
Anna Acra Hostel
Subterranean Crusader City
El-Jazzar St.
Suq El-Abiad
Wall Promenade
Mosque of Ahmed Jezzar Pasha
SAMA Restaurant
Saladin St.
Chaim Parchi Place
Akkotel Hotel
Khan El-Shwarda
Land Gate
Bahji Shrine
Hummus Said
Oriental Souk
Mosque A-Ramal
Burj Es-Sultan
Marco Polo St.
Sea Wall
Beit Elfarasha
Khan El-Faranj
Venezia Sq. (Ha-Dayagim)
Sinian Pasha Mosque
Efendi Hotel
Khan El-Umdan
Clock Tower
Bay of Acre
Uri Buri
Salah Oubashri
Port
Abu Christo
Light-House
Breakwater
Old Akko

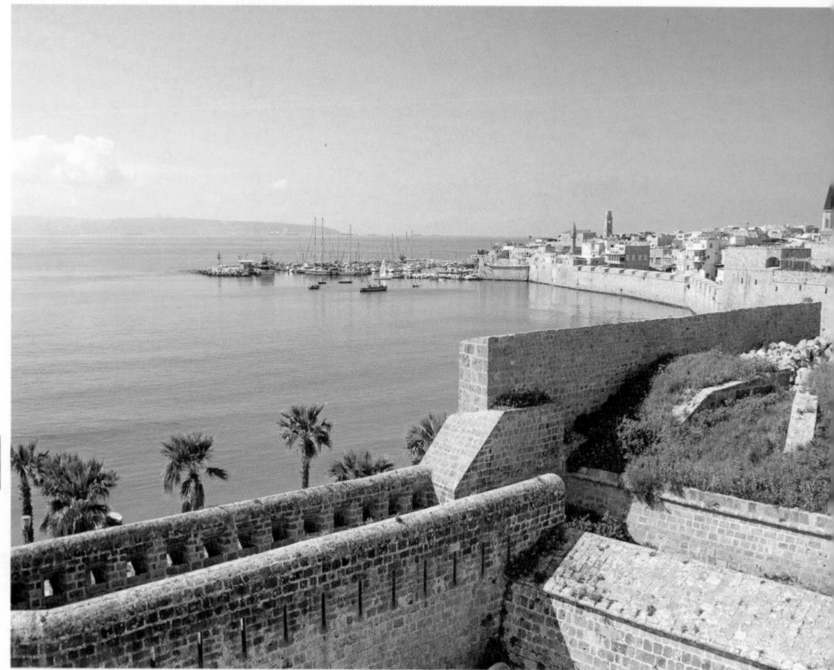

The Old City harbor of Akko.

years. That may be because it's a natural base for touring the northwest quadrant of the country. But we're guessing that many visitors find it difficult to leave Akko itself. With romantic minarets, authentic bazaars, adorable boutique hotels, unusual shops and eateries, and impressive ramparts, Akko (23km/14 miles north of Haifa) has undeniable charm.

It also is loaded with history. Akko has been a port city for more than 4,000 years. It flourished for centuries under the Phoenicians, Romans, and Byzantines and became the capital and last stronghold of the Crusader Kingdom before it finally fell in A.D. 1291. The Crusader city and fortifications lay in ruins until Akko was rebuilt in the late 1700s by the notorious Ottoman governor, Al-Jezzar "the Butcher" Pasha, who constructed a walled city filled with mosques, labyrinthine markets, travelers' inn, bathhouses, and mansions, all on top of the monumental structures of the forgotten Crusader city. Akko is divided into the New City, mainly built after 1948 and home to a mixed Israeli Arab and Jewish population, and the walled **Old City,** which is the main attraction inhabited mostly by Christian and Muslim Israelis.

GETTING THERE **By Tour Bus and Public Transportation:** Both **Egged** (www.eggedtours.com) and **United Bus Tours** (www.unitedtours.co.il) include stops in Caesarea and Akko on tours of the area.

By Railroad and Bus: There is regular train and bus service from Tel Aviv and Haifa to the Akko train and bus stations in the New City of Akko. From there, it's a short taxi ride to the Weizmann Street entrance to Akko's Old City.

By Car: From Haifa, follow signs northward to Akko. The driving distance on the Haifa-Akko road is not long, but heavy traffic can make it an hour trip. Follow signs to Akko, then to Old City. Inside the Weizmann Street entrance to the Old City walls is a pay parking lot.

VISITOR INFORMATION Located just inside the Weitzman Street entrance to the Old City, the excellent **Akko Visitor's Center** (www.akko.org.il; ✆ **04/995-6706;** Mon–Thurs 9am–6pm, Fri 9am–4pm, closed Sun) is the place to buy a combo ticket for Akko's many attractions, or get advice. Their website is also a treasure trove, with a number of free and paid self-guided walking tours of the city. ***Note:*** A combined admission ticket to all major sites and museums is recommended. It costs NIS 49, which is less than you'd pay to enter the attractions most visitors hit here.

Exploring Old Akko

Allow yourself at least a half-day to wander through Old Akko's medieval streets. Unlike the restored Old City of Jaffa, which is filled with tourist galleries, Old Akko is both charming and genuine, and its streets teem with real life. The best place to start your tour is at the **Jezzar Pasha Mosque.** Right across the street from Al-Jezzar Pasha's mosque is the marvelous **Subterranean Crusader City,** and just a few steps farther is the Municipal Museum (exhibits sometimes closed for renovations) housed in Ahmed Al-Jezzar Pasha's **Turkish bath.** Next you'll wander through the pleasant and colorful streets of the **bazaar.** Be sure to see the most picturesque shop in the bazaar, **Kurdy and Berit's Coffee and Spices,** at no. 13/261 (ask around; it's deep in the market). The showcases here are filled with exotic objects and herbal remedies. If you make a purchase at Kurdy and Berit's, the very hospitable owner may invite you to try a cup of thick Arabic coffee. Also look for **Abu Nassar's Oriental Sweets** and **Hummus Said,** both located in the market near the **Khan el Shwardia** and each a legend throughout northern Israel. Akko's "formal" market is **Suq El-Abiad,** but numerous streets within Old Akko serve as shopping areas. You'll pass the **El-Zeituneh Mosque** to the **Khan El-Umdan** caravansary, marked by a tall, segmented tower. A **caravansary,** or khan, was a combination travelers' inn, warehouse, banking center, stable, and factory traditionally built around a lightly fortified courtyard to house caravans, pilgrims, and other visitors.

At the port, you can hire a boat to take you on a **sea tour** of the city walls (about NIS 50–NIS 60 per person, but don't be afraid to bargain). Many boat operators will be glad to take you on a motor- or fishing-boat cruise around Old Akko. Settle on a price in advance (about NIS 150 for an hour is average), and get a boat that looks comfortable.

In Venezia Square (Ha-Dayagim in Hebrew), facing the port, is the **Sinian Pasha Mosque,** and behind it the **Khan El-Faranj** caravansary. Yet another khan, named **El-Shwarda,** is a short distance to the northeast. A few steps back is the Jezzar Pasha Mosque. You'll also want to visit the once-dreaded **Al-Jezzar Wall,** where barbaric punishments were meted out, and the outer wall of the Akko prison, scene of a massive prisoner escape in 1947 (during the British Mandate) engineered by the Jewish underground and dramatized in the film *Exodus.*

Hammam al-Basha (Turkish Bath) ★★ MUSEUM Down at the end of Al-Jezzar Street, just around the corner, these handsome baths were built by Ahmed Al-Jezzar Pasha as part of his mosque complex in the 1780s. Along with an informative interactive show about the baths and their centrality to daily life, the museum's collections include antiquities, an exhibit on Napoleon's attack, the Museum of Heroism, and a folklore exhibit.

Al-Jezzar St. Admission NIS 25 (includes combined ticket to Crusader City). ✆ **04/995-6744.** Sun–Thurs and Sat 9am–6pm; Fri 9am–4pm. Closings are 1 hr. earlier in winter.

Jezzar Pasha Mosque ★ RELIGIOUS SITE Ahmed Al-Jezzar "the Butcher" Pasha was the Ottoman-Turkish governor of Akko during the late 1700s and notorious for his habit of mutilating both those in his government and those he governed. According to legend, on Al-Jezzar Pasha's whim, faithful chamberlains and retainers were ordered to slay their own children as signs of loyalty to him, and the Pasha rewarded government officials and loyal subjects with amputations of hands, arms, eyes, and legs to test their willingness to submit to his desires. If this was how he treated his friends, you can imagine the fate of his enemies. When Napoleon invaded Egypt, the English joined the Ottomans in trying to drive him out. Al-Jezzar Pasha marshaled the defenses of Akko, and the city withstood Napoleon's assault in 1799. Napoleon's forces never recovered, and Napoleon's dream of conquering Egypt died outside the walls of Akko. The Pasha died in Akko in 1804, to everyone's relief.

Ahmed Al-Jezzar Pasha's contributions to Akko included building fountains, a covered market, a Turkish bath, and the harmonious mosque complex that bears his name. Begun in 1781, it's an excellent example of classic Ottoman-Turkish architecture and stands among the Pasha's most ambitious projects. It also illustrates how the traditional mosque complex worked.

As you approach the mosque area, Al-Jezzar Street turns right off Weizmann Street. The mosque entrance is a few steps along Al-Jezzar Street on the left. Before you mount the stairs to the mosque courtyard, notice the ornate little building to the right of the stairs. It's a *sabil,* or cold-drinks stand, from which pure, refreshing drinking water, sometimes mixed with fruit syrups, was distributed—a part of the mosque complex's services. Note especially the fine tile fragments mounted above the little grilled windows just beneath the *sabil*'s dome. Tile-making was an Ottoman specialty.

The ornate interior of the Jezzar Pasha Mosque is open to all visitors, except during prayers.

Up the stairs, you enter the mosque courtyard. Your ticket will enable you to explore the complex of Crusader buildings, including a church (now flooded and used as cisterns) over which the mosque was built. Just inside the entry is a marble disc bearing the *tughra,* or monogram, of the Ottoman sultan. It spells out the sultan's name, his father's name, and the legend "ever-victorious."

The arcaded courtyard around the mosque can be used for prayers during hot days of summer, as can the arcaded porch at the front of the mosque. The *shadirvan,* or ablutions fountain, opposite the mosque entry is used for ritual cleansing five times a day before prayers. You must slip off your shoes before entering the mosque proper.

Inside you'll notice the *mihrab,* or prayer niche, indicating the direction of Mecca, toward which worshipers must face when they pray. The galleries to the right and left of the entrance are reserved for women, the main area of the floor for men. The *minbar,* a sort of pulpit, is that separate structure with a curtained entry, stairs, and a little steeple. Around to the right are a mausoleum and a small graveyard that hold the tombs of Ahmed Al-Jezzar Pasha and his successor, Suleiman Pasha, and members of their families. The mosque is still used by Akko's Muslim population, so when it's in service for prayer, you must wait until the prayers are over to enter the mosque.

Al-Jezzar St. NIS 10. Open daily 8am–11am, 11:45am–3pm, 3:30–6pm.

Museum of Underground Prisoners ★★ This complex of buildings in the Citadel of Akko was used as a prison in Ottoman and British Mandate times. Part of the prison has been set aside in honor of the Jewish underground fighters imprisoned here by the British. With the help of Irgun forces, 251 prisoners staged a mass escape in May 1947. If you saw the movie *Exodus,* that was the breakout featured in the film and this was the prison. The prison is also revered by Arab Israelis and by Palestinians, whose own national fighters were detained and in many cases executed here during the British Mandate.

Among the exhibits are the entrance to the escape tunnel and displays of materials showing the British repression of Zionist activity during the Mandate. Not all prisoners were lucky enough to escape, however. Eight Irgun fighters were hanged here in the 10 years before Israel's independence. You can visit the death chamber, called the Hanging Room, complete with noose.

Inmates here included Zeev Jabotinsky and Dov Gruner, among other leaders of Israel's independence movement. Before the Mandate, the prison's most famous inmate was Bahá'u'lláh (1817–92), founder of the Bahá'i faith (see "Bahjí," below).

Just north of Crusader City. ✆ **04/991-1375.** Admission NIS 20 adults, discounts available for students and children. Sun–Thurs 9am–4:30pm.

Subterranean Crusader City (Hospitallers' Fortress) ★★★ Virtually across the street from the Mosque of Ahmed Al-Jezzar Pasha is this Subterranean Crusader City, the town's unmissable site. In the entrance is a tourism information kiosk, where you can buy a city map and an entrance ticket.

For a look at the life and times of the Crusaders in the 11th century, there's no better site in Israel than the Hospitallers' Fortress.

The Crusaders built their fortified city atop what was left of the Roman city. The Ottomans, and especially Ahmed Al-Jezzar Pasha, built their city on top of the largely intact buildings of the Crusaders. In Ottoman times, the cavernous chambers here were used as a caravansary until Napoleon's attack. In preparation for the defense of his city, Al-Jezzar Pasha ordered the walls heightened, and the Crusader rooms partially filled with sand and dirt, to better support the walls. Today, you get a good look at how the Crusaders lived and worked in the late 1100s, from the ruined Gothic church to the dungeons and massive gathering halls. A highlight is the **Knights' Halls,** once occupied by the Knights Hospitalers of Saint John. In the ceiling of the hall, a patch of concrete marks the spot where Jewish underground members, imprisoned by the British in the citadel (directly above the hall), attempted to break out. Be sure to pick up a headset at the entrance so you understand the significance of what you're seeing.

Across from Jezzar Pasha Mosque. www.akko.org.il/en/attraction/the-knights-halls. Admission NIS 40 adults, discounts for students and children; admission includes entrance to Municipal Museum. Sun–Thurs 8:30am–6pm; Fri 8:30am–5pm; Sat 9am–5pm. Closings are 1 hr. earlier in winter.

Treasures in the Walls Ethnographic Museum ★★ MUSEUM

As you might have guessed from the name, this atmospheric museum is located right in the city walls, in an ancient tunnel. This placement gives the exhibits—all of which explore daily life from the Ottoman period through the founding of Israel—added weight, though even if they were to be housed in a warehouse, the reproduction of a 19th-century market (the museum's showpiece) would be fascinating. A second section of the museum displays exquisite antique furniture (including pieces inlaid with mother-of-pearl in the old Damascus tradition) and decorative items.

In the eastern wall of the Old City (left turn inside the wall at Weitzman St. entrance). ✆ **04/991-1004.** Admission NIS 10 per person, can also be part of a combined ticket for all museums in the vicinity. Sat–Thurs 10am–5pm; Fri 10am–3:30pm; curtailed hours in winter.

AL-JEZZAR'S WALL ★

To appreciate the elaborate system of defenses built by Ahmed Al-Jezzar Pasha to protect against Napoleon's fleet and forces, turn right as you come out of the Municipal Museum/Museum of Heroism onto Ha-Hagana Street and walk a few steps north. You'll see the double system of walls with a moat in between. Jutting into the sea is an Ottoman defensive tower called the Burj El-Kuraim. You're now standing at the northwestern corner of the walled city. Walk east (inland) along the walls, and you'll pass the citadel, the Burj El-Hazineh (Treasury Tower), and cross Weizmann Street to the Burj El-Komander, the strongest point in the walls. The land-wall system continues south from here all the way to the beach.

BAHJÍ ★★

To Bahá'is, this shrine to their prophet Bahá'u'lláh is the holiest place on earth. Bahá'i followers believe that God is manifested to men and women through prophets such as Abraham, Moses, Jesus, and Muhammad, as well as the Bab (Bahá'u'lláh's predecessor) and Bahá'u'lláh himself. The Bahá'i faith proclaims that all religions are one, that men and women are equal, that the world should be at peace, and that education should be universal. Bahá'i followers are encouraged to live simply and to dedicate themselves to helping their fellow men and women. They look forward to a day when there will be a single world government and one world language.

The Bahá'i faith grew out of the revelation of the Bab, a Persian Shiite Muslim teacher and mystic who flourished from 1844 to 1850 and was executed by the Persian shah for insurrection and radical teachings. In 1863, Mirza Husein Ali Nuri, one of the Bab's disciples, proclaimed himself Bahá'u'lláh, the Promised One, whose coming had been foretold by the Bab. Bahá'u'lláh was exiled by the Persian government to Baghdad, Constantinople, Adrianople, and finally to Akko, where he arrived in August 1868. He and several of his followers were imprisoned for 2½ years at the Akko Citadel. The authorities later put him under house arrest, and he was eventually brought to Bahjí, where he remained until his death in 1892. He is buried here in a peaceful tomb surrounded by magnificent gardens. Bahá'is are still persecuted, especially in Iran where the faith was born; the Shiite Muslims in authority today look upon them as blasphemers and heretics.

You can visit the shrine at **Bahjí (Delight),** where Bahá'u'lláh lived, died, and is buried, on Friday, Saturday, and Sunday only, from 9am to noon. The house's beautiful gardens are open to visitors every day, from 9am to 4pm. Catch the 271 bus heading north toward Nahariya, and make sure it stops at Bahjí.

Going north from Akko, you'll see an impressive gilded gate on the right-hand side of the road after about 2km (1¼ mile). This gate is not open to the public. Go past it until you are almost 3km (about 1¾ miles) from Akko, and

For those who follow the Bahá'i religion, this geometrically landscaped shrine is the holiest place on the planet.

you'll see a sign, SHAMERAT. Get off the bus, turn right here, and go another short distance to the visitors' gate. The Ottoman-Victorian house holds some memorabilia of Bahá'u'lláh, and the lush gardens are a real treat.

Where to Stay

Akkotel ★★ This warmly welcoming boutique hotel, run by the very helpful Morani family, is set in a lovingly restored building right inside the walls of the Old City. Everything is comfy and feels like an old inn. Larger rooms (some with sleeping lofts) can fit families; bathrooms have either a tub or a shower. The breakfast is generous and the coffee is strong. What more could you ask—a rooftop cafe, perhaps? They have that, too.

1 Saladin St., Akko. Near Weitzman St. entrance to Old City. www.akkotel.com. ✆ **04/987-7100.** 16 units. From $200 double. Rate includes breakfast. Free limited parking. **Amenities:** Restaurant; free Wi-Fi.

Ana Acre Hostel ★ Also called the Akko Knights Hostel, this efficient and spotlessly clean Israel Youth Hostel Association hostel is housed in a building that blends in with Old City architecture. It's located just inside the main entrance to the walled Old City. The hostel is heavily booked by international groups or Israeli students; however, double or family rooms can be arranged. Meals are kosher.

Weitzman St., Old Akko www.iyha.org.il/akko-hostel. ✆ **02/594-5711** (for English press 2). 76 units. NIS 350–NIS 400 double room, less for dorm beds. Parking nearby (fee). **Amenities:** Free Wi-Fi.

Beit Elfarasha ★★★ Beit Elfarasha is far more than just a hotel. "We believe that by bringing people together, and encouraging small, intimate interactions, we can drive a much broader change and encourage friendships and respect between the local residents of the Old City and our guests," owner Nura Kurdi writes on the website. Towards that goal, she built a state-of-the-art kitchen for workshops led by local cooks, and regularly sponsors cultural programs in the inn's large living room. These are open to all comers, though staying in this evocative, newly renovated Ottoman building (opened in December of 2020), is a special experience. The 200-year-old house (with a few elements dating back to the Crusader era), is situated in a picturesque alley in the heart of the Old City of Akko, overlooking the sea. Guest suites are prettily colorful, and all have fold-out sofas as well as beds, plus such niceties as TVs that can stream Netflix, beamed ceilings, fine bath products, and access to the handsome rooftop terrace.

49 HaBahaim St., Old City. beitelfarasha.com. ✆ **04/625-5551,** 052/609-2996. 2 suites (accommodating up to 3 people each); NIS 684–NIS 850. **Amenities:** Culinary and cultural workshops; free Wi-Fi.

Efendi Hotel ★★★ Few other hotels in Israel match the grace and beauty of this meticulously restored, luxury boutique hotel, set in a pair of conjoined, majestic Ottoman-era mansions on a byway deep in the Old City. Opened in 2012 by the owner of Akko's gourmet **Uri Buri** restaurant (see below), it's a true standard setter. Many of the 12 rooms are palatial in size, some with traditional hand-painted, Ottoman-style ceilings; exquisite wooden latticework; and massive windows with exquisite views. Massages can be had in the 400-year-old on-site hammam, though some find lazing on the rooftop deck with its tremendous sea views to be relaxation enough. Arriving guests can phone from the Uri Buri restaurant and

Baths are an elegant affair at the Efendi Hotel.

arrange for directions and a baggage porter, because the hotel is not car accessible. Breakfast (included) is a gourmet affair not to be missed, and is served under an ancient high-ceilinged room around a long wooden table fit for King Arthur.

Louis IX St. www.efendi-hotel.com. ✆ **074/729-9799.** 12 units. $349–$670. Rates include breakfast. **Amenities:** Rooftop bar and terrace; Turkish bath; wine bar; free Wi-Fi.

Where to Eat

El Marsa ★★★ SEAFOOD One of the top culinary spots in Akko, located in the historic port, El Marsa's atmosphere is a unique blend of contemporary cuisine and ancient architecture. The restaurant is housed in a converted 13th-century home and its Arabic dishes have both Eastern and Western influences, with dazzling with fresh-from-the-water seafood caught right in the port. Try the *siniya* fish baked in lemon and tahini with baked cauliflower florets and caramelized onion over *mujaddara.*

13 Namal HaDayagim. ✆ **04/901-9281.** @elmarsa_akko. Mains NIS 50 up to NIS 225 for an extravagant seafood platter. Open daily noon–11pm.

Hummus Said ★★★ MIDDLE EASTERN It's a strong claim, but the devotees of this 45-plus-year-old restaurant claim it serves the best hummus in the Middle East. Clearly the folks who line up outside the door every day agree, and I think you will too after you taste the tangy, creamy hummus that's hand-mashed here and seasoned with just the right amount of cumin. The other specialty here is *makhlouta,* a Lebanese stew made with caramelized onions, lentils, chickpeas, rice, cracked and whole wheat, and pinto beans, and it, too, is scrumptious.

In the middle of the Old City market—ask any local for directions. ✆ **04/991-3945.** Meals with salad and tea, NIS 18. Hours vary, but typically 5am serving until 2:30pm.

Sama ★★★ ARABIC-SEAFOOD This inviting and trendy rooftop bar-restaurant recently opened to much acclaim. Its expansive views of Akko are as impressive as its food. Start off with a colorful mezze platter of salads, including a varied range of starters to share. Fresh herbs and produce straight from Akko's Old City Market are chopped, diced, cured, and blended to surprise your tastebuds. Then go for any of the just-caught fish or seafood options—in the hands of star chef Hammoodi Okla, they are all expertly flavored and plated.

14 Salah a Din. www.samabar.co.il. ✆ **04/652-7739.** Mains NIS 50–NIS 160. Open Mon–Fri 6–11pm.

Uri Buri ★★★ SEAFOOD This gourmet but relaxed restaurant's secret ingredient is owner/chef Uri Jeremias, who knows how to prepare seafood and fish to perfection. Uri's coquilles St. Jacques, pan-seared according to his special recipe, are like the filet mignon of the sea; his delicate carpaccios are exquisite; and the restaurant's tiny, tender calamari with kumquats and pink grapefruit are without peer. All of this extraordinary food is served in a handsome (and ancient) Turkish home, by an uncommonly affable staff that knows how to make a meal feel like a special occasion. Our advice: If you go as a couple, share one tasting menu, and order another main course, just so nobody goes away hungry.

93 Haganah St., near the lighthouse (on the promenade facing the sea) in the Old City. ✆ **04/955-2212.** Reservations necessary. Main courses NIS 92–NIS 142; tasting menu is NIS 250 per person. Daily noon–11pm.

EILAT & PETRA

By Karen Chernick

At the southern tip of Israel, a 4-hour drive through the Negev from Tel Aviv or Jerusalem, the **Red Sea resort town of Eilat** is a world apart from the rest of the country. It's a place where Israelis and tourists love to unwind and relax. There's no ancient history to absorb, just easily accessible coral reefs to snorkel and plenty of beaches. Even in winter, when Jerusalem can be cold and raw and Tel Aviv can be chilly, Eilat's beaches are usually warm enough for sunbathing and at least a quick swim in the Red Sea. It is packed with hotels at every price point, and although most are not directly on the town's beachfronts, they have large swimming pools, many heated in the winter. Summers in Eilat are blazing hot and usually filled with vacationing Israeli families.

Eilat is also the closest and most convenient border crossing into Jordan if you plan to visit **Petra**—unlike the busy Allenby Bridge Crossing from the West Bank into Jordan (where you must have a visa issued at a Jordanian embassy ahead of time), visas are issued on the spot at the Eilat/Aqaba Crossing, and there are far fewer crowds and processing delays.

Petra (in Jordan), the legendary and extraordinary long-lost ancient city carved from the walls of a hidden canyon, has become a must-see destination for thousands of world travelers. Although 1-day package bus tours from Eilat can give you a 2-hour glimpse of Petra, this amazing site and the dramatic landscape of southern Jordan are well worth several days of your attention.

EILAT ★★★

Eilat's chief claims to fame for the tourist are sandy white beaches kissing calm blue waters, coral reefs filled with prismatic fish, and guaranteed sunshine (no matter when you go). What was once a small, relaxed desert and Red Sea resort town now hosts 50 gargantuan upscale hotels, vast shopping malls, and a boardwalk lined with jewelry shops, sneaker stores, and hawker booths where visitors are exposed to local arts and crafts while enjoying their evenings. (There's no sales tax on retail purchased in Eilat, making it

An aerial view of some of Eilat's resorts and waterfront.

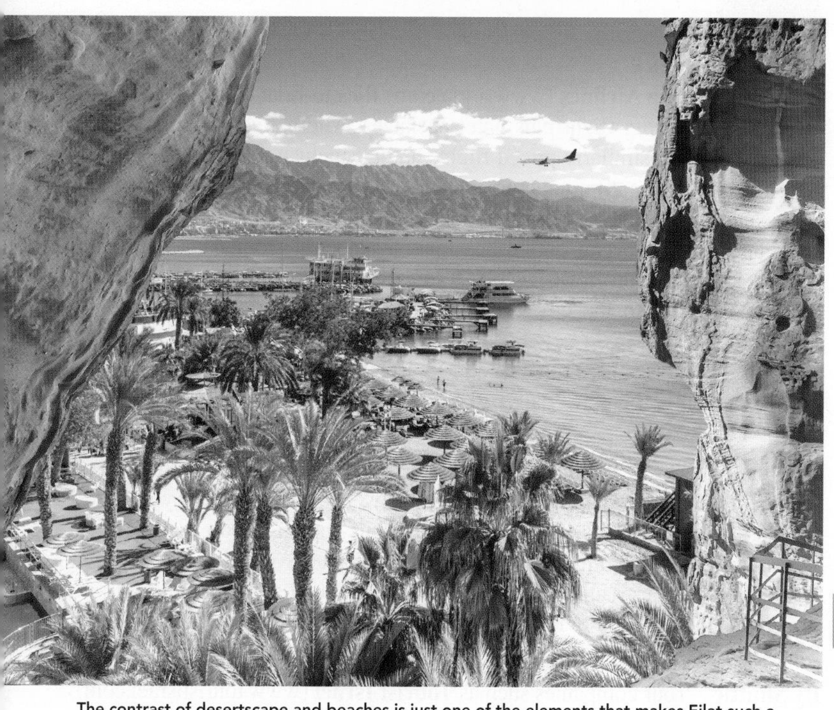

The contrast of desertscape and beaches is just one of the elements that makes Eilat such a unique resort town.

a shopping destination for many.) It's easygoing and fun, and Israelis flock here to forget the pressures of daily life. A number of European tourists jet directly into Eilat (and see nothing else in Israel). Eilat's planners have not emphasized the desert and Bedouin traditions of the region—instead they've aimed for the generic look of a gleaming white international resort, such as Cancún. During Israeli school holidays, Eilat is usually overrun with families and kids.

Eilat is also a military outpost and a major shipping port—you'll see ample evidence of this all along the shoreline. The city's hotel area is less than a mile from the Jordanian border, and you can see the Jordanian port city of Aqaba, with a population of 30,000, across the bay in a haze of desert sand ringed by date palms. Until Israel and Jordan signed a peace treaty in 1994, Aqaba seemed as unattainable as a mirage. There is now a border crossing for tourists just north of Eilat, and from Eilat you can also book excursions to Jordan's fabulous lost canyon city of Petra. Saudi Arabia is 20km (12 miles) south of Aqaba—you can see it from the beaches in Eilat.

During summer, the outdoor afternoon heat in Eilat can exceed 110°F (43°C); it's best to stay in the shade between noon and 4pm. In winter, the weather can be cool to chilly and dry, but the Red Sea is warm enough for swimming, especially if you're used to the waters of the North Atlantic. Pools in better hotels are often heated.

Essentials

GETTING THERE

By Plane **Arkia Airlines** (www.arkia.com) flies to Eilat from Tel Aviv and offers money-saving flight plus hotel packages. Alternatively, **Israir** (www.israir.co.il) offers similarly priced flights and all-inclusive packages. **Ramon Airport** is located a 20-minute drive north of Eilat. One-way flights from Tel Aviv can be as inexpensive as $50, making them a comfortable option within budgetary reach. Several public bus lines leave right from outside Ramon Airport and head into town every 15 minutes; 5 NIS per ride. Taxis from Ramon Airport into the city center cost roughly 85 NIS (before luggage surcharges).

All the local city buses run every 20 to 30 minutes or so, from early morning until about 7 or 8pm, daily except Saturday, stopping early on Friday (about 3 or 4pm).

By Bus There are a number of daily buses (except on Shabbat) from Jerusalem and Tel Aviv to Eilat. The trip takes between 5 to 6 hours. If you arrive by bus, there's a baggage checkroom at the bus station in case you have to seek out a hotel room. It is best not to carry luggage even short distances in Eilat's hot weather. Unlike other bus tickets in Israel, seats on buses from Jerusalem and Tel Aviv to Eilat should be reserved in advance through Egged Buses (www.egged.co.il).

By Shuttle Tour companies such as **Tourist Israel** (www.touristisrael.com) offer daily shared shuttle rides between Tel Aviv and Eilat, with prices starting at $40.

By Car The trip takes approximately 4 hours by direct road from Tel Aviv or Jerusalem. A fun place to pull over for a rest stop is the restaurant at **Neot Semadar** (www.neot-semadar.com), an eco-friendly kibbutz known for its organic juices and other nibbles. Neot Semadar is a little less than an hour from Eilat.

VISITOR INFORMATION

The **Eilat Tourist Information Center** (www.eilat.city/en) is located in a small building called **Bridge House (Beit HaGesher)** on the North Beach Promenade. It's open Sunday to Thursday 8am to 4:30pm, Friday and Jewish holiday eves 8am to 1pm. Pick up English-language maps and free copies of other tourist brochures filled with discount coupons. You can also get help and

Getting to Jordan

Bus and taxi service are now available from Eilat to Aqaba, Jordan border crossing. Once on the Jordanian side of the border, or in Aqaba itself, you can arrange for a private or shared taxi for the 2-hour drive to Petra. The cost can range between $70 and $120 for a shared taxi, depending on your bargaining skills.

advice on booking accommodations and tours, bus schedules, events in the region, diving and snorkeling information, and travel to Jordan.

Tip: Eilat has no VAT, so gasoline for your car will be 18% cheaper there than in the rest of Israel. Be sure to fill up before heading back north.

ORIENTATION

There are three easily distinguishable areas in Eilat. First is the inland, amorphous town itself, built atop hills that roll toward the sea. **Coral Beach,** with its great snorkeling and smattering of hotels, is about 6km (3¾ miles) south of town on the western shore of the harbor, served by bus 15. The **North Beach** district, a 10-minute walk from the center of town on the eastern shore of the harbor, is where most of the hotels are clustered. It is also the site of an elaborate marina system and artificial lagoon, cutting several hundred yards inland. Around this lagoon are hotels, restaurants, and a promenade filled with pubs, discos, shops, and miles of street vendors—a fun way to spend a hot summer evening.

Sports & Outdoor Activities

BEACHES The waters around Eilat are relatively wave-free and safe. The small sharks are not particularly hungry for you; however, stepping on spiny sea urchins can be a major danger.

North Beach ★ is a stony and sandy beach that starts in front of the Leonardo Eilat Hotel and extends to the Dan Eilat Hotel and Herods Palace Hotel complex. Because it's relatively free of coral and sea urchins, this is a good beach for swimming. The nicer part of the beach is at the end near the Dan and Herods Palace hotels. Water skis and boats can be rented, but make sure you know where you're going, because you don't have to ski very far to get into Jordanian or Egyptian territory and hot water.

Mosh Beach ★★ is named for dreadlocked Israeli musician Mosh Ben Ari, who opened this laid-back beachy oasis. Amenities include huts with palm-frond roofs, hammocks, and a shoreside restaurant serving mostly vegetarian food. Mosh Beach is a short drive or bus ride from North Beach, towards the Egyptian border, and if you can't find a wicker sofa available there then go next door to **Dekel Beach.**

Coral Beach ★★, which is a short drive or a no. 15 bus ride around the curve of the bay, is the best beach for **snorkeling** and **diving.** It's blessed with coral reefs just offshore and lots of fish. Snorkeling equipment can be rented. Much of Coral Beach is now a nature preserve, perfect for both first-time and intermediate snorkeling and scuba diving. The best snorkeling is inside the actual **Coral Beach Nature Reserve** (see below).

Dolphin Reef ★★★ is certainly the prettiest beach in Eilat, dotted with palm trees and thatched-roof *palapa* structures for shade. The dolphins, though, are the main attraction. The reef's institute believes in informal, personal contact between humans and dolphins. The dolphins are free to come and go to the open sea as they like, but for years have chosen to attach themselves to Dolphin Reef. As you swim and sun, you can watch them frolicking

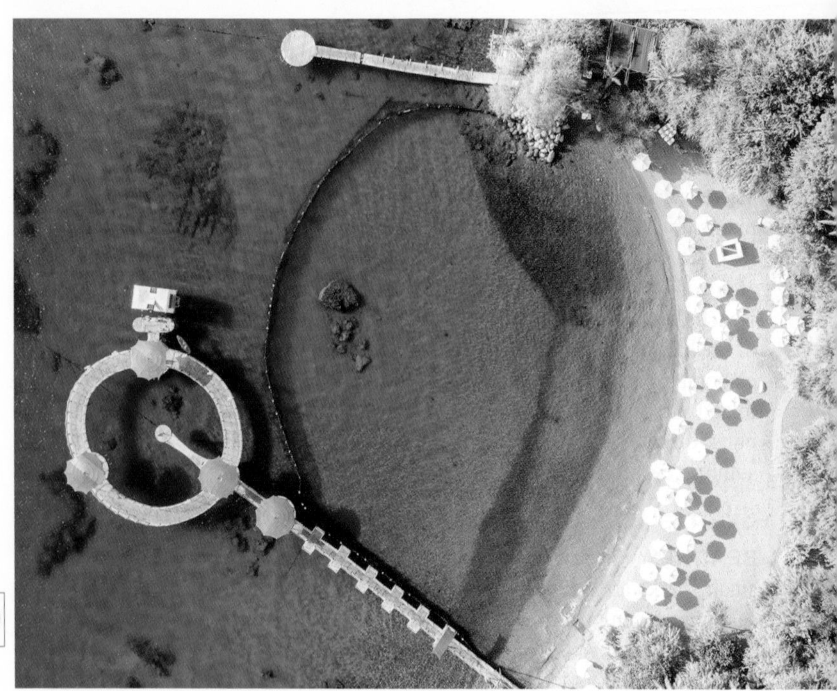

The circular sea pen known as Dolphin Reef.

and being fed just beyond the roped-off human swimming zone; you can also walk out to a wooden observation pier in the dolphins' free-swimming area for a closer look. For NIS 360 per adult above the age of 15 (NIS 330 per child above the age of 8), you can join a guided group of snorkelers for a 30-minute **swim among the dolphins.** (Advance reservations are necessary.) Snorkeling equipment is included in the fee. For qualified divers, guided dives can also be arranged. Sometimes, these swims can bring close encounters, while at other times, the free-swimming dolphins keep their distance. You must be a confident swimmer, and there are no guarantees, refunds, or rain checks. Or you can sit right on a raft while dolphins come up to the trainers for snacks and play sessions. Dolphin Reef also hosts supportive experiences with the dolphins, geared towards children with emotional challenges.

Also offered at the Dolphin Reef are **Relaxation Pools**—one is fresh water, one Red Sea water, and one heavy mineral water not unlike the Dead Sea. Individual or group sessions are available, can last 2 hours, and include New Age music, refreshments, and a botanical habitat for resting. The price is NIS 320 for the one-on-one flotation experience, and otherwise NIS 170 per person and reservations are necessary. General admission to Dolphin Reef is waived for those entering with reservations for snorkeling and diving with dolphins and for the Relaxation Pools.

The International Birding and Research Center offers excellent, and sometimes interactive, tours of its sanctuary.

There is a reasonably priced cafeteria serving hot and cold drinks, snacks, and full meals on the premises, as well as a pub and a program of films on dolphins. Once a month there is live music and dancing at the beach's pub. This is one of the best places in Eilat to spend a day or an evening.

Dolphin Reef is midway between North Beach and Coral Beach (www.dolphinreef.co.il; ✆ **08/630-0111** for activity reservations). It's open Monday to Saturday from 9am to 5pm. Admission is NIS 69 for adults over 15 and NIS 48 for children 3 to 15. Take bus no. 15.

BIRD-WATCHING Eilat is one of the best places on earth for bird-watching, due to its prime location on the Jordan Valley–Red Sea–Great African Rift Valley migration path between Europe and Africa. Migration times are twice a year: From **September through November,** the birds head south to Africa, and from **March through May,** they head back north to Europe.

Eilat's **International Birding and Research Centre** (www.eilatbirds.com/en) is a clearinghouse for information and activities. Entrance to the bird sanctuary is free, but should be coordinated in advance by phone or email. The center also offers guided bird-watching tours for NIS 750 per group of 50, or extended tours that include flamingo pools for NIS 950. Two-hour seminars cost NIS 1,200 per group.

Each year in March, the Center participates in the **Eilat Birds Festival** that has been growing in reputation. Check www.birds.org.il/en for information about the many special programs and discounts on accommodations and car rentals at the time of the festival.

BOATING You can hire boats at all hours of the day at the North Beach marina and lagoon—boats for water-skiing and water parachuting, sailboats, fishing boats, paddleboats, motor sea-cycles, sailboards, and kayaks are all available. GetMyBoat.com is a good resource for larger rentals, with crew or without.

GLASS-BOTTOM BOATS Boats leave from the jetty just north of Coral Beach or from North Beach. **Israel Yam** (www.israel-yam.co.il; ✆ **08/633-2325**) operates daily 1½-hour glass-bottom boat trips, leaving North Beach several times during the day for NIS 70 for adults and NIS 50 for children. Look for a 15% discount coupon, often available in the free Hebrew- and English-language tourist brochures. **Galaxia** (www.galaxy-eilat.co.il; ✆ **050/972-7755**) offers similar glass-bottom tours (every day but Sat) for NIS 60 for adults and NIS 50 for children.

SNORKELING & SCUBA DIVING *Note:* If you want to scuba dive, you must bring your certification from abroad or obtain a license in Israel.

There are 30 different dive spots near Eilat, including a few that encompass shipwrecks.

The best-equipped firms for snorkeling and scuba diving are Aqua-Sport and Red Sea Sports Club. **Aqua-Sport** (www.aqua-sport.com; ✆ **08/633-4404**) is located across the highway from the Isrotel Yam Suf Hotel on Coral Beach. Aqua-Sport also has a program of weeklong adult diving lessons and summer camps for kids ages 10 to 15 during July and August. Aqua-Sport is open daily from 8:30am to 5:30pm.

Red Sea Sport Club's Manta Dive Center, located at the Isrotel Yam Suf Hotel (www.divemanta.com), is another recommended diving center at Coral Beach. It offers facilities similar to those at Aqua-Sport, plus diving courses for divers of all levels. There is even a special sauna facility for divers. It's open daily from 8:30am to 5pm in winter and until 6pm in summer.

Snuba diving, tethered to an oxygen tank on a raft over the coral reef, is an easy, enjoyable way to dive without any extensive training. The **Snuba Diving Center** (www.snuba.co.il; ✆ **08/637-2722**) will arrange a variety of excursions for you. Prices start at NIS 200 for 1½ hours and include training. Look for a discount coupon on the Snuba website.

Sightseeing

Coral Beach Nature Reserve ★★ NATURE RESERVE A small but fascinating chunk of the Red Sea's reef system, teeming with colorful, exotic fish and sea creatures, this nature reserve is a swimmable treasure. Because the wind and current usually move southward, all you have to do is drift and paddle a bit to observe the reef through your mask. At the southern end of the reef, you can head for shore and walk back to the starting point for another round of drifting over the reef!

On site are comfortable changing rooms with showers, and an open-air snack bar (buy an illustrated guide to the swimming trails there). The reserve also rents snorkels, masks, and fins; there is a refundable deposit of NIS 100 for each snorkel set.

Warning: Wear some sort of foot covering every time you enter the water here. Spiny sea urchins lurk almost everywhere you might want to stand.

Bus no. 15 runs from downtown Eilat to Coral Beach and back every half-hour. www.parks.org.il. ✆ **08/632-6422.** Admission NIS 35 adults, NIS 22 children. Mask, snorkel, and fins rental NIS 40. Daily 9am–6pm (except Fri, when it closes at 5pm). Closed Yom Kippur. Bus: 15.

Coral World Underwater Observatory and Marine Park ★★★ AQUARIUM Located just south of Coral Beach, this complex includes two underwater observatories beside a busy, picturesque reef called the Japanese Gardens. In addition to the underwater observatories, you'll also find the **Maritime Museum and Aquarium.** The aquarium is built so that you stand in the middle and the fish swim around you in a huge circular tank. There are also large outdoor observation pools—one for big sharks and another for sea turtles and rays. For an additional NIS 10, you can visit the Aqua Dome, a high-tech simulated "dive" in a small theater that offers the sights and feel of going underwater. Glass-bottom boat cruises are NIS 35. ***Tip:*** Try to plan your visit around the shark and other sea creature feeding times, posted on the observatory's website.

Off Derech Mitzraim. www.coralworld.co.il. ✆ **08/636-4200.** Admission NIS 105 adults, NIS 85 children 3–18. Daily from 9am–4pm. Bus: 15.

Where to Stay

Eilat has an oversupply of comfy, but predictable modern hotels in various price ranges. Most are not directly on Eilat's beachfront, but are short walks to the sea. During holiday periods, Eilat hotels can be mobbed and overpriced, but at other times, at least some of the city's hotels offer great deals online. A lot of Eilat's hotels are all-inclusive, with one to two meals included in the nightly rate.

EXPENSIVE

Dan Eilat Hotel ★★ This is the most unusual of Eilat's top-rank hotels. Along with its neighbor, the Herod's Palace, it's on the nicest stretch of beach on the North Beach waterfront and offers a wide variety of rooms and suites, some with spacious terraces and fabulous Red Sea panoramas. Interior design by Adam Tihany is not the usual five-star hotel generic, but instead plays with lively interpretations of 1940s, '50s, and '60s decor. Food services are strong, and the dinner buffet is the best of any hotel in town. The pools are large and

The Dan Eilat Hotel has a lovely stretch of beach, along with several swimming pools.

face the Red Sea, with the larger (and more kid-friendly) one outfitted with a long waterslide and whirlpool.

North Beach, Eilat. www.danhotels.com. ✆ **08/636-2222.** 378 units. $233–$650 double; surcharge for pool/sea view. Rates include breakfast, and some also include dinner. Parking (fee). **Amenities:** 5 restaurants; cafe; nightclub; children's programs; concierge; fitness center; heated pool and children's pool; spa; squash courts; synagogue; free Wi-Fi.

MODERATE

Orchid Hotel Eilat ★★ Set off Route 90 overlooking the Red Sea, the hotel is just a minute's walk from Coral Beach and a 3-minute walk from Underwater Observatory Marine Park. Rooms have a distinct Thai influence to the decor with lots of slatted wood, and woven grass elements. The resort also offers a slew of cushy villas with private pools and panoramic sundecks. All feature free Wi-Fi, minifridges, and room service. Most have balconies providing direct sea views. Breakfast, parking, and bike rental are all free. A restaurant serves international fare. There's a snack bar by the outdoor pool, and a lobby bar.

Almog Beach, Eilat. orchidhotels.co.il. ✆ **08/636-0360.** 184 units. $150–$255 for 2. Rates include breakfast. Free parking. **Amenities:** Free loaner bikes; gym; spa; pool; arcade/game room; bar/lounge; room service; free airport transportation; free Wi-Fi.

INEXPENSIVE

Abraham Eilat ★ Part of the well-loved chain of Abraham hostels, this clean and friendly budget spot is a good fit for families looking for simple private rooms and kitchen access, or young travelers trying to spend less by sleeping in a dorm-style room. The location isn't shoreside and it's a 15-minute walk to the beach, but what it lacks in Red Sea views it makes up for with complimentary breakfast, a pool, and its own set of guided experiences: sailing in the Red Sea, a jeep tour in the Eilat mountains, or a pub crawl.

3 Shfifon St., Eilat. www.abraham.travel/eilat. 450 beds. From $35 for a bed in a dorm-style room to $125 for a private room with balcony. Prices higher Jewish and Christian holidays. **Amenities:** Pool; free lockers and luggage room; communal kitchen; free Wi-Fi.

The groovy lobby sets the tone at the Abraham Eilat hostel.

Where to Eat

INLAND, NORTH OF HATMARIM BOULEVARD

These choices are away from the almost wall-to-wall restaurants and fast-food places in North Beach, but it's worth the effort to get to them.

MODERATE

The Brewery (Hamivshala) ★★ GASTROPUB If it weren't for Hamivshala's somewhat odd location in an industrial area far from the water, this charming microbrewery would be one of the busiest eateries in Eilat. As you'd expect from a place that brews its own ales, the on tap selection is excellent, and flights sampling their darkest to lightest are available. The menu is a compilation of bar food's greatest hits—mozzarella sticks, sliders, steaks—but they do also cater to vegans, with an excellent cashew labneh and a few other choices.

2 HaOrgim Street, Industrial Zone. www.hamivshala.co.il. ✆ **08/935-0550.** Main courses NIS 70–NIS 150. Daily noon–1am.

The Last Resort ★★ SEAFOOD With its beachfront perch on Coral Beach and slightly over-the-top nautical decor (expect life rafts, wooden helms, and rope), The Last Resort, of course, specializes in fresh fish and seafood. But this veteran restaurant, in business for over 30 years, is not the usual tourist trap catering only to tourists. You'll find plenty of locals at the tables nearby. Order whatever is fresh or on special, and ask for a table by the window for beachy views.

Coral Beach. www.hamiflat-eilat.co.il. ✆ **08/637-2437.** Main courses NIS 48–NIS 150. Daily from 12:30–11pm.

PETRA ★★★

Petra, the legendary lost city carved into the walls of a hidden desert canyon, is the most famous of Jordan's many dazzling sites. This fascinating excursion is best reached from Israel via the Eilat-Aqaba border crossing. There are escorted bus tours that leave Eilat early in the morning, get you to Petra before noon, give you an hour to look around, and have you back at your hotel in Eilat by late afternoon. But for such a short tour, you might do better just watching a video. Petra is one of the wonders of the ancient world, and its antiquities, natural beauty, and ever-changing feel at different times of day are easily worth a stay of 1 to 3 nights or more. In addition, there are beautiful, affordable desert resorts only a few minutes from Petra, which make this a good place to relax and get away from it all.

Essentials

A 2- to 2½-hour drive north of Aqaba, Petra is the jewel in the crown of Jordan's attractions and the main draw for many travelers to the country. The canyon city of Petra is vast, mysterious, and really demands a 1- or 2-night stay and 2 full days of exploring to get a feel for the atmosphere, to say nothing of the contents of the ruins. You could easily spend 3 or 4 very full days exploring Petra and the surrounding countryside.

GETTING THERE

After crossing from Eilat into Aqaba, it's easy to find taxis at the Jordanian side of the border crossing that will take you up to Petra. Some bargaining is required, but the general fare is around JD 55. This is the fastest, safest, and most direct way to make the journey. Splitting a taxi to Petra (or to Wadi Musa, the town at the entrance to Petra National Park) with others you may meet at the border can make the fare per person very reasonable. A taxi to the Aqaba Bus Station, plus bus fare up to Petra, will be less than JD 8, but there are few buses per day and it's hard to find a schedule.

If you want to avoid the hassle of bargaining with taxi drivers, ask your hotel in Petra to arrange for a pickup for you at the border crossing for an agreed price. Most Petra hotels in all price categories will be happy to do this—it ensures you won't be lured somewhere else. Again, the fare will be about JD 55. Such is life in the Middle East that your taxi fare back from Petra/Wadi Musa to the Aqaba/Eilat Crossing should be more like JD 40.

Travel agencies in Eilat can arrange for escorted 1-, 2-, or 3-day tours, or unescorted packages to Petra that will include transportation arrangements.

ENTRY REQUIREMENTS

You must have a passport valid for at least 6 months as of your entry date. The easiest way to get to Petra from Israel is via the Eilat/Aqaba Crossing. First take an Israeli taxi from Eilat to the border (officially around NIS 40, although many drivers will demand a higher rate). Pack lightly, or carry a bag on wheels, as you will have to walk from the Israeli border across a no man's land of approximately .8km (½ mile). There is a $65 USD border crossing fee, and a $60 USD Jordanian visa fee that must be paid at the border.

Important: If you entered Jordan via the Eilat/Aqaba Crossing, you can reenter Israel at the Eilat/Aqaba crossing or at the Sheik Hussein crossing in northern Jordan near the Israeli town of Beit She'an, but you *cannot reenter Israel via the Allenby Bridge/King Hussein Crossing* into the West Bank near Jericho. No entry visas are issued at the Allenby Bridge Crossing from the West Bank into Jordan; if you plan to use this route, you must obtain your Jordanian visa ahead of time from a Jordanian Consulate or Embassy. If you have your Jordanian visa ahead of time, and you exited Israel via the Allenby/King Hussein Bridge (*not* to be confused with the Sheik Hussein Bridge in the north), then you *can* reenter Israel via the Allenby Bridge. ***Note:*** The Allenby Bridge Crossing involves travel through the currently unstable West Bank, and can involve very long delays at the Allenby Bridge due to security. We don't recommend using this route. All border crossings are closed on Yom Kippur and on Eid al Adha.

Good travel agents and reputable tour companies can generally handle the arrangements for their clients' visas. To find the nearest Jordanian diplomatic

Petra's famed Al Khazneh (the Treasury).

Tips: Petra by Night

To the dismay of romantics and adventurers, Petra National Park closes at sunset or earlier, even though this mysterious, long-hidden site is especially evocative in the evenings. In fact, it was once a great place to camp at night, but now camping is forbidden.

At times, the park service offers escorted candlelight tours for an additional fee—a great way to spend the evening if you plan to be in Petra when the tours are available. Night tours are generally available when there's a full moon. Check with the park authorities and reserve in advance. In good weather, a **Bedouin camp dinner** in the mountains is another evening option. Not only do you get a traditional meal, but you also get a feel for the beautiful, wild countryside at night. Check with your hotel or the visitor center. The price is approximately JD 30 for two people.

Bedouin guides can be arranged through the visitor center. The official fee for 4 hours of guiding is JD 50. Or, once inside the park, if you feel you need a guide, you can easily find one to escort you to specific places. ***Tip:*** If you have hired a Jordanian guide before entering the park and the price of his admission is included in the arrangement, you should know that the admission price for Jordanian citizens is only JD 1; don't let your guide add a JD 50 entrance fee for himself to the price of your tour. Many of the guides are colorful, and although they may not have had formal training, most know their stuff (and have picked up great multilingual skills). It's worth it to hire a guide, at least for your first foray into Petra, especially if you plan to do a hike to some of the more off-the-beaten-track parts of the city. A standard 2½-hour Petra city tour costs JD 20. Like camels? Add JD 10 for one to accompany you on the walk from Khazneh to Qasr al-Bint. Seniors (no age limits set yet) and visitors with disabilities can hire a carriage from the entrance gate to Qasr al-Bint for an additional JD 40.

At the Visitor Center, you'll also find a variety of books and maps of Petra for sale. Officially, the park is open daily until 4pm in winter and until 6pm in summer, but in summer the guards may let visitors stay a bit later in order to take in the sunset and twilight.

Tip: To avoid dehydration, bring your own bottle of water when you enter Petra; as the day progresses you'll need to buy more bottled water from the Bedouins who until recently inhabited the site. A number of stands inside Petra sell refreshments and food, though prices will be high. Don't hesitate to shell out for water: It's important to keep drinking even if you're not especially thirsty to avoid the dangers of dehydration. In summer, you'll need four 1.5-liter bottles of water to get through the day.

mission to your location, go to the Jordanian Foreign Ministry website at **www.mfa.gov.jo**.

MONEY

The Jordanian dinar is valued at approximately US$1.40 or 1.19 GBP, so $1 = JD 0.71. The **Jordanian dinar** (JD) is divided into 1,000 **fils:** 10 fils are 1 piaster; 500 fils are generally referred to as 50 **piasters.** Paper currency comes in denominations of JD 1, 5, 10, 20, as well as 500 fils (half a JD); there are silver coins for 25 fils, 50 fils, 100 fils, and 250 fils; copper coins are 5 and 10 fils.

VISITOR INFORMATION

The **Jordan Tourism Board** website (www.visitjordan.com) offers very thorough information about touring Jordan and Petra. Excellent information on Petra can also be found at www.visitpetra.jo.

The **Royal Society for the Conservation of Nature** website (www.rscn.org.jo) has specific information about eco-tourism and hiking in **Petra; Wadi Rum ★★**, south of Petra; the wild, mountainous **Dana Reserve ★**, north of Petra; as well as to other nature and wildlife reserves in the Kingdom of Jordan.

The **visitor center** at the entrance to Petra (www.visitpetra.jo; ✆ **03/215-6029**) is open daily from 6am to 4pm in winter; 6am to 6pm during summer. Admission to Petra is JD 50 for 1 day; JD 55 for 2 days; and JD 60 for 3 days. A fourth day is free of charge. If your passport indicates you are only visiting Jordan for a 1-day excursion to Petra, admission to Petra National Park is JD 90. Children under 12 are free. The fees may seem high, but Petra is a vast area, and the money is needed to preserve and maintain the site.

TOUR OPERATORS

Reputable tour operators that run excursions to Petra (among other locations in Jordan) include **Abercrombie and Kent Jordan** (www.abercrombiekent.com; ✆ **962-06/566-5465** in Amman); **Desert Eco Tours** (an Israeli-based company; www.desertecotours.com; ✆ **972-52/276-5753** outside Israel, or 972/8632-6477 from inside Israel); and **Petra Moon Tourism** (www.petramoon.com; ✆ **962-079/617-0666** in Petra). For further options, check with the Jordan Tourism Board (www.visitjordan.com).

[FastFACTS] PETRA

Banks The Arab Bank and the Housing Bank, in the center of Wadi Musa, and the Cairo Amman Bank, in the Mövenpick Hotel just outside the entrance to Petra, both change money. They also give Visa cash advances. Banking hours are Saturday to Thursday 8:30am to 12:30pm. The Housing Bank has an ATM connected to Cirrus and PLUS.

Emergencies Throughout Jordan, for police dial ✆ **191** or 192. For an ambulance, dial ✆ **193.**

Hospitals The **Petra Emergency Clinic** (✆ **03/215-6694**), across the parking lot from the Petra Forum Hotel, is not a hospital, but it has an X-ray machine, an operating room, and other modern equipment. It's open daily 8am to 8pm. In an emergency, your hotel or the police (✆ **191**) can help get you there. The Petra Polyclinic (✆ **077/733-9209**) is near the main traffic circle and is open 24 hours.

Pharmacies The **Wadi Musa Pharmacy** (✆ **03/215-6444**) is on the main traffic circle in Wadi Musa and is open daily 24 hours. The Modern Petra Pharmacy, a block from the Wadi Musa Traffic Circle, has an English-speaking staff and carries tampons, condoms, and other items not normally stocked by local pharmacies.

Telephones The country code for Jordan is **962.** The area code for Petra is **03.** The area code for Amman is **06.**

Exploring Petra

Petra is only accessible through the Siq, a narrow crevice-canyon lined with niches that once held statues of gods and spirits that protected the city. This incredible canyon winds its way through the rocks for almost 1.6km (1 mile) before opening to Petra's wonders of rock and light. If you walk through the shadowed Siq at twilight, listen for the sound of the evening owl, once the symbol and guardian of the city.

The Nabateans, who carved the elaborate palaces, temples, tombs, storerooms, and stables of their city into the solid rock of this hidden valley, dominated the Trans-Jordan area from the 3rd century B.C. through Byzantine times. A Semitic people from northern Arabia, they moved into the Negev and the southern portions of what is now Jordan in the 6th century B.C. The Nabateans commanded the trade route from Damascus to Arabia; through Petra, caravans passed, carrying spices, silk, jewels, gold, and slaves from as far away as Yemen and East Africa. As a trading people, they developed cosmopolitan tastes and easily incorporated Hellenistic and Roman design into their architecture and into their lifestyle. The fabulous facades carved into the rose sandstone cliffs of Petra are exotically Hellenistic rather than classical Greek or even Roman, and reflect a mixture of Western and Eastern, Semitic and European influences.

Nabatean religion was centered on two deities: **Dushara,** the god of strength and masculine attributes, and **al-Uzza,** also known as Atargatis, the goddess of water and fertility. Slowly, these deities took on the characteristics of Greek and Egyptian gods; al-Uzza, especially, became associated with elements of Aphrodite, the Greek goddess of love; Tyche, the goddess of fortune; and the Egyptian mother goddess, Isis.

In addition to their hidden capital at Petra, the Nabateans developed lucrative trading and caravan cities at **Avdat** and **Mamshit** in the Negev. Using careful methods of conserving dew and rainwater, and developing methods of irrigation that are being studied by modern agronomists, the Nabateans made the desert bloom and managed to sustain a population in the Negev and south Jordan far larger than the population of that region today.

Until the A.D. 1st century, the Nabateans maintained their independence. Nabatean neutrality and aloofness was legendary. In 40 B.C., the young Herod, who had recently been made governor of the Galilee and Judea by the Romans, was overthrown by Jewish insurgents. Desperate and pursued, Herod made his way with a small entourage across the desert to Petra to beg for sanctuary and reinforcements. Despite the fact that Herod's mother had been a Nabatean princess, the ever-cautious rulers of Petra denied him permission to enter the Siq and the confines of the city (the indefatigable Herod eventually made his way to Rome, obtained reinforcements, put down the rebellion, and ruled as Rome's "King of the Jews" until his death in 4 B.C.). In A.D. 106, the Nabateans were finally annexed into the Roman Empire, and it continued to be the center of a profitable trading route, with connections to all parts of the ancient world.

In the early 4th century, Christianity became the dominant religion of the Nabateans. Important churches were built in every Nabatean community; the bishops of Petra participated in ecumenical councils that helped shape the development of the early Church. As the Roman Empire collapsed, and the amount of trade moving on the exotic desert routes through Petra shrank, the city's economy faltered. A series of earthquakes in late Byzantine times hastened the Nabateans' decline. After Petra's conquest by Islamic armies in A.D. 633, it became a forgotten backwater. It was briefly fortified by the Crusaders, but after its surrender to Saladin in 1189, it was abandoned and sank into oblivion. Not until 1812, when the Swiss explorer Johann Ludwig Burckhardt bribed Bedouin tribesmen to take him to Petra, was the long-forgotten, uninhabited city restored to the knowledge of the world. Only since 1958 has a careful exploration of the site been undertaken.

WALKING TOUR: PETRA

START: **The Siq**

FINISH: **Petra Museum**

BEST TIMES: **Early morning, sunset**

WORST TIME: **Midafternoon, when heat is at its worst**

It is important to remember that many of the sites and buildings at Petra were given fanciful names in modern times that have nothing to do with what we now know were their original functions. Also remember that once inside Petra, a fast but reasonably inclusive tour, without hikes to the sacred high places that overlook the city, can take 5 to 6 hours. **Petra deserves at least 2 full days.** Give yourself time to feel the mystery and beauty of the place and to explore at your leisure. Petra changes dramatically as the light of day changes.

Casual lunch and snack spots abound in Petra, so there's no need to pack in food.

---

1 The Siq

Beginning just near the visitor center, the winding 1.2km (¾-mile) walk through the narrow fissure, or canyonlike Siq, that leads into Petra can take from 45 minutes to 1½ hours, depending on your pace. The journey through this mysterious, highly sculptured passageway can be one of the most memorable parts of the Petra experience (especially in the soft twilight as visitors depart from Petra as night falls).

At the entrance to the Siq and at various points throughout the passageway, you'll notice channels cut into the rock that once held pipes for the water system that carried the spring of Ain Musa into Petra. There is a modern dam to prevent flash flooding during the winter rains; it is modeled after the ruins of an ancient Nabatean dam uncovered by archaeologists at this site. According to Nabatean and local Bedouin legend,

Petra's water source, Ain Musa ("the Spring of Moses"), was created when Moses, leading the Israelites through the desert after the Exodus from Egypt, struck a rock with his staff in despair as his people came close to death from thirst. The rock burst forth with cool water. (Petra's Ain Musa is not alone in claiming to be the site of this miracle.) Niches in the walls of the Siq once held the images of gods that protected the city, and intimidated visitors entering Petra.

2 The Khazneh (Treasury)

Suddenly, a turn in the Siq reveals the most famous structure in Petra, a royal tomb that has come to be known as the Treasury. Bedouins believed that the solid urn sculpted into the monument's facade was actually hollow and contained treasure; often they fired bullets at the urn in hopes of having the treasure spill out (you can detect their bullet marks across the magnificent facade). The Khazneh's stone facade changes color during the day: In the morning it can be a soft yellow-rose peach hue; by late afternoon, a pure, soft rose; at sunset, an intense red, before slipping into the dusty twilight.

Beyond the Khazneh (continuing to the right as you face the Khazneh), the Siq widens into what is called the:

3 Outer Siq

Here you'll encounter the busy modern denizens of Petra, sand artists, and water sellers. The outer Siq is lined with carved tomb facades in styles ranging from classical Roman to designs that echo Assyrian and nomadic desert influences. Honoring the dead was an important part of Nabatean culture. The outer Siq also contains caves inhabited until recently by Bedouins—the soft sandstone interiors are as wildly patterned as marbleized paper and are good spots to shelter from the hot summer sun.

A young girl walks into the Siq, the 1.6km entrance to the Nabatean city of Petra.

To the left, opposite the Uneishu Tomb (which an inscription identifies as the tomb of the brother of a queen), is a flight of rough ancient stairs that leads to an uphill trail to the:

4 High Place of Sacrifice & the Tombs of Wadi Farasa

This can be an arduous hike for those out of shape, but it is very worthwhile. A hike to the High Place of Sacrifice and back down to the

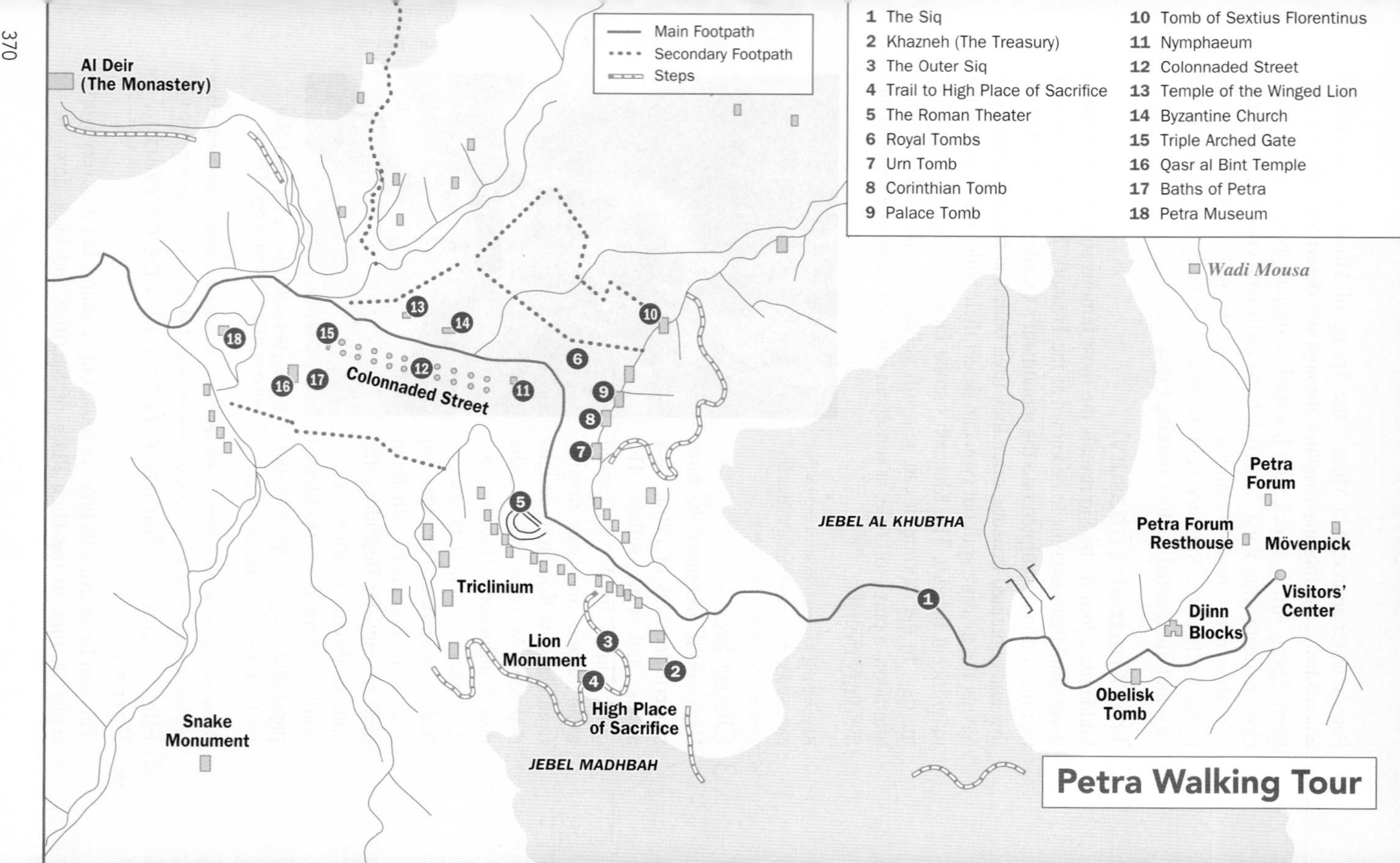
Main Footpath
Secondary Footpath
Steps
1 The Siq
2 Khazneh (The Treasury)
3 The Outer Siq
4 Trail to High Place of Sacrifice
5 The Roman Theater
6 Royal Tombs
7 Urn Tomb
8 Corinthian Tomb
9 Palace Tomb
10 Tomb of Sextius Florentinus
11 Nymphaeum
12 Colonnaded Street
13 Temple of the Winged Lion
14 Byzantine Church
15 Triple Arched Gate
16 Qasr al Bint Temple
17 Baths of Petra
18 Petra Museum
Al Deir (The Monastery)
Wadi Mousa
Colonnaded Street
Petra Forum
Petra Forum Resthouse
Mövenpick
JEBEL AL KHUBTHA
Triclinium
Visitors' Center
Djinn Blocks
Lion Monument
High Place of Sacrifice
Obelisk Tomb
Snake Monument
JEBEL MADHBAH
Petra Walking Tour

colonnaded main street of ancient Petra by a different route can take 1½ to 3 hours. It's wise to invest in a guide if you decide to make the excursion.

Continuing on down what is now the main street of Petra, you come to the:

5 Roman Theater

Originally built by the Nabateans, who were always adapting elements of other cultures into their way of life, the theater facing cliffside facades of tombs may have been used for religious ceremonies. In the A.D. 2nd century, the theater was enlarged by the Romans, who cared little for Nabatean traditions and cut into nearby Nabatean tombs to create a vast 7,000-seat venue. The theater has been restored and, after a 1,500-year hiatus, is occasionally used for performances and other events.

Farther along, on the opposite side of the canyon from the theater, are the:

6 Royal Tombs

The tombs earned this name because of their elaborate facades, not because they were created for royal burials.

Visitors make their way towards the ancient Roman Theater.

The first of these is the:

7 Urn Tomb

It's named for the carefully sculpted urn above its pediment. In A.D. 446, the Byzantines converted the inner chamber of this tomb into a church.

A few facades beyond is the:

8 Corinthian Tomb

The tomb's facade actually includes a small-scale reproduction of the **Khazneh.**

After the Corinthian Tomb is the:

9 Palace Tomb

Its two stories jut out from the side of the canyon. Part of the Palace Tomb was constructed of stone, rather than carved into the canyon rock.

Around to the right is the heavily eroded:

10 Tomb of Sextius Florentinus

The tomb was built around A.D. 130 for a Roman governor of the Province of Arabia who so admired Petra's network of tombs that he asked to be buried in a tomb of his own design in this far outpost of the Roman Empire. A faint Latin inscription and a Roman eagle mark the facade. A route of processional staircases and corridors began here and wound uphill to sacred high places on the mountain beyond.

Staying on the main path to the city center, you come to the:

11 Nymphaeum

This two-story fountain, dedicated to the water nymphs, is a major landmark of Petra. This lavish desert structure of flowing water, piped in from Ain Musa, must have been incredible to travelers approaching for the first time. The Nymphaeum was a place of both refreshment and worship.

The open water channel that fed the Nymphaeum continued on along the:

12 Colonnaded Street

The street, built after A.D. 106 by the Romans, lay over the route of an earlier Nabatean thoroughfare. It was lined with shops but also served as a civic and ceremonial route for processions.

On a rise of land to the right (north), as you walk down the Colonnaded Street, is the:

13 Temple of the Winged Lions

Named for the winged lions that serve as capitals for its columns, this was probably a temple dedicated to the worship of the female deity al-Uzza. Built in A.D. 27, this was one of Petra's major temples until it was heavily damaged, apparently by fire, in the 2nd century. The structure was then used to house families until it was destroyed by an earthquake in 363. That the temple was not rebuilt as a religious structure after the fire in the 2nd century may indicate the old region of Petra had gone into decline under the Roman occupation.

Also several hundred meters to the right of the Colonnaded Street is the:

14 Byzantine Church

Here's a large structure with triple apses and extremely beautiful and well-preserved mosaic floors that have been uncovered by the joint Jordanian-American team excavating the site. On both sides of the Colonnaded Street are the outlines of ruined buildings. According to some theories, the Roman forum of Petra would have been among the structures to the left (south) of the Colonnaded Street.

At the end of the Colonnaded Street is the:

15 Triple-Arched Gate

The gate is adorned with carved panels containing bas-relief busts, animals, and geometric and floral designs. These monumental gateways would have borne wooden doors that opened to the *temenos,* or sacred precincts, of your next stop.

16 Qasr al Bint (Palace of the Pharaoh's Daughter)

Perhaps the most important temple in Petra (again, despite its romantic name, the temple has nothing to do with a Pharaoh's daughter), this massive structure was built of stone, rather than carved from rock. It is the most impressive building in Petra. It faces north, toward the Sharra Mountains, from which the name of the chief Nabatean god, Dushara ("he of Sharra") is derived and may have been a sanctuary for the Dushara cult. This temple was built around the time of Jesus and was most likely destroyed late in the 3rd century.

Just to the south of the Arched Gate, but not accessible at present to visitors, were the:

17 Baths of Petra

These had access to a corner of the *temenos.*

Beyond the ruins of the Qasr al Bint Temple, you'll find the:

18 Petra Museum

There's a small collection of sculptural artifacts, jewelry, and pottery found at Petra. The museum building also houses the Petra Forum restaurant, as well as restrooms. A second part of the museum is housed in a nearby tomb.

A view of Ad Deir.

OTHER HIKES & EXCURSIONS AT PETRA

In addition to the hike up to the High Place of Sacrifice (see stop 4, above), a number of longer walks away from the center of Petra provide important vistas of this extraordinary place. These walks involve some amount of climbing as well as scrambling over rocks and ruined pathways; therefore, it's best to have companions with you. ***Note:*** You're required to have a guide when you go to more remote areas. Guides at Petra will escort you for about JD 35 to JD 50.

Jabal Haroun (the Mountain of Aaron, brother of Moses) is a climbing trek that can take as much as 4 to 8 hours depending on your route and requires a guide. The way passes **Ad Deir** (the Monastery), Petra's largest carved tomb, built in the A.D. 1st century, with an interior adorned by carved and painted crosses from the Byzantine period. Across the canyon from Ad Deir is Jabal Haroun, the highest peak in the area. A small, white church containing the **tomb of Aaron** stands at the top of the mountain. In winter, you might ask your guide to descend on the route that passes **Wadi Siyah,** where winter rains create a waterfall. This difficult but beautiful winter hike will take at least 3 hours, and a few additional hours if you return via Wadi Siyah. **Wadi Turkimaniya** is a pleasant 45-minute round-trip walk down the wadi that starts behind and to the left of the Temple of the Winged Lions. The easy road through the wadi supports rich vegetation in winter and leads to Petra's only tomb with a Nabatean inscription.

Qasr Habis (the Crusader's Castle) is a climb that goes from near Petra's museum to the not-very-impressive ruins of Petra's Crusader stronghold; however, the pathway leads to wonderful vistas that overlook beautiful canyons. The round-trip can run from 1 to 1½ hours.

The **High Place of Sacrifice** is one of the most popular destinations for hikers, heading to the great altars carved from rock (with drainage channels for the blood of sacrificial animals) far above the city. The panorama of Petra is dazzling. The round-trip hike can take from 1½ to 2½ hours and is not for visitors who are out of shape.

Additional treks to the **Snake Monument** and to **Jebal Numair** entail a minimum of 5 or 6 hours and require guides. There are also car tours and hikes available to **Al Madras** and **Al Barid,** nearby satellite towns of Petra. Al Barid is a kind of mini-Petra, entered through a smaller version of Petra's Siq; it's filled with carved canyon structures. Unlike at Petra, some of Al Barid's structures carved into cliffsides seem to have served as houses. Archaeology buffs can also take a taxi excursion (or hike with a Bedouin guide, about a 6-hr. round-trip) to the site of **El Beidha,** a Neolithic village from the 8th millennium B.C. A full-day or overnight-camping tour from Petra to the beautiful desertscapes of **Wadi Rum** is also highly recommended.

Where to Stay

A Bedouin man entertains visitors.

If you're staying at one of the luxury resort hotels near Petra, you can plan for a relaxing, exotic desert holiday amid marvelous surroundings, enjoying local foods, entertainment, and the opportunity to browse shops filled with tribal crafts. For those on a budget, the many less-expensive hotels at Wadi Musa, 5km (3 miles) from the entrance to Petra, are reasonably comfortable and offer the chance to meet fellow travelers. A hard day of exploring Petra will work up your appetite. In the evenings, many budget hotels offer very reasonably priced buffet dinners. In fact, travelers buffet-hop and look for the most interesting and freshest deals being offered each night

Note: As at Israeli accommodations, hotel rates are often quoted in dollars, and bargain rates (often steeply discounted) abound.

EXPENSIVE

Bubble Luxotel Petra ★★ Located farther away from the entrance to Petra National Park (but offering free shuttle service there) is this space age-y glamping option with spectacular views. Each of its 20 free-standing, see-through permanent tents overlooks the Petra Mountains and comes with its own Jacuzzi and terrace, with the transparent (and air-conditioned) bubbles giving the illusion that you're sleeping under the stars.

Little Petra, Petra. www.petrabubble.com. ✆ **03/215-6723.** 20 units. $238–$350 per suite, with some able to accommodate two adults and a child. **Amenities:** Breakfast and dinner; free shuttle to Petra (20-min. distance); private hot tub; free Wi-Fi.

Mövenpick Resort Petra ★★★ This is by far the top hotel in town, and it shares an optimal location with the Petra Guest House (see below)—just steps from the entrance to Petra National Park and close to local shops and eateries. Public areas of this Swiss-managed hotel have finely carved and inlaid furnishings, in the style of upper echelon Jordanian decor; the dinner and lunch buffets are the best in town; and there's a library with reading material about Petra and Jordan. On the roof garden, guests can meet in the evenings over coffee or fruit-flavored hookahs (waterpipes). And instead of a happy hour, they have a chocolate hour every afternoon at which treats are dispensed. The small pool is a blessing after the trek through Petra.

Petra. www.movenpick.com. ✆ **800/344-6835** in the U.S., or 03/215-7111. 183 units. $225–$385 double. Rates include breakfast. Free parking. **Amenities:** Restaurant; bar; fitness center; library; heated pool; spa; free Wi-Fi.

MODERATE

Petra Guest House ★★★ With a perfect location right at the entrance to Petra National Park and a beautifully designed, air-conditioned ensemble of buildings combining ancient and modern structures, this is the best mid-budget choice in the area (the atmospheric Cave Bar lounge of the Guest House is situated inside a Nabatean tomb). Rooms are pleasant, if plain (the mountain views more than compensate for the ordinary decor). The staff is quite knowledgeable.

Wadi Musa, Petra. www.guesthouse-petra.com. ✆ **03/215-6266.** 72 units. $175–$310 double. Rates include breakfast. Free parking. **Amenities:** Restaurant; bar; concierge; free Wi-Fi.

INEXPENSIVE

Al Anbat 1 Hotel ★ Attracting a savvy backpacking crowd, this hotel offers screenings of Indiana Jones films, rooms with balconies, a steam room and small pool (summer only), and free shuttle to the entrance to Petra National Park, 2 miles away. A generous breakfast buffet features freshly baked bread; the dinner buffet is an affordable option. The separate Al Anbat 2 and 3 hotels offer slightly less expensive rooms but without the congenial atmosphere of the Al Anbat 1 original.

Wadi Musa, Petra. www.alanbat.com. ✆ **03/215-6265.** 100 units. $70 double. Rates include breakfast. Free parking. **Amenities:** Restaurant; lounge; pool; Turkish bath; free Wi-Fi.

Excursions South of Petra

WADI RUM NATURE RESERVE ★★★

Also known as "The Valley of the Moon," this extraordinary valley, with its stunning sandstone and granite rock formations, was used as a background location for much of the film *Lawrence of Arabia.* (It also stood in for the planet Mars in the movie *Red Planet* in 2000, which should give you some idea for how distinctive the landscape is here.) Inhabited for centuries, it shelters a number of important Nabatean temples, along with ancient petroglyphs. Today, Bedouins serve as guides to those who wish to explore the Valley's many wonders (or climb the rocks, an increasingly popular activity here). You can obtain information about these extraordinary reserves for camping, escorted tours, and hiking by checking the **Royal Society for the Conservation of Nature** website (www.rscn.org.jo), which contains specific information about eco-tourism to the dramatic desert landscapes of Wadi Rum, south of Petra, as well as about other nature and wildlife reserves in the Kingdom of Jordan. If you're interested in a horseback excursion through Wadi Rum, we recommend Rum Horses (www.wadirumhorses.com), but *only* to experienced riders (this is not an activity for novice riders).

Admission to the park is JD 1 per person, children under 12 free, per vehicle JD 5.

AQABA ★

Aqaba can be a relaxing stop for an overnight or a day or two between Petra and Eilat. If you cross the border from Eilat into Aqaba a day before your excursion up to Petra, you can avoid the morning rush hour at the border and the crush to try to get a taxi (shared or otherwise) up to Petra. Aqaba, though much quieter than Eilat, is a growing resort, and its beautiful luxury hotels are far less expensive than Israeli counterparts. If you want to splurge on a beach break, you'll get much more for your investment in Aqaba, and arrive in Petra refreshed and rested. For the moment, the beaches are less friendly than Eilat's for women traveling alone. The town has inexpensive, interesting restaurants, and its reefs are less damaged than in Eilat.

PLANNING YOUR TRIP TO ISRAEL

11

By Karen Chernick

Israel is a tricky country to visit even when it's at its absolute best. It's a very compact country in a politically sensitive part of the world. Whenever political tensions subside for a while, the floodgates open and the country is awash with a backlog of travelers and religious pilgrims who have been waiting to visit. Because Israel is so small, hotel rates skyrocket during these times, and during the many Jewish, Christian, and Muslim holidays. This chapter helps you get the most out of your stay with a variety of planning tools, including information on how to get there, tips on where to stay, and quick, on-the-ground resources.

GETTING THERE

By Plane

Israel's main international airport, **Ben-Gurion (TLV)** is approximately 20 minutes by train or taxi from Tel Aviv and 45 minutes by private or shared taxi from Jerusalem. The other international airport is in Eilat, at the southern tip of Israel, but it is mainly used for direct charter package flights from Europe and for local flights.

Travelers today have numerous choices when considering their options for air travel to Israel, although the most frequent non-stops still originate from the New York area's major international airports, JFK and Newark. **El Al Israel Airlines** is the country's flag carrier and remains our top pick in terms of frequency of schedule.

Check out the company's website at www.elal.com, or call ✆ **800/223-6700** in the U.S. If you're already in Israel, call ✆ **03/977-1111** or *2250.

It can sometimes be cheaper, if more time-consuming, to consider a European stopover. We've found Athens and Larnaca (in nearby Cyprus) to be good bets in this regard; there are frequent and economical connections from both cities to Tel Aviv on Aegean Airlines (www.aegeanair.com).

From the West Coast, there are more options than in previous years, with United now offering non-stop service from San Francisco to Tel Aviv (in addition to non-stops from Newark International). For updated schedules and fares call ✆ **800/864-8331** or check out www.united.com.

GETTING INTO TOWN FROM THE AIRPORT

FROM BEN-GURION TO JERUSALEM **Trains** leave Ben-Gurion Airport for direct service to Jerusalem twice hourly except in the middle of the night, and the trip takes less than half an hour to reach the central train station. The fare is NIS 18. **Sheruts** (shared taxis) will take you from the airport to any address in Jerusalem for around NIS 70 per person. **Private taxis** are also available at regulated prices from the taxi dispatch outside the terminal; rates are fixed between 250 NIS and 350 NIS (nighttime rides are on the pricier end), whether traveling on the sabbath, and number of bags. See chapter 4.

FROM BEN GURION TO TEL AVIV **Trains** leave Ben-Gurion Airport for Tel Aviv twice hourly except in the middle of the night, and the trip takes 15 minutes. The fare is NIS 9. There is no service starting 3 hours before Shabbat on Friday until after Shabbat is over Saturday night. Tel Aviv railroad stations typically have taxis lined up outside, to make the final leg of your trip to your hotel. **Private flat-rate taxis** run from the airport into Tel Aviv (see chapter 8), and cost somewhere between NIS 110 to NIS 170. The range in rates accounts for extra charges for additional passengers, for each bag, and for night or Shabbat service. Agree on the flat rate and expect around NIS 20 to NIS 30 to pop up in additional charges. Usually, fares will be higher if you choose to pay a meter fare.

GETTING AROUND

By Bus

Intercity buses are the fastest and easiest way of traveling between the major cities of Israel (although traffic jams in recent years have led the country to resuscitate its almost forgotten train service along the Jerusalem–Tel Aviv–Haifa corridor). Buses between Jerusalem, Haifa, and Tel Aviv depart very frequently; at peak times as fast as each bus fills up. The Jerusalem–Tel Aviv fare, bus no. 480, is NIS 16. For less frequent buses, such as Tel Aviv or Jerusalem to Eilat (fare NIS 165 round-trip) or Jerusalem to the Dead Sea (NIS 100 round-trip), you must book your ticket in advance. Buses do not run on Shabbat. **Egged Bus Company** (www.egged.co.il; ✆ ***2800**) connects most cities in Israel and operates buses within Jerusalem and Haifa, as well as working on a cooperative basis with Dan Buses in Tel Aviv.

By Train

Israel Railways (www.rail.co.il) has been undergoing a revival and expansion for more than a decade. **Arlozorov Central Train Station** (Tel Aviv Savidor

Central Railway Station) in Tel Aviv is the rail hub of Israel. The cost of a rail ticket is slightly higher than comparable bus fares. A rail line with frequent service along the Mediterranean coast connects Tel Aviv to Haifa and Nahariya in the north; a second line connects Tel Aviv to Ben-Gurion Airport; a third line goes from Tel Aviv to Beersheba; and a fourth line goes from Tel Aviv to Jerusalem. Trains do not run on the Sabbath.

The **Yitzhak Navon Jerusalem Train Station** is located near the central bus station, and a convenient way to enter Jerusalem from Tel Aviv or Ben-Gurion Airport.

By Sherut

A *sherut* (shared taxi van) is a good way to travel between Jerusalem and Tel Aviv and between Tel Aviv and Haifa. Sheruts from Jerusalem leave as fast as they fill up from the corner of Rav Kook Street and Hanevi'im Street in Jerusalem (across Jaffa Rd. from Zion Square), and deposit you at the New Central Bus Station in Tel Aviv, where you can pick up local sheruts that ply the No. 4 bus route to the Hayarkon Street hotel district or the No. 5 bus route to Rothschild and Dizengoff Boulevards.

Sheruts from Tel Aviv to Jerusalem or to Haifa wait just in front of the Tel Aviv Central Bus Station. Make sure the sherut you enter is going to the right destination. Sheruts to Haifa tend to fill up slowly.

Tip: Intercity sherut fares are virtually the same as bus fares, except on Shabbat, when they double (because no buses run). Because sheruts carry fewer passengers than buses (10 passengers), and there is time to scrutinize passengers, many Israelis feel sheruts are a bit less likely to be terror targets than buses.

By Car

In the main Israeli cities, such as Tel Aviv, Haifa, and Jerusalem, cars are a cumbersome mode of transportation since parking is very difficult. Plus, taxis, sheruts, and buses are efficient and reasonably priced, so you can easily let someone else do the driving.

A car becomes necessary, however, if you want to explore the Galilee or the sites along the coast. Distances are short, so you can take in many sites. Major road signs are almost always in Hebrew and English; don't panic if on a major highway a sign is only in Hebrew—the next sign up or the one beyond will usually have the information you need in English. Most Israeli drivers use the Waze smartphone application as their GPS (and to avoid traffic); if planning to drive, it would be best to make sure you have a good cellphone data plan.

Important note: You cannot take a rental car into or out of Israel. Cars rented in Israel are not generally insured for damages or liability if taken into the West Bank or Gaza. That being said, most companies' rental insurance does permit travel on Hwy. 1, the main east-west highway from Jerusalem to the Dead Sea; and on Rte. 90, the main road along the Dead Sea and the Jordan Valley from near Jericho north to Tiberias. Clarify these regulations each

Driving & Renting Rules

Seatbelt use for drivers and all passengers is mandatory.

Speed limits are 50km (31 miles) per hour in towns and urban areas; 70km (43 miles) per hour on intercity roads unless otherwise posted; 100km (62 miles) per hour on highways.

Age minimums for rentals vary from company to company, but you usually must be 24 years old to rent or drive a rental car in Israel. Seniors over 75 or 80 may have some difficulty finding an agency that will rent to them. You may pay more for insurance if you're under or over a certain age.

Road closures: In the ultrareligious neighborhoods of Jerusalem, such as Mea Shearim or Geula, and in ultrareligious quarters of some smaller cities, public roads are closed to cars for the duration of Shabbat. Usually roads into these neighborhoods are blocked with rocks or boulders or police barriers. DO NOT TRY TO ENTER ANY ROAD BLOCKED OFF IN SUCH A WAY. Back up immediately and try to get away from the area. Drivers who inadvertently wander into such neighborhoods will have stones thrown at them and risk bodily harm.

time you rent a car and get explicit instructions as to how to get to these roads in the West Bank, making sure not to stray anywhere else in the West Bank with your rental car. Also, clarify whether your car is insured for East Jerusalem, should you be planning to drive or stay in that part of the city.

RENTING A CAR

In general, you'll get the most economical rate if you reserve a car in advance of your arrival. Car-rental agencies, both international and local, rent small cars for about $45 to $70 a day, depending on the season and size of the car. If you plan to travel in the summer, or drive to the Negev and Eilat, you'll want a car with powerful air-conditioning.

The largest Israeli car-rental firm is **Eldan** (www.eldan.co.il; ✆ **800/938-5000** or 888/243-5326 in the U.S. and Canada or 08/951-5727 in the U.K.) and is always worth looking into. Its fleet of cars is larger and more varied than those of the international agencies, and it often has discounts. Eldan also offers more offices and service centers throughout the country than any of its non-international Israeli competitors, so if you have a breakdown, you have a better chance of getting a replacement quickly.

Driving is one of the best ways to see Israel, but it can be expensive. **Ways to save:**

- **Find a package** that bundles together the cost of the car with airfare or lodgings.
- **Rent** on an unlimited kilometer basis so there are no ugly surprises. Renting by the week can be cheaper, but it is not a good idea unless you plan to be in countryside areas for the entire 7-day rental period.
- **Rent the cheapest class of vehicle:** There's a shortage of these cars at the rental agencies, which means there's a good chance you'll be bumped up a class, at no extra cost, if you do this. No guarantees though.

WHAT A RENTAL CAR COSTS IN ISRAEL	US$
Basic weekly charge, unlimited kilometers $50/day	$350
Collision Damage Waiver, 7 days at $18 per day	$126
Mandatory Third Party Liability, 7 days at $15 per day	$105
Gasoline, 100 liters at NIS 9.50 per liter (around $10.20 per gal.)	roughly $270 per week for gas
	Total: $851

There are all kinds of online deals and car/hotel/airline packages you can find, but this balance sheet will give you a general idea of what you'll actually end up paying for a lower mid-price-range car rental with automatic transmission:

These figures are an average of going rates, and the total works out to about $122 per day for a simple automatic-transmission car. Do not be misled by firms offering extremely low daily rental rates, such as $6 or $8. The daily rental rate is a small portion of the total rental bill, which includes insurance and the kilometer charge.

PARKING, TOLLS, GASOLINE & BREAKDOWNS

There is **only one toll road** in Israel: Pan Israel Highway (Hwy. 6), which will eventually run the length of the country from north to south. The road roughly spans Zichron Ya'acov in the north to Be'er Sheva in the south. There are no toll bridges in Israel, but there is an **optional toll tunnel under Haifa,** useful during rush hours. There are special Fast Lanes on Hwy. 1 for the distance between Ben-Gurion Airport and Tel Aviv. The **toll for Fast Lane use** ranges from NIS 10 to NIS 75, depending on traffic congestion conditions. Check with your car rental agency as to whether your car is equipped with an automatic scanner for the Tel Aviv Fast Lane that will add the fee to your rental bill. If not, there are heavy fines for Fast Lane use.

In Jerusalem, Tel Aviv, and other main cities, **parking** can be extremely difficult. When you park on streets in downtown areas during daylight hours, you'll need to pay the meter using a smartphone application called **Pango.** If you plan to drive in a large city, either download the Pango app in advance or park in paid lots (the **Waze** navigation app can direct you to the closest parking lot to your destination).

Shabbat Charges

Some smaller Israeli companies offer no rental charge on Shabbat, although you do have to pay Saturday insurance. Others offer free transportation from the airport to your hotel if you want to start the rental later in your trip. Companies offering such services are often more expensive, but you may find these extras worthwhile. ***Warning:*** Beware of companies that offer to waive rental fees and insurance on Shabbat. If your parked car is vandalized or stolen on Shabbat, you're in big trouble.

Parking is permitted where curbs are painted blue and white, although you may need to be a neighborhood resident. It's forbidden where curbs are red and white or gray. Parking on many residential streets in Jerusalem and Tel Aviv will soon be by residential sticker only. At most hotels in major cities, you'll have to pay to park in an often distant municipal lot or the hotel's limited space lot (fees are usually reasonable, but rates vary according to day or night and Shabbat). Most rural hotels offer free parking.

Note: Do not park illegally anywhere or you will get towed; parking enforcement officials in Israel are quick and very thorough. On the Sabbath, parking meter and card regulations are not enforced in Jerusalem and in some cities. Locals may even park on the sidewalks, but unless you know what you're doing, don't follow their example.

Gasoline comes in 91, 95, and 96 octane varieties and costs about $2.70 per liter ($10.20 gal.). Rental cars are often "required" to have the higher-octane gas. These gas prices fluctuate. Gas stations are plentiful enough on main roads, though on Saturday some of them are closed and those that are open often add a surcharge.

Breakdowns: Saturday and Jewish holidays, it's nearly impossible to have a flat tire repaired in many areas, but your rental-car company will provide you with road-service numbers to call in case of emergencies. Bigger companies usually have better service.

Sample Non–Rush Hour Driving Times in Israel

Tel Aviv–Jerusalem: 1 hour
Tel Aviv–Haifa: 1 hour 20 minutes
Jerusalem or Tel Aviv–Eilat: 4 hours 30 minutes
Jerusalem-Tiberias: 2 hours 30 minutes
Nazareth-Haifa: 40 minutes
Tiberias-Nazareth: 30 minutes

By Plane

It is possible to fly between Tel Aviv and Eilat, but keep in mind that the drive takes 4½ hours and with the time you'd spend getting to the airport, passing through security, and going through the arrival process and transfers at your destination, it may not save you much time. But if traveling overland on hot days just isn't your cup of tea, then by all means use Israel's domestic airlines, **Arkia** (www.arkia.com; ✆ **03/690-9698** or *5758 for reservations in Israel) or **Israir** (www.israir.co.il). One-way flights from Tel Aviv to Eilat cost approximately $50.

TIPS ON ACCOMMODATIONS

You'll find a wide range of accommodations in Israel, ranging from hotels to kibbutz vacation guesthouses to great hostels and self-catering apartments.

There has been no official hotel rating system or hotel star system in Israel for more than 20 years, so ignore the star ratings hotels give themselves. We've included our own star ratings in this book, from one to three stars, based on recent, personal visits.

A Note About the Seasons

Israel's hotels fill up during certain seasons and holidays, and you should be prepared with advance reservations, secured by a deposit. Generally speaking, hotels are busiest during July and August, and on the major Jewish and Christian holidays. Rates skyrocket during these times, and rooms can be very scarce if you don't book well in advance. For detailed information, and a full list of holiday dates, see p. 40.

Off-season is generally November through February (except for Hanukkah/Christmas/New Year's). It is, however, a busy season in Eilat, which has almost perfect, sunny weather when it's chilly up north.

Hotels

KIBBUTZ PACKAGES The Kibbutz Hotels network (www.booking-kibbutz.com) is especially enticing. It lets you explore the real Israeli countryside while overnighting at comfortable kibbutz hotels, holiday villages, and less-pricey guesthouses and country accommodations that have swimming pools or beaches, and invariably lovely and often very dramatic settings. There are amazingly well-priced 7-night deals (usually averaging $200 per night), which include a double room, breakfast, and a rental car (with unlimited mileage).

Although all accommodations in the kibbutz hotel and holiday village network are the equivalent of those you'd find in midrange hotels, you'll find great variety in the general setup and character of each facility. The kibbutz system also includes many less expensive **Kibbutz Country Lodgings**, a growing network of smaller kibbutz and moshav communities that run simple guest buildings, or kibbutz families who have guest-room facilities in their homes. Rates for Country Lodgings average $200 per night for a double room with a private bathroom (and do not include breakfast or a rental car). Best of all, you get a chance to see a bit of real kibbutz life.

INDEPENDENT BED & BREAKFASTS & "ZIMMERS" Hundreds of rural accommodations in private homes, ranging from simple to luxurious, are available for tourists today. For a listing of good choices, go to **Zimmeril** (www.zimmeril.com) or the Ministry of Tourism website, www.goisrael.com.

SHORT-TERM RENTAL APARTMENTS If you'd rather be able to cook for yourself and live in an apartment building among locals, another option is either **Airbnb** (www.airbnb.com) or **VRBO** (www.vrbo.com). Both offer a range of accommodations suitable for everyone from solo travelers to large groups, and are an especially comfortable (and often more affordable) hotel alternative in big cities like Tel Aviv and Jerusalem.

YOUTH HOSTELS Israel's wonderful network of official **Israel Youth Hostel Association Hostels,** or IYHA Hostels (iyha.org.il; ✆ **1-599/510-511**) offers simple, inexpensive accommodations in many dramatic sites throughout the country. IYHA hostels often offer the only available accommodations in remote areas of the country, or in areas along hiking routes.

Great Guesthouses

Israel is unique in that many Christian guesthouses that were originally set up for pilgrims have developed into wonderful options for travelers, and most welcome guests of all faiths. Some of the best of these guesthouses are listed in detail in this guidebook, and many other excellent choices may be found on the **Christian Information Centre** website (www.cicts.org). These are among the most atmospheric and unusual accommodations in Israel, often set in historic buildings and enclaves. Rates are very reasonable; rooms are comfortable but simple; atmosphere is quiet; and the staff members are almost always polite.

In the past few years, the IYHA has been busy upgrading its network of facilities. Many hostels are in sleek new buildings set up with a maximum of four to six beds per room. A large percentage of these rooms now have private shower/bathrooms and can easily be converted into private doubles or family rooms. Dining facilities now offer meals far superior to the once-spartan youth-hostel fare.

Age is no barrier to staying at an IYHA Hostel, nor is membership. Having a youth-hostel membership card, however, does give you certain advantages, such as better rates at the hostels, plus discounts at some restaurants, national parks, historical sites, museums, and on buses and trains. It is advisable to book in advance.

Israel Hostels, or ILH (www.hostels-israel.com), is an independent network of more than 30 independent hostels, inexpensive hotels, B&Bs, kibbutz guesthouses, and other unusual, inexpensive places to stay throughout Israel. The managements are almost always friendly, enthusiastic, well-informed, and offer personal attention. Highly recommended!

TOURS & ESCORTED TRIPS

Affordable Escorted Tours

Brilliant, low-budget tours that go from day trips to 8-day packages are offered by **Abraham Tours** (abrahamtours.com/bus), which is affiliated with the network of Abraham Hostels in Jerusalem, Tel Aviv, Nazareth, and Eilat. Routes take visitors to major cities and sites throughout Israel, with brief sightseeing stops at sites along the way that would be hard to get to by public transportation.

Another affordably priced and excellent tour operator is **Tourist Israel** (www.touristisrael.com), which has a range of day trips in Jerusalem, the Galilee, and even Petra. Tours take place daily, including on Saturdays.

For an all-inclusive tour operator that can take care of everything from booking accommodations to multi-day tours including hotel pick-ups, a professional tour guide, entry to ancient and religious sites, and comfortable transportation, **Bein Harim Tours** (www.beinharimtours.com) is a popular and reliable option touring all over Israel and some parts of Jordan. Their day trips begin at $45 per person, and their 10-day whirlwind guided tours of Israel (including hotel accommodations, transportation, and some meals) cost $1,850 per person.

If you don't want to book a private tour—but also don't want to be on a big tour bus surrounded by strangers—**Guided Tours Israel** (www.guidedtoursisrael.com) limits the size of many of its trips to Jerusalem, the Dead Sea, and the Galilee to a max of six people per group. Completely private tours curated to your interests and group size are available through them as well. This tour operator is a favorite among those passing through Israel on cruise ships, since they arrange day trips that begin with a dock pick-up.

Day Tours to the West Bank

Depending on political conditions, a number of independent groups now offer escorted day tours into the West Bank/Palestinian Authority Areas. **Always check State Department and Foreign Office travel advisories before entering the West Bank.** For those who wish to see Bethlehem, Jericho, and other historic and religious sites under Palestinian Administration, these tours (all of which include varying degrees of emphasis on social and political conditions), can be an efficient way to explore. Most day tours range from NIS 200 to NIS 400 per person.

Abraham Tours (abrahamtours.com; see above) is one recommended operator, as is **Green Olive Tours** (www.greenolivetours.com) which offers a heavier emphasis on politics. The meeting point for Green Olive tours is usually the West Jerusalem YMCA on King David Street. **Alternative Tours** (alternativetours-jerusalem.com), based in East Jerusalem, offers tours with a more partisan Palestinian perspective.

Private Guides

Private guides arrange all the logistics of travel during the times they are under hire and can take you to major sites as well as out-of-the-way places efficiently. For those with little time, this can be a restful way to get a great deal done and get an in-depth understanding of the country. The government licensing program has helped to raise the general quality of guides in Israel tremendously, but there's still always a risk in touring with a guide—you never know if they'll be articulate, a compelling storyteller, or a complete bore. So ask for extensive references before booking and, when you can, read online reviews of the guide in question. Many good professional guides have put together a website with videos that will give you an indication of their styles and approaches. At these (or any) prices, you don't want to be stuck with a lemon.

Costs: Approximate rates for a private guide are $300 to $400 per day for a Jerusalem tour by foot and taxi, $500 to $600 a day for a licensed and insured guide with a vehicle within Israel. There can be extra charges for more than 8 hours per day (the Ministry of Tourism recommends the extra charge begin at over 10 hours per day) and for off-road trips and use of off-road vehicles. If your guide accompanies you overnight, the fee should include the cost of their hotel room (in many places, a licensed guide will receive a discount—your guide will know where they can be put up at a discount rate). Some licensed guides are willing to offer lower rates in slow seasons, but most of the best licensed guides won't. This doesn't necessarily mean that some guides with lower rates aren't good, though they may not be as established.

If you engage an Israeli guide to arrange excursions into Jordan, the rate could be $660 to $700 per day, including a vehicle and their hotel accommodations. Israeli guides are not permitted to guide in Bethlehem or in other Palestinian-administered areas.

In Israel, it's illegal for people to guide without a license. Unfortunately, if you go by car with an unlicensed guide, you're probably not insured in case of an accident.

Recommended guides: Following are some guides with unusual background qualifications and specialties. If they're not able to meet your time specifications or interests, they may be able to refer you to guides who will better match your needs, or you can search on **Gateway to Israel** (www.israel-guides.net) which aggregates a list of officially licensed Israeli tour guides along with the languages they speak, specialties, and whether they can drive you as well.

- American-born **David Perlmutter** (www.israeladventure.com; ✆ **054/420-1353**) was a guide for the Society for Protection of Nature in Israel and helped design that organization's hikes and tours. He specializes in mountain-biking, hiking, and off-road tours, as well as photography, wine and culinary, cultural, and general tours.
- **Richard Woolf** (www.safed.co.il/woolfguide.html; ✆ **04/693-5377** or 050/589-4647) specializes in the Galilee, where he has lived for almost 40 years, but guides throughout Israel. Born in the U.K., he is very patient and well-informed.
- **Gila Levitan** (www.walkaboutisrael.com; ✆ **054/5934891**) can guide you all around Israel's predictable tourist destinations, from Masada and the Dead Sea to Jerusalem and Tel Aviv, but her area of expertise is showing visitors the things that aren't on typical itineraries. In the desert this might be a hidden monastery, in Tel Aviv this could be a tour of the labyrinthine Central Bus Station (the second largest in the world) and all the oddities it contains.
- **Sam Salem** (www.sam-salem-tours.business.site; ✆ **054/215-8441**), a member of Jerusalem's Christian community, offers specialties that include Bethlehem, Jericho, the Old City of Jerusalem, and the Temple Mount. He has unusual access and connections to many special sites.
- While many tours will show you around Jerusalem's religious sites, **Naomi Segal** (✆ **052/356-5873**) will guide you around one of Israel's unique (and weekly) religious experiences—the sabbath. In addition to her other tours of Jerusalem, Segal offers a special Friday afternoon tour that is all about watching different Jewish communities and families prepare for Shabbat

according to a variety of Diasporic traditions. The tour ends at the Western Wall, and includes a taste of challah bread and wine.

- **Adam Sela** (www.adamsela.com) is among the most respected guides for the Negev, southern Israel, and the rest of the country.

Escorted Tours, Packages & Trails

Israel is an unusual destination in that there are many major Jewish and Christian organizations that sponsor group tours and missions to the Holy Land. It's always worthwhile to check with your synagogue or church as to what organized group tours they can direct you to. These package tours have the added advantage of zeroing in on sites and events that are of special interest to people who share your traditions and background.

Below, we list a number of special interest tour companies.

ARCHAEOLOGICAL DIGS You can volunteer to work at an archaeological dig if you are 18 or older, prepared to stay for at least 2 weeks, and capable of doing strenuous work in a hot climate. You will have to pay your own fare to and from Israel. Most excavations take place between June and October, but there are off-season digs. Lectures are given at some sites, and some offer academic credit for the work. If you'd like to join a dig, it's best to inquire as far in advance as possible.

The best summary of current digs is found each year in the January/February issue of the magazine *Biblical Archaeology Review,* available at many libraries and newsdealers. *Biblical Archaeology Review*'s listings include exactly whom to contact for information about joining each specific dig, as well as estimates on expenses for volunteers and a description of each dig's recent finds. The **Israel Ministry of Tourism North American Info Center** (www.goisrael.com) will also give you general, updated information about finding a suitable dig.

For those looking to experience just a taste of an archaeological dig, **Dig for a Day** (www.digforaday.com; organized by Archaeological Seminars) allows tourists to dig at their excavation site in Beit Guvrin National Park (a roughly 50-min. drive from either Tel Aviv or Jerusalem). The site includes relics of the Hellenistic period 2 millennia ago, such as water cisterns and the remnants of olive oil production. Unlike closed excavation sites that require credentials and a certain time commitment, Dig for a Day allows budding archaeologists of all ages (yes, even kids) to come play Indiana Jones for a few hours. Excavations take place rain or shine and cost NIS 95 per adult and NIS 72 per child for the public digs; private digs for small groups are also available. Advance reservation strongly recommended.

The **Biblical Archaeology Society** (www.biblicalarchaeology.org), which publishes the *Biblical Archaeology Review,* organizes archaeology-based study tours of Israel and the surrounding region.

BIKING TOURS & HOLIDAYS **Jerusalem Midnight Biking** (www.jerusalembiking.com) offers inventive 3-hour guided nighttime bike tours of Jerusalem's new and old cities for intermediate cyclists. In summer, tours are offered once a week; NIS 115 per person (NIS 230 including rental of mountain bike). Specially scheduled group tours can sometimes be arranged. Highly recommended.

CMBC, the Carmel Mountain Bike Club (https://sites.google.com/site/carmelmtb), is a group of Haifa-area cycling enthusiasts, including Jon Lipman, who maintains a detailed English-language website and will be happy to share advice and info on activities, bike rides, and tours. For further information about mountain-biking in Israel, go to the site for Israel Bike Trails (ibt.org.il/en).

FOOD & WINE TRIPS **Savor Israel** (www.israelfoodtours.com) offers a lively itinerary of day-long tours to Tel Aviv–Jaffa, Jerusalem, the Negev, and the Galilee. The tours include forays into Israeli haute cuisine, ethnic cooking, visits to local wineries, dairies, and Bedouin communities, and offer great insights into the land and the people of Israel. Groups are small, and prices run from $200 to $300 per person per day.

EatWith (www.eatwith.com) lets travelers eat in the homes of vetted Israeli home chefs, together with a small group of other diners. Hosts usually have some form of special draw, whether it be a menu devoted solely to fresh fish, a rooftop garden setting, or homes that are architectural gems. Prices are listed at the time of booking, and these are usually reserved weeks in advance.

Delicious Israel (www.deliciousisrael.com) guides small groups through the major food markets of Tel Aviv and Jerusalem, stopping at a curated selection of vendors to sample local delicacies such as *burekas* (phyllo dough pastries), falafel, malabi pudding, citron juice, and hummus. Some tours can be combined with a cooking class, meaning you tour the market first and shop for produce, then cook at the nearby Delicious Israel kitchen.

HIKING & NATURE TRIPS The Society for Protection of Nature in Israel (http://natureisrael.org), known as SPNI, offers a wide range of excellent nature and camping hikes and tours throughout Israel and beyond. Most tours are in Hebrew, but the guides are among the best in the business, and are generally fluent in English (as are most Israeli participants), so English speakers will not be left out. SPNI offers some tours in English.

Israel National Trail (www.israeltrail.net) is a planned, self-guided, 1,100km (683-mile) network of hiking routes and paths that run from the northern tip of Israel to the shores of the Red Sea and take you through places of natural beauty, historic sites, and a broad range of Israel's many ethnic and religious communities. This is a wonderful resource and great for planning local hiking as well.

Jesus Trail (www.jesustrail.com) is a carefully planned program of walks and hikes through the area between Nazareth and the Sea of Galilee, through the areas that Jesus would have known (p. 197).

Desert Eco Tours (www.desertecotours.com) offers tours and camping trips in the Negev and Jordan's Wadi Musa and Petra National Park.

VOLUNTEER TRIPS **Volunteers for Israel** (www.vfi-usa.org) arranges volunteer support positions in both civilian and military organizations in Israel. Assignments may include hospital work, repair work, and KP duty with noncombat sectors of the Israeli military. After you fulfill your 3-week obligations, you may be eligible for a special El Al discount fare. Application to this program requires a nonrefundable $100 fee.

SPECIAL PROGRAMS

JEWISH-ARAB DIALOGUE PROGRAMS One out of every five Israeli citizens living inside the pre-1967 boundaries of Israel is Arab. There are a growing number of dialogue and intercultural-understanding projects inside Israel for Israeli Arabs and Jews. You will often find Israelis from English-speaking countries, armed with democratic traditions and experience living in multicultural societies at the forefront of these projects. Visitors to Israel may observe these organizations and participate in lectures and tours that illuminate the problems and possibilities that exist for dialogue and understanding. Short-term volunteering is also doable. This can be a good way to encounter one of the most hopeful sides of Israeli society.

Neve Shalom/Wahat al Salaam, 99761 Doar Na Shimshon (visitor programs http://wasns.org; ✆ **02/999-6305**), is a unique Israeli-Palestinian cooperative village near Jerusalem that sponsors programs for visiting youth groups, including meetings with Jewish and Palestinian youth; programs for peace-oriented groups; and tours for pilgrim groups, focusing on religious sites. Neve Shalom/Wahat al Salaam (which means "Oasis of Peace") has a visitor center, guesthouse, and restaurant on its premises, and offers lecture programs.

New Israel Fund & Shatil Volunteer Programs (www.nif.org; U.S. ✆ **202/842-0900**) is concerned with human rights, intercultural understanding, and education programs inside Israel. It sponsors professional exchange, volunteer, and intern projects, social change fellowships, as well as village volunteer-in-residence programs for teaching English and medical, business, and other skills.

PLANT A TREE If you'd like to plant a tree in Israel with your own hands, contact the Jewish National Fund (www.treesfortheholyland.com) for more information. The cost per tree is NIS 36.

SAR-EL NATIONAL PROJECT FOR VOLUNTEERS FOR ISRAEL The Sar-El project offers eligible individuals the chance to volunteer on a short-term basis for the IDF (Israel Defense Forces). The most popular programs run from approximately 1 to 2 weeks; during that time, volunteers stay on an Israeli army base which could be located anywhere in the country and perform basic volunteer work to help with the life of the base. You'll interact not just with fellow volunteers but real Israelis doing their mandatory military service, making this, in our view, one of the more rewarding Israel volunteer programs. For details on how to apply visit www.sar-el.org.

[FastFACTS] ISRAEL

ATMs ATMs are the fastest, easiest way to change money at the best rates. Look for ATMs adorned with international flag decals that accept foreign debit cards. ***Important:*** You'll often need a four-digit PIN to use them. There are fewer international ATMs in smaller towns and in the countryside, and ATMs are not restocked during Shabbat or on Jewish holidays.

Area Codes The telephone country code for Israel is 972. Telephone area codes are 02 for Jerusalem; 03 for Tel Aviv; 04 for Haifa, Caesarea, and the Galilee; 08 for Eilat, the Negev, the Dead Sea, and Rehovot; 09 for Netanya.

Bugs & Wildlife **Scorpions** are always something to be aware of in desert and Mediterranean regions. If bitten by a scorpion, get emergency medical treatment immediately. Scorpions do not go out of their way to attack, but they love damp, warm places, and you can get bitten if you happen to put a hand or foot where one of them is resting. Check carefully when entering showers, bathrooms, or other damp places. Always shake out towels at the beach or pool before drying yourself; shake out shoes and socks before putting them on. If you're staying in simple places in the desert, shake out your sheets before getting into bed. Orange groves may look inviting, but big, mean snakes think so, too; avoid the temptation to stroll or picnic in them. In the Jordan Valley, there is a rare but very ugly skin infection called "Rose of Sharon" that's hard to control and will scar unless you get medical treatment—don't hesitate to see a doctor about any unusual or persistent bug bites or skin eruptions.

There is rabies in the countryside, and wild animals should be avoided. Keep away from stray dogs and cats, no matter how friendly or hungry they may seem.

When snorkeling or diving in the Red Sea, remember that many coral formations are not only sharp, but can burn. It is illegal to touch or walk on any coral—not only for your safety, but for the protection of the coral, which can be easily broken and killed. Spiny sea urchins, covering the underwater floor in many parts of the Red Sea, are the bane of swimmers and snorkelers. It's best to wear foot coverings and try to avoid stepping anywhere near a sea urchin—and note that it's very easy for a wave or current to glide you right onto one. Study photo charts of fish before snorkeling, and memorize those that are poisonous to touch, especially the stonefish or rockfish, with their billowing, diaphanous fins that appear to be so delicate. From June through August, stinging and burning jellyfish plague Israel's Mediterranean waters. Do not swim on days when there is evidence of jellyfish on the beaches.

Business Hours The Israeli work week runs from Sunday through Thursday, with many businesses open on Friday until midday or early afternoon. Government offices are open on weekdays, usually from 8am, and closed to the public on Fridays and Saturdays. Muslim-owned businesses are closed either half the day or all day on Fridays, and Christian-owned shops close on Sunday.

Customs You can bring $200 worth of tax-free gifts into the country. You can also bring in 250 grams (8¾ oz.) of tobacco, and one bottle (⅘ quart) of liquor. When you leave, you can convert up to $3,000 back into foreign currency at the airport, so keep your bank receipts. Note that you cannot take antiquities or archaeological artifacts out of Israel unless you have a certificate identifying the object, which will be provided to you by any licensed antiquities dealer.

Doctors Many (but not all) Israeli doctors speak English. Your hotel can refer you to an appropriate physician or the nearest ***Magen David Adom*** (Red Star of David, Israeli equivalent of the Red Cross) emergency station.

Drinking Laws The legal age for purchase of alcoholic beverages is 18; proof of age is required and often requested at bars, nightclubs, and restaurants, so it's always a good idea to bring ID when you go out. There are no closing times for bars inside Israel. Alcohol is forbidden and considered abhorrent by Islam and so is generally not available in Muslim communities inside Israel or in Jordan or the West Bank except at hotels for tourists. Do not drink or carry alcohol in public in these areas.

Electricity The electric current used in Israel is 220 volts AC (50 cycles) as opposed to the 110-volt system used in America. If your appliance doesn't have the right plug, you can buy a plug adapter in Israel quite easily for approximately NIS 3, or your hotel may have one to lend to you.

Embassies & Consulates **The American Embassy** is at 14 David Flusser St., Jerusalem (il.usembassy.gov; ✆ **02/630-4000**). **The U.S. Branch Office** in Tel Aviv is at 71 HaYarkon Street (✆ **03/519-7575**).

The Australian Embassy is at 23 Yehuda Ha-Levi St., Tel Aviv (✆ **03/693-5000**).

The Irish Embassy is at 2 Ze'ev Jabotinsky, Ramat Gan (✆ **03/696-4166**).

The New Zealand Embassy is served by the British Embassy (see below).

The British Embassy is at 192 Ha-Yarkon St., Tel Aviv (✆ **03/725-1222**). See http://ukinisrael.fco.gov.uk/en for consulates in Jerusalem and Eilat. **The British Consulate-General** in East Jerusalem is in the Sheikh Jarrah neighborhood at 15 Nashashibi St. (✆ **02/671-7724** or 02/541-4100).

The Canadian Embassy is in Tel Aviv at 3 Nirim St., Beit Hasepanut, Yad Eliahu (✆ **03/636-3300**).

Health Concerns Sunburn and dehydration are problems throughout the region, but especially in the desert during summer. Although the air is dry, paradoxically, you often don't feel thirsty. Force yourself to drink a minimum of four 1.5-liter bottles of water a day as you travel the area in summer, more if you are in the desert. Sunscreen is a must, though you need less of it at the Dead Sea because the thicker atmosphere screens out the sun.

Internet & Wi-Fi Downtown West Jerusalem and Tel Aviv are heavily covered with free Wi-Fi zones filled with cafes and restaurants where you can bring your laptop and connect without charge. Almost all accommodations offer free Wi-Fi. Haifa has a free Wi-Fi zone along the Dado Beach Promenade and in Central Carmel.

Language Official languages are Hebrew and Arabic. English is very widely spoken and understood in all hotels and most restaurants. In big cities and on major roads, most signs are in Hebrew, English, and Arabic.

LGBT Travelers Israel has come a long way since the 1980s, when laws regarding homosexual activity were removed from the books. A decision by the government to award pensions of deceased military officers to their surviving partners, regardless of sex or marital status, was a landmark in changing attitudes. However, an open, lively gay scene has only really emerged in trendy Tel Aviv, which *Out* has called the "most gay-friendly city in the Middle East". For the past several years, Eilat, somewhat like Tel Aviv, has developed a general attitude of tolerance; mild-mannered Haifa stands somewhere between Tel Aviv and Jerusalem.

One good resource is the **Association for LGBTQ Equality in Israel** (www.lgbt.org.il; ✆ **03/620-5590**). It offers advice, counseling, and updates on the social scene. For information about the LGBT community in Tel Aviv, visit the website of the **Tel Aviv Municipality LGBTQ Center** (www.lgbtqcenter.org.il).

Note that in the Palestinian/Arabic communities throughout Israel, and in East Jerusalem, the West Bank, Jordan, and Egypt, any kind of openly gay or lesbian behavior is completely forbidden both by custom and by law. Extreme caution and the lowest-possible profile are advised.

Similar discretion must be observed in the ultrareligious Jewish and Hassidic neighborhoods of Jerusalem north of Jaffa Road (such as Mea Shearim); in the Old City of Jerusalem; in Safed, which has a largely religious population; and in small, less-touristy Israeli towns.

Mail The Israeli Postal Service is dependable (but slow). Postal rates are similar to those in the United States and the U.K. Packages must be brought to the post office unsealed for security inspection, and you may be asked to show identification to the postal clerk.

Money & Costs Frommer's lists exact prices in the local currency. The currency conversions provided were correct at press time. However, rates fluctuate, so before departing consult a currency exchange website such as **www.xe.com/ucc** to check up-to-the-minute rates.

THE VALUE OF THE SHEKEL VS. OTHER POPULAR CURRENCIES

NIS	Aus$	Can$	Euro€	NZ$	UK£	US$
Israeli Shekel (NIS)1	A$0.44	C$0.39	€0.28	NZ$0.47	£0.24	US$0.29

Currency: The basic unit of currency is the New Israel Shekel (NIS). The shekel is divided into 100 agorot. The smallest denomination you will encounter are 10-agorot copper-colored coins, and larger, copper 50-agorot (half-shekel) coins.

Packing Tips Israel is a very informal country, so casual, practical clothing is acceptable everywhere. In winter, warm socks and sturdy, rubber-sole walking shoes are helpful. A folding umbrella, and fleece liners and medium-weight jackets that can be layered are essential. Women should pack a multiuse, easy-to-carry shawl for chilly nights in mountain cities such as Jerusalem, and to wrap over shorts, bare shoulders, or short sleeves when visiting holy sites. Men won't need ties; sport jackets are not mandatory at expensive restaurants or at performances. Sun hats are necessary, and men must cover their heads when entering Jewish religious places; if you don't have a head covering, most synagogues will have some at the door to lend.

Passports It is important to check that you have at least 6 months left before your passport's expiration; without that cushion, you won't be allowed into the country.

Pharmacies Pharmacies are well-stocked, and you'll encounter many international name brands, but drug prices outside of Israeli insurance plans—even for nonprescription medicines—are comparatively high. Pharmacies are not open on Shabbat, so plan your purchases accordingly.

Police Dial ✆ **100.**

Safety Israel is a low-crime country. Some of the major dangers you will encounter are car-related. Israeli drivers aren't renowned for sound driving practices. Blatant tailgating is the unnerving way of life here. Car theft and theft of belongings from rental cars is also a problem. Some rental-car companies require you to use a steering wheel lock, and it is never a good idea to leave valuables in your car.

Keeping Flush

Don't wait until you're down to your last shekel if you're using ATMs to keep yourself funded. International ATM connections sometimes go down, and Israeli banks have a way of being open during odd hours. Remember that ATMs will not be restocked during Shabbat, and there's usually a run on ATMs on Friday, so stock up on Thursdays, before the Israeli weekend, and stock up a day before holidays.

WHAT THINGS COST IN ISRAEL	NIS
Taxi from the airport to downtown	250
Double room, moderate	US$240*
Double room, inexpensive	US$140*
Three-course dinner for one without wine, moderate	100
Bottle of beer	25
Cup of coffee	12–18
1 liter of premium gas	9.50
Admission to most museums	25–50
Admission to most national parks	25–35

***Israeli hotel rates are quoted in dollars.**

When traveling in Jordan or in East Jerusalem and Arab cities inside Israel, travelers should not carry or drink alcohol (which is forbidden by Islam) in public, and modest dress is expected of both men and women. Women traveling alone must realize they are visiting Muslim societies, and the fact of being unaccompanied by a man can be regarded as suspicious and provocative. Extremely modest dress is essential.

Security Terrorism is a consideration everywhere in the world, and Israelis have become experts in dealing with it. Despite the news of the past few years, the chance is actually greater that you'll be involved in a traffic mishap while in Israel. In Jerusalem, security guards now prowl the bus stops, checking and intercepting suspicious-looking people before they can board a bus. Guards conduct bag and body checks at the entrances to shopping malls, markets, shops, cafes, restaurants, transportation hubs, and hotels. You'll find security guards at most major restaurants. Always keep alert and be aware of suspicious persons, especially if they are wearing more layers of clothing than the weather warrants.

Note: Get away from and immediately report any suspicious or unattended bags or packages! Any Israeli will know how to summon the police.

Senior Travel Mention the fact that you're a senior when you make your travel reservations. Some Israeli hotels, especially those in international chains, still offer lower rates for seniors, especially during off season.

Smoking Smoking is against the law in all public places, including restaurants, trains, buses, and taxis.

Student Travel Israel is a student-friendly country. There are all kinds of student flights and discount airfares to Israel, and if you're from a Jewish-American family, you may even be eligible for a free trip to Israel under the **Birthright (Taglit) Program** (www.birthright israel.com), which provides the gift of first-time, peer-group, educational tours of Israel (airfare included) to Jewish adults ages 18 to 26. More than 40,000 people have taken advantage of this program, which is designed to encourage Jewish identity and connection with the State of Israel (waiting lists are long).

Even for independent travelers, there are discounts for students at museums, national parks, and railroads, although train discounts are minimal. Check out the **International Student Travel Confederation** (ISTC; www.istc.org) website for comprehensive travel services information and details on how to get an International Student Identity Card (ISIC), which qualifies students for substantial savings. It also provides students with basic health and life insurance and a 24-hour help line. The card is valid for a maximum of 18 months. If you're no longer a student but are still under

26, you can get an International Youth Travel Card (IYTC) from the same people, which entitles you to some discounts. Irish students may prefer to turn to USIT (www.usit.ie; ✆ **01/602-1904**), an Ireland-based specialist in student, youth, and independent travel.

Taxes At press time, there is a value-added tax (VAT) of 17%. This does not apply to Eilat, which is a tax-free zone. Unless otherwise noted on the price tag, all prices automatically include the VAT. Hotel bills (including food and services charged to your room) are not subject to the VAT if you are a tourist with a tourist visa, and if you pay your bill in foreign currency or with a foreign credit or debit card.

For single purchases of over $100, certain shops will give you a form you can use for refund of your VAT as you leave the country at Ben-Gurion Airport. In order to complete this transaction, you have to get to Ben-Gurion well ahead of your flight and hope that the Refund Office will be open and that the lines will not be too long. If the VAT you've paid is substantial, it could be worth the effort.

Telephones **Phoning From Within Israel:** Mobile numbers begin with 05. The major city or area codes inside Israel are:

02 (for Jerusalem)
03 (for Tel Aviv)
04 (for Haifa and the Galilee)
09 (for the coast between Tel Aviv and Haifa)
08 (for the Negev and Eilat)

For calls made within the area code you're calling from, omit the area code, and just dial the local 7-digit number. For calls within Israel that are not within your area code, you must add the 2-digit city or area code to the local number (e.g., from Jerusalem to Haifa, dial 04, plus the local Haifa number).

Major cellphone prefixes are 050; 052; and 054. To call a cellphone, always use the 3-digit prefix, followed by the 7-digit number.

Phoning from Overseas: The international dialing prefix from Australia is 0011; from the U.S. or Canada, 011; from Ireland, New Zealand or the U.K., 00.

The country code for Israel is 972.

To call a number in Israel from overseas, dial the overseas access number (in the U.S., 011) plus 972 and then the Israeli number, omitting the initial 0 in the area code. Thus, to phone a hypothetical number in Jerusalem, you would dial 011-972-2-555-5555. To call a cellphone in Israel, again you must omit the initial 0 in the prefix. So, calling 054-666-6666, would entail dialing 011-972-54-666-6666.

Phoning Overseas: The international dialing code from Israel is 00. Then dial the country code, area code, and local number.

The country code for Australia is 63; for the U.S. and Canada, 1; for Ireland, 353; for New Zealand, 64; for the U.K., dial 44.

For local Israeli directory assistance ("information"), dial ✆ **144;** 1-700 and 1-800 numbers are toll-free. All operators speak some English and if necessary will connect you to a special English-speaking operator.

Time Israel is 2 hours ahead of Greenwich Mean Time, 7 hours ahead of Eastern Standard Time, and 10 hours ahead of Pacific Standard Time. When it's 7pm in Israel, it's noon in New York.

Daylight Saving Time ***Warning:*** Because Israel has its own unique dates for going on and off daylight saving time, there is often a period of 1 or 2 weeks in the spring and a month in September or October when there's only a 1-hour difference between Israel and Greenwich Mean Time and a 6-hour time difference between New York and Israel. Palestinian areas, Jordan, and Egypt keep to their own dates for daylight saving time, and those areas of the West Bank not under direct Israeli control also keep to Egyptian/Jordanian time. This can make border crossings a disaster if both countries are not synchronized. Jordan, Palestinian areas, and Egypt are normally 7 hours ahead of New York time, and 2 hours ahead of Greenwich Mean Time. In the past, because of religious and political considerations, the decision about when to begin and end Israeli daylight saving time has sometimes not been made until the last minute. For this reason, it is

Accessibility Assistance

Yad Sarah (friendsofyadsarah.org; ✆ **972-2/644-4444** from outside Israel) is Israel's largest voluntary organization. It lends medical equipment, crutches, and wheelchairs; arranges airport and intercity transportation; helps prepare and equip hotel rooms for special needs; and offers advice for travelers to Israel with special needs. All services are free, although deposits are required for equipment. Advance planning and reservations are required to get the most help from Yad Sarah, but it's also a great resource for sudden or last-minute emergencies.

very important to reconfirm schedules at these times of year—you could miss your flight, or worse.

Tipping Tip 12% to 15% in restaurants or cafes, unless a service charge is already added to your bill. Taxi drivers do not expect tips unless they have helped you load or carry luggage. An extra NIS 5 per bag is fair. Leave NIS 5 per person per day for your hotel maid, more if she has given you extra help.

Toilets In Israel, public toilets on the street are rare to nonexistent. Try hotel lobbies, bars, restaurants, museums, department stores, railway and bus stations, and service stations. Large hotels and fast food restaurants are often the best bet for clean facilities. Restaurants and bars in resorts or heavily visited areas may reserve their restrooms for patrons. In each quarter of Jerusalem's Old City, there are scattered public restrooms, marked W.C., a tradition from British Mandate times. They're not the cleanest, but they're better than nothing.

Travelers with Disabilities Inside Israel, there's been an ongoing effort to provide access for visitors with disabilities—even at sites famed for their inaccessibility, such as **Masada.** Atop the dramatic plateau of Masada, a network of wheelchair-accessible pathways was completed in 2000. At least some trails in a number of Israel's national parks and nature reserves (www.parks.org.il) have also been made wheelchair accessible.

Street crossings and public restrooms throughout the country rarely offer easy access. Some institutions located in difficult sites, such as the Israel Museum and Jerusalem Cinémathèque, have provisions for handicap access, but you must call in advance to be able to use these facilities.

Visas Visitors from most English-speaking countries will receive a visa for Israel on the spot at Ben-Gurion Airport or at any land border crossing. There is no charge for the visa; however, there is an exit fee if you leave via a land crossing into Jordan.

Citizens of Western Europe, North America, Australia, and New Zealand are issued visas valid for up to 3 months upon arrival at Israel's Ben-Gurion Airport. For security reasons, visitors whose passports indicate extensive travel to countries that are politically unstable or technically at war with Israel (such as Iran, Sudan, Afghanistan, or Lebanon) may be taken aside for questioning upon arrival in Israel, and in some cases denied entrance. Travelers with Israeli visa stamps in their passports may enter Egypt and Jordan, which have peace agreements and diplomatic relations with Israel; however, an Israeli visa stamp or any evidence of travel to Israel will generally preclude entrance into any other Arabic countries, except for Morocco and Tunisia. Travelers entering Jordan by land from Israel are issued a visa at the border for a fee. Travelers entering Sinai by land from Israel will receive a Sinai Only visa at the Taba border crossing. If you wish to travel into Egypt beyond Sinai, you must obtain an All Egypt visa from an Egyptian embassy or consulate ahead of time. If you're spending time in Eilat, the

Egyptian Consulate in Eilat is most convenient.

Note: Visas to Jordan are given on the spot at the Sheikh Hussein Crossing from northern Israel and at the Rabin Crossing from Eilat (southern Israel); however, you must obtain a visa in advance from a Jordanian embassy if you plan to enter Jordan via the Allenby–King Hussein Bridge in the West Bank.

The governments of most Western countries have advised their citizens NOT to travel to the West Bank, which includes Nablus, Ramallah, Jericho, and Bethlehem; however, depending on day-to-day political conditions, many travelers do take pilgrimage or group tours to visit Christian holy places in Bethlehem.

Travelers with Arabic-sounding surnames may also be stopped for questioning. There are some cases of travelers being turned back at the border for reasons of security or without further explanation. Such travelers are not compensated for plane tickets or for canceled hotel reservations. Unfortunately, Israel has no provision for pre-clearance visa interviews before visitors embark on their journeys.

Water Tap water is safe and drinkable in Israel, except at the Dead Sea. There, even luxury hotels have special taps on each floor that provide drinking water. Although Israeli water is safe, the presence of various minerals in the water may make you a bit queasy. For this reason, bottled water could be a good investment, though in small amounts and for brushing your teeth, local water is fine. In Jordan and Sinai, tap water is not drinkable. Bottled water is essential.

Women Travelers It's important to remember to dress modestly when visiting holy places or ultra-Orthodox Jewish neighborhoods. The penalty for immodest dress can be getting spat on, pelted with pebbles, or worse. The police generally do not take action against religious Jews who attack "immodest" visitors to their neighborhoods. The Jerusalem and Tel Aviv suburbs of Beit Shemesh and B'nai Brak should also be avoided unless you dress with **extreme** modesty. In Jerusalem, on the nos. 1 and 2 bus lines, which serve Mea Shearim and the Western Wall, women are relegated to the back of the bus (so as not to tempt the gaze of ultra-religious men in the front rows). Failure to obey this rule may be met with violent protest from religious passengers.

East Jerusalem, the Old City of Jerusalem, and the West Bank are largely Arabic societies, and women travelers should be guarded in their dress and behavior or they may attract insults and unwanted advances. Women in Islamic societies do not venture far from their houses unless they are in the company of a husband, relatives, or at least one other woman; women travelers may seem to be breaking the rules of propriety simply by being alone. It is always best to try to have at least one traveling companion, male or female, with you if possible. Modest dress and behavior also helps to avoid unwanted attention.

Index

See also Accommodations and Restaurant indexes, below.

General Index

A

Abraham Tours, 386
Abu Ghosh, 174–176
Abu Gosh Music Festival, 43
Abyssinian (Ethiopian) Church, 148
Accessibility, 397
Accommodations. *See also* Accommodations index
- Akko (Acre), 347–349
- best of, 10–12
- Caesarea, 321
- Dead Sea, 181–183
- Eilat, 360–361
- Galilee, 227
- Haifa, 335–336
- Jaffa, 285–288
- Jerusalem, 55–74
- kibbutz hotels, 385
- Masada, 191
- Nazareth, 198–200
- Negev, 188–189
- Petra (Jordan), 376–377
- Rosh Pina, 244–245
- Safed (Zefat), 236–237
- saving money, 61
- Tel Aviv, 270–285
- Tiberias, 212–216
- tips for, 384–386

Aderet, 306
Air travel, 379–380
- to Eilat, 354
- in Israel, 384
- to Jerusalem, 46–47
- to Tel Aviv, 250–251

Akko (Acre), 5, 16, 26, 338–350
- accommodations, 347–349
- arrival information, 340–341
- attractions, 341–347
- restaurants, 349–350
- visitor information, 341

Al Aqsa Mosque, 115–116
Alembika, 304–305
Alice, Princess of Greece, 160
Al-jezzar's Wall, 346
Alternative Tours, 387
American Colony Hotel Bookshop, 167
Ancient sites & cities, best of, 5–6
ANU Museum of the Jewish People, 257–259
Apollonia, 17–18, 321
Aqaba (Jordan), 378
Archaeological digs, 389
Archie Granot, Papercuts, 170
Area codes, 54, 392
Armenian Quarter, 107–108
Arrival information, 379–380
- Akko (Acre), 340–341
- Caesarea, 318
- Dead Sea, 178–179
- Eilat, 354
- Galilee, 192–193
- Haifa, 326–327
- Jerusalem, 46–48
- Nazareth, 193–195
- Petra (Jordan), 363
- Rosh Pina, 243
- Safed (Zefat), 232
- Tel Aviv, 250–251
- Tiberias, 207

Art stores, 166
Artists' Quarter (Safed), 235
Ascent Institute of Safed, 235
Ata, 305
ATMs, 392, 394
Aviva Zilberman, 305
Azoulay, Danny, 170–171

B

Bagels, 86–87
Bahá'i Shrine and Gardens, 330–331
Bahjí, 346–347
Baka, 154
Banks in Petra (Jordan), 366
Baptisms in Jordan River, 229
Bar'am National Park, 192
Bar'am Synagogue, 240–241
Barby, 311–312
Bargaining, 170
Barood, 99
Bars
- Jerusalem, 98–99
- Tel Aviv, 311–313

Basilica of the Agony (Church of All Nations), 162
Basilica of the Annunciation, 195–196
Basilica of the Nativity, 6, 175
Baths of Petra, 373
Bauhaus Center, 259
Bauhaus District (Tel Aviv), 2
Beaches
- Eilat, 355–357
- Tel Aviv, 268–269
- Tiberias, 212

Bein Harim Tours, 386
Beit She'arim National Park, 201–202
Beit Shmuel/Center for Progressive Judaism, 96
Beit Ticho (Ticho House), 148–149
Ben-Gurion House, 259
Bet Gabriel Amphitheater, 220
Bet Jamal Monastery, 173
Bet Lessin, 310
Bethlehem, 175
Bezalel Market, 307
Bible Lands Museum, 96
The Bible Lands Museum, 142
Biblical Archaeology Society, 389
Bicycles
- in Tel Aviv, 256, 269
- tours, 389–390

Bird-watching, 357–358
Birim, 241
Boating
- Eilat, 358
- Tel Aviv, 269

Book Gallery/Books on Schatz, 166
Bookshelf, 166
Bookstores
- Jerusalem, 166–167
- Tel Aviv, 304

Bugs, 392
Burekas, 87
Burnt House, 111
Bus tours
- to Akko, 340
- to Caesarea, 318
- to Dead Sea, 178–179

Bus travel, 380
- to Akko, 341
- to Eilat, 354
- to Haifa, 327
- in Haifa, 329
- to Jerusalem, 47–48
- in Jerusalem, 51–52
- to Nazareth, 194–195
- to Tel Aviv, 251
- in Tel Aviv, 254–255

Business hours, 392
Buza, 241
Byzantine church (Petra), 373
Byzantine street (Caesarea), 320

C

Cable cars (Haifa), 329–330
Cadim Gallery, 168
Caesarea, 6, 17–18, 22, 24, 26, 316–322
Caesarea National Park, 318–320
Cafes (Jerusalem), 85
Calendar, 40–45
Cameri Theater, 311
Capernaum (Kfar Nahum), 5, 224–225
Car rental, 382–383
Cardo Maximus, 109
Carmel Market (Shuk Ha-Carmel), 307
Carmel Market (Tel Aviv), 7
Carmelit, 327, 328–329
Ceramics shopping, 167–168
Chagall Windows at Hadassah Ein Kerem Medical Center, 149–150
Chapel of the Archangel Michael, 141
Chelsy True Closet, 306
Children. *See* Family-friendly activities
Chocolates, 168
Chomer Tov Ceramic Co-op, 307
Christian Information Centre, 49, 175
Christian Quarter, 121–127
Church of Saint Anne, 121–122
Church of Saint Joseph, 196
Church of Saint Mary Magdalene, 160, 161
Church of the Holy Sepulchre, 123–125, 142
Church of the Multiplication of the Loaves and Fishes, 222
Church of the Pater Noster, 161
Church of the Primacy of Saint Peter, 223
City of David, 5, 118–121
Clal Center Bookstore, 166
Clandestine Immigration and Naval Museum, 331–332
Climate, 39–40
Clothing stores, 304–307
Clubs
- Jerusalem, 98–99
- Tel Aviv, 311–313

CMBC (Carmel Mountain Bike Club), 390
Coenaculum (Upper Room), 128
Colonnaded Street, 372
Comme Il Faut, 305
The Commonwealth War Cemetery, 159–160
Consulates, 393
Coral Beach, 355
Coral Beach Nature Reserve, 359
Coral World Underwater Observatory and Marine Park, 359–360
Craft stores
- Jerusalem, 168
- Tel Aviv, 307

Cremesan Winery, 173
Cruises (Tiberias), 211–212
Crusader Church of Saint Mary of the Teutonic Knights, 110, 136
Currency exchange, 394
- Jerusalem, 54
- Tel Aviv, 257

Customs, 392

D

Damascus Gate, 105, 126–127
Dancing, 211, 220
Danny Azoulay, 170–171
Darian Armenian Ceramics, 167
Davidson Exhibition Center, 119–121, 136
Day trips
- from Jerusalem, 174–177
- from Safed (Zefat), 239–241
- from Tel Aviv, 313–315
- from Tiberias, 220–221

Daylight saving time, 396–397
Dead Sea, 2, 4, 17, 21, 26, 178–185
- accommodations, 181–183
- arrival information, 178–179
- attractions, 180–181
- Ein Gedi, 183–185
- restaurants, 181–183
- safety, 179

Delicious Israel, 390
Dentists, 257
Desert Eco Tours, 390
Design Museum Holon, 263
Dig for a Day, 389
Dining. *See* Restaurants; Restaurants index
Distillery tours, 98
Diving. *See* Scuba diving
Dizengoff Center Food Fair, 307
Dizengoff Center Young Designers' Bazaar, 307
Doctors, 392–393
- Tel Aviv, 257

Dolphin Reef, 355–357
Dome of the Rock, 2, 114–118
Dominus Flevit, 161
Dormition Abbey, 128
Drinking laws, 393
Drinking water, 398
Driving, 381–384
- to Akko, 341
- to Caesarea, 318
- to Dead Sea, 179
- to Eilat, 354
- to Haifa, 327
- to Jerusalem, 48
- to Nazareth, 193–194
- to Tel Aviv, 251

Drugstores. *See* Pharmacies
Dung Gate, 105, 118–121

E

East Jerusalem, 51
- accommodations, 72–74
- attractions, 155–162
- restaurants, 94–95

EatWith, 390
Eid Al Adha, 44
Eid Al Fitr, 44
8 Ceramists Altogether, 168
Eilat, 26, 351–362
- accommodations, 360–361
- arrival information, 354
- attractions, 359–360
- outdoor activities, 355–359
- restaurants, 362
- visitor information, 354–355

Ein Gedi, 17, 26, 183–185
Ein Gedi Nature Reserve, 183–185
Ein Gev Music Festival, 208
Ein Kerem, 70, 149–150, 155
Electricity, 393
Elia Photo Service, 173
Embassies, 393
Emergencies
- Jerusalem, 54
- Petra (Jordan), 366
- Tel Aviv, 257

Entry fees to Masada, 191
Eretz Israel Museum, 259
Ethiopian Chapel, 140–141
Ethiopian Compound & Monastery, 139–140
Events information (Jerusalem), 54

F

Falafel, 86
Family-friendly activities
Jerusalem attractions, 163–164
Jerusalem hotels, 65
suggested itinerary, 22–25
Tel Aviv restaurants, 294
Ferries (Tiberias), 211–212
Film
Jerusalem, 99–100
Tel Aviv, 313
Food, 36–39. *See also* Restaurants
dining customs, 38–39
saving money, 39
shopping, 168–169
street food, 37, 86–87
tours, 390
Four Sephardic synagogues, 111
Franciscan Mensa Christi Church, 196

G

Galilee, 24, 26, 192–245. *See also* Sea of Galilee
arrival information, 192–193
Bar'am National Park, 192
bed & breakfasts in, 227
Nazareth, 192, 193–205
Rosh Pina, 241–245
Safed (Zefat), 192, 230–241
Tiberias, 205–221
Garden of Gethsemane, 162
The Garden Tomb, 155, 158
Gasoline (petrol), 383–384
General Exhibition (Safed), 235–236
German Colony, 154
Gifts, 169
Ginosar Valley, 222
Glass-bottom boats, 358
Glassware stores, 169
Golden Gate, 105
The Good Samaritan Inn, 180–181
Gottesman Family Aquarium, 163
Granot, Archie, 170
Greek Catholic "Synagogue" Church, 196
Greek Orthodox Church of the Annunciation, 196
Green Olive Tours, 387
Guesthouses, 386
in Jerusalem, 55
Guided tours. *See* Tours
Guided Tours Israel, 387
Guild of Ceramists, 168

H

HaBaron Garden, 243
HaBima National Theater, 311
Hadassah hospitals, 149
Haganah Museum, 260
Haifa, 16, 26, 323–338
accommodations, 335–336
arrival information, 326–327
attractions, 330–334
city layout, 328
nightlife, 338
restaurants, 336–338
transportation within, 328–330
visitor information, 327
Haifa Museum of Art, 332
Haifa University, 332
Halper's Quality Used Books, 304
Hamat Gader, 228–229
Hamat Tiberias National Park, 210–211
Hameiri House, 236
HaMigdalor, 304
Hammam al-Basha (Turkish Bath), 342
Hansen House Center for Design, Media and Technology, 150
Hanukkah, 45
HaOman 17, 312
Health tips, 393
Hebrew University, Givat Ram Campus, 151
Hecht Museum, 332
Hedya Jewelers and the Sarah Einstein Collection, 169
Hemdat Yamim, 238
Herodian Quarter, 135
High Place of Sacrifice, 369
Hiking
Petra (Jordan), 375
tours, 390
Hippodrome (Caesarea), 320
History
of Israel, 29–36
of Petra, 367–368
of Safed (Zefat), 230–232
Holidays, 40–45
Holocaust Memorial Day (Yom Ha-Shoah), 42
Holon, 263
Holy Week, 4
Holyland Sailing Tiberias Marina, 211
Horseback riding, 212
Hospitals
Jerusalem, 54
Petra (Jordan), 366
Tel Aviv, 257
Hostels, 385–386
Hot Springs of Tiberias, 220–221
Hotels. *See* Accommodations; Accommodations index
House of Quality, 168
Hurva Synagogue, 110, 135

I

Ice cream
in Jerusalem, 87
in Tel Aviv, 303
Iconic experiences, 2–4
Ilana Goor Museum, 266
Independence Day, 43
International choir concerts, 45
Internet service. *See* Wi-Fi
Israel
arrival information, 379–380
best of, 1–12
ancient sites & cities, 5–6
experience Israel like a local, 7–8
hotels, 10–12
iconic experiences, 2–4
restaurants, 8–10
calendar, 40–45
climate, 39–40
current population, 28–29
fast facts, 392–398
history of, 29–36
regions in brief, 25–27
suggested itineraries
family-friendly, 22–25
1-week, 19–22
2-week, 13–19
transportation within, 380–384
when to visit, 39–41
Israel and Jerusalem Festivals of the Performing Arts, 43
Israel Children's Museum, 263
Israel Museum, 96, 142–144
Israel Museum Gift Shops, 166
Israel National Museum of Science, Technology and Space (Madatech), 332

Israel National Trail, 390
Israel Philharmonic Orchestra, 310
Israeli Arbor Day (Tu b'Shevat), 41
Israeli Folkdance Festival, 43
The Israeli Opera, 310
Itineraries. *See* Suggested itineraries

J

Jacob's Ladder Country, Folk, and Blues Festival, 43
Jaffa, 13, 19–20, 249
 accommodations, 285–288
 attractions, 263–267
 nightlife, 310–313
 restaurants, 302–303
Jaffa Flea Market (Shuk HaPishpishim), 308
Jaffa Gate, 105–107, 129
"Jaffa Tales" at the Old Jaffa Visitor's Center, 266–267
Jajo Wine Bar, 312
Jerusalem, 18–20, 25–26, 46–177
 accommodations, 55–74
 arrival information, 46–48
 best restaurants, 78
 cafes, 85
 city layout, 50
 City of David, 5
 day trips from, 174–177
 East Jerusalem attractions, 155–162
 fast facts, 54–55
 Holy Week, 4
 neighborhoods in brief, 50–51
 New City, 19, 23–24
 nightlife, 95–100
 Old City, 2, 18, 22–23, 50–51
  accommodations, 55–60
  attractions, 104–128
  markets, 171–172
  restaurants, 75–80
  walking tour, 129–142
 outdoor activities, 165
 restaurants, 74–95
 shopping, 165–174
 tours, 164–165
 transportation within, 51–53
 visitor information, 48–49
 West Jerusalem attractions, 142–155
 when to visit, 18
Jerusalem Archaeological Park, 118–121, 136
Jerusalem Artists' House, 151
Jerusalem Artists' House Gallery, 166
Jerusalem Arts and Crafts Festival (Hutzot Hayotzer), 44
Jerusalem Cinémathèque, 100
Jerusalem Film Festival, 44
Jerusalem International Chamber Music Festival, 44
Jerusalem Light Rail, 52–53
Jerusalem Midnight Biking, 389–390
Jerusalem Performing Arts Center (Jerusalem Theatre), 96
Jerusalem Pottery, 167
Jesus Trail, 197, 390
Jewelry stores
 Jerusalem, 169–170
 Tel Aviv, 307
Jewish Quarter, 108–111, 135
Jewish-Arab dialogue programs, 391
Jezzar Pasha Mosque, 342–344
Jogging
 in Jerusalem, 165
 in Tel Aviv, 269–270
Jordan. *See* Petra (Jordan)
Jordan River baptisms, 229
Jordan Valley, 17, 24
Judaica shopping, 170–171
Judaicut, 171

K

Kassima, 306–307
Kedem Sasson, 305
Kennedy Memorial, 174
Khalifa Shoes, 174
Khazneh (Treasury), 369
Kibbutz Degania, 230
Kibbutz Ein Gev, 227–228
Kibbutz hotels, 385
Kibbutz Sasa, 240–241
Kibbutzim, 26
Kidron Valley, 159–162
Kids. *See* Family-friendly activities
King David's Tomb, 127
Klezmer Festival of East European Jewish Music, 238
The Knesset (Parliament), 151–152
Korazim, 6, 225–226
Kosher food, 38–39, 75
Kuli Alma, 312
Kursi, 226

L

L. A. Mayer Memorial Museum of Islamic Art, 144–145
La Otra, 312
Lag b'Omer, 43
Language, 393
Latrun Monastery, 173
Levitan, Gila (tour guide), 388
Levontin 7, 312
LGBTQ travelers, 393–394
Lido Cruises Sailing Company, 211
Lifeline for the Old, 169
Light Rail (Jerusalem), 52–53
Lions' Gate, 105
Liturgica, 45
Luggage lockers, 54
Lutheran Church of the Redeemer, 125

M

Machane Yehuda Produce Market (Jerusalem), 7, 168–169
Magdala (Migdal), 221–222
Mahroum's Sweets, 202
Mail, 394
Mané-Katz Museum, 333
Manger Square, 175
Markets
 best of, 7
 Jerusalem bazaars, 126–127, 134–135, 136, 138
 Old City (Jerusalem), 171–172
 Tel Aviv, 307–308
Mary's Well, 196
Masada, 17, 21, 26, 185–191
Maskit, 305
Mea Shearim, 154
Mediterranean coast, 26
Melia, 172
Memorial Day, 42–43
Meron, 239–240
Metronit, 330
Mike's Place, 99
Milk Grotto Church, 175
Minzar, 312

Mitzpoor Ha-Shalom (Peace View Park), 333
Monastery of the Cross, 148
Money, 394
- currency exchange, 54, 257
- in Jordan, 365
- typical costs, 395

Mosh Beach, 355
Mosque (and Chapel) of the Ascension, 160–161
Mount Herzl, 145
Mount of Beatitudes, 5, 224
Mount of Olives, 159–162
Mount Scopus, 159–162
Mount Tabor, 202–203
Mount Zion, 127–128
Mount Zion Cultural Center, 96
Museum of Printing Art, 236
Museum of the History of Tel Aviv–Jaffa, 260
Museum of Underground Prisoners, 344
Museum shops, 308
Music, 8
Muslim Quarter, 121–127
MUZA Eretz Israel Museum Shop, 308

N

Na Lagaat, 266
Nahalat Binyamin Arts and Crafts Market, 308
National Maritime Museum, 333
National Park at Bar'am, 241
Nazareth, 16–17, 24, 192, 193–205
- accommodations, 198–200
- arrival information, 193–195
- attractions, 195–198
- city layout, 195
- nearby attractions, 201–205
- restaurants, 200–201
- visitor information, 195

Nazareth Village, 197–198
Negev, 26, 188–189
Nekker Glass Company, 169
Neot Kedumim Biblical Landscape Reserve, 176
Neve Shalom/Wahat al Salaam, 391
New City (Jerusalem), 19, 23–24
New Imperial Hotel, 132–133
New Israel Fund & Shatil Volunteer Programs, 391
New Testament sites (Nazareth), 195–197
Night Spectacular Sound & Light Show, 98
Nightlife
- Haifa, 338
- Jerusalem, 95–100
- Safed (Zefat), 238
- Tel Aviv/Jaffa, 310–313
- Tiberias, 220

Nighttime tours of Petra, 365
North Beach, 355
North Jerusalem accommodations, 71–72
Notre Dame de France, 148
Numero 13, 305
Nymphaeum, 372

O

Old Bezalel Academy of Arts and Design, 151
Old City (Jerusalem), 2, 18, 22–23, 50–51
- accommodations, 55–60
- attractions, 104–128
- markets, 171–172
- restaurants, 75–80
- walking tour, 129–142

Old City Ramparts, 127
Old Jaffa, 4
Old Synagogue of Rosh Pina, 243
Old Yishuv Court Museum, 109
Olive Festival, 44
1-week itinerary, 19–22
Ophir, 169–170
Our Lady of Fright Chapel, 197
Outdoor activities
- Eilat, 355–359
- Jerusalem, 165
- Tel Aviv, 268–270
- Tiberias, 212

Outer Siq, 369

P

Packing tips, 394
Palestinian Armenian Pottery, 167–168
Palestinian Authority areas, 26–27
Palestinian embroidery, 172
Palmachim Beach, 314–315
Park Hayarkon, 310
Parking, 383–384
Passover (Pesach), 42
Passports, 394
Performing arts
- Jerusalem, 96–98
- Tel Aviv, 310–311

Perlmutter, David (tour guide), 388
Petra (Jordan), 6, 27, 362–378
- accommodations, 376–377
- arrival information, 363
- entry requirements, 363
- fast facts, 366
- hiking, 375
- history of, 367–368
- tours, 365, 366
- visitor information, 366
- walking tour, 368–373

Petra Hotel, 133–134
Petra Museum, 373
Petrol (gasoline), 383–384
Pharmacies, 394
- Jerusalem, 54
- Petra (Jordan), 366
- Tel Aviv, 257

Photography studios, 172–174
Police, 394
Pools of Bethesda, 121–122
Population of Israel, 28–29
Post offices
- Jerusalem, 54
- Tel Aviv, 257

Pottery stores, 167–168
The Prince, 312
Private guides, 387–389
Professor Mer's House, 244
Public transportation. *See* Transportation
Purim (Feast of Lots), 41–42

Q

Qasr al Bint (Palace of the Pharaoh's Daughter), 373
Qumran, 181

R

Ralli Museum, 320
Ramadan, 44
Ramban Synagogue, 111
Red Sea Jazz Festival, 45
Regions in brief, 25–27
Rehavia-Talbeyeh, 154–155
Religious services, 54–55
Rental homes, 385
- in Jerusalem, 55
- in Tel Aviv, 271

Renting cars, 382–383

Restaurants. *See also* **Food; Restaurants index**
- Akko (Acre), 349–350
- best of, 8–10, 78
- Caesarea, 321–322
- Dead Sea, 181–183
- Eilat, 362
- Haifa, 336–338
- Jaffa, 302–303
- Jerusalem, 74–95
- Nazareth, 200–201
- Rosh Pina, 244–245
- Safed (Zefat), 238
- Tel Aviv, 288–302
- Tiberias, 216–218

Rockefeller Archaeological Museum, 158
Roman theater (Petra), 371
Rosh Hashanah (Jewish New Year), 44
Rosh Pina, 241–245
Royal tombs (Petra), 371–372
Rubin Museum (Reuven House), 261
Russian Compound, 152
Russian Orthodox Holy Trinity Cathedral, 148

S

Sabbath, 7, 38, 83, 383
Safari Ramat Gan (Zoological Center), 261–262
Safed, 16
Safed (Zefat), 192, 230–241
- accommodations, 236–237
- arrival information, 232
- attractions, 233–236
- city layout, 232
- day trips from, 239–241
- history of, 230–232
- nightlife, 238
- restaurants, 238
- visitor information, 232

Safety, 394–395
- Dead Sea, 179
- health tips, 393
- Jerusalem, 52, 55
- Tel Aviv, 257
- wildlife, 392
- women travelers, 398

Saint Andrew's Church of Scotland, 148
Saint James Cathedral, 107–108
Salem, Sam (tour guide), 388
Sanctuary of the Condemnation, 122
Sanhedrin Tombs, 153
Sar-El project, 391
Saving money
- on car rental, 382–383
- on food, 39
- on hotels, 61
- on tours, 386–387

Savor Israel, 390
Schindler, Oskar, 128
Scooters in Tel Aviv, 256
Scuba diving, 358–359
Sea of Galilee, 4, 16, 22, 26, 221–230. *See also* **Tiberias**
- Capernaum (Kfar Nahum), 224–225
- Ginosar Valley, 222
- Hamat Gader, 228–229
- Kibbutz Degania, 230
- Kibbutz Ein Gev, 227–228
- Korazim, 225–226
- Kursi, 226
- Magdala (Migdal), 221–222
- Mount of Beatitudes, 224
- Tabgha, 222–224

Seasons for hotels, 385
Security, 395
Seekers, 307
Sefer Ve Sefel Bookshop, 166
Segal, Naomi (tour guide), 388–389
Sela, Adam (tour guide), 389
Senior travel, 395
Seven Arches, 110
Sextius Florentinus tomb, 372
Shabbat. *See* **Sabbath**
Shahar Avnet, 305
Sharabati Shops, 174
Shavuot (Pentecost), 43
Shawarma, 86
Shepherds' Field, 175
Sherover Promenade, 220
Sheruts, 46–47, 251, 255, 381
Shoe stores, 174
Shopping
- Jerusalem, 165–174
- Tel Aviv, 303–308
- tips for, 167, 170

Shpagat, 312–313
Shuttle services to Eilat, 354
Silver Print Gallery, 174
Silwan. *See* **City of David**
Simchat Torah, 44
Simon's House, 267
Sinai Coast of Egypt, 26
Sipur Pashut, 304
Siq, 368–369
Smoking, 395
Snorkeling, 358–359
Sorek Stream Nature Reserve, 313–314
Soreq Stalactite Cave/ Avshalom Nature Reserve, 177
Soreq Winery, 173
South Jerusalem
- accommodations, 70–71
- restaurants, 93–94

Southern Wall of the Temple Mount, 119–121, 136
Stations of the Cross, 122–123
Steimatsky, 304
Steimatzky, 166
Stein Books, 166
Stella Maris Lighthouse, Church, and Carmelite Monastery, 333–334
Storage lockers, 54
Street food, 37, 86–87
Street of the Chain, 127
Student travel, 395–396
Stuffed breads, 87
Subterranean Crusader City (Hospitallers' Fortress), 344–345
Succot (Feast of Tabernacles), 44
Suggested itineraries
- family-friendly, 22–25
- 1-week, 19–22
- 2-week, 13–19

Sultan's Pool, 98
Sunbula, 172
Sunsets, 7
Supreme Court Building (Jerusalem), 153
Suq El Attarin, 136, 138
Suq El Hussor, 134
Suq Khan es-Zeit (the Market of the Inn of the Olive Oil), 138–139
Suzanne Dellal Center for Dance and Theater, 311
Sweet 'N Karem, 168
Swimming, 165
Synagogues in Safed (Zefat), 233–235

T

Tabgha, 5, 222–224
Targ (Ein Kerem Music Center), 97
Taxes, 396
Taxis
- in Jerusalem, 47, 53
- to Jerusalem, 380
- to Petra, 354
- in Tel Aviv, 255
- to Tel Aviv, 380

Technion, 334
Tel Aviv, 13–14, 19, 24–25, 26, 246–315
- accommodations, 270–285
- arrival information, 250–251
- attractions, 257–263
- Bauhaus District, 2
- best of, 249–250
- city layout, 252–254
- day trips from, 313–315
- fast facts, 257
- nightlife, 310–313
- outdoor activities, 268–270
- restaurants, 288–302
- shopping, 303–308
- special events, 268
- tours, 267–268
- transportation within, 254–256
- visitor information, 251

Tel Aviv Cinémathèque, 313
Tel Aviv Gay Pride Month, 43
Tel Aviv Museum of Art, 262–263
Tel Aviv Port Organic Farmer's Market, 308
Tel Megiddo (Armageddon) National Park, 203–204
Telephone numbers, 396
- Jerusalem, 55
- Petra (Jordan), 366

Temperatures, 40
Temple Mount (Haram Es Sharif), 2
Temple Mount (Haram esh Sharif)—Dome of the Rock, 2, 114–118
Temple of the Winged Lions, 372–373
Thinkers Distillery, 98
Tiberias, 22, 205–221. *See also* Sea of Galilee
- accommodations, 212–216
- arrival information, 207
- attractions, 208–212
- city layout, 208
- day trips from, 220–221
- nightlife, 220
- outdoor activities, 212
- restaurants, 216–218
- transportation within, 208
- when to visit, 208

Tiberias's Jewish tombs, 209–210
Ticho House, 97
Tickets to Masada, 191
Tiferet Israel (or Yisrael) Synagogue, 111
Tikotin Museum of Japanese Art, 334
The Time Elevator, 163
Time zones, 396–397
Tipping, 397
The Tisch Family Zoological Gardens, 163–164
Tisha b'Av, 44
Tmol Shilshom Bookstore Café, 166
Toilets, 397
- Jerusalem, 55

Tolls, 383–384
Tomb of the Virgin, 162
Tombs of the Kings, 158
Tombs of Wadi Farasa, 369
Tourist Israel, 386
Tours, 386–391. *See also* Bus tours; Walking tours
- of Jerusalem, 164–165
- of Petra, 365, 366
- of Safed (Zefat), 233
- of Tel Aviv, 267–268
- of Tiberias, 212

Tower of David Museum of the History of Jerusalem, 106
Train Puppet Theater, 97, 163
Train travel, 380–381
- to Haifa, 326
- to Jerusalem, 47, 380
- to Tel Aviv, 251
- in Tel Aviv, 255
- to Tel Aviv, 380

Transportation, 380–384
- in Haifa, 328–330
- in Jerusalem, 51–53
- in Tel Aviv, 254–256

Treasures in the Walls Ethnographic Museum, 345
Tree planting, 391
Tres, 305–306
Triple-arched gate (Petra), 373
20th-century memorials (Safed), 235–236
2-week itinerary, 13–19
Tzavta, 311
Tzora Winery, 173

V

Valley of Kidron, 159–162
Varouj Photography Studio, 173
Vegan restaurants (Tel Aviv), 290
Via Dolorosa, 122–125
Visas, 397–398
Vision Gallery, 174
Volunteer trips, 391
Volunteers for Israel, 391

W

Wadi Rum Nature Reserve, 27, 377–378
Walking
- in Jerusalem, 53
- in Tel Aviv, 256

Walking tours
- Jaffa, 264–266
- Jerusalem, 165
- Jesus Trail, 197
- Old City (Jerusalem), 129–142
- Petra (Jordan), 368–373

Water for drinking, 398
Water sports, in Tel Aviv, 270
West Bank, 26–27, 387
West Jerusalem, 51
- accommodations, 61–70
- attractions, 142–155
- restaurants, 80–92

Western Wall, 2, 112–114, 136
White Nights, 43
Wi-Fi, 393
- Jerusalem, 50
- Tel Aviv, 254

Wildflowers, 8
Wildlife, 392
Wineries, 173, 322–323
Wohl Amphitheater, 310
The Wolfson Museum of Jewish Art, 145
Women travelers, 398
Woolf, Richard (tour guide), 388

Y

Yad Sarah, 397
Yad Vashem Memorial and Holocaust Museum, 4, 145–147
Yardenit, 229
Yemin Moshe, 153–154
Yigael Yadin Masada Museum, 189
Yigal Alon Cultural Center and Theatre, 238
Yigal Alon Museum of the Galilee, 222
YMCA, 97, 153
Yom Kippur (Day of Atonement), 44
Youth hostels, 385–386

Z

Zedekiah's Cave, 159
Zichron Ya'acov, 17–18, 26, 322–323
Zion Gate, 105, 127–128
Zippori (Sepphoris), 6, 199–200
Zippori (Sepphoris) National Park, 204–205

Accommodations

Abraham Eilat, 361
Abraham Hostel (Jerusalem), 10, 62
Abraham Hostel Tel Aviv, 284–285
Akkotel, 347
Al Anbat 1 Hotel, 377
Al Hashimi Hotel and Hostel, 60
American Colony Hotel, 10, 72–73
Amirim, 237
Ana Acre Hostel, 347–348
Arthur Hotel, 61
Artist Hotel, 274
Artists' Colony Inn, 236
Assemblage Hotel, 281
Austrian Hospice, 60
Badolina, 183
Bat Shlomo Farmhouse & Winery, 10, 322–323
Beit Elfarasha, 348
Beit Immanuel Hostel, 288
Beit Shmuel Hotel and Conference Center, 69
Beresheet Resort, 188
Best Western Regency Suites Hotel, 274
Brown Beach House Hotel, 275
Brown Urban Hotel, 281–282
Bubble Luxotel Petra, 376
Carlton Hotel Tel Aviv, 10, 271, 274
The Colony Hotel, 335
Dan Boutique Hotel, 70
Dan Caesarea, 25, 321
Dan Carmel Haifa Hotel, 25, 335
Dan Eilat Hotel, 360–361
Dan Jerusalem, 65, 71–72
Dan Panorama, 336
The Dave Gordon—Son of a Brown, 278
David Citadel Hotel, 65–66
Diaghilev LOFT Live Art Hotel, 282
The Drisco, 285–286
Efendi Hotel, 11, 348–349
Eldan Hotel, 68
Elma Arts Complex Luxury Hotel, 25, 323
Fabric Hotel, 282–283
Fauzi Azar Inn, 11, 198–199
Galei Kinneret, 212–213
Gloria Hotel, 58
Harmony Hotel, 62
Herbert Samuel Hod Dead Sea, 181–182
Hotel Montefiore, 278–279
Ink Hotel, 283
InterContinental David Tel Aviv, 279
The Jaffa, 286–287
Jerusalem Hotel, 73–74
Jerusalem Inn Hotel, 64
The Kibbutz Country Lodgings, 227
Kibbutz Ein Gedi Resort Hotel, 182
Kibbutz Ein Gev Resort Village, 215
King David Hotel, 65, 66
The Levee, 280
Little House in Bakah, 71
Loui Hotel, 336
Mamilla Hotel, 66–67
Market House Hotel, 287–288
Masada Guest House and Youth Hostel, 191
Michel House, 199
Mizpe Hayamim Spa Hotel, 244
Montefiore Hotel, 68
Mövenpick Resort Petra, 376–377
Nachsholim, 25
New Imperial Hotel, 58
The Norman, 280–281
Notre Dame de Sion Convent Guest House Ein Kerem, 70
Orchid Hotel Eilat, 361
Orient by Isrotel, 61
Petra Guest House, 377
Pina Barosh, 244
Pod O Hotel, 285
Port Inn Guest House, 336
Ramat Rachel Hotel, 65, 70–71
Rosary Convent Guest House and Hostel, 69
Saint Andrew's Church of Scotland Guest House, 71
Saint Mark's Lutheran Guest House, 59
The Scots Hotel, 11, 213–214
Selina Kinneret, 216
The Setai (Tel Aviv), 287
The Setai Sea of Galilee, 11, 214
Shalom & Relax Hotel, 11, 276
Six Senses Shaharut, 188–189
Spot Hostel, 277–278
St. George Hotel, 74
St. George's Cathedral Pilgrim Guesthouse, 55, 74
Tal Hotel, 275–276
The Vera, 12, 283–284
Vered HaGalil Guest Farm, 215–216
Villa Nazareth Hotel, 199
Waldorf Astoria, 12, 67–68
The Way Inn, 236–237
Yam Hotel, 277
YMCA Three Arches Hotel, 68–69
Zippori Village Guesthouses, 199–200

Restaurants

Abu Assab Refreshments, 79, 139
Abu Shukri, 79
Abu Yussef, 336
Adom, 78, 83, 93
Aldo Ice Cream, 87
American Colony Hotel Arabesque Restaurant, 94
Amigo Emil, 79
Anastasia Vegan Café, 290, 291
Between The Arches, 80
Armenian Tavern, 75
Aroma, 85
Arte Italian Ice Cream, 303
Asif Culinary Institute of Israel, 299
Bagel Cafe, 87
Bait 77, 238
Barbunia, 289–290, 294
Barood Bar Restaurant, 82–83
Bat Ya'ar Ranch Steak House, 238
BlackOut, 266
Breada, 337
Bretonne, 294, 300
The Brewery (Hamivshala), 362
Brut, 293–294
Bucke, 300
Buza, 303
Café Popular, 291
Cafe Rimmon, 85
Caffit, 94

Chakra, 89
Crusaders, 322
Dalida, 294–295
Dallal, 298
Decks, 10, 217
Dok, 299
Douzan, 337
Eats Cafeteria, 292
El Marsa, 349
Eldorado, 85
English Bakery, 87
Eucalyptus, 78, 80–81
Family Restaurant, 79–80
Fat Cow, 294
Fattoush, 337
Focaccia Bar, 83, 84
Four One Six, 290
Galei Gil, 217
Gate Cafe, 86
George and John, 286
Golda, 87, 303
Golda's Restaurant, 287
Goodness, 290
Ha'achim, 300
Hamarakia, 88–89
HaSadna-The Culinary Workshop, 78, 93
Hellena, 10, 322
Hillel Café, 85
Hotel Montefiore, 9–10, 279, 293
House Restaurant, 218
Hummus Abu Hassan, 9, 302–303
Hummus Said, 349
Jaffar Sweets, 80
Jerusalem Hotel, 78
Kangaroo, 84
Kapara Mio, 292
King David Street YMCA, 83
The Last Resort, 362
Luna Bistro, 9, 201
Lux, 337
M25, 295–296
Machneyuda Restaurant, 78, 89–90
Magdalena, 218
Mahane Yehuda Market, 8–9, 87
Mahroum's Sweets, 202
Manta Ray, 301–302
Market Seasonal Kitchen, 290
Marvad Haksamim (Magic Carpet), 94
Menza, 89
Mifgash Rambam, 296
Miznon, 300–301
Mona, 78, 81–82
Moshiko's, 86
Nof Kinneret, 217
North Abraxas, 295
Noya, 78, 88
Opa's, 290
The Pagoda, 217–218
Papa Andreas, 75
Par Derriere, 302
Pasta Banamal, 289
Pastel, 298–299
Piccolino, 83–84
Pizza Brooklyn, 294
Raseef 33, 338
Roast on Fire, 217
Rooftop, 78, 82
Rutenberg, 218
Sabich Frishman, 292
Salimi, 296
Saluf and Sons, 296–297
Sama, 349
Samboosak Bakery/Café, 87
Sami's, 92
Sarwa Street Kitchen, 95
Sea Dolphin (Dolphin Yam), 88
Shanty, 84–85
Shiri Bistro & Wine Bar, 244–245
Shukshuka, 297
Sima's, 91–92
Spaghettim, 83, 85
St. Peter's Restaurant, 225
Suzanna, 298
Talpiot Market, 338
Tmol Shilshom Bookstore Cafe, 85, 86
Tzemah, 9, 78, 91
Uri Buri, 349–350
Veranda, 92
Yulia, 288–289
Zuni Restaurant/Café/Bar, 83, 87

Photo Credits

Front cover: John Theodor / Shutterstock; p. i: Mazur Travel / Shutterstock; p. iii: RnDmS / Shutterstock; p. 3: Beata Bar / Shutterstock; p. 4: xamnesiacx84 / Shutterstock; p. 5: Nina Zorina / Shutterstock; p. 6: Kateryna Mashkevych / Shutterstock; p. 7: Finn stock / Shutterstock; p. 8: irisphoto1 / Shutterstock; p. 9: Courtesy of Tzemah; p. 10: Courtesy of Efendi Hotel / Sivan Askayo; p. 11: Courtesy of Scots Hotel; p. 12: Courtesy of The Waldorf Astoria; p. 15: Hitman Sharon / Shutterstock; p. 17: Courtesy of Israeli Ministry of Tourism / Itamar Grinberg; p. 18: Courtesy of Israeli Ministry of Tourism / Dafna Tal; p. 20: Finn stock / Shutterstock; p. 24: Opachevsky Irina / Shutterstock; p. 27: Bhaven Jani / Shutterstock; p. 33: evantravels / Shutterstock; p. 38: Asya Nurullina / Shutterstock; p. 42: Arkady Mazor / Shutterstock; p. 43: ColorMaker / Shutterstock; p. 49: SJ Travel Photo and Video / Shutterstock; p. 53: Courtesy of Israeli Ministry of Tourism / Noam Chen; p. 59: Courtesy of Gloria Hotel; p. 60: Opachevsky Irina / Shutterstock; p. 62: Courtesy of Harmony Hotel; p. 64: Courtesy of Abraham Hostel Jerusalem; p. 65: Courtesy of David Citadel Hotel / AMIT GERON; p. 67: Courtesy of King David Hotel / Ori Ackerman; p. 69: KiyechkaSo / Shutterstock; p. 73: Courtesy of American Colony Hotel / Mikaela Burstow; p. 78: Courtesy of Eucalyptus; p. 81: Courtesy of Eucalyptus; p. 82: Courtesy of The Rooftop / Adi Gilad; p. 83: Courtesy of Piccolino; p. 88: Courtesy of Hamarkia; p. 90: Kartinkin77 / Shutterstock; p. 91: Fotokon / Shutterstock; p. 92: Courtesy of Tzemah; p. 93: Courtesy of Veranda Restaurant; p. 95: Courtesy of American Colony Hotel; p. 97: Courtesy of Jerusalem Performing Arts Center; p. 99: Courtesy of Abraham Hostel Jerusalem; p. 102: Courtesy of Israeli Ministry of Tourism / Dafna Tal; p. 104: Courtesy of Israeli Ministry of Tourism / Noam Chen; p. 106: Wirestock Creators / Shutterstock; p. 107: Moshe EINHORN / Shutterstock; p. 110: marcobrivio.photo / Shutterstock; p. 112: Boris Diakovsky / Shutterstock; p. 115: Teo K / Shutterstock; p. 120: Altosvic / Shutterstock; p. 122: Berthold Werner / Shutterstock; p. 123: Courtesy of Israeli Ministry of Tourism / Noam Chen; p. 126: Cezary Wojtkowski / Shutterstock; p. 128: Moshe EINHORN / Shutterstock; p. 132: Sean Pavone / Shutterstock; p. 137: Botond Horvath / Shutterstock; p. 138: Frank Fell Media / Shutterstock; p. 139: dominika zara / Shutterstock; p. 141: dominika zara / Shutterstock; p. 143: godongphoto / Shutterstock; p. 146: marcobrivio.photo / Shutterstock; p. 150: mtsyri / Shutterstock; p. 152: Roman Yanushevsky / Shutterstock; p. 158: David McIntosh / Shutterstock; p. 161: LALS STOCK / Shutterstock; p. 164: Courtesy of Archaeological Seminars Ltd / Aner Green; p. 169: Hagen Simon / Shutterstock; p. 170: Courtesy of Ophir; p. 171: Courtesy of Danny Azoulay; p. 176: IgorMarch / Shutterstock; p. 179: Courtesy of Israeli Ministry of Tourism / Itamar Grinberg; p. 180: Opachevsky Irina / Shutterstock; p. 182: Courtesy of Herbert Samuel Hod Dead Sea Hotel / Assaf Pinchuk; p. 185: kavram / Shutterstock; p. 187: mageBank4u / Shutterstock; p. 189: Courtesy of Six Senses Shaharut / ASSAF PINCHUK; p. 190: Nitr / Shutterstock; p. 196: RnDmS / Shutterstock; p. 197: Kobby Dagan / Shutterstock; p. 198: Courtesy of Fauzi Azar / ALON LEVITE; p. 200: Courtesy of Zippori Village Guesthouse / Ben Pershit; p. 201: Barbarajo / Shutterstock; p. 202: StockStudio Aerials / Shutterstock; p. 205: RnDmS / Shutterstock; p. 206: Gil Meshulam / Shutterstock; p. 209: RnDmS / Shutterstock; p. 210: Logan Bush / Shutterstock; p. 213: Courtesy of Galei Kinneret; p. 214: Courtesy of Scots Hotel; p. 215: Courtesy of Vered HaGalil Guest Farm; p. 219: Courtesy of Rutenberg / Afik Gabay; p. 223: Ilan Ejzykowicz / Shutterstock; p. 224: kavram / Shutterstock; p. 226: Barbarajo / Shutterstock; p. 229: ChameleonsEye / Shutterstock; p. 231: RnDmS / Shutterstock; p. 234: David Cohen 156 / Shutterstock; p. 237: Courtesy of Way Inn / Jordan Polevoy Photography; p. 239: David Cohen 156 / Shutterstock; p. 240: Belikova Oksana / Shutterstock; p. 242: Nina Mikryukova / Shutterstock; p. 247: Courtesy of Israeli Ministry of Tourism / Dana Friedlander; p. 249: Courtesy of Manta Ray ; p. 252: Courtesy of Israeli Ministry of Tourism / Dana Friedlander; p. 253: O.Rudenock / Shutterstock; p. 256: Antonio Rico / Shutterstock; p. 258, top: Courtesy of ANU Museum of Jewish People / Roni Cnaani; p. 258, bottom: ChameleonsEye / Shutterstock; p. 260: Courtesy of Eretz Israel Museum / Eli Pozner; p. 261: LevT / Shutterstock; p. 262: Opachevsky Irina / Shutterstock; p. 263: Roofsoldier / Shutterstock; p. 264: Evgeni Fabisuk / Shutterstock; p. 265: Arkady Mazor / Shutterstock; p. 266: Courtesy of Old Jaffa Visitor's Center; p. 268: Courtesy of

Israeli Ministry of Tourism / Dana Friedlander; p. 270: Courtesy of Israeli Ministry of Tourism / Dana Friedlander; p. 275: Courtesy of Brown Beach Hotel / Assaf Pinchuk; p. 276: Courtesy of Shalom & Relax Hotel; p. 277: Courtesy of Yam Hotel / Natan Dvir; p. 280: Courtesy of Levee Hotel / Sivan Askayo; p. 283: Courtesy of The Ink Hotel; p. 284: Courtesy of The Vera / Assaf Pinchuk; p. 285: Courtesy of Abraham Hostel Tel Aviv; p. 286: Courtesy of The Drisco Hotel / Assaf Pinchuk; p. 288: Courtesy of Yulia; p. 289: Courtesy of Pasta Banamal; p. 291: Courtesy of Anastasia / Or Kaplan; p. 295: Courtesy of North Abraxas / Ariel Efron; p. 297: Courtesy of Saluf and Sons / Ariel Efron; p. 301: Courtesy of Manta Ray; p. 302: Courtesy of The Drisco Hotel / HAIM YOSEF; p. 306: Courtesy of Maskit Archive; p. 308: Courtesy of MUZA Eretz Israel Museum Shop; p. 309: Finn stock / Shutterstock; p. 311: Courtesy of Suzanne Dellal Centre / Daniel Tchetchik: ; p. 318: lensfield / Shutterstock; p. 319: John Theodor / Shutterstock; p. 326: Courtesy of Israeli Ministry of Tourism / Itamar Grinberg; p. 327: Opachevsky Irina / Shutterstock; p. 329: YURY LEDENTSOV / Shutterstock; p. 330: Wildnerdpix / Shutterstock; p. 331: trabantos / Shutterstock; p. 333: AlexDonin / Shutterstock; p. 335: Courtesy of Dan Carmel Haifa; p. 340: Nina Zorina / Shutterstock; p. 343: irisphoto1 / Shutterstock; p. 345: trabantos / Shutterstock; p. 347: Eli Schwartz / Shutterstock; p. 348: Courtesy of Efendi Hotel; p. 352: EAZN / Shutterstock; p. 353: Sergei25 / Shutterstock; p. 356: Luciano Santandreu / Shutterstock; p. 357: Courtesy of International Birding and Research Center / Noam Weiss; p. 358: LeonP / Shutterstock; p. 360: Courtesy of Dan Eilat Hotel; p. 361: Courtesy of Abraham Hostel Eilat; p. 364: trabantos / Shutterstock; p. 369: Dietmar Rauscher / Shutterstock; p. 370: trabantos / Shutterstock; p. 374: Georgios Tsichlis / Shutterstock; p. 376: Ruslan Kalnitsky / Shutterstock; back cover: Hrecheniuk Oleksii / Shutterstock.